The Age of Conversation

ALSO BY BENEDETTA CRAVERI

Madame du Deffand and Her World

The Age of Conversation

Benedetta Craveri

TRANSLATED BY
Teresa Waugh

NEW YORK REVIEW BOOKS

nyrb

New York

THIS IS A NEW YORK REVIEW BOOK

PUBLISHED BY THE NEW YORK REVIEW OF BOOKS

THE AGE OF CONVERSATION
by Benedetta Craveri

This edition published in 2006
in the United States of America by
The New York Review of Books
1755 Broadway
New York, NY 10019
www.nybooks.com

First published in Italy by Adelphi Edizioni 2001 as *La civiltà della conversazione*

The Library of Congress has catalogued the hardcover edition of this book as follows:

Craveri, Benedetta, 1942–
    [Civiltà della conversazione. English]
    The age of conversation / by Benedetta Craveri; translated by Teresa Waugh.
       p. cm.
    Includes bibliographical references and index.
    ISBN-10: 1-59017-141-1 (hardcover: alk. paper)
    ISBN-10: 1-59017-214-0 (paperback: alk. paper)

    1. Women intellectuals — France — History.   2. France — Intellectual life —
17th century.   3. France — Intellectual Life — 18th century.   4. Salons — France —
History — 17th century.   5. Salons — France — History — 18th century.
    I. Waugh, Teresa.   II. Title.
    DC121.7.C73 2005
    305.48'96'094409033 — dc 22

                                                                                    2005003059

ISBN-13: 978-1-59017-214-8

ISBN-10: 1-59017-214-0

Printed in the United States of America on acid-free paper.

1 3 5 7 9 10 8 6 4 2

for Benoît

Table of Contents

Illustrations follow page 208

Introduction

THIS BOOK TELLS the story of an ideal—the last one by which the French nobility of the *ancien régime* recognized itself collectively and the last in which it was able to establish itself once more as a symbol and model for the nation. It was an ideal characterized by elegance and courtesy, an ideal that countered the logic of force and the brutality of instinct with an art of living together based on seduction and reciprocal pleasure.

In the first decades of the seventeenth century the aristocracy discovered a still unexplored territory halfway between the court and the Church whose boundaries its members determined. The nobility established its own laws based on a code of behavior marked by the strictest veneration of form. Those within this sphere called it by the generic name *monde*. Soon the term would no longer be used to signify the human sphere opposed to the divine realm—a place of exile and sin in which everything seemed to lead to the soul's damnation—but would describe a carefully circumscribed social reality. In it, a small group of privileged people were united in a strictly secular, ethical, and aesthetic project that could succeed without theological backing. In the course of the seventeenth century, many would ultimately sacrifice this all-too-worldly ideal to a spiritual conversion and a return to God. In the following century, however, once freed from their religious preoccupations, men and women could confidently devote themselves to this purely worldly calling.

It is this project, its motives, and its components that I propose to investigate from its inception to its realization, from the days of the hôtel de Rambouillet until the French Revolution.

But why stop at 1789? Why confine this essentially modern form of sociability to a specific historical period? It would, after all, survive the society that invented it, although passing through further metamorphoses. I stop at the Revolution because only members of the nobility of the *ancien régime*—slaves to a magnificent idleness and with no concern other than to celebrate themselves—could make of social life an art and an end in itself. The Revolution, by terminating the privileges of the nobility, marked a point of no return.

It is hardly surprising that the idea of a history of worldly society dates back to 1835 and that it was a regretful ex-revolutionary, the Comte Pierre Louis de Roederer, who in the spirit of the Bourbon Restoration published the *Mémoire pour servir à l'histoire de la société polie en France*, the first genuinely historical work on the subject. Since that time writers and scholars have continuously studied that lost world, through biography, portraiture, anecdote, and the novel, concentrating for the most part on the central role of salon life and the power that women wielded there. More recently, in the course of the twentieth century, scholars of language, literature, and *ancien régime* culture have gradually paid more attention in their respective spheres of research to the complex web of influence that connected *savants* to socialites, starting with the contribution made by the latter to the birth of the modern French language, to the development of new forms of literature, and to the definition of taste.

What, then, led me to return to a territory already explored by so many distinguished critics, illustrious and extremely well informed scholars, and eloquent and seductive popularizers? First of all, I wanted to confront the well-established but entirely artificial dividing line between the seventeenth and eighteenth centuries. In the academic world these two centuries each have their specialists, usually little inclined to venture beyond their specific fields of competence. Moreover, where the general history of ideas is concerned—or, even more simply, the history of costume and taste—the seventeenth and eighteenth centuries seem to offer two such different worldviews that they often inspire a firm and very personal taking of sides, whatever the fluctuation of historiographic fashion.

Of course, we must recognize that despite the stability of *ancien régime* institutions, important changes were underway as the sixteenth century turned into the seventeenth. What changed primarily was not only man's conception of the society in which he lived but his perception of himself, his way of thinking and his sensibilities, his morality and his idea of happiness.

Any caesura is misleading, however, if we look at the two centuries from the point of view of *la civilisation mondaine*, or high society. The most striking thing about the generations that successively entered the social limelight is, in fact, the strength of tradition, the continuity of style. As the Enlightenment progressed, worldly dilettantism, ever more greedy for knowledge, may have made it a point of honor to side with the avant-garde, but it still obeyed the older formal code of good manners and cultivated the ideal of aesthetic perfection. It was not only a matter of refining the art of self-presentation—by now the hallmark of a nobleman's identity—but of preserving the lingering memory of a utopian dream well suited to a century of utopian ideals, a dream that, despite its many failings, refused to die.

This happy utopia was a blessed island, an innocent Arcadia in which the trials of everyday life might be forgotten and illusory moral and aesthetic perfection cultivated. Here the dramas of life could be corrected, reality reshaped in imitation of art. At the beginning of the seventeenth century, Honoré d'Urfé illustrated this utopia in *L'Astrée*—the novel the French nobility most admired—and Mme de Rambouillet attempted to establish it in her house, making the hôtel de Rambouillet in Paris the archetype of French aristocratic *sociabilité*. But the superficial virtues of style could not always conquer pride, hatred, envy, or violence. Between courtly compliments, noblemen continued to kill one another in duels out of simple spite, to carry off dangerously beautiful or rich young women, to betray, to slander, and to insult one another. Very often courtesy proved to be a fiction, elegance of manners a mere posture. Yet if moralists, novelists, playwrights, and, by no means least, the socialites themselves persisted in tearing off their masks and denouncing the absurdity of the social comedy, it could only be because the authentic ideal of perfection persisted. At the same time, a nostalgia for the past had been part of the myth of polite society since its origins. Already in the seventeenth century, when reviling contemporary society's vulgarity, Jean de La Bruyère—who did not himself belong to the *monde*—nevertheless recalled with infinite regret the brilliant, witty, unique conversations that used to take place at the hôtel de Rambouillet. Similarly, in the years just before the Revolution—those in which the *douceur de vivre*, or the pleasure of society life, reached its peak— Talleyrand, that most worldly of men, thought back to the sublime, never to be repeated conversations of Mme de Lafayette, Mme de Sévigné, and the Duc de La Rochefoucauld.

My wish to reconstruct the history of the *esprit de société* in its entirety goes hand in hand with a desire to do so in a narrative mode unburdened by academic language. Not only does this seem to be the style best suited to the subject, but it also aims to echo that *style moyen*, or middle style, by which the readers of the time liked to recognize themselves. However, the bibliographical notes will bear witness to the great debt I owe to the world of scholarship. If I have been able to accurately bring together the many facets of *la culture mondaine* and the numerous directions in which this culture leads, it is thanks in particular to the richness and quality of the studies that have appeared in the last decades.

To describe a collective ideal of life that lasted for nearly two centuries demands a choice of path and of method, and it is precisely the sharp awareness that this adventure's leading characters had of themselves that showed me the way. Perhaps no society has ever thought about itself as much as the one I propose to evoke here. Certainly none has reflected on its own identity and about the right way to present itself with such care; it seemed natural therefore to describe it from the inside, through its own basic texts, trusting myself to the guidance of some of the era's most distinctive women, allowing them to speak for themselves wherever possible, drawing on the words of their contemporaries, and occasionally pausing to consider some of the larger themes—the female condition, the *esprit de société*, conversation—that show how polite society took account of itself.

But why—it might equally be asked—choose to write again about so many women who have already been portrayed brilliantly and who, thanks to feminist historiography, are now the subject of a growing number of studies? Can it really be that the Grand Condé, the military genius of Louis XIV's wars, is less representative than his sister Mme de Longueville where aristocratic style is concerned? La Rochefoucauld less than his friend Mme de Lafayette? Roger de Bussy-Rabutin less than his cousin Mme de Sévigné? Charles de Saint-Évremond less than his accomplice in epicureanism, Ninon de Lenclos? This is certainly not the case, but one fact must be taken into account: as contemporary observers were the first to point out, in the polite society of the *ancien régime* it was the women and not the men who formed and dictated the rules of the game. What made the French nobility society unique in Europe was the high level of integration between the sexes, the inclusion of the literati, and the concentration of high society life between Paris and Versailles.

Each of the women portrayed here measured herself against a model of ideal behavior that she interpreted and adapted to her own ambitions and interests, to her own social circle, and to her most cherished hopes. In so doing, she established its importance and its central place in the life of the times; she passed it on, enriched by her personal contribution, to the next generation. Here in procession, to give a few examples, are the Duchesse de Longueville, embodying in equal parts the two opposing models of worldly seduction and renunciation; the Marquise de Sablé, initiating the collaboration between polite society and literature; the Grande Mademoiselle, cultivating the whole gamut of noble leisure pursuits; Mme de Sévigné, illustrating in life, as in her letters, the overwhelming power of *enjouement*—the euphoric gaiety essential to success in society; and Mme de Lambert and Mme de Tencin, presiding over a new type of intellectual conversation and preparing the *beau monde* for Enlightenment debate.

But there is a deeper and more personal reason that has led me to revisit a history now so remote that it has the flavor of a legend: an awareness of the fact that, despite the great distance separating us from this vanished world, it continues to exert an irresistible attraction. Here modern man, with an intuitive knowledge of psychology, transformed sociability into an art and brought it to its highest point of aesthetic perfection. Here the elite cultivated the principle of elective affinity between men and women, recognizing their equality, and sought each other out by mutual choice. And in times like ours, when artificial models of behavior imposed from outside follow one another with monotonous regularity, often to the point of caricature, one can only admire the sovereign naturalness of those social beings who, with perfect mastery of word and gesture, interpreted the model they had forged for themselves and by which they were recognized. How can we compare the intimidating, prefabricated notion of "free time" with a culture of leisure in which art, literature, music, dance, theater, and conversation all constituted a permanent training for the body and the mind?

Of all these arts, it is the art of conversation—society's art par excellence—that we miss most and that most demands our admiration, just as it commanded the appreciation of La Bruyère and Talleyrand. Developed as an entertaining end in itself, as a game for shared pleasure, conversation obeyed strict laws that guaranteed harmony based on perfect equality. These were laws of clarity, measure, elegance, and regard for the self-respect of others. A talent for listening was more appreciated than one for speaking. Exquisite courtesy restrained vehemence and prevented quarrels.

The new art was soon raised to a prominent position, becoming central to worldly sociability. Nourished by literature and its own inherent curiosity, it gradually became introspective and brought history, philosophical and scientific reflection, and new ideas within its compass. Since France had neither a representative system nor an institutional forum where citizens could express their opinions, conversation within polite society became a tool of intellectual and political debate—the only ground on which public opinion could be formed. During the Revolution, the representatives of the nobility seated in the Constituent Assembly were distinguished for the quietness of their tones and for their ability to mediate, something for which French diplomacy was celebrated during the *ancien régime*.

This ideal of conversation, which managed to marry lightheartedness with depth, elegance with pleasure, and the search for truth with a tolerant respect for the opinions of others, has never lost its appeal. The more the realities of the present day distance us from it, the more we miss it. It is no longer the ideal of a whole society, but has become a *"lieu de mémoire"*—a realm of memory. No conciliatory powers can revive it under unfavorable conditions; today it leads a clandestine existence and is the territory of the few. Yet there is no reason why it and its pleasures might not one day be revived.

The reader will soon realize that there are many French words which have not been translated or whose translations into English—approximate by necessity—could give rise to ambiguity. The term *mondaine* (translated, for the most part, as "worldly") did not then imply a pejorative judgment, as it might today. I have used the word "salon" to denote the room in which polite society gathered, although the term was not commonly used in France until the end of the eighteenth century. The *ancien régime* had no vocabulary to describe a reception room other than the generic term *maison* (house) or the very specific *ruelle* (little corridor), which denoted the space between the bed and the wall and was made fashionable by the *Précieuses*, who received in their bedrooms. Rather than name a physical space, one referred to the people who occasionally constituted a *cercle, assemblée, société*, or *compagnie*. Yet none of these words (with the possible exception of "circle") lends itself to unambiguous translation.

Another anachronism to which I have occasionally had recourse—for the simple sake of variety—is the word "aristocracy," which was coined as a word of deprecation at the time of the French Revolution. Under the *ancien régime* only the word "nobility" existed to designate the Second Estate.

In the English edition, much as I did in the book's original Italian, we chose to leave certain essentially untranslatable terms in the French. First among these is that key word of seventeenth-century culture *honnêteté*, a word that encompasses both ethics and aesthetics, as readers will realize, with the balance varying enormously depending on the circumstances. In English, "honest" stresses the moral connotations (as in an "honest man"). Terms stemming from the word *galant*—which embodies far more social nuance that the English "gallant"—present the same difficulty. As I discuss in Chapter 13, *galant* can even embody drastically different meanings: from gentlemanly (as in *galant homme*), to flirtatious (*galanterie* or *homme galant*), to compromised (*femme galante*). More subtly resistant to translation is the word *esprit*, which embraces a vast gamut of meanings, from spiritual, intellectual, and speculative to witty, ironic, and brilliant. The list of modifying adjectives attached to it (*bel esprit, esprit railleur, esprit fin*...) are of little help to the translator. We have employed words such as "wit," "intelligence," "mind," and "spirit," where circumstances permit, but in many cases it seemed more suitable to retain the French word, merely specifying the various meanings.

The words *politesse* and *bienséances* present similar difficulties. The former may be rendered in English as "courtesy," "manners," or "politeness," though it is useful for the reader to recall that *politesse* came into use as a more flexible and nuanced alternative to the old-fashioned term *courtoisie*. As for *bienséances*, to simply translate this as "good manners" or "propriety" fails to evoke the complexity of the awareness required to put such manners into practice. Similarly we have almost always kept the French words *raillerie*—denoting everything from "joking" and "jesting" to good-natured "teasing" and "satire"—and *enjouement*, a word related to the ancient Greek *eutrapelia*, which implies a concentration of high-spiritedness, vivacity, and gaiety. For more extensive clarification of the terms and concepts left in French—from *préciosité* to *sociabilité* to the distinction, borrowed from Erich Auerbach, between *cour* and *ville*—we invite the reader to refer to the bibliographical notes.

It is fitting that a book whose theme is conversation should owe so much to conversation, to the exchange of ideas, and to the suggestions of friends. The idea for the book was born of an invitation from Eugenio Scalfari in 1987 to write a series of articles for the newspaper *La Repubblica* on French salons under the *ancien régime* and from Roberto Calasso's suggestion that I collect them into an "instant book" with a small accompanying anthology of texts. Although the "instant book" took more than fifteen years to complete—its pages having multiplied along the way—my publisher at Adelphi never changed his mind, and by entrusting me to the care of Ena Marchi and Pia Cigala Fulgosi, ensured that *La Civiltà della Conversazione* had the benefit of extremely rigorous and competent editing.

An uninterrupted dialogue with friends who are scholars of the seventeenth century has been of great importance to me throughout these years: Marc Fumaroli, whose work has provided a constant point of reference in my research; and Benedetta Papàsogli, Barbara Piqué, and Louis van Delft, all of whom read and discussed what I was writing, offering precious advice as I progressed. Giuseppe Galasso and Bernard Minoret are probably the two whose patience and friendship I put most severely to the test. They were the first to take upon themselves the task of reading the typescript and, as victims of their own knowledge, were subjected to an interminable series of historical, dynastic, and genealogical questions. Robert Silvers's kindness also made it possible for me, through *The New York Review of Books*, to obtain with the greatest ease books and articles that have appeared in the United States on subjects relevant to my research. I am likewise indebted to Francesco Scaglione for his help in checking the texts quoted from the Bibliothèque Nationale de France and to Gaetano Lettieri for his clarification of the Jansenist debate concerning the Augustinian interpretation of grace.

The French edition, elegantly translated by Éliane Deschamps-Pria, has also contributed to the English edition and was ably shepherded by Georges Liébert of Gallimard. In New York, Robert Silvers and publisher Rea Hederman at New York Review Books decided to bring the book to an American audience and chose for the translation to rely on the talent of Teresa Waugh, who also translated my biography of Mme du Deffand. They were assisted by a team that included Sylvia Lonergan, Borden Elniff, Miranda Robbins, and Michael Shae.

To all these friends, I would like to express, from the bottom of my heart, my most affectionate gratitude.

—Benedetta Craveri

I

A WAY OF LIFE

ONE DAY IN 1627, Catherine de Vivonne, Marquise de Rambouillet, received a surprise visit from Père Joseph, the éminence grise of Cardinal de Richelieu, Louis XIII's chief of state. Tallemant des Réaux recounts in his important collection of historical anecdotes how the powerful friar, having paid his initial respects, explained the reasons for his presence at the marquise's home in the rue Saint-Thomas-du-Louvre. Richelieu had charged him with conveying to her his gratification at the important diplomatic negotiations then being conducted in Spain by her husband, Monsieur de Rambouillet, and the cardinal reconfirmed his goodwill toward her and her husband. In exchange, however, he asked that she "grant His Excellency a small satisfaction that he desired of her; a prime minister could not take too many precautions; in a word, Monsieur le Cardinal wished to know, through her, of the intrigues between Madame la Princesse [de Condé] and Monsieur le Cardinal de La Valette."

Mme de Rambouillet's reply was categorical: she firmly believed that the two people in question were innocent of all intrigue, but even if she were mistaken, she "would not be too well suited to the business of spying."[1]

In fact, Richelieu's request was not so outrageous, when we consider the era in which it was made. In an age of plotting, volte-face, and continuous bargaining between the high-ranking nobility and the monarchy, at a time when Louis XIII's minister was busy recalling the rebellious nobility to order with threats of prison and the executioner's ax, the cardinal was suggesting an entirely normal exchange of favors. He was asking the marquise to demonstrate her loyalty to the throne in a tangible way, while offering her and her husband a guarantee of royal favor in exchange. The memoirs of the Cardinal de Retz and the Duc de La Rochefoucauld both offer ample testimony to the nobility's unscrupulousness in matters of

---

1. Tallemant des Réaux, *Historiettes*, edited by Antoine Adam, two volumes (Paris: Gallimard/Bibliothèque de la Pléiade, 1960–1961), Vol. 1, p. 444.

loyalty and obedience to the sovereign and show how family interests generally prevailed over those of king and country. In this case, however, Mme de Rambouillet's flat refusal to spy for Cardinal de Richelieu was not an act of aristocratic defiance. Whatever they may have felt privately about Louis XIII and his chief minister, the Rambouillets were loyal subjects, as they would subsequently prove during the Fronde Rebellion. Their house was no place of intrigue and sedition. The marquise was merely claiming the right to her own private freedom—the right to live as and with whom she pleased in her own home. And yet, her action set an important precedent. Through her, civil society proclaimed its independence from politics and denied the prevailing powers the right to interfere in private life.

Richelieu, for his part, understandably wished to be kept informed of what went on in the marquise's celebrated "Blue Room." Despite his keen political intuition, however, he could not have known that the plot being hatched—for there was indeed a plot—had nothing to do with the old logic of power. It had no need of ministers, armies, or wealth but depended purely on the exchange of ideas. Nor had the plot yet found a name. It would come to be called Opinion, but it was not until a century later that it would threaten the established order.

It may seem arbitrary to attach such symbolic significance to an episode, one of hundreds, recounted by Tallemant; but as a conceit, it corresponds perfectly with Mme de Rambouillet's legend. The marquise's own contemporaries were the first to claim her significance and to realize that a new civilization for fashionable society was being born in her home, a way of life that would serve as a model for the French elites. It was Mme de Rambouillet who, in the words of the poet and novelist Jean Regnault de Segrais, "corrected the wicked customs that went before her [and] taught *politesse* to all those of her time who visited her."[2] The definition of *politesse* that appeared in the first edition of the *Dictionnaire de l'Académie française* of 1694 expresses the full importance of the concept. Rather than consisting of a mere collection of precepts, *politesse* constituted "a certain courteous, honest, and polite way of living, acting, and speaking acquired through usage in society." It could only be learned or taught through practice and a process of initiation. And it was precisely in the hôtel de Rambouillet that this way of life first came to embody an ideal.

Today, the Marquise de Rambouillet is widely granted the distinction of having founded what came to be known as polite society and of presiding over its first center for more than forty years. Reiterated in countless books, the claim has come to be taken for granted and for that very reason deserves to be revisited. How, precisely, did Mme de Rambouillet acquire this honor? More than one private mansion of the sixteenth century had provided a stage for noble pastimes and

---

2. Jean Regnault de Segrais, *Segraisiana ou mélange d'histoire et de littérature* (The Hague: Pierre Gosse, 1722), p. 26.

learned conversation. The marquise was, moreover, hardly the only woman of her day to nourish the ambition of making her house into a cultural and worldly center. The enterprising Vicomtesse d'Auchy, intent on immortalizing her own name, had already held a salon frequented largely by poets. The most illustrious of them, François de Malherbe, celebrated her as "Calliste" in his work. His admiration for her was not, however, entirely platonic, and in 1609 she was banished by a husband to whom literary prestige meant little to the town of Saint-Quentin. Mme d'Auchy's mantle was promptly assumed by Mme des Loges, a Protestant of the recent nobility. In her drawing room, the reputation of which was equal to Mme de Rambouillet's, the cream of the literary world gathered in the 1620s. Malherbe and his followers—Honorat de Bueil de Racan, François Le Metel de Boisrobert, and Antoine Godeau—assembled there, as did the "modernist" writers Guez de Balzac, Nicolas Faret, and Claude Favre de Vaugelas. Mme des Loges's circle in the rue de Tournon, however, did not limit itself to literary interests but was passionate about religion and politics. It did nothing to hide its sympathy for the Duc d'Orléans, Louis XIII's rebellious brother. It was precisely for her salon's standing as a center of opposition that the cardinal ordered Mme des Loges into exile in 1629.

What was novel about Mme de Rambouillet's decision to open her doors to a certain number of regular guests was the fact that a personal idiosyncrasy dictated her decision. She was profoundly ill at ease in the royal receptions at the Louvre. The marquise had abandoned the position due to her by rank at court and withdrawn from public life. Paradoxically, the awakening of her worldly vocation coincided with a *retreat* from the world stage and a conscious distancing of herself from court life. The polemical nature of this initial gesture did not escape her contemporaries. "It was not that she disliked *divertissement*," wrote Tallemant, but that she wanted it to "take place in private. That is quite a strange thing for a young and beautiful person of quality. Mme de Rambouillet had been one of the beauties who took part in the ceremonies when Henri IV had Marie de' Medici crowned."[3] It is not unreasonable to assume that—alongside the explanations offered by successive pregnancies and increasingly delicate health, and despite the marquise's own complaints of the throng and the disorder at the Louvre—the honor of having taken part in the more memorable occasions of Henri IV's reign may have contributed considerably to her detachment.

A closer look at the pleasures, the spirit, and the language of the court of the great king who had brought peace to France after almost four decades of religious strife provides some notion of why Mme de Rambouillet may have wished to withdraw. It was, apparently, a way of life that profoundly disgusted her. Tallemant recounts that at the age of twenty-one, Mme de Rambouillet, along with the

---

3. Tallemant, *Historiettes*, Vol. 1, p. 442.

barely adolescent Mlle de Montmorency and the very young Mlle Paulet—both of whom became her close friends—had taken part in the famous *ballet de la Reine* at Saint-Germain-en-Laye on January 31, 1609, as nymphs in a cortege leading the imprisoned cupid.[4] Neither the splendor of the choreography nor the fact that Malherbe had honored the festivities with his verse could diminish the brutishness of the King's appetites or the scandal that soon became attached to the ceremony. Henri IV, while waiting for his scheme to sleep with Mlle de Montmorency to develop (under cover of a marriage in which he contrived to take the bridegroom's place), turned his attention to Mlle Paulet, who was, as Tallemant tells us, singing exquisitely, half naked, astride a dolphin. Contrary to the popular ditty going around at the time, it was the King himself—and not his son, the Dauphin—who "went to bed with the beautiful singer that she might sing beneath him; and everyone agreed that his wish was satisfied."[5]

To control violent instincts, to build defenses against life's brutality, and to establish a code of behavior that might act as an invisible shield between one person and another so as to protect everyone's dignity—these were not the personal aspirations of one refined noblewoman. On the contrary, an entire caste demanded it—a warring caste that had laid down arms after the long and bloody fratricidal struggle of the wars of religion (1562–1598), without, however, succeeding in eradicating violence from everyday life. Mlle de Gournay, Montaigne's adoptive daughter, musing despairingly on the reasons for such brutality, saw the primary cause as the right to carry a sword—the aristocrat's badge. "The power, and consequently the audacity, conferred on noblemen by this sword, which they wear on their hips, are powers that, except in the case of a few superior minds, go to men's heads."[6]

The civilizing impetus that began to make itself felt in the second decade of the seventeenth century was not motivated by practical necessity alone but belonged to a far broader and more complex notion concerning the identity of the nobility, its social image, and the different role allotted to it within the framework of the modern monarchy. Deprived of its old certainties, the French nobility was obliged to rethink itself and to redefine itself by means of a spectacular metamorphosis.

How could the nobles but question their class identity? They had been deprived

4. Tallemant, *Historiettes*, Vol. 1, p. 69.

5. "*Qui fit le mieux du ballet?/Ce fut la petite Paulet/Montée sur le Dauphin,/Qui montera sur elle enfin.*" ("Who was best in the ballet?/It was the little Paulet/riding on the Dauphin/who in the end would ride her.") Tallemant des Réaux, *Historiettes*, Vol. 1, p. 474. The French word *dauphin* denotes both dolphin and the monarch's son and heir.

6. Mlle de Gournay, "De la Néantise des communes vaillances de ce temps, et du peu de prix de la qualité de la noblesse," in *Les Avis ou les présents de la damoiselle de Gournay*, second edition (Paris: T. du Bray, 1641), cited in Maurice Magendie, *La Politesse mondaine et les théories de l'honnêteté en France au XVIIe siècle, de 1600 à 1660* (1925; reprint, Geneva: Slatkine reprints, 1970), Vol. 1, p. 66.

of the very role that had heretofore constituted their essence: the permanent exercise of arms; royal power had forced them to pull down the walls of their own fortresses and forbidden them to draw their swords to defend their honor; war had become a profession and they, the nobility, had been reduced to the rank of king's officers. And how could they still identify with the monarch? He had ceased to be first among equals and, jealous of his own authority, had excluded the nobility from the world of politics, instead entrusting the kingdom's administration to obscure men who, although ambitious and servile, were arrogantly aware of representing royal authority?

As the American historian Davis Bitton has pointed out, "the French nobles, like the landed aristocrats in other countries, had faced problems of adjustment before. But the period stretching from 1560 to about 1640 was extraordinarily difficult. The transition that the nobility underwent during these years (which was a kind of 'identity crisis' with economic and social as well as psychological dimensions) coincided with the basic changes called to mind by such familiar phrases as the age of religious wars, the commercial revolution, and the scientific revolution."[7] The constantly rising prices that characterized the whole of the sixteenth century had had a disastrous effect on the nobility's revenues. Ever poorer and in ever greater debt, it in fact attempted to recoup its losses at the expense of the peasantry. This only fueled widespread resentment and did nothing to strengthen the position of the nobles within the kingdom.

Indeed, the peasants were not the only Frenchmen to question such privileges. For centuries, in return for the loan of militiamen, the nobility had been exempted from the *taille*, the tax that formed the basis of the French fiscal system from the Middle Ages until the Revolution. Now questions were being asked in various quarters as to whether they still played such an important part in the nation's defense. During the Hundred Years' War, with the creation of large armies permanently mobilized over vast areas, many commoners had had the chance to prove that they too could fight courageously, whereas the noble institution of the *ban et arrière-ban*—the mobilization of vassals on the king's orders—was fast falling into disuse. The nobility seemed increasingly unwilling to mobilize at the king's command, and many of its members hired substitutes to replace them on the battlefield. The very way of going to war, moreover, had changed. The classes were no longer segregated within military units. The role of the cavalry, where noblemen traditionally distinguished themselves, had been redefined by the newly attained importance of the infantry, which the nobility despised.

Affairs were no better for the nobles in the area of public administration and employment. In the courts of justice and local and provincial administration, endemic corruption favored the new rich commoners who were buying their way

---

7. Davis Bitton, *The French Nobility in Crisis, 1560–1640* (Stanford University Press, 1969), p. 1.

into office. The 1604 edict known as "la Paulette" regularizing the sale of offices and designating heirs to these offices constituted a real blow to the nobility's claims. Nevertheless its defensive strategy remained uncertain. If, on the one hand, *class* furnished an argument against corruption, then it also had to be taken into account that money was at the root of the growing number of plebeians infiltrating the nobility. The practice of raising commoners of the Third Estate to the rank of noblemen had always existed, but under Henri IV the phenomenon had grown to hitherto unknown proportions. If, on the other hand, *merit* was to be taken into account, it had to be admitted that many of the positions occupied by the bourgeoisie in the courts required a degree of learning and technical training that the nobility utterly lacked. In all probability, the very awareness of being deprived of a defined and recognizable social function and the difficulty of providing a rational justification for their privileges—combined with the vulnerability of their class to outsiders—persuaded most of the nobility not to contest the *loi de dérogeance*, which forbade them to participate in business or commerce. In fact, many welcomed it as a sign of superiority and distinction. But the law was cold comfort in the face of so dramatic an impasse. There was a time, as the scholar and historian Nicolas Pasquier wrote to Henri IV in 1610, when the nobility could hope to be rewarded for their services with positions of varying kinds. But now that all offices were corrupt, what could a young gentleman aspire to?[8]

In reply to these questions and uncertainties, and in reaction to its difficulties, the nobility redefined its ideology by taking the stress off valor—which it was no longer able to exercise fully—and placing it on the incontestable purity of lineage, thus emphasizing not the superiority of arms but the superiority of breeding. Nevertheless, in order to express itself, even superior lineage required a new code to reinforce the declining authority of the existing one. The outward signs of nobility—titles, positions, lands, palaces, clothing, and jewels—could no longer incontrovertibly indicate membership by right of a certain class, since they had come to be used in the traffic between the crown and the new men. The nobility's traditional prerogatives had lost their exclusivity and the occasions on which to vaunt them were limited to carousels and tournaments. Thus seeing themselves in an entirely new context, the nobility of the sword (the *noblesse d'épée*) chose to define itself through the treacherous domain of style. Henceforth it would be by their way of living, of speaking, of acting, of amusing themselves, of enjoying each other's company that the noble elite would persuade themselves of the unshakeable certainty of their own superiority. In place of arms, their touchstone would be provided by refined manners—*bienséances*—and by a body of unwritten law more powerful than any written one.

---

8. Nicolas Pasquier, in *Œuvres d'Estienne Pasquier*, two volumes (Amsterdam: Compagnie des Libraires associez, 1723), Vol. 2, p. 1072, cited in Bitton, *The French Nobility in Crisis*, p. 45.

It might be expected that the locus of such a metamorphosis would be the Louvre, where the nobility still held the highest honorary positions. It was, after all, in the splendor of her small courts that sixteenth-century Italy had developed a culture of fine manners and thereby earned the admiration of all Europe. The transalpine success of the great Italian pedagogic texts—Giovanni della Casa's *Galateo* of 1560, Baldassare Castiglione's *Book of the Courtier* of 1528, and Stefano Guazzo's *Civil Conversation* of 1574—bore eloquent testimony to France's desire to take the lesson to heart. But it was in looking back to the Valois, as it frequently would in the course of the seventeenth century, that France found closer to home a prestigious example of court society to serve as its national model.

After the death of Henri IV and the turbulent, uncertain years of Marie de' Medici's regency that followed, the monarchy could hardly remain indifferent to the insubordination, arrogance, and violence that continued to mark the nobility's behavior throughout the country. As soon as he appeared on the political scene, Cardinal de Richelieu proposed to reestablish order in the state and to revive the forms of courtesy due to the king and his officers—manners already fully formulated by tradition. But his mission to educate was motivated by something quite distinct from the self-exaltation that motivated the aristocracy. Brushing aside arguments in a debate going back to the Middle Ages concerning the relationship between the monarch and the knighthood and between the king and the state, Richelieu saw to it that the old codes of courtesy were made into an instrument of coercion and control in the service of absolutism. The nobility, first and foremost, would be bridled by a thousand points of etiquette. The cardinal minister was too aware of the symbolic function of the trappings of office not to know that a great monarchy must be reflected in the elegance of its language, the excellence of its cultural and artistic institutions, the prestige of its literature, and, of course, the splendor of its court. As his economic policy shows, Richelieu had no wish whatsoever to deprive the nobility of its standing, provided that that standing reflected the monarchy's own prestige. His sole condition was that the nobility learn to be courtiers.

Given these premises, the nobility was bound to feel the need to regain an area of freedom away from the dominion of the court in which to celebrate only themselves. And it was in this new area, within the social world, that the regeneration of the usages and customs of modern French society began, under the banner of amusement rather than authority.

The eminent Swiss scholar Jean Starobinski has stressed the playful impetus at the origins of the classical doctrine of French *civilité*. In their efforts to palliate the violence of everyday life, the aristocratic elite had in fact discovered that "the *conventional* repudiation of the potential for aggression" could not only make life less dangerous but could also produce pleasure. According to Starobinski, "a protected space is thus created, an enclosed field where by common accord the partners to a relationship refrain from attacking or injuring one another in ordinary commerce as well as in matters having to do with love. The crucial idea, to use an anachronistic terminology, is one of maximization of pleasure. The loss that the amorous instinct incurs owing to repression and sublimation is counterbalanced, according to the theory of *honnêteté*, by the eroticization of everyday intercourse, conversation, and epistolary exchange. The doctrine of *honnêteté* aestheticizes 'instinctual renunciation.'"[9] Well before it culminated in theoretical formulations or found expression in novels, the nobility's uncertain quest to fulfill itself in a new way of life discovered a "protected space" of amusement in which to measure itself for the first time, under the guidance of women, in the complicit and exclusive game of worldliness.

---

9. Jean Starobinski, "On Flattery," in *Blessings in Disguise, or, The Morality of Evil*, translated by Arthur Goldhammer (Harvard University Press, 1993), p. 36.

2

DAUGHTERS OF EVE

THE FIRST FRENCH Renaissance nude (circa 1540–1547), the work of Jean Cousin, braves the curiosity of visitors to the Louvre with sublime indifference. Her face is in profile, like the face on a classical cameo, her glance fixed on something outside our field of vision. The beautiful young woman, lying on her right side, the top half of her body slightly raised, as if she were reclining on a couch, appears remote and inaccessible. An ambiguous veil shields her innocent nakedness. This could be a portrait of Venus if the inscription hanging from the bosky arch that frames the background did not clearly read "Eva Prima Pandora." On close inspection, the painting has no winged putti armed with bows and arrows. Indeed, there is nothing to suggest any association of amorous fantasy with this splendid body. Instead, the woman's symbolic trappings are decidedly disturbing. The little apple branch she holds in her right hand could, of course, seem innocent. She rests her elbow on a skull; a serpent encircles her left arm. Two elegantly carved funerary urns provide the grotto's only ornaments.

Not Venus, then, but Eve and Pandora are symbiotically embodied in this perfect nude. Two cultural traditions—the classical mythological tradition and the biblical one—unite and evolve in Cousin's painting to warn sixteenth-century man of the insidious nature of feminine beauty. Woman is the fount of all evil, bearer not only of life but also of death, bringing with her devastation and sin. Cousin's precise historical references seem to confirm that her malice is stronger than the chains by which society attempts to discipline her, and that her seduction is more powerful than the interdicts circumscribing her actions. The Louvre's Eve-Pandora is close in style to Benvenuto Cellini's bronze lunette of a nymph-huntress reclining on a stag, the celebrated *Nymph of Fontainebleau* (1543). This work, commissioned by François I, soon found its way to Diane de Poitiers's château at Anet. *Eva Prima Pandora* accentuates its own metaphysical misogyny by alluding to the greatest scandal of the day: Diane, the most seductive of all the seductive women of her times, was the extremely powerful mistress of the future Henri II.

Surprising as it may seem, the French Renaissance did not mark a step forward for the female condition. On the social plain, the return to Roman law was distinctly unfavorable to women, gravely weakening their legal position. On the spiritual plain, women, who had long been active in religious life through their charitable works and in the proliferating minor religious orders, found themselves deprived of both spontaneity and autonomy. The Counter-Reformation forbade women to make public display of their religious vocation. Nor could they organize themselves into communities. They could now serve God only inside convents, under the rigorous spiritual control of male clerics.

Misogyny, deeply rooted in religious thinking, now found authoritative corroboration in the rediscovery of classical ideas. Aristotle had theorized about the congenital imperfections of the female nature. The Pythagorean tradition saw in woman the lunar, dark face of the universe, in contrast to man's sunny, positive nature—a scientific and philosophical view of woman seen to be perfectly in keeping with Christian theology's antifeminism. Not only did the "daughters of Eve" separate man from the rational order; they kept him from divine grace as well. "The power of the devil is in [their] loins," wrote Montaigne, citing Saint Jerome.[1] Woman, in short, was a negative force that needed to be dominated. But the fear she inspired was also an acknowledgment of her importance in social life.

At the dawn of the sixteenth century, however, neither control nor prohibition nor suspicion had prevented the daughters of Eve-Pandora from hatching a new plot that, within a century, would bring them unprecedented power, a power that would remain unique in the history of Europe. It is true that Renaissance Italy had made room for women—as much within the courts as in the worlds of prostitution and illicit pleasure—but they had been kept well away from civil society. The presence of women in the public arena remained extremely controversial and was always couched in ambiguous formulas such as "honest courtesan," an expression whose very history speaks for itself. In *The Book of the Courtier* (1528), the great book on courtly style that served as a model of behavior for the elite of Europe, Baldassare Castiglione never used the term *cortegiano* (courtier) in the feminine form. Women—even those whose presence had contributed to making the pastimes of the small ducal court of Urbino into works of art—were generally described indirectly as "palace ladies." Indeed, Castiglione could not have used the expression *cortegiana* (courtesan) without implying the exact opposite of the courtly ideal. With the exception of a few isolated noblewomen—Giulia Gonzaga, Vittoria Colonna, or Isabella d'Este, for example—the only women in Italian Renaissance society permitted to make a public display of their beauty or intellect

---

1. Saint Jerome, *Contre Jovinien*, II, cited in "On Some Lines of Virgil," Book III, Chapter 5, in *The Essays of Montaigne*, translated by E. J. Trechmann, two volumes (Oxford University Press/Humphrey Milford, 1935), Vol. 2, p. 319.

were prostitutes. The closer they came to Castiglione's ideal of the palace ladies in refinement, culture, and elegance, and the further removed they were from vulgar whores, the more they became part of the superior social class of the "honest courtesan." There was, in fact, only one basic difference between the "palace lady" and the "honest courtesan." The former was permitted to play with love so long as it remained sublimated; the latter, choosing to be more down to earth, disposed as freely of her body as of her soul. Both ways of life, however, remained in blatant contrast to the customs of the ruling social classes, which ordained the separation of male and female realms, with woman's field of action confined to her private life.

In sixteenth-century France, where the Renaissance was at least fifty years behind Italy, noblewomen were more liberally treated. There, unlike in Italy and Spain, women did not live in traditional isolation from men, nor were they excluded from social life. Although their role in public was essentially a decorative one, they were not exiles. Several women had already contributed to true centers of humanist culture, and the feminine presence had made a real contribution to the splendor of the Valois monarchy. In the reign of François I (to the indignation of François de Fénelon, one of the outstanding writers and theologians of the seventeenth century), the court had begun to expand beyond the King's narrow family circle and was increasingly open to women. Their beauty, elegance, and grace destined them to preside as much over courtly splendor as over the weakening moral order that characterized Catherine de' Medici's long period of influence. They were mothers, wives, sisters, and lovers who, within the closed world of the court, and in keeping with an old tradition, enjoyed a certain freedom—and sometimes an abusive power—based on the ability to impose by persuasion and seduction.

During the first decades of the seventeenth century, however, the significance of women in French society changed. They were no longer obliged to fight gradually for a questionable sphere of influence beyond the confines of domesticity, but took upon themselves the leadership of society. Henceforth, women would decide matters of manners, language, taste, and *loisirs*—the array of noble pastimes that included reading, conversation, theater and the arts, games, and dancing. In short, they would define the outstanding characteristics of aristocratic style. It was a spectacular revolution, rich in consequences and destined to characterize French society until the end of the *ancien régime*. Many contemporaries welcomed its purifying and civilizing process, but certain observers immediately perceived its dangers. From the beginning of the 1640s, the writer François de Grenaille sounded the alarm. The conversation of women "polishes men," he wrote, "but softens them."[2] Jean-François Sarasin, in his five-voice dialogue *S'il faut que un jeune homme soit*

2. François de Grenaille, *L'honneste garçon* (Paris: T. Quinet, 1642), p. 229, cited in Peter Burke, *The Art of Conversation* (Cornell University Press, 1993), p. 116.

Amoureux, had one of the interlocutors—his friend the Abbé Gilles Ménage—sketch the caricature of some *petits-maîtres*—young fashionable nobles: "We find them occupied, like women, in doing their hair and in dressing up, and all this with such indecent softness that they leave us to wonder not only whether they are men, but whether they are not themselves looking for other men."[3] Fénelon perceived as serious the far deeper and more widespread phenomenon, which Louis XIV was able to turn to good political advantage: the feminization of a society through idleness and *loisirs*. "Softness," he wrote, "removes from a man anything that may contribute to outstanding qualities. A soft man is not a man but a half-woman."[4] Jean-Jacques Rousseau in his renowned *Lettre à d'Alembert sur les spectacles*, written exactly a hundred years after Ménage's disparaging remarks, described this female appropriation of power in the severest terms: Parisian society had turned upside down; the natural relationship between men and women appeared to be totally subverted. "Meanly devoted to the wills of the sex which we ought to protect and not serve, we have learned to despise it in obeying it, to insult it by our derisive attentions; and every woman in Paris gathers in her apartment a harem of men more womanish than she."[5] Had the misogynist fears dreamed up in the past by theologians and moralists finally been realized? Having seduced the sons of Adam by their diabolical art, had the daughters of Eve-Pandora succeeded in perverting their very nature? Had they enfeebled them and reduced them to slavery?

It is highly unlikely that the increasing influence of women in high society arose from any conscious plot against traditional male authority. From the legal, religious, and moral point of view, women continued to live in France, as they did in the rest of Europe, under conditions of crushing inferiority compared to men. Subjected first to paternal and then to marital authority, they could neither dispose of themselves as they pleased nor offer their opinion with regard to the basic decisions that determined their existence. The only freedom allowed them was that of renouncing the world and retiring to a convent. Some could see no alternative to taking their own lives. The very establishment of women in society, far from constituting a bid for power, reflected, in the first place, the attitudes of male culture.

Seen in the light of the old feudal traditions, woman's position of objective inferiority lent itself to an unexpected reversal. Precisely because of their delicacy,

---

3. Jean-François Sarasin, *Les Œuvres de Monsieur Sarasin publiées par Ménage, Préface de [Paul] Pellisson*, second edition (Rouen, Paris: Augustin Courbé, 1658), p. 176.

4. François de Salignac de La Mothe Fénelon, *Lettres spirituelles de Fénelon*, letter 34, in *Œuvres complètes, précédées par son histoire littéraire par M. Gosselin, 1851–1852* (Geneva: Slatkine Reprints, 1971), Vol. 8, p. 472.

5. Jean-Jacques Rousseau, "Letter to d'Alembert," in *Letter to d'Alembert and Writings for the Theater*, translated by Allan Bloom, Charles Butterworth, and Christopher Kelly (University Press of New England, 2004), p. 236.

defenselessness, and need of protection, women, according to the nobility's concept of chivalrous honor, were the ideal objects of homage. Manners had, of course, changed considerably since the days of the medieval *cours d'amour* (courts of love), but when it came time to redefine its lifestyle and behavioral codes, the French nobility looked back to the ideal of its origins. It also turned to the more recent discovery by the Renaissance elite of the Neoplatonic, idealizing conception of love as an instrument of spiritual elevation, illustrated by Honoré d'Urfé in his extremely successful pastoral novel *L'Astrée*. Unlike the antifeminism typical of popular opinion and narrow-minded bourgeois morality, the aristocratic ethic pledged faithfulness to a feminine model that, instead of representing the dangers of the fallen woman, presented an exalted ideal. There was no room here for base instinct. Only the civilizing power of culture was recognized.

In this tradition, then, homage offered to women represented first and foremost an important means of establishing masculine honor and was, at the same time, evidence of social distinction. Mythologized, revered, and adulated, a woman became an indispensable component of the nobleman's lifestyle: masculine pride's finest trophy. After the barbarous, fratricidal wars of religion, to revive the chivalrous tradition and to reestablish it within the antifeudal framework of a centralized and modern monarchy presupposed, above all, the cooperation of the fair sex. But French womanhood had reacted to the previous century's endemic violence by closing in on itself and withdrawing within the confines of its own culture. It remained, moreover, excluded from political and civil responsibilities as well as from learning.

Men were the first to realize the risks of female isolation, which deprived them of a joyful, sportive element to their existence. It was essentially in the name of a stricter concept of masculine pleasure that Montaigne wished for an exchange between the sexes based on equality and understanding: "Let us teach the ladies to make the most of themselves, to observe self-respect, to keep us in suspense and fool us.... He who finds no enjoyment except in enjoyment, who wins nothing unless he sweeps the stakes, who loves the chase only for the sake of the quarry, has no business to intrude into our school."[6]

Montaigne's thinking anticipated the future. Before long, men and women of the French nobility would be practicing the same game together, the game of *galanterie*—"gallantry." What was that game if not "the chase," divested of all violence and deprived of the joy of possession? In it, masculine valor was measured against his ardor as a hunter and woman's valor by her capacity to escape the desires of her pursuer. Contrary to what Montaigne thought, however, it was a game in which women had no need of instruction. The men had only to consent for the women to be ready, not only to "put themselves forward" but also to

6. "On Some Lines of Virgil," in *Essays*, translated by E. J. Trechmann, Vol. 2, p. 341.

become mistresses of their art. This was true to such a degree that only a few decades later, the gist of the problem as Montaigne had described it had been turned upside down. Opinion almost unanimously held that only women were capable of teaching the art of gallantry and good manners and of teaching men how to behave in society.

In a fine book about the education of aristocratic girls under the *ancien régime*, Paule Constant has described in detail the feminine culture handed down from mother to daughter, which prepared girls to proudly accept the immutable destiny due to their sex and social standing:

> The world is certainly made for men; in it they take priority. Young ladies must consent to this.... Yet they learn that they have their place among the men, that they are the gentle contrast to man's violence and the strength to their weakness. The difference does not imply exclusion but is presented to them as being complimentary and sometimes, on condition they carry out all their duties, crucial. They are therefore dispensers of happiness, guardians of virtue, protectors of morality, and, by dint of circumstance, mistresses of the world in which men are masters.[7]

Before belonging to themselves, aristocratic girls belonged to their families, the history and importance of which they had learned at an early age. They thus compensated for the inferior condition of their sex by stressing their superiority of rank. Education contributed toward the development in young women of an awareness of aristocratic identity. In her diary begun in 1773 when she was just ten years old, the little Polish princess Hélène Massalska, a pupil at the Parisian convent of l'Abbaye-aux-Bois, recorded a telling exchange between the abbess and one of her pupils. "When I see you do that, I could kill you," said Mme de Richelieu to her nine-year-old pupil, Mlle de Montmorency; to which the child replied, "It would not be the first time that the Richelieus were executioners of the Montmorencys."[8] The death of an illustrious ancestor, sent to the scaffold 150 years earlier by Cardinal de Richelieu, was ingrained in the child's memory, merely awaiting an opportunity for passionate acclaim.

At home, as in the convent, the education given to women was decided by the position they would occupy in society. And this education, so strongly influenced by an awareness of and a pride in social standing, usually persuaded the *demoiselles* calmly to accept arranged marriages based not on love but on lineage. In fact, unlike the daughters of the bourgeoisie, aristocratic young women were totally

7. Paule Constant, *Un Monde à l'usage des demoiselles* (Paris: Gallimard, 1987), p. 22.

8. Lucien Perey, *Histoire d'une grande dame au XVIIIe siècle, la Princesse Hélène de Ligne* (Paris: Calmann-Lévy, 1887), p. 76.

unaccustomed to questioning their feelings. In Mme de Lafayette's novel, Mlle de Chartres, on being consulted by her mother, readily accepted becoming the Princesse de Clèves although she had not the slightest attraction to her future husband.[9] Indeed, such feeling would have had an element of impropriety about it, to say nothing of the ridiculous. In a union designed to strengthen family prestige, to preserve fortunes, and to perpetuate the name and the line, sentiment could even be damaging. For those bound even in the most unhappy unions, there was comfort in joining an illustrious family. But in the education of girls, the social imperative and moral integrity went hand in hand with warnings against the dangers of "society."

Here we are faced with the first of the obvious contradictions inherent in the condition of noblewomen, one which helped to make them the virtuosos of social appearance. From a religious and moral point of view, girls' education concentrated on obedience, modesty, chastity, reserve, fear of men, and guarding against the passions. At the same time that traditional misogynist thinking continued to characterize women as irrational and impure, feminine society now saw itself in a completely opposite light. In the maternal home and within the convent walls, generation after generation of girls could live out a few utopian years, chaste and virtuous, according to the model of the cult of Mary. Generally, this age of innocence ended abruptly with a young woman's debut in society. But since everyone knew such a debut to be essential, infinite care was taken to see that *demoiselles* were equipped to resist the flattery of society while gaining both its admiration and its homage.

If infinite pains were taken to strengthen the spirit against inevitable assault, no less attention was paid to refining girls' minds and molding their bodies. Corsets, bodices, and whalebones corrected too undistinguished a figure and reproduced a distinct shape with sloping shoulders, narrow hips, and a straight back. Dancing and deportment lessons imparted a deftness of bearing, since heavy court dress, long trains, and precarious hairstyles required an artful gait and considerable training. The obligations of "appearance" were, of course, not limited to producing physical style and elegant gestures but placed equal emphasis on the art of speaking. Here too, the apprenticeship began in early childhood, drawing on the purity of the mother tongue and a system of transmitting feminine culture, which was essentially oral and suited to pedagogic conversation.

There remained the problem of what to say. Women's learning was limited, and any personalization in discussion was considered dangerous. It was essential to avoid drawing attention to oneself, since individual identity depended primarily on social identity and every word could be treacherous: "Whatsoever the distinction, it attracts the attention of men; their interest engenders talk, and such talk, whether advantageous or disagreeable, flatters or tickles the vanity, thus giving

9. Mme de Lafayette, *The Princesse de Clèves* (1678), translated by Robin Buss (Penguin, 1962), p. 39.

rise to temptations capable of leading to various mistakes."[10] There was, however, one language common to both sexes capable of resolving, at least on a formal level, the first of the two great contradictions facing noblewomen, who were expected not only to devote themselves to God while living in the world but to provide a spectacle while giving nothing of themselves away. This was the language of *politesse*, a subtle language involving both the body and the mind, both voice and gesture. The fair sex would use it as a sign of belonging to the nobility, as a shield for their own reputation, and as a measure of worth.

The *Introduction à la vie dévote*, written by Saint François de Sales in 1609 for a woman of high birth called upon to live in society, went so far as to propose making *politesse* a Christian virtue. Until then, he wrote, "those who treat of devotion have nearly all considered the instruction of persons entirely withdrawn from worldly commerce, or have at least taught a kind of devotion that leads to such total retreat."[11] The time had come, he continued, to take into account that for many, such "commerce" seemed an inevitable choice and that women needed help in leading a worldly life in harmony with their religious faith, not in antithesis to it. Expressions of *politesse*, "the face and words embellished by joy, gaiety and civility,"[12] could then become the expression of the soul and bear eloquent witness to the presence of God. Destined to a great future, the *Introduction* did not merely legitimize from a religious point of view the active participation of women in society. It also contributed toward typifying such a life by the attributes of feminine virtue.

A great deal thus predisposed noblewomen to play an important part in strengthening aristocratic identity. Their values and their virtues were at the service of a class culture and complemented the heroic, warrior qualities of the male world. With traditional male values in a period of crisis, however, women found themselves unexpectedly in the limelight. There were two reasons for this: because the chivalrous deference paid them was a conscious gesture of loyalty to the old feudal ways, in implicit conflict with contemporary attitudes; and because, with the redefinition of the aristocratic way of life, traditionally feminine values like *politesse* became of critical importance for men as well.

Women were therefore allowed to take control of the new social environment that had come into being halfway between the official life of the court and the straightforwardly domestic world of the private house. The territory required continual guarding, and its autonomy had to be protected—as much from the

10. Pierre Nicole, letter 3, *Lettres choisies* (Liège: J. F. Bronkart, 1706), p. 15, cited in Constant, *Un Monde à l'usage des demoiselles*, p. 233.

11. Saint François de Sales, preface to *Introduction à la vie dévote* (1609), in *Œuvres*, edited by André Ravier (Paris: Gallimard/Bibliothèque de la Pléiade, 1969), p. 24.

12. Saint François de Sales, *Introduction à la vie devote*, p. 201.

unwarranted pressures of the outside world as from the intimate disorders of the heart.

Women's new-found prestige, destined as it was to be exercised over an extremely changeable and treacherous terrain, had an inherent ambiguity. Its authority was based on simple convention and depended more or less on obligatory choices. Was it by virtue of their excellence or their weakness that women merited the homage of men? The fact remains that in the new cultural climate, their frailty could be turned to strength and their initial disadvantages to unexpected opportunities for recognition. For instance, the correct use of *bienséances*—decorum—was primarily a weapon of defense and only secondarily a mark of social distinction. Women had become the most faithful custodians of the rules of behavior, since only those rules —consecrated by usage—could better their inferior position. Noblewomen were skilled at maintaining a delicate balance between custom and the law and were used to entrusting their prestige and reputation to their ability to interpret what today would be termed a collective class or caste sensibility. They thus acquired the consummate art of nuance, which naturally allowed them to excel in the game of society.

Madeleine de Scudéry, the seventeenth-century novelist, denounced in no uncertain terms the conditions of ignorance in which women were purposely held: "Those who own slaves instruct them for their [own] convenience; and yet they whom Nature or custom has given us as masters would have us extinguish in our minds all the brilliance that Heaven has put there and would have us live in the heaviest shadows of ignorance," she wrote in *Les Femmes illustres* (1642).[13] Even after a century of female social successes, this situation had not basically altered. Mme du Deffand, celebrated for her mordant and outspoken wit, complained bitterly about it in her correspondence with her good friends Voltaire and Horace Walpole; and again, in 1771, an indignant Mme d'Épinay echoed Mlle de Scudéry, in a beautiful letter to the Abbé Galiani:

> I am very ignorant; that is the fact of the matter. My entire education was concerned with developing talents to make me agreeable.... The reputation of a woman with a *bel esprit* seems to me no more than a mockery invented by men to avenge the fact that women generally have more wit than they do; so much so that to this epithet [witty] is almost always added the idea of the learned woman, and the most learned woman has—can indeed only have— very superficial learning.... So I say that a woman, by the mere fact of being a woman, is not able to acquire sufficient knowledge to be of use to her

---

13. Madeleine de Scudéry, "Sappho to Erinna," in *Selected Letters, Orations, and Rhetorical Dialogues*, translated by Jane Donawerth and Julie Strongson (University of Chicago Press, 2004), p. 91.

kind, and it seems to me that it is only by being of such use that she might reasonably be proud. In order profitably to apply knowledge of whatever kind, the practice must be linked to theory, without which ideas are perforce imperfect.... Let us conclude then from all this that a woman makes a great mistake and earns only ridicule when she claims to be learned or to have a fine mind and believes that she can keep up that reputation; nevertheless she has good reason to acquire as much learning as she can. She has good reason, once she has fulfilled her duties as mother, daughter, and wife, to give herself up to study and work because this is a sure way of her being sufficient unto herself, of being free and independent and of consoling herself for the injustices of fate.[14]

These dense "shadows of ignorance" were, in fact, to prove extremely fruitful in the development of the French language and its literature. Precisely because women received no humanist education, their limpid natural French, devoid of both popular vulgarity and of learned jargon, presented itself, in the great language debate, as a model for the nation. Ever since François I had made French the official language of the administration and the courts of justice, cultivated minds had been fascinated by the problem of a national language suited to illustrating the full glory of the kingdom. How could French equal Latin in prestige and replace it in the world of learning and literature? Should its "natural" character be allowed to develop, or should it be latinized and, through assimilation, become a scholarly imitation of an ancient model? Gallic pride was assured at the beginning of the seventeenth century when France boasted of supplanting Italian cultural supremacy in Europe, making the *translatio studiorum francorum* an undeniable reality. French should preserve its own purity, reject foreign adornment, and fully realize its vocation as a universal language. Malherbe was the first to confront the problem with regard not only to the written language but to the spoken one as well. Despite his love of the classics, he professed that the musicality of a language could not be born of archaeological distillation but should develop from the daily practice of the elite. Above all, it was to stem from the conversation of women, raised as they were away from the world's corrupting influences. His reform thus did not involve merely a small circle of specialists and scholars. It appealed to the court nobility as well. The poet, writes Marc Fumaroli, "succeeded in sharing his concern for the language with a whole articulate milieu.... From then onward, the art of conversation became inseparable in France from a quasi-musical delicacy and a precise curiosity concerning the enunciation of the language. Women,

---

14. Mme d'Épinay to the Abbé Galiani, May 4, 1771, in Ferdinando Galiani and Louise d'Épinay, *Correspondance*, edited by Georges Dulac and Daniel Maggetti, five volumes (Paris: Desjonquières, 1992–1997), Vol. 2, pp. 24–26.

though 'ignorant' as any picklock, have still a better ear with which to judge this music and to play it."[15] From Claude Favre de Vaugelas and Dominique Bouhours to Jean de La Bruyère, official culture would almost unanimously recognize in women a linguistic competence superior to men's. The honor was conferred upon them by the very virtue of their not having studied and of knowing no language other than their own.

But this peculiar paradox implied another, even greater one. With Cardinal de Richelieu's ascent to political power, the promotion of the royal language initiated by Malherbe became one of the key issues in the monarchy's cultural politics. A modern, elegant French would allow a great national literature to dawn and enable court society to express the sovereign's magnificence with refinement. French would, moreover, become the lingua franca of Europe. Academies were established, beginning in the 1630s with the Académie française, designed specifically to supervise the purity of the language. Concurrently, state patronage of the arts flourished, and Richelieu set up a far-reaching system of cultural promotion and control. But such measures were not enough for the realization of this grandiose plan. As Malherbe had shown, civil society's collaboration was required, and society had the total freedom to make the revolution its own. Without realizing it, the nobles contributed positively to the success of the hated cardinal minister's cultural politics by distancing themselves from the court and making the art of speaking a distinctive badge of their own identity. And women, whom the State and the Church had condemned to obedience and ignorance, actually acquired the authority to lay down the law on the foremost institution needed to support the State, namely, language.

That was not all. Since women were deprived of academic culture and primarily sought amusement in literature, they became the new, important public, which writers soon learned to take into account. A vast literature of entertainment grew up to meet their demand. Minor genres like literary portraits, aphorisms, letters, the game of posing *questions d'amour*, and novels were all designed to fill the idle hours of a noblewoman's life. These entertainments, disdained by the learned and condemned by the Church, would in the long term become pillars of the French literary tradition.

If, by virtue of their ignorance, women influenced modern culture, they were obliged to compensate by carefully concealing what they did know. Decorum abhorred female "pedantry," preferring playfulness and gallantry instead. But even the general rules of the game imposed self-control and dissimulation: women were supposed to please but at the same time subjugate themselves; they must seduce without allowing themselves to be conquered. Once again, in order to

---

15. Marc Fumaroli, "Le génie de la langue française," in *Trois Institutions littéraires* (Paris: Gallimard, 1986).

comply with the specific demands of their condition, women were obliged to excel in the complex art of appearances. The feminine requirements of seduction, ease, and lightheartedness were the very preconditions of *honnêteté*—the new secular ethic that would regulate social behavior in polite society.

The growing prestige of women and the importance they had assumed within society were destined to cause both sexes to reexamine the particular characteristics of the female nature and to question women's legitimate field of action. The first half of the seventeenth century saw a marked revival of the points of view that had since the Middle Ages characterized the *Querelle des femmes*—the ongoing literary, scholarly, and theological debates about the nature of women. But Saint François de Sales's *Introduction à la vie dévote* represented, as we have seen, a radical change of position by proposing the compatibility of devout and worldly ways of life. Women were to prove their devotion by their behavior. Moralists and churchmen, aware of this revolution, which invested women with a spiritual mission in the heart of civil society, hastened to proclaim this mission a duty. The burgeoning instructive literature of the time bears eloquent witness to this haste. Following the Italian example of the preceding century, a succession of tracts on good manners now appeared in France. The first and most important, *L'honneste homme ou l'art de plaire à la cour* (1630) by Nicolas Faret,[16] departed in interesting ways from Castiglione's great treatise. It no longer taught the courtier how to shine at court but how to make a career there. It ushered in a vast literature on the subject of *honnêteté*. Only two years later, the fair sex was treated to its first handbook, *L'honneste femme* (1632–1636) by Jacques Du Bosc. These were soon followed by Grenaille's more specific *Honneste fille* (1639–1640) for girls and *Honneste veuve* (1640) for widows.

It must be admitted, however, that *honnêteté* could take on a different meaning depending on the sex to which it was applied. For men *honnêteté* represented a thoroughly lay ideal of social behavior: the art of pleasing. For his female counterpart, however, it was inseparable from the religious values of devotion, piety, and chastity. Her role in society was essentially passive and her conduct obeyed far stricter norms of behavior than those prescribed for the *honnête homme*. Rather, preceptors of morality advised women to be ever watchful of their honor and reputation and to rebuff all gallantry.

In the new social reality, however, women were less prepared to heed such advice or to remain in their passive roles, at least insofar as taste and entertainment were concerned. They wanted their visitors to write, to converse, and to invent rhymes —all in an unexpected, lighthearted, quick, brilliant, flirtatious fashion. The favored themes were psychology and love, the two subjects in which women could excel without training, thanks to their sensibility, intuition, and awareness of the ways of the world.

---

16. Published in London as early as 1632 as *The Honest Man: or, the Art to Please in Court.*

The Church continued to preach against the dangers of games and the feminine imagination but found itself unable to update the old arguments, which the nobility's evolution had rendered redundant. A new and far fiercer attack was to come from the quarter of the *savants*—whom noblewomen had traditionally treated as accomplices in their *loisirs*. These learned men saw the citadel of true literature as seriously threatened by the increasing power of feminine taste, a taste both superficial and frivolous. Women, ignorant of even the rudiments of humanist culture, were said to be incapable of understanding beauty, grandeur, or true artistic quest. In the wake of the Fronde Rebellion, that is, just after the seventeenth century's midpoint and its most serious political crisis, a certain creeping hostility developed among irritated and jealous society writers toward a now considerable group of literary women. These had, with their collections of verse, their tragedies, novels, and stories, managed to establish themselves firmly in the literary arena.

No one at that time in the world of letters, however, could allow himself the luxury of ignoring the fact that feminine taste now determined the success of a literary work, confirmed the reputation of a writer, and steered the course of literature. And it was not only unscrupulous hacks who cultivated the new reading public. Descartes himself chose to write his *Discours de la méthode* (1637) in French rather than Latin and to give up the idea of dealing in depth with the far too difficult problem of the existence of God. He, too, wanted to be read by women.

Not content with their "tyrannical" hold over the world of letters, women advanced new ideas and even aspired to reshape life in the image of literature. About halfway through the century, with the appearance of the so-called *Précieuses*—of which we shall read more in future chapters—the female condition became for the first time the subject of systematic analysis by a group of women. For the first time, it was not men who studied, interpreted, and directed the opposite sex, but women themselves who loudly declared who they were and how they wished to be treated, aspiring to a high degree of social polish and purity of language. This obvious strain on convention brought about by the game society played provided the *savants* with a long-awaited opportunity to settle old scores. No longer protected by the code of *bienséances*, these outspoken women united representatives of the Church, politicians, and men of letters in resentment against them, even if they were of such high social standing that they could not be criticized openly. Reduced to type, the *Précieuses* found themselves exposed and defenseless not only against second-rate parodies but against the satiric genius of Molière and the misogyny of Nicolas Boileau and La Bruyère. The backlash, moreover, was tied up in the heated contemporary "quarrel of the ancients and the moderns"—the famous literary *Querelle*. For the "ancients," who embraced the classical tradition and despised the "modern" trends in contemporary literature, the mockery they reserved for women was a powerful weapon in their arsenal.

For a period of more than twenty years beginning around 1620 (before the *Pré-cieuses* had defined a feminine ideal typified by delicacy), a host of mounted "Amazons" in breastplates and helmets, sword in hand, made a striking appearance in the literature of the day. The literary origins of these *femmes fortes* were a mix of Christian and pagan, mythological and historical, but their reappearance was initiated by men, the product of male fantasy. It is not easy to decipher the meaning of such a remarkable pageant, and the inevitable question arises as to whether or not it was intended to revive the traditional image of the weaker sex or if it merely revisited old forgotten stereotypes. It was, however, no accident that during the years of Anne of Austria's regency (1643–1652), two churchmen, the Jesuit Pierre Le Moyne and the Franciscan friar Jacques Du Bosc, both celebrated the archetype of the *femme forte*. In less than a century, three queens had ruled France in the name of their young sons.[17] These, along with several grand ladies who subsequently participated in the insurrections of the Fronde, provided proof enough that when the occasion arose, women were not lacking in manly attributes. These were, of course, exceptional cases demanded by extraordinary circumstances. The idealized Amazons of Le Moyne and Du Bosc were, above all, both Christian and chaste, in fact superior to men by virtue of their beauty and charity. They could be accused of neither inconstancy nor indolence, neither hypocrisy nor any of the other vices generally imputed to women. Their exceptional nature did not excuse them from the obligations of ordinary women, nor could their actions dispense them from obeying the rules of the Church. Nor did such figures question the norm or revise the opinions of traditional antifeminism. But even this noble model was foreign to most current thinking, which saw women as an incitement to male heroism, and the actions of the real regent queens, princesses, and Fronde "adventuresses" belied the longed-for figure of the compassionate and pious Amazon.

Throughout the seventeenth century, two constant, if not always compatible, preoccupations appeared to dispose literature in favor of women. In order to gain the respect and approval of men, they had either to shine by their moral qualities or to give proof of a perfect understanding of the usages of society. Full of good intentions, the Le Moynes, Du Boscs, and Grenailles of the world wanted to demonstrate the equality of the sexes but remained prisoners of the innate contradictions in a discourse that persisted in bowing to the rules of order and social conformity. But although in 1673 the philosopher François Poullain de La Barre had the audacity to propose women as the intellectual equals of men,[18] it was the

---

17. Catherine de' Medici (for Charles IX), Marie de' Medici (for Louis XIII), and Anne of Austria (for Louis XIV).

18. In *De l'égalité des deux sexes, discours physique et moral où l'on voit l'importance de se défaire des préjugéz* (Paris: Jean Du Puis, 1673).

Précieuses in the 1660s who would persuade members of the fair sex that their strength lay in their difference from, not their equality with men. And although this difference could give rise to conflict and vindication, it constituted one of the immutable characteristics of civilized society.

Without a deep understanding between the sexes, chivalry, gallantry, and *honnêteté* were in fact impossible ideals. Nobility and the elegance of French aristocratic life developed from a single challenge. Proud of their differences, rich in their various experiences, men and women were united in their passion for society life. For its sake they showed themselves willing to sacrifice the most violent individual feelings, sometimes even their profoundest aspirations, receiving in exchange the right of belonging to a world of pleasure, diversion, and entertainment. A world of like-minded people where beauty and worth were newly allied and where the only laws to be respected were those agreed by common accord.

By the end of the seventeenth century, even a prolific writer of manuals like the Abbé de Bellegarde was obliged to admit that spending time in the company of polished women proved more beneficial than his own specialized books: "It is only by frequenting ladies that we acquire that society air and that *politesse* that no counsel and no reading can teach."[19] From the time of Mme de Rambouillet onward, and from one generation to the next, high society women took it upon themselves to educate the men. The activity was to be the touchstone and the most significant proof of their success. Twenty years after the "incomparable Arthénice"—Mme de Rambouillet—Mme de Sablé received what might be thought a unique compliment: "Never has anyone brought *politesse* to a higher point of perfection."[20] And yet, similar tributes continued to be paid to women at regular intervals for the duration of the *ancien régime*. A description by the Duc de Lévis (1764–1830) of the Maréchale de Luxembourg, the last glorious example of her times, is evidence enough. In teaching the new generation the art of good manners, this great lady took upon herself the civilizing mission that would subsequently involve the entire nation. *Politesse* had for some time ceased to be a mark of social distinction and had come to be a characteristic of French cultural identity:

> With the help of a name, considerable audacity, and above all a fine house, she managed to cause the more than frivolous, earlier behavior to be forgotten, and to establish herself as the supreme arbiter of *bienséances*, of good taste, and of the good form that serves as the basis of *politesse*. She held

---

19. Jean-Baptiste Morvan de Bellegarde, *Réflexions sur la politesse des mœurs*, in *Œuvres diverses*, four volumes (Paris: Robustel, 1723), Vol. 2, p. 621.

20. Nicolas d'Ailly, preface to *Maximes de Madame la marquise de Sablé et pensées diverses de M. L. D.* (Paris: Sébastien Mabre-Cramoisy, 1678), p. 6.

absolute sway over the young of both sexes; she controlled the giddiness of young women, obliging them to be generally coquettish; she induced young men to be reserved and respectful; in fact she maintained the sacred flame of French sophistication; at her house she preserved intact the tradition of noble, easy good manners that the whole of Europe came to Paris to admire and tried in vain to imitate.[21]

As guardians of an inherited set of rules recognized by an entire elite, and as guarantors, by their very presence, of refined behavior and the purity of language, noblewomen would have seemed to side with continuity and tradition. But the understanding of *bienséances* was in no way mechanical. Rather it was a cognitive process, an initiation rite that depended on individual attitudes and sensitivity. It was not necessarily tied to birth. Based on the principles of both co-option and exclusion, the social art could be used as an instrument of social advancement as much as a bulwark of aristocratic identity. This double dynamic was responsible for a singular sequence of events. Studied, copied, and interiorized, the aristocratic model of behavior became the object of constant imitation by the most enterprising and ambitious of the bourgeois elite. But every time the object of desire appeared to be within their grasp, the code of behavior was slightly modified. In clothing, as in entertainment, in intellectual enthusiasms, and in the most frivolous of attitudes, new fashions changed the rules of the game and reestablished the distance between the chosen and the excluded, until such time as the ability to adapt forced the latter to begin the cycle all over again. If emulation, wealth, lessons in deportment and dancing, the study of formative literature, and the reading of fashionable novels were not enough to guarantee social acceptance, there remained the possibility of acquiring the style of a gentleman through the living practice of *bienséances* and direct participation in society life. This process of initiation had, as its means and its goal, the realm ruled over by women in their salons. These salons provided not only a training ground for the aspiring, constituting both tribunal and theater, but were at the same time an end in themselves.

With the authority to preside over society and to determine an individual's right to participate based on qualities such as amiability, refinement, and wit, women came to bear a notable power to delineate nobility. But in making behavior a distinguishing mark of its own social identity, the French aristocracy had thrown down a dangerous challenge.

By changing the criterion of belonging from birth to merit, by identifying merit with the values of a worldly culture, and by entrusting women with the dissemination and control of that culture, the nobility seemed to betray the old traditions

---

21. *Souvenirs-Portraits du Duc de Lévis* (1813) edited by Jacques Dupaquier (Paris: Mercure de France, 1993), p. 101.

of caste and to renounce the belief in their own genetic superiority, accepting to mix with people of humble origins. The playful realm of the salon might have seemed remarkable for the confusion of rank and alarming social mobility, representing a threat as much to traditional aristocratic values as to the bourgeois ethic. And since the most salient fact about the new social comedy was the pride of place held there by women, it was they who acted as scapegoats in an ideological conflict that went far beyond the boundaries of a discussion on female identity.

It is from exactly this point of view that the American scholar Carolyn C. Lougee has analyzed the fresh wave of antifeminism that assailed women from the second half of the seventeenth century on, and it is significant that her argument has less to do with the nature of women than with their social position.[22] If contemporaries made fun of the social ambitions and cultural aspirations of women, of their insistence on courtesy, urbanity, and gallantry, and if men admonished them to remember their domestic duties and recalled them to restraint and obedience, it was precisely because the "ridiculous" claims of women represented so many threats to the forces of tradition, to custom's sway, and to the stability of the social order. The extramarital practice of *amour galant* in the guise of idealism was more and more widespread and went against the concept of Christian marriage; women gave precedence to the new social virtues over those handed down by breeding. Their pedagogic authority and their ability to "make gentlemen" made women the arbiters of the social composition of the salons. For the most part, they were responsible for the mixture of rank that resulted. But their aspirations to luxury and *loisirs* borrowed from both aristocratic and bourgeois values, causing, in the eyes of their detractors, irreparable harm to both social orders.

Lougee has made a careful analysis of the social origins of the women whose names figure in Antoine Baudeau de Somaize's *Grand dictionnaire des Prétieuses*[23] —that is, the most prominent women in society around 1660. She has shown that from the start a mixed society frequented the Parisian salons. If half the women mentioned in the *Dictionnaire* belonged to the old nobility, or *noblesse d'épée*, the rest—despite titles acquired by marriage—were either from the *noblesse de robe* or even of plebeian origin. Contrary to whatever indignant conservatives like La Bruyère and the Duc de Saint-Simon would have us believe about the decline this inspired, the welcome was far from hostile for those wealthy young brides whose

---

22. Carolyn C. Lougee, *Le Paradis des Femmes: Women, Salons, and Social Stratification in Seventeenth-Century France* (Princeton University Press, 1976).

23. There are two slightly different editions of Somaize's *Grand dictionnaire des Prétieuses*. The first is *Le grand dictionnaire des Prétieuses ou la Clef de la langue des ruelles* (Paris: Jean Ribou, 1660); the second is the two-volume *Le grand dictionnaire des Prétieuses, historique, poétique, géographique, cosmographique, chronologique et armoirique* (Paris: Jean Ribou, 1661).

dowries swelled the coffers of the old, impoverished feudal classes. The newcomers were not only rich but were generally young, willing to please, and zealous to learn. Their social regeneration came about by osmosis through direct experience of life in society. The great families of the court nobility might turn up their noses at such mixing of classes, or *mésalliance*; but society as a whole seemed disposed to open its arms to those who could add to the capital of gaiety, elegance, and wit, all of which constituted its most authentic hallmark. The tendency, which became evident in the 1660s, for the nobility—old or new, of "the robe" or of "the sword"—to integrate with bourgeois financiers was to become more pronounced with time, developing into an irreversible process.

The salon, conceived as a utopian place "apart from the world," in the words of Elizabeth Goldsmith, "yet able to encompass all that was best in it,"[24] proved in the end to be a threat to the old caste spirit from which it had sprung. Modern culture had perfected a distinctive model of behavior, but its frankly elite ideology went hand in hand with a distinctly pedagogic calling. And to whom was its civilizing message addressed? Certainly to the nobility. But it was also open to anyone who could understand it and make it his or her own. With social inclusion now based on aesthetic and moral grounds and founded on better behavior, the arrangement of a hierarchical, rigidly stratified society was now questioned. Rank was fixed, but at the same time, the original composition altered. And since it was women who assumed the sensitive pedagogic mission, it was they who were largely responsible for the social mobility triggered by the civilizing process. They were doubly responsible in that they had suggested the criteria that opened the doors to good society, and it was they who helped the young bourgeois women, suddenly ennobled through marriage, to integrate swiftly into the aristocracy. By the speed of their success, the new arrivals only confirmed the superior ability of women to excel in the social arts.

---

24. Elizabeth C. Goldsmith, *"Exclusive Conversations": The Art of Interaction in Seventeenth-Century France* (University of Pennsylvania Press, 1988), p. 45.

3

THE BLUE ROOM

IT IS IMPOSSIBLE to establish exactly when Catherine de Vivonne de Rambouillet first opened the doors of her salon, although we know from a letter by the poet Malherbe that by 1613 she was already receiving regularly at her house.[1] That year, the great reformer of modern French poetry became a habitué of the Marquise de Rambouillet's house, and it was he who, in deference to the Arcadian tradition, coined the name Arthénice—an anagram of Catherine—for his hostess.[2] Nevertheless, 1618 is the year that suggests itself as the true date of inauguration. In that year reconstruction work began on the house in the rue Saint-Thomas-du-Louvre, work that would furnish a setting appropriate to Mme de Rambouillet's new way of life. Two complementary facts coincided to make the event memorable. The building was to prove important in the history of taste and interior decoration; the marquise herself had taken on the role of architect. Tallemant des Réaux recounts:

> Dissatisfied with all the drawings made for her, ... one evening, after having reflected at length, she began to shout: "Quick, some paper! I have found the way to do what I wanted." Within the hour she had done the drawing, for naturally she knows how to draw.... Madame de Rambouillet's drawing was followed to the detail. It was from her they learned to put the stairs to one side in order to allow for a great suite of rooms, to raise the floors, and to make the doors and windows high and wide and opposite one another. This is so true that when the Queen Mother [Marie de' Medici] had the Luxembourg built, she sent the architects to see the hôtel de Rambouillet, and

---

1. Nicole Aronson, *Madame de Rambouillet ou la magicienne de la Chambre bleue* (Paris: Fayard, 1988), pp. 98–99.

2. Honorat de Bueil de Racan, *Vie de Monsieur Malherbe*, edited by Marie-Françoise Quignard (Paris: Gallimard/Le Promeneur, 1991), pp. 57–59.

such attention did not prove to be useless. She was the first to think of painting a room a color other than red or tan, which is how her great room came to have the name "Chambre bleue."[3]

The two main architectural innovations that Tallemant attributed to the marquise were not entirely new. Nor was it a new idea to create a sense of unity in a room by coordinating the colors and the materials. What was without precedent, however, was the overall effect of the house when the work was finished. Admiring Parisians went so far as to consider it to be the "most celebrated in the kingdom."[4] The hôtel de Rambouillet, which was immediately copied, became the perfect prototype for the décor that would form the backdrop to the rituals of French society for nearly three centuries.

The house in the rue Saint-Thomas-du-Louvre was surprising in its "regularity," but its Italian-inspired, light, harmonious look was infused with a quite new feeling of intimacy and comfort. In designing the archetypal setting for society life, Mme de Rambouillet seemed to have conceived of her own home as a refuge from the world, a *locus amoenus* in which to forget the roughness of the real world and escape the stench of mud and the disorder of the Parisian streets. What most struck the marquise's contemporaries and what continues to strike those who read their accounts is the sense of surprise and disorientation experienced by visitors to the rue Saint-Thomas-du-Louvre. Tallemant tells how Arthénice managed to plant an avenue of sycamores and sow a field in front of her house so that she could boast of "being the only one in Paris to be able to see from her cabinet a field of hay being scythed."[5] The novelist Mlle de Scudéry, who depicted the marquise as Cléomire in *Le Grand Cyrus* (1649–1653), her thinly veiled portrait of high society, described the house's illusory effect and magical atmosphere: the marquise had

> discovered the art of building a vast palace in a modest space. Order, regularity, and cleanliness permeate all the apartments and all the furniture; everything in her house is magnificent, even singular; [even] the lamps there are different. . . . Her cabinets are filled with a thousand rarities, each revealing the taste of she who chose them. The air is always scented . . . various magnificent baskets of flowers impart a continuous springtime to her chamber,

3. Tallemant des Réaux, *Historiettes*, Vol. 1, p. 443.

4. Henri Sauval, *Histoire et recherches des antiquités de la ville de Paris* (Paris: Charles Moette, 1774), Vol. 2, Book 3, p. 100, quoted in Peter Thornton, *Seventeenth-Century Interior Decoration in England, France and Holland* (Yale University Press, 1990), p. 337, note 1.

5. Tallemant, *Historiettes*, Vol. 1, p. 450.

and the room where one usually sees her is so agreeable and so well conceived that one imagines oneself in an enchanted place.[6]

The enchanted place in which the marquise usually received her intimate friends was the famous Chambre Bleu—the Blue Room. The walls were hung with blue brocade interwoven with threads of silver and gold; the chairs were upholstered in blue; the curtains on the bed were blue. In addition to this enchanting unity of color, another surprise was the unusual purpose to which the room was put. Breaking with convention, Mme de Rambouillet had transferred her actual bedroom to a little closet and had turned the big bedroom into an official reception room. The decision, taken for reasons of convenience and health, allowed Arthénice to receive her guests as she lay stretched on the daybed in the most protected corner of the room. The practice set an example and was to become a social ritual. The *ruelle*—as the space between the bed and the wall came to be known— was to become par excellence the part of the room where seventeenth-century ladies received their guests. Brought to the heart of the social scene, the alcove became a "virtuous" place, a place of prestige, devoid of all suggestion of intimacy. Homage that had heretofore been reserved for the King of France would henceforth be paid symbolically to the most obscure *Précieuse*. Only in the eighteenth century did the alcove become central to the world of erotic fantasy, a world on which Mme de Rambouillet had decidedly turned her back.

Although the marquise's taste may have been dictated by a deep-seated desire for beauty and harmony, it is impossible not to sense from the permanent animation in her house her continuous need for distraction and amusement. The first discipline to be practiced at the hôtel de Rambouillet was the art of entertainment.

It may well be asked what the driving force was that gave the fragile marquise such abundant energy and, with the passing years, withstood misfortune and sorrow. Perhaps it was due to a much-loved and spoiled child bride's refusal to grow up. Despite being an exemplary wife and the mother of seven, she often professed her wish to have remained "a maiden."[7] Perhaps it was the awareness that idleness was an essential element of aristocratic life, that to know how to cultivate it nobly was a mark of identity and of belonging. Perhaps it was the fear of the void and of solitude—the same void that Pascal would soon describe in his *Pensées* as defining social life from its earliest beginnings. Each of these explanations has an element of truth. The sum of them imparted a frankly utopian quality to the hôtel de Rambouillet.

---

6. Mlle de Scudéry, *Artamène ou le Grand Cyrus*, ten volumes (1656; reprint, Geneva: Slatkine Reprints, 1972), Vol. 7, Part 7, Book 1, pp. 298–299.

7. "She swears that had she been left until she was twenty, and had she not been obliged to marry, she would have remained a maiden," Tallemant, *Historiettes*, Vol. 1, p. 442.

Arthénice's house was "another place," a world apart. Its primary characteristic was beauty; the weather there was always temperate, the spring perpetual, and the only climate one of diversion. In this world of games, social differences were ignored and all the players were considered equal. As Jacques Revel put it, "at the hôtel de Rambouillet, one elects oneself, or rather, one recognizes oneself." But few were granted access to this world, and at times, in order to gain entry, the favored one was subjected to initiation rites and obliged to "patiently respect the rules of the game."[8]

Life in the marquise's house was easy, open, untroubled, and free of passion. Eros had been stripped of his arms, purged of desire, and reduced to a fiction, a mere pleasantry. And if, as occasionally happened, someone forgot and was carried away by the game, they were sharply called to order. "At the hôtel de Rambouillet, gallantry was allowed, but not love," the Abbé de Ménage is reported to have said. "Monsieur de Voiture, giving his hand one day to Mademoiselle de Rambouillet, the future Madame de Montausier, and, wanting to show himself to be unfettered by convention, kissed her arm. But Mademoiselle de Rambouillet reacted so severely to his audacity that it prevented him from ever again wishing to brave a similar impertinence."[9] Of course, regular visitors had only to leave the house in the rue Saint-Thomas-du-Louvre for real life to reassert itself and for them to take up their usual activities of lusting, loving, hating, conspiring, killing, fighting—indeed, even praying, preaching, and looking after the diocese. "We conversed with each other, we made polite talk . . . but we were on the point of strangling one another," Cardinal de Retz recalled of the years during the Fronde Rebellion, of which he was a leader.[10] But the memory of a utopian fiction remained, and if the temptation to go back and play was so great, it was probably because playing was becoming second nature. This dual life was a phenomenon that was to have a profound effect on the very identity of the French nobility until the Revolution. It was the only possible answer to and an impossible choice between court life and society life. Thus, for nearly two centuries, the nobility played two different, if parallel, parts, sometimes adopting the courtier's uniform, at other times donning the dress of a man of the world.

During Louis XIV's reign, of course, court life monopolized everyone's attention, but already before the Sun King's death, the double rhythm had resumed. The Comte de Roederer, in his *Mémoire pour servir à l'histoire de la société polie*

---

8. Jacques Revel, "Les usages de la civilité," in *De la Renaissance aux Lumières*, Vol. III of *Histoire de la vie privée*, edited by Philippe Ariès and Georges Duby (Paris: Éditions du Seuil, 1985–1987), p. 196.

9. Gilles Ménage, *Menagiana, sive excerpta ex ore Ægidii Menagii* (Paris: Florentin et Pierre Delaulne, 1693), pp. 223–224.

10. Cardinal de Retz, *Mémoires, La conjuration du comte Jean-Louis de Fiesque, Pamphlets*, edited by Maurice Allem and Édith Thomas (Paris: Gallimard/Bibliothèque de la Pléiade, 1956), p. 328.

en France, published in 1835, claimed that this double life originated at the hôtel de Rambouillet: "Society and the court were two different worlds, where the very people who frequented them no longer resembled themselves when they passed from one to the other.... At the hôtel de Rambouillet, politics and intrigue were left at the door; at court, the manners of the hôtel de Rambouillet were disguised and ceded to the dominant note. The more agitated and corrupt the court, the more recherché and flourishing the Rambouillet society."[11] About halfway through the seventeenth century, by which time the salon in the rue Saint-Thomas-du-Louvre was a past glory, the acute observer Antoine Gombaud, Chevalier de Méré, explained how the marquise's utopian wager had come to be that of an entire society. By distancing itself from the court and resisting the court's almost limitless power, by imposing itself as the arbiter of judgment and choice, this society made itself the supreme tribunal of the *Grand Monde,* or high society. "This court [of Louis XIV], although the finest and perhaps the greatest on earth, still has its limitations and its faults. But the *Grand Monde,* which extends everywhere, is more perfect; so where the ways that we love of living and behaving are concerned, the *Grand Monde* and the Court must be considered separately, and it must not be forgotten that the Court, by custom or by caprice, sometimes approves of things that the *Grand Monde* would not allow."[12]

The *Grand Monde* was the only aristocratic institution to maintain its prestige until the end of the *ancien régime.* And that prestige, as novelists like Honoré de Balzac and Marcel Proust in his *À la recherche du temps perdu* show, was to survive through a thousand metamorphoses until this day. "This *grande société* or *bonne compagnie,*" Mme de Genlis wrote in her late-eighteenth- and early-nineteenth-century memoirs,

> did not limit itself to pronouncing frivolous decrees on tone and manners but exercised a severe, very useful control of morals; by means of censure, it suppressed the vices which are not punished by the law: ingratitude and avarice. Where justice was in charge of punishing bad actions, society punished bad behavior. Its general disapprobation removed something of his personal standing from one who was its object; to be excluded from society's heart had the most fatal effect on a person's destiny. An existence was turned upside down by the words: *everyone closed their doors to him.*[13]

11. Pierre-Louis de Roederer, *Mémoire pour servir à l'histoire de la société polie en France par M. le Comte de Roederer* (Paris: F. Didot frères, 1835), p. 51.

12. Antoine Gombaud, Chevalier de Méré, "Discours de la conversation," in *Œuvres complètes,* edited by Charles H. Boudhors, three volumes (Paris: Fernand Roches, 1930), Vol. 2, p. 111.

13. Mme de Genlis, *Mémoires inédits sur le XVIIIe siécle et la Révolution française,* ten volumes (Paris: Ladvocat, 1825) Vol. 2, pp. 207–208.

Myths began to be woven about the hôtel de Rambouillet from its first splendid beginnings, contemporary accounts being a prelude to Mlle de Scudéry's absolute idealization of the marquise in *Le Grand Cyrus*. Tallemant should be consulted for a clear idea of the daily life of the time and a more realistic picture. His *Historiettes*, written for private entertainment and with no thought of publication, are characterized by their lack of respect for anyone and by the iconoclastic delight with which they treat even the most illustrious. Tallemant penned his portraits from a whirlwind mixture of history, slices of private life, physical traits, psychological detail, anecdote, gossip, indiscretions, and calumny. He picked up information wherever he could: from books, witnesses, hearsay, and, above all, from his own personal experience. In this case, his description of Mme de Rambouillet and her world is firsthand. Despite his affectionate admiration for her, he portrays her just as he found her, without the slightest trace of hagiography. Because it shows us Mme de Rambouillet and her circle unencumbered by the trappings of legend, Tallemant's *Historiettes* is thus the most valuable document for understanding the extraordinary contradictions of a changing society that, while open to modernity and elegance in certain privileged circles, remained to a great extent both brutal and barbaric.

The marquise, Tallemant tells us, was "inclined to make fun of everything" and loved to jest.[14] Laughter—as a primary, instinctive distancing from the world—must have been therapeutic for a woman who, by her own admission, tended toward pessimism. The house employed a few Italian servants whose main job was to entertain the marquise and her husband by their eccentricities. As Voltaire would ask a century later, did not a primitive taste for buffoons go hand in hand with a love of theater?[15] Accounts of life at the Rambouillets tell of a succession of practical jokes that, despite the elegance of the setting, suggest that the taste of the lady of the house and her guests was inclined toward the burlesque, not to say the surprisingly elementary. Thus the Comte de Guiche was, for example, invited to supper and offered all the dishes he most disliked, to general hilarity. It was only after he had been severely tested that he received solace in the form of a splendid banquet. M. de Chaudebonne—the Duchesse d'Orléans's knight-in-waiting—was persuaded that he had eaten poisonous mushrooms and that his body had swollen monstrously because he could not fit into his clothes, which had been secretly removed and taken in. In her turn, Arthénice was herself the butt of certain jokes, as when she was alone in a room and a huge trained bear suddenly appeared from behind a screen. By no means did this love of farce exclude more sophisticated passion for *coups de théâtre* and feats of scenography. Tallemant records some of

---

14. Tallemant, *Historiettes*, Vol. 1, p. 444.

15. Voltaire, *Vie de Molière avec des petits sommaires de ses pièces* (1739), in *Œuvres complètes*, edited by Louis Moland, fifty volumes (Paris: Garnier, 1877–1885), Vol. 23, *Mélanges* II, p. 97.

the most memorable. On one occasion, the marquise had secretly had a new room built over the garden, which she furnished completely. "One evening, when there was a large gathering at the hôtel de Rambouillet, suddenly a noise came from behind the tapestry, a door opened, and Mademoiselle [Julie] de Rambouillet, now Mme de Montauzier, superbly dressed, appeared in a large, magnificent, marvelously well-lit closet. I leave you to imagine how surprised everyone was. They knew that behind that tapestry there was only the garden of the Quinze-Vingts, and without their having had the least suspicion of it, they saw such a beautiful, finely painted closet, almost the size of a room, which seemed to have been brought there by magic."[16] On another occasion, Philippe de Cospeau, the bishop of Lisieux, was the privileged spectator at a pastoral tableau vivant that might have come straight from the pages of Honoré d'Urfé's novel *L'Astrée*. The bishop, who was visiting Mme de Rambouillet in her country château, was invited to walk with her. Conversing affably, they reached a part of the garden where they could see a circle of large rocks partly hidden by trees. As he approached, the bishop had the impression of a strange shimmering and thought he glimpsed nymph-like figures. Indeed, when he reached the rocky clearing, he discovered "Mademoiselle de Rambouillet and all the maidens of the house, dressed as nymphs and sitting on rocks, thus forming the most graceful spectacle in the world." As Tallemant noted, one of the marquise's "greatest pleasures was to surprise people."[17] The scene, with its typically baroque taste for effects of illusion, brings to mind the marquise's Italian origins, and particularly her connection to the distinguished Roman Savelli family, to which she belonged on her mother's side.

In fact, of all the entertainments whose rhythm interrupted the idle hours at the hôtel de Rambouillet—receptions, balls, concerts, outings, parlor games, conversation, readings—the passion for the theater dominated in every way. This did not pass unnoticed by contemporaries. The writer Jean Regnault de Segrais tells us that Jean Desmarets in his play *Les Visionnaires* (1637), written under Richelieu's influence, portrayed Mme de Rambouillet as Sestianne, a virtuous young girl whose only love is the theater.[18] Not only did the marquise invite great actors—Montdory and Molière among them—to entertain her guests, but she also staged proper performances at the hôtel, with her regular guests improvising as actors. In 1636 Jean Mairet's tragedy *Sophonisbe* was put on at the country château de Rambouillet, with the marquise's eldest daughter—thirty-one-year-old Julie d'Angennes—in the main role and the austere Abbé Arnauld as Scipio. Mlle Paulet,

16. Tallemant, *Historiettes*, Vol. 1, p. 450.

17. Tallemant, *Historiettes*, Vol. 1, pp. 444–445.

18. Charles-Louis Livet, *Précieux et précieuses, caractères et mœurs littéraires du XVIIe siècle* (Paris: Didier, 1859), p. 65.

dressed as a nymph, sang during the intermission. A 1639 letter by Jean Chaplain describes Arthénice "busy preparing a performance in the style of the commedia dell'arte."[19] Even the great playwright Corneille recognized the theatrical competence of Mme de Rambouillet and her guests by asking their opinion of his tragedy *Polyeucte*.[20]

By her taste for theater, the marquise was not only expressing a marked inclination to disguise reality by making a spectacle of it. She was also taking a stand on a controversy that raged in France during the 1630s. One of the main aims of Richelieu's cultural policy was to dignify the theater by removing it from Church jurisdiction and placing it directly under the King's protection. Hence the importance of his artistic statute and of the debate about the kind of rules that would guarantee literary excellence. The cardinal, himself a failed playwright, made it the duty of the theater to reflect and exalt the prestige of the monarchy. Mme de Rambouillet, meanwhile, contributed to its success in civil society by bringing to it an aristocratic public that would support the theater until the end of the *ancien régime*, even against its own interests, as, for example, when Beaumarchais's *Mariage de Figaro* saw the light in 1780.

Society at the hôtel de Rambouillet thus fell in love with the theater, appropriating it and making it central to its entertainment. Soon the powerful Nicolas Fouquet, as a genial patron of the arts, would show, albeit briefly, how private entertainment and artistic excellence could go hand in hand. But such lavish private splendor would be the superintendent's downfall in 1661. By the middle decades of Louis XIV's reign, theater would be a royal monopoly, and under the sovereign's jealous eye, the nobility would concentrate its entire efforts on participating in the daily spectacle of court life.

This passion for theater would erupt fully at the beginning of the eighteenth century. Not satisfied with an endless round of professional theater—from the Opéra, to the Théâtre Français, Les Italiens, and L'Opéra Comique—society figures would invite actors to their houses for private performances. They commissioned miniature theaters both in their Paris houses and on their country estates. There, away from prying eyes, they could, for their own exclusive pleasure, organize theatrical seasons in which they themselves were often not only the instigators but also the authors, spectators, and actors. From the princes of the blood and the old court nobility down to the minor aristocracy and the rich parvenus from the financial world—not to mention Voltaire's productions at his château at Ferney or the royal mistress Mme de Pompadour's spectacles in the *petits appartements* at Versailles—the privileged world used and abused the theater like a drug.

---

19. Aronson, *Madame de Rambouillet ou la magicienne de la Chambre bleue*, p. 226.

20. This took place in 1640. See Émile Magne, *Voiture et les années de gloire de l'hôtel de Rambouillet (1635–1648)* (Paris: Mercure de France, 1912), pp. 226f.

Perhaps this irresistible fascination with the stage was due to the fact that life as it was presented in the theater obeyed the same rules as the real life it mirrored. Society life had been growing more and more to seem like one great, uninterrupted theatrical performance in which the most celebrated protagonists were those who, like the best actors, knew how to disguise their art with a semblance of simplicity and ease. The first theorist of society, the Chevalier de Méré, had claimed that a man of society, like an actor, must be able to distance himself from the part he intended to play: "It is a rare talent indeed to be a good actor in life; much wit and precision are needed if perfection is to be found.... I am convinced that on many occasions it is not without its uses to regard what one does as a Play and to imagine that one acts a part in the theater. This thought prevents anything from being taken too much to heart and so imparts a freedom to language and action that one cannot have if one is troubled by fear and anxiety."[21]

Mme de Rambouillet's most original production, the plot of which she conceived and the style of which she dictated, was certainly that of society life itself. "The hôtel de Rambouillet," wrote Tallemant, "was, so to speak, the theater of all their entertainments and was the rendezvous for all the most honorable gentlefolk at Court, as well as for the most polished of the century's wits."[22] The Jesuit Pierre Le Moyne called her salon "the court of the court," in which the demands of etiquette had given way to mutual attraction.[23] "Princesses frequented [Mme de Rambouillet] although she was not a duchess," remarked Segrais.[24] Society life at the hôtel de Rambouillet saw itself from the start as representing freedom of choice, with the criteria of affinity and understanding taking precedence over rank. A telling example was the behavior of the royal bride Marie-Louise de Gonzague-Nevers, who left the chapel where her marriage to the King of Poland had just been celebrated and went straight to take her leave of Mme de Rambouillet—"with the crown still on her head."[25] The gesture anticipated Stanisław Augustus Poniatowski's renowned remark to the bourgeois Mme de Geoffrin in 1764— "*Maman*, your son is king"—with which he informed her that he had come to the throne of Poland.

The first to accept the rules of the new game and discard her legendary haughtiness on entering the Blue Room was Charlotte de Montmorency, known as Madame la Princesse. She was the daughter of the last constable de Montmorency

---

21. Antoine Gombaud, Chevalier de Méré, Discours VI, "Suite du Commerce du Monde," in *Œuvres posthumes*, Vol. 3 of *Œuvres complètes*, pp. 157–158.

22. Tallemant, *Historiettes*, Vol. 1, p. 443.

23. Pierre Le Moyne, *Galerie des femmes fortes* (Paris: Antoine de Sommaville, 1647), pp. 252–253; quoted in Magne, *Voiture et les années de gloire de l'hôtel de Rambouillet*, p. 212, note 2.

24. Segrais, *Segraisiana, ou mélange d'histoire et de littérature*, p. 26.

25. Tallemant, *Historiettes*, Vol. 1, p. 585.

and wife of a prince of the blood, Henri de Bourbon, Prince de Condé. In her celebrated memoirs, the much younger Mme de Motteville described Madame la Princesse as a shining example: "Among the princesses, the first in rank was also the most beautiful; and, though no longer young, she still inspired the admiration of all who saw her. . . . She was blond and white; she had perfectly beautiful blue eyes. Her expression was lofty and full of majesty, and her manners agreeable. Her powers of seduction were absolute, except when, with unmannerly pride and abundant ill will, she set herself against those who dared to displease her."[26]

It must be said that Madame la Princesse had paid dearly for the privileges of beauty and rank. At age fifteen, the victim of Henri IV's lust, Charlotte was given in marriage to Henri de Bourbon, a man with whom she was never compatible.[27] Contrary to what might have been expected, the Prince de Condé—who had been carefully chosen as her spouse only so that he might renounce his conjugal rights in favor of the King—opted to salvage his honor and flee with his young wife to Brussels. Henri IV's death in 1610 put an end to the young couple's exile. Then, in 1619, as a result of a violent quarrel with Marie de' Medici, the Prince de Condé was locked up in the Bastille, and his wife felt obliged to share his prison out of respect for decorum. (Without this forced cohabitation, their daughter Anne Geneviève, future Duchesse de Longueville, might never have seen the light of day.) Finally, in 1632, Charlotte's brother, the glorious Duc de Montmorency, was beheaded for supporting Louis XIII's rebellious brother, Gaston d'Orléans. More realistic, if less courageous, than his brother-in-law, Monsieur le Prince chose to adapt to the times and compromise the grand family bloodline by consenting to the marriage of his eldest son, the future Grand Condé, to one of Cardinal de Richelieu's nieces.

The friendship between Madame la Princesse and Mme de Rambouillet was deep and of long standing. Catherine, who was five years older than Charlotte, had surely followed the events of the persecuted Condé couple's life with sympathy, all the more so since her father had been the young Condé's tutor. From the beginning of the 1620s until the midcentury eruption of the Fronde, Madame la Princesse was a regular visitor to the Blue Room, as was her most assiduous admirer, "her little husband," Cardinal de La Valette—the very pair Cardinal de Richelieu suspected of plotting against him in 1627. With time, the children of the princess and the marquise also became friends, sharing festivities and

---

26. *Mémoires de Madame de Motteville sur Anne d'Autriche et sa cour*, edited by M. E. Riaux, four volumes (Paris: Charpentier, 1855), Vol. 1, pp. 37–38.

27. "She did not despair at his death; the illustrious Madame de Rambouillet was esteemed to have said, on that occasion, that Madame la Princesse had had only two good days with Monsieur le Prince, which were the day she married him because of the high rank he bestowed on her, and the day of his death because of the freedom he gave her and the great wealth he left her." *Mémoires de Madame de Motteville*, Vol. 1, p. 300.

entertainments and contributing their cheerfulness and youth to the hôtel de Rambouillet's period of greatest splendor.

For the marquise's contemporary Angélique Paulet, on the other hand, it was anything but simple to become part of the select circle in the rue Saint-Thomas du-Louvre. The 1609 *ballet de la Reine*, the occasion of her first meeting with Mme de Rambouillet and Mlle de Montmorency, had also borne consequences that proved fatal to her reputation. Tallemant maintains that Henri IV's assassination by Ravaillac in 1610 took place while he was on his way to visit her with one of his illegitimate sons, the Duc de Vendôme, whom "he wanted to introduce ... to love; perhaps he had already noticed that this young gentleman did not like women."[28] Having fallen prey to royal conquest at an early age, Angélique saw little reason to refuse her favors to the men who pleased her, and so she collected a series of lovers and scandals until, at about the age of thirty, she decided to change her life and become devout.

Tallemant recounts that Mme de Rambouillet had always liked her and, "to restore her reputation," thus "received her as a friend, and, if it may be said, Mademoiselle Paulet was purified by this lady's great virtue, and thereafter cherished and esteemed by everyone."[29] This conversion was providential for the glory of the Blue Room, since Angélique was one of the most original and attractive women of the time.[30] Other guests at the hôtel de Rambouillet might compete with her in beauty, grace, and wit, but none had a voice like hers. And none had gained in life's battle so splendid a nickname: "The ardor with which she loved, her courage, her pride, her bright eyes, her too golden hair were what earned her the name of Lioness."[31]

Another of the marquise's guests who, in keeping with the spirit of the place, attempted to disguise her imperious manners was Mme de Combalet, who became the Duchesse d'Aiguillon in 1638. Her pride derived not from noble birth but from the power of her uncle, Cardinal de Richelieu. The marriage of his favorite niece had greatly helped the cardinal's social advancement. According to Tallemant, Mme de Combalet had such an aversion to her husband that when she was unexpectedly widowed in 1621, "for fear of being sacrificed once more to the *raison d'état*, she made a rather sudden vow never to marry and to become a Carmelite nun."[32] Having placed herself strategically under God's protection, Mme de Combalet could at last begin to enjoy her life on earth. (Not much later,

---

28. Tallemant, *Historiettes*, Vol. 1, p. 474.

29. Tallemant, *Historiettes*, Vol. 1, p. 476.

30. Mlle de Scudéry depicted her as Élise, and dedicated to her "L'Histoire d'Élise" in *Artamène ou le Grand Cyrus*, Vol. 7, Part 7, Book 1, pp. 132–361.

31. Tallemant, *Historiettes*, Vol. 1, p. 476.

32. Tallemant, *Historiettes*, Vol. 1, p. 304.

Mme de Sévigné's own jubilation upon being widowed attested that this was the only condition that allowed a woman in the seventeenth century to do as she wished. And Mme de Sévigné had not disliked her husband.)

From the day on which she took her vows, says Tallemant, Mme de Combalet

> dressed as modestly as a votary of fifty. Not a hair was out of place. She wore a dress of worsted wool and never raised her eyes. In this garb, she served as lady-in-waiting[33] to the Queen Mother [Marie de' Medici] and never left the court; her beauty was in full flower. This behavior lasted for quite some time. Finally, as her uncle became more powerful, she began to wear little fringes; then she made a ringlet or put a small black ribbon in her hair; she donned silk dresses and, little by little, went so far that, because of her, widows [now permit themselves to] wear all sorts of colors, apart from green.... Madame de Combalet renewed her Carmelite vows every year; as many as seven times.[34]

Mme de Combalet's influence with Cardinal de Richelieu was obvious to everyone. The cardinal rarely refused his niece a favor, and her friends—beginning with Mme de Rambouillet—often asked her to intervene with the minister on their behalf. Madame la Princesse was the first to seek her friendship in order "to have the Cardinal's protection, for she feared her husband might confine her at [the ancestral château of] Bourges."[35] The close bond between uncle and niece was in fact open to some malicious interpretation. "Great slander has been spoken of her uncle and her; he loved women but feared a scandal. His familiarity with his beautiful niece, on the other hand, could not be judged out of place. In fact she profited from it with little modesty, for knowing him to like bouquets, she always wore them, and she used to visit him décolleté."[36] This suspicion of incest nevertheless did nothing to protect the beautiful widow from insinuations of her inclination toward women. Tallemant refers to rumors about her relationship with another Blue Room habitué, Anne de Neufbourg, a rich bourgeoise who had married the Baron du Vigean in 1617.[37] La Barre, the du Vigeans' beautiful country property, was, like the various Condé estates and the Richelieus' château, destined to become part of the regular circuit for the Rambouillet set.

Vincent Voiture gave this account of their playful, spectacular, and utopian way of life in a letter to Cardinal de La Valette, presumably written in about 1630:

---

33. The duties of the *dame d'atour* included supervising the dressing ceremony of the princesses of royal blood.

34. Tallemant, *Historiettes*, Vol. 1, pp. 304–305.

35. Tallemant, *Historiettes*, Vol. 1, p. 310.

36. Tallemant, *Historiettes*, Vol. 1, p. 306.

37. Tallemant, *Historiettes*, Vol. 1, p. 309–310.

Madame la Princesse, Mademoiselle de Bourbon, Madame du Vigean, Madame Aubry, Mademoiselle de Rambouillet, Mademoiselle Paulet, Monsieur de Chaudebonne, and I left Paris at six o'clock in the evening to go to La Barre, where Madame du Vigean was to give supper for Madame la Princesse.... We entered a room strewn only with roses and orange blossoms. Having admired this magnificence, Madame la Princesse wished to [take a turn around] the walks before the hour for supper.... At the end of a path stretching as far as the eye could see, we discovered a fountain from which jetted more water than all the fountains of Tivoli. Around it were arranged twenty-four violinists.... On approaching, we discovered in a niche in the wall a Diana; [she was] about eleven or twelve years old and more beautiful than the forests of Greece and Thessaly had ever seen.... In another niche was a nymph pretty enough to belong to her suite. Those who do not believe in fables thought it was Mademoiselle de Bourbon [that is, the daughter of Madame la Princesse] with the maiden Priande [her friend Mademoiselle d'Aubry].... No one could utter a word, so great was the admiration at so many things that astounded at once both the eyes and the ears. All of a sudden, the goddess sprang from her niche and began to dance with indescribable grace around the fountain, a dance which lasted for some time.... This might have lasted too long had not the violins quickly struck up a saraband so gay that everyone rose as joyfully as if nothing had happened. Thus jumping, tumbling, pirouetting, and capering, we reached the house, where we found a table that could well have been laid by fairies.... As we rose from table, the sound of violins called everyone upstairs, where we found a room so well lit that it seemed as though the day, which no longer covered the earth, had entirely taken refuge there.... The ball continued most pleasurably when all at once a great noise from outside brought all the ladies to the window, and we saw rising from the wood some three hundred paces from the house such a number of fireworks that it seemed that every branch and tree trunk had become a rocket.[38]

In accordance with Mme de Rambouillet's dictates, aristocratic idleness aimed to redeem itself through artistic expression. For this to happen, however, the performers in this unending metamorphosis required a mirror in which to see their actions reflected. Paradoxically, it was a bourgeois, Vincent Voiture, who supplied that mirror in his writings. No one can help us better than Voiture to comprehend the spirit of the hôtel de Rambouillet, since no one contributed more than he to adding artistic dignity to the "cultural revolution" underway in the Blue Room.

---

38. Voiture to Cardinal de La Valette (late 1630), letter 10 in *Œuvres de Voiture, Lettres et poésies*, edited by M. A. Ubicini, two volumes (Paris: Charpentier, 1855), Vol. 1, pp. 45–50.

His verses and letters, all written in the name of ephemeral fun, constituted a manifesto for the new social aesthetic. Despite their lighthearted playfulness, they assured Arthénice's salon its presence in literary history.

The hôtel de Rambouillet had always enjoyed an excellent relationship with the literary world. Malherbe was a habitué of the house, as was Jean Chapelain, the best critic of the day, from the time of his first success with the preface to Giambattista Marino's *Adone* (1623). Other literati to be admitted to the Blue Room included the poet Jean Ogier de Gombauld, the grammarian Vaugelas, the poets Racan and Saint-Amant, and Jean Desmarets de Saint-Sorlin (literary friend of Cardinal de Richelieu and the first champion of the "moderns"). For professional writers, the social world was an ideal hunting ground for possible patrons. For the Marquise de Rambouillet and her guests, literature—like dancing, theater, music, parlor games, and conversation—was another form of entertainment. Slightly earlier, Mme d'Auchy and Mme des Loges might have aspired to making their houses into distinguished intellectual centers; but for Arthénice, the faintest hint that she cultivated literary ambition would have insulted her. Jean Chapelain, aware of the marquise's aversion to academic pretensions, thought it wise to alter the text of a letter from the writer Guez de Balzac—the best-known letter-writer of the day—before showing it to her. As the diplomatic editor explained to the letter's author,

> In one place alone where you refer to her room as a nest where so many rare spirits gather every day, or the equivalent, Monsieur de Chaudebonne, Monsieur Vaugelas, and I thought it appropriate, before showing her the letter, to put "and some excellent persons who meet frequently at her house," by which means, without changing your meaning, we hint that we know we owe it to her to be more agreeable, confirming at the same time your intention that her house should be seen rather as a resort for the chosen court and purified great society, which you so well describe, than as a place for regulated discussion, which in fact it is not and which would be less honorable than otherwise.[39]

The view of literature as a kind of specialized interest was rejected, in keeping with aristocratic dilettantism. Nevertheless, literature made a considerable contribution to the process of "purification of high society" that Mme de Rambouillet promoted. Her insistence on cleaning up and disguising real life before allowing it to cross her threshold certainly arose from deeply personal feelings, although she was not alone in devising either the form or the practice of this playful fiction.

---

39. Quoted in Aronson, *Madame de Rambouillet ou la magicienne de la Chambre bleue*, p. 32.

Paradoxically, the hôtel de Rambouillet drew most of its inspiration for its ethical and aesthetic ideals from the literary genre so despised by *savants* and moralists: the novel. And at a time when the learned, wishing to impose French supremacy throughout Europe, were engaged in bitter anti-Italian polemic, the Italian born Mme de Rambouillet had, according to Segrais, "trained her mind by reading good Italian and Spanish books."[40] This was entirely in keeping with modern cultural tastes. In fact the nobility's treasured heroic aspirations, forever trampled on as they were by the new monarchist ideology, found solace in the Spanish literature of the preceding century. A peculiar historical discrepancy meant that while contemporary Spain was busy substituting its new heroes for old, the French aristocracy continued to admire and to model itself on the Spanish sixteenth-century courtly ideal. Thus, both in the original and in translation, the faultless heroes of courtly novels, of which the best known was *Amides*, were admired together with the idealized love in Montemayor's *Diana* (circa 1559) and Lope de Vega's *Arcadia* (1598). As Lionello Sozzi has noted, courtly poems of the Italian Renaissance also had a strong influence on the French nobility. On a theoretical level, the Italian authors made a decisive contribution to opening the debate on the use of the "marvelous" in the epic. At the same time, they helped to point the aesthetic thinking of French literati toward a conception of an art obedient to the laws of verisimilitude and reason. But in practice, the reading of Ariosto's *Orlando furioso* and Tasso's *Gerusalemme liberata* continued to conquer the hearts and imaginations of the nobility, showing them a chivalrous, noble, and passionate ideal in which "kindness espoused strength and courtesy espoused vigor."[41]

For the small circle of the chosen gathered around Mme de Rambouillet, this taste for the past reflected the discomfort felt by much of the nobility in the present. It went back even further than the Italian and Spanish Renaissance, to the French Middle Ages and the very origins of chivalric civilization. Thus long-forgotten novels of Chrétien de Troyes were reopened in the Blue Room, and courtly love and courtly virtue were rediscovered with the legends of the Round Table. Chapelain made himself the spokesperson for the hôtel de Rambouillet by promoting the *Lecture des vieux romans* in a dialogue dedicated to Jean François Paul de Gondi, the future Cardinal de Retz. *Lancelot*, he wrote, was "a book of marvels and of history all in one." It expressed the quintessence of the feudal ethos by which the French nobility had never ceased to recognize itself. In it one could read "how they [the knights] conversed; that they were imbued with principles and true honor; how they stood by their word religiously; how they wooed; just how far they could take an honorable friendship; the gratitude they expressed

---

40. Segrais, *Segraisiana, ou mélange d'histoire et de littérature*, p. 26.

41. Lionello Sozzi, "L'Influence en France des épopées italiennes et le débat sur le merveilleux," in *Mélanges offerts à Georges Couton* (Lyon: Presses Universitaires de Lyon, 1991), p. 72.

for good deeds; the high opinion they had of valor; and finally, what they felt about Heaven and what respect they had for holy things."[42]

All this reading may well have added to the wealth of images, gestures, and emotions that the marquise could draw on in setting up the mise-en-scène of her own life. But there was also a more recent French novel, which appeared just as she was forming her salon. Honoré d'Urfé's *L'Astrée* provided a very real model for the habitués of the Blue Room.[43]

Using the proven formula of the pastoral novel, Urfé describes, in open contrast to court society, an ideal community of a few privileged people disguised as shepherds. The forest of Forez is the scene of a utopian experiment in which a small, free elite seeks moral perfection through amorous quest by returning women to the prestige once accorded them in chivalric society and later in the poetic tradition launched by Petrarch and his followers. When the outside world, with its ambition, cupidity, and abuse of power, comes to disturb the forest's peace, the shepherds prove to be valiant knights, ever faithful to the aristocratic ideal of honor.

Honoré d'Urfé belonged to the old provincial nobility and had wide experience of people and of the world. He had fought courageously for the Catholic League during the religious wars, had experienced both court life and exile, and had been involved in a long, difficult love affair. Yet it is interesting to ask to what extent the novel reflects the real aristocratic elite's way of life and how much of it was born of fantasy. *L'Astrée*'s huge success implied the existence of a public capable of sharing the innocent, noble aspirations of the inhabitants of the forest of Forez. Urfé's saga certainly did not win enthusiastic readers by merely recounting one adventure after another, and love affairs in succession. Almost like a moral tract, it taught manners, gallantry, and the ways of the world, edifying the sensibilities, tastes, hearts, and intellects of its readers. In the form of a novel, French society found, almost from the beginning, a national model, a "breviary" of behavior to be compared to the classic texts on manners that had been imported from Renaissance Italy.

Mme de Rambouillet would have been the first to recognize in *L'Astrée* the expression of her own dearest aspirations. After all, she too was looking for a *locus amoenus*, a protected space, far from the poison of the court, wherein to surround herself with compatible people. Her guests came of their own free will, thus guaranteeing their shared pleasure. In such a place, love nourished itself on

---

42. *De la lecture des vieux romans par Jean Chapelain*, first published with notes by Alphonse Feillet (Paris: Aubry, 1870), p. 31.

43. The first part of *L'Astrée* was published in 1607, the second appeared in 1610, the third in 1619, and the fourth posthumously in 1627. *La conclusion et dernière partie d'Astrée* by Balthasar Baro was sent to press in 1628.

expectation rather than gratification, and women inspired admiration and respect. Why, then, should Arthénice not make Urfé's Arcadian fiction her own? Why not try to introduce the innocence, grace, and pretty ways of those shepherds and shepherdesses into the beautiful rooms of the house in the rue Saint-Thomas-du-Louvre? So began in the Blue Room the frantic game of mirrors in which literature and life reflected one another, a game that was soon to become a characteristic of all worldly culture. The hôtel de Rambouillet was especially noticeable, for in taking its inspiration from *L'Astrée* and providing in turn the model for Mlle de Scudéry's idealized society depicted in *Le Grand Cyrus*, it placed itself between the century's two most successful novels. But this was far from unique.

From the start, the most distinctive characteristic of this world proved to be the acute self-awareness of its members, particularly their need to check their own reflections in the eyes of others. Thus bent on constant introspection and self-analysis, French society gradually, almost involuntarily, slipped from the spoken to the written word. One aspired to capture the fleeting word and gesture, the short-lived incident, in anecdotes, in letters, in written portraits, or in the thousands of verses intended not to be read silently but to be listened to, though they nevertheless ended up circulating in manuscript and published in collections.[44] Social presentation—*paraître*—prompted the complete "exteriorization" of self. For some of its most distinguished critics, like the Chevalier de Méré or the Duc de la Rochefoucauld, it also became a subject of theoretical reflection, leading to disturbing questions about the identity of the ego.

The habitués of the hôtel de Rambouillet walked and conversed as if they were Urfé's shepherds. They discussed the moral dilemmas of love, composed verses and songs, and wrote dashing letters. Under Arthénice's rule, the different literary forms that in *L'Astrée* added depth to the narrative served only to make life more agreeable, more entertaining. Yet by a strange trick of fate, it was through a man from the realm of *negotium* (business) that the Blue Room's celebrated *otium* (leisure) came to be embraced as literature. That man was Vincent Voiture.

---

44. There were, in addition to collections and anthologies, also the *-ana*—collections of aphorisms and thoughts of an author or well-known person, and of anecdotes about their life, usually designated by the name followed by the suffix *-ana*, as in the *Segraisiana* and *Menagiana* referenced in these notes.

4

VINCENT VOITURE:

THE *ÂME DU ROND*

Voiture was the son of a wine merchant who followed the court.... He already had a certain reputation...when Monsieur de Chaudebonne met him at someone's house and said to him, "Monsieur, you are too gallant a man to remain among the bourgeoisie. I must get you out of it." He talked of him to Mme de Rambouillet and took him to see her some time later, which is what Voiture refers to in a letter where he writes, "Since M. de Chaudebonne regenerated me with Madame and Mademoiselle de Rambouillet."[1]

IF WE ARE to trust Émile Magne's scholarly imagination, we may suppose that Vincent Voiture first crossed the threshold of the hôtel de Rambouillet in 1625, on the occasion of a reception held there in honor of the Duke of Buckingham.[2] Buckingham, who had come to Paris to fetch the King of England's bride, Princess Henrietta Maria of France, had expressed a wish to hear Mlle Paulet's celebrated voice, and the Rambouillets had offered to satisfy his curiosity. A memorable reception was given in the house in the rue Saint-Thomas-du-Louvre. And on that very night, in the house illuminated by a thousand candles, shimmering with crystal and silver, and teeming with the full flower of the French nobility, Voiture was presented for the first time to Mme de Rambouillet and her eldest daughter, Julie d'Angennes. Arthénice was thirty-seven, Julie twenty, and it is hard to say which of the two subsequently had the greatest influence over the newcomer. That evening, however, everyone's attention was turned to the English visitor, a favorite of Charles I. Voiture's imagination was probably struck by the magic of the place, as the guest arrived in a suit of gold cloth embroidered with pearls, in the company of the Duc and the Duchesse de Chevreuse.

---

1. Tallemant des Réaux, *Historiettes*, Vol. 1, pp. 48–85.

2. Émile Magne, *Voiture et l'hôtel de Rambouillet: Les origines, 1597–1635*, second edition (Paris: Émile-Paul frères, 1929), pp. 39–57.

Tallemant de Réaux had little sympathy for Voiture and, in a lengthy portrait of him, points out precisely why this man, whose manners often betrayed his humble origins, was welcomed so unreservedly in the Blue Room and ended up becoming its very emblem. Voiture's looks were pleasing, but he was extremely small, vain, moody, sensual, and ruled by a passion for gambling.

The seventeenth century is said to mark the moment when France discovered wit, or *esprit*. Voiture was certainly the first example of a man who owed everything—his social rise, success, friendships, reputation, and fame—to that quality. Tallemant was explicit: "As he had a great deal of wit and was more or less born for the court, he soon became the great joy of society and all those illustrious persons; his letters and poetry are proof enough of it."[3] Of course, those "illustrious persons" had no doubt about the reasons for their preference. As Mme de Rambouillet remarked to someone who had read the posthumous collection of Voiture's letters and praised their wittiness, "But, Monsieur, did you think that it was for his birth or fine figure that he was received, as you saw, everywhere?"[4]

Esprit is an almost untranslatable term that, being both vague and precise, can only be defined by its nuances. Forty years after Voiture's debut in society, the Duc de La Rochefoucauld made a survey of the many different uses of the word *esprit*, among them, *bel esprit, esprit adroit, esprit enjoué, esprit moqueur, esprit de raillerie, esprit fin, esprit de finesse, esprit de détail*. It is difficult to provide exact English equivalents for each nuance. For example, *bel esprit*, depending on the speaker's intention, can be either complimentary or ironic. *Esprit de raillerie* (bantering) can imply a gentle teasing, or it may denote the desire to make someone the butt of cutting sarcasm; if *esprit fin* was usually used to describe a refined mind, *esprit de finesse* generally referred to intellectual subtlety. La Rochefoucauld himself found it impossible to provide precise general definitions for the rest, beyond each particular context: "Although several epithets for *esprit* appear to have the same meaning, the tone and the manner of pronouncing them makes the difference, but since tone and manner of speaking cannot be put on paper, I will not enter into details that it would be impossible to explain well."[5]

Turning to La Rochefoucauld's guide, despite the anachronism of being written a generation later, the epithets best suited to Voiture would probably be *esprit enjoué* (merry) and *railleur* (bantering). His was a gay, ironic wit, capable of making fun of everyone and everything while maintaining a delicate balance between impertinence and adulation. Voiture was to become a virtuoso in this difficult art,

---

3. Tallemant, *Historiettes*, Vol. 1, p. 485.

4. Tallemant, *Historiettes*, Vol. 1, p. 499.

5. François de La Rochefoucauld, "De la différence des esprits," *Maximes, suivies de Réflexions diverses, du Portrait de La Rochefoucauld par lui-même et des Remarques de Christine de Suède sur les "Maximes,"* edited by Jacques Truchet (Paris: Garnier, 1967), pp. 218–220.

which required quickness, psychological intuition, and a precise understanding of the times. He knew his public, and he knew exactly what was expected of him. By spreading surprise and amusement day after day, he would fulfill his obligation to those who had welcomed him as an equal. "He took care to amuse the company at the hôtel de Rambouillet. He had always seen things that the others had not seen; so, as soon as he arrived, everyone gathered around to listen to him.... In gatherings at the hôtel de Rambouillet and the hôtel de Condé, Voiture always amused people, at times with his ballads, at times with some foolish thing that came to his mind."[6]

Amid all the fantasy, extravaganza, sketches, tales, and continuous invention, there was one main subject of conversation of which the small, privileged circle around Voiture never tired: the idealized story of their own daily lives. In verse or in prose, written or spoken, this cheerful, affectionate, saucy, dashing saga not only reflected the tastes of the hôtel de Rambouillet but determined, updated, and redirected them.

Since one of the favorite subjects of entertainment in the Blue Room was love, the use of verse was more or less obligatory. The well-established Petrarchan convention, with its codified poetic language and wide choice of situation and imagery, guaranteed that desire remained platonic and virtue remained protected. And Voiture would not hesitate to adopt it. In fact, Petrarchism was for him a purely formal solution, a screen behind which he could desanctify love. "Everyone has always known quite well," wrote Mlle de Scudéry immediately after his death in 1648, "that in his heart he adored Venus Anadiomene [earthly love] more than Venus Urania [heavenly love], since, in the end, he could not understand that passion might be detached from the senses, and he was even at great pains to believe that any completely pure affection existed in the world."[7] Woman remained the focus of Voiture's poetry. She was celebrated, admired, adulated, and courted with due respect, but she was no longer a sacred figure. Thus the poet made a fiction of Petrarchan idealization. Voiture wrote of love elegantly and with light-handed grace. Despite the profusion of declarations, oaths, palpitations, and sighs, however, he never claimed to be believed:

> *Lors tout à coup je revins en moy-mesme,*
> *Le Repentir, et la Peur au teint blesme,*
> *Les prompts Souhaits, les violens Desirs,*
> *La fausse Joye et les vains Desplaisirs,*
> *Les tristes Soins, et les Inquietudes,*

6. Tallemant, *Historiettes*, Vol. 1, pp. 489–491.

7. Mlle de Scudéry, portrait of Voiture as Callicrate in *Artamène ou le Grand Cyrus*, Vol. 6, Part 6, Book 1, p. 81.

> Les longs Regrets, amis des solitudes,
> Les doux Espoirs, les bizarres Pensers,
> Les courts Dépits, et les souspirs legers,
> Les Desespoirs, les vaines Défiances,
> Et les Langueurs, et les Impatiences,
> Et tous les biens et les maux que l'Amour
> Tient d'ordinaire attachez à sa Cour....[8]

This accumulation of the traditional formulas of love poetry, with the hurried introduction of all the possible states of mind that attend passion, may tempt the reader to smile. Elsewhere Voiture shows more sincerity by exposing the classic literary conceit "to die of love." "You can rest assured," he wrote to an unknown woman, "that neither love nor sorrow ever caused anyone to die, since neither the one nor the other has yet killed me, and having been two days without the honor of seeing you, I still have some sign of life. If anything had induced me to accept your absence, it was the belief I held that I would only die, and that so bitter a pain as that would not allow me to languish long. However, I find, against all hope, that I am lasting far better than I had imagined, and whatever mortal blows I may have suffered, I think my soul is unable to detach itself from my heart on account of what it contemplates there, which is your image."[9]

The ambiguous grace of Voiture's poetry, which was primarily addressed to women, immediately appealed to them. The hôtel de Rambouillet wanted to play the game of love without taking any real risks. Voiture made that possible by forging, for the exclusive use of a small elite, a model of chivalry that, through infinite variety and nuance, would become essential to an entire civilization. Mlle de Scudéry herself had to recognize that Voiture "wrote so agreeably in prose and in verse and in so chivalrous and unusual a manner that he could almost be said to have invented it."[10] Tallemant had already stated without a shadow of doubt that Voiture was to be recognized as "the father of witty foolery" and credited with "having shown others how to talk agreeably."[11]

---

8. "When I suddenly came back to myself,/Repentance and pale-faced fear,/The hasty wishes and violent desires,/The false joy and vain chagrin,/The sad cares, and the anxieties,/The long regrets, friends to solitude,/The sweet hopes and strange thoughts,/The short vexations, and the soft sighs,/The despair, the empty suspicions,/The languor, and the impatience,/And all the good and ill that Love/Normally keeps attached to its Court...." Vincent Voiture, *Poésies*, edited by Henri Lafay, two volumes (Paris: Didier, 1971), Vol. 1, pp. 21–22.

9. Voiture to Mme ***, letter 15 of *Lettres amoureuses*, in *Œuvres de Voiture, Lettres et poésies*, Vol. 1, p. 192.

10. Mlle de Scudéry, *Artamène ou le Grand Cyrus*, Vol. 6, Part 6, Book 1, p. 77.

11. Tallemant, *Historiettes*, Vol. 1, p. 489.

The poet of the Blue Room, however, could boast of another, more important stylistic discovery, one that would not only characterize aristocratic behavior but would denote the very essence of French classical literature: the aesthetic of the *naturel*—what the Italians, after Castiglione coined the term *sprezzatura*, regarded as the very cornerstone of social grace. Castiglione wrote:

> But I, imagining with myself oftentimes how this grace cometh, leaving apart such as have it from above, find one rule that is most general, which in this part, I think, taketh place in all things belonging to man in word or deed above all other. And that is to eschew as much as a man may, and as a sharp and dangerous rock, Affectation or curiosity and (to speak a new word) to use in everything a certain recklessness [*sprezzatura*], to cover art withall, and seem whatsoever he doth and sayeth to do it without pain, and, as it were, not minding it. And of this do I believe grace is much derived.... Therefore that may be said to be a very art that appeareth not to be art, neither ought a man to put more diligence in anything then in covering it.[12]

It was another Italian, Stefano Guazzo, who defined the aesthetic of this hidden art, this disguised artifice that the French would a century later style as *naturel*. Mlle de Scudéry would later call it "subtle negligence" and "pleasing nonchalance."[13] For the author of *Civil Conversation* (1574), the "natural" did not relate to nature on an equal footing, but rather revealed its intrinsic potential; what was natural was "everything that nature allows one to do best and to carry to perfection."[14]

Nearly a century later, the great French theorist of *honnêteté*, the Chevalier de Méré, illustrated the aesthetic of naturalness along the same lines as Guazzo had. "Nature is to be imitated and followed in all things, that is, everything most perfect and most accomplished in nature; everything that is seen to be most beautiful, most lovely, most delightful must be observed and taken from it, not only in the realm of the senses and the intellect, but also in the realm of the understanding, the invisible and the spiritual."[15] This dictate, obeyed as much in the drawing rooms as it was in Nicolas Boileau's *Art poétique*, was handed down through the generations: from Mme de Sévigné to Mme du Deffand to Julie de Lespinasse,

---

12. Baldassare Castiglione, *The Book of the Courtier*, translated by Thomas Hoby (1561), edited by Virginia Cox (Everyman, 1994), Book 1, Chapter 26, p. 53; translation modified.

13. Mlle de Scudéry, "Épître aux Dames," in *Les femmes illustres ou les Harangues héroïques*, p. 29.

14. Stefano Guazzo, *La civil conversazione*, edited by Amadeo Quondam (Modena: Panini, 1993), Vol. 1, Book 2, p. 87.

15. Letter 42 to Mr de ***, in *Lettres de Monsieur le Chevalier de Méré*, two volumes (Paris: D. Thierry & C. Barbin, 1682), Vol. 1, pp. 223–224.

until culminating at the end of the eighteenth century in the famous saying of the Prince de Ligne, *"du naturel, surtout du naturel!"* (naturalness, above all naturalness!).

Well before being expressed as a theory, the aesthetic of the natural became living practice. Voiture, the favorite of the Blue Room, led the way. The Jesuit Dominique Bouhours, one of the most influential critics of the 1670s and 1680s, stated that Voiture had taught the French to write with "naturalness."[16] But even here, Voiture restricted himself to interpreting Mme de Rambouillet's taste and that of her house. Guez de Balzac wrote with a hint of paternalism to his friend and frequent correspondent Jean Chapelain about one of Voiture's *divertissements*—literary amusements—composed for the marquise's circle: "If it has been said that Nature was never greater than in little things, let us apply that to the advantage of his notes [*ses billets*], and let us prefer them to the volumes of Asiatic authors!"[17] Guez de Balzac, the great French master of French Atticism, did not yet realize that this very naturalness would threaten his own prestige as a writer.

Unlike Guez de Balzac, Voiture did not aspire to be a *savant*, even less an "author," but merely a *galant homme*—a gentleman—who wrote with the sole purpose of pleasing his friends. Composed for the very people who inspired it, his poetry mimicked their style; it was brilliant, discursive, anecdotal, swift, and conspicuously lighthearted. Voiture easily adopted minor poetic genres—stanzas, ballads, sonnets, letters, madrigals, and rondeaux. He was, in Tallemant's words, "libertine" with meter and disdainful of *labor limae*—laborious polish—relying instead on immediacy for effect.[18] The drawing-room poetry he invented depended, like conversation, on improvisation—a difficult art that reached its apotheosis with the eighteenth-century impromptu. While drawing from a wide mnemonic repertoire and presupposing a considerable amount of preparation, it made it a point of honor to disguise any trace of effort and to capture the fleeting moment. It was, in fact, very hard work. As Tallemant commented dryly, Voiture "made it look like he extemporized. That may have happened many times, but many other times he brought things with him, composed at home."[19] Tallemant goes on to

---

16. Dominique Bouhours, "La langue française" (entretien 2) and "Le bel esprit" (entretien 4), in *Les Entretiens d'Ariste et d'Eugène* (1671), edited by Ferdinand Brunot (Paris: A. Colin, 1962), p. 79, p. 133.

17. Guez de Balzac to Chapelain, March 15, 1640, letter 6 in Book 5 of *Lettres de Monsieur de Balzac à Monsieur Chapelain* (Paris: Augustin Courbé, 1656), p. 464. Balzac refers here to the two great rhetorical currents of antiquity that gained importance in erudite discussions in seventeenth-century France. The term "Atticism" in this context points to a purity of language and to a clarity, elegance, and conciseness of style pertaining to the great authors of the fifth century BC. In contrast to it is the "flowery" style of "Asianism" (a term introduced by Cicero to refer to the language spoken in the Aegean Isles).

18. Tallemant, *Historiettes*, Vol. 1, p. 490.

19. Tallemant, *Historiettes*, Vol. 1, p. 489.

recount an anecdote that perfectly reveals the sense of irony that presided over the Blue Room and the degree to which its habitués were aware of the complicated game of balancing the written with the spoken word, dilettantism with the literary tradition:

> Madame de Rambouillet tricked him successfully. He had written a sonnet with which he was quite pleased; he gave it to Madame de Rambouillet, who had it printed with great attention to the page number and everything else and then had it cleverly stitched into a collection of verse that had been printed quite some time ago. Voiture found the book, which had been left purposefully open at that page. He read the sonnet several times; he quietly repeated his own to see if there was any difference; in the end, he became so confused that he thought he must have read the sonnet before and, instead of having written it, had simply just remembered it. Finally, when the laughter was over, he was disabused.[20]

Voiture's lighthearted verse was so popular that a number of professional writers followed his example—not merely minor, success-seeking authors like the Abbé Cotin and the poet Isaac de Benserade but also distinguished writers like Chapelain and the erudite Abbé Ménage and Valentin Conrart. All contributed to a collective game that produced unlimited verses year after year, continually enriching them with variations along the way. In 1636, for instance, Voiture launched a fashion for rondeaux, and the following year Cotin had tremendous success with riddles. In 1638, "metamorphoses" in prose came into fashion. In 1640, as Y. Fukui writes, letters in verse "become the genre par excellence for the exchange of news, gallantry, and the requesting of favors."[21] Here too, as might be expected, Voiture proved his mastery.

But it was not in dedicatory verse letters so much as in prose letters that Voiture showed the full measure of his talent. From the beginning, the epistolary genre had been an essential component of society life. Letters were conversation at one remove, which meant not only that the absent were remembered but also that they could shine from a distance, entertaining the recipients and providing news. Read aloud, commentated on, and often copied, a letter, if sent to the right person, could reach a very wide circle indeed. The letters of Guez de Balzac are a case in point. Though he had retired to his château in the Charente, "the father of hyperbole" still made his presence felt in Paris, mostly thanks to his prolific correspondence with Chapelain. Through him, Balzac continued to keep up-to-date about

---

20. Tallemant, *Historiettes*, Vol. 1, p. 492.

21. Y. Fukui, *Raffinement précieux dans la poésie française du XVIIe siècle* (Paris: Nizet, 1964), pp. 214–215.

what was going on in the capital, and with the help of his friend he managed to orchestrate a long-distance campaign of self-promotion. Balzac's own relationship with the hôtel de Rambouillet perfectly demonstrates the link between letter-writing and drawing-room life. Although it is highly unlikely that he ever actually set foot in the rue Saint-Thomas-du-Louvre, he can be considered a genuine habitué of the house. Through Chapelain, he knew its ways, its tastes, and its guests. As Chapelain wrote to him on March 22, 1638, "Nothing merits your curiosity more than the hôtel de Rambouillet. Conversation there is not learned, but it is reasonable, and nowhere in the world is there more good sense and less pedantry.... [It is] the one place in the world where your virtue would find itself most agreeably at home, as I am sure you will agree when you come here and have made several visits. Until now, you are honored, esteemed, and cherished and held present by the perpetual souvenir we have of your merit."[22] The "hermit of the Charente" would do everything in his power to keep that "perpetual souvenir" alive.

Thus aware of the Blue Room's prestige and its ability to influence fashion, Balzac cultivated the goodwill of its hostess and her circle by means of a conscious strategy of letter-writing. His correspondence with Chapelain allowed him to praise Arthénice tactfully, elegantly, and indirectly in the certain knowledge that his friend would be pressed to read the letters aloud at the first opportunity. And, always through Chapelain, the hôtel de Rambouillet promptly reciprocated with appreciation and praise. Thus encouraged, Guez de Balzac tested the ground to see if he might pay public homage to the marquise. On receiving a reply in the affirmative, he dedicated to her four of his discourses, including his masterpiece, *Le Romain* (known as *De la vertu romaine*), an excellent opportunity to point out that Arthénice was a descendant, through her mother, of the illustrious Roman Savelli family.

This long-distance flirtation between two "powers"—a distinguished writer and an influential social circle—proved to be extremely profitable to both and heralded further correspondence along the same lines. Many distinguished exiles—from Roger de Bussy-Rabutin to Voltaire and the Italian Abbé Galiani in the following century—would write letters as a means of keeping their connections to Parisian society and defending their own interests. Thus, even when they were cruelly excluded from it, letter-writers contributed to society's variety and prestige from afar.

For Balzac, as it was later for Bussy-Rabutin and Voltaire, exile was also to be a choice—a period of *otium studiosum* (studious leisure) in which to recover oneself in silence, study the ancients, and eventually reestablish contact with the world through the medium of writing. While a playful utopia of pleasure and amusement was being launched at the hôtel de Rambouillet, Guez de Balzac

---

22. Jean Chapelain, letter 151, in *Lettres de Jean Chapelain de L'Académie française*, edited by Ph. Tamizey de Larroque, two volumes (Paris: Imprimerie nationale, 1880–1883), Vol. 1, pp. 215–216.

embraced a symbolically studious solitude and literary creativity in his forced exile. The two cultural models were profoundly different but would henceforth increasingly interact and enrich one another. Even Voiture was to suffer the pain of separation and exile on several occasions. As "usher" to the "ambassadors" of the King's rebellious brother Gaston d'Orléans in the 1630s, he was obliged to follow him from place to place.

For Voiture, before letter-writing became a practical necessity imposed by physical circumstance, it was a means of seduction and entertainment.[23] Whereas Guez de Balzac was full of a sense of his own literary dignity (his splendid letters give the impression that he is already thinking of the printed work and future readers), Voiture cared not a fig for posterity, and true to the aristocratic ethos of the group that adopted him, he disdained all thought of publication, addressing his readers in a familiar, conspiratorial way. But when, in 1650, two years after Voiture's death, his nephew, Étienne Martin de Pinchêne, produced the first collection of his letters, it became obvious that it was he, not Balzac, who had blazed the path for the genre. "Voiture taught us the easy, delicate way of writing that now holds dominion," wrote Père Bouhours twenty years later. "Before that it was presumed that to be witty was quite simply to talk like Balzac, to express great thoughts with great words."[24]

Voiture's main ambition was to please and entertain those to whom he wrote. To succeed in this, he did not hesitate, first and foremost, to play the card of self-mockery. A brilliant example of this is the long letter he addressed to Mlle de Bourbon, the future Mme de Longueville. The little eleven-year-old princess was ill, and Voiture, on being sent to her bedside, had failed to distract her:

> Mademoiselle,
> After dinner on Friday I was tossed in a blanket because I had not made you laugh in the time allotted to me for that purpose, which punishment was decreed by Madame de Rambouillet at the request of Mademoiselle her daughter [Julie d'Angennes] and Mademoiselle Paulet. They postponed the execution of this plan until Madame la Princesse [the addressee's mother] and you yourself should return. But they then decided to delay no longer and desired the agony not to be postponed to a season that should be destined for joy. I shouted and defended myself in vain. The blanket was brought and four of the strongest men were chosen. All I can say, Mademoiselle, is that

---

23. In 1629 Voiture joined Gaston in Lorraine; from July 1632 to October 1636 he was in Spain on diplomatic missions for his master; in 1638 the King sent him as special ambassador to the Grand Duke of Tuscany to announce the birth of the future Louis XIV and he reached Florence by way of Turin, Vercelli, Genoa, and Livorno.

24. Bouhours, "Le bel esprit" (entretien 4), in *Les Entretiens d'Ariste et d'Eugène*, pp. 133–134.

never was anyone so high up as I, nor did I ever think fortune would raise me so high. Every time I was lost to view and sent higher than eagles can fly. I saw the mountains bow down below me; I saw the winds and the clouds passing under my feet; I discovered countries I had never seen and seas I had never imagined. Nothing is more entertaining than to see so many things at once and to discover half the world at a single glance. But I can assure you, Mademoiselle, that one only perceives all that with anxiety when one is in the air and certain to fall back down. One of the things that frightened me so much was that when I was really high up and I looked below, the blanket appeared so small that it seemed impossible for me to fall back into it, and I must say that this fact caused me some emotion. But among the many different objects that struck me at the same time, there was one which for an instant removed my fear and caused me real pleasure. This, Mademoiselle, was that on wishing to look toward Piedmont to see what they were doing there, I saw you crossing the Saône at Lyons. At least I saw a great light on the water and many beams shining around the most beautiful face in the world. I could not easily discern who was with you, because I was upside down at the time, and I think you did not see me, for you were looking in the other direction. I tried to make a sign, but just as you began to raise your eyes, I fell back down, and one of the peaks of the Rhône-Alps prevented you from seeing me. As soon as I landed, I wanted to give them news of you, and I assured them that I had seen you. But they began to laugh as though I had said something impossible and they started to bounce me again, higher than before. A strange accident happened, which would seem unbelievable to anyone who had not seen it. On one occasion when they threw me so high that I found myself, on falling back, in a very thick cloud and, being very light, I was caught for some time without falling. So they stood below for a long time holding out the blanket and looking up, unable to imagine what had happened to me. Fortunately there was no wind at all, for, had there been, the cloud would have carried me from side to side and I would have fallen to the ground, which could not have happened without my hurting myself badly. But a more dangerous accident occurred. The last time they threw me into the sky, I found myself amid a flock of cranes. They were at first astonished to see me so high up. But on coming closer, they took me for one of those pygmies with which, as you well know, Mademoiselle, they have always been at war, and they thought that I had come to spy on them up in the sky. They immediately fell on me, attacking me so violently with their beaks that I thought I had been stabbed by a hundred daggers, and one of them would not leave me alone at all until I was back in the blanket. This warned my tormentors against putting me once again at the mercy of my enemies, for they were gathered in great numbers, and were hanging in the air waiting for me to be sent back. So I was carried home, wrapped in the same blanket and feeling as faint as could be. To tell the truth, this exercise is a little violent for a man as weak as I. You can judge for yourself, Mademoiselle, how tyrannical this business is, and for how many reasons you are obliged to disapprove of it. And without lying, it absolutely behooves you, who are born with so many qualities of leadership, soon to accustom yourself to the hatred of injustice and to taking the oppressed under your protection. I beg you therefore, Mademoiselle, first of all to declare this affair to be an assault that you disavow, and to order, so as to satisfy my honor and restore my strength, that a great gauze pavilion be erected for me in the Blue Room at the Hôtel de Rambouillet where I will be waited on and treated magnificently for two days by the two maidens who have been the cause of this misfortune. In one corner of the room sweetmeats will be made at all hours; one of the maidens will blow on the stove, and the other will do nothing but put syrup on plates to cool it and bring it to me from time to time. Thus, Mademoiselle, you would perform a just action, and one worthy of the great and beautiful a princess that you are.[25]

Here, in fact, the buffoonery and self-mockery very delicately disguise a moving declaration of total devotion. The miniature man, bounced up and down like a clown on the outstretched blanket, has given himself entirely to the tyrannical ladies, whose plaything he has become. For one who could then claim the right to sit under a gauze canopy in the middle of the Blue Room, however, no trial seemed too arduous.

Voiture's letter-writing skills were based on a thorough knowledge of his audience, their psychology, their tastes, and their habits, all of which went to making him a true master of flattering statements. His letters were enchanting mirrors in which the recipients could see the sublime reflection of themselves. They were enjoyed equally by all the habitués of the hôtel de Rambouillet because they allowed them, over and over again, to evoke precious moments from their own lives. Ultimately, in applauding Voiture, the Blue Room was applauding itself; such mirroring resulted from fierce reciprocal conditioning. In becoming the chronicler of the hôtel de Rambouillet, Voiture did not merely interpret its spirit but also enhanced its awareness of himself by providing a definitive display of style through his writing. Voiture was, after all, one of the hôtel de Rambouillet's most brilliant creations, the irrefutable proof of its power to educate. Writing in praise of him, but with some reserve, the man of letters Paul Pellisson stressed the interdependency between Voiture and the Blue Room: "May he have eternally the advantage of belonging to the finest and most gallant society ever, from which he received much

25. Voiture to Mlle de Bourbon (circa 1630), letter 9 in *Œuvres de Voiture*, Vol. 1, pp. 40–44.

and to which he gave much; may he eternally charm all that is most delicate in Society; may he be eternally inimitable: but may we not be accused eternally of imitating him."[26]

It was the women who, in repayment for his admiration, made Voiture's work "inimitable." He may well have been the first modern French writer to dedicate himself to a female public. "I am mistaken if the opinion of any man, however qualified by fortune or ability, is of greater advantage to him than the approbation of these illustrious women, who have made of his conversation and writing one of their most agreeable pastimes," wrote his nephew in the preface to the 1650 edition.[27] In exchange for their goodwill, Voiture appealed precisely to the extraordinary qualities of these women—their expectations, their sensibilities, and their judgment. In his letters, as in his verse, Voiture excelled in *badinage*—flirtatious banter—a delicate courtly art that struck a fine balance between sincerity and insincerity, between impertinence and respect, between the mind and the heart.

How could one woman after another be raised higher than perfection itself, refreshing the stereotype that, even if it succeeded in flattering, could only bear a semblance of truth? How could the bubbling excitement of love and courtship be reconciled to society's lucid awareness of fiction? How, finally, could conniving, vulgar discourse ever be the means of both proclaiming and denying the same message? The art of *badinage* was exactly the ability to reconcile all these contradictions in the name of fun, and to produce a brilliant comedy of courtship without ever confusing it with real life. One inherent ambiguity made this courtly banter particularly attractive: Could not this blatantly artificial love serve as a smoke-screen to disguise feelings that dared not reveal themselves? Voiture's letters to Julie d'Angennes certainly arouse suspicion. If his witty exchanges with the Marquise de Rambouillet's eldest daughter reached the heights of virtuosity, it could only be because he had never wished so intensely to please any woman. Voiture probably really loved her with a love that could never be openly expressed. *Badinage* presented him with the only way of courting her without giving offense.

The two following letters are rightly celebrated as absolute models of the genre. Both were written for entertainment and both were designed to have a double meaning: a private one for Julie and a public one for the Blue Room habitués.

The *Lettre à Mademoiselle de Rambouillet, sous le nom du roi de Suède*, dated March 1632, has its origins in a typical instance of Rambouillet fun. There was much talk in the Blue Room of Julie's passion for the King of Sweden, whose military prowess was admired throughout Europe. Julie had been the first to encourage the chatter by hanging a portrait of Gustav Adolph in her bedroom. It

---

26. Paul Pellisson, Preface to *Les Œuvres de Monsieur Sarasin*, p. 42.

27. Étienne Martin de Pinchêne, preface to *Les Œuvres de Monsieur de Voiture*, second edition (Paris: Augustin Courbé, 1650), p. 7.

would be hard to imagine a subject more likely to provoke *badinage*. This time Chapelain was the first to react. Two anonymous poems appeared mysteriously in succession in the rue Saint-Thomas-du-Louvre: *La Couronne impériale* ("The Imperial Crown") and *L'Aigle de l'Empire* ("The Eagle of Empire"). In both, Gustav Adolph expressed his gratitude to and tenderness for Julie. Everyone admired the verses and was fascinated by the mystery; several visitors even competed in the literary game. The last to arrive on the scene, after it seemed that everything had been tried, Voiture furnished proof of his supremacy. The Rambouillets were astonished when one day a large carriage stopped in front of their house and various people in Swedish dress descended from it, bearing a portrait of Gustav Adolph as a gift. Had the fame of the hôtel de Rambouillet really reached Sweden? The letter handed to Julie soon made it clear that this was a joke that could only be of Voiture's making:

> Mademoiselle,
>
> Here is the Lion of the North, the conqueror whose name has sounded throughout the world, who comes to place trophies from Germany at your feet and who, having defeated Tilly and crushed the power of Spain and the forces of the Empire, comes to join your ranks. Among the cries of joy and songs of victory that I have been hearing for many days, I have heard nothing so agreeable as the news that you wish me well, and since hearing it, I have changed my plans and limited my ambition, which embraced the whole earth, to you alone. This is not so much to have attenuated my designs as to have elevated them. For the earth still has its limits, and the desire to rule it has sometimes befallen souls other than mine. But the wit that is admired in you, which can be neither measured nor understood; your heart, which is so much more than scepters and crowns; and the grace by which you rule all wills are benefits of infinite value to which no one but I have ever dared lay claim. And those who wished for several worlds have, in so doing, wished for less than I. If my wish could triumph and if the fortune with which I conquer everywhere should accompany me to you, I would not envy Alexander all his conquests, and I would believe that those who have ruled over all men have not had so vast an empire as I. I would say more, Mademoiselle, but I am at this moment about to fight the imperial army and six hours later to take Nuremberg. I am, Mademoiselle, your most passionate servant.
>
> Gustav Adolph[28]

Voiture's gallantry conformed to the tradition of the *laudatio*, declaring Julie's intelligence, heart, and beauty to be incomparable. But its true success depended

---

28. Voiture to Mlle de Rambouillet [March 1632], letter 22, in *Œuvres de Voiture*, Vol. 1, pp. 73–75.

on invention and surprise. Repetition was the greatest intrinsic threat to *badinage*, and the risk was particularly high in the case of the eldest Rambouillet daughter, the most fêted young woman of her day. Instead of bothering to think up original compliments, Voiture decided to pay homage by means of a performance in two parts. The initial coup de théâtre—the arrival of the Swedish delegation and the presentation of the portrait and letter—was to capture the general attention and turn it toward Julie. The letter then praised the young woman in the most flattering terms. Such praise was exceptional less for the compliments themselves than because of the reputed sender. In it, the "conqueror of Europe" bowed down to one who had declared herself unconquerable. Only he dared to express publicly the hope of a love that Voiture himself was obliged not to mention.

Another means by which Voiture employed the element of surprise was by introducing a delicate hint of genuine melancholy to one of the most overused themes of amatory rhetoric: the indifference of the "cruel beauty." In 1637 a letter from Julie to Voiture, who was away from Paris at the time, gave rise to a magnificent subject for flirtatious banter. Purists in the Académie française had condemned the use of the conjunction *car* ("because") in favor of *pour ce que*, and Arthénice's daughter had come down on the side of the former. The controversy, widely debated in Parisian high society, provided a splendid double opportunity to celebrate Julie, while at the same time engaging the interest of all the hôtel de Rambouillet habitués. Thus, despite the distance, Voiture could remind his public that no one was wittier than he, that he, more than anyone, possessed the secret of laughter:

> Mademoiselle,
>
> *Car* being of such great importance in our language, I very much approve the resentment you feel at the ill wished upon it.... At a time when fortune has wrought much tragedy throughout Europe, I can see nothing so worthy of pity as a word that I see is about to be banished and put on trial, one which has so usefully served this monarchy and which, in all the kingdom's disputes, has ever proved itself a good Frenchman.... I do not know for what reason they attempt to take from *car* that which belongs to it in order to give it to *pour ce que*, nor why they wish to say with three words what they could say with three letters.... But it is principally you, Mademoiselle, who are obliged to protect it. Since the great strength and most perfect beauty of our language is spoken by you, you should have sovereign power over it and cause words to live or die as you please. Therefore I believe that you have already saved this one from the danger it incurred and that, by enclosing it in your letter, you have given it refuge and a place of glory, where time and envy cannot reach it. Amid all that, I confess that I was astonished by the whimsical nature of your goodness, and I find it strange that you, Mademoiselle, who would pitilessly leave a hundred men to

perish, could not see one syllable die. Had you cared as much for me as you do for *car*, I would have been very happy despite my misfortune. Poverty, exile, and anguish would barely have touched me.... Grant me more consideration another time, if you please; and when you undertake to defend the afflicted, remember that I am of that number. I will always use that same word [*car*] to oblige you to confer me with that favor.[29]

Voiture's pen turned the linguistic debate to parody, making *car* into the persecuted hero of a tragicomedy. But at the height of his tale, with Julie's protective intervention, Voiture unexpectedly introduced a personal, sorrowful note. If only the illustrious, all-powerful lady had granted to him a little of the mercy she showed toward a simple syllable!

The linguistic controversy was in fact not merely a pretext for *badinage* but an opportunity to pay Mlle d'Angennes the most coveted compliment: that she was the absolute arbiter of language. For once, this was no exaggerated tribute but a precise assessment of merit. Like her mother and the other noblewomen who frequented the Blue Room, Julie spoke perfect French. She had an instinctive awareness of the language, and her authority in the matter was considered indisputable. It was to the hôtel de Rambouillet that the grammarian Claude Favre de Vaugelas went in preparation for his *Remarques sur la langue françoise, utiles à ceux qui veulent bien parler et bien écrire*, there to check on the "good usage" and "pure" French spoken by the "most wholesome part of the court."[30] By seeing Arthénice's eldest daughter as the supreme linguistic authority at the hôtel de Rambouillet, Voiture was raising her as a symbol of the new rule of women in matters of language and taste.

For all his literary success, however, Voiture was not a nobleman and never would be. As Mme de Staal-Delaunay wrote a century later, neither exceptional skills in the art of pleasing nor the ability to amuse had the power to redeem the "original sin" of humble birth.[31] The process of initiation by which Voiture had been accepted in the Blue Room was by its nature incomplete and gave him no permanent right of belonging. If "King Chiquito" tended to forget this, there was always someone ready to remind him.[32]

---

29. Voiture to Mlle de Rambouillet [circa 1637], Letter 101 in *Œuvres de Voiture*, Vol. 1, pp. 293–296.

30. Claude Favre de Vaugelas, preface to *Remarques sur la langue françoise* (1647), edited by Jeanne Streicher (anastatic reprint Paris: Droz, 1934), p. 2.

31. *Mémoires de Madame de Staal-Delaunay* (1775; reprint Paris: Mercure de France, 1970). The author was first a maid, then a lady-in-waiting to the Duchesse du Maine.

32. Because of the poet's small size and his passion for Spain, Julie's nickname for Voiture was "King Chiquito," derived from the story of a gnome who became king of Granada.

Among the many fashionable society games, a very popular one at the time consisted of collective "rigmaroles"—rhymed verses formed by each participant adding a line. Some time around 1633–1634, Mme de Loges, according to Tallemant, launched one such rigmarole rhyming on the syllable *-ture*, destined to become "*le portrait du pitoyable Voiture.*" Her intent had been entirely playful, but as the game progressed, someone saw it fit to change the tone from good-natured irony to brutal rudeness:

> *C'est une aimable créature*
> *Si sa race estoit sans rature,*
> *Et sa naissance sans roture.*[33]

Voiture's letter to the Abbé Costar, a scholar and Latinist with whom he was friendly, revealed the depth of the wound:

> I send you some verses that have been composed against me, in which Voiture is made to rhyme with *roture* [plebeian].... Though we resemble each other in nothing else, [Horace and I] are alike in our plebeian descent..., and it seems to me that when I have written a book, I will be able to say of it, as Horace did of his: "*Me libertino natum patre, et in tenui re/Majores pennas nido extendisse loqueris.*" I would not dare to add what follows: "*Ut quantum generi demas, virtutibus addas.*"[34]
>
> Tell me if you think I deserve it. In truth, Monsieur, those who reproach me thus know me very little if they think that this vexes me. I can assure you that I would like everyone to know who I am. They would despise me less if I were of little value, and if I had merit, they would appreciate me all the more. Undoubtedly the nobility occupies an important place in the hierarchy of our blessings and constitutes an advantage whereby we are able to gain many others. But there are so many other more desirable things in life, and this is one of the last that I would dare desire. If one could not be generous without being what the Latins call *generosus* [someone belonging to a *genus*, or noble family], if one could not have a fine mind, a superior, strong and great soul; if health, reputation, and riches necessarily depended on birth, then there would be no possible consolation for either Horace or me. But this is not so, thanks be to God, and I know that there is an entire satire

---

33. "He is an amiable creature,/If only his race were not impure,/And his birth not plebeian." Tallemant, *Historiettes*, Vol. 1, p. 488.

34. "You will tell [o little book] that I was born of a freedman father in a poor house, and that I flew far beyond my little nest. I can attribute little to birth, but as much again to merit." Horace, *Epistles*, I, 20, lines 20–22.

by Juvenal on that subject and Sallust devotes an entire speech by Marius to it.[35]

But perhaps you do not know the Castilian proverb whereby everyone is the child of his own deeds, or the reply given to an Italian gentleman by a *bravo* of that country: "I and my right arm, which I now recognize as my father, are worth more than you." Allow me to point out that in Spanish *hidalgo*, which means "gentleman," comes from *hijo d'algo* or "son of something," thus underlining the fact that true nobility derives from virtuous deeds which give us a second birth, better and more glorious than the first.

Things being thus, Monsieur, he who is born a plebeian can be reborn as a gentleman and flood his life with light, despite his obscure beginnings. But to do so, extraordinary qualities which I lack and will always lack are required. My good luck is that they are not indispensable for your friendship or I would lose the hope of preserving it, and this is one of the thoughts that most cheers me.[36]

Wounded to the quick, Voiture had changed his tone and dropped his guard. There is neither a trace of irony nor are there any jokes in this fine letter in which, by adopting a moral tone, he stands on his intellectual, bourgeois dignity. For him the word "gentleman" did not merely describe a social condition but had moral overtones. As Stefano Guazzo had opined in *Civil Conversation*, there is a nobility of the soul that ignores birth and is forged through the exercise of virtue.[37] With a semblance of obligatory modesty and, in his indignation, forgetting his dilettante's detachment, Voiture implicitly defends the value of his own work. But he knew from experience that this "second birth, better and more glorious than the first" was not always recognized and involved a challenge, destined to recur from generation to generation.

Once again Voiture seems to symbolize the future. With him, the writer made his entry on the social scene and became an integral part of it, while retaining a strong element of ambiguity. Sought after, spoiled, argued with, the "intellectual" was treated by the nobility both as an equal and as a very different being. Equal in the salon's utopian surroundings, he could not but hold an inferior position in the general context of a hierarchical society based on birth and wealth. Years later, not even the enormous prestige of men of letters in the Age of Enlightenment could entirely eradicate the social differences. The situation would remain static even on the eve of the Revolution. Sainte-Beuve recounts a story about Nicolas

---

35. Juvenal, *Satira* VIII; Sallust, *Bellum Jugurthinum*, Chapter 85.

36. Voiture, *Correspondence de Voiture avec Costar*, letter 4, in *Œuvres de Voiture*, Vol. 2, pp. 148–150.

37. Guazzo, *La civil conversazione*, Vol. 1, Book 2, pp. 124ff.

Chamfort, who, as the illegitimate son of a nobleman, experienced more fully than anyone the drama of this double sense of belonging:

> One day the Marquis de Créqui said to him, "But Monsieur de Chamfort, it seems to me that today a man of wit is everyone's equal, and the name does not matter." "You speak very easily, Monsieur le marquis," replied Chamfort, "but imagine that instead of being called Monsieur de Créqui, you were called Monsieur Criquet. Then see if the effect would be the same when you entered a salon."[38]

The Italian *bravo* that Voiture quoted to his friend as saying "I and my right arm, which I now recognize as my father, are worth more than you" foreshadows an exchange that took place between the young Voltaire and the Chevalier de Rohan toward the end of January 1726, an exchange that was repeated first at the Opéra and again two days later in the foyer of the Comédie française. To Rohan's provocative question "Monsieur de Voltaire, Monsieur Arouet, what are you called?" Voltaire replied in the same tone, "And you, are you called Rohan or Chabot?" The difference between the two of them, Voltaire continued, was that the chevalier was dishonoring an illustrious name, while he was making his own immortal.[39] As with Vincent Voiture almost a century before him, worldly success had led Voltaire to suppose that birth and merit could meet on equal terms and be held in the same regard. One privileged man's rudeness suddenly made him realize that this was not the case. A notary's son could not reply with impunity to the insults of the scion of one of France's proudest houses. Rohan made sure he knew it, by having his servants beat him. The act was in keeping with the chevalier's reputation for degeneracy, yet none of Voltaire's aristocratic friends came openly to his defense. In the end, as the Maréchal de Villars is supposed to have said, "he was no more than a poet."[40] In spite of everything, the poet, intent on behaving like a gentleman, took fencing lessons and challenged Rohan to a duel. Once again, Voltaire was put back in his place, this time by the forces of law and order, which sent him to the Bastille.

Dueling had held a great fascination for Voiture as well, almost to the point of obsession. At a time when the right to defend one's honor by the sword had been defended by the nobility at its very peril, dueling, a symbol of aristocratic excellence, seemed able to provide a man of the Third Estate with a passing illusion of

---

38. Charles Augustin Sainte-Beuve, "Chamfort," in *Causeries du lundi*, third edition, sixteen volumes (Paris: Garnier, 1857–1870), Vol. 4, p. 540, note 1.

39. René Pomeau, *D'Arouet à Voltaire, 1694–1734* (Oxford: The Voltaire Foundation/Taylor Institution, 1985), p. 204.

40. Pomeau, *D'Arouet à Voltaire*, p. 206.

social advancement. Thus, wishing to model his behavior on that of the marquise's noble friends, Voiture added to his contempt for money a contempt for life.
It was a duel—and a ridiculous one at that—that would have him banished from
the Blue Room shortly before his sad demise. Not only did he have the audacity,
after Julie d'Angennes's marriage, to fall in love with the marquise's youngest
daughter, Angélique Clarice, and to show his jealousy of her, but he was mad
enough to fight for her with Chavaroche, the Rambouillets' intendant. This inad-
vertently comic situation represented a confusion of roles quite unacceptable
to the good reputation of the hôtel de Rambouillet. Indeed, verbal dueling was
the only dueling allowed to Voiture, and perhaps, even in this case, his great openness of speech, not to say insolence, was an indication of inequality rather than
equality. "If Voiture were one of us," said Monsieur le Prince, "it would be intolerable."[41] It leads one to ask whether the indulgence Voiture enjoyed at the hôtel
de Rambouillet was not, in the end, the age-old indulgence with which grandees
had always treated their buffoons.

---

41. Tallemant, *Historiettes*, Vol. 1, p. 489.

5

LA GUIRLANDE DE JULIE

NEITHER VOITURE'S IMPUDENCE, nor his cheerfulness, nor his laugh amused Charles de Montausier, who had been a regular visitor to the hôtel de Rambouillet since 1632. Julie d'Angennes's suitor had long been the butt of jokes by the *corps*, the small band of young scoundrels led by the Rambouillets' only son, Léon Pompée, Marquis de Pisani. Although decidedly unlettered, the young marquis was unreservedly friendly to the house poet and had co-opted him into his clique. Their fellowship was not entirely haphazard. Pisani's irreverence and his taste for farce, salacious turn of mind, and audacity were all employed to disguise, as they did in Voiture, the deep mortification of one who felt himself excluded. Small, hunchbacked, and misshapen, Pisani exorcised his tragedy through laughter. So, at the hôtel de Rambouillet, the refined, worldly Voiture did not devote himself just to pleasing the ladies. He also allied himself with the *enfant terrible* of the house, who, indifferent to the revolution taking place in his mother's drawing room, sneered at good manners and boasted of his ignorance.

In contrast, Charles de Sainte-Maure, later Duc de Montausier, was an austere, introverted man. He had served dutifully as a soldier and loved both study and erudite conversation with distinguished literati. For him, culture was not, as it was for Pisani, a sign of pedantry incompatible with noble pride. Montausier's position as suitor for Julie's hand made him especially vulnerable to attack from the *corps*'s noisy irreverence and Voiture's petulance, both of which he found distasteful. But Montausier took his revenge on Voiture in the subtlest way: by beating him at his own game. The king of gallantry was excluded from "from the greatest gallantry there ever was."[1]

Waking on her name day, May 22, in 1641, Julie d'Angennes discovered an extraordinary present on the dressing table in her bedroom. Enclosed in a case of sweet-smelling wood was the most beautiful book she had ever seen. The book

---

1. Tallemant des Réaux, *Historiettes*, Vol. 1, p. 461.

celebrated her on every page, a delicate, heart-melting declaration of love. The manuscript, bound in red morocco with her initials stamped in gold on the spine, contained forty pages of the finest parchment on which as many short poems were written in exquisite handwriting, interspersed with twenty-nine paintings on vellum. A marvelous garland of flowers adorned the frontispiece, giving the book its title and announcing its theme: *La Guirlande de Julie*. Together, the twenty-nine flowers would form a wreath to crown the brow of the most admired *demoiselle* of her day. Inside, each flower had a plate to itself and spoke in madrigals of Julie's beauty and virtue. This precious tour de force was no mere literary exercise. Behind the conventional amorous rhetoric and the virtuosity of the allusions throbbed the Duc de Montausier's all too real feelings, which he had been nursing for more ten years.

Aged thirty-seven—at a time when her contemporaries were already grandmothers—Julie d'Angennes still considered herself young and had no wish to face reality. She had declared herself invincible to amorous advances. Her true vocation was society life. To be generally admired, never to allow that admiration to wane, and to increase the number of her conquests daily seemed a far more exciting undertaking than to reign over one heart alone. But what else could be expected of the Marquise de Rambouillet's daughter? If Arthénice had managed to make her drawing room a model for the new French *sociabilité*, and if, thanks to her example, the art of good manners and the religion of taste were to become the inalienable patrimony of aristocratic culture, how could her eldest child not represent, in her own eyes and those of the world, the perfect incarnation of that *esprit de société* which so embellished the Blue Room? As a favorite daughter who had grown up at her mother's side, Julie was a masterpiece of the marquise's creation. Her bearing was regal, she danced incomparably, her tact was exquisite, her taste infallible. She conversed on varied subjects with wit and brilliance, but never interrupted others. Everyone competed for her love. "After Helen," wrote Tallemant des Réaux, "there has been no one whose beauty has been more widely sung; yet she has never been a beauty.... Dancing admirably, as she did, with the spirit and grace which was always hers, she was an admirable person."[2]

But as we have already seen, Eros, with all his passion and turbulence, was unwelcome at the hôtel de Rambouillet. There, gallantry had to be loveless, and language stripped of any impurity. There, life was to direct itself toward a pure artistic image. Mme de Rambouillet often declared that if she could put the clock back, she would not have married, and in Julie, the mother's hopes were realized. Why forgo a free and pleasant life only to embrace the prosaic reality of marriage? It would, however, be wrong to suppose that Mlle d'Angennes was the perfect image of her mother. Even contemporaries and habitués of the hôtel de

---

2. Tallemant, *Historiettes*, Vol. i, p. 457.

Rambouillet noted the marked difference in character and style between the two women, a difference that signaled subsequent developments of French *sociabilité*.

For Julie, worldliness was not, as it was for her mother, a mere opportunity for entertainment, a flight toward Arcadia, a gratuitous game. The Marquise de Rambouillet had created a world in her own likeness, but Julie had no intention of limiting her conquests. The marquise had turned her back on the court, whereas her daughter would one day solicit favors there, using seduction as the most effective way of achieving her goals. Mlle d'Angennes was driven to seek the approval of all, not so much by love, friendship, or her own moral integrity as by an all-commanding wish to please. Mlle de Scudéry, in her 1651 portrait of Julie in *Le Grand Cyrus*, intimates as much. How does Philonide[3] manage to cultivate such a vast number of friends? Mlle de Scudéry, more conscious than anyone of society's artificial nature, was well aware that everyone's success depended on the ability to act naturally and convincingly in accordance with a strictly codified mode of behavior. Julie's behavior and desire for acclaim manifested such virtuosity that it almost called her credibility into question. What feelings might lie behind such infinite amiability? As Mlle de Scudéry concluded diplomatically, "only she knows for certain whom she loves and how much."[4]

Mme de Motteville was far more explicit and direct in her *Mémoires*—which were not written with her contemporaries in mind. She captured all the potential moral ambiguity of Julie's art of pleasing, the same *art de plaire* that Rousseau would denounce a century later as the supreme expression of "vanity" and of the arrogant wish to dominate. Julie

> treated her men and women friends in such a courteous fashion [*d'une manière si honnête*] that it was impossible not to wish to please her.... Her obliging displays of friendship flattered all those who saw her; and everyone found them to their advantage. Nevertheless, it was said that she had one failing, and sometimes she was told of the whispering against her. She was blamed for always wishing by her manners to please even those for whom she had no esteem. Those who believed themselves deserving complained that she treated everyone equally. They said that she took an interest in so many, and that in wanting too many friends, she had not one.[5]

Mme de Motteville, writing around 1661, describes a fully mature Julie at a time when the magnificence of the hôtel de Rambouillet had already passed into

---

3. Julie had adopted this "precious" pseudonym.

4. Mlle de Scudéry, *Artamène ou le Grand Cyrus*, Vol. 7, Part 7, Book 1, p. 302.

5. *Mémoires de Madame de Motteville*, Vol. 4 (for the year 1661), p. 303.

legend. Nevertheless, from the moment forty years earlier, when the marquise's favorite daughter first appeared in the Blue Room, it was obvious that she would not be a mere ornament in her mother's drawing room but one of its main attractions. Within their closed circle, mother and daughter complemented each other admirably. The elder was more collected, poised, and alert; the other, more communicative and extroverted but, at the same time, more indifferent to others.

Had Mlle d'Angennes ever considered leaving that magic circle and accepting the idea of marriage, who could have competed with her romantic dreams? Only one suitor worthy of her ever presented himself, and that was not Charles de Montausier but his elder brother, Hector. Handsome, gallant, brave, and extremely elegant—he was always dressed in red—Hector would not have been out of place in the chivalric novels so beloved of the Blue Room. Julie might have considered him had he not died heroically in battle. With the loss of the elder Montausier in 1635, the second presented himself. Charles, three years younger than Mlle d'Angennes, had none of his brother's gifts, but he had loved her since he was a boy. He was bitter, intransigent, and sincere to the point of brutality. He hated falseness, never disguising his intolerance for even that element of hypocrisy so essential to society life. Molière is said to have taken Montausier as his model for *The Misanthrope*. Indeed, the real-life clash between his and Julie's personalities can hardly have been less than that between Alceste and Célimène on the stage.

Unlike Molière's character, however, the Duc de Montausier had no intention of withdrawing from the world, or of giving up the woman he loved. For years he had battled the twin afflictions of his own uncouth, antisocial nature and Mlle d'Angennes's proud resistance. By dint of determination and application he had triumphed surprisingly over the first, gradually becoming the most perfect of lovers, one almost worthy of a chivalric treatise. He fought courageously in the Thirty Years' War, but during the winter truces in Paris, he followed in the steps of his goddess like a humble and respectful shadow. As for the second obstacle, the duke could draw comfort only from the fact that instead of refusing him point-blank, Julie remained enigmatic and vague.

By 1641, in order to escape from a situation that had been static for too long, Montausier decided to play a last card and to entrust his sentiments to the language of flowers. A perfect book in which the symbolism of real flowers was illustrated by the rhetorical flowers of poetry would finally reveal the perfection of his love for Julie and the perfection of the loved one herself. Montausier had sought the collaboration of the Blue Room's most gifted habitués—among them Desmarets, Tallemant, and Georges de Scudéry—to compose the madrigals. For the calligraphy and illustrations, he had turned to two artists: the calligrapher Nicolas Jarry, whose writing was remarkable in that it was impossible to tell at what point he had dipped his pen in the ink; and the botanical painter Nicolas Robert, a discovery of the duke's who would soon be employed by the kings of France.

At a time when illuminated manuscripts had been replaced by printing, Montausier decided on the manuscript form because he wanted to give Julie an absolutely unique object whose fame would spread. With his erudition and his magnificent library, Montausier was fully aware of the rich variety of symbols that each flower could bring to a lover's discourse. It is probable that during the siege of Casale he had had a chance to admire the garland of madrigals dedicated to Angela Bianca Beccaria in 1595 by Stefano Guazzo, a distinguished citizen of that Piedmontese town. But Montausier's choice of flowers was also a specific tribute to the hôtel de Rambouillet. It was the marquise who introduced into France the habit of decorating the house with baskets of flowers and scenting the rooms with potpourri.

By combining the rigors of educated culture with the taste for word games, puzzles, and symbolism, Montausier managed to offer Mlle d'Angennes an irresistible reflection of her own splendid apotheosis. The news of the duke's project caused a sensation. The verses from the collection gave rise to more verses, and finally parody confirmed the exceptional nature of the affair. In the *Guirlande*, the tender violet addresses Julie, in a madrigal composed by Desmarets, as follows:

> *Franche d'ambition, ie me cache sous l'herbe,*
> *Modeste en ma couleur, modeste en mon séjour;*
> *Mais si sur votre front ie me puis voir un iour,*
> *La plus humble des Fleurs sera la plus superbe.*[6]

In an anonymous ballad, however, reference was made to a flower that did not appear in the *Guirlande* but which urgently needed picking: the flower of the celebrated *jeune fille*'s virginity:

> *Cette fleur vive, rouge et belle*
> *Dure au monde si longuement*
> *Que l'on peut dire justement*
> *Que c'est une fleur immortelle.*
>
> *La recherche en eût été prompte;*
> *Ou si tu la laisse vieillir*

---

6. "Free of ambition, I hide in the grass,/Modest in my color, modest in my abode;/But if on your brow I can see myself one day/The humblest of Flowers will be the proudest." *La Guirlande de Julie*, edited by Irène Frain (Paris: Laffont, 1991), p. 129.

Pas un ne voudra la cueillir
Et son honneur sera ta honte....[7]

Without securing Julie's immediate consent, the *Guirlande* managed to breach the wall of her indifference. Finally, her closest friends—and even Cardinal Mazarin, Anne of Austria, and, above all, her mother—managed to persuade her to take the great step. Montausier, for his part, abjured his Protestant faith in order at last to marry her. Tallemant tells how Julie suddenly capitulated in May 1645, on the eve of her fortieth birthday.[8] He hints that she may simply have understood that it was preferable to be a new bride than an old maid. Montausier's courtship had lasted for fourteen years.

Two people who did not join in rejoicing at the festivities were Voiture and the Marquis de Pisani. Julie's brother had gone to join his regiment, announcing that since Montausier was so happy, he would certainly go and get himself killed. His prophesy came true three months later, on August 3, at Nördlingen. His disabilities had not prevented him from being a courageous soldier. As for Voiture, without Julie and without Pisani, he began to display signs of instability. The people he had loved so much had gone, and Mme de Rambouillet no longer wished to laugh. Among the paintings described in Georges de Scudéry's poetic "gallery"[9] is one painted by Pieter van Mol, which depicts Arthénice in an Italian Pietà, deep in the contemplation of her son's dead body.[10]

---

7. "This bright flower, red and beautiful/Has lasted so long in the world/That it can justly be said/That it is an immortal flower./It would have been quickly sought;/But if you let it grow old/No one will wish to gather it/And its honor will be your disgrace...."; *La Guirlande de Julie*, p. 49.

8. They were married on July 5, 1645, by Godeau, the bishop of Grasse, at the château de Reuil, which belonged to Mme d'Aiguillon. The Queen lent the King's twenty-four violinists for the occasion.

9. Georges de Scudéry, *Le Cabinet de Monsieur de Scudéry*, edited by Christian Biet and Dominique Mocond'hui (Paris: Klincksieck, 1991), p. 157.

10. Victor Cousin, *La Société française au XVIIe siècle d'après le Grand Cyrus de Mlle de Scudéry*, fourth edition, two volumes (Paris: Didier, 1873), Vol. 1, p. 250.

6

MADAME DE LONGUEVILLE:
A PERFECT TRANSFORMATION

ANNE GENEVIÈVE DE BOURBON-CONDÉ was sixteen years old when she made her first official appearance at court. Until then she had grown up in the apartments of her mother, Madame la Princesse, under her vigilant eye, spending much of her time in the Carmelite convent in the neighboring rue Saint-Jacques. The serenity and austere kindness of the convent had made a profound impression on her, and during her innocent, chaste adolescence, Anne Geneviève had often wondered if she did not prefer the peace of the cloister to the tumult of the outside world. But the illustrious Condé family had other plans for their very beautiful daughter, and on February 18, 1635, heedless of her reservations, they took her to a ball held at the Louvre in the sovereign's presence. Like many other girls of her caste, Mlle de Bourbon dreaded going out into the world. It was not only from the nuns that she had learned of the risks to which she would be exposed. In spite of the religious injunction against novels, she had read too many of them not to fantasize about the infinite seductions of society life. So in order to force herself to stick to her principles, Anne Geneviève acquired a hair shirt, which she wore under her ball gown.

Her fears proved to be well founded and her precautions useless. While the court paid homage to the young princess's "angelic" beauty,[1] Anne Geneviève discovered a new self in the admiring glances turned toward her and thus became captivated by her own image. As her friends at Port-Royal would later say, her soul became idolatrous in yielding to that subtlest of temptations: the cult of self. From the evening of the ball, she abandoned her dreams of hiding away in a convent and sought instead to become the supreme arbiter of morals and aesthetics on the world stage, a position to which she felt destined by her beauty and rank.

No one had a happier youth than Mlle de Bourbon. With her slightly younger brother the Duc d'Enghien (her other brother, the Prince de Conti, was still a child), Anne Geneviève was at the center of a cheerful group of *petits-maîtres* and

---

1. *Mémoires de Madame de Motteville*, Vol. 1, p. 37.

petites-maîtresses consisting of the children of Madame la Princesse's closest friends: the Rambouillets, the Clermonts, the du Vigeans, the Boutevilles. For several years life seemed like a continuous round of fêtes, balls, concerts, spectacles, hunting parties, picnics, luncheons, "tiltings for rings," and society games. Friendships, exchanges of confidences, and chaste courtships were enough to fill the heart, and there was no time to think about the future. Mme de Rambouillet's Blue Room, where Anne Geneviève's mother loved to take her, did everything to nurture the hope that serenity and harmony would prevail in the adult world.

The enchantment lasted until she was twenty. In 1642, *comme une rose en la saison nouvelle...tombe entre les mains d'un passant malappris,*[2] Anne Geneviève was given in marriage to Henri d'Orléans, Duc de Longueville—the first gentleman of France after the princes of the blood. The duke, who had an immense fortune, was a widower, twenty-four years older than his bride. Despite the promise he made to his new mother-in-law, however, he seemed unready to put his passion for his mistress, the Duchesse de Montbazon, behind him. For the new duchess, in any case, dynastic considerations counted for more than the heart, and never was her pride more gratified than at the time of her splendid marriage.

With the death in 1642 of Cardinal de Richelieu, followed swiftly by that of Louis XIII in 1643 and the beginning of Anne of Austria's regency, the Condés regained all the political clout that Richelieu had removed from the princes of the blood. With the King's brother, Gaston d'Orléans, they became the crown's chief guarantors. Moreover, Anne Geneviève's father, Monsieur le Prince, by declaring his support for Cardinal Mazarin from the start, assured himself of both the Queen's and the new minister's gratitude. But that was not all. On May 19, 1643, at the age of only twenty-two, the Duc d'Enghien proved his military genius for the first time, crushing the Spanish army at Rocroi and saving the French from the threat of foreign invasion. Henceforth Condé pride knew no bounds. The kingdom's other grandees soon took issue with it.

The Vendômes and their supporters, Mme de Chevreuse and her lover, the Marquis de Châteauneuf, together with a large number of other eminent malcontents, found the new understanding between Monsieur le Prince and Mazarin worrisome. They were suspicious of the cardinal minister's increasing "tyranny" and embittered by the ingratitude of a queen to whom they had remained loyal through difficult times but who had failed to reward them adequately. These parties lost no opportunity to oppose the Condés and advance themselves. When one such opportunity was presented to them under the guise of a female vendetta, the "*Importants*" seized it.

---

2. "As a rose in the new season...falls into the hands of an uncouth passerby." Lines written for the occasion by Jean-François Sarasin, quoted in Michel Pernot, *La Fronde* (Paris: Éditions de Fallois, 1994), p. 104, note 2.

The Duchesse de Longueville had been married for nearly two years when Mme de Montbazon, her husband's former lover, launched a bitter attack on her virtue—the one quality, other than her rank, that was unassailable. "The universal admiration to which Madame de Montbazon aspired" was quite different from the chaste respect inspired by her young, angelic rival. If the Duchesse de Montbazon's virtue had long since been sacrificed without regrets "to her extreme desire to please," her seductive appeal was nonetheless without comparison. Few men were not bowled over by her majestic, sensual beauty, which, now that she was in her thirties, was in its full glory. So much so that the rigorous Mme de Motteville felt obliged to award her, for the entire century, "the first place for beauty and *galanterie*."[3]

A letter, which probably fell from the pocket of a distracted guest at one of Mme de Montbazon's receptions, opened hostilities in 1644. It was an unsigned love letter in what appeared to be a woman's handwriting. Who had written it, and to whom? The small mystery would have enlivened any social gathering, and under the knowing direction of the lady of the house, "gaiety turned to curiosity, curiosity to suspicion, and from suspicion, the decision was reached that it had fallen from the pocket of [the Comte de] Coligny, . . . who, it was whispered, had a passion for Madame de Longueville."[4] These beginnings could hardly have been more romantic, and it could barely have been by chance that they were so faithfully reproduced in the century's finest novel, *La Princesse de Clèves*. Surely, in writing the main episode, Mme de Lafayette was thinking about Mme de Longueville—who had once loved La Rochefoucauld, the man whom she now loved—and of the tragic events in which the duchess had been the protagonist thirty-four years earlier.

In fact, until the Duc de La Rochefoucauld came to capture her heart a few years later, Mme de Longueville's behavior had been unimpeachable. Like the word *esprit*, the word *galanterie* expressed a whole range of nuances, even to the point of assuming opposite meanings, as it did for Mme de Longueville and Mme de Montbazon. For one, *galanterie* was an open, innocent game in keeping with aristocratic and courtly traditions; for the other, the boundaries were there to be crossed, and the gallant game could be the prelude to a full-blown affair. If the proud Mme de Longueville publicly accepted the devoted admiration of a handsome young knight like Maurice de Coligny, this was part of the *honnête galanterie* she had learned at the hôtel de Rambouillet. Nonetheless, the insinuations of Mme de Montbazon and her circle cast a shadow of doubt on her shining reputation.

What in other cases would have been passed off as an amusing piece of gossip became, in the eyes of the Condés, an "affair of state." In tears, Madame la

---

3. *Mémoires de Mme de Motteville*, Vol. 1, pp. 135–136.

4. *Mémoires de Mme de Motteville*, Vol. 1, p. 137.

Princesse begged the Queen that suitable reparation be made for the affront to her daughter. Anne of Austria ordered a public apology for the insinuations against Mme de Longueville. Obliged to obey, the Duchesse de Montbazon came to the hôtel de Condé at the appointed hour with a little piece of paper pinned to her fan on which were written the sentences that she had been asked to pronounce. "She did it in the proudest and haughtiest way possible, with a face that seemed to say: 'I disdain what I am saying.'"[5] The matter was closed to the dissatisfaction of both sides, and the quarrel remained unsettled. Madame la Princesse asked Anne of Austria to be excused from appearing in places where Mme de Montbazon might be expected, and Mme de Montbazon eventually took daring to the point of insolence by refusing to leave a reception at which the Queen had requested the Princesse de Condé's presence.

Until now the Queen Regent's politics had been one of conciliation and tolerance, but Mme de Montbazon's disrespect made her very angry. It was only too obvious that behind this story of women's backbiting lay the increasing antagonism between the Condés and their enemies, who amounted to the enemies of Mazarin. It was equally obvious that Mme de Montbazon's insubordination represented that of her new lover, the arrogant Duc de Beaufort, who was extremely handsome but lacked even basic common sense. He had offered his services to the Queen as Louis XIII lay dying and now could not hide his irritation at seeing her prefer Mazarin. And behind the Duc de Beaufort—brother of the Duc de Mercoeur and son of the Prince de Vendôme—could be sensed the increasingly threatening ill-humor of the *cabale des Importants*. All this would have been absorbed in the patient game of politics, however, had Anne of Austria not felt that her dignity as sovereign had been insulted. It was the one thing about which she was intransigent. Mme de Montbazon was ordered to leave the court at once. Her departure marked the beginning of Mazarin's rule. By taking advantage of his opponents' quarrels and cleverly exploiting the Queen's indignation, he took the opportunity to rid himself of his enemies. One after another, the most dangerous of the *Importants* were condemned either to prison or exile.

According to the chivalric code, the king had the power to banish or otherwise punish, but he could not intervene to resolve a dispute based on honor. When a woman had been insulted, it was up to her knight to avenge her, even at the cost of his life. While *honnête galanterie* exempted women from love, it did not exempt men from death. According to this logic and unable to confront Beaufort, who was in prison, the Comte de Coligny challenged Beaufort's friend Henri de Guise to a duel. The latter had aligned himself with Mme de Montbazon's camp. But what was the point of all this where Mme de Longueville was concerned? No one doubted her innocence. She was a married woman in an advanced stage of pregnancy,

5. *Mémoires de Mme de Motteville*, Vol. 1, p. 142.

expecting the son of her legitimate consort and with an illustrious family ready to intervene in her defense. The count, her admirer, had not compromised her in any way. The rash woman who had dared to cast the rumor had been soundly, not to say excessively, punished, and the Duc de Guise had had no part in the slander. So why force matters beyond all reason? Perhaps Coligny really loved Mme de Longueville and wanted to earn her gratitude; perhaps he, too, had read too many novels and the memory of the ancient enmity between his family and the house of Guise made his gesture all the more dramatic.[6] Indeed, it was nothing short of a suicidal gesture, for Coligny was just recovering from a long illness and it was well known that Guise was the finer swordsman. The meeting took place on December 1, 1643, at three o'clock in the afternoon in the place Royale, a location favored by duelists since it allowed this illegal activity maximum visibility. "The fight was soon over," recounts La Rochefoucauld. "Coligny fell, and the Duc de Guise, to affront him, removed his sword and struck him with the flat side of his own.... Coligny, overwhelmed by the anguish of having so ill-defended such a worthy cause, died four or five months later of a languishing sickness."[7]

In the whole affair, Mme de Longueville's behavior is the most puzzling. What were her true feelings for Coligny?[8] Was it really she who asked him to fight, as Mme de Motteville claims? And if that was not the case, why did she not oppose the duel instead of watching it, hidden behind a window in the hôtel de Rohan? Perhaps Anne Geneviève was incapable of distinguishing between truth and fiction, and her overactive imagination led her to see herself as a Corneillean heroine. Perhaps her behavior was dictated by a self-love to which everything seemed fitting homage, including death.

Many years later, in her "general confession," Mme de Longueville admitted to having "always sought pleasure in all that flattered my pride, and offering to myself what Satan offered our first parents: 'You will be as Gods.'"[9] In her longing for expiation, the penitent allowed the remembrance of her sin to overwhelm her, until it took over her whole life. Yet there was a story attached to that "always," as Lucifer advanced step by step.

The Condés, starting with Madame la Princesse, were united in the belief that they were different from the rest of the world, a belief confirmed by their mutual

---

6. François de La Rochefoucauld, *Mémoires*, in *Œuvres complètes*, edited by L. Martin-Chauffier, chronology and index by Jean Marchand (Paris: Gallimard/Bibliothèque de la Pléiade, 1957), p. 85.

7. La Rochefoucauld, *Mémoires*, p. 85.

8. Unlike La Rochefoucauld, Cardinal de Retz maintains that Mme de Longueville was in love with Coligny. See Retz, *Mémoires,* p. 132.

9. J. F. Bourgoin de Villefore, *La Véritable Vie d'Anne Geneviève de Bourbon, duchesse de Longueville, par l'Auteur des Anecdotes de la Constitution Unigenitus,* two volumes (Amsterdam: J-F. Jolly, 1739), Vol. 2, p. 50.

admiration. As immensely rich and powerful princes of the blood, they not only demanded implacably what they saw as their rights, but they were equally intransigent with regard to what they judged to be their duty. They believed in excellence: the Duc d'Enghien was a masterpiece of Jesuit education, and his sister, that of the Blue Room. They basked in the traditional values of their class—courage, pride, ostentation—and in becoming arbiters of the new spirit of the times they distinguished themselves not only as patrons of art but also by their elegant style and infallible taste. Of course they all had their weaknesses and vices, but individual failings were compensated for by the sum of the qualities of the various family members. The Condés formed a whole. Each life was interwoven with that of the others. From her earliest youth Anne Geneviève had been at the center of this mirror game. Loved and spoiled by the entire family, she soon established a seductive relationship with the Duc d'Enghien, over whom she had a vaguely incestuous hold.[10] This was repeated later with her younger brother.[11] Admiration and jealousy, quarrels and reconciliation were the extremes in a process of identification and self-aggrandizement that reinforced the Condés' certainty of being a race apart with their own code of behavior and unmistakable style.

Marie d'Orléans, the daughter of M. de Longueville's first marriage—whose *Mémoires* show how little she loved her stepmother—describes the Condé spirit during those happy years in the 1640s. After a series of boisterous victories and having become the prince in 1646, the Duc d'Enghien earned the name the Grand Condé. At that time the family delighted in laying down the law in society through the peaceful medium of conversation. The topics they preferred, according to Marie, were the "gallant and merry" ones that allowed them to discuss "the delicacy of the heart and the sentiments. . . . Those who shone most were, in their eyes, the most *honnêtes*, and the cleverest; whereas they treated as ridiculous and clumsy anything with the slightest hint of seriousness."[12]

Just as the *esprit de société* was establishing itself as the common ideal, it was obliged to contend with the different attitudes of various aristocratic circles. The *esprit* of the Condés, the Mortemarts, and the *Précieuses* are famous examples of the desire for diversification that denied homogeneity and questioned the rules of social conformity. But after the first half of the century, with the triumph of classical taste, moralists and writers were united in condemning as ridiculous and dangerous any desire for "distinction." As in literature, good taste in society must consist in constantly maintaining the balance between naturalness and the norm, between being true to oneself and obedient to the demands of "good company."

10. La Rochefoucauld, *Mémoires*, p. 86.

11. Retz, *Mémoires*, p. 132.

12. *Mémoires de Marie d'Orléans, duchesse de Nemours (1625–1707)* (1709; Paris: Mercure de France, 1990), p. 78.

Mme de Longueville was fully aware of this and could, whenever necessary, forget the Condé *esprit* and adopt that of the hôtel de Rambouillet. At Münster, where she joined her husband in 1646, she showed how well she understood what an important part that ideal, perfect, worldly courtesy could play, not only on the social scene but in diplomacy and politics as well. Away from the hôtel de Condé for the first time, Mme de Longueville discovered the pleasure of having a role of her own. M. de Longueville had since 1645 served as French ambassador plenipotentiary in the small German town where European diplomacy sought to reach an agreement that would put an end to the Thirty Years' War. While her brother was stamping French supremacy on the battlefields and her husband sought to establish it at the negotiating table, Anne Geneviève was exemplifying her country's superiority in civilization and elegance. There, by attentive mediation, and with a natural ability to smooth over differences while showing the greatest regard for the self-respect of her interlocutors, the young ambassadress, accompanied by a brilliant entourage of gentlemen and literati, confirmed the highly diplomatic quality of French conversation.

On December 6, 1646, the Comte d'Avaux—a master of the art of diplomacy and personification of all the virtues of the ideal man of the world—wrote to Vincent Voiture asking him to inform the Blue Room of Mme de Longueville's popularity in Germany. Singing her praises, he described her as

> a person so *précieuse*, who has come two hundred leagues to rejoin an old husband; who has left the Court for Westphalia; who is continuously gay; who was recently delighted to see a play at the Jesuits (in truth it was in good Latin); who gives many audiences; who converses peaceably with Monsieur Salvius, Monsieur Vulteius, Monsieur Lampadius; who is no longer afraid of a big Dutchman who kisses her regularly twice an hour every time he visits; who agreeably receives the compliments of another ambassador who advises her to learn German for amusement; who, with all that, is growing plumper in Münster and has a satisfied expression; who divides her time between good reading and audiences; who advances the cause of peace as much by her counsel as by her prayers; who has not only a great many womanly virtues but many others besides: *Quas sexus habere/Fortior optaret.*[13]

The long-awaited peace was not concluded in Westphalia until October 24, 1648, without Mme de Longueville's presence. She had been back in France for

---

13. Letter from Claude d'Avaux to Voiture, December 6, 1646, quoted in Victor Cousin, *La Jeunesse de Madame de Longueville*, second edition (Paris: Didier, 1876), pp. 282–283. D'Avaux cites Ausonius' description of his virtuous sister Julia Dryadia in the *Parentalia*: "She had many [virtues] which the stronger sex and the nobler heart of men would gladly have" (translated by Hugh G. Evelyn White, 1919; Loeb Classic Library, 1988), p. 75.

over a year, "crowned in myrtle."[14] At Münster the princess had discovered the world of politics and had shone in high diplomatic circles. She had promoted urbanity and French elegance and had gained the admiration of the representatives of all the European powers. In fact she had contributed to the glory of the Condés with an entirely personal victory. A triumphal Parisian welcome only reinforced her desire to take center stage. "She became the object of all desires; her drawing room became the center of all intrigue, and those she loved immediately became fortune's favorites," Mme de Motteville recounts. "Her courtiers were revered by the minister; before long, we shall see her as the cause of all our revolutions and all the squabbles that have threatened to destroy France."[15]

Love did the rest. Although physically cold, in imagination she had always been inclined toward romance, and when she finally recognized her hero in the brilliant Duc de La Rochefoucauld, she gave herself to him wholly. "She grew ambitious on his account; for his sake she no longer sought repose; and in her sensibility to this fondness, she became too insensible of her own honor."[16] This may well have been a congenital character defect, according to a cruel portrait of her that has been unjustly attributed to the pen of La Rochefoucauld.[17] Perhaps it was, as Sainte-Beuve suggests, "a desire to shine again."[18] Or it may have denoted a perfect identification with the loved one, a desire to raise him to a level worthy of her. Certainly, by shaking her out of her languor, passion gave her a feeling of omnipotence. For further temptation, Lucifer turned to the Fronde.

Although modern historians do not always attach importance to Mme de Longueville, contemporary witnesses all see her as having played a significant part in the disruption that overwhelmed France between 1648 and 1653. The Fronde was the major civil crisis of seventeenth-century France and the last time the country's nobility would rise in armed rebellion against a king. Its immediate cause was widespread discontent with mounting taxes and other financial burdens incurred by a lengthy period of war with France's neighbors. More deeply, however, it was an expression of the nobility's frustration with the growing power of the crown and particularly the current regency government, which had begun five years

14. Letter from Antoine Godeau, bishop of Grasse, to Mme de Longueville, quoted in Cousin, *La Jeunesse de Madame de Longueville*, p. 287.

15. *Mémories de Mme de Motteville*, Vol. 1, p. 334.

16. *Mémoires de Mme de Motteville*, Vol. 1, p. 335.

17. "Far from imposing her will on those who particularly adored her, she adopted their sentiments so much as no longer to recognize her own," quoted in Charles Augustin Sainte-Beuve, "Madame de Longueville," in *Portraits de femmes*, in *Œuvres*, two volumes (Paris: Gallimard/Bibliothèque de la Pléiade, 1950–1951), Vol. 2, p. 1280.

18. Sainte-Beuve, "Madame de Longueville," in *Œuvres*, Vol. 2, p. 1280.

earlier when Anne of Austria annulled her husband's will and, in alliance with Cardinal Mazarin, enlarged the powers of her regency for the nine-year-old Louis XIV. Historians usually divide the Fronde into two distinct parts—the Fronde of the Parlement (1648–1649), set off by the regency's proposal that government officials give up four years' salary, and the Fronde of the Princes (1650–1653), characterized by conflicting personal grievances and ambitions among the nobility.

Mme de Longueville was not the only woman to invade the masculine world of politics. The Fronde, more than any other conflict in French history, seems to have been a woman's war. Like Mme de Longueville, the Duchesse de Chevreuse, the Princesse de Palatine, and the Grande Mademoiselle, along with other noblewomen, hatched plots, instigated rebellion, sowed discord, and even took up arms.[19] Was this an "upside-down world," as it has been described, or was it, rather, the last spectacular occasion on which men and women of the French nobility fought together to have their particular interests of class and family prevail over those of the state? It might be more to the point to speak in terms of lineage and clan. In the Fronde of the Princes, the nobles were united only in their opposition to the increasing centralization of power in the monarchy and to Mazarin, whom they considered corrupt, duplicitous, and despotic. Far from constituting a single block, they were permanently squabbling among themselves. Under the *ancien régime*, individual ambition depended on family support, which in turn needed to be reinforced through the dense network of marriages. Brothers, sons, nephews, and cousins with their various positions, connections, and spheres of influence were the essential allies of anyone who aspired to lasting power. The first person to be aware of this was the hated Mazarin himself, who, in order to give himself family support, had brought an army of nephews and nieces with him from Italy.

Noblewomen had long been accustomed to putting whatever strengthened the family position before themselves and knew no greater ambition than that of belonging to an illustrious family. Female ingenuity was traditionally concentrated on the display of magnificence, beauty, and elegance while, behind the scenes, they were intriguing and planning marriages. The Princesse de Guéméné, although she cared little for domestic affairs, had declared herself "prepared to draw a dagger" in the "interests of her line," even for a young sister-in-law's right to the *tabouret*.[20] In times long past, with their husbands away at war, some noblewomen had not hesitated to take up arms to defend their lands from powerful

---

19. The Duchesse de Chevreuse had been Anne of Austria's great confidante but was exiled under Louis XIII. Anne de Gonzague-Nevers Palatine, the sister of the Polish Queen Marie, was famous for her wit and her intrigues. Chapter 9 will be devoted to the Grande Mademoiselle, Louis XIV's cousin.

20. Tallemant des Réaux, *Historiettes*, Vol. 2, p. 229. Only duchesses, princes of the blood, and pregnant women had the right to sit (usually on a *tabouret*, or folding stool) in the Queen's apartments or when admitted to the King's meals. Anne de Rohan, Princesse de Guéméné, married her first cousin, Louis de Rohan Guéméné.

neighbors. Only a few years before the Fronde, when her husband was away, the Comtesse de Saint-Balmon, dressed as a man and riding a horse, had led an army of peasants to keep her Lorraine property from being ravaged by Austrian and French forces. In inciting the provinces governed by their fathers, husbands, and brothers to rebel against the King's authority, the Grande Mademoiselle, Mme de Longueville, and even the Princesse de Condé, the Grand Condé's timid, much-disliked wife, were acting, according to feudal logic, in the name of their absent or imprisoned men. Thus, even as she made La Rochefoucauld's Frondist ambitions her own, Anne Geneviève was fighting just as determinedly for the interests of her husband and her brothers.

Should we not speak of the Amazons of the Fronde in terms of continuity rather than rupture with the past? The civil war did not transform the aristocratic code of behavior but merely exacerbated its character and exaggerated its excesses. If the memory of classical female heroism had faded, it was now revived in litera-ture in the image of the *femme forte*, with characters like Bradamante, Clorinda, and Semiramis, to say nothing of Joan of Arc's shining bravery in Chapelain's *Pucelle*. It did not take long, however, for identification with literary models to take a dangerous turn for both sexes. Too many of the *Frondeurs* were passionate about novels and convinced that life mirrored them. Mme de Longueville, for one, was sure of it in Paris in the winter of 1649, just at the time of the Fronde of the Parlement. Cardinal de Retz describes her in his memoirs as giving the impression of a heroine straight from the pages of Honoré d'Urfé's *L'Astrée*.[21]

Mme de Longueville may have indulged her romantic fantasies, but she in turn inspired the great new narrative success of the times, one that was greatly to influ-ence the collective imagination. Not only did Mlle de Scudéry dedicate all ten vol-umes of *Artamène ou le Grand Cyrus*—her contemporary fictional account of the Fronde—to Mme de Longueville, she also made her the story's main heroine. No contemporary reader had any trouble in recognizing the Grand Condé in the exotic guise of the heroic Cyrus or in identifying the beautiful Mandane as his sister.

Long before La Rochefoucauld appeared in her life, Mazarin had sensed Anne Geneviève's potential threat to politics. "The lady in question has absolute power over her brother," the cardinal minister wrote in one of his notebooks. "She would like to see this brother in charge of and dispensing all favors . . . she suggests to the brother high ideas to which he, therefore, is naturally drawn . . . like her brother, she believes that all favors granted to her person, house, relations, friends, are her due."[22] The explosion of the Fronde of the Parlement confirmed the minister's fears. At Mme de Longueville's instigation, first her younger brother, the Prince de Conti, and then the Grand Condé rebelled against royal authority

---

21. Retz, *Mémoires*, pp. 153–154.

22. Quoted in Cousin, *La Jeunesse de Madame de Longueville*, p. 272, note 1.

and declared war on Mazarin, wishing to show the full measure of their power and to assume the country's leadership. This tragic ambition was destined to radicalize the Fronde and engulf France in a new civil war.

Memoirists of quite different views—among them Cardinal de Retz, La Rochefoucauld, the Grande Mademoiselle, Mme de Motteville, and Mme de Nemours—all level an imposing list of accusations at Mme de Longueville. None, however, failed to respect her fearlessness. Perhaps Mme de Longueville was in fact merely the instrument of La Rochefoucauld's ambition, as Mme de Motteville suggests. Perhaps she was no more than an "adventuress" of the Fronde, as Retz described her.[23] It is impossible not to be impressed by the iron determination with which she dominated her husband, stirred up her brothers, quarreled with them, won them back over, allied herself with the Paris Parlement, threw herself with the help of her secretaries into civil rhetoric and political invective, rode a horse across France, incited Normandy to rebellion, took to the sea in a storm to find refuge in Holland, conducted negotiations with Mazarin from the small town of Stenay, the rebels' only remaining stronghold, and allied herself in Bordeaux with the popular Ormée movement. Reputation, morality, friendship were all subordinated to the heroic affirmation of self and the hunger for power. For her, gallantry became a tool of vanity and domination. In his scandalous collection of anecdotes, the *Histoire amoureuse des Gaules*, Roger de Bussy-Rabutin recounted her conquest of the Duc de Nemours, who had followed Condé to Guyenne. The duchess

> made such advances that this prince, although much in love with another, could not resist her; but he yielded through weakness of the flesh rather than attachment from the heart. The Duc de La Rochefoucauld, who had been the Duchesse de Longueville's much-loved lover for three years, observed his mistress's infidelity with all the rage that such an encounter might provoke. Filled with a grand passion for the Duc de Nemours, she took no trouble to accommodate her first lover.... This commerce did not last, for this duke [Nemours] could not oblige himself to show friendship he did not feel, and it is easy to believe that the princess, who was dirty and smelled bad, was unable to hide her defects from a man who was hopelessly in love elsewhere.[24]

In sacrificing La Rochefoucauld to the Duc de Nemours, Anne Geneviève let herself fall from her pedestal. The "precious" heroine of the *Grand Cyrus* joined the degraded world of the "gallant" women populating Bussy's racy satire. Nor

---

23. Retz, *Mémoires*, p. 158.

24. Roger de Bussy-Rabutin, "Histoire d'Angélique et de Ginotic," in *Histoire amoureuse des Gaules*, edited by Jacqueline and Roger Duchêne (Paris: Gallimard, 1993), p. 108. The coded names have been replaced by the real ones.

would the *Mémoires* of her betrayed lover serve as a vehicle for restoring her ideal kingdom to her.[25] Yet so long as the struggle was possible, no failure, no adversity, no disappointment could restrain her.

Once she was finally obliged to admit to the wreck of all her ambitions, Mme de Longueville displayed an equally extraordinary strength and dignity. The terrible energy that had supported her until then gave way to a new form of courage: resignation. The exalted Amazon recognized her husband's authority, reconciled herself with the court, and put herself back on the Carmelite path, attempting by her exemplary conduct to expiate her past. And as though a blindfold had fallen from her eyes, "all the charms of Truth presented themselves together in front of me: Faith, which had remained dead and buried beneath my passions, renewed itself. I felt like a person who, after a long sleep in which she had dreamed of being great, happy, honored, and esteemed by all, had suddenly awoken to find herself shackled by chains, covered in sores, overwhelmed by languor, and enclosed in a dark prison."[26]

Chateaubriand describes the ailing Madame la Princesse's reaction to her daughter's predicament. In 1650, far from her daughter and close to death, she told the Comtesse de Brienne, "My dear friend, send to that poor misery...news of the state in which you see me, and let her learn how to die."[27] From 1654 on, Mme de Longueville seems to have conducted herself in accordance with her mother's admonishments.

At the Carmelite convent in the rue Saint-Jacques—where she had been educated and to which she returned for comfort and advice—she found a few of the nuns she had known as a child and with whom she had always remained in contact. There were also some old friends who, older and wiser than she, had chosen the heroism of renunciation and discovered inner peace by consecrating themselves to God. Behind the veil of Sister Anne Marie de Jésus, for example, was Anne Louise Christine de La Valette d'Épernon, who had entered the convent in 1649 at age twenty-five after the death on the battlefield of the Chevalier de Fiesque, to whom she was bound by a tender, chaste love. That same year, Mlle du Vigean, having abandoned all hope of one day marrying the Grand Condé and determined to love none other, had also taken the veil. Nor was Mme de Longueville alone at the convent of Port-Royal, which became the second great point of spiritual reference in her life in 1660. Other society women, too, had turned their backs on the world to seek refuge in the Jansenist stronghold.

25. Beginning in 1662 La Rochefoucauld's *Mémoires* were pirated, and different editions with a great many variations and additions were published in Holland.

26. Bourgoin de Villefore, *La Véritable Vie d'Anne Geneviève de Bourbon*, p. 5.

27. François René de Chateaubriand, *Mémoires d'Outre-Tombe*, edited by Jean-Claude Berchet (Paris: Classiques Garnier/Bordas, 1989–1998), Vol. 2, p. 16.

The same tools that Anne Geneviève had used to cultivate the sense of her own superiority were needed now to humble her pride. She no longer used her psychological subtlety to expatiate on delicate matters of the heart and on sentiment, but directed it instead to implacable self-denigration. Shameful secrets were hidden at "the bottom" of her troubled and treacherous "heart" that evaded ever closer introspection, thus preventing the certainty of guilt. Where in the past Anne Geneviève had vigilantly claimed whatever she considered her due, now she was careful not to overlook the slightest occasion for self-mortification. All the diplomacy, all the powers of persuasion she had displayed at Münster, in her dealings with the Fronde, and in Holland at Stenay were now used for the "Peace of the Church"—the truce that in 1669 provisionally put an end to the theological dispute between the Church authorities and the *solitaires* at Port-Royal.[28] Based on an analysis of Mme de Longueville's writings, the scholar Benedetta Papàsogli suggests that her allegiance to Jansenism "was paradoxically defined without doctrinal connotations but rather as a profound expression of a religious sensibility and of a historical meeting of association and the sentiments. Her personal theology represented an anguished search for signs of salvation. . . . It was the solitaires' somewhat obsessive rigidity in itself that coincided with her need for moral rectitude and obsession with scruple."[29]

Unable to forget her betrayal, La Rochefoucauld did not believe in the sincerity of Mme de Longueville's conversion and ironically referred to her as the "mother" of the Church.[30] Perhaps he had forgotten that she was also the mother of his son, the Comte de Saint-Paul, later Duc de Longueville. His baptism, conducted by Cardinal de Retz in 1649 in the besieged capital, was an occasion for the entire Fronde of the Parlement to rejoice. The name chosen for the child, Charles Paris, reflected the euphoria of the moment as well as a demagogic intent similar to that which, 140 years later, inspired another Orléans to call himself Philippe Égalité. Intelligent, brave, and very like his natural father, the Comte de Saint-Paul was dearly loved by both his parents, and his death at the age of twenty-three on the battlefield united them in the last terrible ordeal of their lives. Like one of La

---

28. The *solitaires* were followers of the theological doctrine of Jansenism, who chose to live in retirement as part of the community of Port-Royal des Champs, devoting themselves to prayer and study. As soon as she died, it became clear how much Jansenism owed to Mme de Longueville. Less than a month later, a royal injunction ordered the ecclesiastics and solitaires of Port-Royal to leave the convent and forbade the nuns from welcoming further novices. As Louis XIV declared to Condé, it was only respect for Mme de Longueville that had persuaded him to put off closing the convent until then.

29. Benedetta Papàsogli, "Ritratto di Madame de Longueville" in *La lettera e lo spirito: Temi e figure del Seicento francese* (Pisa: Libreria Goliardica, 1986), pp. 110–111.

30. Réné Rapin, *Mémoires du Père René Rapin de la Compagnie de Jésus sur l'église et la société, la cour, la ville et le jansénisme*, edited by Léon Aubineau, two volumes (Paris-Lyon: Librairie Catholique Emmanuel Vitte, 1865), Vol. 2, p. 420.

Rochefoucauld's two legitimate sons, Longueville was killed, a victim of his own "burning ardor,"[31] on June 12, 1672, during the famous "crossing of the Rhine," the military exploit that Bossuet called the "marvel of our century and of Louis le Grand's life,"[32] whereby Louis XIV, at the head of his troops, led the invasion of the Netherlands. The Grand Condé, who was directing operations, brought the body of his nephew home, wrapped in a coat.

> Madame de Longueville's heart, they say, is broken. I have not seen her, but here is what I know. Mademoiselle de Vertus [a friend and confidante of Mme de Longueville] returned two days ago to Port-Royal, where she almost always stays. They went to fetch her together with Monsieur Arnauld to bring the terrible news. Mademoiselle de Vertus had only to show her face; [her] sudden return marked something sinister. In fact, as soon as she appeared: "Ah! Mademoiselle, how is Monsieur my brother?" She dared think no further. "Madame, he is well despite his wound. There was fighting." "And my son? My dear son! Did he die straight away? Did he not have a single moment? Ah! My God! What sacrifice!" and thereupon she fell on her bed and through her convulsions, her fainting, her mortal silence, her stifled cries, her bitter tears, her outbursts to Heaven, and by her tender, pitiful moaning, she experienced everything that the keenest pain can inflict. She sees certain people. She drinks some broth because God wishes it. She has no rest. Her health, which is already very bad, has visibly worsened. For my part, unable to understand how she can live after such a loss, I wish for her death.
>
> There is one man in the world who is no less affected; I believe that if the two of them had met in those first moments, and if no one but the cat had been with them...all other sentiments would have given way to the weeping and the tears that would have been redoubled from the heart: it is a vision.[33]

Mme de Sévigné's "vision" derived from La Rochefoucauld's assiduous visiting and her close friendship with Mme de Lafayette. Everything points to the fact that on hearing of his former lover's pain, the duke was at last able to perceive what it meant to Mme de Longueville to be a "mother."

La Rochefoucauld was not alone in doubting the authenticity of Mme de Longueville's religious conversion. In his memoirs, the Jesuit Père Rapin also

---

31. Mme de Sévigné to Mme de Grignan, July 3, 1672, in Mme de Sévigné, *Correspondance*, edited by Roger Duchêne, three volumes (Paris: Gallimard, 1972–1978), Vol. 1, p. 547.

32. Bossuet quoted in François Bluche, *Louis XIV* (Paris: Fayard, 1986).

33. Mme de Sévigné to Mme de Grignan, June 20, 1672, in Mme de Sévigné, *Correspondance*, Vol. 1, pp. 535–536.

expressed misgivings, albeit dictated by other reasons, which are of considerable interest. Why, the Jesuit wondered, did the Duchesse de Longueville, the Princesse de Guéméné, the Marquise de Sablé, the Comtesse de Maure, Mlle de Vertus, and countless other aristocratic ladies allow themselves to be attracted to Port-Royal? Why, instead of appreciating the Jesuit efforts to reconcile religion with worldly pursuits, did a refined society—dedicated to pleasure and in love with appearances—respond to the call of rigorous Jansenism? Père Rapin's explanation is brilliantly reductionist. Port-Royal's success in high society was exclusively worldly: a taste for novelty and the desire to attract notice. Whereas in Flanders, the land of its origins, Jansenism had remained within the confines of theological discussion, "in France, it was only persons of quality, the *beaux esprits*, and the ladies" who propounded the new doctrine.[34] Considering her high rank, Mme de Longueville was a dangerous example, and Rapin turned to the subtle art of denigration to discredit her: "This party had long since begun to please her on account of the moral severity taught at Port-Royal, because, being naturally severe in sentiment, she judged that to be admirable, although she was not at all so in her conduct, in addition to which, the intellectual refinement that reigned in that cabal, more than elsewhere, was greatly to her taste since she was herself very refined and greatly esteemed those who were so."[35] A hostage to appearances, Mme de Longueville might well have changed her behavior, Rapin implied, but in throwing herself into theological discussion, she was indulging a far more dangerous libertinism than that of the senses: "spiritual gallantry."[36]

Jansenist counterpropaganda, on the other hand, saw Anne Geneviève's conversion, without her having renounced either "delicacy" or *esprit*, as in perfect harmony with her fervid religiosity. One *solitaire*—perhaps Pierre Nicole, one of Port-Royal's most important intellectual figures—wrote that worldly perfection and Christian humility surprisingly reflected one another:

> The way in which Madame de Longueville conversed with the world was something to be studied.... She never said anything to her own advantage, this without exception; without affectation she took every opportunity she could to humiliate herself. Everything she said, she said so well that it would have been difficult to say it better whatever concentration was brought to the matter.... She spoke modestly, charitably, and without passion.... The air she adopted least was a decisive, abstract one, and I know some people, very amiable too, whom she never liked because they had something of that

34. *Mémoires du Père René Rapin*, Vol. 1, p. 36.
35. *Mémoires du Père René Rapin*, Vol. 2, p. 151.
36. *Mémoires du Père René Rapin*, Vol. 2, p. 147.

air.... Finally, her whole appearance, her voice, her face, her movements, were like perfect music, and her mind and her body served her so well in expressing everything she wished to communicate that she was the most perfect actress in the world.[37]

After her son's death, conversation became increasingly rare for Anne Geneviève. If the search for truth in human commerce was pure illusion, she seemed to find it better to remain silent. There is no such thing as an innocent word, as the Trappist Abbé de Rancé had in fact cautioned her in 1675. The very act of communication implies a lie. "Not only does one offend God by the word when one communicates with men," Rancé wrote, "but one sins even more in thought when one is no longer with them by virtue of ties and liaisons from which one cannot defend oneself; and there is no one who, on looking closely at himself, does not find great differences between what he is in conversation, however holy he may be, and what he is when alone."[38]

Anne Geneviève abandoned the hôtel de Longueville and went to live at Port-Royal des Champs in a house next to the convent, which she only left in order to visit the Carmelite convent in the rue Saint-Jacques: "It would seem that she wished to unite, in one supreme embrace, the remembered abbey of her young innocence and the monastery that bore witness to her holy repentance," wrote Cécile Gazier.[39] She never wanted it to be forgotten that she was a sinner with grievous sins to expiate. She was as faithful in her mortification as she was in her pride. The two apparently opposite phases of her life obeyed Providence's one design; the gravity of her sins was an eloquent sign of divine mercy.

Fallax pulchritudo; mulier timens Deum laudabitur (Beauty is vain; but a woman that feareth the Lord, she shall be praised): in taking this text from the Old Testament, Gabriel de Roquette, bishop of Autun, evoked the two seasons of Mme de Longueville's life in his funerary oration at the Carmelites on April 11, 1680, a year after her death.[40] Emotions ran high in the church in the rue Saint-Jacques, and many wept. The Prince de Condé was unable to hold back his tears at the memory of his sister; Mme de Lafayette cried as well, thinking of La Rochefoucauld, who had died a few months earlier, as did those of his sons who were present. Death

---

37. Quoted in Sainte-Beuve, "Madame de Longueville," in *Portraits de femmes*, in *Œuvres*, Vol. 2, p. 1303.

38. L'Abbé de Rancé to Mme de Longueville, [December?] *1675*, in Armand Jean de Rancé, *Correspondance*, edited by Alban John Krailsheimer, four volumes (Paris: Les Éditions du Cerf/Citeaux, *Commentarii cistercienses*, 1993), Vol. 1, pp. 727–728.

39. Cécile Gazier, *Les Belles Amies de Port-Royal* (1930; Paris: Librairie Académique Perrin, 1954), p. 110.

40. Mme de Longueville died on April 15, 1679.

reunited the two erstwhile lovers in one last, unexpected assignation. In order to write to her daughter, Mme de Sévigné observed the reactions of those present and reflected with fascination on the coincidences and network of memories, for "there was much to dream about where those two names were concerned."[41]

---

41. Mme de Sévigné to Mme de Grignan, April 12 [1680], in Mme de Sévigné, *Correspondance*, Vol. 2, p. 903.

7

THE DUCHESSE DE MONTBAZON AND
THE REFORMER OF LA TRAPPE

WHEREAS MME DE LONGUEVILLE had twenty-five years to prepare herself for death, Mme de Montbazon had only a few hours to repent of a life full of scandal.

With their overwhelming terror of damnation, seventeenth-century men and women considered a good death to be crucial to their existence. They thus had a morbid curiosity about the way in which their contemporaries confronted the end. "That illustrious society lady had only three hours to prepare for the great journey," wrote Mme de Motteville. "It seemed nevertheless that she employed them well. She confessed and received all the sacraments with many signs of piety and repentance for not having followed the strictest and most Christian maxims, telling her daughter, the Abbess of Caen, who was there at her side, that she was sorry not to have been, like her, always in a cloister, and that feeling the approach of her judgment hour, she was horrified by her past life."[1]

Marie de Bretagne-Avaugour, of the family of the Comtes de Vertus, left the convent at sixteen, in 1628, to be married to Hercule de Rohan, Duc de Montbazon, who was then aged seventy-two. Like a character in a story by Sade, her old husband relished introducing his wife to libertinage while calling her "his nun."[2] The young duchess made her début within the family by taking as her lover her husband's son-in-law, the Duc de Chevreuse. Her new lover's wife, Mme de Chevreuse, was Montbazon's daughter by his first marriage and herself a great adventuress. According to Cardinal de Retz, however, Mme de Chevreuse "loved without choosing and simply because she had to love someone . . . but as soon as she had taken a lover, she loved him singly and faithfully." Mme de Montbazon, in contrast, "loved nothing but her own pleasure, and beyond her pleasure, her interest. I have never seen anyone retain so little respect for virtue in her vice."[3]

---

1. *Mémoires de Mme de Motteville*, Vol. 4, p. 94.

2. Tallemant des Réaux, *Historiettes*, Vol. 2, p. 217.

3. Retz, *Mémoires*, pp. 158–159.

Contemporary accounts of Mme de Montbazon allow us to see how distant the Blue Room's utopian world was from the brutal habits of the day. The duchess knew no law other than her own desire. She loved love, sex, money, and power, which she high-handedly demanded, bowling men over with her sumptuous, sensual beauty. Always prepared to betray, she knew nothing of discretion or of the value of a word given. Insolent and impertinent to everyone, even to the Queen, the duchess did not bother to disguise her vices or to moderate the crudity of her language; Tallemant recounts that when she was pregnant, she "went all around Paris in her carriage at a fast trot, saying: 'I have just broken a child's neck.'"[4]

The license of the civil war gave full rein to Mme de Montbazon's own license. The power she had over the Duc de Beaufort, one of the leaders of the Fronde—known as "the King of Les Halles" because of his ability to win popular sympathy—allowed her to intrigue endlessly, to bargain with favors, to make and break alliances. Their common struggle against Cardinal Mazarin did nothing to attenuate the hatred between Mme de Longueville and Mme de Montbazon nor to assuage the longstanding enmity between the Condés and their rivals the Rohans and Vendômes. At times, though, they were obliged to reach some kind of agreement; on one such occasion, the Grand Condé asked Retz to pass the following message to Mme de Montbazon: "The only condition I require for our reconciliation is that when she cuts off Monsieur de La Rochefoucauld's I-know-not-what, she should not send it to my sister in a silver basin, as, over the last two days, she has told twenty people she will."[5] Even in her recourse to metaphor, the duchess was none too delicate.

It was toward the end of April 1657 that an unexpected fever carried off Marie de Montbazon, leaving her barely enough time to receive the sacraments. Few mourned her. "Her old lovers regarded her with disdain, and those who still loved her were untouched because each one, jealous of his rival, left the tears and the pain to the Duc de Beaufort as his prerogative, since he was the best-loved at the time,"[6] Mme de Motteville affirmed dryly. But Mme de Motteville did not know that among all those lovers, there was one who was broken by grief and anguish and tortured by the doubt that Mme de Montbazon's repentance in extremis would not be enough to save her from eternal damnation. He was a churchman who had until then remained deaf to the word of God and to whom the unexpected death of the woman he loved suddenly revealed "that there is nothing here below to which to become attached since the world has nothing so great or so glorious that it does not pass in a flash, nor that cannot be snatched away in a moment."[7]

---

4. Tallemant, *Historiettes*, Vol. 2, p. 220.

5. Retz, *Mémoires*, pp. 307–308.

6. *Mémoires de Mme de Motteville*, Vol. 4, p. 94.

7. Rancé to Mme de Longueville [July 1672], in Rancé, *Correspondance*, Vol. 1, p. 467.

Armand Jean Le Bouthillier, the Abbé de Rancé, was destined for the Church from childhood. Born in Paris on January 9, 1626, into a family of the *noblesse de robe*, the young abbot was intelligent and ambitious. By the age of twelve he had translated Anacreon. He graduated first in theology, coming even before Jacques Bénigne Bossuet, who would become a major classical figure and great writer. Rancé's awareness of his own merit and passion for study went hand in hand with a taste for the high life. Sole heir to a considerable fortune, Rancé had adopted the ways and fashions of the aristocratic Parisian world to which he was so strongly drawn. Without a qualm, the young abbot simultaneously managed to play the part of a pleasure-seeking *petit-maître* and an ambitious career ecclesiastic. "I am going this morning to preach like an angel, and tonight to hunt like a devil," he replied to a friend who inquired about his plans.[8] For him it was important to excel in both roles, and to do so elegantly.

During the *ancien régime*, dress was an immediate sign of belonging, and Rancé paid the utmost attention to his wardrobe:

> A violet close coat of precious material, silk stockings of the same color, tightly drawn; a dotted cravat of the most fashionable kind; long hair, always curled and well powdered; two large emeralds at his cuffs and a very valuable diamond on his finger; this was then the Abbé de Rancé's dress. But when he was in the country or out hunting, it was quite different. There was no sign in him of a man devoted to serving at the altar: a sword at his side, two pistols on the saddle bow, a fawn-colored habit, and a black taffeta cravat embroidered in gold. If, when in the most serious of company, he donned a black velvet close coat with gold buttons, he thought he had done well and was dressed according to the rules.[9]

Meeting Mme de Montbazon must certainly have helped to push Rancé in the devil's direction. He was then twenty; she was at least fourteen years his senior, and it is easy to imagine the hold such a great seductress of inalterable beauty must have had over the young libertine. It is not known with how many others Rancé shared the lady's favors, nor if the matter troubled him. Cardinal de Retz insinuates that the Duc de Beaufort was hardly a rival to be feared. But the fascination exercised by the high-ranking adventuress whom Rancé followed through the tumult of the Fronde was not of an exclusively erotic nature. The young abbot's embrace of the ideology and style of the high-ranking nobility may well have been accomplished at the hôtel de Montbazon, but that adopted home also

---

8. Blandine Kriegel, *La Querelle Mabillon-Rancé*, second edition (Paris: Quai Voltaire, 1992), p. 26.

9. Dom Gervaise's description, repeated by Chateaubriand and quoted in Kriegel, *La Querelle Mabillon-Rancé*, p. 23.

became the most important point of reference for his emotional life. And it was, paradoxically, in his mistress's house, too, that he experienced the beginnings of a spiritual metamorphosis that would lead him to abandon the world to join the monastery of La Trappe. Saint-Simon, the great chronicler of Louis XIV's reign, provides two different accounts of Rancé's conversion, and both have the hôtel de Montbazon as their backdrop.

The first version is that on hearing the news of Mme de Montbazon's illness, the abbé immediately returned from the country to Paris, ignorant of the fact that she had already died. Hurrying to her side, Rancé found himself confronted by a terrible sight: "The first thing he saw was her head, which . . . the surgeons had severed; to learn of her death this way, the surprise and horror of the sight, together with the pain suffered by a passionate and until then happy man, converted him, drove him into retreat, and from thence to the order of Saint Bernard and to reform."[10] The second account is the one that Rancé himself gave to Saint-Simon many years later: "Madame de Montbazon died of German measles in a very few days. Monsieur de Rancé was by her side, he did not leave her at all, saw her take the sacraments, and was present at her death. The truth is that, already touched and torn between God and the world, he had been thinking for some time of a retreat; the effect that this so sudden death had on his heart and his soul finally convinced him."[11]

Two centuries later, Chateaubriand, who had been persuaded by his confessor to write a biography of the famous Trappist reformer, claimed that poets believed the first version but that all churchmen denied it. For Chateaubriand, however, poetic and official truth were not irreconcilable, and in his *Vie de Rancé* the two stories are woven together in a single dramatic sequence. Rancé had been present at Mme de Montbazon's death and at her deathbed confession, and only when she had breathed her last did he leave her. A few hours later, the abbé was unable to resist the urge to pay his last respects to the body of the woman he loved and, going back, found himself confronted by the macabre spectacle of her mutilated body. Chateaubriand also lends credence to the legend that Rancé brought Mme de Montbazon's decapitated head with him to the monastery of La Trappe. Marie de Bretagne, once the incarnation of the triumph of beauty and the senses but now no more than a miserable death's head, was to fortify the man who had loved her so much in his rejection of the world.

It took Rancé six years to break off all his ties with the world before finally retiring to Notre-Dame-de-La-Trappe, of which he was commendatory abbot. The dark, insalubrious monastery was lost in the depths of the Perche valley, surrounded

10. Saint-Simon, *Mémoires (1691–1701). Additions au Journal de Dangeau*, edited by Yves Coirault, eight volumes (Paris: Gallimard/Bibliothèque de la Pléiade, 1982–1987), Vol. 1, p. 522.

11. Saint-Simon, *Mémoires*, Vol. 1, p. 522.

by ponds and marshland. La Trappe and its moral standards were in decay. Rancé immediately decided to reform it, subjecting it so vigorously that the religious authorities themselves objected to the harshness of his rule.

Taking its inspiration from the anchorite monasticism of the desert, the new Trappist rule departed from the contemplative, scholarly tradition of Western monasticism and imposed an unprecedented program of penitence and expiation. To be dead to one's own humanity, to forget the world, to remain silent, to obey, to humiliate oneself, to pray, and to live in the expectation of appearing before the Creator were certainly all central to seventeenth-century theological debate. But Rancé brought them together in a program for monastic life that sounded like a challenge: not even Jansenism had taken such an extreme position. In his fever of mortification and self-denial, Rancé, contradicting the great Benedictine scholar Dom Mabillon, forbade monks to study because, he said, "their condition is to weep and not to instruct, and God's design in making recluses in the Church is not to make scholars but penitents."[12] In the name of God, the reformer of La Trappe condemned history. "Rancé's spiritual thinking," Bernard Beugnot has written, "is pervaded by the myth of original essential purity and by the idea that time engenders decadence."[13] Nothing was further from the euphoric certainty of many of Louis XIV's subjects, who believed they lived in a privileged age quite unlike any other, in which progress in the arts and science allowed both belief in the superiority of the new and trust in the future. Rancé's departure from the world must have made a profound impression on a society that still sustained a constant dialogue with the idea of retreat. Like Mlle de La Vallière, who fled the court for a convent when she lost Louis's favor, Rancé "admirably incarnated the contrast between a worldly period, lived in the name of dissipation... and a nonetheless spectacular entry into the religious life."[14] Unlike the Sun King's delightful mistress, however, Rancé was turning his back not merely on the century's miseries but on his personal glory as well.

For thirty-seven years, as Chateaubriand wrote, Rancé lived in solitude, "to expiate the thirty-seven years he had spent in the world."[15] This did not prevent the world from making his monastery into a place of permanent pilgrimage. Despite polemic and adverse opinion, and as Rancé gradually increased the severity of his rule, the court was won over by the fame of his terrifying sanctity. La

---

12. Rancé, *De la sainteté et des devoirs de la vie monastique*, two volumes (Paris: F. Muguet, 1683), Vol. 2, pp. 370–371; quoted in Kriegel, *La Querelle Mabillon-Rancé*, p. 65.

13. Bernard Beugnot, *Le Discours de la retraite au XVIIe siècle: Loin du monde et du bruit* (Paris: Presses Universitaires de France, Paris, 1996), p. 254.

14. Beugnot, *Le Discours de la retraite au XVIIe siècle*, p. 253.

15. François René de Chateaubriand, *Vie de Rancé*, preface by Roland Barthes (Union Générale d'Éditions, 1965), p. 183.

Trappe became a fashionable phenomenon in the 1670s just as the Jansenist Port-Royal had been twenty years earlier. "People rush there from nearby monasteries, and soon, in Paris and at Versailles, the talk is all about the Trappist silence. To go to La Trappe, says a great grandee, is the passionate desire of all gentlemen. Six to seven thousand pilgrims go there every year."[16] Among the visitors were Mme de Guise, Louis XIV's cousin and the younger half-sister through her father of the Grande Mademoiselle; Monsieur, the King's brother; James II of England; the Maréchal de Bellefonds; the Duc de Saint-Simon and his son, the future memoirist; and Bossuet, bishop of Meaux and Rancé's former schoolmate, who had become a leading figure of the French Church at the time of the Gallican Church.[17]

A glance at the list of his correspondents—250 people from all social backgrounds to whom he addressed thousands of letters—suffices to convey an impression of the breadth of the network that Rancé continued to weave, albeit from his place of solitude. Such a correspondence—one of the seventeenth century's richest, and of which only a minimal part remains—begs the question of whether it constitutes "a denial of the solitary life by bearing witness against an otherwise exemplary existence."[18] Was it surprising that Rancé felt he had the right to communicate, even as he forbade his monks to do so? Two considerations must have overcome his scruples. Good relations with the ecclesiastical world and the court were indispensable to the order's survival and support, and to refuse to reply to those who turned to him for help would have been to deny his religious duties.

Unlike Port-Royal, the monastery at La Trappe excluded women although they figure largely among Rancé's correspondents. Some, like Mme de Longueville and the Duchesse de La Vallière, were illustrious penitents; others, like Mme de La Sablière and Mme de Lafayette, were women of the upper ranks of society who sought refuge in religion, having spent their lives cultivating their intelligence and a worldly knowledge. Rancé refused the role of serving as their spiritual guide, but he supported them with advice and words of encouragement. Although he regarded monastic life as the best way for man to serve God, Rancé believed that salvation could be gained and sanctity achieved through a secular existence as well, provided worldly values were abjured.

In *La Princesse de Clèves*, Mme de Lafayette tells the story of a woman's retreat from the world and her refusal, for the sake of inner peace, to yield to passion. Yet in appearance at least, the reasons for the heroine entering a convent are not religious so much as sentimental and moral: the logic that compels her to leave

---

16. Kriegel, *La Querelle Mabillon-Rancé*, p. 53.

17. The term "Gallican" was first used in the nineteenth century to denote the autonomist attitude of the French Parlement and Church.

18. Lucien Aubry, "Introduction à la spiritualité de Rancé," in Rancé, *Correspondance*, Vol. 1, p. 30.

the world is a secular logic. In 1686, sixteen years after the publication of her masterpiece, sad, ill, and tormented by the loss of her close friend La Rochefoucauld,
Mme de Lafayette herself sought tranquility. Unlike her heroine, she turned to
religion to help detach herself from an intensely lived life from which she was
about to depart. However, "intelligence, reason, honor, and probity" could not
replace the gift of faith, and she was tormented by doubts and uncertainty. Called
on to support her in her hour of tribulation, Rancé asked for a total metamorphosis of the self, without which there could be no salvation; for God to speak to her
and to tell her what He had not yet told her, there needed to be "a radical conversion of her mind and heart."[19]

Mme de Lafayette's faith in her correspondent did not prevent her from seriously doubting herself. How could she possibly change in the way she had been
asked to? How could she find the courage to turn her back on her own life, to
sacrifice to the unknown the few certainties she had acquired? She was tired, a
prisoner of her own fears, and acutely aware of her own weaknesses. Unlike the
Princesse de Clèves, she was incapable of any exceptional undertaking. What, she
asked, had induced Rancé to turn his back on everything and to shut himself up in
silence and solitude? Mme de Lafayette certainly knew about Mme de Montbazon,
about Rancé's religious crisis after her death, his conversion, and his decision to
bury his past forever. Nevertheless she boldly dared to question him. And even more
extraordinarily, after thirty years of silence, the famous abbé consented to reply.
"I don't know why I have given you so much detail, which I have never given to
anyone; I could have refrained from doing so without your having any further say,
but I thought it better to explain these things sincerely that you might reflect upon
them, since you gave me your word that the secret would be inviolable."[20]

Had Chateaubriand known about this letter, his Vie de Rancé might have been
very different indeed. In Rancé's account there was not a trace of fatality or sudden illumination. Nor was there any place for "poetry." He wrote that his conversion was brought about only by dissatisfaction and disgust with life. With one
stroke of the pen, the abbé seemed to deny his past and to establish a new version
of the truth. Did he wish to put an end once and for all to the scandalous rumor
that was circulating about him, which might harm La Trappe? Or, more simply,
had he finally blotted out a memory that would prevent him from living, in accordance with seventeenth-century spirituality, "in the narrow space of the present
moment . . . illuminated by the Absolute"?[21] The real reason is probably something
else. If Rancé had decided to talk about himself, it was because his experience

19. Rancé to Mme de Lafayette, November 27, 1686, in Rancé, *Correspondance*, Vol. 3, pp. 403–406.

20. Rancé to Mme de Lafayette, November 22, 1686, in Rancé, *Correspondance*, Vol. 3, p. 405.

21. Benedetta Papàsogli, introduction to Chateaubriand, *La vita di Rancé* (Milan: San Paolo, 1993), p. 35.

might help his correspondent. He was not appealing to the romantic imagination of a novelist, but to the lucidity of a moralist. God had no need to resort to extraordinary events in order to speak to people's hearts. Disgust with the world was something everyone could understand. It required only a recognition of its intrinsic misery and an awareness of its inadequacy:

> You ask, Madame, the reasons that determined me to leave the world. I will tell you simply that I left it because I did not find there what I was seeking. I wanted a peace that the world could not give me, and if, unfortunately for me, I had found it, I would perhaps not have looked any further. The reasons for which I would have lived longer in the world displeased me so that I was ashamed to accept them or to be attached to them. Finally, agreeable conversation, worldly pleasures, plans for a career and a fortune, seemed to be such vain and hollow things that I began to look on them with disgust. To that was added the disdain I had for most men, seeing that they had neither good faith, nor honor, nor loyalty, all of which combined, led me to flee what could no longer please me and to search for something better.[22]

Rancé had agreed to talk about himself in order to present Mme de Lafayette with a mirror in which to recognize herself. The different ways in which they had led their lives was unimportant compared to the shared aim, the yearning for inner peace, and the longing for detachment from the world. In the light of what we know about Mme de Lafayette, the obstacles to be overcome were surprisingly the same. The same worldly civilization had seduced them both with its agreeable talk and its pleasures, and the same aristocratic pride had made them slaves to social ambition. To gain inner peace, the Princesse de Clèves sacrificed her passion for the Duc de Nemours; Rancé now showed Mme de Lafayette a far simpler way to be receptive to the word of God: to live her disenchantment with life to the depths of her being.

---

22. Rancé to Mme de Lafayette, November 22, 1686, in Rancé, *Correspondance*, Vol. 3, pp. 403–404.

8

THE MARQUISE DE SABLÉ:
THE SALON IN THE CONVENT

I. Foundresses of Jansenism

IT WAS NOT so much the terror of damnation that tormented Magdeleine de Sablé as, quite simply, the fear of dying. It was a panic fear that the marquise had had since youth and which she did not attempt to confront with the usual weapons—good sense, reason, or Christian resignation—but rather with the absolute determination to live as long as possible. She waged a cunning, defensive war against death. She never exposed herself to drafts, insalubrious air, storms, or travel. For fear of contagion, she carefully avoided the sick, and she always had a well-stocked pharmacy and team of doctors at hand. At night, in order to avoid sleeping too deeply —with the attendant risk of never waking up again—she required someone to be by her bedside and watch over her slumbers with the precise duty of shaking her at regular intervals. She was not the least troubled by the bewilderment she caused, and once said, "I fear death more than others do, because no one has ever understood better than I do what nothing is."[1] And the marquise would probably have replied to Tallemant des Réaux, who did not fail to point out the incongruity of all this with her devotions and professed belief in another life, just as she had once replied to the Jansenist Arnauld d'Andilly: "I assure you that I consider each thing separately and put each thing in its proper place without overlooking anything."[2] She was fully aware both of her obsessive pathology and of her religious faith. Side by side, the two might have seemed incompatible, but for her the important thing was "in every case to give a truthful answer, that is to say, one that conformed to the rules of necessity and duty, however contradictory they might be."[3]

---

1. Tallemant des Réaux, *Historiettes*, Vol. 1, p. 517.

2. Andilly quoted in Jean Lafond, "Madame de Sablé et son salon," in *L'Homme et son image* (Paris: Champion, 1996), p. 264.

3. Lafond, "Madame de Sablé et son salon," in *L'Homme et son image*, p. 264.

"To consider each thing separately and put each thing in its proper place." This classic formula might have been Mme de Sablé's motto. The marquise had an independent, curious mind and did not like to be trapped by accepted logic or enforced opinion. As a leading player in the social, intellectual, and moral life of her times, she refused to delegate the responsibility of decision. In order to be able to judge for herself, she wished, above all, to understand—a requirement that was not self-evident at a time when access to learning was still the prerogative of a male elite, and the Church judged it opportune to limit women's religious education, emphasizing humility and obedience instead. Possessed of the two vices typical of her sex—frivolity and curiosity—Mme de Sablé confirmed the theory of those who believed in the satanic nature of the daughters of Eve and so reignited the discord within the Church.

One day in 1642—the precise date is unknown—Mme de Sablé was preparing to go to a ball with her friend Anne de Rohan, Princesse de Guéméné. The princess expressed considerable surprise when she heard that her friend had taken communion that morning; in the eyes of her confessor, taking communion meant refraining from all profane activity. Made curious by the princess's display of rigor, Mme de Sablé questioned her own confessor. He, in turn, inquired after the rules by which Mme de Guéméné lived and wrote a commentary that, passing from Mme de Sablé to Mme de Guéméné, ended up in the hands of that lady's confessor. Delighted to have hit upon such a fascinating subject of conversation, the two friends could never imagine that they had launched a potentially explosive theological debate.

Both women had reached a stage in life when religious concerns naturally tended to be of more importance than affairs of the heart. Whereas Mme de Sablé had always been an excellent advocate for her own wishes, however, Mme de Guéméné had experienced the transition in a more dramatic mode. Married in 1618 at the age of fourteen to her first cousin, Louis VII de Rohan—a son of M. de Montbazon's first marriage—Anne de Rohan rivaled her mother-in-law Mme de Montbazon in both beauty and libertinage. Her affairs were publicly known, and "it was said that all her lovers came to a bad end."[4] In fact, at least three of them—the Duc de Montmorency, the Comte de Bouteville, and M. de Thou—had been beheaded. Jean François Paul de Gondi, the future Cardinal de Retz, had fared a little better, although during one of their disputes, he is said to have tried to strangle her and she threw a candelabrum at his head. Nevertheless the relationship continued for some time. When, finally racked by remorse and threatened by her confessor with the flames of hell, Anne sought to end it, Gondi showed her a devil of his own whose form seemed "more benign and more agreeable" to her.[5]

---

4. Tallemant, *Historiettes*, Vol. 2, p. 228.

5. Retz, *Mémoires*, p. 15.

The princess was an uncertain penitent. "She would have outbursts of devotion; then she would return to the world."[6] And yet she was not afraid to entrust herself to the guidance of the Jansenist Abbé de Saint-Cyran, "the Christian director par excellence . . . strict and a sure doctor of souls."[7] In 1638 her "examination of conscience" reached the spiritual director of the convent of Port-Royal, imprisoned at Vincennes at the time. With the help of Arnauld d'Andilly, Father Singlin, and Mother Agnès, Saint-Cyran tried to strengthen the princess's faintheartedness, which was described as resembling "the spark from a fire lit on icy terrain and exposed to all the winds."[8] Their charitable act was destined to reap an unexpected reward. Mme de Guémené would always be a mediocre penitent, but thanks to her, Saint-Cyran came into possession of a document that allowed French Jansenism to come out into the open and to set out in search of souls.

The letter that Mme de Sablé's confessor had written to her in reply to her questions proved to be an example of extreme religious laxity, of that "convenient devotion" later denounced by Pascal, and to which the Jesuits owed their popularity in court circles. "Among other outrageous instances of complacency, it said that the more one lacks in grace, the more ardently one should approach Jesus Christ in the Eucharist."[9] It was a private letter, and the Abbé de Saint-Cyran would never have known about it had it not been for the indiscreet exchange of confidences between two noble women on their way to a ball. Imprisoned in his tower, the persecuted abbé understood that the time had come to act. He asked Antoine Arnauld to write a public refutation of it in the light of Jansenist doctrine on sin and grace. Published in August 1643, Arnauld's *De la fréquente communion* was intended, in the words of Sainte-Beuve, to "revolutionize the way of understanding and practicing piety and the way of writing theology. . . . No devotional book since the *Introduction à la vie dévote* by Saint François de Sales, published at the beginning of the century, had had so great an effect nor attracted such a following; it may be said, however, that the books differed in one way. While François de Sales's work intended to reconcile society people to an amiable and consoling religion, Arnauld showed them its severity and terror."[10]

Jansenist pessimism, Augustinian in origin, denounced worldly values, power, and grandeur as inauthentic and called for introspection and retreat. The answer it gave to the religious and moral crisis that shook the privileged classes was radical.

6. Tallemant, *Historiettes*, Vol. 2, p. 279.

7. Charles Augustin Sainte-Beuve, *Port-Royal*, edited by Maxime Leroy, three volumes (Paris: Gallimard/Bibliothèque de la Pléiade, 1953–1955), Vol. 1, p. 361.

8. From a letter to Mother Agnès from Saint-Cyran, quoted in Sainte-Beuve, *Port-Royal*, Vol. 1, p. 378.

9. Sainte-Beuve, *Port-Royal*, Vol. 1, p. 634.

10. Sainte-Beuve, *Port-Royal*, Vol. 1, pp. 633–635.

Richelieu had crushed the ardently Catholic party led by Bérulle—the *parti dévot*—and in doing so, had also suffocated one of the most genuine expressions of a desire for religious revival in Counter-Reformation France. The success of the centralized monarchy had spread disappointment and incertitude in the heart of two social categories that had always been closely associated with power but were now being gradually deprived of important positions: the high nobility and the parlementary magistrature. To these two elite classes, both nurtured on worldly culture, Arnauld addressed his message, not in scholastic Latin but—an important novelty where theological discussion was concerned—in clear and elegant French, following in the tradition of the simplicity and clarity of Gallican rhetoric.

An essay by Jean Delumeau helps in assessing the Jansenist position in the great debate on confession initiated by the Council of Trent.[11] What should the Church's attitude be toward the millions of Christians called upon to confess at least once a year? What position should be adopted to encourage believers in a practice that brings all their behavior into question and confronts them with divine justice? Should it opt for quantity or for quality, for indulgence or intransigence, for generous absolution or for the strictest conversion? Until the second half of the seventeenth century, the leaning, supported mainly by the Jesuits, had been toward indulgence; Port-Royal, on the other hand, sided with rigor.

This rigor was not an end in itself but was born of a total disbelief in man's ability to contribute to his own redemption. Only grace could save a fallen and irredeemably corrupt creature, and this grace came from on high, unforeseeably and gratuitously. To suppose that it could be assuaged by the exercise of worldly virtues was laughable, the Jansenists held, mere delusions of vanity and pride. Suspended between the fear of damnation and the hope of belonging to the small number of the elect, man must fight his own humanity and annihilate himself in faith. In this terrible uncertainty, rigor was both useful and necessary; man must "pray as if everything depended on God and act as if everything depended on ourselves."[12]

The first step toward salvation was, obviously, penitence. This could be of two kinds, born either of a love of God and despair at having offended him (contrition) or from entirely human shame, an objective disgust of sin and fear of punishment (attrition). In the confessional, the Jesuits encouraged attrition as a prelude to contrition. The Jansenists, on the other hand, denied its validity, considering it to be a human invention. According to Jansenius, the Flemish-born theologian

---

11. Jean Delumeau, *L'Aveu et le Pardon: les difficultés de la confession XIIIe–XVIIIe siècle* (1964; Paris: Fayard, 1992).

12. Mathieu Feydeau, "Catéchisme de la Grâce," Art. 44, in Antoine Arnauld, *Œuvres*, thirty-eight volumes (1650; Paris-Lausanne: S. d'Arnay, 1775–1783; reprint, Brussels, 1967), Vol. 17, p. 845.

who gave the reform movement its name, there was nothing supernatural about the fear of hell.

The Jesuits regarded a dialogue with sinners to be of primary importance, however imperfect that dialogue might be, in order to lessen the demands of an ideal that, for many, were too exacting and too difficult. By easily granting absolution and authorizing frequent communion, the Jesuits put their trust in the powers of salvation intrinsic to the sacraments. In *De la fréquente communion*, Arnauld took the opposite position. It did not faze him that he was speaking only to the few—since only the few were chosen. In his view, the laxity of confessors resulted in "deceiving sinners with false mercy and a cruel sweetness that merely covered up the wounds that could be healed by iron and fire alone."[13] Absolution could be given only where there was unreserved contrition and an undertaking not to fall back into sin. Where there was no such guarantee, it must be deferred. As for communion, it should be given only sparingly, as a reward and not as encouragement.

Arnauld's deadly onslaught, together with Pascal's, is partly responsible for the pejorative epithets of "laxity," "casuistry," and "probabilism" still in use today. But the Jesuit theological-moral position resulted from apostolic zeal dictated by the "conviction of belonging to a civilization on the move, to a new age where complex, unprecedented problems presented themselves, and to which the fathers of the Church could provide no answer."[14] Pilloried by Pascal in *Les Provinciales*, the "casuist theologians" were attempting to reconcile religious imperatives with the economic, moral, and social necessities of modern life. Carried away by a passion for classification and a baroque imagination, they no doubt created monstrosities and terrible compromises, but they were seeking a solution to the problem of the incompatibility of religion with the world. For their part, the Jansenists chose to make this incompatibility their byword and to force the conflict to its very limits.

Mme de Sablé was the first to turn her back on the Jesuits and to allow herself to be won over to the cause of Port-Royal. La Rochefoucauld called her and the Princesse de Guéméné the "foundresses of Jansenism," a paradox that contained an element of truth. The success of the new doctrine, the way it spread throughout cultivated social circles, would be difficult to explain were it not for the passionate support of a small female elite. Such a belief was widely held by Port-Royal's detractors and provided them with an excellent polemical weapon. Not only was the Jansenists' manifest regard for women dictated by self-interest, they claimed, but it had damaging results. To gain support and protection in society, the apostles of

---

13. Antoine Arnauld, *De la fréquente communion* (Paris: A. Vitré, 1643), p. 480, quoted in Delumeau, *L'Aveu et le Pardon*, p. 73.

14. Delumeau, *L'Aveu et le Pardon*, p. 109.

asceticism and rigor appealed to the vanity of women, dangerously encouraging their curiosity and their critical ability, pushing them to take part in theological discussions without taking into account the natural limits of the female intellect.

All these accusations were knowledgeably formulated by the worldly, amiable Jesuit Père Rapin in his *Mémoires* and expressed in tones ranging from apparent good nature to cunning insinuation, from subtle criticism to violent denigration. Rapin was a dangerous enemy to the Jansenist cause. With his "goodness" and "sweetness,"[15] he was master of the art of persuasion, and had a perfect knowledge of the world and remarkable psychological insight. According to Rapin, the Jansenist "plot" was far more successful in France than it was in Flanders because in France, thanks to women and the influence they had over society, it became a fashionable phenomenon. "Women...were won over by the brilliant, flowery style [of *De la fréquente communion*], which greatly pleased all the *beaux-esprits*, whose opinions are of such weight in a country where so much importance is attached to refinement."[16]

This would have been all right, Rapin continued, if the women in question had not been seduced by form, had they not embraced a doctrine whose significance they were unable to understand fully, and had they not wished to preach it in order to demonstrate their own intellectual superiority and their good taste. Conversion to Jansenism resulted from an ambiguity, if not an imposture; the co-option was based on seduction and the conversion dictated by vanity and pride —the very vices that Port-Royal claimed to combat above all others. What was still to be explained, however, was why so many distinguished women made the same "mistake," but he knew every one of them—after all, drawing rooms were his hunting ground—and he had an answer for them all:

> The great theater where the gospel according to Port-Royal was most loudly proclaimed and with the greatest applause was, at the time,[17] the hôtel de Nevers, home of the Comtesse du Plessis. . . . The good manners of the house where the countess did the honors, good living—for the table was sumptuously prepared with great delicacies—the most select Parisian society, there being as many from the magistrature as from the court, and all sorts of witty and intelligent entertainments attracted so many people of quality that it became the most frequented rendezvous of the whole cabal: the Bishop of Comminges, the countess's first cousin; the Prince de Marcillac, later Duc de

---

15. Mme de Sévigné to Bussy-Rabutin, December 2, 1678, in Mme de Sévigné, *Correspondance*, Vol. 3, p. 338.

16. *Mémoires du Père René Rapin*, Vol. 1, p. 36.

17. Rapin's description refers, very inaccurately however, to the Paris of the 1650s, immediately after the Fronde.

La Rochefoucauld; the Maréchal d'Albret; the Marquise de Liancourt; the Comtesse de Lafayette; the Marquise de Sévigné; d'Andilly de Pomponne; the Abbé Testu, an intimate friend of the Comtesse du Plessis, and a fine speaker, but subject to fashionable vapors; the Abbé de Rancé, an agreeable and witty man who later became the famous abbot of La Trappe.... Not everyone who went there belonged to the party, since most of them went there through a spirit of intrigue and curiosity characteristic of the hostess, to make remarks that might be of use to interested parties, and to favor spreading the new ideas, because Paris was full of refined people.[18]

There were two sides to society life at the hôtel de Nevers, both of which would evolve during the next century. Disguised within the varied and brilliant spectacle of a wide circle of distinguished guests lurked a secret group, a small circle of initiates, united by a common cause. The same thing occurred a hundred years later in the Baron d'Holbach's sumptuous house in the rue Royal, on the days when the baron was not receiving Parisian high society. There, behind closed doors, free from the self-censorship imposed by the conventions of the salons, the baron and his *philosophe* friends had taken to speaking quite objectively of politics, religion, and philosophy. Likewise, the Jansenist cabal at the hôtel de Nevers was weaving a plot against the established order, creating a climate of expectation and of assent to the new doctrine, while remaining wisely reserved about the conspirators' personal convictions.[19]

In Père Rapin's view, the beautiful hostess's concerns were decidedly not of a religious nature. If Port-Royal was using her to gain sympathy in society, she was using Port-Royal politically, to weaken Mazarin—who was guilty of not having shown her husband sufficient consideration. For his part, the Comte du Plessis-Guénégaud "left the trouble of avenging himself to his wife; and she entered willingly into whatever was against the court. She only became a Jansenist through aversion to the Cardinal."[20]

According to Rapin, Mme de Longueville , too, was motivated in her choice of the Jansenist cause by hatred and vengeance far more than by Christian charity. Only the "secret desire to avenge herself of the contempt in which she was held at court" in the years after her involvement in the Fronde pushed Mme de Longueville into the arms of the Jansenists.[21] And her support would cause "the new doctrine to make more progress than would all the discourses and writings

---

18. *Mémoires du Père René Rapin*, Vol. 1, pp. 403–404.

19. *Mémoires du Père René Rapin*, Vol. 1, p. 218.

20. *Mémoires du Père René Rapin*, Vol. 1, p. 218.

21. *Mémoires du Père René Rapin*, Vol. 2, p. 446.

of Port-Royal put together."[22] Rapin did not deny the sincerity of her later involvement, "a devotion without equal and devoid of circumspection,"[23] but claimed that self-love was still her main characteristic. The extreme rigor of the "new morality" provided her with "glittering opportunities to show her piety and to display her spirit, which she did not like to conceal."[24] In her pride, she had discovered a new model of heroism against which to measure herself: that of the perfect penitent.

To withstand the enemy advance, Rapin was quite happy to resort to the old, commonly held misogynist opinions that, as Mme de Motteville's *Mémoires* reveal, were still deeply rooted in the consciousness of both sexes. Woman's hunger for knowledge and excessive curiosity lay at the root of all evil. Her longing for learning could only be born of pride. Jansenism, by distancing itself from traditional Church attitudes, authorized grand ladies—who under any other circumstances would have thought it highly unsuitable to show off their knowledge—"to concern themselves with matters that occupied the most sublime of minds and about which they were consulted as if they were doctors."[25] And since they were exceptionally intelligent and high-ranking, their example was particularly harmful. For the motives that inspired society ladies to become Jansenists were mainly "imitation—or fashion, which is nothing if not incitement to imitation—and emulation."[26]

Misogyny apart, however, the new doctrine's detractors drew particular attention to the reaction of a female public only because women had become symbolic of high society. By addressing themselves directly to them and winning their support, the Port-Royal writers had outwitted their adversaries and won an important initial victory. Arnauld, followed by Pascal, sensed the growing importance of society opinion, and turning their backs on the rules of traditional religious debate, they abandoned Latin for French, as Descartes had already done. They discussed theology without overlooking its complex theoretical problems, and by appealing to the believers' own judgment, they made them wholly responsible for their decisions. They knew the tastes of an aristocratic, cultivated public that demanded style and language. Readers were, in the words of Mme de Motteville, captivated with "such beautiful French that they put down their novels."[27]

Contrary to what Rapin thought, however, not only the form was appealing. The moralism and intellectualism that characterized Port-Royal spiritualism from the 1640s, to the detriment of Saint-Cyran's "affective and mystic tendencies,"[28]

---

22. *Mémoires du Père René Rapin*, Vol. 3, p. 429.

23. *Mémoires du Père René Rapin*, Vol. 2, p. 424.

24. *Mémoires du Père René Rapin*, Vol. 2, p. 447.

25. *Mémoires du Père René Rapin*, Vol. 1, p. 402.

26. *Mémoires du Père René Rapin*, Vol. 1, p. 356.

27. *Mémoires de Mme de Motteville*, Vol. 1, p. 321.

were also perfectly attuned to the moral and psychological interests of society with its constant leanings toward introspection. This was established before the advent of the classical writers—Molière, Racine, La Fontaine, La Rochefoucauld, and La Bruyère. *Préciosité*, which was seen as a social phenomenon as well as a literary one, already proved that a certain number of aristocratic women wished to be distinguished by their culture, their refinement, their rejection of physical love and all sensuality, and to keep to a pure and rigorous ethical and aesthetic way of life. By describing the *Précieuses* as the "Jansenists of love," the worldly courtesan Ninon de Lenclos clearly expressed the belief, quite widely held by Port-Royal's enemies, in the existence of a secret affinity between the two "sects." Whether expressed through the exaltation of human nature or its mortification, the same need to stand out or to present a challenge must have driven, as Jean Lafond writes, "a not inconsiderable part of the aristocracy to feel in moral harmony with an extremism beyond the reach of ordinary people."[29]

In her youth Mme de Sablé had been a passionate "casuist" for love. Even Mlle de Scudéry, who feared no rival in her knowledge of the heart's pathology, paid homage to the marquise's psychological insight, depicting her in *Le Grand Cyrus* as the Princesse de Salamis:

> Never had anyone so perfectly understood all the different aspects of love as the Princesse de Salamis understood them; and I know nothing more agreeable than to hear her distinguish between a wholly pure love and a coarse, earthly love; between sincere love and pretend love; self-interested love and heroic love. For in fact she takes you into the hearts of all those who are capable of love; she describes the most horrifying jealousy in such words as to evoke serpents destroying the heart; she knows all love's innocent tenderness, and all its agony; and everything which concerns this passion is so perfectly known to her that Venus and Uranus know no more than she.[30]

For Mme de Sablé, love was not simply passion, but "a passion necessary to bienséances."[31] Influenced like all the ladies of her generation by Urfé's novel *L'Astrée*, the marquise maintained that love had a highly educative function and that "all men should love and all women be loved."[32] Her moralizing Platonism

---

28. See Lafond, "Madame de Sablé," in *L'homme et son image*, p. 265.

29. See Lafond, "La Rochefoucauld d'une culture à l'autre" (1978), in *L'Homme et son image*, p. 150.

30. Mlle de Scudéry, *Artamène ou le Grand Cyrus*, Part 6, Book 1, Vol. 6, pp. 72–73.

31. Mlle de Scudéry, *Artamène ou le Grand Cyrus*, Part 6, Book 1, Vol. 6, p. 70.

32. Mlle de Scudéry, *Artamène ou le Grand Cyrus*, Part 6, Book 1, Vol. 6, p. 70.

led her to believe that, as in the golden age of courtesy, "men could, without sin, have tender feelings for women; that the desire to please led them on to the greatest and finest actions, encouraged their wit, and inspired generosity and all sorts of virtues."[33]

Mme de Sablé's behavior was not always in keeping with her principles. She is known to have yielded to the Duc de Montmorency, a man "recommended for his courage, his good looks, and his magnificence,"[34] with whom she fell in love at first sight. "She was very young when he came to see her for the first time," Tallemant recounts. "She was in a ground-floor room, one of whose windows was open. Instead of coming through the door, he leaped through the window and, by a certain agreeable air of his, he immediately charmed her and she felt herself to be captivated."[35] The apparition would certainly have been irresistible for anyone indulging in romantic fantasy. Mme de Lafayette may have had it in mind when she wrote the famous ball scene at the Louvre in *La Princesse de Clèves*, when the heroine recognizes the Duc de Nemours at first sight as he comes toward her to invite her to dance, leaping with athletic grace over the row of chairs between them.

Unlike the Princesse de Clèves, however, Mme de Sablé did not end her relationship with Montmorency because of a sense of guilt toward her husband. He was brutal and unfaithful in addition to being profligate with the family fortune. Rather it was her unyielding pride that caused the break. The duke was deeply in love with her, but vanity led him to pay court to the young queen, Anne of Austria, and for Mme de Sablé, this lack of consideration was incompatible with the respect she considered her due. Even Mme de Motteville's *Mémoires* reflect this scorn: "I heard her say... that such was her pride with regard to the Duc de Montmorency that at the first sign he might give her of any change, she would not wish to see him anymore, since she would be unable to accept with grace respects that she had had to share with the greatest princess in the world."[36] Although the duke continued to offer proof of his devotion for a long time, he was never forgiven. If we are to believe Tallemant, the marquise's resentment survived even Montmorency's death on the scaffold in 1632, a death that she claimed gave her no displeasure.[37]

The adventure, however, did nothing to discourage Mme de Sablé from taking other lovers nor from, at the same time, promoting "honest gallantry" at the French court. Her beauty and intelligence gave her an authority that her love affairs never jeopardized. The "high idea" she had conceived that the Spanish had

33. *Mémoires de Mme de Motteville*, Vol. 1, p. 13.

34. *Mémoires de Mme de Motteville*, Vol. 1, p. 12.

35. Tallemant, *Historiettes*, Vol. 1, p. 514.

36. *Mémoires de Mme de Motteville*, Vol. 1, pp. 13–14.

37. Tallemant, *Historiettes*, Vol. 1, p. 515.

learned gallantry "from the Moors"[38] was supported by the great regard in which Spanish chivalric literature was held at the time. The Queen herself, who had arrived from Madrid in 1615, "did not understand how fine conversation, which is ordinarily called honest gallantry, ... where no particular promises are given, could ever be blameworthy."[39]

Considering the circumstances, Mme de Sablé's welcome at the hôtel de Rambouillet was thus a warm one. She had begun to frequent the Blue Room in about 1620, by which time her marriage had already proved to be a disaster. For the next twenty years she was to make it her favorite place. She was ten years younger than Mme de Rambouillet and seven years older than Julie d'Angennes. Thus astride the two generations, Mme de Sablé would live with equal intensity through two successive seasons of the new social culture. No one illustrates better than she the path that led from the "moralizing idealism" fashionable at the hôtel de Rambouillet to the puritanical Jansenism of Port-Royal, from the cult of love and friendship and a social world dedicated to literature as primarily a game to the new "gallantry dressed in black,"[40] wherein the perfect practice of the *bienséances* went hand in hand with rigorous reflection on moral and intellectual problems.

The crisis of the Fronde, with all its dramatic taking of sides and everyone's passions laid bare, had brought to an end the golden era of Rambouillet-style *sociabilité*. With a return to order and to the principle of royal authority, few would relive the utopia of a *locus amoenus* where men and women could still freely express their ideal of a perfect aesthetic. The abrupt downfall in 1661 of the minister of finance, Nicolas Fouquet, seemed to symbolize the fate that awaited too independent a spirit. Most aristocrats, having firmly transferred themselves to the Sun King's court, would adapt themselves to the service of the sovereign, to seeking his favor, to intrigue, and to dissimulation. Those who could not swallow this too bitter pill found refuge in religion and withdrew from society.

Mme de Sablé—in public as in private life, during the difficult years of the Fronde and those of the restoration of royal authority, when faced with advancing old age and personal sorrow—showed great courage, a marked intellectual independence, and, despite appearances to the contrary, a rare sense of balance. Throughout the civil war she had remained loyal to the King even while keeping in close contact with her Frondist friends, attempting to mediate disagreements and to suggest peaceful reconciliation between the rival parties. Even in her conversion to Jansenism, she avoided the extreme; she adopted the new doctrine and helped considerably in its diffusion without taking on its enemies or its interdictions. Although settled in an apartment within the walls of the convent

38. *Mémoires de Mme de Motteville*, Vol. 1, p. 13.

39. *Mémoires de Mme de Motteville*, Vol. 1, p. 15.

40. Giovanni Macchia, *La Letteratura francese* (Milan: Mondadori/I Meridiani, 1987), p. 795.

at Port-Royal, she kept in touch with the court and society and would never have sacrificed her friends, her interests, her tastes, or her habits.

The marquise's contemporaries were struck by this combination of marked individualism and self-indulgence. Within a code of manners that tended toward conformity of behavior, Mme de Sablé attached importance above all to the respect she owed herself. The friends and lovers she chose did much to compensate for her conjugal disappointments, while curiosity, reading, and conversation all helped to fill the lacunae left by her education and to broaden her horizons. She was admired by the most elevated minds. "Her mind becomes more refined from day to day to an astonishing degree," Jean Chapelain wrote to Guez de Balzac in 1640, adding, "it must be admitted that she writes most delicately and that she has, in her letters as in her conversation, the most lucid quaintness desirable."[41] Mme de Sablé paid as much attention to looking after her body as she did to developing her intelligence and to affairs of the heart. She nourished her well-being with delicate morsels, infusions, jams, and syrups and avoided exposing herself to inclement weather or to the dangers of the street.

In attempting to adapt her way of life to her sensibilities and intimate aspirations, the marquise never took refuge in dreams but started from an awareness of what was owed to her on account of her merit. Such an assertion of a sublime ego was of course not exclusive to Mme de Sablé; several of her friends and acquaintances would have adopted similar attitudes, more or less explicitly, and would have reached the same decisions and experienced the same fears. There was a widespread "neurosis" in high society in which Philippe Sellier has discerned the presence of the essential characteristic of the "precious" woman long before satire made her "ridiculous."[42] Mme de Rambouillet and her daughters Julie and Angélique Clarice, Mademoiselle de Montpensier and the members of her small court, Mme de Lafayette and her friend Mme de Sévigné, and finally Mlle de Scudéry were surely the most luminous stars in the new constellation of women. They were aristocratic rather than bourgeois, individualistic rather than part of the clique, more bold than conformist, usually remarkable for their great psychological and moral insight, for their impeccable taste, their style, and their language. They deserve to be remembered for their masterpieces rather than reflected in the distorted mirror of caricature. And if Mme de Sablé shines in this illustrious company, it is doubtless because, of all the genuine *précieuses*, she was the one who dared the most.

---

41. Chapelain to Balzac, April 2, 1640, letter 387, in *Lettres de Jean Chapelain*, Vol. 1, p. 596.

42. See Philippe Sellier, "La névrose précieuse: une nouvelle pléiade?" in *Présences féminines: littérature et société au XVIIe siècle français*, Actes de London (Canada), 1985, directed by Ian Richmond and C. Venesoen, Biblio 17 (Paris-Tübingen-Seattle: PFSCL, 1987), pp. 95–125.

II. *Friendship as a Passion*

For years, the Blue Room habitués had laughed at the extremity of the Marquise de Sablé's phobias. Mme de Rambouillet's paled in comparison, even though the latter was reduced to living in semi-darkness because of her inability to bear the light. A letter from Julie d'Angennes to the marquise, written sometime in the early 1640s, when Mlle de Bourbon had smallpox, gently spoofs the inventive lengths to which Mme de Sablé would go in order to avoid any contact, however indirect, with the illness. As usual, Julie addressed herself not only to Mme de Sablé but to a whole group of shared friends who would have been amused and who would have admired her panache: Mlle d'Angennes knew how to write—in fact, according to Vincent Voiture, there was not a man in France whose style was better than hers.[43]

Having begun by advising the marquise's lady companion to read her the letter from the "lee side," Julie immediately embarked on her "treatise":

> I am certain that between the first proposal that will be made about my coming to see you and the realization of a visit, you will have so many things to consider, so many doctors to consult, so many fears to overcome, that I will have had plenty of time to be aired. The conditions I offer are: to come to your house only if I have not been to the hôtel de Condé for three days, to entirely change my clothes, to choose a day when there has been a frost, not to come within four paces of you, to sit always on the same seat. You could also make a great fire in your room and burn juniper in the four corners, surround yourself with imperial vinegar, rue, and absinthe. If you can find reassurance in these propositions without requiring me to cut my hair, I swear to execute them most religiously; and if you require examples to fortify you, I will tell you that the Queen was happy to see Monsieur de Chaudebonne who had just left Mademoiselle de Bourbon's room, and that Mme d'Aiguillon, who knows about such things, and who is beyond reproach in these matters, has just sent word that if I would like to visit her, she will come and fetch me.[44]

Despite their close friendship, Mme de Sablé could not help being wounded by Mlle d'Angennes's sarcastic tone and decided to reply with an elegant morality lesson destroying her mocking arguments. Mme de Sablé knew only too well that

---

43. Voiture, letter to Mlle de Rambouillet, January 6, 1634, in *Œuvres de Voiture, Lettres et poésies*, Vol. 1, p. 205.

44. Victor Cousin, *Mme de Sablé: Nouvelles études sur les femmes illustres et la société du XVIIe siècle* (1858; Paris: Didier, 1869), pp. 37–38.

by exposing the views of whoever resorts to it, irony can become a double-edged weapon:

> I found you so well instructed in all the cowardly precautions that I rather doubt if I was right two days ago to contend with one of your friends that you had visited Mademoiselle de Bourbon without fear. It is not, as you can judge, that I wish to detract the credit it deserves from your generosity, for I know full well that, if necessary, generosity would cause you to overcome all those things so as never to fail in your duty; but I admit that I am no more convinced of the friendship you have for your friends than I am of your courage. However, you have commented so finely on timidity as to lead me to hope that since you know the dangers so well, you may one day fear them, and that finally you will give your friends the pleasure of conserving yourself more carefully in the future. Besides you have said everything that can be thought about fear and you have never written anything more delicate, but I reply that, whatever you think, you have gone far beyond my precautions. I am no more reassured by my doctor than I am by your promising to change your clothes, for, when I need him, I will resolve to see him even after he leaves a patient with smallpox, provided he changes out of a greasy habit, which is more likely to attract sickness than nice clean clothes are. And, all said and done, I have read your letters to Mme de Maure and mine without fumigating them.[45]

From the way in which Julie mocked her precautions, Mme de Sablé saw that she had no understanding of fear. What was the point in doing something that did not require the slightest effort? Generosity springs from the warmth of the heart, not from insensitivity. Seen objectively in Julie's elegant parody, the manifestation of the neurosis depended on a rapid succession of superstitious rites. Mme de Sablé replied in quite a different vein with a subtle moral analysis, more in keeping with the discussions soon to take place in her drawing room at her *hôtel* in the place Royale than with the spirit of the Blue Room. Then, having struck her blow, she returned to a lighter tone, showing herself to be the first to laugh at her own peculiarities.

In a small enclosed world, where the private ego and the social ego often coincided, and everyone's speech and behavior was bound to be reported and commented upon, letters were always risky. Already ten years earlier, Julie had been at the center of an epistolary dispute, but on that occasion, it was Mme de Sablé who put herself on the spot. Writing to Mme de Rambouillet in 1632, Mme de Sablé expressed her affection for her daughter, declaring that she would have been happy to spend her entire life with Mlle d'Angennes alone. It has to be said that

45. Cousin, *Mme de Sablé*, pp. 38–39.

the formula for courtesy at the time considered hyperbole a part of good manners. And in any case, where Mme de Sablé was concerned, the rhetoric came from the heart. She loved Julie dearly, had known her as a child, and was aware that no greater pleasure existed for Arthénice than to hear her eldest daughter praised. Presumably Mme de Rambouillet was particularly pleased to circulate the letter, and Mme de Sablé's "compliment" did not pass unnoticed by the faithful at the *hôtel*. But this ritual of manners was soon interrupted. Anne d'Attichy's anger flashed like lightning from a clear sky.

This bosom friend of Mme de Sablé's judged the betrayal to be so serious that she refused an invitation to spend several months at the Sablé estate. Her violent reaction threw Mme de Sablé into despair. Her friendship with Anne d'Attichy went back to earliest youth when they were both maids of honor to Marie de' Medici. They were about the same age, and Mlle d'Attichy, who was lucky enough to still be unmarried, had been a great comfort at the time of Mme de Sablé's marital problems. But in the dark days of 1632, it was Mlle d'Attichy who needed comfort. Richelieu was in the process of reestablishing order in France, forcing the King's rebellious brother Gaston d'Orléans to take refuge in Lorraine and dispensing punishment to his political enemies as an example to others. An uncle on her mother's side, the Maréchal Louis de Marillac, had ended his days, like Montmorency, on the executioner's block, while another, the keeper of the seals, Michel de Marillac, died in prison. It was just at this time that Mme de Sablé's letter expressing her affection for Julie d'Angennes began to circulate.

Mme de Sablé tried in vain to defend herself, claiming that her words were not to be taken literally, but Mlle d'Attichy was not in a forgiving mood. For her, the words retained their full significance no matter the context in which they had been used:

> I have seen the letter in which you tell me [all this] is so much nonsense, and I assure you that I found everything in it all too well explained. You know that no one is more convinced than I of her [Julie's] worth; but I admit that this does not prevent me from being surprised to see that you could have a thought that should so injure our friendship. For to believe that you said [such a thing] to the one and wrote it to the other, just for the sake of paying an agreeable compliment, I have too great a respect for your courage to suppose that the desire to please could make you so betray the feelings of your heart. . . . The affection I have for you being so well known by everyone, and above all Mademoiselle de Rambouillet, that I cannot doubt that she will have been more sensible to the wrong you do me than to the praise you give her. The chance that caused this letter to fall into my hands reminded me strongly of Bertaut's lines:

Malheureuse est l'ignorance,
Et plus malheureux est le savoir.[46]

Having thus lost a trust that alone helped me to bear life, the journey which
you have so often suggested [to Mme de Sablé's country estate] becomes
unthinkable; for what is the likelihood of traveling sixty leagues in this season to burden you with so little pleasing a person, of whom you could not
prevent yourself from saying, after so many years of unequaled passion, that
the greatest pleasure in life would be to spend it without her? I return to my
solitude to examine the failings that make me so miserable, and, unless I am
able to correct them, I could not have so much joy in seeing you but that my
confusion would be greater.[47]

This astounding letter would be considerably less so had it been written by the
Marquise de Sablé to the Duc de Montmorency. But here an " unequaled passion"
is seen to be aroused by the double affront of an emotional betrayal and a public
humiliation. The supposed crime is not one of behavior but of a wish belonging
to the world of dreams. Yet this unrealizable wish—for a happy life away from
the world in the company of one person, Julie d'Angennes—which might be
the childish expression of a strong preference, was interpreted by Mlle d'Attichy
as an absolute sentimental engagement, the sign of an exclusive friendship, unlike
any other.

   The preference claimed by the young Mlle d'Attichy was not necessarily of an
illicit nature, since her affection for Mme de Sablé was in the "public domain."
But her jealousy and her violent recriminations inevitably put a question mark
over the nature of her friendship with Mme de Sablé. During the *ancien régime*,
female solidarity often compensated for estranged marriages and questionable
maternal love—somewhat uncertain at the time, as women had to contend continually with unwanted, risky pregnancies and a high infant-mortality rate that
did not always encourage mothers to become attached to their children.
Galanterie, whether *honnête* or not, could make amends for marriages that disregarded feelings, but it was still a dangerous game, full of unknown hazards. It is
hardly surprising that in describing marriage, war metaphors were used with
increasing frequency.

---

46. "Unhappy is ignorance,/And more unhappy is knowing." This somewhat inaccurate quotation
comes from song 27 in *Recueil de quelques vers amoureux* by Jean Bertaut, first published in 1600 and
in 1603 by Guillemot, and reprinted with variations in 1606. See *Le Recueil de quelques vers amoureux*,
edited by Louis Terreaux (Paris: Didier, 1970), p. 142.

47. The Comtesse de Maure to Mme de Sablé, October 1631, letter 1, in *Mme la comtesse de Maure, sa
vie et sa correspondance suivies des Maximes de Mme de Sablé et d'une étude sur la vie de Mademoiselle de Vandy*, edited by Édouard de Barthélemy (Paris: J. Gay, 1863), pp. 77–79.

Little by little, as their worldly prestige increased, however, some women began to express their aspirations, their likes and dislikes. Whether married or single, they did not disguise the violent repulsion they felt for marriage and sex, while both in private and in society, they hallowed the typically feminine qualities of reserve, refinement, and emotional sensibility. Men were also asked to respect and share these values, but women were able to find understanding and an emotional security sufficient in itself within their own world.

The exaltation and sublimation of female friendship typical of the "precious" ideal could, however, present a threat to society's equilibrium, since they were bound to be in competition with gallant love. And if ridicule was used as a weapon to discredit them, so too was the accusation of unnatural sexuality. The Abbé Cotin had already alluded in vague terms to "the strange habits of a cabal who wish to oblige women to be content with themselves,"[48] but Saint-Évremond dotted the *i*'s in this polemical campaign:

> *Nous ne vous plaignons point, ô chères Précieuses,*
> *Qui dans les bras aimés de quelque tendre sœur,*
> *Savez goûter les fruits des peines amoureuses*
> *Sans intéresser votre honneur.*[49]

Up until the fall of the *ancien régime*, the language and expressions of female friendship, in contrast to society manners, which knew nothing of the joys of abandon, provided ample opportunity for satire and insinuation. Marie-Antoinette would be the most famous victim. But the striking thing about Mlle d'Attichy's outburst against Mme de Sablé is the unyielding conception of friendship, of its rights and its duties, surprisingly similar to those of love. Well before Molière's *Le Misanthrope* (1666), the young woman attacks society language's lack of authenticity for sacrificing sincerity to manners. Mlle d'Attichy was ready to agree with Mlle de Scudéry, who considered obligingness (*complaisance*) to be indispensable to the pleasantness of civil living,[50] but here she reminded Mme de Sablé of what a pedagogue of manners like Ortigue de Vaumorière would have felt it his duty to

---

48. Charles Cotin, *Œuvres galantes* (Paris: E. Loyson, 1663), p. 65, quoted in Sellier, "La névrose précieuse," p. 115.

49. "We do not pity you at all, oh dear *Précieuses*,/Who in the loved arms of a tender sister,/Know how to taste the fruits of love's anguish/Without endangering your honor," Saint-Évremond, *Œuvres*, seven volumes (London: J. Tonson, 1725), Vol. 4, pp. 113–115, quoted in Sellier, "La névrose précieuse," p. 114.

50. "It unites, softens, and binds society, . . . without it the opinionated, the ambitious, the angry, and, in fact, all those people with violent, contrary temperaments, would be unable to live together"; Mlle de Scudéry, "De la différence du flatteur et du complaisant," in *Conversations sur divers sujets*, two volumes (Paris: C. Barbin, 1680), Vol. 1, p. 353.

point out to his readers: that "there are many kinds of obligingness that one should never have," and above all, that the wish to please must not betray "one's feelings in essential matters."[51]

Unlike in the outcome of her affair with Montmorency, Mme de Sablé overcame her pride in this case, as did Mlle d'Attichy, and the two remained friends for life. The latter's late marriage in 1637 to Henri Louis de Rochechouart, Comte de Maure, in no way came between them, but rather brought them closer together. At thirty-six, Anne d'Attichy remained the sole heiress to a vast fortune. Her marriage, arranged for financial reasons, turned out to be an immediate success. The bride may have lost some of the beauty that Mme de Motteville described as having "caused such commotion," but she had retained "a shining, spotless virtue, generosity with extraordinary eloquence, an elevated soul, noble sentiments, [and] great insight and perception," all gifts that were bound to command the respect of a man like the Comte de Maure, a man with "a spirit as intrepid in hatred as in friendship."[52] (Mazarin's refusal to allow the posthumous retrial and rehabilitation of his wife's uncle, the Maréchal de Marcillac, was enough to drive Maure into the arms of the Fronde.)

The Maures were well suited, not only because of their shared ideals but on account of a shared inclination to extravagance. Disorganized, spendthrift, and extraordinarily scatterbrained, the couple would leave for the country just as the season came for the return to the city and would go visiting at an hour when everyone was already in bed. Indeed, they proved themselves constitutionally incapable of "subjecting themselves to the clock."[53] And since Mme de Maure shared many of Mme de Sablé's phobias, the couple went without hesitation to live with the marquise: a most novel and unusual cohabitation.

Even so, weeks could pass without the two hypochondriacs seeing one another. A hint of indisposition, each one's fear of the other's germs, the drafts lying in wait in the corridors and the hall often confined them to their respective rooms. On one occasion, fearing that the countess had quarreled with her husband, Mme de Sablé, protected by a mobile tent held up by servants, bravely visited Mme de Maure in her bedroom. Usually, however, the two friends preferred to communicate by letter, and they wrote to one another many times a day.

Given the circumstances, their correspondence was of a totally unprecedented nature. Sometimes they wrote a few lines with no heading or formal introduction, which had the immediacy and naturalness of a conversation between friends.

---

51. Ortigue de Vaumorière, "De la conversations des Dames, et jusqu'à la flatterie on peut porter la complaisance que l'on doit avoir pour elles," in *L'Art de plaire dans la conversation* (1688; Paris: Jean and Michel Guignard, 1701), p. 63.

52. *Mémoires de Mme de Motteville*, Vol. 2, pp. 395–396.

53. "Portrait de Mme la Comtesse de Maure, fait par Monsieur le Marquis de Sourdis," in *Divers Portraits* (Mademoiselle de Montpensier's *Recueil*, edited by Segrais) (Caen: 1659), p. 160.

These notes were circulated just as much as the endless anecdotes about the eccentricities of two lady letter-writers, and were thus to determine the aesthetic of the society letter. Society's liking for irony did not put an end to admiration; cultured, brilliant, fanciful, entertaining, with a perfect knowledge of the language, the two friends had discovered the epistolary tone to suit society, a tone that could only be adopted between equals who saw "the person to whom one was writing as another self, treating that person without affectation, in a familiar honest way."[54]

"It was in their time that letter-writing became usual," declared the Grande Mademoiselle in her *Histoire de la Princesse de Paphlagonie*, at a time when people enjoyed playing games with literature. "Before then, only marriage contracts were written, and nothing was heard of letters; thus we are obliged to them for such a convenient [development] in communication."[55] And in 1675, the scholarly Abbé Ménage unhesitatingly named the two friends in his *Observations sur la langue française*: "To write notes to one another is very convenient and was introduced as such thirty or forty years ago by Madame la Marquise de Sablé and Madame la Comtesse de Maure."[56]

Only Mme de Maure's notes have survived. Undated, written in haste, often scribbled, full of now incomprehensible references, they leave us with fragments of extravagant, secretive conversations, the strangeness and emotional tension of which are disconcerting. "Your thanks, my love, are worth more than all that I can ever do for you. Do you not know full well that I owe everything to you and that I am repaid by your hand when I serve you? You made me laugh over your anguish concerning the letter which your servants never sent me. It is well known that in such matters, you are rather more likely to exaggerate than not."[57]

Every letter was meant to express affection and gratitude, to give advice, to suggest a therapy, or to accompany the gift of an infusion, an ointment, or some delicacy. Mme de Sablé and Mme de Maure never tired of nurturing their shared neuroses through shared confidences, indulging in the pleasure of discussing them as often as possible, and despairing at the very thought of one of their missives going astray. "No letter has been lost my love.... I have had the one in which you tell me that Monsieur de Valens was raving; it is just that I thought he had

---

54. *Nouveau recueil contenant la vie, les amours, les infortunes et les lettres d'Abailard et d'Héloïse, les lettres d'une religieuse portugaise et du chevalier * * *, celles de Cléante et Bélise, avec l'histoire de la Matrone d'Éphèse* (Brussels, 1709), *remarque* VII, p. 476, quoted in Roger Duchêne, *Mme de Sévigné et la lettre d'amour*, edited by Geneviève Haroche-Bouzinac (Paris: Klincksieck, 1992), p. 111.

55. Mademoiselle de Montpensier, *La Relation de l'isle imaginaire et l'histoire de la Princesse de Paphlagonie* (Bordeaux: 1659), pp. 81–82.

56. Gilles Ménage, *Observations sur la langue française*, two volumes (Paris: C. Barbin, 1675–1676), Vol. 1, p. 395.

57. Comtesse de Maure to Mme de Sablé, November 1662, letter 55, in Bartélémy, *Mme la comtesse de Maure, sa vie et sa correspondance*, p. 182.

recovered. I send you a thousand thanks, my dear, my love, for everything you say about the water. It is well known that it is always your wish to give. I am a little better, thank God, my dear, my love, but I am not yet well."[58]

Because of the profound understanding that each expressed for the other's obsessions, the two could also try to exorcise their agonizing hypochondriac fantasies by listing their symptoms and their illnesses one by one. "I sympathize with you very much, my love, about the pain in your eyes, which gives you the discomfort you speak of. As for me, my love, I would be quite well, if I did not suffer from nausea; as for my cold, I am not concerned about it any longer since I have no catarrh and not even much of a cough."[59]

But we should not be deceived by such sweet, melodious terms of affection. Despite their intimacy, their shared phobias, and their similar habits, Mme de Sablé and Mme de Maure both retained an absolute independence of judgment and a respect for the beliefs of the other. The Comte de Maure was a fiery Frondist and a convinced Molinist,[60] and his wife never embraced Port-Royal's doctrines; but in Mme de Sablé, who was both a realist and a Jansenist, tolerance was combined with an intellectual curiosity about how other people reasoned. And in any case, the Comtesse de Maure was perfectly capable of voicing her own opinions:

> My love, what you write to Monsieur de Sourdis—that by your reasoning you take his side, although your faith does not allow you to do so—and what Monsieur le Comte [de Maure] told me about the dispute you had with him the day before yesterday makes me think that you take as an article of faith what Saint Augustine says in the *Treatise on Grace*.[61] And I, far from believing it to be an article of faith, would be very angry if I had to believe it, since it is such a harsh opinion, and in my understanding so contrary to God's goodness, that I believe it would lead to atheism rather than to anything else. So I most willingly hold to the Bull that, without condemning Saint Augustine, condemns the opinions I found in that work, so that, without ever having been able to understand the reasoning used to explain sufficient grace, I keep to it since that means holding to the Bull, and that I

---

58. Comtesse de Maure to Mme de Sablé, letter 55, in Bartélémy, *Mme la comtesse de Maure, sa vie et sa correspondance*, p. 182.

59. Comtesse de Maure to Mme de Sablé, letter 71, in Bartélémy, *Mme la comtesse de Maure, sa vie et sa correspondance*, p. 220.

60. Much attacked in France by the Jansenists, the Molinists were followers of Luis Molina (1535–1600), a Spanish Jesuit whose teachings aimed at reconciling free will with the doctrines of grace and divine prescience.

61. See the Bibliographical Essay for an explanation of the letter's many references, especially the discussion of predestination, a central point of the Jansenist polemic.

want to know nothing more about the matter. I do not know for whom it can be useful to believe in the necessity of the damned and that God has not given us the grace needed to accomplish what he has commanded; but I certainly believe that that creed would be very dangerous to me. I also well know that were the most learned men in the world gathered together in one place where I might easily go, I would like to hear them only to hear who spoke best; for where doctrine is concerned, I am convinced that the simple know as much as the learned, and I have always been horrified when I have seen those on both sides become so heated over so obscure a matter; not because of the matter disputed, for I understand well the heat that derives from the desire to win, but because so many people come to hate each other because their opinions on it differ. And I have had the joy of seeing you always as zealous as I.[62]

III. In the Shade of Port-Royal

With her conversion to Jansenism, Mme de Sablé renounced festivities and entertainments but not the pleasures of society. The marquise continued to receive friends and acquaintances at her house, and in the years following the collapse of the Fronde, her drawing room became one of the most creative meeting places in French cultural and society circles. In 1640 her husband had the good taste to die, and she to receive the news with great composure. In a letter to the Marquis de Montausier, Chapelain portrays her as a genuine *honnête femme*, capable of obeying all the demands of social decorum without betraying her own integrity: 'So Mme la Marquise de Sablé is a widow and one of the most dignified widows I have ever seen; she neither laughs nor cries; without overplaying her mourning nor displaying a scandalous indifference to such an important change, she behaves in the very way necessary to allow no one to have a hold over her.'[63]

Another death had certainly affected her more deeply. That was the death in 1639 of the Marquis d'Armentières, killed in a duel. He was, according to Tallemant, her last lover. "After that loss, the marquise no longer made love, she decided the time had come to be devout."[64] Then, in October 1646, the marquise suffered another misfortune, the loss of her younger son, the bold, valorous, cultured Guy de Laval, who perished aged twenty-four at the siege of Dunkerque.

---

62. Comtesse de Maure to Mme de Sablé, letter 60, in Bartélémy, *Mme la comtesse de Maure, sa vie et sa correspondance*, pp. 189–191.

63. Chapelain to the Marquis de Montausier, June 15, 1640, letter 407, *Lettres de Jean Chapelain*, Vol. 1, p. 640.

64. Tallemant, *Historiettes*, Vol. 1, p. 516.

The ensuing family quarrel, during which her other sons obliged her to sell the Sablé property, can have offered little consolation.

According to Père Rapin, it was precisely for economic reasons that Mme de Sablé had a house built for herself within the walls of the convent of Port-Royal.[65] Anxious to gain her goodwill, the nuns agreed to a request that would have seemed unacceptable to other religious institutions. Despite the numerous problems that resulted, their calculations turned out to be far-sighted. The marquise was to win much sympathy for the Jansenist cause. Above all, she attracted the Duchesse de Longueville to Port-Royal.

Mme de Sablé's decision set a precedent. Right up until the end of the *ancien régime*, a great many convents would provide accommodation for noblewomen— whether single, widowed, or separated—giving them the opportunity to benefit both from the comforts of religion and total independence in the name of respectability and economy. It was for precisely these very practical reasons that a century later Mme du Deffand would move to an apartment in the convent of Saint-Joseph, there to open her famous salon. Unlike Mme du Deffand, however, Mme de Sablé was genuinely religious. She wanted to detach herself from the profane but she had not the strength, and she was well aware that hating the world did not necessarily make it possible to forgo it: "To abandon the world, a grace is needed," she would say. "To hate it, none is needed."[66]

The location of her house within the convent, facing the church on one side and the street on the other, was symbolic of her inner self, suspended as she was between retreat and the world. It is not known how often the marquise used the key that allowed her direct access to her private tribune in the church where she could follow religious services at a safe remove from any unhealthy contact. The correspondence she had with the nuns, despite her many and often comical practical concerns, indicates a genuine interest in the life of the community and a profound religious sentiment.

Although they had embraced the strictest of rules, the nuns, beginning with the convent's legendary reformer Mother Angélique, were continuously obliged to compromise over the marquise's demands, her phobias, and her *grande dame* requirements. Sickness and death were common enough in the convent; the nuns subjected themselves to privations, vigils, and endless chores; and if they weakened they entrusted themselves to God's hands. But such was Mme de Sablé's

---

65. In the 1640s (and certainly before the year 1648—the year of Voiture's death) Mme de Sablé lived with the de Maures in a *hôtel* in the place Royale. In 1656, she moved to a house contiguous to the convent of Port-Royal. In 1665, when persecution of the Jansenists dispersed the religious community and Church authorities installed a new abbess at Port-Royal, the marquise left the convent and was taken in by her brother, the Commandant de Sauvré, on the rue des Petits-Champs. In 1668, after the "Peace of the Church," she returned to live at Port-Royal until her death.

66. Quoted in Sainte-Beuve, *Port-Royal*, Vol. 3, p. 72.

reaction one day when, on entering the choir of the church, she happened upon the body of a nun awaiting burial that the sisters made sure no such thing should ever happen again. In vain did Mother Angélique remind the marquise: "The day advances, twilight approaches."[67] From that point onward, the corpses of nuns were laid out far from the marquise's eyes and buried as quickly as possible.

The nuns of Port-Royal—Mother Angélique, Mother Agnès, Sister Angélique de Saint-Jean, and others—did not bow to Mme de Sablé's inadmissible requests out of sheer opportunism. They were sufficiently aware of her psychology and they knew her well enough to understand her suffering and the uncontrollable panic that gripped her at the thought of death. They believed that was the cross she had to bear, and they felt deeply for her. But they were not always prepared to give way to her. When Mme de Sablé was offended that the convent confessor had not sought her out first, Mother Angélique told her firmly that faith took no account of society's *bienséances*. Yet Port-Royal's reformer, who had sacrificed her dearest love to God, carried the memory of her difficult lodger in her heart to the bitter end. Only two days before she died, when she could barely speak, Mother Angélique was heard to whisper quite clearly: "My poor marquise!"[68]

Although installed within the Jansenist stronghold, Mme de Sablé remained on excellent terms with society. The only conditions the nuns set were that they should be protected from the curiosity of her guests and that the shutters over the windows facing the convent garden should remain locked when she was receiving. In fact a great many visitors came to the rue de la Bourbe, attracted by both the pleasure of the marquise's conversation and the refinement of her table. It was the latter that particularly delighted the King's brother, Monsieur, and La Rochefoucauld, who shared Mme de Sablé's taste for coining maxims. Her Jansenist friends also honored her table without fear of flaunting their rigid rules.

The Marquise de Sablé had, above all, a supreme genius for mixing her guests around discussions of communal interest. Great aristocrats, magistrates, scientists, Jesuits, Jansenists, doctors, men of letters, diplomats, and society ladies would all gather at her house to hear theological discussions, watch scientific experiments, and talk of metaphysics, morality, psychology, and medicine. These were probably small gatherings because, in so far as she could, the marquise avoided physical contact and kept to the spirit of Guazzo's famous formula that a conversational circle should never include more than ten people.[69] Presumably these receptions

---

67. Letter from Mother Angélique to Mme de Sablé, November 11, 1655, quoted in Cousin, *Mme de Sablé*, p. 184.

68. Gazier, *Les Belles Amies de Port-Royal*, p. 49.

69. "... That the banquet should begin with the Graces and end with the Muses, that is to say that the number of guests should never be less than three nor more than nine," Guazzo, *La civil conversazione*, Book 2, Vol. 1, p. 175.

did not occur regularly (a practice introduced by the *Précieuses*), since Mme de Sablé became more and more eccentric as she grew older and tended to isolate herself for weeks on end, refusing to receive even her closest friends and interrupting all correspondence.

Paradoxically, it is because of the hostess's hypochondria that the names of her guests as well as the nature and tone of their conversation are known. When she went to live at Port-Royal, the marquise wanted her doctor, Vallant, permanently at hand. He may not have prevented her from dying, but by preserving her letters and a record of the literary games, topics of discussion, and verses, he managed to preserve her from oblivion.

The marquise remained interested in love even at Port-Royal, despite her years and preoccupation with religion. As a subject of conversation, it interested socialites and moralists equally and lent itself as much to frivolity as it did to profound reflection. Mlle de Scudéry, with the publication of the third part of her novel *Clélie* in 1658,[70] made *questions d'amour* fashionable, so that for about ten years they and *maximes d'amour* were "all the rage in the salons." The game —almost as old as French aristocratic civilization—consisted of raising various points concerning love or suggesting maxims on the subject so that players could display such valued social virtues as psychological acumen, wit, and refinement. Even the young Louis XIV loved this form of entertainment and considered it a useful school of elegance for the court. Roger de Bussy-Rabutin tells how, when asked to read out his *Maximes d'amour* in front of the King's brother, he was struck by the wit with which, despite her youth, Françoise Athénaïs de Roche-chouart—the future Marquise de Montespan and mistress to the King—gave the best answers.[71]

Mme de Sablé's habitués, too, joined in the game. In November 1667, the Marquis de Sourdis, putting theology aside for the moment, read out his thirty-two *Questions sur l'amour* in the marquise's drawing room. These, along with Mme de Brégy's *Cinq Questions d'amour*, were transcribed into Volume XIII of Dr. Vallant's *Portefeuilles*. Among other questions, the marquis asked "whether it was better to lose a loved one through death or infidelity"; "if great jealousy is a sign of great love"; and "if it is possible to love something more than oneself."[72] Mme de Brégy asked "if the presence of the loved one occasioned joy that was greater than the pain caused by indifference"; what should a person choose when "his

---

70. Mlle de Scudéry, "Morale galante de Térame," in *Clélie, Histoire romaine* (1654–1660) reprint of the 1658–1662 Paris edition, Part 3, Book 3, Vol. 4 (Geneva: Slatkine reprint, 1973), pp. 1360–1379.

71. See Roger de Bussy-Rabutin, *Mémoires de Roger de Rabutin, comte de Bussy*, edited by Ludovic Lalanne, two volumes (Paris: C. Marpon and E. Flammarion, 1882), Vol. 2, p. 60.

72. Quoted in Nicolas Ivanoff, *La marquise de Sablé et son salon* (Paris: Les Presses Modernes, 1927), pp. 138–139.

heart inclines to one side and his reason to the other?"; "should we hate someone we find too pleasing and whom we cannot please?"; "is it sweeter to love a person whose heart is elsewhere engaged, or another whose heart is insensible?"; and lastly, "whether the pleasure of being loved compensates for the displeasure in not being loved."[73]

The five questions posed by the Comtesse de Brégy—who had been lady-in-waiting to Anne of Austria—had been addressed to the King, who had been so kind as to charge Philippe Quinault with formulating replies in verse. For their part, Sourdis's questions seem to have inspired some of the more ardent declarations in the extremely successful novel *Lettres portugaises*. The recent discovery of the "privilege to publish" granted to the publisher Barbin on November 17, 1668, reveals that both the *Lettres portugaises* and a volume of gallant verses called *Valentins* were penned by a habitué and friend of Mme de Sablé's, the Vicomte de Guilleragues.[74] Published separately and anonymously, the novel and *Valentins*—whose verses were very similar to the *questions d'amour*—were received very differently, in absolute keeping with their differing literary quality. The first greatly impressed its readers and was established as a masterpiece, while the second had the passing success of a fashionable game. Yet, as was discovered two centuries later, both bear indubitable signs of the same authorship. Frédéric Deloffre's textual and thematic analysis shows an obvious link between the *Lettres portugaises* and *Valentins*; both can be read in the light of the *questions d'amour* so fashionable in Mme de Sablé's drawing room. Published with *Valentins*, there was also a real letter, probably written years earlier, in which Guilleragues did not disguise his admiration for the marquise:

Madame,

I know that I do not deserve your letters; but for all that, I want them. Here is an opening which is not at all contrived and that will doubtless surprise you. In fact such a precious thing should be requested with less effrontery, particularly to someone like you, who has all the imaginable worth and as much delicacy as worth. But, Mme, you know that one is carried away in speech when one desires violently, and that the words *I want* are not always reserved for the mouths of mistresses and kings. These two kinds of people

---

73. *Cinq Questions d'amour, proposées par Mme de Brégy, avec la réponse en vers par M. Quinault, par l'ordre du Roy* (Leyden, 1666), pp. 130–132.

74. According to the *Registre des Privilèges*, the full title of the book whose authorization was reported on November 17, 1668, was *Les Valantains Lettres portugaises Epigrames et Madrigaux de Guilleragues*. See Frédéric Deloffre's preface in Guilleragues, *Lettres Portugaises, suivies de Guilleragues par lui-même* (Paris: Gallimard, 1990) p. 27.

who confuse reason with will, do not always want things that are very reasonable, and should not often say *I want*. For myself, what I desire is so excellent, and I desire it with such passion, that if there were something more than *I want*, I should be forgiven for saying it. Allow me, therefore, Mme, to finish my note if possible more madly than I began it, by saying, *like the King to his sergeant and the Queen to her son*, which are the most absolute orders of which you have ever heard tell, that I *want* you to do me the honor of writing to me.[75]

The social graces are perfectly exemplified in this letter, probably written in the early 1650s, when Guilleragues had known Mme de Sablé only a short time. In it, a young provincial, newly arrived in Paris, attempts to join the circle of the marquise's correspondents and to snatch one of her famous replies from her. Its elegance, immediacy, delicate flattery, and boldness, its originality and element of surprise, overwhelm and draw the reader into the game. The writing retains the enthusiasm and communicative power of the request with all the spontaneity and naturalness of the spoken word.

Born in Bordeaux into a family of several generations of the *noblesse de robe*, Gabriel de Lavergne, Vicomte de Guilleragues, would remain faithful to the style of this letter throughout his life. He was cultivated, witty, and clever, and he knew how to exploit his ability to please in the interests of his career. He managed to infiltrate smart Parisian society, becoming an habitué of the hôtel d'Albret and the hôtel de Richelieu, and of Mme de Sablé's and Mme de Sablière's salons. Nor did he forget to pay his respects to Mme de Montespan, her sister Mme de Thianges, and Mme de Maintenon. Eventually he arrived at court, where he gained favor with Monsieur and with Louis XIV himself. Guilleragues was a soldier, secretary to the King, diplomat, ambassador to the Sublime Porte, and a lifelong literary dilettante who, as the years went by, wrote verses, rhymes, and lyrics. *Valentins* illustrates better than anything the lightheartedness so in tune with the taste of the time. But none of his aristocratic, amateur scribblings could have hinted at the literary marvel of the *Lettres portugaises*.

This marvel took shape in Mme de Sablé's drawing room. There the game of *questions d'amour* was accompanied by a systematic discussion of the nature of feelings, and the lady of the house, as Mother Angélique knew only to well, was "well learned in the passions, revulsions, and the occasions of worldly cunning."[76] Although the study of the heart remained one of the marquise's main interests as much when she was seventy as when she was twenty, her point of view changed considerably with time.

---

75. Guilleragues, *Lettres Portugaises*, p. 117.

76. Sainte-Beuve, *Port-Royal*, Vol. 3, p. 82.

The chivalric conception of love that Mme de Sablé had cultivated in her youth represented a form of morality based on metaphysics. As *L'Astrée* declared, devotion to the beloved woman, to her beauty and her virtues, was seen as an instrument of spiritual elevation, essential to the mystical process. Jansenist Augustinianism, on the other hand, taught that man's nature was too corrupted by sin for him to put faith in the authenticity of his own ideals. Two irreconcilable loves existed: the love of God and the love of self, and the choice was simply between the two. Unless a morality of love was rejected, it became "impossible to agree on its bases,"[77] because the very idea of love became confused.

Many of the discussions in Mme de Sablé's drawing room thus took place between those who supported "love by choice and election" and others who supported "love by inclination." The first camp, led by the Marquis de Sourdis, believed in the possibility of virtuous love based on a knowledge of the qualities of the loved one—not unlike "love through esteem" (*l'amour d'estime*) to which Mlle de Scudéry had given pride of place on her *Carte de Tendre*.[78] The other group followed the Jansenist Jacques Esprit, who denounced the mysterious, irrational nature of passion with all its attendant dangers. Apparently the marquise hesitated for a long time before taking sides and definitively turning her back on the Spanish idea of gallantry, which, as Lafond points out, had meanwhile "become one of the ideals of *préciosité*."[79] Ultimately "love by inclination" seemed to hold sway. "Love, wherever it is, is always master," wrote Mme de Sablé. "It shapes the heart, the soul, and the mind, in accordance with what it is. Its smallness or its greatness depends not on the heart or mind that it occupies, but on what it is itself. And it truly seems that love is to the soul of the lover what the soul is to the body it animates."[80]

This all-encompassing conception of love was lived out to the extreme in the *Lettres portugaises*. The novel consists of five unanswered letters written by the nun Mariane—long monologues that reminded Leo Spitzer of the five acts of a classical tragedy—describing a blind passion obliged to face up to betrayal and abandonment until it finally became disillusioned and detached. Scholars have shown, in minute analysis of each sentence, how much Guilleragues owed to the ideas of some of Mme de Sablé's habitués; but the place where the marquise lived probably influenced the author's imagination too. Although they had no direct contact with the convent, Mme de Sablé's guests could hardly forget that only a few meters away from the room in which they conversed, there existed a world

---

77. Jean-Michel Pelous, *Amour précieux, amour galant (1654–1675)* (Paris: Klincksieck, 1980), p. 122.

78. See Chapter 9 for more discussion of Mlle de Scudéry's *Carte de Tendre*.

79. Lafond, "L'amitié selon Arnauld d'Andilly, " in *L'Homme et son image*, p. 267.

80. Maxim 74, in Bartélémy, *Mme la comtesse de Maure, sa vie et sa correspondance*, pp. 38–39.

that lived by absolute faith. Religion, however, was entirely absent from the Portuguese convent in which Guilleragues set his story; tolerance and human understanding allowed the nun who was in love to yield to her passion with impunity.

A long literary tradition, from the letters of Abélard and Héloïse to Boccaccio's novellas, had made convents highly erotic places, and only a few years before the *Lettres portugaises*, in 1665, La Fontaine, in his *Contes et nouvelles en vers*, had told stories in which sacred and profane love lived happily side by side. Guilleragues chose to take quite a different line. The religious context that formed the framework of his novel provoked no malice, no louche fantasy, no moral indignation. Like Port-Royal, the Portuguese convent was a place apart, where an absolute experiment was being lived. In Mariane's letters there was no place for faith, morality, modesty, guilt, or, even less, for the outside world. Only passion counted. Like Port-Royal, Guilleragues's convent was a laboratory in which to test extreme theories. In the first, earthly love was subsumed into the love of God; in the second, the flame of "love by inclination" was free to burn itself out and thus reveal its deceptive nature, leaving in its wake nothing but a pile of ashes.

On his visits to Port-Royal, Guilleragues must have heard Mme de Sablé's friends discussing—not merely for the pleasures of abstract argument—these opposing yet interrelated forms of love. Some of them, like Mme de Sablé, Mme de Guéméné, or Mme de Longueville, had lived through experiences similar to those of Mariane, and were attracted by the extreme spiritual challenge Port-Royal presented. Others, like La Rochefoucauld, tempered their disappointments with irony. Guilleragues knew their stories and, as the nuns' muffled singing reminded the guests in the drawing room that only a wall separated them from a radically different world, he must sometimes have wondered about their past loves as well.

Perhaps such considerations led Guilleragues to go further and to wish to bring love back to the real world. With a stroke of genius he moved from the abstract casuistry of *Valentins* to creating a totally convincing character and plot. From the depths of her convent and from her own vivid experience, Mariane illustrated the stages in a sentimental journey that disregarded *bienséances* and the good taste of Mlle de Scudéry's *Carte de Tendre*. The latter had argued that women were better at writing love letters because "when a lover has decided to write quite openly of his passion, there is no longer any art in always saying, 'I am dying of love': but for a woman who never admits quite how much she loves, and who makes a greater mystery of it, the love which is only glimpsed, pleases more than that which shows itself brazenly."[81]

Turning this logic on its head, Mariane had the audacity to shout her feelings out

---

81. Mlle de Scudéry, "De la manière d'écrire des lettres, " in *"De l'air galant" et autres conversations (1653–1684): Pour une étude de l'archive galante*, edited by Delphine Denis (Paris: Champion, 1998), p. 157.

loud and did not mind declaring that she had been the first to fall in love. "I had only to see you, to dedicate my life to you," she declares.[82] Before the publication of *La Princesse de Clèves*, the amiable, skeptical Guilleragues taught women to use sincerity as a weapon and to take their destinies into their own hands. But Mariane, unlike Mme de Clèves, did not give up her love affair for fear of being disillusioned; in the name of clear thinking and courage, she lived out her idyll to the bitter end.

Some of the women who read this novel were not content merely to admire Guilleragues's heroine. As time went by, bolder readers went so far as to follow her example. A century later, Mme de La Popelinière was inspired by her passion for the Maréchal de Richelieu to write harrowing letters; Horace Walpole would accuse Mme du Deffand of writing "Portuguese" letters to him; and in hundreds of letters, Julie de Lespinasse would repeat the same challenge that Mariane had sent to her unknown officer: to love for love's sake.

The novelty of the *Lettres portugaises* lay also in the form, and even in this, Guilleragues managed to use the means of expression with which, as a bold amateur, he was most familiar. Like all socialites, he loved novels, and like some, he excelled in the art of letter-writing. By cheerfully combining the two genres, Guilleragues reacted to the crisis into which novel-writing had fallen at the beginning of the 1660s with a winning combination of brevity, topicality, and authorial subjectivity. Once again with no intention other than to amuse himself, an aristocratic amateur described society life in a masterpiece that was to have a considerable influence in opening the way for the French eighteenth-century novel. Only La Rochefoucauld could offer Mme de Sablé's salon a greater compliment.

Another ideal that Mme de Sablé was not prepared to sacrifice to her religious conviction was the ideal of friendship. Rather than being a topic for discussion, friendship for her was primarily a real affection that occupied a central position in her life. "She loved her friends, company, and life above everything," wrote Père Rapin. He recognized that the respect and consideration the marquise enjoyed in society were due to the "*honnêteté* of her behavior" and to "the pleasure she took in pleasing all those who were close to her; for it is true that no one has ever been more faithful to her friends."[83]

Theoretically, the discussion of friendship involved everyone in the marquise's intimate circle. In reply to one of them—La Rochefoucauld perhaps?—who chose "to imagine that true friendship was based on something as frail as common interests and similar occupations,"[84] the marquise wrote a *Traité de l'amitié* in which

---

82. Guilleragues, *Lettres portugaises*, p. 75.

83. *Mémoires du Père René Rapin*, Vol. 1, pp. 175, 405.

84. Quoted in Lafond, "L'amitié," in *L'Homme et son image*, p. 268.

she maintained in eight "sentences" that friendship conformed perfectly with reason and virtue. The position was rather more Aristotelian than Cartesian and would be echoed by Arnauld d'Andilly when writing on the same subject.

Robert Arnauld d'Andilly was, as Marc Fumaroli has called him, one of the "*gens* Arnauld, a breed of Christian lawyers of solid stamp . . . an eloquent family . . . more prestigious in its own right than the Parlement or the Académie."[85] Son of a great prince of the legal profession, champion of Gallican virtues, Robert was the brother of Antoine Arnauld—the Grand Arnauld who had composed *De la fréquente communion*. Mother Angélique was his sister. His own two daughters were nuns at Port-Royal. He had frequented society in his youth and had known Mme de Sablé since the days of the hôtel de Rambouillet. Unlike Mme de Sablé's, his conversion to Jansenism had been radical. In Louis XIII and Richelieu's France there was no room for civil eloquence, and like other members of his family, d'Andilly chose "the eloquence of exile and Christian faith." From 1645 he lived in retirement at Port-Royal des Champs, a monastery southwest of Paris closely connected to the convent of Port-Royal, which had moved in 1625 to larger quarters in Paris. Here he translated, among other things, the *Confessions* of Saint Augustine. But he still maintained a correspondence with his friends and was a careful reader of the reflections and "sentences" written by Mme de Sablé in those early years of the 1660s. Considering their provenance, the compliments he addressed to the marquise after reading her *Traité de l'amitié* are of great significance.

"In truth," he wrote to her on January 28, 1661,

> it is I who can say, without flattering you, that however well you have always written, you write even better than you have ever done. Which, to my mind, comes from the fact that judgment grows ceaselessly, and thus the intelligence applies itself with greater art and more care. There is no better proof of friendship than that which you have done me the honor of sending me, nothing more beautiful, more just, or more true. But what makes me esteem it even more, is that, however great your judgment and your intelligence, they play a much smaller part in it than does your heart. Such things have to be felt for them to be thought and spoken.[86]

The marquise wrote well because she thought clearly, and above all because her eloquence reflected her true feelings. Her style was not artificial but sprang from her deepest convictions. It was "the eloquence of the heart" that Saint-Cyran had taught at Port-Royal.

---

85. See Marc Fumaroli, *L'Âge de l'éloquence, Rhétorique et 'res literaria' de la Renaissance au seuil de l'époque classique* (Geneva: Droz, 1980), pp. 624–625.

86. Letter of January 28, 1661, in Cousin, *Madame de Sablé*, p. 357.

IV. The Maxim Game

La Rochefoucauld and his friend Jacques Esprit did not, however, share the marquise's rationalized certainties and those of Port-Royal des Champs *solitaires* like Arnauld d'Andilly. For La Rochefoucauld, even friendship was subject to the laws of *amour-propre*,[87] and for Esprit, it was a false virtue.[88] But although Mme de Sablé and her two guests may not have agreed, it did not upset their friendship. Rather, their differing points of view constituted one of the strongest elements in the unusual project on which all three had been working for some years, "a shared fund of sentences," a collection of their thoughts about mankind, human nature, and social behavior.

La Rochefoucauld first mentioned sending Mme de Sablé some "sentences" in a short note to her in 1658 or 1659, but in a later letter to Esprit of uncertain date, the reference is more explicit: "I beg you to show Mme de Sablé our latest sentences; that will perhaps renew her wish to write some, and, for your part, think about it too, if only to fill out our volume."[89] The three friends continued to write, to pass their compositions back and forth, and to comment upon them until 1663, when they went their separate ways. La Rochefoucauld made a collection of all his maxims; Mme de Sablé, aware of La Rochefoucauld's crushingly superior talent, decided not to persevere with her own "sentences," which only appeared posthumously; whereas Esprit chose to crystallize his thoughts more systematically into a treatise.[90]

This new pastime elaborated by Mme de Sablé, La Rochefoucauld, and Esprit was certainly not a game to rival the *maximes d'amours*, which was still being played during those years in that same drawing room. The "sentences" of the three main players were neither improvised nor publicly discussed but written "in solitude" and afterward debated. All the same, there were obvious analogies to be drawn between the two games; both were evidence of the new fortunes of the literary fragment as a privileged expression of ideas of morality and psychology.

In the wake of Montaigne, many seventeenth-century French writers questioned the nature of man. Some of them entrusted themselves faithfully to the

---

87. Maxim 81: 'We cannot love anything except in terms of ourselves, and when we put our friends above ourselves we are only concerned with our own taste and pleasure. Yet it is only through such preference that friendship can be true and perfect." La Rochefoucauld, *Maximes*, edited by Jean Lafond (Paris: Gallimard, 1976) p. 25; translation from La Rochefoucauld, *Maximes*, translated by Leonard Tancock (Penguin, 1959).

88. Jacques Esprit, "L'amitié," in *La Fausseté des vertus humaines* (1678), preceded by the *Traité sur Esprit* by Pascal Quignard (Paris: Aubier, 1996), pp. 127–146.

89. La Rochefoucauld to Jacques Esprit, 1662, in *Maximes*, p. 545.

90. *La Fausseté des vertus humaines*, which discussed fifty-four virtues in as many chapters systematically denouncing imposture, did not come out until the summer of 1678, coinciding with the author's death.

moral order and to typology; others turned to the revelations of a new, much-accepted psychological analysis; still others were sustained in their search by the light of faith. Unlike preachers, they did not arrogate to themselves any superior moral authority, and they brought a subtle ambiguity to their judgments of behavior. Regardless of different points of view, they all aimed to study man at "man's level" and to help him to know himself through simple analysis and the straightforward representation of reality—which is why we tend to describe them nowadays as "anthropologists." But in seventeenth-century terminology they were first and foremost "moralists," that is, writers who concerned themselves with *mœurs* —customs. Many of them had a preference for the short form: sayings, maxims, aphorisms, and *caractères* (typologies based on Theophrastus). They avoided both the treatise and sweeping Ciceronian prose and distanced themselves from erudite culture; they confined themselves to gleaning from the "great book of the world," and their deliberations were intended for an essentially social public. If the moralists preferred short forms to the treatise—which presupposed a coherent vision, systematic knowledge, and a pedagogic engagement with the reader—it was partly because their vision of the world had been shattered.

The ancient genre of "sayings," or "sentences," imposed a general order of truth on the reader. The new ideas brought into fashion by the maxim in modern literature, in contrast, depended less on moral authority than on a surprise effect and a seductive style. The intention was not to instruct but to provoke. As though in conversation, maxims addressed active readers who were capable of reacting to the questions in the text and assimilating their meaning.

With the *questions*, the *maximes*, and the *sentences*, socialites discovered a literature that demanded neither a study of rhetoric nor any other specific erudition. Rather, it explored mankind, its passions, its weaknesses, and its anomalies. To practice it, however, a knowledge of the world was needed, knowledge of its visible face and of its hidden mechanisms—of both the *paraître* (appearance) of the actors on the stage and of their private thoughts. Perhaps this had always been the only learning that nobles required in order to occupy their allotted position, a learning of which they had always been proud and which they cultivated in order to distinguish themselves. The systematic observance of behavior, acute psychological insight, constant self-analysis, punctilious *politesse*, and the art of conversation were all manifestations of this knowledge. With the great novels of the first half of the seventeenth century, professional writers had contributed to the cultivation of this self-awareness, and society itself soon learned to make use of literature, to write verses, letters, and literary portraits, with no aim other than shared enjoyment and no authority other than their own taste. In the case of the *questions d'amour*, a novel written by a society lady—Mlle de Scudéry—had started the fashion. Where the maximes were concerned, a few dilettante aristocrats— Mme de Sablé, La Rochefoucauld, and Esprit—initiated this exercise in reflection and self-analysis that corresponded perfectly with the concerns of the readership to whom it was addressed.

"By about 1660," writes Jean Lafond, "society had wearied of the heroic pose whose decline had been precipitated by the failure of the Fronde."[91] Henceforth, literature was expected to represent man in his reality. As La Fontaine recounted in his *Fables*, La Rochefoucauld turned the myth of Narcissus upside down:

> *Notre âme, c'est cet Homme amoureux de lui-même;*
> *Tant de miroirs, ce sont les sottises d'autrui;*
> *Miroirs de nos défauts les Peinteurs légitimes;*
> *Et quant au Canal, c'est celui*
> *Que chacun sait, le Livre des Maximes.*[92]

Instead of being enchanted by his own image, man is horrified by the discovery of his moral ugliness. The *Maximes* "snatched" readers "out of a deadly enchantment" while still allowing them to indulge their love of self.[93]

What really drove La Rochefoucauld to write his masterpiece? The symbolic events in his life, combined with the ambiguity of his work, lead to a variety of interpretations. Did the defeat of the Fronde with the resulting ruin of his ambitions cause him to change? Did the writer then fill the void left by the soldier, or was the Augustinian pessimism of the *Maximes* another form of confrontation? Despite being a spectacular work of demolition, La Rochefoucauld's "substitutive morals" may, in the long run, have revived the image of the old values among the ruins of the former system. In renouncing heroism, did he make way for a new form of courage?

Jacques Esprit's thinking was also based on the belief that men lived by lies and that all generosity of spirit was motivated by egoism. Which of the two writers first launched the idea of negating all virtue? Victor Cousin claims the dark vision dominating the *Maximes* was inspired in La Rochefoucauld by Esprit. Sainte-Beuve, on the other hand, without denying Esprit's influence, held that La Rochefoucauld wrote his book from personal experience, while developing a literary style that perfectly reflected his style of life. Whereas Esprit protected himself by returning

---

91. Jean Lafond, Preface to *Moralistes du XVIIe siècle* (Paris: Laffont, 1992), p. xxii.

92. "All souls hide this man, rapt in love's dream;/To us, so many mirrors show others' imperfections;/Mirrors that paint our own flaws in true tableaux;/And the stream? Its pure reflections/Are *The Maxims*, the book that everyone knows." Jean de La Fontaine, "L'homme et son image," fable XI of the first book of *Fables* (1668) dedicated to La Rochefoucauld, in *Œuvres complètes*, edited by Jean-Pierre Collinet, two volumes (Paris: Gallimard/Bibliothèque de la Pléiade, 1991), Vol. 1, pp. 46–47; translation by Norman B. Spector, from *The Complete Fables of Jean de La Fontaine* (Northwestern University Press, 1988), p. 25.

93. Lafond, preface to *Moralistes du XVIIe siècle*, p. xxii.

to religion at the end of each chapter, La Rochefoucauld eliminated God from his maxims entirely.

La Rochefoucauld—unlike the Abbé de Rancé, Mme de Longueville, his Port-Royal friends, and the many well-known people who converted in a century accustomed to great personal transformations—remained above all a man of the world. In a self-portrait written in 1658, he describes his features precisely without making any reference to the fact that his face bore a disfiguring scar caused by a musket shot he received at the time of the Fronde. "It missed its object with great grace," writes Louis van Delft, "and, in its most elevated sense, society culture is that: wisdom, the art of bearing life's humiliations gracefully."[94] His friendship with Mme de Sablé was certainly a very helpful in this. There had never been a hint of gallantry in their relationship, which was nevertheless of a very intimate nature. The marquise was fifteen years his senior, had been his father's mistress, and was a close friend of the Duchesse de Longueville. She had probably listened to confidences about his earlier relationship with the duchess and had attempted to alleviate his bitterness. He never managed to forgive or forget that "dead woman" on whom he avenged himself in his *Mémoires* but who still continued to fascinate him. In June 1662 he asked the marquise, "I would certainly like to know, from someone who understands the secrets of the heart as you do, what her real feelings for me are. I mean, whether she has ceased to hate me through devotion, through lassitude, or because she has learned that I was not so much in the wrong as she believed."[95]

La Rochefoucauld and Mme de Sablé both possessed exquisite manners and were both fascinated by modern, eclectic culture. They were curious, intellectually open, but above all, they shared an interest in psychology and morality. The pleasure they derived from their exchange of ideas must have encouraged them to write them down. The initiative came from La Rochefoucauld. Mme de Motteville had said of Mme de Sablé that "her intellect was so great and so fine that I have seen learned men ignorant of the things she knew."[96] La Rochefoucauld dragged her into the game advisedly: "You know that I believe only you where certain chapters are concerned, and particularly about the secrets of the heart."[97] Mme de Sablé returned the compliment by defining his maxims as "a treaty on the movements of the heart of a man, which until this moment, it might be said, were unknown to the heart of the one who produced them."[98] This was a beautiful definition of

94. Louis van Delft, *Le Moraliste classique: Essai de définition et de typologie* (Geneva: Droz, 1982), p. 160.

95. La Rochefoucauld to Mme de Sablé, June 21, [1662], in *Œuvres complètes*, p. 608.

96. *Mémoires de Mme de Motteville*, Vol. 1, p. 12.

97. La Rochefoucauld to Mme de Sablé, circa end of 1662/1663, in *Maximes*, p. 550.

98. Planned article for the *Journal des Savants* on the *Maximes*, in La Rochefoucauld, *Œuvres complètes*, pp. 702–703.

something that, despite the anachronism, might be termed an analysis of the sub-conscious, which, once discovered, caused havoc, scorned virtue by questioning its hidden intentions, discovered the existence of "unthought thoughts," called into account the unsaid, and denounced the secret life of desire.

Not all the "heart's impulses" commented on by La Rochefoucauld in his *Maximes* had tragic overtones. A man of the world who continued to live in the world could hardly fail to realize that life was also a comedy. In writing to Mme de Sablé, he would quite naturally send her, together with some "sentences," a request for jam, for a recipe, or even for a powder made of vipers; so it was only natural that in the *Maximes*, the bitterest disillusionment shared the page with *préciosité*, irony, and a straightforward desire to provoke. Maxims such as "Simplicity put on is a subtle imposture" (289), "Over-subtlety is false delicacy; true delicacy is sound subtlety" (128), and "Nothing makes it so difficult to be natural as the desire to appear so"(431),[99] which could just as well have been written by Mlle de Scudéry, are solidly entrenched in values that were part of society's aesthetic, like refinement and naturalness. Readers admired these maxims for their subtlety of nuance and their finesse of observation. They provided, moreover, ideal points of departure for conversation, giving habitués of the circle the opportunity to show off their own psychological and worldly knowledge. La Rochefoucauld took pleasure in making fun of the old, commonly held, misogynist opinions, and had the nerve to announce, "True love is like ghostly apparitions: everybody talks about them, but few have ever seen one" (76); or "Prudery is a sort of make-up with which women enhance their beauty" (204); and again: "Few virtuous women are not tired of their way of life" (367). Thus he appealed directly to the readers, asking for their reaction.

It was precisely because La Rochefoucauld knew his public so well that he realized it would need preparation for a book that might appear scandalous. He asked for Mme de Sablé's help. The marquise had always loved working behind the scenes, patching up quarrels and favoring friends—to the point that she had aroused Mazarin's suspicion, although he had never had reason to doubt her loyalty. In those very years, Mme de Sablé's support was proving decisive in the campaign for Jansenism. The *messieurs* of Port-Royal had a genius for propaganda and in addressing nobles, they appealed to their autonomous judgment, their interest in psychological and moral problems, and their taste for elegance and purity of language. And in such politics of seduction, no outside support proved more valuable than that offered by Mme de Sablé.

The launching of a book in polite society was not a novelty. Mme du Plessis-Guénégaud, for example, had contributed to promoting Pascal's *Les Provinciales*, but that work was backed by the Jansenist movement, whereas the *Maximes*

---

99. Numbers and translations are from Tancock's edition of the *Maxims*.

constituted one individual's arraignment of an entire society. Like *Les Provinciales*, the *Maximes* were supposed to appear anonymously—not, however, for reasons of caution but as a matter of style. For a gentleman to officially recognize authorship of a book meant lowering himself socially. In aristocratic circles, writing might be a leisure activity but not a profession, and the writer's condition was incompatible with the nobleman's. But this was not to prevent two dilettantes like La Rochefoucauld and Mme de Sablé from preparing for the success of the *Maximes* by drawing up a promotional strategy such as modern publishers use to this day: sounding opinion and guiding the criticism. Although protected by a much more rigorous anonymity, Mme de Lafayette used the same methods in launching *La Princesse de Clèves* some fifteen years later, and it too, was crowned by an enormous success. For the first time, the rarefied aristocratic ideology of dilettantism had come up against the more vulgar desire for success, which won the day.

In 1663 Mme de Sablé arranged for several copies of the Liancourt manuscript, in which La Rochefoucauld's maxims were collected, to be read to a number of distinguished people in order to elicit their comments on the work. This sounding of different opinions revealed that the book's savage pessimism could only be tolerated in the light of faith—to such an extent that some of those present saw in it an implicit invitation to "turn to God."[100] La Rochefoucauld decided quite impartially to use this interpretation to defend his work against the indignation of the *bien-pensants*. And it was only too obvious that despite alterations to the text —additions, cuts, changes in the order of maxims—the book remained ambiguous. La Rochefoucauld made use of what was to become an exemplary expedient: a prudent preface to set the reader's mind at rest. When the first edition of the *Maximes* finally saw publication in 1665, it was in fact prefaced by a "Discours sur les Réflexions ou Sentences et Maximes morales," written on commission by a lawyer and literary amateur, Henri de La Chapelle-Bessé, that obviously diverged from the tone of the maxims themselves. Anticipating the criticism that had emerged from Mme de Sablé's opinion poll two years earlier, La Rochefoucauld had himself indicated points that needed defending.

The severest and most precise criticisms came from the women who had been consulted on that occasion. First of all, on March 3, 1661, the Comtesse de Maure, on reading the maxims that Mme de Sablé and La Rochefoucauld were exchanging, wrote to the marquise the famous sentence, "It seems to depict man's soul in colors too somber."[101] Two years later, when asked for her opinion on the whole work, and despite her strict adherence to Jansenism, the Princesse de Guéméné refused to believe that there was no one "who desired nothing but to do good,"

---

100. See Jacques Truchet, introduction to La Rochefoucauld, *Maximes*, p. xxii.

101. Mme de Maure to Mme de Sablé, March 3, 1661, in La Rochefoucauld, *Maximes*, p. 561.

and she accused the author of judging "everyone by himself."[102] But a long letter of 1663 from the Duchesse de Schomberg to Mme de Sablé shows especially well how even a strict assessment of the morality of the *Maximes* was no impediment to being caught up in the game. In 1646—after having rejected Louis XIII, who was captivated by her—the beautiful Marie d'Hautefort had married the Duc de Schomberg, Maréchal de France, which brought her great social prestige. By age sixty, with her season of ambition and intrigue behind her, the duchess was remarkable for her deep religiosity and, having spent much time developing moral reflections, was immediately aware of the risk inherent in the *Maximes*. They could, she wrote, persuade the reader that "there is neither vice nor virtue in anything, and that all the actions in life are performed of necessity. If it is thus that we are unable to prevent ourselves from doing all that we desire, we are excusable and you may judge from that how dangerous these maxims are."[103] All the same, Mme de Schomberg understood them all marvelously, as if she had written them herself, and found some of them enchanting. "The head is always fooled by the heart" (102), for example, immediately appealed to her. How did she interpret it? That "the mind always believes that by force of reason and cunning it can make the heart do as it wishes, but it is mistaken; it is always the heart that dominates the mind and the mind that is deceived." She also found maxim 48 to be quite apt, whereby "felicity dwells in taste and not in things," and number 266 to be extremely perceptive in its affirmation that "laziness, for all her langour... eats away and destroys passions and virtues alike." Whereas the crucial maxim 256 on dissembling, "Each man puts on a personality and outward appearance so as to look what he wants to be thought," reminded her of how she had always thought that in society life, everything was deception and disguise.

In spite of its basic tone of condemnation, Mme de Schomberg's letter predicted how society would react to the *Maximes*. The book was sure of success because it was impossible for the reader to remain indifferent. By shocking, maltreating, surprising, and amusing the reader, by stimulating his intelligence, and by saying better than he could what he may already have thought, it inevitably made him complicit. It spoke to him and induced him in turn to speak to others of what he had read, thus broadening the circle of initiates.

At the time of publication, and once opinion had been successfully sounded, the book had been corrected. A climate of expectation and curiosity reigned in society. The reception of the *Maximes* had been pointed in the right direction with a first article hinting at a reading that conformed with Christian doctrine. Once again La Rochefoucauld turned to Mme de Sablé for help, asking her to review his collection of maxims for the *Journal des savants*.

---

102. Mme de Guéméné to Mme de Sablé, 1663, in La Rochefoucauld, *Maximes*, p. 570.

103. Mme de Schomberg to Mme de Sablé, 1663, in La Rochefoucauld, *Maximes*, p. 565.

Certainly a *grande dame* like Mme de Sablé would not have agreed to be labeled a *femme savante*. But here she was writing at the request of a dilettante aristocrat who had never concerned himself with "studying,"[104] writing an article, albeit anonymously, for a paper that addressed a learned public. It was an exceptional case, doubtless a product of Mme de Sablé's extraordinary personality. But it shows the impossibility of drawing clear lines between society culture and the world of the pedants. It can only be supposed that the editors of the *Journal des savants* felt honored by the attention of such illustrious individuals.

It is easy to imagine why La Rochefoucauld picked Mme de Sablé. No one knew the *Maximes* better than she; she could even consider herself to be the co-authoress of many of them. No one was better able than she—versed in theology as she was, and used to writing very naturally—to explain elegantly and simply the book's moral use. By revealing mankind to himself, she wrote, the *Maximes* taught him that there could be no virtuous action without religion. And in the end, no one else would be so accommodating or more complicit, allowing La Rochefoucauld to correct what she had written to the point of creating an ideal cover. The review appeared in the March 9, 1665, *Journal des savants* The nineteenth-century scholar Victor Cousin was the first to publish Mme de Sablé's original article alongside La Rochefoucauld's edited version.[105] The comparison is revealing. Like the ideal modern publicist, La Rochefoucauld had simplified the message, cutting the paragraph in which she warned of the criticism the book might provoke and at the same time strengthening it and clarifying it with several small changes. Mme de Sablé's article, "planned," entrusted to safe hands, revised, and corrected, once and for all set the stage for the comedy of literary editing, which remains the same to this day. What is singular is that this comedy was set in motion not by an poor writer struggling to succeed but by a great nobleman, a *pair de France*—a peer—who preached absolute detachment. "The true gentleman [*honnête homme*] never claims superiority in anything" (203), wrote the man who scorned to put his name to the book whose success he so keenly desired. But behind the scenes, the critic of self-love brilliantly exemplified one of its most odious manifestations: authorial vanity. Mme de Sablé was more consistent than La Rochefoucauld himself when she allowed him a free hand with her article. For she remembered that writing for her was always a game.

Among the letters sent to Mme de Sablé at the time of the prepublication "opinion poll," there was one from another exceptional reader, one who was destined to play an ever more important part in La Rochefoucauld's life. In the summer of 1663 Mme de Lafayette had read a copy of the manuscript of the *Maximes* while staying alone with her hostess at Fresnes, the du Plessis-

---

104. Mme de Sablé to La Rochefoucauld, 1663, in La Rochefoucauld, *Maximes*, p. 552.

105. In Cousin, *Mme de Sablé*.

Guénégauds' country estate, an ideal oasis in which to meditate. There could hardly have been a more interested or more informed conversationalist in matters of psychology and morality.

Her reaction was one of total disgust. "Ah, Madame," she wrote to Mme de Sablé from Fresnes, "the mind and the heart must be terribly corrupted to be able to imagine all this!"[106] Such a statement of dismay suggests that she did not know La Rochefoucauld at the time. But this is hardly plausible. In 1659 Mme de Lafayette had returned from a long absence in the provinces to live in Paris, where there had been plenty of opportunities to meet the duke. Both were regular guests of the du Plessis-Guénégauds, and there would have been many occasions for intimate conversations at both the hôtel de Nevers and at Fresnes. Nor could the ideas expressed in the *Maximes* have been totally new to her. It is perhaps more likely that, while waiting to "reform" her friend's "heart,"[107] Mme de Lafayette amused herself by joking with him through a third person, feigning surprise and indignation that she was in fact far from feeling.

What radical change of mind could otherwise have persuaded the Marquise de Lafayette two years later, in 1665, to present the sixteen-year-old Comte de Saint-Paul with the very text that had so profoundly shocked her? She used the *Maximes* as an indirect way of telling the child of Mme de Longueville and La Rochefoucauld of the special sympathy that had blossomed between herself and the duke. The same book that ruthlessly revealed the truth of love's illusions bore the message of a delicate and secret feeling about whose real nature there can be no certainty. But Saint-Paul's visit was hardly over before Mme de Lafayette, anxious that she had gone too far, wrote in haste to Mme de Sablé, asking for her help.[108]

She did not want the young man to think that there was anything other than a simple friendship between her and his father, and she insisted on pointing out that there was nothing she hated more than the thought that the young might still credit her with love affairs. These are revealing sentences, which literary historians interpret as the first definite signs of her relationship with La Rochefoucauld. In fact, at the time, Mme de Lafayette had not yet turned thirty and she was discovering for the first time that love need not be "a troublesome thing."[109]

---

106. Mme de Lafayette to Mme de Sablé [August–September 1663], in Mme de Lafayette, *Œuvres complètes*, edited by Roger Duchêne (Paris: Bourin, 1990), p. 582.

107. "*Monsieur de La Rochefoucauld m'a donné de l'esprit, mais j'ai réformé son cœur*": well-known pronouncement attributed to Mme de Lafayette by Segrais, quoted in La Rochefoucauld, *Œuvres complètes*, p. 709.

108. The undated letter was written some time between 1665 and 1667. Mme de LaFayette, *Œuvres complètes*, pp. 605–606.

109. Mlle de La Vergne [Mme de Lafayette's maiden name] to the Abbé Ménage, September 18, [1653], in Mme de Lafayette, *Œuvres complètes*, p. 513.

9

LA GRANDE MADEMOISELLE

I. The Heroine of the Fronde

MME DE RAMBOUILLET may have taught the French nobility to be content by themselves away from the court, but the Blue Room style gradually infiltrated the Louvre, converting even members of the royal family.

Anne of Austria, once she became regent in 1643 and was at last free to follow her natural inclination for *l'honnête galanterie*, reintroduced the palace to the old traditions of sociability, which had been banished by Richelieu's authoritarianism and Louis XIII's tormented loneliness. In setting a first good example, she quickly reestablished the old custom of the *cercle de la reine*—the queen's circle. From the time of Eleanor of Aquitaine, the queens of France had made a habit of inviting the ladies of the retinue to pass time with them. The conversations, which took place with the doors open so that anyone admitted to the royal apartments might participate, set the tone for the court. Seated in a circle around the queen, ready to respond to her requests, the ladies vied in the art of the spoken word, discussing psychology, love, and literature, or merely commenting on recent events and the latest fashions. Here, instead of being spectators of men's prowess, they suddenly became protagonists in a tournament of words where insight, verve, and felicity of expression replaced courage and strength. But the Queen's goodwill was not enough for this tradition to be reinstated. Anne of Austria had to contend with the ignorance and awkwardness of many of her ladies as well as with the misogyny of Cardinal Mazarin, whose very presence was enough to freeze any light conversation.[1]

When François de Bassompierre—who had been one of the Queen's boldest suitors—left the Bastille in 1643 after a twelve-year imprisonment, "that man, formerly so *galant* and who had been judged a marvel at the old court, seemed like

---

1. "He despised the most *honnêtes femmes*, literature, and anything that might contribute to men's good manners," *Mémoires de Mme de Motteville*, Vol. 1, pp. 292–293.

a German," so foreign were his style and manners to those of the court, which had changed completely over the decade.[2] Gallantry had gone out of fashion, and poor Bassompierre "was accused, as if of a great crime, of liking to please, of being dignified, and of coming from a court where civility and respect for ladies ruled; of continuing to live by the same principles in one where, to the contrary, men saw it as almost a disgrace to pay them some civility."[3] In spite of her ardent piety and a jealous sense of her dignity, Anne of Austria, too, remained faithful to her youthful tastes—so faithful that she smiled indulgently when, in 1644, Vincent Voiture extemporized for her some "pleasing and daring" verses in which he reminded her of her former love for the Duke of Buckingham.[4]

Anne persevered with her plans, and her circle became a school for courtesy and manners to young girls who visited the court, starting with Mazarin's own nieces. There Maria Mancini learned not only to appreciate literature but also the ways of society and the sense of elegant deportment with which she later impressed Roman society as the Principessa Colonna. Louis XIV, the first and most affectionate of her admirers, must have resigned himself regretfully to the fact that his shy, ignorant young wife, Marie-Thérèse, the Infanta of Spain, was not equal to Anne of Austria's example and would not create a circle of her own.

Despite Anne's efforts, however, the court never regained its old prestige in matters of culture and taste; the big Parisian houses continued to set the tone. So it is hardly surprising that Mademoiselle de Montpensier, the first and the proudest princess of the blood, brought up in the heart of the royal family and educated to be queen, often left the Tuileries to go and amuse herself at the hôtel de Rambouillet in the rue Saint-Thomas-du-Louvre. She could not then have imagined the degree to which the Blue Room ideal would be of help to her in years to come.

Anne Marie Louise d'Orléans, daughter of Louis XIII's brother, Gaston d'Orléans, inherited the biggest fortune in France from her mother, Marie de Bourbon-Montpensier, who died giving birth to her in 1627. Pride in her exceptional breeding—not even the King was more French or more of a Bourbon than she—became her dominating passion and marked her destiny.

She was the first woman in the French royal court to be addressed by the honorific title Mademoiselle, without a proper name following it. Her father was known simply as Monsieur, and she alone, she felt, had the right to be called

---

2. *Mémoires de l'abbé Arnauld contenant quelques anecdotes de la Cour de France depuis 1634, jusqu'en 1675* (1756); quoted in Magendie, *La Politesse mondaine*, Vol. 1, p. 292.

3. *Mémoires de Mme de Motteville*, Vol. 1, p. 292.

4. The exchange took place in the summer of 1644, when the Queen was Mme d'Aiguillon's guest at Rueil. The Queen asked Voiture what he was thinking as he walked dreamily in the park, and he replied "without really thinking" with the verses about Buckingham, who was known in 1625 to have inspired the Queen's affections. *Mémoires de Mme de Motteville*, Vol. 1, pp. 182–183.

Mademoiselle and have the title serve as an explicit symbol of her royal status. Only later, with the death of Louis XIII, did it become necessary to add La Grande to her title in order to distinguish her from a new, younger Mademoiselle, whose father, Philippe, Duc d'Orléans, brother of Louis XIV, also had the rank of Monsieur. Yet because of the remarkable personality and life of La Grande Mademoiselle, what was merely an identifying label became an acknowledgment of her formidable qualities.

Primarily Mademoiselle was not a woman but a princess of the blood, which freed her from all the banal preoccupations of other women, like those concerning attractiveness. This is evident from the calm objectivity of her famous self-portrait, which she wrote at the age of thirty: "I am tall; neither fat nor thin; with a handsome, graceful figure. I have a good complexion; a well-formed bust; my hands and arms are not beautiful but the skin is beautiful like that of my breasts. I have straight legs and well-formed feet; my hair is ash blond; my face is long, the shape is beautiful; my nose is large and aquiline; my mouth is neither large nor small but shaped in a most agreeable fashion; my lips vermilion; my teeth are not beautiful, but not horrible either; my eyes are blue, neither big nor small, but shining, soft, and proud like my countenance."[5] In any case, she considered the usual rules of aesthetics to be inadequate in judging her own appearance. When she was forty, the Duc de Lauzun had the impertinence to tell her one day that she was too old to wear a bright red ribbon in her hair, to which Mademoiselle replied sharply that persons of her condition were always young.[6]

As the granddaughter of Henri le Grand, her imagination was fired by heroism and glory rather than feminine vanity. What she saw as her sublime vocation had its roots in the mystique of royalty, with which she had been indoctrinated in childhood, and followed the example of a long line of illustrious ancestors. She must have been particularly aware of the cult of the three great Marguerites—Marguerite de Navarre, Marguerite de Savoie, and Marguerite de Valois—renowned for their learning, their courage, and their political acumen. Similarly, she would have been impressed by her paternal grandmother, Marie de' Medici, who was exiled too early for her granddaughter to have been able to remember her, but whose achievements she could have contemplated a thousand times in Rubens's huge canvases, which hung in her father's residence at the Luxembourg Palace. Even so, in her eyes, Queen Christina of Sweden was the prototype of female heroism, the living proof of how a woman could combine great culture with political and military talent.[7]

---

5. "Portrait de Mademoiselle, fait par elle mesme," in *Divers Portraits*, p. 30.

6. Michel Le Moël, *La Grande Mademoiselle* (Paris: Éditions de Fallois, 1994), p. 171.

7. Daughter of Gustav Adolphe, Christina of Sweden (1626–1689) had received an excellent education that developed her intellectual curiosity and made her broadly cultured. Corresponding with all of

Between 1630 and 1640, the theater contributed enormously to the heroic exaltation of the female ego. Corneille's plays honored womanly courage, breathing new life into Roman heroines. Fashionable novels pointed to women's moral superiority, and an array of panegyrists and churchmen advocated a model of behavior based on the fearless and chaste ideal of the *femme forte*. Since many of these texts were dedicated to Anne of Austria or Mademoiselle herself, it is reasonable to suppose that they suggested an image of female sovereignty with which the two princesses identified.

Chivalric ideals and the cult of noble deeds were also nurtured at the hôtel de Rambouillet, but in her early youth, Mademoiselle de Montpensier was drawn there above all by the attractions of a society that was infinitely freer and more cheerful than that at the Louvre. Her taste, formed since birth by the Renaissance splendor of the Tuileries and the grandeur of the Luxembourg and other royal palaces, responded to a different, more modern conception of an architecture adapted to the new demands of private life. Everything in Mme de Rambouillet's house—from the layout of the rooms and the furniture to the service—seemed designed to encourage sociability and good cheer, to create a refined atmosphere of well-being, to put the guests at their ease rather than to intimidate them. Later, the Grande Mademoiselle herself wrote one of the most evocative descriptions of Mme de Rambouillet in the half-light of the Blue Room:

> I seem to see her in an alcove where the rays of the sun do not penetrate but from whence the light is not entirely banished. This den is surrounded by large crystal vases filled with the most beautiful spring flowers that last forever in the gardens around her Temple to provide her with what she likes best. Around her are many paintings of all the people she loves: looking at these portraits, she confers every blessing on the Originals. There are also many books on the little tables in the grotto. It is clear that they do not contain anything commonplace; only two or three people may enter this place at one time, since confusion displeases her.[8]

The Blue Room left an important mark on the young Mademoiselle. More than once, she sought to recreate the conditions for such enchantment in her castles and palaces. Not even the jealous defense of what was due to her rank stopped her from cultivating the dream of a happy "elsewhere," an egalitarian utopia under

---

intellectual Europe, she attracted Descartes to her court. The singularity of her conduct shocked her Protestant and puritan compatriots. In 1654, she abdicated in favor of her cousin Charles X, left her country, converted to Catholicism the following year in Innsbruck, and moved to Rome, where she created an academy that encouraged painters, writers, and musicians.

8. Mademoiselle de Montpensier, *Histoire de la Princesse de Paphlagonie*, pp. 120–121.

the banner of spiritual affinity. Her father, Monsieur, was a great collector and a cultivated, liberal patron of the arts, but his intellectual entertainments influenced her less than the Blue Room did. Mademoiselle certainly knew the small group with which Gaston d'Orléans surrounded himself at the Luxembourg, and she was present at several conversations there about politics, history, and philosophy; there are, perhaps, distant echoes of those discussions in some of the remarks she makes in her *Mémoires*. However, this gathering of men only, steeped in humanist culture and inclined toward libertinism, could not have a lasting hold over a young woman deprived of classical learning; moreover, the scurrilous, erotic verses of Gaston's protégé poets were incompatible with her own unyielding morality. At the hôtel de Rambouillet, on the other hand, Mademoiselle could be in touch with a more modern and more accessible worldly culture based on conversation. It was precisely there that Vincent Voiture, a man of her father's set, transformed by the magic of the place, became the *âme du rond*—the soul of the circle.

Until the age of twenty, while waiting for her hand to be asked for by a great sovereign—the King of England, perhaps the Holy Roman Emperor, or, better still, her young cousin Louis XIV—Mademoiselle daily walked the long gallery that connected the Tuileries to the Louvre to participate with the regent, Anne of Austria, and the young King in all the most important court ceremonies, balls, concerts, and theatrical performances. As soon as her duties permitted, she went, like her Condé cousins, to be entertained in the rue Saint-Thomas-du-Louvre, to breathe the exhilarating air of an exclusive gathering in which everyone was asked to give his best.

In 1652, however, her vocation for the heroic took precedence over society life. The Fronde put it to the test. In the early stages of the rebellion, Mademoiselle had supported the royal family, but, suddenly, with the Fronde of the Princes, she sided with the rebels. Like the fictional heroines Bradamante and Clorinda, Mademoiselle, in a helmet adorned with a splendid feather, entered the arena and finally proved the full measure of her courage.

What could have persuaded her to take part in so disastrous an adventure, an adventure that could only bring exile and Louis XIV's lasting hostility? Could it have been caste solidarity against the abuses of the minister Mazarin, a foreigner guilty of, among other things, not having found her a husband who met her expectations? Was it a wish to redeem the family honor, brought low by Gaston's cowardly indecisiveness? Was it the hope of forcing a marriage with her royal cousin? It is difficult to say. Certainly in the royal family's eyes, Mademoiselle's expedition to Orléans—the first of her two great undertakings—could be justified as an act of filial obedience. But responsibility for the second—her order in Paris to fire the Bastille's cannons on the royal troops laying siege to the rebellious capital—was to have disastrous consequences for her.

In March 1652, the city of Orléans, frightened by the approach of the royal army and the news of the violence and sacking perpetrated by the soldiers along the way, turned to Gaston, its titular prince, to negotiate with the court and to safeguard the city's right to remain neutral. But the King's brother, who for all his other gentlemanly qualities lacked "only courage," according to Cardinal de Retz,[9] seemed most concerned with protecting himself, and preferred to stay in Paris, which was threatened at the time by Turenne's troops. He sent his twenty-five-year-old daughter in his place.

Mademoiselle had nothing of her father's indecision, and she hurried to Orléans to confront the advancing royal army. Like one of Le Moyne's Christian Amazons, she acted in the name of a superior absent authority for a noble and just cause: the defense of a peaceful community threatened by the horrors of war. It is easy to imagine her thinking of Joan of Arc as she hurried to the aid of the city where the Maid of Orléans had won her first battle.

To her enormous disappointment, the city was not prepared to give her the triumphal welcome she expected. The city notables, divided over policy and intimidated by the King's injunctions, had had the gates of the city closed and refused entry to Gaston's daughter, beseeching her to go and wait in a safe place until the situation was clarified. It was certainly a wise decision, though it failed to take the princess's temperament into account. Without losing heart, Mademoiselle—followed by her two "aides-de-camp," Mme de Frontenac and Mme de Fiesque[10]—took to the ditches and inspected in turn all the gates to the city, which they found firmly bolted. On the side of the city overlooking the Loire, however, she detected, thanks to some boatmen, a small unused door, which once opened led to a passage; climbing a ladder, she thus managed to penetrate the city walls, where she was met by an enthusiastic populace that had witnessed the various phases of this extraordinary spectacle. Confronted with this fait accompli, the city council realized that it would have to refuse entry to the King's delegation. Mademoiselle meanwhile hastened to show herself at the ramparts, surrounded by her officers and wearing her father's blue sash to prove to the royal representatives, who had reached the other side of the Loire, that Gaston's city had passed into the hands of the Fronde.

"My daughter, You can imagine the joy that your recent action brought me; you have saved Orléans for me and secured Paris. It is a matter for public joy, and everyone says that your action is worthy of Henri le Grand's granddaughter. I did not doubt your heart, but I see that in this action you heeded prudence more than advice. I tell you again that I am delighted by what you have done, as much for

---

9. Retz, *Mémoires*, p. 152.

10. After the entry into Orléans, Monsieur complimented his daughter's ladies-in-waiting in a letter addressed as follows: "To mesdames les comtesses, field marshals in my daughter's army against Mazarin"; see *Mémoires de Mademoiselle de Montpensier, petite fille de Henri IV*, edited by A. Chéruel, four volumes (Paris: Charpentier, 1858), Vol. 2, p. 47.

love of you as for love of myself."[11] Gaston would soon learn that prudence and obedience were hardly Mademoiselle's primary virtues. The adventure was too exciting to end at Orléans. Ignoring her father's orders, the princess headed for Paris.

The capital, which Turenne was preparing to besiege at the head of the royal army, was in the hands of the Grand Condé's rebel troops. Clearly, the future of the country would be decided here, and Mademoiselle did not want to be late for the appointment. There were many key actors on the scene. Orléans, Condé, Retz, Beaufort, and La Rochefoucauld were all competing—even coming to blows—for the leading role. There were many women too, all just as bold, intriguing, and ambitious as their husbands, brothers, and lovers—mad Amazons who obeyed nothing but personal whim. It was definitely no place for a virtuous heroine, and Gaston, for one, would gladly have forgone the presence of his brave, impulsive daughter, her extraordinary behavior being incompatible with his own purposefully ambiguous tactics.

During that frantic Parisian summer, with the Fronde sinking beneath the weight of individual passions and betrayals, Mademoiselle was aware of no other duty than that of being faithful to the high ideal she had of herself. She alone was fully responsible for her actions. Unlike her cousin Mme de Longueville, Mademoiselle knew nothing of the pitfalls of love, treachery, or the will to dominate. But her pure aspirations to glory can hardly have been less dangerous. The deeds of her ancestors filtered through epic romances provided Mademoiselle's primary models. Reality was useful only to the extent that it allowed her to prove herself the equal of her illustrious forbears. In the climate of excitement and theatricality, punctuated by the fêtes and military parades in which she found herself immersed, Mademoiselle had no time to question the plans behind histrionic gestures or the passionate eloquence of the leaders of the Fronde. She had taken sides and was waiting, in blissful ignorance, for events to decide her behavior. On July 2, 1652, the day of the fighting in the rue Saint-Antoine, Condé's men were routed by Turenne. Mademoiselle was appalled to see the Grand Condé, covered in dust and blood, weeping for his fallen friends. For the first time in her life she had glimpsed the sublime, and she was carried away by an uncontrollable desire to emulate her hero. His tears showed her clearly the path to take. She put her own house and the regiment of which she was so proud at Condé's disposal, hastened to the Bastille, and gave the order to fire the cannon on the royal troops in order to allow whatever remained of the rebel army to retreat to safety. She is even reputed to have lit the fuse herself.

The fourteen-year-old Louis XIV, who watched the scene from the top of a hill, would never forgive the unheard-of affront to himself, especially by one whom he had always regarded as an older sister. Less than three months later,

---

11. *Mémoires de Mademoiselle*, Vol. 2, p. 16.

with the capital restored to royal control, the King informed Mademoiselle de Montpensier that she had twenty-four hours to leave the Tuileries, and he ordered Gaston to leave Paris. There was no need for further orders for Mademoiselle herself to realize that it would be wise to leave the capital. Because her father refused to take her with him to his estate at Blois, Mademoiselle, fearing arrest, had no choice but to ask the King's permission to retire to her Burgundian château of Saint-Fargeau, near Auxerre, a three-day journey from Paris.

Monsieur's last conversation with his daughter was tempestuous. Mademoiselle reproached him for having abandoned Condé. He rebuked her for her imprudence. She proudly reminded him of her expedition to Orléans. The exchange that followed, according to Mademoiselle's version, is revealing:

> The father: "As for the Saint-Antoine affair, do you not think, Mademoiselle, that it did you considerable harm at court? You were so pleased to play the heroine and to be told that you were on our side that you saved us [notre parti] twice, and whatever happens to you, you will be able to console yourself with the memory of all the praise you were given."
>
> The daughter: "I do not know what it is to be a heroine; my birth is such that I can do nothing without grandeur and authority playing a part in it, and—call that what they will—for my part, I call it following my inclination and my path; I am born to take no other."[12]

Just as the father knew the daughter's weaknesses, so the daughter knew his. What Gaston saw as girlish vainglory was, for Mademoiselle, the only behavior compatible with her birth. Each and every individual was fully responsible for his or her moral choice. Was this not a subtle way of reminding the father of his lack of generosity and courage?

II. The Trials of Exile

Mademoiselle was now faced with a new and greater test. For her, as for Mme de Longueville, the time had come to define herself with the heroism of the defeated. To accept fate, to put up with misfortune, to face up to disgrace: Was this not the irrefutable characteristic of a noble soul?

Mme de Longueville had sought solace in religion and chosen the path of penitence, asceticism, and exaltation, turning her back forever on her past idols. Unlike her cousin, Mademoiselle de Montpensier chose the path of aristocratic stoicism rather than Christian resignation. She had no intention of changing her

---

12. *Mémoires de Mademoiselle*, Vol. 2, p. 197.

way of life and was neither persecuted by remorse nor did she have any sins to expiate. The only blame that could be laid at her door was that of having made a legitimate choice, one that perfectly suited the ethics of her class.

Exile, therefore, hit her where it hurt most, by preventing her exercise of prerogatives that belonged to a princess of the blood. Banished from the intimacy of the royal family, far from the court and any power strategy, life lost all meaning for her. What use were privileges if there was no one to share them with and no opportunity to exercise them? But Mademoiselle was determined to preserve her dignity and worldly prestige to the bitter end. It is said that during his imprisonment after the Fronde, the Grand Condé whiled away the time by cultivating carnations on the window sill of his cell.[13] More fortunate than he, the Grande Mademoiselle confronted isolation, loneliness, and the sorrow of exile from the depths of her estate at Saint-Fargeau by cultivating all the *loisirs*—the leisure pursuits—that aristocratic idleness had long used to ornament itself.

Forced against her inclinations to renounce public life, alone and rejected by her family, the twenty-five-year-old princess managed, by virtue of her birth, extraordinary character, and enormous inheritance, to transform her forced retreat into an archetypal place of private pleasures. In fact, in her disgrace Mademoiselle discovered the inestimable value of the last free realm the monarchy allowed to the French nobility, and she celebrated it through all the means her imagination and culture could muster. The Grande Mademoiselle's five-year stay at Saint-Fargeau provides a perfect example of the myriad activities and pastimes that an aristocracy could enjoy when free of court duties; it helps us understand the variety and the kinds of occupations available to an idle nobility.

As Mademoiselle discovered, Saint-Fargeau was surrounded by great forests, which meant that during her exile she could continue to ride and to hunt all year. More than anything else, these two activities—from the king to his humblest vassal —represented the aristocratic lifestyle. Built in polygonal form in the thirteenth century, the imposing castle was in an advanced state of decay and required urgent repairs. As soon as she arrived, Mademoiselle renovated one wing for her private apartments; then, quite taken with the fun of it, she summoned the architect François Le Vau from Paris and entrusted him with the task of enlarging the old building with a new wing that opened onto the courtyard. Thus, under Mademoiselle's magic wand, the old castle was transformed into a magnificent modern dwelling, light and elegant. The old, overgrown park underwent the same metamorphosis. Avenues, alleys, paths, terraces, waterfalls, and views made it an enchanting setting for walks, picnics, and concerts, and a pall-mall court made open-air exercise possible.

A taste for architecture was of course very much part of royal family tradition —Marie de' Medici had shown it with the Luxembourg; but Mme de Rambouillet,

13. *Mémoires de Mme de Motteville*, Vol. 3, p. 239.

followed by Mme du Pléssis-Guénégaud, had already proven how important the design and decor of a house could be to society life. Thus at Saint-Fargeau Mademoiselle discovered the pleasures of building: to construct, to enlarge, and to beautify, these contributed to the splendor of one's family and would leave a lasting trace in stone and marble, all perfectly natural ambitions for a great princess. Over and above any appreciation of its practicality, Mademoiselle found in architecture a delicious source of fantasy: "If one is bored at court, one goes to one's country estates, where one has one's own court. There one orders things to be built and one is amused."[14]

The princess was not the only person to indulge in this expensive pastime. Building soon became an unbridled passion for Louis XIV, one which, along with his passion for women and hunting, he was to pass down to Louis XV. Nicolas Fouquet, the King's superintendent of finance, had already given pride of place to architecture in his personal aesthetic program. The sumptuousness of his château and gardens at Vaux-le-Vicomte, however, represented an unpardonable challenge to the King's supremacy, and it is no coincidence that the minister's disgrace and arrest in September 1661 followed Vaux-le-Vicomte's opening festivities by less than three weeks. In the eighteenth century, under a more tolerant political climate and during a time of remarkable social mobility, the craze for building was to become a hallmark of the aristocracy, carrying away noblemen and parvenus alike, and contributing as much to the ruin of old fortunes as to the worldly success of the newly rich. In towns as in the country, homes eloquently reflected the fortunes, ambitions, and taste of their owners.

At Saint-Fargeau, by transforming a "wild place" into a palace worthy of Ariosto's Alcina, Mademoiselle was able to express in solid architecture and on a large scale a taste for both change and illusions, which was typical of contemporary aristocratic culture. Of the many innovations at the castle, at least three—the portrait gallery, the theater, and the library—were especially typical of Mademoiselle's culture and interests.

The gallery, annexed to the princess's bedroom, housed some thirty portraits of family members. The habit of assembling family portraits, widespread since the fifteenth century, had become easier with the invention of various methods of printmaking and reproduction, and it was almost obligatory for Mademoiselle to collect them, so proud was she of her family history. In the loneliness of exile, however, those rows of princes and kings, in addition to bearing glorious witness to her breeding, could, like guardian angels, comfort Mademoiselle in her tribulations. By this time it had also already become customary to collect portraits of friends as well as of family, to remember and honor social acquaintances and

---

14. *Mémoires de Mademoiselle*, Vol. 3, p. 537; quoted in Claude Mignot, "Mademoiselle et son château de Saint-Fargeau," in *La Grande Mademoiselle (1627–1693)*, PFSCL, Vol. 22, No. 42 (1995), p. 99.

friendships as well as ancestors and relatives. We know from Mademoiselle herself that Mme de Rambouillet collected portraits in her studio of people she liked and admired.[15] Far from Paris, Mme des Loges, too, had decorated the walls of her room with portraits of friends. Not fifteen years later, another famous exile, Roger de Bussy-Rabutin, had the walls of a room in his château hung with portraits of Parisian society ladies to console himself with the illusion of being able to converse—and squabble—with them.

Until she was banished from court, Mademoiselle had been too occupied with thoughts of her own dynastic superiority and her own glory to pay much attention to others. Now, isolated at Saint-Fargeau, she turned her back on heroes in order to focus on her neighbors; to the portraits of her ancestors, she soon added those of her friends and acquaintances, although she would change the medium—substituting writing for painting.

In deciding to use one room in the château as a theater, Mademoiselle displayed a passion for spectacle that was typical of the aristocratic society in which she had been raised. Since girlhood she had loved music, the theater, and dancing. An excellent dancer herself, she had performed in some of the great *ballets de cour*. Her favorite playwright was of course Corneille, but she also appreciated Desmarets's lively caricature and Paul Scarron's comedy, in which tragedy alternated with burlesque. In fact, she loved the baroque theater for its varied forms, bold inventiveness, and expressive virtuosity; this theater that had to learn to obey rules and order, much as she did. In Paris, Mademoiselle had been an enthusiastic spectator, but at Saint-Fargeau, in order to continue to enjoy a pleasure made even more precious by solitude, she became a patron.

During a visit to her father at Blois, Mademoiselle had the opportunity to enjoy the actors who performed for Gaston and decided to engage them herself. The itinerant company of "Son Altesse Royale the Duc d'Orléans and Mademoiselle" performed for some thirty years. The troop, which included several actors from the Illustres Français, a company in which the young Molière had cut his teeth, were to have a particularly fortunate season under the direction of the great Dorimond, who first introduced the story of Don Juan to France.

The company performed regularly at Saint-Fargeau during Mademoiselle's exile and later benefited from her protection even in Paris. Such illustrious protection, in the mold of royal patronage, was much needed by the theater as it faced attacks from the Church and the *dévots*, that ardently Catholic and extremely influential party; it was also a visible sign of the liberality of a princess of the blood. There is no record of the plays performed at Saint-Fargeau, but it must certainly have been important for the exiled princess and her retinue to rediscover

---

15. *Mémoires de Mademoiselle*, Vol. 3, p. 151.

the pleasures of the theater.[16] Elegantly dressed, sporting fur hats adorned with feathers, the ladies of the château erased the distance from Paris. Forgetting isolation, rivalry, and jealousy, they could enter the illusory world of the great magic lantern with its vast repertory of characters, images, and romantic situations. They could again hear heroic soliloquies, passionate declarations of love, subtle disquisitions, sparkling dialogue, gallant conversation, and brilliant, irresistible wit on which to model their own sentiments and language. For them the theater was not merely a means of ignoring reality and indulging in dreams. It also provided useful instruction for life and a great review of possible situations to be found in the world.

Music, which Mademoiselle had loved from earliest youth, became a daily entertainment for the château's inhabitants. Among her instrumentalists was a young Italian called Gian Battista Lulli, who was soon to become the King's composer at court.

More than anything else, it was the creation of a library that signified the beginnings of a new, important experience for Mademoiselle. Only at Saint-Fargeau did she discover the pleasures of reading. At the time, society culture, as it generally applied to aristocratic women, had been essentially oral and extremely eclectic. It derived in equal measure from conversation, the pedagogic charms of the literati in attendance, the theater, music, and poetry, and the almost uninterrupted flow of verse and prose designed for the instant diversion of society. Of course, all this could have led to a direct engagement with literature, but for it to bear fruit the quiet of a country château was needed. "It was at that time that I began to love reading, which I have much loved ever since," Mademoiselle was to write in her *Mémoires*.[17] "She passionately loved stories," according to Pierre Daniel Huet, "and above all novels, as they are called. While the women dressed her hair, she wanted me to read to her, and, whatever the subject, it prompted a thousand questions from her. I thereby easily determined the fineness of her mind and erudition, rare in one of her sex."[18]

Strange though it may seem, before she even discovered reading, Mademoiselle had experimented with writing. It is true that in the society of her day, improvising verse or dictating a polite letter was a natural extension of conversation, an occasion like any other for playing the social game. But right in the middle of the events of the Fronde, while still supposedly preoccupied by thoughts of heroism, Mademoiselle had written something considerably more original than the usual

16. The theater was more essential than ever to her well-being, Mademoiselle writes. "I listened to the plays with greater pleasure than I had ever done," *Mémoires de Mademoiselle*, Vol. 2, p. 250.

17. *Mémoires de Mademoiselle*, Vol. 1, p. 259.

18. *Mémoires* (1718), edited by Philippe-Joseph Salazar (Toulouse: Société de Littérature Classiques, 1993), p. 76.

verses: *Histoire de Jeanne Lambert d'Herbigny marquise de Fourquesolle*, an ironic, ferocious *divertissement* in prose. Using the form of a fake confession —"Mme de Fourquesolle" tells her story of dishonesty and intrigue to a friend— Mademoiselle settled the score with her former lady-in-waiting Mme de Fouquerolles. Indeed, this woman had a tendency to get into trouble; it was she who, ten years earlier, had penned the infamous lost love letter that Mme de Montbazon had been so eager to attribute to the Duchesse de Longueville.

The brief story of some seventy pages was intended for Mademoiselle's close friends and invited them to laugh off an intrigue that could have had disagreeable consequences for everyone. Through Mme de Fouqucrolles, however, the princess revealed something of herself, her temperament and tastes, as the lady-in-waiting's hypocritical, disloyal behavior showed Mademoiselle's proud character and love of truth in brilliant contrast. Mademoiselle was probably influenced in her choice of the confessional formula by the *mazarinades*—lampoons that were all the rage in Paris at the time. There were undoubtedly violent overtones to the *Histoire de la marquise de Fourquesolle* and a vague sense of "going for the kill" that belonged to thc Fronde.

Written at one sitting, the *Histoire* had no literary ambitions. It was part of an amusement that involved other authors: a collection of short texts, letters, and verses, to which Mademoiselle's ladies-in-waiting Mme de Fiesque and Mme de Frontenac had also contributed. Nevertheless, the *Histoire* introduced on the literary scene a key figure in French civilization: the person who tears away the mask. This figure would have its apotheosis in the next century with Versac's famous soliloquy in *Les Égarements du cœur et de l'esprit* by Crébillon *fils* and in Mme de Merteuil's even more famous letter in Chodcrlos de Laclos's *Les Liaisons dangereuses*.

In exile, writing was to play an increasingly important part in Mademoiselle's life, although, at least at first, it remained mere entertainment, useful as a social tool or as an aide-mémoire, and not as an end in itself. Mademoiselle liked to display the ease and speed of her writing and her contemptuous refusal to reread or correct it, which made these written words conform to Castiglione's aesthetic of *sprezzatura*, the very hallmark of aristocratic conversation.

Now that the season of action was over, the time had come for Mademoiselle and the Fronde's other distinguished activists to look back. Gathering ideas from her small court, which included Mme de Fiesque, Mmc de Frontenac, and her confidential secretary, Préfontaine, Mademoiselle set about writing her memoirs. Once more, she was obeying the rules of her class in a model fashion.

The King's glory had long ceased to coincide with that of the nobility. Who, then, could recount the facts truthfully for future generations? Neither men of letters in the pay of the crown nor official historiographers could give any guarantee of objectivity, let alone competence. So the task of telling the true history fell to those who had witnessed it and shaped it. The task belonged to the nobility and not the bourgeoisie or the clerics, who had spent their lives shut up in libraries and who did not know what a battlefield was. Since the sixteenth century—a century marked by a series of tragic political and religious conflicts—the nobility had understood the need to preserve its honor and the honor of its descendants by writing memoirs. Here nobles described the reasons for their actions and the events in which they had taken part. These memoirs were intended to reinforce oral histories that were being handed down from generation to generation. The most recent work of this kind was the *Journal de ma vie* by Bassompierre, who had been imprisoned in the Bastille between 1631 and 1643 on Cardinal de Richelieu's orders.

After a civil war that had disturbed the whole country and in which she herself had openly defied the royal family, Mademoiselle must have felt very strongly the need to establish the legitimacy of her own behavior and to give her personal version of the facts. It was no easy task. The princess wished to be forgiven by the Queen Regent and by her royal cousin and to be readmitted to court, but she had no desire to apologize; the memory of the cannonade from the Bastille filled her with both remorse and pride. She felt that her mistakes, if mistakes they were, resulted less from her behavior than from fortune's whim, and they were not such as to cast the slightest shadow on her reputation.[19]

Mademoiselle confronted the undertaking as only she could have done. Her *Mémoires* tell of the heroic exploits of a princess of the blood capable of shouldering the entire responsibility imposed on her by birth and of making herself the guarantor of the most sacred values of the French monarchy—and all this with the naturalness, lightness of touch, playfulness, resourcefulness, and psychological curiosity of a lady of the *Grand Monde*.

Unlike the traditional memoir writer who hid behind events, Mademoiselle put herself center stage, with all the theatrical gusto of which she was capable, describing events according to the extent to which she was either a protagonist or a witness. Combining authority with worldly naturalness, she spoke in the first person, reaffirming, by the very act of writing, her freedom and the reasons for her decisions, confirming her own values, and not hiding her satisfaction with what she had been able to accomplish. The *Mémoires* represented not only an act of faith in her public self but also allowed her to unveil a private, sensitive, refined self that would gradually assert itself more and more in her conscience. Such a new and agreeable method of thinking about oneself was encouraged by society's growing interest in all forms of psychological analysis. The publication in 1649 of the Jansenist Arnauld d'Andilly's translation of Saint Augustine's *Confessions*

19. "I have been less deficient in behavior, than fortune has been in judgement," in "Portrait de Mademoiselle, fait par elle mesme," in *Divers Portraits*, p. 36.

paradoxically made introspection into a society game—with an old, disillusioned Frondeur like La Rochefoucauld preparing to sacrifice heroism to "unthought thoughts."

Of the many pastimes at Saint-Fargeau, there was one on which all the others depended. It alone could lend unity and style to the life of the château. Did not conversation prolong the pleasure of theatrical performances and of reading? Did it not lead to thinking out loud and to the exchange of opinion? Was not the solitary act of writing itself concerned with an almost immediate reaction on the part of the first small circle of readers to whom it was addressed? Did it not anticipate the comments, the applause, and the new wave of conversation to which it would in turn give rise? And what was the point of the various *cabinets*—tranquil, elegantly furnished spaces that Mademoiselle had arranged all over the house—if their harmonious climate of perfect intimacy did not create the ideal conditions for conversation to unfold?

Conversation, like the theater, needed performers, and Mademoiselle had assured herself of the presence at Saint-Fargeau of two real virtuosi: Mme de Fiesque and Mme de Frontenac. Those two ladies-in-waiting were the quintessence of that Parisian worldliness to which Mademoiselle had been so drawn since her earliest visits to the Blue Room. Beautiful, cheerful, witty, and brilliant, they had already enjoyed the company of the princess on her expedition to Orléans in 1652. Neither of the two had lost her good humor when, obliged to pay for the consequences of that adventure, they followed Mademoiselle into exile.

Eight years Mademoiselle's senior, Mme de Fiesque had taken as her second husband the son of Mademoiselle's own governess. Her seductive powers must have been considerable indeed, for even Bussy-Rabutin, a man known for his spite, praised her enthusiastically:

> She was an admirable woman. She had brown, luminous eyes, a good nose, a pleasant mouth of a beautiful color, her skin was white and smooth and her face long; she was the only woman in the world whom a pointed chin made more beautiful. Her hair was ash blond. She was always very clean and finely dressed, but her attractiveness lay in her manner more than in the magnificence of her dress. Her mind was lively and natural. Her disposition cannot be described, for with the modesty of her sex, she was amiable with everybody.[20]

Born for the *esprit de société* to which she dedicated herself passionately and exclusively, Mme de Fiesque was destined to remain eternally young. Saint-Simon said as much in writing her obituary: "She was the best woman in the world, the

---

20. Bussy-Rabutin, *Histoire amoureuse des Gaules*, pp. 54–55.

gayest, the most unusual, and one who, having died aged eighty, never aged except between the ages of fifteen and eighteen."[21]

In the same way her great friend Mme de Frontenac brought to Saint-Fargeau a real gift for society life. She too earned the praises of Saint-Simon when she died: "She had been beautiful and gallant, very much [a part] of high society and most sought after."[22] When she arrived at Saint-Fargeau, Mme de Frontenac was only twenty and trying in every possible way to rid herself of her husband, the Comte de Frontenac. He was "amiable," "witty," and not unaware of the "ways of the world,"[23] but this was not enough to induce the young bride to welcome him to the marital bed or to yield to his demands. Still, Monsieur de Frontenac had no rivals, and even after he left providentially for Canada, his wife never took a lover. At Saint-Fargeau she met a friend—Madeleine d'Outrelaize—with whom she could serenely and happily enjoy the pleasures of both society life and a sentimental attachment. It was Mme de Fiesque who had summoned the young lady from the provinces and introduced her to Mademoiselle. "She was a young woman of great spirit whose many friends called her 'the Divine,' a name that she then gave to Madame de Frontenac . . . with whom she spent the rest of her life without separation."[24] Thirty years after their first meeting, they were still living together in such perfect happiness that Mme de Frontenac declined the offer to become a lady-in-waiting to the Queen, declaring that "her peace and 'the Divine' were worth more than so brilliant and such an agitated life [at court]."[25] It is useless to question the nature of their relationship, since neither Mme de Sévigné, Saint-Simon, Loret, nor any of the anonymous versifiers comments on it. We only know that everyone called them "the Divine ones" and that "they were people whose approbation needed to be sought."[26]

Mme de Fiesque's and Mme de Frontenac's presence was thus essential to the lightheartedness and worldly gaiety of the château. Mademoiselle had wanted to make Saint-Fargeau an oasis of beauty, culture, and peace, a happy Arcadia that mirrored the novel *L'Astrée* and the pastoral poetry she loved so much. Here, under the protection of a great princess, life could flow, serene and noble, far from ambitions for power and Machiavellian politics. Of course, her inspiration was the Blue Room, and now that Mme de Rambouillet no longer received,

21. Saint-Simon, *Mémoires*, Vol. 1, p. 1114.

22. Saint-Simon, *Mémoires*, Vol. 1, p. 609.

23. Saint-Simon, *Mémoires*, Vol. 1, p. 609.

24. Saint-Simon, *Mémoires*, Vol. 1, p. 470.

25. Mme de Sévigné to Mme de Grignan, January 9, [1680], in Mme de Sévigné, *Correspondance*, Vol. 2, p. 783.

26. Saint-Simon, *Mémoires*, Vol. 1, p. 609.

Mademoiselle was ready to inherit her role. Exiled from court, disappointed in her aspirations for the crown, Mademoiselle turned her attention to the Parisian *beau monde* and prepared herself to become its leader once she returned to the capital. For this to be really possible, the princess, however, would have had to be able to believe utterly in her utopia; she would have had to renounce her royal destiny and betray her own ambitions of glory. This was not, in fact, possible for her. But for several years, in "another place," suspended between the past and the future, infected by the gaiety of her lady companions, Mademoiselle was able to throw herself unreservedly into the pleasures of society. Mme de Fiesque's and Mme de Frontenac's gaiety was both euphoric and contagious, capable of making every moment of the day pleasant and entertaining. It depended on a perfect forgetfulness of ego and on the ability to be, as Bussy-Rabutin wrote, "amiability itself." Good humor was a discipline that took no account of mood and needed no special reason to exist. More than a century later, Pierre Louis Moreau de Maupertius would say of Mme de La Ferté-Imbault—Mme Geoffrin's delightful, frivolous daughter—"that her gaiety would last indefinitely because it was based on nothing."[27] Only a consummate art, handed down from generation to generation could lend that *nothing* an illusion of reality.

Paris already had newer salons and patrons, but it looked toward Saint-Fargeau with curiosity and admiration. Mademoiselle's rank and exceptional personality and the presence at her side of two such social luminaries as Mme de Fiesque and Mme de Frontenac induced many court and society people to set out for Burgundy. In the summer of 1655, besides Mme de Sully and the Comte and Comtesse de Béthune, two young stars of the Parisian world made their way to the château: Mme de Montglas and Mme de Sévigné. Even Mme de Sablé's bosom friend the Comtesse de Maure, on her way to the thermal spa at Bourbon, near Auxerre, stopped at the château to pay her respects. The countess was accompanied by Catherine d'Asprémont de Vandy, a young relative who, being orphaned and penniless, lived with her. Mademoiselle knew Mme de Maure, as she knew Mme de Sablé, from the hôtel de Rambouillet and admired her intelligence and worldly courtesy. She also knew that, like herself, Monsieur and Madame de Maure were paying bitterly for their loyalty to the Fronde. The meeting was so successful that the following year, when Mme de Maure went again to Bourbon, Mlle de Vandy remained with the princess at Saint-Fargeau, and Mme de Maure returned alone to Paris.

Mademoiselle was certainly not the first to be struck by Mlle de Vandy's personality. The young woman came from an old and noble family of the Lorraine, but as an orphan with no dowry, she preferred to remain unmarried rather than

---

27. From *Mélanges de Mme Necker*, quoted in Pierre-Marie de Ségur, *Le Royaume de la rue Saint-Honoré: Mme Geoffrin et sa fille* (Paris: Calmann-Lévy, 1897), p. 118.

marry beneath her rank. She compensated for this decision dictated by pride with *préciosité*, sometimes betraying an exaggerated emotionalism that bordered on hysteria. Mlle de Vandy had the same phobia of love that her protectresses, Mme de Maure and Mme de Sablé, had of illness. It was said that the Grand Condé never failed to pay her court when he visited Mme de Sablé, and once, catching her by surprise, he kissed her on the cheek. Mlle de Vandy practically fainted and shuddered so violently that no one ever dared do the same again. It was not only the idea of physical contact that disgusted her. Even the word "love" was banished from her vocabulary. If she ever was obliged to refer to it, she spoke of it as "the Other."[28] Once sheltered from the threat of eros, however, Mlle de Vandy became amiability personified, her unyielding virtue never preventing her from behaving in the true Rambouillet style. Mlle de Scudéry sang her praises in *Le Grand Cyrus*, depicting her as Télagène, Princesse de Paphlagonie: "She had not only great beauty, great gentleness, and great wit, she also had her memory filled with everything agreeable that had ever been written...and nothing excellent ever produced by the muses had escaped her curiosity.... This wide reading therefore endowed Télagène with an ability to write well and to write gallantly.... Her conversation was sweet, flattering and agreeable."[29]

Mlle de Vandy's talents all came from an exemplary training. Growing up alone in the provinces, she had learned about the world from a distance, through books, and especially through fashionable novels. These were at the root of that happy blend of reading, conversation, and writing from which so many would benefit. Although social expertise was primarily taught through the *bienséances* and conversation, it could also be imparted through the written word, provided that that reading was then reinforced by firsthand experience and "corrected by several years in Paris or at Court, or by both together."[30] This is just what happened when Mlle de Vandy accepted Mme de Maure's hospitality. The countess took her by the hand and introduced her into the world. She "was the person most suited to forming people and teaching them to be very agreeable."[31] This pattern—by which a genuine talent was matched with an exceptional mentor who provided initiation into the mysteries of a certain *je ne sais quoi*—was the process by which a perfect society know-how developed. It would be repeated until the end of the *ancien régime*. A century later, a skeptical, blind old lady, Mme du Deffand, transformed another provincial orphan, Julie de Lespinasse, into a star in the Parisian firmament. Like Mme de Maure, she had no children and excelled in

---

28. Mademoiselle de Montpensier, *Histoire de la Princesse de Paphlagonie*, p. 74.

29. Mlle de Scudéry, *Artamène ou le Grand Cyrus*, Part 9, Book 2, Vol. 9, p. 334.

30. "Portrait de Mlle de Vandy, escrit par Mademoiselle," in *Divers Portraits*, pp. 72–73.

31. "Portrait de Mlle de Vandy," p. 73.

the arts of conversation and letter-writing, but she was not as generous as the countess, and her protégé paid for her initiation with her freedom.

Whereas Mme de Maure encouraged the Grande Mademoiselle's friendship with Mlle de Vandy on account of the advantages the friendship would bring her young cousin, the latter's entourage was planning a merciless attack on the newcomer. This virtuous, knowledgeable virgin whose pride and haughtiness were natural sentiments, "the sickness of her race,"[32] had far too great an affinity with her new protectress not to give rise to alarm. Generous and loyal, Mlle de Vandy had no interests beyond those of her new patroness and no object but to serve her faithfully. She obeyed only the dictates of her conscience and conducted herself quite without prejudice en philosophe. Mme de Fiesque and Mme de Frontenac, on the other hand, were grand ladies whose main preoccupation was their own social position and, after four years at Saint-Fargeau, the pleasures of retraite had been eclipsed by their wish to return to Paris. The two friends immediately came to a secret agreement with Gaston, with whom they often plotted behind Mademoiselle's back, to persuade the princess to agree to the conditions necessary for a speedy reconciliation with the royal family.

For all their endless intrigues, the charming countesses were unable to gain control of the princess's household. Nor were they able to prevent the rise of the new favorite. Within a few months there was an electric atmosphere at Saint-Fargeau, and on January 1, 1657, after a final noisy scene, Mme de Fiesque left the château, followed a few months later by Mme de Frontenac. Mademoiselle took her revenge on both of them, just as she had already on Mme de Fouquerolles, by pillorying them two years later in a satirical novella, L'Histoire de la Princesse de Paphlagonie, whose heroine—Mlle de Vandy, of course—is finally assumed into heaven by Diana the Huntress, to the eternal confusion of her rivals.

By good fortune, in November 1656, just as Mademoiselle's Arcadia was becoming a disordered, unharmonious place—a suffocating prison from which to escape—Segrais's Les Nouvelles françaises appeared. It presented a picture of idealized château life, naming Saint-Fargeau as the locus of the ideal marriage of princely and worldly culture. Mademoiselle was ready to take Arthénice's place, and Segrais that of Voiture.

A native of Caen, educated by the Jesuits, Jean Regnault de Segrais was deeply immersed in humanist culture. He was a pupil of Malherbe's and eager for success in the world of letters. Though prepared to meet the demands of a new, available, and curious literary public, he was quite untempted by any form of specialization. Once admitted to the hôtel de Rambouillet, he proved himself by his elegiac poetry, much in vogue in the Blue Room, and by excelling in eclogues, to which he had been introduced by his friend and fellow native of Caen, Pierre Daniel Huet.

33. "Portrait de Mlle de Vandy," p. 73.

Then, with the end of the Fronde, he discovered in Mademoiselle the patroness he had long sought. His presence at Saint-Fargeau turned out to be invaluable. Under Segrais's guidance, the princess broadened her knowledge of literature, discovered the pleasure of reading, concentrated on her writing, and brought some order to her hitherto fragmentary, eclectic culture. Above all, she found a writer who could celebrate her, making her the personification in poetry as in prose of the elevated idea she had of herself, her ambitions, and her dreams.

The first work Segrais dedicated to Mademoiselle was a pastoral poem, *Athys*, the tragic story of a love affair between a shepherd and a chaste, unobtainable nymph. The plot could not have been more banal, but it sounded the Arcadian myth that with d'Urfé's novel *L'Astrée* had become so deeply rooted in aristocratic imagination. The conventional form and symbolism were in fact well suited to the noble huntress banished to her lands.

Les Nouvelles françaises et les divertissements de la princesse Aurélie of 1656 was a far more innovative way of enhancing the princess's glory and marked an important milestone in the evolution of French narrative writing. This time, too, Segrais drew on a literary form with a long tradition, describing a small group of people gathered together in an isolated, tranquil place, who entertained each other by telling stories. Only in the case of *Les Nouvelles françaises*, the setting and narrative framework were as important as the stories themselves, and were the basic inspiration. The *locus amoenus*, "the seven-towered château" with its aristocratic *loisirs*, its conversations, theatrical performances, and games, was none other than an idealized Saint-Fargeau, and Mademoiselle and her ladies were easily recognized in the Princesse Aurélie and her entourage.

Les Nouvelles françaises was not only a celebration of Mademoiselle as the Marquise de Rambouillet's spiritual heir. It also demonstrated the necessity of bringing the tastes of the Blue Room into line with more contemporary literary culture. It was time to abandon the exotic settings, the distant times, and the unusual adventures of the novels that had so delighted the hôtel de Rambouillet. The Fronde had recently proved that reality could be far more exciting than fiction. Readers who had lived through it now demanded shorter, more credible stories set in France, preferably in a more recent past, and no longer described in the mannered, cloying fashion of yesteryear. Madeleine de Scudéry's style had had its day, and in saying so, however indirectly, Segrais was attacking her social authority, her reputation as a *précieuse*, and her claim to be the custodian of *politesse* and good manners. Mademoiselle did not hesitate to take up the polemic in the first person, either in her *Portraits* or in her *Histoire de la Princesse de Paphlagonie*. Meanwhile Segrais launched a new aesthetic debate that would prepare the way for the birth of the modern French novel. The choice of Saint-Fargeau and its noblewomen as a point of departure was by no means a casual one. Fifteen years later his friend Huet made the connections in his treatise on the novel among "the high level of elegance and art to which the French have brought the novel," the "refinement of gallantry," and the supreme authority of women in matters of style and taste.[33]

At the same time, the princess's *retraite* at Saint-Fargeau was drawing to a close. In the wake of her domestic crises, the spring of 1657 had brought Mademoiselle two pieces of good news: a royal decree ended in her favor her quarrel with Gaston concerning her mother's vast inheritance; and Champigny, ancestral fiefdom of the Montpensiers—iniquitously appropriated by Richelieu—was restored to her in a decree by the Parlement. Furthermore, at the end of July, the princess was granted permission to go to Sedan to receive the royal family's pardon.

Thus the happiest period in her life began. Having nobly withstood the trials of exile and strengthened with a more mature understanding of herself, Mademoiselle looked optimistically toward the future. Expecting to fully reestablish her position in the royal family and to find a solution to the delicate problem of her marriage, the princess returned to Paris. She lost no time in rediscovering the joys of society life and, by launching the "portrait game," proved herself capable of dictating fashion.

III. The Portrait Game

Madeleine de Scudéry was the first to divine public taste and introduce the fashion for literary portraits. With her extraordinary powers of observation, she continued under various disguises to tell the same story in one novel after another: the story of the society of her day. It may be said that she lacked imagination and knew only how to describe the people she knew. Sometimes her characters were so recognizable that her brother, the writer Georges de Scudéry, was obliged to intervene to water down the likeness. But in the ten volumes of *Artamène, ou Le Grand Cyrus*, Mlle de Scudéry intentionally displayed a talent of which she might not have been aware until then. She had begun to attract attention with a series of thinly disguised portraits of well-known society people, from the Grand Condé to Mme de Rambouillet and her daughter, Julie d'Angennes. She took advantage of the instant public success and gradually, volume after volume, over four years of publication (1649–1653), added to the number of portraits in the novel as she went. In the wake of her success, Mlle de Scudéry completed her census of contemporary society with a new book, *Clélie: Histoire romaine*. Between 1654 and 1660, almost everyone of note in Parisian society would meet their perfect "double" in that novel's ten volumes.

---

33. *Lettre-traité de Pierre Daniel Huet sur l'origine des romans*, tricentenary edition 1669–1969, edited by Fabienne Gégou (Paris: Nizet, 1971), p. 139.

The idea of a profile or *médaillon* was not new; distinguished writers had used it before, and exactly a century before Mademoiselle was writing, Amyot's fine translation of Plutarch's *Lives* brought it to a public beyond the *savants*. Society literature had already turned to the commemorative portrait in both prose and verse. When, about 1640, Voiture started the fashion for *métamorphoses*—in which he was soon followed by Chapelain, Malleville, and Saint-Amant—the *âme du rond* amused himself by likening Julie d'Angennes to a diamond and Mademoiselle to a pearl. In *Athys*, written in the early 1650s, Segrais described Mademoiselle and her lady companions dressed as nymphs. In *Les Nouvelles françaises*, however, they wore contemporary clothes.

If Segrais's works gloried exclusively in the search for a great princess, Mlle de Scudéry's novels became the coded *Who's Who* for Parisian high society. All the ladies, starting with the Comtesse de Fiesque, longed to figure in Mlle de Scudéry's fictional Elysium. Although she worked tremendously hard, however, she had difficulty keeping up with all the requests. A much less refined but equally well informed writer, Antoine Baudeau de Somaize, soon took advantage of the situation. His *Grand dictionnaire des Prétieuses* (1660) was the very first example of an idea fundamental to modern society: the social register—a register of those belonging to the privileged world which, nevertheless, became an object of fascination to the excluded, making voyeurs of them. It was a register to be studied regularly and revised by anyone cultivating social ambitions from that time onward. The criteria for such a register may change depending on the mood of the times, but its main purpose will always be to establish a list of people who count.

In a society where the individual was developing an ever-increasing awareness of his own image, it was not merely a narcissistic pleasure to see oneself through the eyes of others; it was a valuable opportunity to observe oneself from the outside, to compare the self-image with outward social success. Contemplating an idealized picture of oneself, one might quite possibly wish either to emulate or correct it.

Until now only professional writers had played the game, but the time had come for it to pass into the hands of the ones who had the sole right to judge themselves or others. Mademoiselle took the initiative. With a contemptuous disregard for Mlle de Scudéry's example, she decided to write her own self-portrait. She had already read those self-portraits of her two friends the Princesse de Tarente and the Princesse de La Trémoille, who had discovered the game in Holland, where it was at the height of fashion. Removed from its literary context, the written portrait became simply an entertainment, a flight of fancy, and an explicit affirmation of the self.

For a long time it was the exclusive privilege of the nobility to have their portraits done. By choosing the form of the self-portrait, and encouraging her friends to follow suit, Mademoiselle took it upon herself to contravene one of the basic rules of *bienséances*, which forbade talking about oneself. As she had already done in her *Mémoires*, Mademoiselle opted for sincerity, knowing full well that such portraits were immediately circulated among large numbers. The openness with which the princess described herself also guided her pen when she described others. In her portraits, Mlle de Scudéry had used her great psychological insight to flatter the self-respect of her subjects. With tact and delicacy, and never abandoning her inborn optimism, she brought out their hidden qualities while ignoring or disguising their worst flaws. Mlle de Scudéry beautified, sweetened, and praised. The Grande Mademoiselle, on the other hand, was not worried about pleasing anyone except the King, and she used the privilege of birth as an excuse to indulge her capricious imagination to the full.

For twelve months—from November 1657 to November of the following year, at Champigny, at Saint-Fargeau, in Paris, at Forges, and at Fontainebleau—Mademoiselle, her friends, and the friends of her friends amused themselves by writing and exchanging portraits, only to be emulated by a growing number of society people. As the fashion spread, Mademoiselle felt the need to end the game, wishing it to remain an exclusive entertainment for a small circle of initiates. Having freed the portrait from its literary context, the princess now wished to protect it from the dangers of fleeting fashion. She wanted to give it a new framework as a *recueil*, or collection, which would be perfectly compatible with the autonomy of each of the individual pieces. The printing of *Divers Portraits* was entrusted to the editorial hands of Segrais and Huet, who produced a limited number of copies— thirty according to Segrais, sixty according to Huet—in Caen during the first weeks of 1659. They formed not just *a* collection, but *Mademoiselle's* collection. It was her idea. She had chosen the contributors—most of them nobles. And she had penned more portraits than anyone else—fifteen out of fifty-nine. Above all, she had organized the material collected according to her own criteria alone.

For reasons of courtesy, the first three self-portraits in the collection were those of the three most important people to have taken part in the game: the Prince and Princesse de Tarente and the Princesse de La Trémoille. These were followed by Mademoiselle's long self-portrait, representing the boundaries of a world that revolved entirely around her. There were two more portraits of her in verse, one in the middle of the collection by the Comtesse de Suze, and the other, considerably longer and more demanding, by Segrais at the end of the volume.

Mademoiselle begins by describing her ladies sitting in a circle around the portraitist as if in a painting by Watteau. On further reading, it becomes clear that, for the author, the portrait game was more than a simple entertainment. It depended on a logic entirely her own. A portrait could result from a rush of sympathy for someone; it could be a mark of admiration, a proof of friendship, a reward for a faithful servant; it could console someone in disgrace or pay homage to the royal family; but it could also punish, be used in vengeance, to mock, or quite simply to discredit.

At last, Mademoiselle had a kingdom of her own: the *pays de portraiture*.[34] Only she conferred citizenship; only she dictated the moral, social, and aesthetic rules. Her sovereign liberty was expressed through writing. Mlle de Scudéry's portraits followed a fixed format that was easily imitated, even by dilettantes. It began with a physical description of the person in question and went on to speak of his or her social attitudes, ending with "spiritual qualities"—care having been taken to subtract from this the incidental details of time and particular personal events. In contrast, the Grande Mademoiselle had no respect for the established order and from time to time invented a different format. She approached her character with absolute freedom, talked to him or her, allowing her subject to speak from center stage. She described the person moving and in the context of time; she spoke of qualities and defects alike, of the full bloom of youth, of faded beauty, and of maturity and old age.

Nothing about this approach was in the least bit objective or detached. In describing others, Mademoiselle continued to talk about herself, her taste, her moods, her unshakeable belief in her own judgment, and her social superiority. Her disdain for rules and models drove her to literary experimentation that boldly illustrated the permutations of the new genre to both society and the literati. Despite these innovations, the portrait nevertheless remained a game for Mademoiselle. Throughout the collection, her voice alternates with the voices of her guests, and her skills encouraged widespread emulation.

In all, sixteen people in the *Divers Portraits* accepted the challenge of writing about themselves. The others preferred to describe their friends; it was possible to appear in the collection both as artist and model. Two people might describe one another, and someone might be described more than once without figuring among the writers. The Duchesse de Montbazon's virtuous daughter, the Abbess of Caen, contributed a self-portrait and a description of her fellow townsman, Huet. He in turn described her. But although Mme de Brégy contributed five pieces, she was not herself portrayed. Mme de Choisy, on the other hand, was comforted, following the shock of exile, by two affectionate portraits in the collection. In turn, she consoled the Duchesse d'Épernon, about whom Mademoiselle had written one of her more stinging profiles. The noble Brienne family was the most widely represented, with the Comtesse de Brienne portrayed by Mademoiselle and the Comtesse herself daring to write about the Queen. Her daughter the Marquise de Gamaches described both her parents, whereas her daughter-in-law, the young Comtesse de Brienne, decided on a self-portrait.

Not unlike a conversation piece, Mademoiselle's collection shows all the contributors intent on talking about themselves, about others, and, to a considerable

---

34. See Charles Sorel's satire *La Description de l'Isle de portraiture et de la Ville des portraits* (Paris: C. de Sercy, 1659).

extent, about the problems concerning their social position. It is mainly a conversation among women—only nine of the thirty-five writers are men—whose subject matter is primarily the women themselves. Thirty-six of the fifty individuals portrayed are women, and, of the sixteen self-portraits, only four are authored by men.

For the most part, the portraits concentrate on the way in which their subjects expose themselves to the judgment of others. Several recurring themes clarify for us how already, by the end of the 1650s, the *bienséances* no longer reflected a body of clear, immediately recognizable rules, but needed to be continuously interpreted, depending, as they did, on an ever more complex system of nuance.

In the *Divers Portraits*, the quality of the individual's conversation is almost always seen as one of the most important keys to character, and in the context of women in society, "cheerful" conversations among friends were more appreciated than serious ones or learned ones. Yet it emerges that lightheartedness evidently needed to be continually supervised if it was not to become offensive. "There is a delicate, flattering style of mockery," La Rochefoucauld wrote, "that touches only on the failings that the people of whom one speaks are pleased to have, that knows how to disguise praise behind an appearance of blame, and that reveals their amiable qualities while feigning to wish to disguise them."[35] To tease someone gently could thus be the most subtle way of praising that person, as it made him or her the center of attention and provoked a generally friendly and sympathetic attitude. Success in picking out an amusing trait, a penchant, or a weakness required a lightness of touch, psychological insight, and tact. The comic element had to remain perfectly in keeping with the individual's dignity. This was *la belle raillerie*—the art of polite mockery—which Mademoiselle admired in Mme de Montglas[36] and which could hardly fail to bring a smile to the faces of those involved. And it was precisely through that gentle *raillerie*, of which she herself had been the subject, that Mme de Montglas acquired her great "knowledge of the world and of how to live."[37] "To understand the mockery," or to get the joke, was quintessential to the *esprit de société*, so that even the Queen willingly gave a good example,[38] and Louis XIV himself knew how to joke pleasantly.[39]

Even when practiced with the best intentions in the world, however, joking still could be a dangerous game. It was like "dancing on the flowers by the edge of a

---

35. La Rochefoucauld, "De la différence des esprits," in *Réflexions diverses*, XVI, in *Maximes*, p. 219.

36. "Portrait de Mme de Montglas, fait par Mademoiselle," in *Divers Portraits*, p. 111.

37. "Portrait de Mme de Montglas," p. 110.

38. "Portrait de la Reyne, fait par Madame de Motteville," in *Divers Portraits*, p. 245.

39. "Portrait du Roy, fait par Mademoiselle," in *Divers Portraits*, p. 268.

precipice"—and everyone knew it.[40] The Princesse de Tarente preferred to shun excess by avoiding "cutting mockery.[41] The young Comtesse de Brienne admitted enjoying jokes, but immediately pointed out—as did the Marquise de Maulny[42]— that she was not "slanderous."[43] An element of moodiness was all that was needed for Mme de Fiesque's inexhaustible verve to become dangerous,[44] and a change of humor could turn "fine and witty jokes" to spite.

Another ambiguous word, which society language could not do without and which recurs frequently in the *Divers Portraits*, is *complaisance*—obligingness. In its originally accepted form, *complaisance* was inseparable from *politesse* and indicated the wish, common to most of society, not to enter into an argument but to be unreservedly obliging to an interlocutor, even at the expense of one's own character. "I am cheerful with those who please me," Mademoiselle de Montpensier quoted Mlle Melson as saying, "and my *complaisance* toward them is so great that, even though I have a melancholy temperament, I appear to be naturally very merry."[45]

But soon, as this general attitude came into conflict with the differing conditions that fundamentally constituted society under the *ancien régime*, the word *complaisance* became suspect, and "flattery" took its place.

In *De l'Allemagne*, published in 1814, Mme de Staël claimed that in France until 1789, conversation alone had regulated social relations, attenuated differences, and given to each his due by setting itself up as the highest arbiter of institutions.[46] In this complex system of relationships, the manner of addressing others constituted an explicit utterance of identity, imposing prudence and measure. Among equals, *complaisance* implied a rivalry in education, but if one of two interlocutors was socially superior—or thought he was—an excess of courtesy could suddenly be risky. One small false step and *complaisance* came dangerously close to flattery— just as joking could degenerate into slander. In either case, there was a fine distinction, and only by subtlety and worldly know-how could the balance be kept.

---

40. Ortigue de Vaumorière, "Avec quelle précaution il est permi de railler, " in *L'Art de plaire dans la conversation*, p. 183.

41. See "Portrait de Mme la Princesse de Tarente, fait par elle-mesme," in *Divers Portraits*, p. 7.

42. See "Portrait de Mme la Marquise de Mauny, fait par elle-mesme," in *Divers Portraits*, p. 129.

43. See "Portrait de Madame la Comtesse de Brienne la fille, fait par elle-mesme," in *Divers Portraits*, p. 136.

44. See "Portrait d'Aramanthe, escrit par Mademoiselle," in *Divers Portraits*, p. 89.

45. "Portrait de Mlle Melson," in *La Galerie de portraits de Mlle de Montpensier*, edited by M. Édouard de Barthélemy (Paris: Didier, 1860), pp. 204–206, quoted in Pelous, *Amour précieux, amour galant*, p. 206.

46. Mme de Staël, *De l'Allemagne*, chronology and introduction by Simone Balayé, two volumes (Paris: Garnier-Flammarion, 1967), Vol. 1, pp. 105–106.

If Mademoiselle, seated on her pedestal, could solve the problem easily by announcing in her self-portrait that she would not oblige while expecting others to do so,[47] the profiles of her friends show how some of the key words in society's idiom could be interpreted in remarkably different ways, even within the most exclusive circles.

The Princesse de La Trémoille had no doubts: "I have as great an aversion for it [flattery] as I have praise for *complaisance*," she claimed, without appearing to think that there was any ambiguity where the two were concerned.[48] Her daughter was less confident, and her behavior was conditioned by the fear of being misunderstood: "The fear I have of being accused of it [flattery] often makes me less *complaisante* than I ought to be."[49] For the Princesse de Tarente, who took pride in "being entirely *complaisante*, but not to the point of flattery,"[50] the latter was no disgrace, but a pointless excess of zeal. The Abbess of Caen was the only one to confront the problem from the point of view of *honnêteté*, much as the Chevalier de Méré did. She gave *complaisance* a moral value: "I do not like to contradict even though my opinions are contrary to those being expressed: this comes from my *complaisance*: I can even say this complaisance is one of my virtues; for although I tend to have this quality, I make use of it reasonably and not out of cowardice...and if *complaisance* causes me sometimes to be silent, it never causes me to contradict what I feel."[51]

The Duchesse de Vitry looked at it from another angle and admitted she was "sensitive to *complaisance* while not liking flattery."[52] She thus implied that flattery was put to the severest test by the pride of the person praised. In order to please, the compliments had to be credible or they risked giving offense.

Finding themselves torn between two barely reconcilable demands—"to present oneself and to occupy one's place in the world with dignity"[53] and "to be really what one wishes to appear"[54]—the women in these portraits imagine themselves and see themselves through the eyes of others. They say nothing of their private feelings. While waiting for "God to touch their hearts,"[55] the only passionate

---

47. "Portrait de Mademoiselle, fait par elle mesme," in *Divers Portraits*, p. 33.

48. "Portrait de Madame la Duchesse de la Trimoüille, fait par elle-mesme," in *Divers Portraits*, p. 19.

49. "Portrait de Mlle de la Trimoüille, fait par elle mesme," in *Divers Portraits*, p. 10.

50. "Portrait de Madame la Princesse de Tarente, fait par elle-mesme," in *Divers Portraits*, p. 4.

51. "Portrait de Madame l'Abbesse de Caen, escrit par elle-mesme," in *Divers Portraits*, p. 59.

52. "Portrait de Madame la Duchesse de Vitry, fait par elle-mesme," in *Divers Portraits*, p. 141.

53. "Portrait de Madame la Princesse de Tarente, fait par elle-mesme," in *Divers Portraits*, p. 7.

54. "Portrait de Madame la Duchesse de la Trimoüille, fait par elle-mesme," in *Divers Portraits*, p. 17.

55. "Portrait de Madame la Duchesse d'Espernon, escrit par Mademoiselle," in *Divers Portraits*, p. 80.

feelings allowed are pride, the longing for glory, and family ambition. On the social scene, however—where people were what they seemed, albeit behind a veil of good manners—they could talk and laugh, make friends, cultivate their taste for beautiful things, seduce, and perhaps even, if only for a fleeting moment, be happy.

Among the portraits collected by Mademoiselle, the most delightful is a child's self-portrait. In a time without children, as Molière would say, a little girl of five and a half comes onto the scene and confronts the public for the first time; she still prefers the company of her parents and her confidence in God is still intact. She seems perfectly spontaneous and yet already conscious of how she appears and who she is. She expresses herself in a simple and direct manner—I am, I love, I hate—her syntax is elementary, but as a child of her time, she has already learned to analyze herself, to speak of moods and inclinations, to distinguish intuition from judgment, temperament from will:

> I have black eyes that are a little too small; a round face; too large a fore-head; a bit of a pug nose; well-shaped eyebrows; a very pretty mouth; a cleft chin that is a little square; a very white complexion when it's scrubbed; a head that's slightly too big but that is shrinking little by little; beautifully colored hair, very fine; and I'm a little too tall. I have more spirit than judg-ment. I would rather give than receive. I'm very sweet-tempered, but some-times however I'm a bit piqued. I'm very charitable. I love to read, especially the word of God. I love my parents. I am not at all greedy. I don't like peo-ple to make fun of me. My mood is very gay. I'm not opinionated. To tell the truth, I'm a little bit cowardly. I love to play, to amuse myself, to run. I love to see things done, and I very much hate doing nothing. I'm totally reserved. I very much love those who serve me. I don't like those who lie, and I hate myself when I've lied. I love rare things. The company I like best is that of my parents. I am not at all proud. I will never be coquettish. I don't like to fight at all, or to be defeated. I am not at all bad-tempered, but I am a bit rash. I very much fear God, I love to do his will, and I hope that he will bless me.[56]

In the *Divers Portraits*, Mademoiselle alone, imbued with the idea of her natu-ral superiority, indulged in the luxury of sincerity, although the facts often belied her most emphatic declarations. How is it possible, for example, to reconcile the fact that she was the author of a cruel satire, even as she described herself as "nei-ther malicious nor mocking, although ... more aware than anyone of the ridicu-lousness of people"?[57]

---

56. "Portrait de la fille de Madame la Princesse de Tarente, agée de cinq ans et demy, escrit par elle-mesme," in *Divers Portraits*, pp. 64–65.

57. "Portrait de Mademoiselle, fait par elle-mesme," in *Divers Portraits*, p. 31.

Mademoiselle's bold new idea for a "collective portrait" (also attempted by Tallemant des Réaux) was born of a desire to settle a series of old scores. She certainly did not spare Mme de Fiesque, whom she described as beautiful but dirty, a brilliant conversationalist who lacked any talent for writing, a woman devoid of taste and "delicacy of mind," whose outbursts of religious feeling did not last long enough for the making of a hair shirt, and who, preoccupied with pleasure, was frivolous and superficial. This list of perfidies did not, however, soothe Mademoiselle, who was vexed to have to conclude, "for all this, to see her is to love her."[58] Before reopening hostilities against her ex-lady-in-waiting, however, Mademoiselle took her revenge on Mlle d'Aumale and Mlle d'Haucourt, two members of her circle who had betrayed Mlle de Vandy for the Comtesse de Fiesque. They served as the models for her satirical portrait of the *Précieuses*. Here her personal dislike coincided with a popular polemic attacking society behavior and a whole way of life:

> ...They lean their heads on their shoulders, simper with their eyes and mouths, look disdainful, and have a certain affectation in all their behavior, which is extremely offensive. If there is only a single *Précieuse* in a gathering, she seems bored and very weary with chagrin; she yawns, doesn't respond to anything said to her, and if she responds, it's all wrong, to show that she's not paying any attention to what she's saying; if there is anyone not afraid to challenge her, or better yet, kind enough to point out to her what she's saying, she bursts out laughing, saying, ah, well, I'm not paying any attention to what I'm saying, ah Jesus, can it be otherwise? If another *Précieuse* joins this gathering, they joke together, and without dreaming that they might not be in the strongest position, they provoke again, and no one is exempt, and it's all done very boldly, with bursts of laughter in people's faces, which are the most unbearable in the world. They have something like a private language, since unless one spends time with them, one cannot understand them. They find fault with everything one does and everything one says, and generally disapprove of the conduct of everyone. Some of them pretend to be devout, since they have family reasons that oblige them to be, in order to make life easier than if they did otherwise; there are some that would have you believe that the only thing that prevents them from having an easier life is not having the right religion. It's all politics, since husbands are a rarity for these women, and among them a marriage is something that only happens once in a century; most of them having less of value in their coffers than they imagine they have in their minds.
>
> They regard matters of friendship the same as they regard matters of love, for they have none for anyone; they are polite enough to endure the

---

58. "Portrait de Amaranthe, escrit par Mademoiselle," in *Divers Portraits*, p. 93.

friendship of others, and to accept their favors when they need them; but fearing that those who endure them will tire of them, they claim to honor some with the glory of serving them, each in his turn, and their grand judgment has its usual effect, since they don't remember anything. They are very mocking and joking even about those who give them no reason to be. I think I've said enough to make them very recognizable.[59]

Mademoiselle's "Portrait des Précieuses" in the *Divers Portraits* brings to the fore one of the most discussed problems of French seventeenth-century culture: that of the *Précieuses* and their real historical identity. Paradoxically, the only trace left of these women who caused a scandal by not being prepared to renounce their own intrinsic merit is in satirical literature, of which Mademoiselle's scathing portrait is one of the basic texts. Anyone interested in the *Précieuses* as a group must confront this paradox. A letter from the Chevalier de Sévigné, dated April 3, 1654, might be taken as the birth certificate of their set. "There is a kind of young lady and woman in Paris known as '*précieuses*'; they have their own jargon, their own grimaces, and a marvelous way of swinging their hips: a map has been made to show how to navigate through their land."[60]

The map to which he referred was probably the work of the Marquis de Maulévrier, a regular visitor of Gaston d'Orléans's circle. It was not published until 1659, when the vogue for the *Précieuses* was at its height. Between 1654 and 1661 the habits and intellectual aspirations of the group became the subject of a fierce campaign marked by the Abbé de Pure's novel *La Prétieuse* (1656–1658), Molière's *Les Précieuses Ridicules* (1659), and two successive editions (1660 and 1661) of Somaize's *Le Grand dictionnaire des Prétieuses*. For seven years they were discussed intensely for good or ill, as a phenomenon of fashion, only to vanish into nothing.

This body of work, mostly very ambiguous, has been interpreted in various ways. Through learned literary research, attempts have been made to identify the original models, taking for granted the existence of the *Précieuses*. But it has also been suggested that they only represented an abstract idea, the personification of a lack of judgment that might threaten society, or a pure invention of male misogyny.

What is certain is that from the 1640s, a Pléiade of women held positions of prime importance in the social life of the capital. More than 130—most of them nobles—have now been identified and each of them described in the singular by the adjective "precious," which had no pejorative connotation and was synonymous with delicacy, refinement, and distinction.

---

59. "Portrait des Précieuses," in *Divers Portraits*, pp. 303–306.

60. *Correspondance du chevalier de Sévigné et de Christine de France, duchesse de Savoie*, edited by Jean Lemoine and Frédéric Saulnier (Paris: H. Laurens, 1911), p. 246, quoted in Pelous, *Amour précieux, amour galant*, p. 309.

In 1638, Voiture was already addressing Julie d'Angennes as "the most precious thing in the world."[61] The word undoubtedly still meant "amiable," "gracious," and "dear," as it did with the Spanish *prezioso*, without the connotation subsequently assumed by the noun. But the very fact that Voiture used it to praise a woman, and that this woman was Mme de Rambouillet's daughter, shows that it was frequently used in the Blue Room to praise women. Tallemant des Réaux did not hesitate to point to Arthénice's second daughter, Angélique Clarice, as one of the original inspirations for Molière's farce; she openly expressed an aversion to marriage and embraced a "purism" in language that prefigured the excesses imputed to the *Précieuses ridicules* in the 1650s.

Society life was of its nature fluid, and the noblewomen who came to be described as "precious" naturally preferred to visit the same places and were often friends among themselves. It is enough to point out the uninterrupted chain of friendship that united Julie d'Angennes, Mme de Longueville, Mme de Sablé, Mme de Maure, Mlle de Vandy, Mme de Lafayette, and Mme de Sévigné—to name but the best known. They all shared an interest in literature, a love of language, and a passion for conversation. They had psychological insight and were refined and unyielding in matters of taste. But none of these characteristics was exclusive to the typical *précieuse*. Rather, they were elements of the new worldly culture. Even the cult of heroism and glory, which was a hallmark of the Fronde's feminism, was not a complete novelty for aristocratic women; a great literary tradition had long encouraged their warlike fantasies.

There is no doubt that some of them rebelled more or less openly against marriage. Some found the idea of love repulsive. Not all were equally intransigent, and some had yielded to their admirers. Many of them were hypochondriacs, neurotics, or manifested signs of hysteria. But there were also those who, like Mademoiselle, boasted an iron constitution. All these different attitudes in the *Précieuses* could be traced back to a communal desire to give their behavior an unmistakable character of its own.

Whether robust or delicate, austere or frivolous, libertine or phobic about sex, the *précieuse* cultivated a high idea of herself and of the respect due to her. This was based not merely on class but resulted from a tragic awareness of the fragility of the female condition. The privileges she enjoyed in the heart of aristocratic society did nothing to alter her inferior position in the eyes of the law, nor did it prevent the fact that, in the overwhelming majority of cases, her fate was decided by others. But to find oneself at the mercy of an unloved husband or to risk one's life for an unwanted pregnancy did not necessarily imply resignation. In fact, the *précieuse* remained faithful to herself. She listened to herself, analyzed herself, and was in control of herself. Strengthened by the power

---

61. See Alexandre Cioranescu, "Précieuse," in *Baroque* 3–4, December 1969, p. 82.

conferred on her by the *bienséances*, she proved her worth in the duty-free zone of high society. There she was free to use her intelligence, to dictate according to her sensibilities, and to indulge the abstract pleasures of the mind. There she was allowed to choose, to make demands, to seduce, or to refuse her favors, and finally, to triumph over reality, treating it as metaphor. For this reason literature and language were of overwhelming importance to the *précieuse*; they not only represented a dreamlike, aesthetic escape and helped to refine her taste and sensibilities, but they also taught her the fundamental power of the word. Talking and writing were creative acts for her: nothing existed for her except what she chose to name.

At the hôtel de Rambouillet, the Grande Mademoiselle discovered both the *précieuse* sensibility and the art of distinguished social behavior. She cultivated the feminine ideal of heroism and chastity, preferred the company of women, was not susceptible to seduction, and her women friends and her intimacy with Mme de Fiesque, the "Divine Ones," and then Mlle de Vandy placed her at the center of the constellation of *Précieuses* that was formed in the early years of the Regency. Why, then, by means of the portrait—that most "precious" of literary genres—did she so forcefully betray herself and declare war on the new *Précieuses* just as they were finding the strength publicly to proclaim their aspirations? Or was the stand she took really all that surprising?

To answer these questions, it is necessary to look at the word *précieuse*, to understand its development from an adjective to a noun and how it came to be used not in the singular but the plural. From that time on, it ceased to indicate an individual but rather referred to a type. It also lost any complimentary connotation, gaining, to say the least, a suspect one. What had happened? Beginning in 1654, with the return of peace and stability after the Fronde, Parisian society lived through a period of intensity equaled only by the period following Louis XIV's death: salons multiplied, more and more of the nobility and the bourgeoisie became passionate for *sociabilité*, new forms of entertainment were introduced, and the *cercles* widened their interests. The nobility had definitively renounced its dreams of autonomy and glory and took refuge in social pleasures. The *haute bourgeoisie* took advantage of all this to narrow the distance between themselves and the privileged world whose lifestyle they imitated. Hitherto warlike Amazons were obliged to withdraw from the political scene and to transfer their ambitions to the world of literature. Whereas in the first half of the century it was considered quite unsuitable for women to think of writing, in the ten years following the Fronde there were more and more women writers, and society's very conception of literature encouraged them to take up the pen. Women took an active part in literary games that once would have been the monopoly of writers like Voiture, Cotin, and Benserade: "*bouts-rimés*, conundrums, riddles, *métamorphoses*, rondeaux, madrigals, collective letters in verse and prose, gazettes and chronicles, and portraits."[62] As their decisive contribution to the birth of the modern novel goes to show, writing was, for women, not necessarily just a pastime.

Mlle de Scudéry was in many ways responsible for this development. In the "Harangue de Sapho à Érinne," published in *Les Femmes illustres* (1642), she was the first, discreetly but firmly, to claim the right of women to write verse. Her novels promote a model of society that encourages intellectual curiosity and a taste for psychological analysis. Because of her modesty, diplomacy, and tact, she was able, with barely disguised anonymity, to publish her books and earn her living by her pen untroubled by malicious critics. But by the beginning of the 1650s, freed at last from her brother's tyranny and fortified by success, Mlle de Scudéry was no longer satisfied with the role of society's novelist.[63] She wanted the pleasure of a salon all her own. Her Saturdays in the rue de Beauce, in the Marais, were quite unlike the Blue Room gatherings. Mlle de Scudéry's habitués were not aristocrats but literati. They were *savants*, critics, and poets whose conversation and entertainments were epitomized by literary experimentation. A small group of women —not all of them noble—was invited to admire this weekly display of cheerful intellectual discussion, sensibility, and *bel esprit*.

Before propounding the joys of platonic love in *Clélie*, the "Marais nymph" was to discover them in person. The initiation rites to which Mlle de Scudéry, who represented herself under the name of Sappho in that book, subjected her young admirer Pellisson-Acante before giving him the title of "friend of her heart" took place one day in 1653. Pellisson himself has described the origins of romantic literature's best-known geographical allegory—the *Carte de Tendre*—which would soon delight readers of the first volume of *Clélie*:

> On the subject of friendship during a Saturday conversation, Sappho having made a distinction between new friends, her special friends, and her tender friends, Acante asked what his own rank was, and he was told he was a special friend. He decided to ask if the distance was great between Special and Tender, and if a man always walking diligently could hope to arrive between the month of November, which [month] it was, and the month of February, by which time the six-month trial by Sappho would be up. He was told that he would succeed by following the route, for if he missed the path he would never arrive. He asked how many paths there were: he was told that he could travel by water, by land, or by air, and that he should choose which of

---

62. Linda Timmermans, *L'Accès de la femme à la culture (1598–1715): Un débat d'idées de Saint-François de Sales à la Marquise de Lambert* (Paris: Champion, 1993), p. 181.

63. The Scudéry siblings lived together for many years and collaborated on works up until the publication of *Artamène, ou Le Grand Cyrus*, which was signed by Georges de Scudéry. After that Georges moved away from Paris and Mlle de Scudéry published under her own name.

THE AGE OF CONVERSATION

the three he preferred. He said that the last was the shortest and that he would find a way to fly. Whereupon several persons were spoken about who had understood that it was not impossible.... This gallantry, furthermore, having gone so far, gave rise to the *Carte de Tendre*.[64]

This wonderful game invited imitation, and Sappho was bound to be the model. Mlle de Scudéry's pedagogic talent, combined with the way her literary universe increasingly reflected reality, helped to make manuals of her books. They were particularly useful for bourgeois women who had not been initiated into society and who had usually suffered from a far less liberal education than that reserved for their aristocratic sisters. Thus, albeit without ever mentioning the word "precious" in her work, the writer and her character came to represent an ideal in the public eye.

Mlle de Scudéry was too intelligent and knew the world too well not to realize the dangers threatening her model. One false note and she, an intelligent woman, would become a figure of ridicule, lacking in any moral or social credibility. So when, at the end of *L'Histoire de Sapho*, the tenth and last part of *Le Grand Cyrus*, she presented herself to her readers, she was careful to distance herself from her imitators. By contrasting Sappho's modesty and discretion with the pretentious Démophile's lack of judgment, she anticipated future criticism by distinguishing between the real and the false *Précieuses*, leaving the latter to ridicule.

But Sappho's followers loved provocation and braved excess. In the *ruelles* of the Marais where these overstated *Précieuses* were so exhilarated with the idea of their own omnipotence, noises were stifled, lights were filtered, and the world was presented as a place where will and intelligence triumphed over nature and instinct. "The Abbé de Pure comically imagined that joining the *précieuses* was like joining a monastic order and that the second vow pronounced by a *précieuse* is that of 'method in desire.'"[65] They sought inner peace and freedom through emotional tranquility and absolute control of the heart.

In 1656, when the movement was still in its infancy, Charles de Saint-Évremond described the *Précieuses* with discernment:

> The Queen of Sweden was told one day that "the *Précieuses* were love's Jansenists"; and she was not displeased by the definition. Love is still a God for the *Précieuses*. It excites no passion in their souls but forms there a kind

---

64. "Documents inédits sur la société et la littérature précieuse: extraits de la 'Chronique' du Samedi, publiés d'après le registre original de Pellisson (1652–1657)," published by Luc Belmont, in *Revue d'histoire littéraire de la France*, IX (1902), 9, p. 671.

65. See René Bray, *La Préciosité et les Précieux, de Thibaut de Champagne à Jean Giraudoux* (Paris: Nizet, 1968), p. 153.

of religion. But to speak on a more serious note, the body of the *Précieuses* is no more than a gathering of a small number of persons in which several truly refined women have led others into ridiculous attitudes of affected refinement.

These falsely refined women have removed all that is most natural from love, thinking thereby to give it something "precious." They have removed a passion from the heart and lent it to the mind, and converted feelings to thoughts. This great purification arose from an honest disgust of sensuality; but they are no closer to the true nature of love than were the voluptuous; for love has as little to do with speculation as with brutish appetites.[66]

The libertine Saint-Évremond took care not to condemn all the *Précieuses* out of hand, however; in his eyes many of them were not ridiculous, and their concerns were far from incomprehensible. But suffering as they did from an excess of intellectualism, none of them understood the real nature of the divinity they celebrated within their cult.

For the noblewomen trained at Mme de Rambouillet's salon, the "precious" ideal was perfectly in keeping with social convention. On the one hand, aristocratic women were allowed considerable freedom in choosing a way of life compatible with their most personal aspirations; on the other hand, the *précieuse* sensibility found that in society it could assert itself in the name of refinement and elegance and under the protective umbrella of the *bienséances*. In fact, in the 1650s, many *Précieuses* imagined they could turn their backs on the *bienséances* with impunity, thus depriving themselves of their one weapon of defense. Most of them came from the bourgeoisie and, not having enjoyed the privileges of the nobility, were uncertain of society's ways. They wished to proclaim their demands for freedom and emancipation in loud voices, without regard to discretion or taste. United by an *esprit de corps*, they counted on their strength as a group and were encouraged in their audacity by the euphoria of society and by reading novels. In noisily drawing attention to themselves, they exposed themselves to satire.

La Grande Mademoiselle, unlike Molière, understood neither the originality nor the significance of a movement that made culture the keystone of female emancipation. The subjects of her pitiless portrait prompted her disapproval mainly for reasons of style. Nothing annoyed her more than their collectively pretentious and artificial behavior, which she saw as the antithesis of true aristocratic distinction and the aesthetic of the natural. If Mademoiselle did not spare her enemies the full force of her attack—in her caricature, they are uneducated, ugly, and poor—it was because she wished to teach them a lesson of classical simplicity. "I am one of those people who is convinced that one must live among the living,

---

66. Saint-Évremond, "Sur les Précieuses," in *Œuvres*, edited by René de Planhol, three volumes (Paris: La Cité des livres, 1927), Vol. 1, p. 45.

THE AGE OF CONVERSATION

and that one must not stand out in any way by affection or choice; and if one belongs to the world, the world's approbation of our behavior must depend on our virtue and not on a thousand useless affectations, which are never to be found in genuine people."[67]

Mademoiselle's optimism was not destined to last. The triumph of the portraits was to be her last great worldly success; from then onward, both in Paris and at court, her star was in the descendant. Both the *Précieuses'* taste and that of Mademoiselle herself went out of fashion. Little by little she realized that no more crowns awaited her and that her position in the heart of the royal family was definitively losing importance. Soon a new queen and a new Madame would be seated beside the Queen Mother, taking precedence over her. In the frivolous, gallant young court that was building up around Louis XIV, the austere morality of an aging virgin and her Rambouillet-style society culture suddenly seemed outdated.

By the summer of 1660, Mademoiselle found herself waiting with the rest of the court at Saint-Jean-de-Luz near the Spanish frontier for Louis XIV's marriage to the Infanta to be negotiated. At age thirty-three, Mademoiselle probably realized that there would be no more central roles for her. Forgetting that barely two years earlier she had preached to the despised *Précieuses* that one must "live with the living and not be conspicuous in any way," she hastened to take refuge in the most precious of all utopias. In a letter to Mme de Motteville, she described a plan for an Arcadian retreat, halfway between Saint-Fargeau and the world depicted in *L'Astrée*. Dressed as shepherdesses, living in the solitude of uncultivated countryside, a few ladies of merit would spend their lives reading, meditating, and chatting. The presence of one or two *honnêtes hommes* would serve to make the conversation more interesting and more varied, but not the slightest hint of gallantry would be introduced. Based on the perfect equality of the sexes, Mademoiselle's Arcadia strictly forbade marriage and love—and not only for reasons of prudence. In her utopia, disillusioned by politics, the former Amazon rediscovered her taste for battle and thus incited women to fight for their freedom and to rebel against custom and patriarchal laws. "What gave men superiority was marriage, and the reason for our being called the weaker sex is the dependency to which we have been subjected by sex, often against our will, and for family reasons of which we have been victims. Finally, let us free ourselves from slavery; let there be a corner of the world where it can be said that women are mistresses of themselves and that they do not have all the failings attributed to them. Let us extol ourselves in future centuries with a life that allows us to live forever!"[68]

---

67. "Portrait des Précieuses," in *Divers Portraits*, p. 302.

68. Mademoiselle to Mme de Motteville, letter 3, in *Lettres de Mademoiselle de Montpensier, des Mesdames de Motteville et de Montmorency, de Mademoiselle Du Pré et de Madame la marquise de Lambert*, with biographical and explanatory notes (Paris: A. Colin, 1806), p. 35.

172

IV. The Discovery of "The Other"

Ten years later Mademoiselle was obliged to betray herself and to dream of her own married servitude. Armed with an instinctive mistrustfulness and scornful of the strategies practiced in the *ruelles*, having already reached the age of forty, she unexpectedly came face to face with "The Other." Having already met him in literature, she immediately recognized him.

He was Antoine Nompar de Caumont, Comte de Puyguilhem, later Duc de Lauzun, a man six years her junior. He was neither a king, nor an emperor, nor a hero. He was of mediocre birth, and his only advantages were his ability to please women and the fact that he was the King's favorite. Mademoiselle would in the course of time humiliate herself, cover herself with ridicule, and relinquish her titles and her riches for his sake. Two days before the wedding, the King told her he would not permit the marriage. The much-dreamed-of union did not take place until 1680, after Lauzun was released from prison, and only then in secret. It proved to be a terrible disappointment. Incensed by her lover's extreme arrogance, rudeness, and ingratitude, Mademoiselle broke with him definitively in 1684.

At a time when Mlle de Scudéry had long stopped writing the novels on which the princess poured scorn, Mademoiselle de Montpensier had set out on the most unbelievable of adventures. Mme de Sévigné's celebrated letter to Coulanges of December 1670 encapsulates the surprise felt by all of society at the fall of the last and most inaccessible of all the Amazons:

> I am about to tell you the most astonishing thing, the most surprising, the most marvelous, the most miraculous, the most triumphant, the most bewildering, the most unheard of, the most extraordinary, the most incredible, the most unforeseen, the greatest, the smallest, the most rare, the most common, the most dazzling, the most secret until today, the most brilliant, the most enviable; in short, a thing whose parallel is only to be found in bygone centuries; and even this comparison is not exact; a thing which we cannot believe in Paris (so how could it be believed in Lyon?); a thing which makes everyone exclaim Merciful Heavens! a thing which fills Mme de Rohan and Mme d'Hauteville with joy; a thing, finally, which will take place on Sunday, when those who witness it will think their eyes have tricked them; a thing which will take place on Sunday and which will perhaps not have taken place by Monday. I cannot bring myself to give it away. Guess. I will give you three guesses. Has the cat got your tongue? Do you give up? Well then, I must tell you: Monsieur de Lauzun is going to marry, on Sunday, at the Louvre—guess who! I give you four guesses; I give you ten; I give you a hundred. Mme de Coulanges says, That's easy; it is Mme de La Vallière. No, absolutely not, Madame.—Then it is Mlle de Retz?—No, not so; how

provincial you are!—Ah! you say, how silly we are; it is Mlle Colbert!—
Even less likely.—Then, it must assuredly be Mlle de Créquy?—No, wrong
again. So, finally, I shall have to tell you: Monsieur de Lauzun is going
to marry, on Sunday, at the Louvre, with the King's consent, Mademoiselle,
Mademoiselle de . . . Mademoiselle . . . guess the name! He is marrying Mademoiselle, my faith, by my faith, my sworn faith! Mademoiselle, the Grande
Mademoiselle, Mademoiselle daughter of the late Monsieur, granddaughter
of Henri IV; Mademoiselle d'Eu, Mademoiselle de Dombes, Mademoiselle
de Montpensier, Mademoiselle d'Orléans; Mademoiselle, first cousin of the
King; Mademoiselle destined to a throne; Mademoiselle, the only match in
France really worthy of Monsieur. Now there's a fine topic for discussion. If
you cry out, if you are beside yourselves, if you accuse us of having fabri-
cated this story, of having made it up, if you call it a lie, if you feel you are
being made fools of, if you conclude that it's all a big joke, impossible to
imagine; if, at last, you insult us, we will feel that you have reason to; we
had the same reaction when it was told to us.[69]

---

69. Francis Mossiker, *Madame de Sevigné: A Life and Letters* (Knopf, 1983), pp. 70–71. For the original French, see Mme de Sévigné to Coulanges, December 15, 1670, in Mme de Sévigné, *Correspondance*, Vol. 1, pp. 139–140.

10

MADAME DE SÉVIGNÉ AND MADAME DE LAFAYETTE: A LASTING FRIENDSHIP

Des ouvrages du Ciel le plus parfait ouvrage,
Ornement de la cour, merveille de notre âge,
Aimable Sévigné dont les charmes puissants
Captivent la raison et maîtrisent les sens....

IN THE SUMMER of 1652, when the Fronde was in its dying throes and the Grande Mademoiselle was preparing for her period in exile, *Miscellanea*, a newly published collection of Gilles Ménage's writings, established the reputation of a rising star in the social firmament with a poem of some two hundred lines, *Le Pêcheur ou Alexis*, dedicated to the Marquise de Sévigné.[1] The following year, with peace restored, the young widow was to return to the capital, glowing with the pleasure of being in Paris.

The marquise descended on her father's side from the old Burgundian house of Rabutin-Chantal, and on her mother's side from the Coulanges, a rich Parisian bourgeois family. She was orphaned of both parents in earliest childhood. Two apparently irreconcilable codes of behavior, two different mentalities, and two cultural traditions managed nevertheless to combine to produce the "perfect work." In addition to a considerable fortune and an excellent education, the beautiful blond Marie received from the Coulanges the gifts of stability, optimism, and common sense. From the Rabutin-Chantals she inherited family pride, the wit that had already made her father irresistible, and an innate grace. Her writing would eventually reveal the presence of what Proust described as her "*côté* Dostoevsky," which would remain concealed from most of her acquaintances.

---

1. "Of all heaven's works, the most perfect work / Ornament of the court, marvel of our age, / Lovely Sévigné whose powerful charms / Captivate reason and master the senses..."; from Gilles Ménage, *Le Pêcheur ou Alexis. Idylle à Mme la marquise de Sévigné*, in *Miscellanea* (Paris: A. Courbé, 1652), quoted in Roger Duchêne, *Mme de Sévigné ou la chance d'être femme*, new revised edition (Paris: Fayard, 1982), p. 105.

In 1644, at the age of eighteen and in compliance with the demands of the Rabutin family, the orphaned girl confronted the second difficult trial of her life: marriage. Henri de Sévigné, the husband chosen for her on the basis of his ancestry, was in fact an attractive young Breton marquis, a perfect, fashionable *petit-maître*. The bride had no illusions about marital bliss—"Monsieur de Sévigné esteems but does not love me; I love him, but do not esteem him," Tallemant reports her as saying.[2] But marriage did not last long enough for her to shed too many tears, nor long enough for her husband to spend all her fortune. In 1651, he was killed by the Chevalier d'Albret in a duel over a woman who had long since lost her reputation.

Widowed at twenty-five, with two magnificent children and the support of her uncle the Abbé de Coulanges—her providential *"bien bon,"* who helped her look after her fortune—the marquise discovered the pleasure of being her own mistress. Family connections and friendships linking her husband to the powerful Gondi clan—grouped around the future Cardinal de Retz—meant that from the earliest years of her marriage, Mme de Sévigné had frequented the hôtel de Condé and from there, under Mme de Longueville's wing, had been admitted to the Blue Room. She arrived just in time to admire it in the last days of its splendor. She could not pass unnoticed, and Jean Chapelain, distinguished writer that he was, took credit for having forged the friendship of the young bride with Mme de Rambouillet and her daughter Julie.[3] According to tradition Chapelain also, together with the Abbé Ménage, contributed to completing the education of the charming marquise and refining her taste.

But Mme de Sévigné's establishment in Parisian society really took place after the Fronde, coinciding with the fashion for *préciosité*. Her presence under the name of Sophronie in Somaize's *Grand dictionnaire des Prétieuses* should not deceive us. Her jealously guarded independence, her sexual coldness, her marked preference for female friendships, and her passion for literature had no need of group support or declarations of shared principles. Her realism and her taste for life were too marked for her to require the screen of metaphor. Mme de Sévigné's legendary naturalness was the antithesis of the language of the *ruelles*, with its euphemisms and "precious" conceits. According to Tallemant, she tended to sacrifice the restraint that propriety demanded of her sex in favor of frankness.[4]

So far, we have depended on the judgments and words of others in an attempt to define the distinctive characteristics of the women we have encountered. Not a single

---

2. Tallemant des Réaux, *Historiettes*, Vol. 2, p. 429.

3. See Duchêne, *Mme de Sévigné et la lettre d'amour*, p. 125.

4. "She is blunt and cannot refrain from saying what she thinks is amusing, even though they may often be quite light-hearted; she even creates the opportunity to say them"; Tallemant, *Historiettes*, Vol. 2, p. 429n.

visual image of Mme de Rambouillet remains, and the few lines there are from her own hand are of little help in getting to know her. Sometimes the portrait paintings that do survive appear remote, incomprehensible, and openly to contradict contemporary assessments. A different concept of feminine beauty—or simply an inadequate portrait painter—can be enough to paralyze our imaginations and to give us an overwhelming sense of distance from the subject. One seeks in vain for confirmation of Mme de Longueville's irresistible attractiveness in her portraits. The adoration her admirers expressed is of greater account; and if we are to have any idea of her wit—the famous Condé wit—it can be detected only in the sarcasm of her detractors or the implacable self-denigration of the penitent after she had withdrawn from the world. Mme de Sablé, with her fat face, pointed nose and chin, and short, crimped hair in Du Moustier's portrait of her as a no-longer-young woman, is bound to disappoint. But in her case, despite the difficulty of associating the portrait with the image of one of the most renowned beauties of the day, something in her expression attracts attention: the penetrating eyes that stare fixedly out from under the too-heavy eyelids are perfectly in keeping with one who best knew all the ways of the heart. From her *Maximes* it can be inferred that this gaze was mostly turned toward the observation of the psychological and moral behavior of mankind in general. Society favored appearance, whereas talking about oneself was forbidden, and even those who left an account of their lives, like the Grande Mademoiselle, did so by hiding as much as possible behind personality, indulging in private revelations only insofar as they did not appear to contradict the public image, and, above all, never forgetting what they owed to their rank and its glory.

Suddenly, with Mme de Sévigné, the distance seems to diminish. For the first time we find ourselves face to face with someone with whom it is possible to establish a direct rapport and who spontaneously opens her heart, confiding her feelings, her joys and sorrows, her worries and hopes. She tells us what she thinks, informs us of her friendships, her reading, and her entertainments. She gives us day-by-day accounts of her life and what is happening around her. With her pen, the daily life and public events of Louis XIV's reign acquire a reality that defies distance, so that we laugh and shudder as though listening to her living voice.

On reading her letters, we can claim to know Mme de Sévigné intimately, as a friend, and thus we recognize her too in the words of others. We recognize her spirit, her vivacity, her will to please, while at the same time believing that behind the objective reasons for her success, we can understand the subjective, psychological, and moral imperatives that drove her so forcefully into society. Society life represented for her, as it did for many of her contemporaries, more than an entertainment and an opportunity to assert oneself; it provided a moment of absolute well-being, a rite that could, for the space of several hours, overcome the pain of living while awaiting death. Few in the seventeenth century could claim freedom from the fear of the last judgment and eternal damnation.

There are several reliable portraits of Mme de Sévigné that make it possible to see her face as it changed from adolescence to maturity. The same intense luminosity can be seen in the shy, astonished charm of early youth as in the irresistible attraction of her twenties and the serenity of maturity: the luminosity of the wispy, blond ringlets, of the famous "flecked" eyes, and of "the most beautiful complexion in the world"[5] enhanced by the mother-of-pearl tone of the necklace.

It may seem curious that this creature of light, who brought with her life and joy, could not bear the idea of one day returning to the darkness. She knew only too well that her attachment to the world was stronger than her attachment to God. She even claimed that horror at what awaited her caused her to regret not having died "in the arms of her wet nurse." That same love of life and fear of losing it sometimes drove her to hate it: "I find death so terrible that I hate life even more because it leads me there by the thorns along the way."[6] But luckily for her and for us, the instinctive love of life was stronger in her than the moments of distress, and it was in worldly entertainment that Mme de Sévigné discovered the formula for immediate happiness without risk—the same *divertissement* that her much-loved Pascal would soon denounce as one of the greatest obstacles to an awareness of the human condition.

Mlle de Scudéry was the first to sing the praises of Mme de Sévigné's wit, depicting her as Clarinte in *Clélie*.[7] But it was Mme de Lafayette who, in her first and only signed work—a portrait of Mme de Sévigné in the Grande Mademoiselle's collection of literary portraits—pointed clearly to the mutual advantage that began to evolve as soon as a highly gifted person arrived in a social circle: "Your presence enhances every occasion, and every occasion enhances your beauty. In sum, joy is the true state of your soul, and sorrow more alien to your spirit than to that of anyone else."[8]

The marquise's verve helped to create an atmosphere of euphoria around her, a euphoria that then infected her, stimulating both her mind and body. "There is none other on earth so delightful as you when you are carried away in animated conversation from which restraint has been banished," Mme de Lafayette continued. "Everything you say has such charm, and so well becomes you that your words invoke spontaneous laughter, bring smiles to the lips of those who surround you, and the brilliance of your mind brings such a glow to your face and

5. Bussy-Rabutin, *Histoire amoureuse des Gaules*, pp. 152, 156.

6. Mme de Sévigné to Mme de Grignan, March 16, 1672, in Mme de Sévigné, *Correspondance*, Vol. 1, p. 459.

7. Mlle de Scudéry, *Clélie*, sequel to Book 3, Part 4, Vol. 6, pp. 1,324–1,335.

8. "Portrait de Madame la marquise de Sevigny, par Madame la Comtesse de Lafayette sous le nom d'un inconnu," in *Divers Portraits*, p. 315. English translation in Mossiker, *Madame de Sévigné: A Life and Letters*, p. 521.

such a sparkle to your eyes that—although it would seem that wit should strike only the ear—it is certain that yours dazzles the eye as well."[9] Mme de Sévigné's mind, as lively and expressive as her eyes, easily grasped people and circumstances. "You are the most polite and obliging person in the world and, thanks to that sweet and easy way of yours, the simplest compliment prescribed by social custom sounds—coming from you—like a protestation of friendship, and all the people who leave your presence leave convinced that they have won your esteem and consideration although they cannot recall, even to themselves, precisely what token you gave them of the one or the other."[10]

Was it really like this? Others suspected her of not wishing to reveal herself. A little later, in his *Histoire amoureuse des Gaules*, the Comte de Bussy-Rabutin—Mme de Sévigné's cousin—amused himself by writing a satirical version of a "precious" portrait. His description of 1659 is far from flattering. Brilliant libertine that he was, Bussy-Rabutin's sole intention had been to entertain his sick friend Mme de Montglas by describing through a series of coded portraits the less edifying habits and characteristics of some of the court ladies most in view. The fact that many of them—Mme de Châtillon, the Comtesse d'Olonne, the Comtesse de Fiesque, and Mme de Sévigné herself—had had the honor of being included in the Grande Mademoiselle's collection only goes to show that Bussy's game consisted precisely in turning the "precious" image on its head. His portraits laid bare all that the *bienséances* chose to ignore. The entertainment had been intended for a small circle of friends but, to Bussy-Rabutin's shame and the shame of the ladies he mocked, the game became a public scandal when the manuscript fell into the wrong hands in 1665. Bussy soon learned that to laugh too freely under Louis XIV was very risky indeed.

In his description of Mme de Sévigné as "Mme de Cheneville," Bussy was in fact carrying out a vendetta. Despite their kinship and their long friendship, the marquise—spurred on no doubt by the Abbé de Coulanges—had firmly refused her cousin a loan when he was in dire financial straits. So he paid her back in kind: by describing her character as false. "Mme de Cheneville's main preoccupation is to appear to be everything that she is not."[11]

Both Mlle de Scudéry and Mme de Lafayette had, in their portraits, insisted on the young widow's invulnerability and on her firm intention to distance herself from any suitor. Her virtue was unquestionable; her adherence to the hôtel de Rambouillet's much-loved formula "gallant without *galanterie*" was impeccable. In his portrait, Bussy-Rabutin had tried to tear the mask of respectability from his

---

9. *Divers Portraits*, pp. 314–315; Mossiker, *Madame de Sévigné*, p. 521.

10. *Divers Portraits*, p. 316; Mossiker, *Madame de Sévigné*, p. 522.

11. Bussy-Rabutin, *Histoire amoureuse des Gaules*, p. 156.

cousin's face and turn her morality upside down. There was nothing virtuous in Mme de Sévigné's behavior, he claimed; her chastity did not stem from moral choice but resulted from frigidity, which lent overtones of immodesty to her particular game of *galanterie*. Protected by her own inadequacy, the marquise was satisfied by the act of seduction, her pleasure in it becoming so great that she lost control of herself. In treating his cousin as a teasing flirt, Bussy happily bolstered his case by arguing the morality of his intention: if the late Marquis de Sévigné's conjugal honor might seem unimpeachable in the eyes of the world, he was certainly "a cuckold in the eyes of God."[12] Perhaps the hypocrisy Bussy denounced in Mme de Sévigné was that of a whole society, one which avoided love's pitfalls by sublimation.

Bussy-Rabutin, more than anyone, embodied the prototype of the aristocrat in search of military glory who amused himself as a literary amateur. At thirteen he had been obliged to leave school and to join his father's regiment. As so often happened to young men of his background, he had completed his education in the school of society, between military campaigns. He therefore delighted in sharing the reading and tastes of the society ladies to whom he paid court. As his *Portraits* and his *Maximes d'amour* show, he excelled at fashionable literary games.[13] However, in keeping with the new *galanterie* of the 1660s, his psychological insight and literary talent were not put to the service of an idealized, chaste love but rather, quite simply, employed in playing the game. Before even attempting the subtle casuistry of the *maximes d'amour*, Bussy threw himself into parodying Mlle de Scudéry's *Carte de Tendre* with a *Carte du pays de braquerie*—a parody of amorous conquest. Written to entertain the Prince de Conti during the siege of Villafranca in 1654, Bussy's *Carte* produced a detailed map of fortresses and citadels with names very like those of the most "gallant" court ladies, each of whose surrender was humorously illustrated. *L'Histoire amoureuse des Gaules* followed the same lines with its gallery of satirical portraits that obviously mocked Mlle de Scudéry's systematic idealization of society figures in her novels.

Without scandalous gossip to use as a basis for his portrait of Mme de Sévigné, Bussy-Rabutin used all his psychological and social insight in order to identify her weakest point. In a bold strike, he aimed at what appeared to be her most unassailable quality: her intelligence. "There is not a woman in France with more spirit than she, and there are very few who have as much. She is lively and amusing.

---

12. Bussy-Rabutin, *Histoire amoureuse des Gaules*, p. 154.

13. At least two of the portraits in *Recueil des portraits et éloges, en vers et en prose, dédié à son Altesse royale, Mademoiselle*, published by Charles de Sercy and Claude Barbin in Paris in 1659, are attributable to Bussy. (This was an expanded, commercial edition of the original *Recueil* that Mademoiselle had assembled.) The *Maximes d'amour* appeared for the first time anonymously in Part I of *Recueils de pièces en prose, les plus agréables de ce temps composées par divers Auteurs*, published by Charles de Sercy in 1658.

There are those who say that for a woman of quality, her character is a little too waggish [*badin*]. When I used to see her, I found that judgment somewhat ridiculous, and I admired her burlesque style in the name of gaiety; now that I no longer see her I am not dazzled by her fire and agree that she attempts to be too agreeable."[14]

Bussy freely admitted that the marquise was mistress of the difficult art of *badinage*—the very bantering that, from Voiture's time, had become one of the greatest pleasures of social intercourse—and that she, more than anyone else, was able to attract the company's attention. He claimed, however, that she lacked the judgment to recognize the precise boundaries appropriate to a real gentlewoman's conversation. Mme de Sévigné's mounting euphoria, which Bussy-Rabutin describes, in fact echoes Mme de Lafayette's account of her friend, although evoked with a very different effect.

Giving way to changing moods and carried away by the excitement of the game, Bussy continues, Mme de Sévigné could sometimes lose all restraint. Then the high spirits turned to boldness and the desire to laugh became uncontrollable. Then the careful widow revealed a hidden sensuality, happily indulging in conversations that decency should have forbidden. In fact, Bussy was attacking his cousin's *esprit* itself: "With so much fire, it is hardly surprising if her discernment is mediocre, since the two things are ordinarily incompatible."[15] So it was not surprising, he said, if Mme de Sévigné preferred the high-spiritedness of fools to the thoughtfulness of intelligent people. Her overwhelming good cheer was simply at odds with *honnêteté* and all the values that went with it.

Written in satirical mode, just when the literary genre was at the height of fashion, the portrait aptly drew on all the social skills that had, until then, been used to flatter the self-respect of others: a precise knowledge of the *bienséances*, psychological insight, and the "precious" taste for nuance, all of which proved helpful in divining the secrets of personality. Even before La Rochefoucauld opened the season for the great classical moralists with his *Maximes*, Bussy-Rabutin showed how merciless an observer a man of the world might be. With his portrait of Mme de Sévigné, Bussy made of this genre a perfect weapon for settling scores. Many were those who followed his example. Cardinal de Retz, an admirer of the marquise's, concentrated all his poison in a few searing lines; Saint-Simon knowingly spread his out to more spectacular effect. But there were plenty of extempore portraits dictated by dislike or personal resentment or which resulted from brooding vendettas and were written in a moment of rage. Others embodied the pure pleasure of vilification, as did Célimène in Molière's *Le Misanthrope*. For generation after generation these brilliantly cruel attacks continued, with women proving

---

14. Bussy-Rabutin, *Histoire amoureuse des Gaules*, p. 135.

15. Bussy-Rabutin, *Histoire amoureuse des Gaules*, p. 135.

themselves to be no more merciful than men. Proof enough is Mme de Staal-Delaunay's portrait of the Duchesse du Maine, written nearly a hundred years later, not to mention Mme du Deffand's caricature of Mme du Châtelet or Mlle de Lespinasse's detailed bill of indictment against Mme du Deffand. Compared with what followed, Bussy-Rabutin seems quite good-natured.

Most contemporary sources describe Mme de Sévigné as witty, cheerful, vivacious, extroverted, temperamental, chameleonlike, and determined to please, all qualities that explain the reasons for her success, a success which appears to have opened all doors to her. Yet this indefatigable socialite who was received in the best society, from the hôtel de Condé to Mademoiselle's court—from the hôtel de Gondi and the château de Vaux-le-Vicomte to Versailles itself—was not in the habit of receiving in her own house. Unlike the *Précieuses* of the Marais district, the marquise had no ambition to surround herself with a circle of her own chosen guests, but preferred to flit from drawing room to drawing room, visiting different groups.

Was the choice made for financial reasons, or did it betray a lack of confidence in her ability to preside over her own group? Might it have been made through prudence? Mme de Sévigné had only too often seen her friends struck by misfortune as a result of tying themselves to one group with which they totally identified. During the Fronde, the Sévignés had been driven by their relationship to the Gondis to take the losing side, and Cardinal de Retz, the young couple's friend and protector, was forced to flee. With the return of peace, the marquise had, without hesitation, taken the opposite side and sought the support of a man not only loyal to Mazarin but connected to both the Jesuits and the *dévot* party: the powerful superintendent, Nicolas Fouquet. But Louis XIV's deadly and unexpected wrath struck him, too. It is true that Mme de Sévigné also frequented the du Plessis-Guénégauds, who were ardent supporters of Jansenism and would not remain for long in the King's favor. Persecution also awaited the Arnauld family, with whom Mme de Sévigné became ever more closely connected, and a tragic fate hung over the Jansenist stronghold of Port-Royal. As for Bussy-Rabutin's disgrace, it not only weakened the marquise's family standing but hurt her so deeply that she was prepared to forgive her cousin the joke that had cost her so dearly.

Mme de Sévigné was realist enough to resign herself to the inevitable. She knew the art of adapting to circumstance. Alone, without a husband, father, or brothers, with two children to establish in the world, the marquise could not afford to forgo the support of influential people, and society life presented the best opportunity for cultivating them. Steadfastness was not her strong point, but this did not prevent her from sincerely loving her friends, fearing for them, and, if she could do nothing else, secretly weeping for their misfortunes.

The famous sequence of letters from Mme de Sévigné on the subject of Fouquet's trial and the emotion she expresses in them—"our dear friend," "the poor unfortunate man," "our dear, unfortunate friend," "our dear unfortunate one," "our poor friend"—leaves no doubt that she and the persecuted superintendent were close. Fouquet, a great financier with a solid legal background, had been one of Cardinal Mazarin's men. He had given proof of absolute loyalty during the Fronde. Beginning in 1653 he held the important position of superintendent of finance. In the hope of one day succeeding the cardinal as prime minister, he pursued a policy of reconciliation designed to put an end once and for all to the quarrels, the spite, the disappointments, and the struggles that had for too long riven the country. Those hopes were dashed in 1661, when the King suddenly had him arrested and put on trial for high treason.

We know from Bussy that Fouquet, having courted Mme de Sévigné assiduously, only resigned himself to making do with a simple friendship in 1657. And in that very year some lines dedicated to her by a young poet, a protégé of Fouquet's, confirm her presence in the superintendent's circle. The poet who paid that compliment—which ended in the lines *"Entre les dieux, et c'est chose notoire,/En me louant Sévigné me plaça"*—was Jean de La Fontaine.[16] The marquise had contributed to the success of one of his compositions in verse, "La lettre à l'abbesse de Mouzon,"[17] and he was quick to express his gratitude. "The only lyric poet in the century of Louis XIV," as Marc Fumaroli has called him,[18] and the gentlewoman who, unlike any other writer of the time, could speak of her own feelings and express her emotions, were born to be friends. Both had a talent for joy and radiated good cheer. But for them gaiety was not so much the result of natural inclination as an antidote to life's dramas and a determined refusal to give way to grief. La Fontaine was presenting himself as a new Voiture. His epistle in verse, dedicated to a young nun whom the Graces, laughter, and Cupid all wished to follow into the convent, perfectly reflected the tone of pleasant epicureanism and gallant libertinage that held sway at Fouquet's court.

In the fascinating pages on Fouquet in his book on La Fontaine, Fumaroli shows how this political vision went hand in hand with a humanistic dream of peace, pleasure, and beauty. This utopian dream had blossomed in the small sixteenth-century Italian courts and found philosophical expression in Lorenzo Valla's *De voluptate*, and poetic illustration in Tasso's *Aminta* and Guarini's *Pastor fido*. The Valois court would later adopt it, as would some of the most noble circles in Louis XIII's time. Fouquet's policy of patronage and his artistic taste stemmed from the conviction that art was "capable of creating harmony,

---

16. "Among the gods, and it is a well known thing/With her praises Sévigné has placed me..."; La Fontaine, "Pour Mme de Sévigné," in *Œuvres complètes*, Vol. 2, p. 493.

17. La Fontaine, "Lettre à M.D.C.A.D.M.," in *Œuvres complètes*, Vol. 2, pp. 491–493.

18. Marc Fumaroli, *The Poet and the King: Jean de La Fontaine and his Century*, translated by Jane Marie Todd (University of Notre Dame Press, 2002), p. 24.

sweetness, and an appetite for true happiness."[19] His château de Vaux-le-Vicomte was the visible embodiment of that aesthetic program.

Determined to encourage the new literary and artistic talent emerging at the time and not trusting solely to his own judgment, the superintendent turned for advice to Paul Pellisson, a knowledgeable man of letters and connoisseur of classical poetry, who helped him gather a real academy of artists and scholars. And it was precisely at Pellisson's suggestion that he welcomed La Fontaine. There was nothing pedantic about this refined and extremely erudite culture, which lent itself to elegance and good-humor, to society games, and to the fashionable *préciosité*.

Rich, powerful, intelligent, handsome, elegant, and gallant, Fouquet possessed all the qualities needed to make both his house in Paris and his estate at Saint-Mandé into influential centers of Parisian society. For him, society life was undoubtedly an instrument of advancement and self-promotion, but the worldly utopia was also absolutely in keeping with his political vision. Both private and public happiness required harmony, and this harmony depended on man's ability to express his own aspirations and to open his mind to those of others. After the violence and hatred of the Fronde, the French nobility became reconciled by sublimating its wish for supremacy in a desire for pleasure, and so took to meeting again in the same places, sharing the same entertainments, and conversing together, while taking care to deal with the unavoidable obstacles of real life by resorting to the "precious" language of euphemism.

This moment of grace was idealized in Mlle de Scudéry's *Clélie*. The ten-volume novel went to press between 1654 and 1660—that is to say, during the brief, intense period between the end of the civil war and the beginning of Louis XIV's personal reign. The author, after exalting the heroes of the Fronde in *Le Grand Cyrus*, now celebrated the new social season in the capital, describing its workings with contagious enthusiasm. Again society's leading lights were portrayed under coded names. "*Clélie* was the last literary attempt to represent, in a single harmonious fiction, the private and public lives of the kingdom, in an ideal city that included the court," Fumaroli writes. And by glorifying society not merely as a spectacle in which everyone was called on to give his best but as a center of communication, tolerance, and empathy, Mlle de Scudéry supported Fouquet's policy. "The kingdom as Foucquet and Pellisson foresaw it would have reconciled the state inherited from Richelieu and the flavor and virtues proper to private life."[20]

The superintendent was the first to show how the duties of great office were not incompatible with the pleasures of *sociabilité* or the sweetness of friendship. Beginning in 1657, the year in which Pellisson presented both Mlle de Scudéry

---

19. Fumaroli, *The Poet and the King*, p. 141.

20. Fumaroli, *The Poet and the King*, p. 230.

and La Fontaine to his protector, the "illustrious Sappho" would have been able to see that for herself. But Fouquet did not await her arrival before leaving his mark on the field of *belle galanterie*.

The superintendent's social life—if not his choice of lovers, as some gossips claimed—was influenced not by the timid, devoted Mme Fouquet but by a seductive young widow, Suzanne de Bruc, Marquise du Plessis-Bellière. This country neighbor of Fouquet's knew how to combine the delicacy of "precious" taste with the traditionally masculine virtues of courage and business acumen. Her husband had been a brilliant soldier who shared her passion for games and entertainment, but having had the misfortune to die shortly after his wife's parrot, he was given second place after the bird. Of course it was the fashion to pay tribute in light but moving verse to the domestic animals to which society ladies had dedicated so much tender care. To name but a few, there were Mlle de Scudéry's warbler, her dove, and her chameleon, Mme de Montglas's dogs and cats, the Duchesse de Bouillon's Barbary ape, and the animals kept by Cardinal Mazarin's nieces. None of these, however, enjoyed funerary honors equal to those of Mme du Plessis-Bellière's parrot. At least twenty-eight sonnets and set-rhymes were composed to console this parrot's noble mistress. Such a gallant tour de force had not been seen since the days of *La Guirlande de Julie*. And it was mainly instigated by Fouquet, who himself contributed a sonnet. Thus the great, erudite maecenas with infallible taste, the protector of La Fontaine and Molière, showed his love for "precious" pastimes and amateur poetry. "Sitting on his bed, by candlelight, with the curtains closed," he continued to find time to write witty, ingenious, cheerful, tender, gallant verses, perfectly in keeping with the mood of the day.[21] The Parisians loved him, and when he was removed from office, they missed his carefree gaiety, as witnessed by these anonymous lines:

> *Quand vous l'aviez, Fouquet, on ne parlait en France*
> *Que de paix, que de ris, que de jeux, que d'amour.*[22]

From the beginning of the 1650s, Mme de Sévigné was a frequent guest at the hôtel de Nevers, where, following the example of the Blue Room, Mme du Plessis-Guénégaud had gathered a prestigious and brilliant social circle around her. The marquise was probably introduced there by Arnauld d'Andilly's son,

---

21. *Mémoires pour servir à l'histoire de Louis XIV par feu M. l'abbé Choisy, suivis des Mémoires de l'abbé de Choisy habillé en femme*, edited by Georges Montgrédien (1966; Paris: Mercure de France, 1979), p. 65.

22. "When you had it, Fouquet, one only spoke in France/Of peace, of laughter, of games, of love"; anonymous, in ms. 22559 of the Bibliothèque Nationale, quoted in Urbain-Victor Chatelain, *Le Surintendant Nicolas Foucquet* (1905; Geneva: Slatkine Reprints, 1971), p. 83.

Simon Arnauld de Pomponne, a country neighbor of the du Plessis-Guénégauds. In her correspondence with him she often refers back to this friendship "by reverberation," which, despite a growing sympathy and mutual respect, was never to become very close.[23] Again in 1664, Mme de Sévigné was anxious to find out what Mme du Plessis-Guénégaud felt about her, and she enlisted Pomponne to woo his "admirable neighbor": "You send me some welcome news in telling me that I am making some progress in her heart; there is none in which I am gladder to advance; when I wish for a moment of joy, I think of her and her enchanted palace."[24]

Like Mme de Rambouillet, the Comtesse du Plessis-Guénégaud was of "unstained virtue,"[25] and, as was the case with the illustrious Arthénice, her wish to make her house a social center came from her attitude toward the court. According to her great friend Mme de Motteville, "the Queen, who did not know her particularly well, did not treat her with the distinction that her good qualities might merit. And her heart, filled with that noble pride that human reason justifies, made her wish to establish for herself and at her home a kind of domination that might console her for her privations; for she could not suffer them without anguish when she was at court."[26]

But unlike the Blue Room, the countess's salon was no retreat from the world but a center of political opposition. Here, for the first time since the Fronde, and as the result of a wise strategy, public opinion proved itself capable of contesting the established power. Mazarin was perfectly aware of this, and in 1660, Père Rapin tells us, he "sent Gourville to the countess to beg her to cease speaking ill of him so freely and criticizing his ministry."[27] The Sorbonne and the Jesuits also realized it when Pascal's *Les Provinciales* appeared and the sixth and seventh letters were read at the hôtel de Nevers prior to publication.[28] As a true woman of the world, Mme du Plessis-Guénégaud knew the power of vanity. The convinced Jansenist did not hesitate to take advantage of it for a two-way promotional exercise. Given the powerful mobilization of the forces against Port-Royal, it was necessary to act in anticipation in order to ensure the support of a certain number of *habiles*—cultivated people of authority capable of influencing public opinion and of winning it over.

---

23. Mme de Sévigné to Mme de Grignan, August 10, 1677, in Mme de Sévigné, *Correspondance*, Vol. 2, p. 519.

24. Mme de Sévigné to Pomponne, November 18, 1664, in Mme de Sévigné, *Correspondance*, Vol. 1, p. 57.

25. *Mémoires de Mme de Motteville*, Vol. 3, p. 147.

26. *Mémoires de Mme de Motteville*, Vol. 3, p. 146.

27. *Mémoires du Père René Rapin*, Vol. 3, p. 72.

28. The sixth letter is dated April 10, 1656, the seventh April 25 (See Pascal, *Œuvres complètes*, edited by Michel Le Guern, Paris: Gallimard/Bibliothèque de la Pléiade, 1998–, Vol. 1). A detailed account of the reading of the sixth letter is to be found in *Mémoires du Père René Rapin*, Vol. 2, pp. 368–369.

The first part of her campaign was also the most delicate, and Mme du Plessis-Guénégaud conducted it in the name of *amour-propre*. The people whose help she wished to guarantee had to feel that they belonged to the chosen few. There was an agreeable invitation to attend the house of a great lady with the accompanying "privilege" of a prepublication reading of a fiery, still secret text on which guests would be invited to comment. How could anyone thus favored not feel naturally inclined to share the hostess's opinion, gaining her lasting respect and goodwill? It is thus thanks to Mme du Plessis-Guénégaud that Pascal's radically intransigent text—pillorying all those who believed in the possibility of a compromise between God and the world—reached a privileged public. Her greatest tool was the most dangerous of all worldly idols, one which no one had yet thought to name, but which two centuries later would come to be called snobbery.

Neither political ambition nor religious conviction prevented Mme du Plessis-Guénégaud from loving society life for its own sake. It was undoubtedly the duty of one of her social status to receive nobly and magnificently, and the countess was not in the habit of ignoring her duty. She was an exemplary mother and wife and, in rigorous obedience to the *bienséances*, knew how to disguise her desire for perfection behind a veil of modesty. She was equally discreet about her charitable works and even "made a secret of her curiosity"[29]; nor did she wait for maturity before renouncing the pleasures of youth—the balls and festivities and all the ornaments that might have enhanced her blond beauty. Yet like Arthénice, this austere woman who made "ruling her passions into her greatest pleasure"[30] loved to amuse herself. When in the company of her friends, she proved capable of analyzing everyone in society most elegantly.

In the tradition of the Blue Room, the hôtel de Nevers took a lively interest in literature and counted a whole new generation of writers among its many guests. Simon Arnauld de Pomponne contacted his society friends as soon as he returned to Paris, his friendship with Fouquet having cost him a year in exile. On the evening of February 4, 1665, without even changing out of his traveling clothes, he went straight to the hôtel de Nevers. "There," he immediately wrote to his father, Arnauld d'Andilly,

> I found only Madame and Mademoiselle de Sévigné, Madame de Feuquières and Madame de Lafayette, Monsieur de La Rochefoucauld, Messieurs de Sens, de Xaintes, and de Léon; Messieurs d'Avaux, de Barrillon, de Châtillon, de Caumartin, and several others; there was also Boileau, whom you know and who had come to read some of his satires, which I found admirable; and Racine, who recited three and a half acts of a play about

29. Mlle de Scudéry, *Clélie*, Part 3, Book 2, Vol. 6, p. 817.

30. Mlle de Scudéry, *Clélie*, Part 3, Book 2, Vol. 6, p. 819.

Porus, renowned for his rivalry with Alexander, which was assuredly of very great beauty. It would be hard to describe how I was received by all these people, for they were so agreeable and so full of friendship and pleasure at my return.[31]

It is worth noting that the works read by Boileau and Racine that evening were newly written. *Alexandre le Grand* was first performed in December of that year, and the first edition of the satires only came out a year later. Once again, following the example of the Blue Room and its authors' readings, the hôtel de Nevers provided a meeting place for society and the literary world, arrogating to itself the role of mentor in matters of taste.

At the beginning of the next century, in another hôtel de Nevers—which no longer stood by the Pont-Neuf but near the Louvre—the Marquise de Lambert resurrected the habit of inviting writers to read their latest works before they were sent to the printers. This practice, handed on from drawing room to drawing room throughout the eighteenth century, naturally had its parallel in academic circles. But while the latter addressed a specialist public, provoking scholarly discussion, the readings designed to entertain society allowed writers to launch both their ideas and their writing, to test the public, and possibly to bear in mind its reaction when completing their work.

Even more than in Paris, it was at the du Plessis-Guénégauds' country house at Fresnes that the hostess gave free reign to her *enjouement, flatterie, tendresse,* and *galanterie*.[32] The masterpiece by the architect François Mansart is no longer standing. Far from the capital, in an idyllic setting, with the collaboration of a select group of friends, social life could once more turn its back on duty, ambition, and the cares of the world and abandon itself to the pure pleasure of the game. Nothing encouraged this happy transformation more than the company's passion for acting and disguise. Mlle de Scudéry was the first to give the lady of the house a literary name in *Clélie* by including portraits of the state minister and his wife as Amalthée and Alcandre.[33] The stories to which they most liked to refer in their society games were the heroic legends and old chivalric romances that had so delighted the hôtel de Rambouillet. Echoes of this can be found in the correspondence of their distant "Quinquoi."[34] Posted as ambassador to Sweden, Arnauld de Pomponne wrote nostalgically to his dear Alcandre of the "enchanted palace"

31. *Mémoires de Monsieur de Coulanges, suivis de lettres inédites de Mme de Sévigné, de son fils, de l'abbé de Coulanges, d'Arnauld d'Andilly, d'Arnauld de Pomponne, de Jean de La Fontaine, et d'autres personnages du même siècle* (Paris: M. de Monmerqué, J.-J. Blaise, 1820), pp. 470–473.

32. Mlle de Scudéry, *Clélie*, Part 3, Book 2, Vol. 6, p. 814.

33. Mlle de Scudéry, *Clélie*, Part 3, Book 2, Vol. 6, pp. 812–829.

34. The nonsense nickname that the habitués of Fresnes used for themselves.

surrounded by ditches and canals, rising up in the middle of the valley at the confluence of the Brevonne and the Marne. Recalling the river that had been the scene of so much entertainment, he wrote that even "with all the Baltic sea at my disposal" he felt "a real fish out of water."[35]

Pomponne's absence was felt as much by his friends as by himself, and they, from Mme du Plessis-Guénégaud down, kept him informed:

> Nothing seems stranger than a note from Fresnes received in the north. It brings enormous joy and enormous sorrow; it alleviates and increases the sorrow of separation; it helps to support the weight of the embassy by making it still heavier. You understand clearly in fact, incomparable Amalthée, and you, illustrious Alcandre—for God save me from separating you—how sensible one is to the pleasure of seeing in the same letter the names of Sévigné, of Lafayette, and La Rochefoucauld, and how much one suffers at the same time, having hardly missed any of the most memorable events at Fresnes, from not having been at one of the most notable. On more than one occasion I have seen the Brevonne rise from its grotto; I played my part there in the Comtesse de Bourgogne's surprising adventure; I witnessed Louis Bayard's different transformations.... In fact nothing remarkable had passed me by since the birth of the Quiquoix; but today, and I have a great desire to complain about it to the embassy, I missed Mademoiselle de Sévigné's [reference to] *salement*. But are you not cruel, all of you, insofar as you do not explain such words to me?[36]

New games were added to the old, games that were incomprehensible to anyone not present, which were bound to intensify the feeling of distance. On August 1, Mme de Sévigné described for him a typical moment of aristocratic *loisir*. Several like-minded people were gathered together in an absolutely beautiful place apart. Sunk in the peaceful happiness of *dolce far niente*, they talked, sketched, thought, and dreamed while waiting to continue their childish game of dressing up once again as knights and ladies of yore:

> With respect to the King's service, I think that you, Monsieur l'ambassadeur, would be very glad to be here with us rather than in Stockholm looking at the sun out of the corner of your eye only. I must tell you how I am placed at

---

35. Arnauld de Pomponne to M. de Guénégaud, April 17, 1666, quoted in Chatelain, *Le Surintendant Nicolas Foucquet*, p. 64.

36. Quoted in *Mémoires de M. de Coulanges, suivis de lettres inédites*, pp. 497–499. In "*J'ai manqué le salement de Mademoiselle de Sévigné*," the reference to *salement* ("dirtily") surely depended on some inside joke whose meaning is lost to the modern reader, as much as it was to the distant Pomponne.

the moment. I have Monsieur d'Andilly on my left, that is to say on the side of my heart; I have Mme de Lafayette on my right; Mme du Plessis is in front of me, amusing herself by scribbling some little drawings; Mme de Motteville a little further off is in a deep reverie.... I am certain, Monsieur, that this company would greatly please you, particularly if you knew how we remember you, how much we love you, and of the bitterness we are beginning to feel against Your Excellency, or rather on account of your worth, which for so long keeps you four or five hundred leagues distant from us.[37]

We should not allow such elegant dilettantism to deceive us. All the players in the scene described by Mme de Sévigné had a profound understanding of human nature and of the world; they were unusually cultured, and they brought a surprising degree of theological understanding to bear on their Christian faith and on the examination of their doubts. At least three of them excelled in the art of writing.

Mme de Motteville, lady-in-waiting to Anne of Austria, was by then over fifty and busy finishing her *Mémoires*. The Queen she had so faithfully served had died a few months earlier, leaving her with a last duty—to defend her mistress for posterity. But discretion and loyalty were not enough to disguise the tragic reality of court life. The memoirs Mme de Motteville was writing in her retreat were not only an invaluable, irreplaceable firsthand account of Louis XIII's reign, of the Regency, and of aristocratic motivation and crown decisions. They were also a serious reflection on the marked incompatibility of worldly and Christian values, and on a kind of great baroque "vanity" in which magnificence and splendor brought moral misery and the soul's perdition in their wake.

Mme de Lafayette, on the other hand, was at court during the very years Mme de Motteville was writing. Unlike Mme de Motteville, she had no official position but owed her presence there to Anne of Austria's young daughter-in-law, Henrietta of England—wife of the King's brother, Monsieur—who favored the countess with her friendship and often sought her company. Mme de Lafayette, too, might have written her *Mémoires* to do justice to the enchanting princess who died in the first flower of youth. But for her, the closed, claustrophobic court life was primarily a privileged place in which to observe the passions—love, jealousy, ambition—and vendettas. Their attendant disasters would be carefully analyzed in her novels.

But on that peaceful August afternoon, she was probably engrossed in thoughts of her own love affair with La Rochefoucauld. We know how determinedly Mme de Lafayette pursued him, seeking to engage the sympathy of both Mme de Sablé

37. Mme de Sévigné to Pomponne, August 1, [1667], in Mme de Sévigné, *Correspondance*, Vol. 1, p. 87.

and the Comte de Saint-Paul, the duke's son by Mme de Longueville. Fresnes was probably the scene of their first tête-à-têtes; such a beautiful place, with its relaxed, playful atmosphere and its gathering of shared friends, must have seemed from the beginning like the ideal place in which to attempt to conquer the moralist duke. So close to success, the countess must have congratulated herself on her tenacity. And La Rochefoucauld would surely have been there with her that day, had he not judged it opportune to volunteer for the Flanders campaign in order to please Louis XIV.

The third member of the group who was on her way to becoming a great writer was Mme de Sévigné. At the time she had just turned forty and, capable of expressing her extraordinary conversational talents on paper, had already established herself as a gifted letter-writer. She had amused herself by carrying on a gallant intellectual friendship with the Abbé Ménage; with her cousin Bussy-Rabutin she had launched a lively display of letter-writing of which they were both proud, and which they named *rabutinage*; she had sent an uproarious account of Fouquet's trial to the same Pomponne to whom she now wrote from Fresnes.

Where Fouquet was concerned, however, her deftness as a writer ended up getting her into trouble. The superintendent cherished her letters and carefully kept them in a box along with those of the women he courted. When the contents became public at the time of his arrest, this was enough for Mme de Sévigné to be included on the list of his mistresses. Royal whim, in its eagerness to discredit Fouquet, was prepared to plunder his private life, and Mme de Sévigné had thus become its indirect victim. She turned to some of her more influential friends for help. Quite unexpectedly, it was Bussy—with whom she had broken off relations three years earlier—who came to her assistance and loudly proclaimed her virtue and innocence. In the face of scandal, Bussy rediscovered his sense of family solidarity, forgot his resentment, and saved her reputation. To those who remembered what he had written of her in his famous portrait, he replied that he had criticized the young widow's character, not her behavior.

Such chivalry brought about a reconciliation: Bussy solemnly promised to destroy the notorious portrait and Mme de Sévigné agreed to forgive him. The hatchet seemed to have been buried, but worse was to come. In 1665, at the instigation of a malicious troublemaker, several copies of the manuscript of the *Histoire amoureuse des Gaules* (which Rabutin had shared only with his closest friends) began to circulate in both Paris and Versailles. One of them ended up in the hands of an unscrupulous printer. Mme de Sévigné was at last able to read the offensive portrait about which she had heard for so long. "I read and I reread that cruel portrait; I would have judged it very pretty had it been about someone other than myself and by someone other than you," she wrote to her cousin three years later in the course of an epistolary duel. "I even found it so well placed, holding its own so well in the book, that I did not have the consolation of being able to flatter myself that it was by anyone other than you. I recognized it from several things I had heard said about it, rather than from the description of my feelings, which I was quite unable to recognize.... To be in everybody's hands; to be printed; to be part of the book that is the delight of all the provinces, where such things do irreparable harm, to come across oneself in libraries...."[38]

In spite of her justifiable anger, Mme de Sévigné was prepared to forgive again, knowing that Bussy-Rabutin had been even more hurt than she by the book's clandestine publication. On April 17, as the scandal broke, Bussy was sent to the Bastille, and on August 7, exile definitively put an end to his military career. It was a harsh punishment that would last for sixteen years and that, like Fouquet's persecution, sounded a warning note. For a long time censorship had proven powerless to control what was published in France. Printed matter had never been as free—to denounce, insult, slander, and ridicule people regardless of position or rank—as it was during the Fronde. With the beginning of Louis XIV's personal rule, however, the situation changed rapidly. In the King's new politics of control and order, the irreverence and license displayed in the *Histoire amoureuse des Gaules* undoubtedly deserved to be condemned as an example. Nevertheless Bussy's treatment seemed excessively severe, and Mme de Sévigné was the first to protest.

Her feelings of pity and solidarity were understandable, but Bussy's disgrace and his consequent marginalization from society were damaging to the ambitions Mme de Sévigné cherished for her family. "I will admit to you that I am not in the least humble, and it would have been a great joy to me had you made of our name everything of which you were capable,"[39] she wrote to her cousin in exile. Furthermore, she lacked family support at the very moment in which she had to confront the delicate problem of her children's future. Eighteen-year-old Charles needed help establishing a brilliant career, and a good match had to be found for the beautiful Françoise Marguerite, already in the flower of her twenty-first year.

For the third time since Retz's flight and Fouquet's imprisonment, Mme de Sévigné lost someone essential to her in the game of favors and influence that shaped the destinies of the scions of the French nobility. Left on her own to defend the Rabutin reputation, she was determined to acquire the Comte de Grignan for a son-in-law. He was a widower twice over, syphilitic, and fourteen years older than his bride—whose fortune was inadequate for his grandiose tastes. But the count boasted an ancient lineage, a large château in the south of France, good prospects for an important position in the King's administration, and the honor of having been married to Mme de Rambouillet's youngest daughter, Angélique Clarice. In December 1668, with the black humor of which she was always a

---

38. Mme de Sévigné to Bussy-Rabutin, July 26, 1668, in Mme de Sévigné, *Correspondance*, Vol. 1, p. 93.

39. Mme de Sévigné to Bussy-Rabutin, January 23, 1671, in Mme de Sévigné, *Correspondance*, Vol. 1, pp. 147–148.

master, Mme de Sévigné informed Bussy of the lengthy episodes of mourning that had made Grignan such an excellent choice: "All his wives have been considerate enough to have died to make way for your cousin, and his father and son have likewise obliged, so that richer than he has ever been—and furthermore, by his lofty lineage, by his connections as well as his good qualities, he is just such a husband as we could wish for, and, therefore, we are not haggling over terms, as is customary, but instead are taking the word of the two illustrious families into which he married earlier."[40]

The marquise's enthusiasm did not last long. Appointed governor of Provence, Grignan soon removed Françoise from the all-encompassing maternal embrace and carried her off to the remote south. Had Bussy not incurred the King's anger, "the prettiest girl in France"[41] would probably have found a better match in Paris—but we would have neither Mme de Sévigné's letters to her daughter nor those she wrote to her exiled cousin. Bussy's disgrace in fact forced her to forget her bitterness and to continue a brilliant and affectionate correspondence under the old banner of *rabutinage*. It was a real display of bravura by two conversational stars that revolved around mutual admiration. In her correspondence with Bussy, the marquise remained faithful to the aristocratic dictates of the art of pleasing for its own sake. In her letters to Mme de Grignan, however, she put all her talent in the service of passion.

When Françoise de Grignan left, the marquise discovered the intolerable pain of separation. Until then she had carefully avoided the snares of love—"the Other"—and would certainly not have suspected that it would take her by surprise in her tranquil family surroundings just as she turned forty-five. But her daughter's absence shattered Mme de Sévigné's wise equilibrium. It was almost as if tender maternal love had morphed into Eros, driving her into treacherous "unknown territory," into that tragic, passionate area of experience from which she had always distanced herself. It was not only the physical distance between Paris and the château de Grignan in Provence—seven hundred kilometers of bad roads—that distressed her. What Mme de Sévigné required of her daughter was a totally interdependence, and she was quite unable to accept that the countess had other ideas. For one thing, Mme de Grignan was foolish enough to love her husband, to share his ambitions, and to welcome him frequently to her bed despite the many difficult pregnancies this incurred. But above all, she wished to "live her own life" without her mother acting as a "screen" between her and the rest of the world.

---

40. Mme de Sévigné to Bussy-Rabutin, December 4, 1668, in Mme de Sévigné, *Correspondance*, Vol. 1, p. 105; Mossiker, *Madame de Sévigné*, p. 58.

41. Mme de Sévigné to Bussy-Rabutin, December 4, 1668, in Mme de Sévigné, *Correspondance*, Vol. 1, p. 105; Mossiker, *Madame de Sévigné*, p. 58.

Mme de Sévigné thus brought all her bewitching talent into play, but this time not in order to attract admiration for herself or applause for a piece of bravura in some amusing social game. This time her intention was to keep alive, day after day, the interest of the loved one—a loved one who was far away, distracted by other occupations, and needed to be stimulated, moved, and seduced exclusively by means of the written word.

To succeed, Mme de Sévigné set about collecting stories. Twice then three times a week she would send as a gift to her adored daughter stories of Paris, of Versailles; of the glories, the intrigues, and the miseries of the Sun King's reign; of literary masterpieces; of illustrious men and their heroic deaths, and of the horrible ends of criminals and rebels. She would tell of the small details of everyday life, social gossip, conversations with friends, and occasions of fun and laughter. It was an extraordinary feast of information in exchange for news about one thing: Mme de Grignan in her distant Provençal château, her health, her thoughts, and her preoccupations.

On that fatal February 6, 1671—the day on which her daughter left to join her husband, thus preparing the way for the most celebrated correspondence in the French language—Mme de Sévigné dragged herself "weeping" and "dying" to the rue Saint-Jacques to take refuge in the convent of the daughters of Sainte-Marie.[42] The convent belonged to the Order of the Visitation, founded sixty years earlier by Mme de Sévigné's paternal grandmother, Jeanne de Chantal. The nuns always kept a room ready for their foundress's granddaughter.

The marquise's behavior certainly did not appear to be modeled on the austere fortitude of her ancestress, for whom Saint François de Sales had written the *Entretiens spirituels*. On the death of her husband in 1601, Jeanne de Chantal had decided to give up family life for a religious vocation. Unmoved by her thirteen-year-old son's desperation, she left the house by stepping over the poor boy as he lay on the threshold trying to bar her way. Mme de Sévigné had chosen the opposite path, preferring worldly affairs and domestic affections. Just as her father had suffered the cruelty of separation and abandonment as a child, so she felt it now. Unable to stop the carriage that bore her daughter away, she could only weep bitter tears in solitude. After five hours of uninterrupted sobbing at the convent, the marquise regained her grip on life and went to seek comfort from Mme de Lafayette. The broken-hearted mother was not yet ready to accept the designs of Providence. She needed sympathy. And so she turned for consolation to her intimate friend who loved and knew her well.

The Marquise de Sévigné and the Comtesse de Lafayette had met twenty years earlier, in 1651, when the countess's widowed mother had married an uncle of M. de Sévigné's. The natural sympathy felt by the two young women was cemented

---

42. Mme de Sévigné to Mme de Grignan, February 6, [1671], in Mme de Sévigné, *Correspondance*, Vol. 1, p. 149.

with Mme de Lafayette's definitive arrival from the provinces in Paris in 1659. Their friendship lasted for forty years, ending only in death. "Believe me, my dearest," the countess wrote to Mme de Sévigné in 1692, as her end was approaching. "You are the one person in the world whom I have most truly loved."[43]

This friendship, exceptional for both its quality and its duration, perfectly illustrates an entire society's attitude toward friendship. The nobility's longstanding belief in friendship as a disinterested gift of the self had survived the post-Fronde crisis of heroic values far better than love. We have seen Mme de Sablé and Arnauld d'Andilly defending the belief in friendship based on virtue against La Rochefoucauld's cynical doubts. The duke himself, despite having analyzed the flawed nature of friendship in his *Maximes*, negated his theory in practice. In his self-portrait he wrote, "I love my friends and I love them in such a way that I would not hesitate for one moment to sacrifice my interest to theirs."[44]

Noblemen and noblewomen had always claimed to cultivate friendship in accordance with the sensibilities and values quintessential to their education. From the man's point of view, friendship represented the highest expression of a caste morality that saw loyalty, solidarity, and honor as the principle guarantees of strength and belonging. Friendship among women, on the other hand, allowed them to cultivate their own values, to confide in one another, to express warmth, and to comfort one another without risk to their reputations.

It was Montaigne who in the previous century had profoundly altered the thinking on friendship, freeing it from the realms of social class, transporting it into the free zone of intellectual affinity, and giving it a central position in the moral and emotional life of modern man. In welcoming his teaching, seventeenth-century society culture had broadened the field to include women in the communal experiment, and suggested friendship as the best meeting ground between the sexes. *Honnête galanterie* had ceased to be a myth and instead became a form of protocol in the meeting between two different mentalities and two ways of dealing with life, both of which were destined to compromise and change. In the world of the nobility, love had always exalted the dichotomy between reality and the ideal; friendship now allowed for a noble compromise. It became the sign of a successful marriage. With passion pushed to the geographic margins of the *Carte de Tendre*, the "precious" movement, in the name of elective affinities, paradoxically found itself coming to the same conclusions as those of the institution—marriage—it meant to confront.

If we are to trust Mlle de Scudéry and see *Clélie* as an accurate representation of Parisian life circa 1650, we will see that the dominant moral value in the novel

---

43. Mme de Lafayette to Mme de Sévigné, January 24, [1692], in Mme de Lafayette, *Œuvres complètes*, p. 661.

44. La Rochefoucauld, "Portrait de M.R.D. fait par lui-même," in *Maximes*, p. 257.

is no longer heroism but friendship. Her famous descriptions of her characters give us an image of a society in which the greatest merit lies in building relationships and putting them to the service of friendship. Such mutual support was in keeping with the ideals of solidarity and harmony typical of various groups, from Mlle de Scudéry's Saturday gatherings, to the "solitaries" at Port-Royal des Champs, to the du Plessis-Guénégauds' habitués and Fouquet's court. In whatever milieu, friendship was a means of co-option and a medium whereby individuals could distinguish themselves and establish their identities. But it could also be, as in Fouquet's case particularly, a school of tolerance—"an opening," in the words of Chantal Morlet-Chantalat, "to the diversity of opinions that, in many ways, announce the best of the eighteenth century."[45]

Soon a jealous, controlling Louis XIV would summon the nobility to court, proving that he valued admiration and obedience far more than friendship. But even before the Sun King's reign had run its course, Mme de Lambert founded the first eighteenth-century salon, in which she welcomed the heirs of that ideal society in the belief that "all the duties of *honnêteté* were incorporated in the duties of perfect friendship."[46] When she was asked "if friendship could exist between persons of different sexes," she replied as a true society lady and as a true *précieuse*. Not only was it possible; such friendship was even superior in intensity, complicity, and seduction to a friendship between two people of the same sex.[47] Mlle de Scudéry had already said as much when she wrote that "the sweetest and most sensitive [friendship] is that which unites an *honnête homme* to an intelligent and noble-hearted woman, so long as neither one nor the other is in love."[48]

Mme de Sévigné was proud of her talent for friendship. "Monsieur de La Rochefoucauld says that I satisfy his idea of friendship in every circumstance and instance,"[49] she wrote in one of her first letters to her daughter. Everything indicates that Mme de Lafayette shared the duke's judgment. In his *Mémoires* Talleyrand describes the conversations of this formidable trio as one of the high points of civilization under the *ancien régime*. We know that beginning in the

45. Chantal Morlet-Chantalat, *La "Clélie" de Mademoiselle de Scudéry: De l'épopée à la gazette: un discours féminin de la gloire* (Paris: Champion, 1994), p. 497.

46. Mme de Lambert, "Avis d'une mère à son fils," in *Œuvres*, edited by Robert Granderoute (Paris: Champion, 1990), p. 60.

47. Mme de Lambert, "Traité de l'amitié," in *Œuvres*, pp. 168–170.

48. Mlle de Scudéry, *Entretiens de morale*, two volumes (Paris: J. Anisson, 1692), Vol. 1, pp. 81–82; quoted in Nicole Aronson, "Les femmes dans les 'Conversations morales' de Mademoiselle de Scudéry," in *Onze Nouvelles Études sur l'image de la femme dans la littérature française du dix-septième siècle*, edited by Wolfgang Leiner (Tübingen: Gunter Narr/Paris: Jean-Michel Place, 1984), p. 87.

49. Mme de Sévigné to Mme de Grignan, February 25, [1671], in Mme de Sévigné, *Correspondance*, Vol. 1, p. 169.

1670s, when the two ladies and La Rochefoucauld were all in Paris, these conversations took place almost every day in Mme de Lafayette's salon or, depending on the season, in her sweetly scented garden. From what La Rochefoucauld has told us about himself, we can imagine the infinitely courteous nobleman delighting in the company of the two women, refraining from taking the lead but backing them up and spurring them on with his witty comments and ironical interjections. So too, can we imagine Mme de Sévigné in all her different moods contributing her repertoire of news and irresistible comment. Whether melancholy or laughing gaily, she would be ready to give her best for the sheer pleasure of seeing the merriment she provoked in others.

It is, however, next to impossible to penetrate Mme de Lafayette's reserve or to establish any degree of intimacy with her. Whereas Mme de Sévigné was ready to open her heart to others, the countess avoided talking about her feelings and jealously guarded her secrets. Not only does comparison between these two attitudes throw light on the characters of the two friends, it also reveals two different ways of establishing oneself in society. Both were rich heiresses and far better educated than other women of their social position. Mme de Sévigné had advanced her learning "in the field" by taking part in Parisian life, attending the salons, listening to the opinions of dilettanti and *savants* alike, going to the theater, reading the literature of the day, and training her ear and her taste in the school of polite society. Mme de Lafayette, on the other hand, had prepared herself for society in solitude, priming herself for future experience through meditation and study.

Marie-Madeleine de La Vergne had left Paris with her mother and stepfather after the Fronde and in 1655 married the Comte de Lafayette, who took her away with him to his estate in the Auvergne. She had thus lived in provincial isolation from 1653 to 1659. These were years of tremendous change in fashion and taste in the capital, and Mme de Lafayette was obliged to educate herself, by reading, writing, and trusting to the epistolary advice of the erudite Abbé de Ménage—also a longtime admirer of the Marquise de Sévigné's. The friendship between the two women, which began before Mlle de La Vergne's forced departure from the capital, had not escaped Ménage's notice. Already in August 1652, the marquise had delighted in teasing the abbé, accusing him of pretending to take offense at her "giving herself entirely to Mademoiselle de La Vergne."[50] Mme de Sévigné's rival for the abbé's attention could not claim to be as beautiful, but she was eight years younger and prepared to make advances to Ménage that could be excused only by her lack of worldly experience and her distance from Paris. The marquise laughingly predicted that the abbé would within ten years stop dedicating his verses to her in order to pay homage to Mme de Lafayette.

---

50. Mme de Sévigné to Ménage, August 19, [1652], in Mme de Sévigné, *Correspondance*, Vol. 1, p. 19.

Far from interrupting her correspondence with the abbé, Mme de Lafayette's marriage transformed it into an accepted gallant friendship.[51] Her correspondence with Ménage allowed the young woman, relegated as she was to the Lafayettes' ancestral château, not only to join the game of the *Carte de Tendre*, but to follow the distant cultural developments in Paris during the years immediately after the Fronde. Mme de Lafayette could have found no better guide than the abbé. With Pierre Costar, Sarasin, Pellisson and Segrais, he was one of the *nouveaux doctes* who, despite an erudite education, sought to address a wider, non-specialist readership. He might even be said to have led the revival of the minor genres and the literature of entertainment that had once flourished in the Blue Room. This began with the veritable rediscovery of Voiture, whose nephew published his letters posthumously, while Costar devoted various writings to him and Sarasin praised his humor in *Pompe funèbre*. It was precisely the kind of news Ménage sent his young friend, along with a copy of Pascal's *Les Provinciales* and, of course, the last, long-awaited volumes of *Clélie*. In Mlle de Scudéry's novel, Mme de Lafayette recognized, in their Roman disguise, those leading lights of Parisian society whom she had met as a girl in her mother's drawing room. Thus she learned to recognize before meeting them the new, high-profile personalities and to conjure up various social itineraries; she learned, too, of the currents of sympathy and hostility running in different circles and about the style and subjects of the conversation of the day. Proud of decoding the portraits, she did not hesitate to check her accuracy with Ménage and ask for his help in identifying characters whom she did not know. But Mme de Lafayette was not interested in mere gossip. As she was to record years later, she read with Ménage's guidance "in order to learn something."[52] Nor should we be mislead by her characteristic understatement, which she would use widely in her novels. There was nothing vague about the countess's interest in literature; she was driven to reading to fill the lacunae in her knowledge. It was also at the abbé's suggestion that she studied Italian and Latin. Unlike Mme de Sévigné, Mme de Lafayette decided early to try her hand at writing, and she pursued her ends with methodical determination—albeit with the inevitable circumspection and restraint of an aristocratic woman. Again, it was Ménage who encouraged her to perfect her knowledge of the French language and, as she claimed, "taught her how to write."[53]

In her faraway château, Mme de Lafayette thus came to imagine polite society long before she had any experience of it. At the same time, she learned to harness her own talent. But writing was never a lonely occupation for her; Ménage had

51. See Roger Duchêne, *Mme de Lafayette la romancière aux cent bras* (Paris: Fayard, 1988), Chapter 12: "Une espèce de Mme Laure," pp. 102–112.

52. Mme de Lafayette to Ménage [spring 1692], in Mme de Lafayette, *Œuvres complètes*, p. 661.

53. Mme de Lafayette to Ménage [October 12, 1691], in Mme de Lafayette, *Œuvres complètes*, p. 656.

taught her to turn to him for advice and to listen to his criticism. Even after their friendship faded, Mme de Lafayette remained faithful to this collaborative working method in everything she wrote, from *La Princesse de Montpensier* (1662) to *Zaïde* (1669–1671) and *La Princesse de Clèves* (1678).

While Mme de Sévigné, forced by life's vicissitudes to face up to the problems of correspondence, wanted her writing to perfectly reflect her personality and her moods so that her letters absolutely expressed herself, Mme de Lafayette chose to touch the hearts of unknown readers by attempting an experimental genre—that of the *nouvelle*, or novelette—with all its attendant problems. She did so with the active advice of writers and *savants*.

Naturally the countess took great care to preserve her anonymity, but the precision with which she revised her work and her desire to bring it to public attention obliges us to reflect on the professionalism of amateurs. And it is hardly an accident that the successful launch of *La Princesse de Clèves*—with its prepublication readings, articles in the *Mercure*, and organized reviews—was comparable in efficacy and success only to the promotion of La Rochefoucauld's *Maximes*.

When she returned definitively to Paris in 1659, just as the fashion was changing again and women's intellectual ambitions were becoming the butt of merciless satire, Mme de Lafayette temporarily put her literary aspirations aside and concentrated on establishing herself in society. She was twenty-five and, like Mme de Sévigné, her own mistress. Her husband was not dead, but he much preferred living in the country with his friend Jacques de Bayard and merely paid the occasional, most courteous of visits to his wife and their two children. If Mme de Sévigné's driving force was her *joie de vivre*, Mme de Lafayette's was ambition. In the first place, the countess appeared to attach little importance to love. While still unmarried, she had declared that she not only had no illusions about love but that she had none about affection either. Her absolute priority was social standing: family success and prestige, inheritance, and the careers of her children. Marriage had allowed her to join an illustrious family, albeit one in decline, and it was now up to her, with her money, intelligence, and determination, to readorn the ancestral escutcheon. Once settled in her house in the rue de Vaugirard, Mme de Lafayette immediately displayed both a know-how in the art of social relations and remarkable business savvy—with surprising energy for one in such delicate health. In any case, the two were closely connected. It would have been difficult for the countess to manage her family affairs, bring lawsuits, throw herself into risky investments, and see to her children's future without the support of well-placed friends.

So Mme de Lafayette set out in the Marquise de Sévigné's footsteps. She paid her respects to the Grande Mademoiselle and contributed to her celebrated *Recueil* with a portrait of the marquise; she became a close friend of Mme du Plessis-Guénégaud's, a frequent visitor to her hôtel de Nevers and château de

Fresnes; with Ménage, she looked in on the fashionable literati and *savants*: Mlle de Scudéry and Pellisson, Segrais and Huet. She did not need to be part of Fouquet's court for La Fontaine to dedicate to her some verses in the "precious" style, in which he compared the game of love to billiards. Clearly determined to please, but without Mme de Sévigné's natural attraction and contagious cordiality, Mme de Lafayette was seductive for her psychological insight and intellectual elegance. She is known to have had a liking for playful irony and to have excelled at *belle raillerie*—skillful teasing. She had learned it from reading Voiture alone in Auvergne, and used it now to disguise her breadth of reading and to protect herself from the ridicule that threatened the *femmes savantes*.

Parisian society was the scene of Mme de Lafayette's self-advancement until 1661, but with Henrietta of England's marriage to the King's brother, Monsieur, the countess's social network extended even to the court. In his well-known essay "La cour et la ville," Erich Auerbach was the first to theorize the dualism of civil and court society—first Paris and the Louvre, then Paris and Versailles—which represented two different realities, two mentalities, two parallel lifestyles. They could either ignore one another, live together harmoniously, or fight, but neither could gain ascendancy over the other.[54] Mme de Lafayette is one of the privileged few who was accepted as a citizen of both worlds, crossing the boundaries as she pleased.

Unlike Mme de Sévigné (who was typical of the *ville*), Mme de Lafayette was to have direct experience of the court, taking more than a moral lesson from it. Madame's affection and Monsieur's liking for her, together with Louis XIV's respect, meant that she was able to make friends with princes of the blood and ministers and to penetrate the world of intrigue and of politics. She could turn this not only to her social advantage but to the advantage of her business affairs as well. Her house became a center of power, and she was able to ask for and dispense favors to a vast number of friends and acquaintances. Her relationship with La Rochefoucauld, duke and peer de France, was perhaps part of this social awareness. The old Frondeur, back again at court, could not but rejoice at the countess's success, and for her part, Mme de Lafayette used her most distinguished connections to attract his. Mme de Sablé might well persist in treating her coldly, but on the day her young rival brought Monsieur for a visit, she was obliged to treat her with some respect.

In 1663, after thirteen years, Mme de Lafayette's friendship with Ménage underwent a terrible crisis. Ménage may have been resigned to keeping within the bounds of his position as intellectual mentor and gallant abbé, but he could not bear his friend's growing intimacy with La Rochefoucauld. As Voiture had

---

54. Erich Auerbach, "La cour et la ville," in *Scenes from the Drama of European Literature: Six Essays* (Meridian, 1959), pp. 133–182.

already felt obliged to remark, the social utopia encouraged dangerous illusions of equality, which sometimes made it more difficult to accept reality. Thus driven by both jealousy and a sense of social inferiority, Ménage began to lose touch with the countess, although he helped her to write and publish her first story, *La Princesse de Montpensier*, or "notre Princesse," as Mme de Lafayette wrote to him in an expression of sincere gratitude.[55]

At the time of Mme de Lafayette's arrival in Paris, Mme de Sévigné was already a star in the social firmament and so served as a model for the newcomer. Ten years later, the situation seemed more or less to have reversed, so that it was the countess who called the tune. From the 1670s on, Mme de Lafayette not only enjoyed a social position the likes of which Mme de Sévigné had never achieved, but it was also the younger woman who, in their friendship, adopted the more mature, more protective role. At least this is the impression given both by Mme de Lafayette's letters to the marquise when the latter was staying with her daughter in 1673 and those written in the last years of her life. Unlike the marquise, Mme de Lafayette did not like letter-writing and attached little importance to it. All her attention, perfectionism, and stylistic rigor were concentrated on her secret activity as a novelist. Letters for her were no more than a simple and practical means of communication, essential to her many social relationships. The extent to which they were either elaborate or complimentary depended on circumstances and obeyed the inevitable rules of *bienséances*. No effort of the imagination was required, so there was no pleasure in the telling. The functional, laconic style she adopted was the antithesis to Mme de Sévigné's. "So do not measure our friendship in letters. Were I to write you one page a month I would love you just as much as you would love me were you to write ten pages in eight days,"[56] she assured the marquise, who complained of receiving few letters.

Despite this declaration, the desire to reaffirm her friendship with Mme de Sévigné and to express her displeasure at their separation is evident in every one of her letters. She knew that the marquise suffered from a secret weakness at which none of the portraits of her hinted, including her own. This unique fault—"the only thing about you that can displease me"—was "mistrust."[57] Perhaps the marquise's need to attract and to entertain disguised a fear of not being really loved—a fear that her daughter's withdrawal had greatly exacerbated, which extended even to her closest relationships.

---

55. Mme de Lafayette to Ménage, [end of August 1662], in Mme de Lafayette, *Œuvres complètes*, p. 573.

56. Mme de Lafayette to Mme de Sévigné, June 30, [1673], in Mme de Lafayette, *Œuvres complètes*, p. 617.

57. Mme de Lafayette to Mme de Sévigné, June 30, [1673], in Mme de Lafayette, *Œuvres complètes*, p. 617.

Mme de Lafayette made use of a surprising medical metaphor to persuade the marquise of how vitally important their friendship was to her. Mme de Sévigné's presence acted like a tonic on the countess, combating the vapors and depression and "refreshing her blood."[58] The eternal invalid who shared the obsession of her times for purification of the body, bleeding, purges, and emetics could not have described the regenerative power of her friendship with the marquise more emphatically or more precisely.

But Mme de Lafayette was not only concerned repeatedly to prove her own attachment. She also occasionally interfered affectionately though decisively in the marquise's private affairs, which reveals much about the extent of their intimacy. She counseled Mme de Sévigné to be more indulgent with her son, Charles, and not to favor her daughter; not to ruin her life by worrying too much about money and condemning herself to long and lonely exile on the family estate in Brittany in order to spend a little less; not to force herself into isolation; to show more consideration for herself—at least so as not to alarm her friends.

In her letters to the marquise, Mme de Lafayette's directness is proof of their closeness. The two women knew each other well enough to be able to read between the lines, and when, three years after Henrietta of England's death, the countess wrote to her friend, "Yesterday I reread several of her letters, I am quite full of her,"[59] she knew that Mme de Sévigné, with whom she must often have talked about the poor princess, would understand the strength of her emotion.

Society life was the only subject on which Mme de Lafayette was prepared to write expansively. She knew from personal experience how important it was for anyone out of Paris to be kept in touch with society news. She was, moreover, so used to discussing it with her friend that she could hardly resist writing about it. So from time to time she sent her pieces of news and gossip, raw material that their conversation would have transformed into precious jewels and on which Mme de Lafayette had no desire to work alone. Just a few lines can reveal the tendency for psychological and moral observation and the satirical genius that presided in her home in the rue de Vaugirard:

> Your son is madly in love with Mlle de Poussai; he aspires only to be as trans-
> fixed as La Fare. M. de La Rochefoucauld says that [Charles] Sévigné's ambi-
> tion is to die of a love he does not feel, for we do not believe him to be made
> of the stuff of passion. I am disgusted by La Fare's passion. It is too great
> and too slavish. His mistress does not respond to the least of his feelings. She

---

58. Mme de Lafayette to Mme de Sévigné, April 15, [1673], in Mme de Lafayette, Œuvres complètes, p. 614.

59. Mme de Lafayette to Mme de Sévigné, June 30, [1673], in Mme de Lafayette, Œuvres complètes, p. 617.

supped with Longueil at a concert on the very evening of his departure. To sup in company when your lover leaves, and when he is leaving to join the army, seems like a capital crime to me; but I doubt I am well versed in such matters.[60]

Mme de Sévigné was the first to make fun of her son's love affairs, his sentimental attachments and his failed affairs alike, and La Rochefoucauld's acid comment would certainly have provoked a smile. But we do not know whether she shared the countess's indignation about La Fare's indifferent lover; this was the same La Fare who had broken Mme de La Sablière's heart. Interaction in love and the refinement of lovers' behavior were two of the great subjects of "precious" argument and gave rise to unending discussions, but in this instance, at least, Mme de Lafayette seems to have been talking mainly to herself, recording a slice of life that struck her novelist's imagination. The heroine of *La Princesse de Clèves* makes her first implicit admission of love for the Duc de Nemours by refusing to go to a ball that he cannot attend, knowing that for him there is "no affliction comparable to that of seeing one's mistress at a ball, except knowing that she is there, when one is not there oneself."[61]

There has been endless discussion about the authenticity of and the interpretation of the well-known sentence attributed to Mme de Lafayette about her relationship with La Rochefoucauld: "He gave me *esprit*, but I reformed his heart."[62] There is certainly no sign of this metamorphosis in La Rochefoucauld's work. Indeed, the increased misogyny in the second edition of the *Maximes* (1666) was so obvious that it caused the Abbess de Malnoue to write to the author: "It seems to me that Mme de Lafayette and I clearly deserve that your opinion of our sex in general should be a little better."[63] It is out of place to question whether the "precious" valetudinarian and the scar-faced old Frondeur with his wounded pride ever shared a bed. Their union was, rather, a perfect illustration of that *amitié amoureuse* about which an entire generation fantasized. It was neither a prudent choice nor a sublimated love nor a worldly game. It was a meeting between two people who shared the same interests, tastes, ambitions, and prejudices and who preferred a deep, quiet friendship to passion. They were two people without illusions, both equally determined to cultivate the sensitive plant of their friendship with loving care. Mme de Sévigné claimed that La Rochefoucauld had never been in love,[64] and her testimony could not be more precise: "A companionship filled

---

60. Mme de Lafayette to Mme de Sévigné, May 19, [1673], in Mme de Lafayette, *Œuvres complètes*, p. 615.

61. Mme de Lafayette, *The Princesse de Clèves*, translated by Robin Buss (1962; Penguin, 1992), p. 53.

62. Segrais, *Segraisiana*, p. 28.

63. Letter from Mme de Rohan to La Rochefoucauld [1671–1674], in La Rochefoucauld, *Maximes*, p. 589.

64. Mme de Sévigné to Mme de Grignan, October 7, [1676], in Mme de Sévigné, *Correspondance*, Vol. 2, p. 416.

with all the friendship and trust possible between two people of unusual worth; add to that the circumstance of bad health, which made them necessary one to the other.... I do not believe that any passion could be greater than the strength of such a liaison."[65] In this "so delicious companionship," the intellectual and sentimental exchange enriched the psychological understanding and emotional experience of both while tying them ever more closely together.

While Mme de Lafayette continued to observe human behavior, La Rochefoucauld never stopped working on his census of the ambiguities on which human behavior was based. In 1673 he was preparing the fourth edition of the *Maximes*, which was due to be published at the end of the following year; from the salon in the rue de Vaugirard he continued to ask Mme de Sablé, Mme de Rohan (formerly Abbess of Caen, now Abbess of Malnoue), and of course Mme de Lafayette what they thought of his new sentences. Mme de Lafayette then sent them to Mme de Sévigné, who was with her daughter in Provence at the time. "Here is a question about two maxims: 'Infidelity is forgiven, but never forgotten'; 'Infidelity is forgotten, but never forgiven.' Would you prefer to have been unfaithful to your lover whom you still love, or that he had been unfaithful to you whom he too still loves?"[66] It is difficult in the midst of such casuistry to see where acute observation ends and the taste for abstract formula begins. (We certainly know that La Rochefoucauld was not speaking from his own experience, since he had neither forgiven nor forgotten Mme de Longueville's betrayal.)

Three months later, conversation was fired by another of La Rochefoucauld's reflections: "There are those who have more wit than taste, and others who have more taste than wit; but taste is more capricious and more varied than wit."[67] By virtue of hairsplitting, even the cleverest commentators ended up losing their way:

> I do not know if Mme de Coulanges has written to you about a conversation we had after dinner at the Gourville house with Mme Scarron and the Abbé Testu about people whose taste is superior or inferior to their wit. We threw ourselves into discussing all the subtleties until we could no longer understand anything. If the Provençal air, which refines everything further, adds to your view of such things, you will be in the clouds. "Your taste is superior to your wit, so is Monsieur de La Rochefoucauld's, as is mine, although not so much as both of yours"; here are some examples to guide you.[68]

---

65. Mme de Sévigné to the Comte de Guitaut, April 5, [1680], in Mme de Sévigné, *Correspondance*, Vol. 2, pp. 896–897.

66. Mme de Lafayette to Mme de Sévigné, July 14, [1673], in Mme de Lafayette, *Œuvres complètes*, p. 618.

67. La Rochefoucauld, "Des goûts," in *Réflexions diverses*, X, *Maximes*, p. 201.

68. Mme de Lafayette to Mme de Sévigné, September 4, [1673], in Mme de Lafayette, *Œuvres complètes*, p. 619.

Mme de Lafayette and her friends were not the only ones to contemplate the notion of taste, attempting to understand its every nuance. It was no coincidence that two years earlier Père Bouhours had included the word "taste" in a list of fashionable words. The metaphorical use of the term, meaning a kind of immediate judgment that anticipated every thought, went back to the preceding century, but it was only in the last decade that it had become established as one of the fundamentals of *honnêteté*. Those who first promoted it—from Mlle de Scudéry to the Chevalier de Méré, La Rochefoucauld, and Saint-Évremond—had immediately understood how important the idea of taste could be to an élite in search of some kind of redress. Heroic morality loved a challenge and encouraged extremes of action, whereas the morality imposed by *honnêteté* taught realism and prudence and limited the field of action to society life. But confidence in his own taste allowed the man of the world to be indisputably in charge of his own senses and thereby peacefully to affirm his natural superiority.

"True beauty of spirit consists in just and refined discernment," Bouhours wrote; and this type of discernment, which "makes things be seen as they are in themselves," was at all times an essential quality of the *honnête homme*.[69] There was nothing mechanical about a perfect education; it demanded tact and discretion and depended largely on intelligence and intuition. Psychological understanding and a precise grasp of ambience went hand in glove with the ability to divine the most appropriate tone and topic, to fit in harmoniously whatever the circumstances, and to always please, regardless of what happened.

If the concept of taste, seen as much as a perceptive ability as a social and moral quality, was inextricably linked to *honnêteté*, its function, from the 1660s on, was extended by the demands of social life to include the arts. Since literature, the theater, music, dance, and conversation all played so important a part in a society man's *loisirs*, a growing aesthetic awareness was inevitable. But in a nonpedantic culture of leisure, such awareness could not depend on doctrine or abstract rules; it was acquired by instinct, thanks to infallible intuition. This intuition was born of intelligence and sensitivity, a certain *je ne sais quoi* not governed by reason alone, which discovered in a fashionable word—*goût*—the means of defining itself.

In trusting faithfully to his own senses, the man of taste did not, however, intend to affirm his own diversity. He had no wish to stand out. What he aspired to was to feel at one with the aesthetic and ethical values of his world and to interpret them perfectly. His selection was therefore quite arbitrary, for as Claude Chantalat writes, "There is only one way of having good taste, since all things have but one form of beauty, which an upright mind cannot fail to recognize in the light of reason."[70]

---

69. Bouhours, "Le bel esprit," in *Les Entretiens d'Ariste et d'Eugène*, p. 115.

70. Claude Chantalat, *À la recherche du goût classique* (Paris: Klincksieck, 1992), p. 43.

Saint-Évremond claimed that taste was inborn and could neither be learned nor taught; Méré thought that it could be handed down; but the most commonly held belief was that it was a gift of nature to be enhanced through education—a natural education not unlike an education in the *bienséances*, which occurred through osmosis, observation, conversation, reading, and the contemplation of beautiful things. Whatever its origins, however, taste was "the supreme mark of acquired refinement and of social belonging," in the words of Jean-Pierre Dens. "Its edicts [had] the force of the law," and whoever ignored them incurred general disapproval.[71]

By including the arts within its jurisdiction, taste ceased to be society's exclusive property but became a matter for the consideration of writers and critics, establishing itself as one of the key concepts of the classical aesthetic. As with every area of human experience, taste was subjected to reason. "Compared with wit and judgment," Chantalat writes, "its function was to rein in genius and to control bursts of inspiration,"[72] bringing it into mutually supportive agreement with the rules. But the denizens of polite society were not prepared to be intimidated by scholars. They needed neither Aristotle nor Plato to appreciate the beauty of a work of literature, and so they continued to stand by what appealed to their own sensibilities and by their own sense of the appropriate.

There were two equally important reasons why the literati could not ignore society's dictates. Good taste could only be studied by frequenting *bonne compagnie*, and without its approval no work could hope to be successful. Thus, paradoxically, aristocratic dilettantism found itself spreading discord among the *savants*. Many of them, following the example of Voiture, who had always been his own man, opted for society culture—and not just for practical reasons. The nobility's antihumanistic, antidogmatic position, which held that its way of life and its taste were superior to those of any other time, encompassed an idea of liberty and a faith in the present that some writers—the Moderns—recognized as their own. Thus began the systematic collaboration between society and literature whose remarkable interaction created the conditions necessary for the triumph of the Enlightenment.

With the famous literary *Querelle* between the Ancients and the Moderns, France became aware of her intellectual superiority. Right until the approach of the Revolution in 1789, it would claim a cultural hegemony that descended straight from the Latin literary and humanist *res publica*. For this to happen, criteria had to change, society had to adopt new parameters, and "taste and

---

71. Jean-Pierre Dens, *L'honnête homme et la critique du goût: Ésthétique et société au XVIIe siècle* (Lexington: French Forum Publishers, 1981), p. 89.

72. Chantalat, *À la recherche du goût classique*, p. 95.

honnêteté à la française," as Emmanuel Bury writes, had to be inscribed "as models of civilization and culture for the modern man."[73]

No one exemplified this new way of thinking more illustriously than the Comtesse de Lafayette, the Marquise de Sévigné, and the Duc de La Rochefoucauld. For them, the rigorous aesthetic made no distinction between literature and life. All three were gifted with the highest degree of *esprit*; yet, as we have seen, they preferred to express their personalities through taste, perhaps because, as La Rochefoucauld explained, true good taste retained the imprint of a lost truth. Few possessed it, but, as La Rochefoucauld also wrote, those who do, "by some kind of instinct of whose cause they remain ignorant, always make the right decision."[74] And the three greatest exponents of society culture were first among the few.

---

73. Emmanuel Bury, *Littérature et politesse: L'invention de l'honnête homme (1580–1750)* (Paris: Presses Universitaires de France, 1996), p. 6.

74. La Rochefoucauld, "Des goûts," in *Maximes*, p. 202.

School of Abraham Bosse: *The Women's Dinner*, circa 1610–1640
(Musée de la Renaissance, Écouen, France/
Réunion des Musées Nationaux/Art Resource)

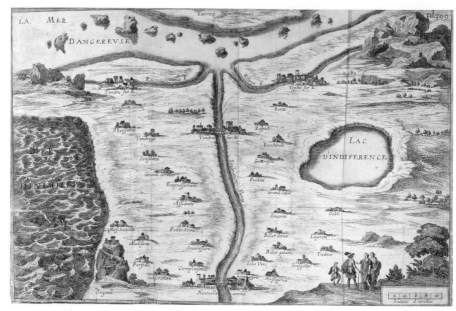

La carte de Tendre, from Madeleine de Scudéry, *Clélie*
(Bibliothèque nationale de France)

Frosne: *The Duchesse de
Longueville* (Bibliothèque
nationale de France)

Daniel Du Moustier: *The Marquise de
Sablé* (Musée du Louvre/Réunion des
Musées Nationaux/Art Resource)

Philippe de Champaigne: *Robert Arnauld d'Andilly*, 1667
(Musée du Louvre/Réunion des Musées Nationaux/Art Resource)

Charles Beaubrun: *La Grande Mademoiselle*
(Musée de la Ville de Paris, Musée Carnavalet, Paris/Bridgeman Art Library)

LEFT: Claude Lefebvre: *Marie de Rabutin-Chantal, Marquise de Sévigné*
(Musée de la Ville de Paris, Musée Carnavalet, Paris/Bridgeman Art Library)

Louis Elle: *Ninon de Lenclos*
(Musée du Louvre/Réunion des Musées Nationaux/Art Resource)

Claude Lefebvre: *Roger de Rabutin,*
Comte de Bussy
(David Bordes/Centre des
Monuments Nationaux, Paris)

Nicolas de Poilley, le Vieux:
The Grand Condé
(Bibliothèque nationale de France)

Jean Petitot the Elder: *Madame de Maintenon*
(Musée du Louvre/Réunion des Musées Nationaux/Art Resource)

François, Duc de La Rochefoucauld (Château des Rochers-Sévigné, Vitré)

Marie-Madeleine Pioche de la Vergne, Comtesse de Lafayette
(Château des Rochers-Sévigné, Vitré)

François de Troy: *The Duchesse du Maine's Astronomy Lesson*
(Musée de l'Île de France–Sceaux)

Anicet Charles Gabriel Lemonnier: *Reading of Voltaire's Tragedy*
'L'Orphelin de la Chine' at the salon of Madame Geoffrin, 1755
(Châteaux de Malmaison et Bois-Preau, Rueil-Malmaison, France/
Réunion des Musées Nationaux/Art Resource)

Madame de Tencin (Musée de Grenoble)

Jean-Marc Nattier: *Madame Geoffrin*, 1738
(Fuji Art Museum, Tokyo/Bridgeman Art Library)

Jean-Marc Nattier: *The Marquise de La Ferté-Imbault*, 1740
(Fuji Art Museum, Tokyo/Bridgeman Art Library)

Michel Barthélémy Ollivier: *Supper of the Prince de Conti*, 1766
(Châteaux de Versailles et de Trianon, Versailles, France/
Réunion des Musées Nationaux/Art Resource)

Élisabeth Louise Vigée Le Brun: *Madame de Staël as Corinne*, 1807
(Chateau de Coppet, Switzerland/Erich Lessing/Art Resource)

I I

MADAME DE LA SABLIÈRE:
PURE SENTIMENT

MME DE LA SABLIÈRE, too, was remarkable for her absolute adherence to the dictates of instinct and taste. For the most enchanting of all the *Grand Siècle*'s distinguished women, however, the two terms did not merely imply aesthetic and social superiority. They proclaimed the demands of a new sensibility, a sensibility inclined to favor the emotions and the heart. In the following century, the Marquise de Lambert described her as the perfect prefiguration of the eighteenth-century ideal of an *âme sensible*:

> One single sentiment, one single transport of the heart, does the soul more credit than all the sayings of the philosophers. . . . A lady who was a model of agreeableness proves my claim. A witty man of her acquaintance was asked one day what she did and what she thought about in her retreat. "She has never thought," he replied, "she only feels." Everyone who knew her agreed that she was the most bewitching person in the world, and that her tastes, or rather her passions, made themselves masters of her imagination and her reason, so that her tastes were always justified by her reason and respected by her friends.[1]

For ten happy years in the 1670s Mme de La Sablière devoted herself to friendship and intellectual inquiry. These two passions did much to alleviate the misery of her marriage and contributed to making her house the freest and most stimulating center of Parisian society of its day. Though initially endowed with many gifts, Marguerite Hessein Rambouillet de La Sablière was cruelly treated by life. Beautiful, intelligent, and extremely cultivated, she was the daughter of a rich Huguenot banker and well connected to the nobility. At the age of fourteen she was married to Antoine Rambouillet de La Sablière, the younger son of another very rich banker,

---

1. Mme de Lambert, *Réflexions nouvelles sur les femmes*, in *Œuvres*, pp. 321–322.

Nicolas Rambouillet du Plessis. Despite the surname, Marguerite's father-in-law was no relation to the family of Arthénice. He belonged to the nouveau riche, and was a somewhat unrefined man who had built a house surrounded by magnificent gardens just outside Paris. This house, the so-called Folie-Rambouillet, would became just as well known as the Blue Room.

Everything pointed to a good match. M. de La Sablière was cultivated, galant, and a tireless versifier. Who better than he could have appreciated the qualities of his wife, described by Marc Fumaroli as "the joint masterpiece of nature, fortune, the republic of letters, and the court aristocracy"?[2] But the "great French madrigalist" was not of that opinion and subjected his wife to every form of maltreatment, despite the three children she bore him. She was obliged to seek a separation. It was 1668. "La belle Sablière," as Mme de Sévigné called her, was nearly thirty and preparing for the best years of her life.

In her new house in the rue Neuve-des-Petits-Champs, Mme de La Sablière gathered around her a mixed elite.[3] She was helped in this by her brother, Pierre Hessein, a friend of Boileau's and Molière's, and by Antoine Menjot, her doctor-philosopher-theologian uncle who was well respected by Pascal, Racine, and Huet. Attracted by their hostess's urbanity, noblemen, elegant women, ambassadors, galant poets, philosophers, doctors, and scientists came to discover the pleasure of discussing their experiences. From the very beginning, eclecticism had been a characteristic of society culture. Several scientific discussions had already taken place in Mme de Sablé's convent drawing room. But the climate in the rue Neuve-des-Petits-Champs was quite different. There was no sign of a society game or of any pastime other than conversation, which, in anticipation of the eighteenth-century salon, completely absorbed the habitués' attention. It was the first time a society circle had included so many philosophers and scientists. And for the first time, it was not the specialists who confronted the amateurs, for the amateurs proved themselves equally ready, not only to apply themselves to the most arduous discussions but also to learn the rudiments necessary to understanding the great philosophical and scientific discoveries of the modern world. For the first time, a society lady—albeit with the modesty of an honnête femme[4]—attracted

---

2. Fumaroli, The Poet and the King, p. 387.

3. Among the women were Mme de Sévigné, Mme de Lafayette, Mme de Coulanges, Mme Scarron, Mme de La Suze, Ninon de Lenclos; among the diplomats, Barrillon d'Amoncourt, Monsieur de Bonrepaus, the Abbé de Chaulieu; among the literati, Mlle de Scudéry, Méré, Pellisson, Conrart, Benserade, Chapelle, Charles Perrault, Fontenelle; among the scientists, Dalancé, Du Verney, Roberval, Sauveur. And there was of course La Fontaine, who lodged in her house.

4. "She loved poetry, and even more so philosophy, but without ostentation," from Pellisson and d'Olivet, Histoire de l'Académie française, two volumes (third edition; Paris: J.-B. Coignard, 1743), Vol. 2, p. 253; quoted in Samuel Menjot d'Elbenne, Mme de La Sablière, ses pensées chrétiennes et ses lettres à l'abbé de Rancé (Paris: Plon, 1923), p. 71.

admiration for her knowledge in all intellectual fields. She brought out the best in her guests by encouraging them to talk about what interested them. The only other woman who could have competed with her was Mme de Montespan's sister, Mme de Fontevrault. "Look at Mme de Fontevrault and Mme de la Sablière," wrote Corbinelli to Bussy-Rabutin, "they understand Homer as we understand Virgil."[5] Of course, Mme de Fontevrault was an abbess.

Mme de La Sablière was not only versed in literature. As a convinced Cartesian, she had studied mathematics, geometry, and astronomy with the best teachers, the most distinguished of whom was François Bernier. The well-known scientist and Orientalist dedicated the *Abrégé de la philosophie de Gassendi* to her in 1678. Six years later, he dedicated his *Doutes* to her. According to Bayle, Mme de La Sablière's reputation was such that Bernier "did not doubt that the illustrious name he put at the top of that treatise would immortalize his work more than his work would immortalize that name."[6] Before long this exchange of favors between intellectuals and socialites would go beyond mere dedications and become a basic business of society life. In eighteenth-century salons, the quality of the guests depended on the prestige of the lady of the house, but she herself guaranteed the distinction of her habitués. "He certainly has great wit; I do not know him, but he has entrée to Mme de Geoffrin's," the Marquis de Chastellux once said of an unknown man. No doubt the same claim could have been made for the guests of Mme de La Sablière.

Not everyone shared this view, however. By allowing her intellectual interests to be known, Mme de La Sablière defied society's conventions and provided satire with an easy target. According to legend, it was with her and her guests that Molière devised the doctor's macaronic Latin in *Le Malade imaginaire*,[7] although he nevertheless caricatured her in *Les Femmes savantes*. And after her death, Boileau—although he had been a frequent guest at her house—used her as his model for the *savante ridicule* in his *Satire X* against women:

> *Qui s'offrira d'abord? Bon c'est une savante*
> *Qu'estime Roberval, et que Sauveur fréquente.*
> *D'où vient qu'elle a l'œil trouble et le teint terni?*
> *C'est que sur le calcul, dit-on, de Cassini,*

5. Letter from Corbinelli to Bussy-Rabutin and to Mme de Coligny of July 30, 1677, *Lettres de Mme de Sévigné*, in *Correspondance*, Vol. 2, p. 511.

6. "Nouvelles de la République des Lettres," Amsterdam, September 1685, p. 233; quoted in Menjot d'Elbenne, *Mme de La Sablière*, p. 74.

7. See the *Notice au Malade Imaginaire*, in *Œuvres de Molière*, edited by Eugène Despois and Paul Mesnard, Vol. 9 of *Les Grands Écrivains de la France* (Paris: Hachette, 1873–1900), pp. 230–231. See also Émile Magne, *Ninon de Lenclos* (1912; Paris: Émile-Paul frères, 1948), pp. 204–205.

Un astrolabe en main, elle a, dans sa gouttière,
À suivre Jupiter passé la nuit entière.
Gardons de la troubler. Sa science, je croi,
Aura pour s'occuper ce jour plus d'un emploi,
D'un nouveau microscope on doit, en sa présence,
Tantôt chez Dalancé faire l'expérience;
Puis d'une femme morte avec son embryon
Il faut chez Du Verney voir la dissection.
Rien n'échappe aux regards de notre curieuse.[8]

It was in fact because of Mme de La Sablière's great reputation that, despite herself, she became involved in a battle of opinions that went quite beyond her. In the *Querelle des Anciens et des Modernes*, the side of the Ancients, led by Boileau, refused to recognize that society—and above all women—had any critical authority. This was the sole prerogative of men of letters. On the other hand, the Moderns, led by Charles Perrault, encouraged the amateur's freedom of judgment and pragmatism in matters of taste—questioning the indisputable authority that the Ancients claimed for themselves. Boileau thus saw fit to undermine the prestige of a woman who had doubly transgressed. Her learning and perfect manners had given the lie to traditional misogyny, and her salon encouraged an interest in science that was so inseparable from progress. Perrault took the initiative to defend his late friend in the *Apologie des femmes*, a reply to the *Satire X*:

The character of the *Savante Ridicule* is said to have been taken from a lady who is no longer with us and whose extraordinary merit should attract nothing but praise. This lady was pleased during her leisure hours to hear talk of Astronomy and Physics; and she even had a very great understanding of these sciences, and of several others with which the beauty and ability of her mind had made her familiar. It remains true that she had no ostentation, and she was no less esteemed for the care she took in hiding her gifts than for her advantage in possessing them. . . . Twenty years ago, when the author of the satire included the two following lines in his work—

---

8. "Who will offer themselves first? Ah well, it is a woman scientist/Whom Roberval esteems and Sauveur visits./Why is her look so troubled and her complexion dulled?/It is, they say, that on Cassini's calculus,/an astrolabe in her hand, and sitting on her roof,/She spent the whole night following Jupiter./Let us take care not to trouble her. Her science I believe,/Will be occupied this day by more than one thing,/A new microscope has in her presence,/Later on at Dalancé's to be tried out;/Then a dead woman with her embryo/Must be seen being dissected at Du Verney's./Nothing escapes the eyes of our curious lady," in *Œuvres complètes de Boileau*, edited by A. Ch. Gidel, four volumes (Paris: Garnier frères, 1870–1873), Vol. 2, pp. 81–82.

Que l'Astrolabe à la main un autre aille chercher,
Si le soleil est fixe ou tourne sur son axe[9]

—this lady had the goodness to point out to him that when one deals in
satire one should know what one is talking about; that those who maintain
that the sun is fixed and immovable are the same as those who claim that it
turns on its axis, and that these are not different opinions, as he seems to say
in his verse. . . . It seems that the vexation he felt on being so corrected
caused him to write this portrait of a *Savante Ridicule*. But the Lady who
instructed him could not be blamed for his ignorance, nor for the mistake he
made in talking of things he knew nothing about.[10]

The Moderns won the day, and Mme de La Sablière led the way for the sister-
hood of the next century. In 1686, Fontenelle chose Mme de La Sablière's second
daughter, the Marquise de La Mésangère, as the interlocutress for his *Entretiens
sur la pluralité des mondes,* a book popularizing science that was destined to be as
successful as the novel *L'Astrée* was in its day. Fifty years later, another marquise,
Mme du Châtelet, introduced Newton to France and set Voltaire on a scientific
path. And in the eighteenth century, society men and women collected minerals and
fossils and set up observatories for astronomy and laboratories for chemistry. They
took a passionate interest in Mesmer's experiments and applauded the launch of
the first hot-air balloon—in the blissful belief that science and progress went hand
in hand with the triumph of reason and the perfection of human nature.

Mme de La Sablière, a daughter of her times, did not yet hold such certainties.
It was, rather, her capacity for feeling that led her to tackle the two existential
themes of greatest concern to seventeenth-century man: the absolute experience of
love and the absolute of God. At thirty-six, having turned her back on the humiliations she had suffered in her marriage, and surrounded by the admiration and
affection of her friends, Mme de La Sablière abandoned herself to love. She loved
with all "the tenderness, the passion, the earnestness, and perfect faithfulness"
that her heart was capable of.[11] The man of her choice, Charles Auguste de La
Fare, had all the talents necessary to shine in society, but none of the virtues—
devotion, strength of character, constancy—required for a love affair. Both sentimental and voluptuous, he distinguished himself mainly by "that amiable lack of

---

9. "With an astrolabe in hand, let another go to find/If the sun is fixed or if it turns on its axis";
Boileau, "Epistle V," lines 28–29, in *Œuvres complètes,* p. 185.

10. Charles Perrault, *Apologie des femmes* (Paris: chez la veuve de Jean-Baptiste Coignard, et Jean-
Baptiste Coignard fils, 1694), f. 1v.

11. Mme de Sévigné to Mme de Grignan, August 4, 1677, in Mme de Sévigné, *Correspondance,* Vol. 2,
p. 515.

vigor and easy morality which made him fully indulgent about whatever men did,"[12] according to Chaulieu, the most epicurean of the society abbés.

Primarily indulgent with himself, La Fare grew tired of Mme de La Sablière, and while continuing to accept her adoration, he made no secret of his increasing indifference. His mistress finally drew the inevitable conclusions. Their relationship, which had lasted about four years, had taken place in full view of society, where there little room for intimacy or secrecy. Membership was based on appearance and the individual's behavior was implacably observed by the group as a whole. A wish to control went hand in hand with a taste for spectacle, all the more so since judgment was based on the same criteria as *honnêteté*. A love affair was condemned or forgiven not in the name of morality but in the name of style. This is made quite evident from Mme de Sévigné's letter to her daughter on the subject of Mme de La Sablière's separation from La Fare:

> You ask me what caused the separation of La Fare and Mme de La Sablière: it was basset [a card game], would you believe it? It was in the name of basset that faithlessness was declared; he abandoned religious adoration for the sake of the prostitute, basset. The moment had come for this passion to cease, even to be transferred to another object; can one believe that basset could be anyone's path to salvation? It is well known that it can open up five hundred thousand paths. She looked first at this distraction, this desertion; she examined all the bad excuses, the insincere reasoning, the pretexts, the embarrassed self-justification, the uncomfortable conversations, the impatience to leave her company, the journeys to Saint-Germain where he gambled, the weariness, the no longer knowing what to say; finally, when she had carefully observed the eclipse that was taking place, and that alien body which little by little obscured all that brilliant love, she resolved to do something; I do not know what this cost her; but, finally, without a quarrel, without reproach, without a scene, without sending him away, without explanation, without wishing to confound him, she eclipsed herself; and without having left her house, to which she still sometimes returns, without having said that she would renounce everything, she finds herself so well at the [hospital of the] Incurables that she spends almost all her life there, feeling with pleasure that her pain is not like that of the invalids she cares for. The superiors at this house are charmed by her wit; she manages them all; her friends visit her; she is always very good company. La Fare plays basset: *Et le combat finit faute de combattants.*[13]

---

12. *Œuvres de Chaulieu*, two volumes (The Hague and Paris: C. Blouet, 1774), Vol. 2, p. 46, note 1, quoted in Menjot d'Elbenne, *Mme de La Sablière*, p. 133.

13. Letter from Mme de Sévigné to Mme de Grignan, July 14, 1680, in Mme de Sévigné, *Correspondance*,

Mme de La Sablière had thus behaved as a perfect *honnête femme*, and there is not a word of blame for La Fare; what is really remarkable is not Mme de La Sablière's pain so much as the elegance of her behavior and the drollness of the story.

Mme de La Sablière left the scene discretely, but the price she paid was a total metamorphosis of self. To escape the anguish of an unhappy affair, the abandoned mistress cut herself off from everything that had until then given her the will to live—her religion, her culture, her friends—and spent ever more time helping people in a place of real suffering. It would have been hard to find anywhere in Paris more terrible than the hospital, which took in the sick and dying poor.

Society at the time was used to this sort of transformation, whether caused by a need for expiation, fear of death, or quite simply ardent spirituality. Six years earlier another woman disappointed in love, Mlle de La Vallière, had left the court to shut herself up with the Carmelites. Unlike the royal mistress, however, Mme de La Sablière did nothing to draw attention to herself but withdrew on tiptoe. "She is devout, really devout," wrote Mme de Sévigné again. "She makes good use of her free will. But is it not God who makes her act so? Is it not God who makes her want to act so? Is it not God who has delivered her from the Devil's dominion? Is it not God who has given her a change of heart? Is it not God who guides and supports her? Is it not God who shows her the path and gives her the desire to be His? It is that which is the glory; it is God who crowns her gifts."[14]

With her conversion Mme de La Sablière gradually discarded her worldly background to become a living proof of divine goodness. Her example was a comfort to Mme de Sévigné in her difficult attempt to accept Providence. And for Mme de Lafayette, who was unable to resign herself to La Rochefoucauld's death, Mme de La Sablière's particular victory over a lost love made her feel "that her pain was not incurable."[15]

In Mme de La Sablière's case, Père Rapin was the chosen instrument of Providence. Having been often defeated, and having seen all the most brilliant women embrace Port-Royal—from Mme de Longueville to Mme to Sablé—the learned Jesuit at last reaped the rewards of his long dedication to society life. Like Père Bouhours, he frequented the salon in the rue Neuve-des-Petits-Champs and had helped Mme de La Sablière fill the void left by the man she loved by teaching her to have hope in the love of God. Rapin, mistrusting extreme gestures, hoped instead

---

Vol. 2, p. 1012. As often happens, the quotation of Corneille from memory is slightly inaccurate: "*Et le combat cessa faute de combattants*" ("And the battle ended for lack of combatants"), *Le Cid*, Act IV, Scene iii.

14. Letter from Mme de Sévigné to Mme de Grignan, June 21, 1680, in Mme de Sévigné, *Correspondance*, Vol. 2, p. 982.

15. Letter from Mme de Sévigné to Mme de Grignan, June 21, 1680, in Mme de Sévigné, *Correspondance*, Vol. 2, p. 982.

for his penitent's gradual conversion. Once she had discarded her Protestantism, he encouraged her to practice self-mortification without breaking her ties with society. By continuing to live with her past, she would make her renunciation all the more worthy and her example would be the more obvious and edifying.

But Mme de La Sablière's anguished sensibilities demanded something more radical, and in 1687, on Rapin's death, she immediately entrusted herself to the Abbé de Rancé's guidance. She was by then forty-seven and had six years left to live. God continued to test her harshly. Louis XIV's revocation of the Edict of Nantes forced her Huguenot son and her sons-in-law to leave France. Then a tumor on the breast forced her to face an illness she had always dreaded. Little time was left for her to expiate—in accordance with the key concept of Trappist faith—her life's mistakes, which she "trembled" to think about. She must now renounce everything to do with that life, beginning with the empty pleasures of conversation at which she had been supreme. "Having flaunted myself too much, I must hide; having listened too much, I must hear nothing more but that which it would please Our Lord to tell me; and having talked too much, I must remain silent."[16]

But perhaps even her worldly success was founded on deception. Being fundamentally artificial, society was satisfied with superficial virtues. Mme de La Sablière had seen her changed life as an act of humility and modesty, whereas the choice was dictated by the subtlest form of *amour-propre*: "I have always been devilishly proud, and all the more so in that I disguised it so well that the world did not notice it, because I seemed modest and humble in the way that the world, which judges only by appearances, understood; but presently I feel strongly that I was all the more abominable in the eyes of He who sounds the depths of all hearts, for I disguised myself *alio fastu* [with a different pride]."[17]

Yet hidden away in the hospital, deaf to the voices of the past and enclosed in silence, Mme de La Sablière did not forget her friend and protégé La Fontaine. Twenty years earlier she had welcomed the poet, then in financial trouble, to the rue Neuve-des-Petits-Champs; then, at the time of her "reformation," she took him with her to the rue Saint-Honoré and arranged for him to continue to live there even after she retired to the Incurables.

She had not wanted to interrupt the flight of the "butterfly of Parnassus"[18] although she was concerned with saving his soul, and she probably had something to do with his conversion if, as Marc Fumaroli suggests, the following words were addressed to him: "I believe that silence, suffering, and peace are all that is necessary to me. So then, Sir, I have shown you my heart of hearts and have produced

16. Mme de La Sablière to M. [Maisne] (the spiritual director to whom Rancé had entrusted her), June 28, 1688, quoted in Menjot d'Elbenne, *Mme de La Sablière*, p. 284.

17. Mme de La Sablière to Rancé [1688], quoted in Menjot d'Elbenne, *Mme de La Sablière*, p. 285.

18. La Fontaine, "Discours à Madame de la Sablière" in *Œuvres complètes*, Vol. 2, p. 645.

in your own the peace I ask for. . . . I ask you again, Sir, to remember me before the Lord. It is only in that way that we must love each other, simply: all the rest is mere illusion, and only the greater when we believe we are practicing charity."[19]

Before remembering her before God, La Fontaine kept his friend's name alive among men with his portrait of her in the prologue to the fable he dedicated to her, "Le Corbeau, la Gazelle, la Tortue et le Rat." The poet dreams of building in verse a temple to Iris[20] and of placing in the sanctuary a statue to the goddess, with "her smiles, her charms,/Her art of pleasing all without knowing it,/Her graces, which the world does praise," adding that "In her eyes I would show each treasure/Of her bright soul." But the attempt was in vain:

> Car ce cœur vif et tendre infiniment,
> Pour ses amis, et non point autrement;
> Car cet esprit qui né du firmament,
> A beauté d'homme avec grâces de femme
> Ne se peut pas comme on veut exprimer.[21]

"To be astonished, to feel, to see reality in its surprising diversity, were gifts common to that superior woman and to the author of Fables."[22] The finest of all seventeenth-century portraits shows us a woman quite unlike any other, but it is also the picture of a *grande dame* who clearly represents the ultimate in half a century of polite society.

---

19. Letter from Mme de La Sablière of August 12, 1692, quoted in Fumaroli, *The Poet and the King*, p. 463.

20. The choice of goddess was highly symbolic. Iris, as Fumaroli reminds us, was the daughter of the god Thaumas, the Wonder, "who had driven the first philosophers to philosophical speculation."

21. "For that heart, sensitive, tender, wholly wise/For her friends' sake, and never otherwise;/That wit which, born as the firmament's prize,/Has man's virtues, woman's grace in full measure/Cannot as one would like be expressed or portrayed." La Fontaine, "The Crow, the Gazelle, the Tortoise, and the Rat," in *The Complete Fables of Jean de la Fontaine*, translated by Norman B. Spector, pp. 639–640.

22. Fumaroli, *The Poet and the King*, p. 389.

12

MADAME DE MAINTENON
AND NINON DE LENCLOS:
THE IMPORTANCE OF REPUTATION

NINON DE LENCLOS was among those who had followed Mme de La Sablière's love affair with the Marquis de La Fare with the greatest sympathy. As a friend of both, she was sensible to the dazzling gentleman's attractiveness and his polished poetry, and admiring of the great culture, intellectual refinement, and graciousness of Mme de La Sablière. She knew, moreover, the source of that noble lady's conjugal unhappiness. Twenty-five years earlier, Ninon had had an affair with Antoine de La Sablière, to whom she yielded with the immortal phrase, "I think I will love you for three months. That is infinity for me!"[1]

From the very beginning, however, Ninon had tried to caution Mme de La Sablière against the violence of her passion, exhorting her in vain to prudence. The clear-sighted courtesan was able to understand how Mme de La Sablière, for all her admirable qualities, could yield to some terrible weakness. On seeing her friend's despair she remarked sorrowfully, "An excess of sensibility is a cruel gift from heaven, and affairs of the heart cause more suffering than they bring joy in the end."[2] But although the conversion of the betrayed mistress and her retreat to the Hôpital des Incurables did not appeal to Ninon's libertine morality, she continued to take an interest and to sympathize sincerely with her poor penitent friend's agonizing misfortunes until the end.

Mme de La Sablière's unhappy fate could only reinforce the disenchantment with which Mlle de Lenclos viewed the feminine condition. Many years earlier, she had taken control of her own destiny, with the declaration, "From this moment on, I am becoming a man."[3] She never regretted her choice. Like the *Précieuses*, Ninon

---

1. Quoted in Émile Magne, *Ninon de Lenclos*, p. 103.

2. Magne, *Ninon de Lenclos*, p. 236.

3. Quoted in Émile Colombey, *Introduction to Correspondance authentique de Ninon de Lenclos comprenant un grand nombre de lettres inédites et suivie de "La Coquette vengée"* (1886; Geneva: Slatkine Reprints, 1968), p. 12.

had a very high opinion of her own worth, and like them she dictated her own conditions and imposed her taste. Yet her way of life seemed diametrically opposed to theirs. She believed not in the religion of love but in the cult of pleasure and in pure friendship, free from any sentimental ambiguity. When she declared that love was nothing more than "a taste based on the senses,"[4] she certainly did not imagine that seventy years later, men and women of good Parisian society would find it perfectly natural to submit to the whims of *amour-goût*—love by attraction.

The lofty composure with which Ninon embraced the career of a courtesan was a reflection of her seasoned hedonism. In early youth her formative reading had been Montaigne, and frequenting libertine circles, she had counted the most impious of them all among her lovers: the Sieur Jacques Vallée Des Barreaux. It was to Charles de Saint-Évremond, however, that she owed her moral and philosophical education. He remained a friend for life and, in old age, dedicated his discourse *Sur la morale d'Épicure* to her, calling her "Léonce moderne."

Even in the free climate of the Regency, an open display of godlessness was imprudent and could be severely punished. As early as 1647 Bussy-Rabutin had been exiled for carousing and singing sacrilegious songs during Lent. When this sort of provocation came from a woman—and a libertine at that—it was intolerable. Ninon had made the mistake of taking a house near the parish of Saint-Sulpice, where the priest, Jean-Jacques Olier, supported by the Compagnie du Saint-Sacrement, was conducting a moralizing campaign against heretics and unbelievers. During Lent in 1651, when a bone fell on the head of a priest passing under a window at dinner time, a scandal broke out, the consequences of which would have been far more severe but for Ninon's presence of mind and Anne of Austria's sense of humor. The indignation of the *dévots*—the "devout" party— was such that the Queen Mother was obliged to send Ninon that most feared of royal documents, a *lettre de cachet*, commanding her to withdraw to a convent of her choice. Unfazed, Ninon quipped that her preference was for the Grand Cordeliers—the most notorious, undisciplined, and debauched male order of the day. Anne of Austria could not help laughing and so opted for indulgence. Ninon thus kept her friends and did nothing to alter her lifestyle.

Five years later, with the restoration of royal authority, the *dévots* were able to take their revenge on the unrepentant libertine, shutting her up in the Madelonettes, a convent for the reform of women of easy virtue. The nuns there treated her kindly. As she wrote to François de Boisrobert, the dramatist known for his homosexual leanings, "I think that in emulation of yourself, I will begin to love my own sex."[5] She could not but be worried for her future, however. Once again help came from a queen. Hearing of her confinement from the Maréchal d'Albret,

---

4. Quoted in Magne, *Ninon de Lenclos*, p. 226.

5. Quoted in Magne, *Ninon de Lenclos*, p. 155.

Queen Christina of Sweden, then visiting France, asked to meet in person the woman whose intellectual reputation was known throughout Europe. It was during a conversation with her at the Madelonettes that Ninon famously described the *Précieuses* as the "Jansenists of love."[6] According to Mme de Motteville, "of all the women whom Christina of Sweden saw in France, Ninon was the only one to whom she showed any sign of respect."[7] Indeed, the Queen went so far as to petition Louis XIV for her immediate release.

Into a rigidly hierarchical society where everyone's fortune depended on family and friends, the new culture had introduced another criterion of judgment based on the recognition of personal merit. For an outsider, a brilliant reputation could, although not easily, be a passport to the world of privilege wherein to try his or her luck. Ninon de Lenclos's case was symbolic of this, as was, albeit quite differently, that of her friend Mme Scarron, later the Marquise de Maintenon.

Ninon de Lenclos and Françoise d'Aubigné were born fifteen years apart. Although both belonged to the minor nobility, their fathers had committed serious crimes and had been imprisoned or exiled. Poor, alone, and with nothing but their beauty to depend on, they chose to invest their only capital in quite different ways. Ninon opted for freedom and pleasure, Françoise for respectability and virtue. The first delighted in collecting men and ridding herself of them with casual frankness; the second knew the art of being admired and refusing herself without offending the *amour-propre* of her admirers. One was a nonbeliever who enjoyed challenging the Compagnie du Saint-Sacrement; the other was the niece of the great Huguenot poet Agrippa d'Aubigné but had been converted to Catholicism as a child. She was religious and, by placing herself under Anne of Austria's protection, aligned herself automatically with the *dévots*.

They were not driven in opposite directions simply by opportunism but by the aspirations of their profoundly different natures. Ninon's wish to enjoy life freely and to be in control of her life went hand in hand with an absolute intellectual autonomy and a taste for challenge. Françoise d'Aubigné, on the other hand, wanted to be accepted and loved; she wished to be appreciated and would sacrifice anything to please her neighbor: "I did not wish to be loved by anyone in particular, I wished to be so by everyone and to be spoken well of; I made a great effort, but it cost me nothing provided that I had a good reputation; therein lay my folly; I cared not at all for riches, I was infinitely above self-interest, but I wanted honor."[8]

---

6. See Magne, *Ninon de Lenclos*, p. 238 and note 2.

7. *Mémoires de Mme de Motteville*, Vol. 4, p. 74.

8. "Entretien particulier avec Mme de Glapion" (extract), 1707, in Mme de Maintenon, *Comment la sagesse vient aux filles: Propos d'éducation*, edited by Pierre E. Leroy and Marcel Loyau (Paris: Bartillat, 1998), p. 38.

This difference didn't prevent the two women from liking each other and becoming friends. They were brought together by a shared passion for the art of conversation, an interest in moral and psychological problems, and a taste for literature. They met in 1652 when, in order to avoid ending up in a convent, Françoise, at just sixteen, had agreed to marry Paul Scarron. The well-known libertine writer was paralyzed and deformed by arthritis, deeply in debt, bad-tempered, and had a marked talent in life, as in his writing, for provocative conversation and obscene narrative. On the other hand, he was genial, clever, culti-vated, amusing, and in his house in the rue Neuve-Saint-Louis, which he called the hôtel de l'Impécuniosité, the conversation sparkled continuously, so that all Paris came to admire the "king of burlesque" in action. Françoise managed to profit enormously from the intellectual and social side of her marriage without allowing herself to be carried away by the license and liberty of her surroundings. Her dig-nified reserve and the care she took of her invalid husband earned respect and formed the basis for her "good reputation."

Was there a secret liaison between Françoise and Ninon? Had the young prude whose marriage everyone knew to be unconsummated and who was continuously being propositioned yielded to a moment of abandon in the arms of her friend who knew everything there was to know about love? Should we believe La Fare when he says that "for whole months" they shared "the same bed"?[9] It is far more likely that after Scarron's death, and with Ninon's complicity, she succumbed to the handsome Marquis de Villarceaux, a longtime lover of her friend. In a letter written to Saint-Évremond toward the end of her life, Ninon was quite explicit: "Scarron was my friend, I had much pleasure from conversation with his wife, and, in time, I found her too gauche for love. About the details I know nothing, I saw nothing, but I often lent my yellow room to her and to Villarceaux."[10]

As a widow, Françoise went on seeing some of Scarron's friends and increasing her circle of acquaintances. Ninon's old lover the Marquis d'Albret helped to introduce her to the hôtel de Richelieu, where she soon managed to make herself welcome by the suspicious and difficult duchess. Both the Albrets and the Riche-lieus received often, and in their houses Françoise was able to meet some of the most distinguished people from both the court and society.

Beautiful, modest, ingratiating, and pleasing, Mme Scarron was blessed not only with the delicacy of "precious" taste but also with the psychological insight of one who knew everything about life. She knew how to create an atmosphere of admiration and respect around her. Mme de Sévigné's letters describe her dining every night either with the marquise herself or with Mme de Coulanges,

9. See Magne, *Ninon de Lenclos*, p. 164, note 1, and p. 167.

10. Ninon de Lenclos to Saint-Évremond, undated, in Saint-Évremond, *Lettres*, edited by René Ternois, two volumes (Paris: Didier, 1968), Vol. 2, p. 260.

conversing with Mme de Lafayette, with La Rochefoucauld, with Guilleragues, and with the Abbé Têtu, and being admired for her "amiable and marvelously upright mind," her gift for storytelling, and the enormous tact with which she "knew how to flatter."[11] When presented to Louis XIV's mistress—Françoise Athénaïs de Rochechouart, Marquise de Montespan—she impressed her with prompt replies well suited to the *esprit Mortemart*, the wit for which Athénaïs and her sisters were famous. The Marquise de Montespan would remember her when it came time to find a governess for the children born of her relationship with the King.

Thus began an extraordinary adventure that, within the space of thirteen years, would make Paul Scarron's widow into the Marquise de Maintenon and the Sun King's morganatic wife. For several years Françoise led a double life, divided between Paris and Versailles. Finally, having shown the King "a new country which was unknown to him and whose commerce is friendship," she was swallowed up by Versailles, and Louis became the only one fortunate enough to hear her straightforward, honest conversations.[12] On January 1, 1675, she must have had a great surge of pride at feeling herself to be a citizen of both worlds in her own right. Mme de Thianges had presented her four-year-old nephew, the recently legitimized Duc du Maine, with a sumptuous miniature theater, and Mme Scarron was depicted within it, near the tiny duke who was being crowned by the nation's greatest writers, moralists, and arbiters of taste: Racine, Bossuet, Boileau, La Fontaine, La Rochefoucauld, and Mme de Lafayette. Mme Scarron's presence in the renowned "Chambre du Sublime" among such company did not as yet ring false. She was there in that extraordinary context because the Duc du Maine was her masterpiece, her star pupil, and because she too, like Mme de Lafayette and La Rochefoucauld, was the product of the particular worldly culture that alone could have shaped her destiny.

More than half a century later, in a dialogue entitled *Mme de Maintenon et Mademoiselle de Lenclos*, Voltaire happily imagined an improbable conversation taking place between the two old friends after Mme de Maintenon's extraordinary metamorphosis.[13] Françoise asks Ninon to pretend to be devout and to settle at Versailles to help her bear the weight of her new grievous way of life. Having come to rule over the greatest court in Europe, the one-time *précieuse* found nothing but loneliness and boredom there. "My heart is empty," she confides to her friend, "my spirit is constrained. I play the part of the first person in France; but it is only a part. I lead a borrowed life. Ah! If you knew what a burden it is for a

---

11. Mme de Sévigné to Mme de Grignan, January 13, 1672, and March 9, 1672, in Mme de Sévigné, *Correspondance*, Vol. 1, pp. 414 and 456.

12. Mme de Sévigné to Mme de Grignan, July 17, 1680, in Mme de Sévigné, *Correspondance*, Vol. 2, p. 1016.

13. Voltaire, *Mélanges II*, in *Œuvres complètes*, Vol. 23, pp. 488–499.

languishing soul to revive another soul, to amuse a mind which is no longer able to be amused!" Mlle de Lenclos was obviously unable to accept the invitation. True to herself, she was preparing to confront the evils of old age with serenity, convinced that "with friends, freedom, and philosophy, one is as well as one's age will allow. The soul suffers only when it is out of its own sphere." And inviting her friend to follow her example, she concludes by saying, "Believe me and come and live with my philosophers."[14] Written in 1751 (the same year in which Voltaire handed Le Siècle de Louis XIV to the printers, after working on it for twenty years), the dialogue serves as a small apologia for the happiness of the intellectual's free and independent way of life—a way of life that the "patriarch of philosophy," having finally given up all ambition as a courtier, was about to exemplify by settling at Ferney on the shores of Lake Geneva.

The choice of two female interlocutors was, however, significant. Voltaire could remember as a child seeing the aged Ninon lined and ravished by the years. He knew enough about the famous courtesan from the Abbé de Châteauneuf's stories to understand the continuity that existed between the gallant epicureanism that Ninon had exemplified in the Sun King's day and the spirit of the libertine circles under the Regency that he had frequented in his youth. Perhaps Châteauneuf had also repeated Ninon's remarks about her former friend. Beyond the stereotype of the false prude, the dialogue hints at a profound personal drama, also reflected in Mme de Maintenon's reflections, which she wrote around the turn of the century for the instruction of the boarding girls at Saint-Cyr. "One no longer has friends when one is in favor; the position one occupies becomes an object of envy, and everyone wishes to take advantage of it; there is no more society, no more freedom, no more simplicity; it is all craft, plotting, forced agreeability, unlimited flattery, and bitterness at heart."[15] The art of pleasing, which had carried Mme de Maintenon to the steps of the throne, turned out to be incompatible with the goal once it was achieved.

Whereas society manners could no longer protect Françoise, not even court etiquette could sustain her. Her position was certainly "unique in the world," as Mme de Sévigné wrote in 1684, but it was also profoundly ambiguous.[16] She was neither a wife nor officially a mistress, treated in private as a queen but with no title to give her standing on official occasions. She who had known how to gain everyone's respect came to embody hypocrisy by, as Simone Bertère writes, "playing two distinct parts, one of which blurred the outlines of the other despite her

14. Voltaire, Œuvres complètes, Vol. 23, p. 500.

15. Mme de Maintenon, "Conversation sur la faveur," in Portraits, Souvenirs, in Comment la sagesse vient aux filles, p. 59.

16. Mme de Sévigné to Mme de Grignan, September 27, 1684, in Mme de Sévigné, Correspondance, Vol. 3. p. 143.

efforts to make them coincide; and she made people ill at ease by affecting an incompetence, where court affairs were concerned, in which no one believed."[17] Only the belief, inculcated in her by her confessors, that she was the humble instrument chosen by Providence for the spiritual salvation of the King prevented her from losing herself in the contradictions and uncertainties of her new position. Perhaps, as Chamfort suggests, gazing on the large goldfish who had difficulty adapting to the too limpid waters of the new fountains at the château of Marly, she too sometimes "regretted her hovel."[18] But it would have been a momentary weakness. Françoise knew she had a mission that alone could justify her presence at the King's side, and she would have done anything to prove herself equal to the task.

It was a century in which people were admired for finding the strength to turn their backs on immense privilege and embarking on the path of obscurity and silence. But those who remained in the world were expected to follow the rules, to choose a "part," and to remain faithful to it. *Honnêteté* was concerned with appearance alone, but the appearance had at least to seem to coincide with the individual's private reality. The part that Mme de Maintenon found herself playing had no precedent either in society or at court. The difficulty may have been insurmountable, but in the eyes of the "public," her decision to claim religious legitimacy was perhaps the least convincing explanation of all. Nothing was more reprehensible, in art or in life, than the adulteration of style or genre—the success of Molière's *Tartuffe* was proof enough of that. By adopting a devotional tone from her triumphant position, Mme de Maintenon laid herself open to suspicion, and instead of burying her past for good, she reminded people of all the gray areas and contradictions of which, by persuasive grace as a society lady, she had rid herself.

The only place in which Mme de Maintenon enjoyed a perfectly legitimate position was at the Institution Royale de Saint Louis at Saint-Cyr. The school owed its very existence to her, and its creation in 1686, which came about rapidly and at vast expense, was the only official recognition paid her by Louis XIV— "a visible sign of that mutual engagement contracted in secret."[19] The idea of providing for the education and dowries of 250 girls of impoverished aristocratic families must have stemmed from her own experience. She too came from that background, and, having known poverty, was quick to realize the importance of education and a knowledge of society to a girl without means. Furthermore, during

---

17. Simone Bertière, *Les Femmes du Roi-Soleil* (Paris: Éditions de Fallois, 1998), p. 301.

18. Chamfort, "Caractères et anecdotes," in *Produit de la civilisation perfectionnée: Maximes et pensées, Caractères et anecdotes*, with a preface by Albert Camus, edited by Geneviève Renaux (Paris: Gallimard, 1970), fragment 888, p. 249.

19. Pierre-E. Leroy, introduction to Mme de Maintenon, *Comment la sagesse vient aux filles*, p. 21.

the years in which she had been governess to Louis XIV and Mme de Montespan's children, she had discovered a genuine vocation for teaching and wished to demonstrate her belief in the virtues of education.

Under her direction, the first state institution designed to see systematically to the practical and theoretical education of girls of good family, from childhood to adulthood, thus came into being. With great insight, Mme de Maintenon planned down to the last detail a bravely innovative educational model of lasting duration. Saint-Cyr also stood for a kind of utopia, for it represented Mme de Maintenon's last attempt to reconcile the irreconcilable: public and private life, spontaneity and discipline, religion and society. Created by will of the sovereign but far from the poisoned atmosphere of the court, Saint-Cyr was meant to be a laboratory in which virtue and innocence were not incompatible with worldly sophistication, where Christian morality could profit from reading the novels of Mlle de Scudéry, and where the theater was a school of beauty and truth.

In the first months of 1689, with a series of performances of *Esther*, the biblical tragedy Racine wrote expressly for the pupils of Saint-Cyr, the utopia seemed to be fully realized. The King welcomed the guests like an ordinary person, using his walking stick to hold open the door to the room where the performance was to take place; Mme de Maintenon, at last at home and out of the way of etiquette, received the great of the kingdom on an equal footing; the spectators were delighted, and Racine was moved by the superb performances of the young actresses; the denizens of the *ville* and the *cour* conversed together as they had in the golden age of Parisian society.

Many descriptions survive of those extraordinary evenings—by Mme de Caylus, the Abbé de Choisy, and the Marquise de Sévigné, who wrote to her daughter on February 21 of that year:

> I paid court at Saint-Cyr the other day, it was a great deal more agreeable than I would ever have imagined. We went out there on Saturday, Mme de Coulanges, Mme de Bagnols, the Abbé Têtu, and I. Seats had been reserved for us.... The attention the Maréchal de Bellefonds and I paid in listening to the tragedy did not pass unnoticed, nor did certain words of praise spoken quietly and at the right moment.... I cannot speak too highly of this play: it is one which is not easy to perform and which will never be imitated; it is a marriage of music, verse, song, and characters so perfect and so complete that nothing is left to be desired. The girls who play roles of the kings and other characters seem made for the parts.... I was quite charmed by it, as was the maréchal, who left his seat to go to tell the King how much it had pleased him that he sat beside a lady who was quite worthy of having seen *Esther*. The King came to where we were sitting and, turning, addressed himself to me, saying, "Madame, I have been assured that you were pleased."

Keeping my composure, I replied, "Sire, I am charmed. What I feel is beyond words." The King said to me, "Racine has great talent." "Sire," I replied, "he has indeed, but—in truth so do these young people; they play their roles as if that was all they had ever done." "Ah, that is true indeed," he said. And then His Majesty moved away, leaving me the object of envy. Since I was almost the only one who had not seen it before, he took some pleasure in my sincere and simple expression of admiration. Monsieur le Prince and Madame la Princesse came to have a word with me; Mme de Maintenon stopped by for a fleeting moment, then was gone, leaving with the King. I replied to everything because I was happy. We returned [to Paris] by torchlight. I supped with Mme de Coulanges, to whom the King had also spoken in an easy manner, which lent him an agreeable gentleness.[20]

This happy state of affairs at Saint-Cyr was not to survive the triumph. Once they became the subject of interest and admiration of the whole court, it was hard for the girls to return to their old routines without complaining. As a wind of frivolity, insubordination, and *galanterie* swept through the college, and the parish priest at Versailles thundered against the dangers of the theater, Mme de Maintenon was obliged to take steps to redress the situation. The curriculum was severely revised, as much in spirit as in form. Henceforth, Saint-Cyr would aim to prepare its pupils for their roles as Christian wives and mothers in a spirit of humility and obedience. Anything that might distract them from this end—a taste for elegance or distinction, independence of mind, a desire for learning or knowledge—was to be firmly resisted. Mlle de Scudéry's *Conversations*, the product of too secular a morality, was struck off the reading list and substituted with dialogues and observations written expressly by Mme de Maintenon. Besides, for her, the reform of Saint-Cyr went hand in hand with an internal development and an ever more rigorous religiosity. A striking example of this was the intransigent advice that, in old age, she hammered into her beautiful niece, that same Mme de Caylus whom she had educated in the perfect ways of polite society. "Don't return to the world," she wrote after the Comte de Caylus's death, "mistrust the wisest, mistrust yourself."[21] And a month later she insisted, "Let the world talk; you can never hate, fear, and despise it too much."[22] By now even her acquaintance with the poor Abbé Têtu, with whom she had happily discussed the

---

20. Mme de Sévigné to Mme de Grignan, February 21, 1689, in Mme de Sévigné, *Correspondance*, Vol. 3, pp. 350–351.

21. Mme de Maintenon to Mme de Caylus, December 30, 1704, in Mme de Maintenon, Mme de Caylus, and Mme de Dangeau, *L'Estime et la Tendresse: Correspondances intimes*, with a preface by Marc Fumaroli, edited by Pierre-E. Leroy and Marcel Loyau (Paris: Michel, 1998), p. 86.

22. Mme de Maintenon to Mme de Caylus, February 12, 1705, in *L'Estime et la Tendresse*, p. 88.

differences between *esprit* and *goût* thirty years earlier, had become "a dangerous friendship."[23]

In shutting herself off from the society culture of her youth, denying her past, and adopting the mantle of austerity, Mme de Maintenon let herself down and allowed herself to be misunderstood by the world on which she was turning her back. Instead of commanding respect, her devotion was seen as a mask that barely disguised an implacable desire to dominate. Of all Saint-Simon's poisonous portraits, there is one which pinpoints this comparison:

> She was a woman of great intelligence who had been greatly polished and educated in the ways of society by the best company, which had initially suffered her presence but which she so soon captivated, and to whom, polished by *galanterie*, she had become most agreeable. Her various situations had made her flattering, insinuating, courteous, seeking always to please.... An incomparable grace, an easy manner, though cautious and respectful at all times, which had become natural to her after many years in a humble condition, helped her talents marvelously. She spoke gently and straightforwardly, expressed herself well, and was naturally eloquent and precise. Her finest hour—for she was three or four years older than the King—had been in the days of fine conversation, fine *galanterie*, in a word, the days of what were called the *ruelles*, and they meant so much to her that she always retained the flavor and a strong coloring of them. To the precious, affected style of that day, which had remained with her a little, had been added a glow of importance and subsequently devotion. The latter became her main characteristic appearing to swamp all else. This was essential to maintaining herself in the position to which it had brought her, and no less so in order for her to govern. This last was her reason for existing; everything else was unreservedly sacrificed to it.[24]

While Françoise d'Aubigné, having reached the pinnacle of society, was losing the fine reputation that had borne her so high and becoming the subject of every kind of calumny, Ninon de Lenclos, having remained true to herself, was enjoying an ever greater public respect. With the passing of time, and without her having made the slightest attempt to deny them, people were forgetting the scandals of her youth, only to admire the elegance of her intellect and her perfect manners. Ninon, the once "dangerous Ninon," had made way for Mlle de Lenclos.

In keeping with the spirit of the times, she no longer—after turning fifty—sorted men into the categories of "payers," "passing fancies," and "lovers." Now

---

23. Mme de Maintenon to Mme de Caylus, January 11, 1705, in *L'Estime et la Tendresse*, p. 87.

24. Saint-Simon, *Mémoires*, Vol. 5, pp. 548–549.

she had only friends whom she received with exquisite grace. Even ladies of good society permitted themselves to visit her house in the rue des Tournelles, proving that her past had been forgotten. Mme de Sévigné—who had, in her day, seen both her husband and her son succumb to Ninon's charms—could not resist remarking with a touch of acidity, "Corbellini tells me wonders about the excellent company of men he finds at Mademoiselle de Lenclos's house; thus in her old age she gathers everyone together, men and women, but when presently she has only women, she should console herself with the arrangement, having had the men at the "right age to plead.""[25] Of course old age brought with it its share of melancholy and regret, but for Ninon, life deserved to be lived to the bitter end. "How I envy those who go to England and how glad I would be to dine with you once more!" she wrote when nearly eighty to Saint-Évremond, who was living in exile in England. "But is it not gross to wish for a dinner? The mind has great advantages over the body; yet the body often satisfies little tastes, which recur and which relieve the soul of its sad reflections. You often made fun of mine: I have banished them all. There is no more time when one reaches the last stage of one's life. One must be content with the day in which one is living."[26]

The hours of the day that gave her most pleasure were now devoted to conversation; the realm of ideas was the only one in which she could satisfy her passion for variety and her taste for collecting:

> Beauty strikes her equally wherever she finds it; and her taste enables her to discover it wherever it may be, for it is a kind of instinct, surer and truer than reason.... In leading her from flower to flower, like the bees to whom Plato compares poets, it causes her to cross all countries and all centuries indifferently, but such lightsome and brilliant kinds of imagination scorn work and application as ordinary. A spirit born for pleasure that has made sacrifices to the graces alone is far from subjecting itself to the patience needed to compare the beauty of one time with that of another, to studying the similarities and differences, of looking at them from every imaginable angle.[27]

In writing these lines, the Abbé de Chateauneuf—author of the *Dialogue sur la musique des Anciens*—may have looked back on conversations he had had many years earlier with his friend who had, in old age, developed an increasing interest

---

25. Mme de Sévigné to Mme de Coulanges and to Coulanges, February 22, 1695, in Mme de Sévigné, *Correspondances*, Vol. 3, p. 1088. The citation from is Jean Racine, *Les Plaideurs*, Act 1, Scene vii.

26. Mlle de Lenclos to Saint-Évremond, (April or May) 1698, in *Lettres*, Vol. 2, pp. 276–277.

27. Abbé de Châteauneuf, *Dialogue sur la musique des Anciens* (Paris: chez la veuve Pissot, 1725), pp. 8–9.

in music while maintaining a typically dilettante attitude toward it. But it was precisely for their variety and wonderful lightness of tone that conversations with Ninon were so sought after. The sacred and purifying fire of her *esprit* had made an *honnête femme* of Mlle de Lenclos—even in the eyes of the formidably outspoken Princesse Palatine, sister-in-law of the King himself—and had turned the house in the rue des Tournelles into the last sanctuary for society of the dying century.[28]

---

28. See the letter from the Duchess of Hanover dated May 18, 1698, in *Lettres de Madame, duchesse d'Orléans, née Princesse Palatine*, edited by Olivier Amiel (Paris: Mercure de France, 1982), p. 154.

13

L'ESPRIT DE SOCIÉTÉ

I. The Character of the Nation

"IT IS SAID that man is a social animal. On that basis it strikes me that a Frenchman is more of a man than anyone else; he is a man par excellence, for he seems to have been made solely for society."[1] Thus the youngest of Montesquieu's Persian travelers, with Furetière's dictionary[2] in hand, paradoxically defines the culmination of a spectacular process. In 1721, a hundred years after Mme de Rambouillet's first initiative, close observers saw the art of living in society as a characteristic of French identity. Even before the publication of the *Lettres persanes*, the Swiss writer Béat Louis de Muralt—the first in a long line of genuine foreign visitors—observed: "In every way the French seem made for society.... What they want us to admire in them, above all, is their wit, their vivacity, courtesy, and manners."[3] But it was not only foreigners who commented on this national trait. In dedicating his tragedy *Zaïre* to the English merchant Everard Fawkener, Voltaire declared that, without a shadow of doubt, "since Anne of Austria's regency, the French have been the most sociable and the most polite people on earth."[4]

With the passage of time, however, the very idea of "society" was undergoing a profound transformation. In the seventeenth century, the word was generally used

---

1. Charles-Louis de Secondat de Montesquieu, *Lettres persanes*, letter 87, in *Œuvres complètes*, edited by Roger Caillois, two volumes (Paris: Gallimard/Bibliothèque de la Pléiade, 1949–1951), Vol. 1, p. 261.

2. "Man is the only naturally social animal, who can establish a link of friendship with another and offer mutual support"; *Dictionnaire Universel*, three volumes (The Hague–Rotterdam: A. and R. Leers, 1690), Vol. 3, p. 1112.

3. Béat Louis de Muralt, *Lettres sur les Anglais et les Français et sur les voyages* (1725), pp. 176–177.

4. Voltaire, *Seconde Épitre dédicatoire à Zaïre, Théâtre* I in *Œuvres complètes*, Vol. 2, p. 553.

to mean a small group of chosen people,[5] whereas during the following century it came more clearly to have the modern meaning of "social milieu." And from the first decade of the eighteenth century on, *sociabilité* indicated just as much the *philosophe*'s benevolent sympathy for the whole human race as it did the worldly attitude typical of the *honnête homme*. The *Encyclopédie* says that for the true *philosophe*, "civil society is, so to speak, a divinity for him on earth; he praises it, honors it by probity, by exact attention to duty, and by a sincere wish not to be a useless or embarrassing member of it."[6]

In *De l'esprit des lois*, twenty-seven years after the publication of the *Lettres persanes*, Montesquieu again reflected on his compatriots' sociability, hypothesizing the existence of "a country whose inhabitants were of a social temper, open-hearted, cheerful, endowed with taste and a facility in communicating their thoughts; who were sprightly and agreeable; sometimes imprudent, often indiscreet; and besides had courage, generosity, frankness, and a sure sense of honor."[7] The tone was very different from what it had once been, and parody was replaced by a more tender meditation, but the characteristics he describes of a nation easily recognizable as France were the same as the ones he had made fun of in his youthful novel. The frivolity, gaiety, gallantry, love of theater and of self-presentation, the tyranny of fashion, the pervasive influence of women, the cults of honor and *esprit*—all of which the two visitors from the East had ridiculed for their artificiality—were merely the unrelinquished characteristics of an aristocratic lifestyle that had become the collective model for the country's elite. The style was by now a hundred years old. It had withstood the Enlightenment conscience to enjoy a brilliant renewal under the Regency, and its prestige would survive until the end of the *ancien régime*.

How had a pattern of behavior designed for the select few reached so wide a public that it represented the spirit of an entire nation? The *Lettres persanes* refers with a hint of irony to "certain books that are collections of witticisms composed for the use of those who have no *esprit*, and want to fake it."[8] These primers in the art of pleasing, conversation, and social advancement were consulted by those who wished to master the rules of the social game.

The vast number of manuals on manners that appeared in France throughout the seventeenth century and for a large part of the eighteenth leads one to

---

5. "A company of people who normally gather for pleasurable pastimes," *Dictionnaire de l'Académie française*, p. 1694.

6. *Encyclopédie*, thirty-five volumes (1765; reprint, Stuttgart–Bad Cannstatt: F. Frommann Verlag, 1967), Vol. 12, p. 510.

7. Montesquieu, *The Spirit of the Laws*, translated by Thomas Nugent (1752; London: G. Bell & Sons, Ltd., 1914), Book 19, Chapter 5.

8. Montesquieu, *Lettres persanes*, letter 54, in *Œuvres complètes*, Vol. 1, p. 210.

suppose that there must have been an extensive and varied readership. The example for this kind of pedagogy came from Italy, and although none of the many French manuals could begin to compare with the three great "instruction" treatises of the high and late Renaissance—*The Book of the Courtier, Galateo*, and *Civil Conversation*—they had all adapted their teaching to the requirements of French society.

In fact, neither the model of the *Courtier* nor of *Civil Conversation* corresponded exactly to the demands of the new French social ideal. Castiglione's book pointed to the court as the only place in which Renaissance man's dream of perfection could be fulfilled. In the first decade of the seventeenth century, however, the French nobility had become aware of the need to distance itself from the court in order to rediscover its identity. The first French treatise on the subject, Nicolas Faret's *L'Honneste homme ou l'art de plaire à la cour* (1630), attests to the degree to which the conception of the court had changed profoundly. Faret, though he pillaged Castiglione's book ruthlessly, nevertheless betrayed its fundamental thesis. It was not his goal to initiate a small aristocratic elite of courtiers into an ideal of aesthetic and moral perfection. Rather, he proposed teaching the rules of a new profession—the profession of courtier—to a far from homogenous social group made up of aristocrats and commoners, bourgeois and people who had come up from nothing. And the field of action was no longer the private apartments of princes but the crowded and labyrinthine corridors of one of the greatest European palaces, a place where all the political, administrative, and military interests of the French monarchy converged. The game was no longer to identify with the prince but to obtain favors for one's career. Nor could Guazzo's book act as a model for the French aristocracy. With its clearly anti-courtier approach, *Civil Conversation* preferred the city to the palace, encouraged gentlemen to be themselves, and proposed a broadening of knowledge and a betterment of social relations through conversation. Where Castiglione turned to the courtly culture of the past, Guazzo anticipated the bourgeois culture of the future.

The reasons for the extraordinary success of the *Courtier* and *Civil Conversation* throughout Europe depended not on their historical or cultural background so much as on the breadth and novelty of the teaching process that evolved and on the strength of their arguments. The two treatises could be read as two succeeding elements of the same program: teaching elite men how to express their social identity through the perfect command of word and gesture. The "manifesto" can be traced to a passage in the second book of the *Courtier* when, discussing the pastimes and company most suited to the perfect gentleman, Gasparo Pallavicino remarks how, in Lombardy, "young gentlemen upon the holy days come dance all day long in the sun with them of the country, and pass the time with them in casting the barre, in wrestling, running, and leaping," and Federigo Fregoso declares, "This dancing in the sun . . . does not please me in any way, and I can not see what a man shall gain by it."[9] This was an outright declaration of war against the old ways, and it sanctioned a break with tradition that was initiated at the dawn of the Renaissance. From then onward, the gentleman and the peasant would no longer cultivate a common meeting place or shared gestures and habits, as they had done in medieval society. From that moment on, the nobleman's first objective would be to make himself instantly distinguishable from the nonnoble. The gentleman turned his back on popular culture and the physiological world of smells, sounds, and tastes and adopted an aesthetic outlook whereby nature was reinterpreted through art. This new *paideia* was born of Humanism and obeyed the classical ideal of *kalòs kaì agathós*—the beautiful and the good. Art and virtue were united, with art understood first and foremost as "competence"—a perfect command of technique and of the powers of expression—and virtue as the Aristotelian "middle way." A gentleman's education aimed precisely at knowing how to master emotions, words, and gestures through different degrees of rhetoric. This delicate balancing involved not only choosing words carefully for the best possible exchange in the social economy, but also maintaining the perfect bearing of the body when coming into contact with other bodies.

In this process of dramatizing the self, conversation became crucial. The individual was at his most socially exposed in conversation, which required a conscious command of all his means of expression: tone of voice, gesture, bearing, and facial expression were as important as the spoken word. And whatever the outcome, conversation had to take the general rule of convenience into account— the *aptum*—and adapt itself to people, places, and circumstances, without which it could aspire to being neither urbane nor civil nor courteous.

Although inspired by the same criteria of convenience, the French manuals had no great theoretical ambitions. They were intended, rather, to codify a set of rules and to illustrate them practically. Their authors—churchmen, soldiers, diplomats, aristocrats, and obscure writers on various subjects—had different motivations, and despite the growing number of works devoted to the subject, we remain almost entirely ignorant of the audience they addressed. Were the manuals written for noblemen to perfect the educations given them by their families and to correct their provincial ways? Or were they intended for the commoner who wished to understand the ways of the nobility?

Certainly Jean-Baptiste de La Salle's *Les règles de la bienséance et de la civilité chrétienne divisées en deux parties à l'usage des écoles chrétiennes* (1703) was meant for teaching purposes, to preach a model of noble behavior to the lower social classes. But are we to believe the claims of most authors of such manuals when they announced they were addressing young, inexperienced gentlemen and future tutors? It may well have been a promotional ploy to boast of readers of

---

9. Castiglione, *The Book of the Courtier*, Book Two, Chapter 10; Hoby translation modified.

quality. What need had noble scions of books to verify what they had already learned by imitation and through everyday practice? Were not all the manuals alike in stating that no theoretical teaching could replace direct experience for acquiring that "certain *je ne sais quoi*"? That natural gift was considered to be the essence of social grace—an inexplicable, indispensable subtle charm, "that little extra" which entirely escaped analysis, as noticeable in its presence as in its absence.

What were objectives of such didactic literature? To inquire into the readership of these manuals raises the inevitable question of whether the exact codification of behavior was meant to protect or to open up the frontiers of the social hierarchy. Did the *bienséances* aim to maintain the status quo or to encourage change? Were they used by the monarchy as an instrument of control and repression, or were they a shared code that allowed civil society a space for freedom independent from power? Did *politesse* conform to a moral imperative or was it merely hypocrisy? Was it a social virtue or a front? Did it respect the distinctions of a society based on inequality or did it encourage the smoothing out of differences?

For Faret, a bourgeois of modest origins, *L'Honneste homme ou l'art de plaire à la cour* was a definite manual for rising in society. For Antoine de Courtin, on the other hand, word and deed had to take account of the slightest nuances of a hierarchical society and emphasized them.[10] Courtin built a brilliant diplomatic career from nothing and was ennobled by Christina of Sweden. There were different models too: for Courtin, the *cour* was the absolute authority on behavior; for Faret, François de Callières, the Chevalier de Méré, and the defenders of conversation, only the *ville* could set the tone in matters of elegance and style.

Whatever the author's didactic intentions, however, *politesse* was at stake. Initially synonymous with *civilité*, *politesse* ultimately replaced it and imposed itself in manual after manual on an ever wider public. For the Baron d'Holbach, who in the 1770s analyzed the phenomenon of sociability from the point of view of natural law and universal morality, *politesse*, along with *douceur* and *complaisance*, now seemed, as Daniel Gordon puts it, to be "constitutive of 'social life' or 'society' as a general field of human interactions, whereas the courtesy literature had defined the same qualities as constitutive of a select company of refined individuals."[11]

The enormous importance of *politesse* was not limited to manuals of behavior. It occupied the minds of the greatest eighteenth-century thinkers. For Montesquieu, it was born of aristocratic indolence and could only flourish under an absolute monarchy. In a free country like England, where the citizens were busy with their own concerns, he wrote, they had no time to cultivate refinement and

10. Antoine de Courtin, *Nouveau Traité de la civilité qui se pratique en France parmi les honnestes gens* (Paris: H. Josset, 1671). Eight revised and corrected editions were published within thirty years.

11. Daniel Gordon, *Citizens Without Sovereignty: Equality and Sociability in French Thought, 1670–1789* (Princeton University Press, 1994), p. 67.

good manners. In fact in England, "those who govern have a power which, in some measure, has need of fresh vigor every day, they have a greater regard for such as are useful to them than for those who only contribute to their amusement: we see, therefore, fewer courtiers, flatterers, and parasites; in short, fewer of all those who make their own advantage of the folly of the great."[12] Manners, however, did not have to be reduced to an elegant form of servility, nor did noblemen have to be reduced to courtiers. Even before they obeyed their sovereign, French nobles submitted to the religion of honor, which buttressed their individualism and guaranteed them a sphere of unrestrained freedom. The virtues the nobleman displayed —courage, gallantry, frankness—were primarily of his own creation. Courtesy, too, was born of the wish to be distinguished—"It is out of pride that we are polite: we feel flattered to have manners that prove we are not base"[13]—but it needed at the same time to remain an art of living, which was a credit to the entire nation.

The discovery of an admiration for England's constitutional monarchy had a profound effect on both Montesquieu's and Voltaire's view of France. Both tended to see aristocratic culture as a kind of resistance to the monarchy's absolute power and aristocratic custom as a corrective to the law. Refinement, luxury, the art of conversation, and an acute awareness of fashion were not merely the whims of a caste excluded from political activity. They also constituted a dynamic force for the benefit of civil society.

It was the Scotsman David Hume, observing France through the eyes of a British citizen, who provided the most intelligent and subtle analysis of French courtesy. In the service of the British ambassador to Louis XV from 1734 to 1737 and again from 1763 to 1765, Hume had learned to know and love French society, which had welcomed him especially warmly. The liberal reformer could not help but affirm the superiority of English political life, but that did not prevent him from appreciating the unequaled splendor of French society. In his essay "Of Civil Liberty," Hume recognizes that if commerce, science, and the intellectual and artistic life needed a free state in order to develop,

> the most eminent instance of the flourishing of learning in absolute government is that of France, which scarcely ever enjoyed any established liberty, and yet has carried the arts and sciences as near to perfection as any other nation. The English are, perhaps, greater philosophers; the Italians better painters and musicians; the Romans were greater orators: but the French are the only people, except the Greeks, who have been at once philosophers, poets, orators, historians, painters, architects, sculptors, and musicians. With regard to the stage, they have excelled even the Greeks, who far excelled the English.

12. Montesquieu, *The Spirit of the Laws*, Book 19, Chapter 27.

13. Montesquieu, *The Spirit of the Laws*, Book 4, Chapter 2.

And in common life, they have, in a great measure, perfected that art, the most useful and agreeable of any, *l'Art de Vivre*, the art of society and conversation.[14]

But Hume went even further, claiming that whereas the dynamic of *civilité* and *politesse* definitely sprang from inequality, it ended up producing an unexpected form of equality. While preserving the virtues of an aristocratic society, it did not aim to enforce the differences so much as to attenuate them through "a long train of dependence from the prince to the peasant, which is not great enough to render property precarious, or depress the minds of the people; but is sufficient to beget in every one an inclination to please his superiors, and to form himself upon those models which are most acceptable to people of condition and education. Politeness of manners, therefore, arises most naturally in monarchies and courts; and where that flourishes, none of the liberal arts will be altogether neglected or despised."[15] The desire to please one's "superiors" was paralleled by the courtesy the more powerful felt they owed to the weak, and nothing illustrates the subtly primed dialectic of *politesse* more than the way in which aristocratic women were treated: "Gallantry is nothing but an instance of the same generous attention. As nature has given *man* the superiority above *woman*, by endowing him with greater strength both of mind and body, it is his part to alleviate that superiority, as much as possible, by the generosity of his behavior, and by a studied deference and complaisance for all her inclinations and opinions."[16]

Despite political disagreements, different social practices, and different institutions, there were many people in England who shared Hume's opinion. Philip Dormer Stanhope, the fourth Earl of Chesterfield, was so convinced of the superiority of the French way of life that he considered it essential to finish his son's education with a stay in Paris under the guidance of a society lady. Lord Chesterfield's choice did not denote an admission of inferiority but sprang from the belief that the French monarchy had been able to make its own and to pass on the model of the perfect Italian Renaissance gentleman.[17] From Italy to Russia to Scandinavia, the eighteenth-century aristocracy followed Lord Chesterfield's example, but no one explained his reasons with the same luxury of detail.

"Paris is indisputably the seat of the GRACES; they will even court you, if you

---

14. David Hume, "Of Civil Liberty," in *Essays, Moral, Political and Literary*, in *The Philosophical Works*, edited by Thomas Hill Green and Thomas Hodge Grose, four volumes (1878; reprint, Darmstadt: Scientia Verlag Aallen, 1964), Vol. 3, pp. 158–159.

15. Hume, "On the Rise and Progress of the Arts and Sciences," in *Essays, Moral, Political and Literary*, p. 187.

16. Hume, "On the Rise and Progress of the Arts and Sciences," p. 193.

17. See Marc Fumaroli, preface to Lord Chesterfield, *Lettres à son fils à Paris (1750–1752)* (Paris: Rivages, 1993), pp. 19–22.

are not too coy," Lord Chesterfield wrote to his son on July 9, 1750.[18] A few
months later, he pointed out: "Your great point at present at Paris, to which all
other considerations must give way, is to become entirely a man of fashion: to be
well-bred without ceremony, easy without negligence, steady and intrepid with
modesty, genteel without affectation, insinuating without meanness, cheerful
without being noisy, frank without indiscretion, and secret without mysterious-
ness; to know the proper time and place for whatever you say or do, and to do it
with an air of condition all this is not so soon nor so easily learned as people imagine, but requires observation and time."[19] And where more than one foreigner
may have remarked that the excessive importance attached to wit and manners
caused the French to "overlook substance," "to attach importance to things of little account," and "to put the pleasure of appearances before the reality of being,"[20]
Lord Chesterfield knew French society too well to judge it superficially. The widespread reputation, from which even the *émigrés* suffered during the Revolution,
that France was "a whistling, singing, dancing, frivolous nation;... is very far from
being a true one, though many *'petits maîtres'* by their behavior seem to justify it;
but those very *'petits maîtres,'* when mellowed by age and experience, very often
turn out very able men."[21] In the hands of an artist, fatuity itself can become a
successful strategy: "You cannot conceive, nor can I express, how advantageous a
good air, genteel motions, and engaging address are, not only among women, but
among men, and even in the course of business; they fascinate the affections, they
steal a preference, they play about the heart till they engage it. I know a man, and
so do you, who, without a grain of merit, knowledge, or talents, has raised himself
millions of degrees above his level, simply by a good air and engaging manners."[22]

The best practical illustration of the French *art de vivre* is probably to be found
in this English grandee's private letters to his illegitimate son, who was little suited
to life in society, and to a godson equally indifferent to good manners:

> I daresay you have heard and read of the *je ne sais quoi*, both in French and
> English, for the expression is now adopted into our language; but I question
> whether you have any clear idea of it, and indeed it is more easily felt than
> defined. It is a most inestimable quality, and adorns every other. I will

18. Lord Chesterfield to his son, July 9, 1750, in *Letters of Philip Dormer Stanhope, 4th Earl of Chester-field*, edited by Bonamy Dobrée, six volumes (London: Eyre and Spottiswoode, 1932), Vol. 4, p. 1,564.

19. Lord Chesterfield to his son, January 14, 1751, in *Letters*, Vol. 4, p. 1655.

20. Muralt, *Lettres sur les Anglais et les Français et sur les voyages*, pp. 180–182.

21. Lord Chesterfield to his son, [undated] November 1750, in *Letters*, Vol. 4, p. 1611.

22. Lord Chesterfield to his son, June 10, 1751, in *Letters*, Vol. 4, p. 1,748. Lord Chesterfield refers to the Maréchal de Richelieu.

endeavor to give you a general notion of it, though I cannot an exact one; experience must teach it to you, and will, if you attend to it. It is in my opinion a compound of all the agreeable qualities of body and mind, in which no one of them predominates in such a manner as to give exclusion to any other. It is not mere wit, mere beauty, mere learning, nor indeed mere any one thing that produces it, though they all contribute something towards it. It is owing to this *je ne sais quoi* that one takes a liking to some one particular person at first rather than to another. One feels oneself prepossessed in favour of that person without being enough acquainted with him to judge of his intrinsic merit or talents, and one finds oneself inclined to suppose him to have good sense, good nature, and good humour. A genteel address, graceful motions, a pleasing elocution, and elegancy of style, are powerful ingredients in this compound. It is in short an extract of all the *Graces*. Here you will perhaps ask me to define the Graces, which I can only do by the *je ne sais quoi*, as I can only define the *je ne sais quoi* by the Graces. No one person possesses them all, but happy he who possesses the most, and wretched he who possesses none of them. I can much more easily describe what their contraries are. As for example, a head sunk in between the shoulders; feet turned inwards instead of outwards; the manner of walking or rather waddling of a macaw, so as to make Mrs. Dodd very justly call you her *macaw*. All these sorts of things are most notorious insults upon the Graces and indeed upon all good company. Do not take into your head that these things are trifles; though they may seem so if singly and separately considered, yet when considered aggregately and relatively to the great and necessary art of pleasing, they are of infinite consequence. Socrates, the wisest and honestest pagan that ever lived, thought the Graces of such vast importance that he always advised his disciples to *sacrifice to them*. From so great an authority, I will most earnestly recommend to you to sacrifice to them. Invite, entreat, supplicate them to accompany you, in all you say or do; and sacrifice to them every little idle humour and laziness.[23]

At the time, neither the teaching ploys of the manuals nor the history of the origins of *politesse* with all its political and social implications were of any interest to society's leading lights. According to Karl Vossler, "The spiritual activity of good society could be summarized by two occupations: the study of self and the describing of self."[24] In its blind self-confidence, its belief that it represented the "norm of all humanity,"[25] and its effort to consider itself down to the smallest

23. Lord Chesterfield to his godson, August 9, 1768, in *Letters*, Vol. 6, pp. 2854–2855.

24. Karl Vossler, *Frankreichs Kultur und Sprache* (1913; second edition, Heidelberg: Carl Winter, 1929), p. 331.

25. Vossler, *Frankreichs Kultur und Sprache*, p. 332.

detail, the *parfaitement bonne compagnie* turned only to literature for guidance. Never was collaboration more fruitful.

In order to please the socialites, who resisted anything with a hint of learnedness about it, the literati managed from the earliest decades of the seventeenth century to "civilize the doctrine" and adapt it to the demands of a new public.[26] French erudition had definitively supplanted Italian learning; with *translatio studiorum* a *fait accompli*, it was possible to turn to Italian Humanism on equal terms in order for the ancient *paideia* to become French. The classical canon suggested, through its literary memory, its rhetoric, and its collection of *exempla* and *loci communes*, an ideal of a totally lay morality grounded in a belief in man's excellence and in his dual vocation for both private and public life. In outline, the model coincided perfectly with the demands of the worldly ideal; but clever grafting was needed to give the impression of an entirely French invention, an invention so French that the word coined to describe it, *honnêteté*, had no equivalent in any other language. Its principal theorist, the Chevalier de Méré, made it "the science of man" par excellence because it consisted in "living and communicating in a humane and reasonable fashion."[27]

The assimilation of the ancient *paideia*, as Marc Fumaroli writes, passed almost unnoticed:

> Through preaching, the novel, the theater, poetry, learned humanist works that influenced indirectly, through translations, and more directly, whole sections of the humanist encyclopedia, fathers of the Church, philosophers, orators, and poets from Antiquity insinuated themselves into society's consciousness, providing it with a *copia rerum*, certainly lightweight if compared to that of the scholars, but which allowed Descartes or Pascal, for instance, to raise the most difficult questions of philosophy and moral theology with the "*honnestes gens.*"[28]

Honoré d'Urfé led the way in *L'Astrée*, marrying the Neoplatonic vision of love and beauty to the national consciousness by means of the adventures of a group of shepherds from ancient Gaul. *L'Astrée*, Emmanuel Bury writes, "while laying the foundation for the modern novel, lent credibility to the very idea of literature, suggesting that its aim should be to instruct mankind, not merely to amuse it."[29] Writers and socialites came to share experiences and expectations in a way that

---

26. Bury, *Littérature et politesse*, p. 75.

27. Méré, "De la vraie honnêteté," in *Œuvres complètes*, Vol. 3, p. 72.

28. Marc Fumaroli, "Le 'langage de la Cour' en France: Problèmes et points de repères," in *Europäische Hofkultur in 16. und 17. Jahrhundert*, II (Hamburg: Dr. Ernst Hauswedell & Co., 1981), p. 30.

29. Bury, *Littérature et politesse*, p. 93.

created an unprecedented osmosis between literature and life. Half a century later, in the first critical essay on the novel, the celebrated *savant* Pierre Daniel Huet recalled this phenomenon, affirming that narrative in France reflected the interests of gallant society, and that the reading of good novels was a preparation for society life.[30]

Love, introspection, moral reflection, *esprit*, and the art of communication were seen more as the essential qualities of *sociabilité* than as individual experiences; thus they constituted the touchstone of *sociabilité* both for those who enacted them on the world's stage and for those who wrote about them. The public was exactly the same. It would be impossible to read Voiture's letters or Mlle de Scudéry's novels without thinking about their intended readership; impossible to draw an accurate line denoting the counterpoint between society life and worldly poetry; impossible to say who imitated whom in the general effort to please, in the aesthetic of the *naturel*, the elegance of expression, and the construction of sentences by which people spoke as they wrote and wrote as they spoke. In any case, literature's importance in making society aware of itself is unquestionable. The contemplation of his or her own image elevated by poetry, or in complimentary letters, prose portraits, and novels, allowed the reader to judge the distance between the real and the ideal while encouraging an attempt at narrowing the divide. Without ever feeling they were being preached at, readers could thus review the behavior expected of society, take in its aesthetic and moral implications in order to correct their own behavior, improve themselves, and memorize themes, examples, and anecdotes for use in conversation. Literature, because of its optimism, its ability to exaggerate, and its entertaining side, contributed, above all, to an atmosphere of contagious euphoria, of fun and laughter, thus providing that escape to a happy utopia on which the *esprit de société* was based.

By the second half of the seventeenth century the *paideia* had experienced a double assault: that of Cartesianism, which made a tabula rasa of past knowledge, and that of Jansenism, which condemned the false values of humanism. The greatest of society writers—La Rochefoucauld—was inveighing against any form of illusion in the *Maximes*. But society still had its classical writers—Voiture, Corneille, Racine, Pascal, La Fontaine—its own language and style, and absolute confidence in its superior taste. Basically, the victory of the Moderns in the famous *Querelle* that began in the 1680s was also a victory for the nobility, which, convinced of its aesthetic and moral superiority, had arrogated to itself the right to choose and to judge "in ignorance" whatever suited it, without the slightest reference to the authors of antiquity. The new female culture so mocked by Boileau and Molière took its revenge on classical misogyny. It legitimized the new literary genres, which were despised by scholars but which delighted men and

30. *Lettre-traité de Pierre Daniel Huet sur l'origine des romans* (1669).

women of high society. Twenty years before, with the beginning of Louis XIV's personal rule, the nobility had hoped for a different, more important victory. It had cherished the thought of sharing with the young sovereign the worldly ideal it had elaborated for its own glory. After so many tragic misunderstandings court life would once again become a shared undertaking for the nobility and the monarchy, as it had been in the days of the Valois.

At the time of Mazarin's death, Louis was twenty-three years old. Never had France rejoiced in so handsome, so affable, or so courteous a king. He excelled in the exercise of arms, was a skilled horseman and an exceptionally elegant dancer. Unlike his father, Louis enjoyed the company of women. He owed his impeccable manners to his mother, Anne of Austria, and her ladies-in-waiting, whose conversation had been his only school. Maria Mancini had introduced him to love and to novels, and his marriage to the Infanta of Spain in 1660 would not prevent him from indulging his taste for gallantry.

While remaining essential to aristocratic style, gallantry was changing significantly. The ideal of a noble, chaste *parfait amour* of courtly descent that had prevailed from the Blue Room through the time of the Fronde made way during the 1650s for the *précieux* model of Mlle de Scudéry's *Carte de Tendre*. The tendency toward minute analysis had replaced the metaphysical view of love; the casuists had replaced the theologians. With the return of peace, a freer and more relaxed attitude toward relations between the sexes set itself up in contrast to the *précieux* model of *l'amour galant*. Love was no longer seen as a gift of self but as an exaltation of reciprocal desire that retained the delicate elegance of *Tendre* while benefiting ironically from the whole gamut of ambiguities implicit in the very idea of *galanterie*. *Galant* and *galanterie*—keywords in seventeenth-century society—escaped precise definition and changed their meanings according to the context or the verb used. Neither referred exclusively to matters of love. *Galanterie*, for instance, encompassed every nuance of social behavior. It was synonymous with *politesse*, urbanity, and courtesy, and indicated a desire to please and to delight that typified the gaiety of social life. But *l'air galant* meant something a little more. For Mlle de Scudéry it meant that inexpressible, intangible *je ne sais quoi* that could "complete the making of society people . . . causing them to be amiable and to love." An *air galant* was possible in everything: in dress, in attitudes, and in behavior, but above all in a person's manner of speaking. "In fact," Mlle de Scudéry went on, "there is an oblique way of saying things that gives them a different value; it is always the case that those who have a gallant turn of mind can often say things which others only dare to think."[31]

From the 1650s on, with the crisis of the Fronde behind it and having renounced all political ambition, Parisian society experienced a new intense

---

31. Mlle de Scudéry, "De l'air galant," in *"De l'air galant" et autres conversations (1653–1684)*, p. 53.

worldly season, daring not only to think about but to practice a joyful epicureanism and pleasure-seeking elegantly disguised by the conventions of *Tendre*. Having lost its innocence, the flirtatious banter of the *Précieuse* lent the protection of style to a whole range of bold double meanings. With its poets and artists and the prestigious example of its patrons, the Académie Fouquet—the circle surrounding Louis's glamorous minister of finance—actively promoted this new lifestyle. The golden age of gallantry had been inaugurated. After the superintendent's abrupt disgrace in 1661, the King with his young court adopted the vogue for gallantry as their own, attracting all the attention and dictating the rules of fashion and style.

II. The Court as Theater

The court really was young, beautiful, and gallant. In 1661 Louis was twenty-three, as was his wife, Maria Teresa; his brother, Monsieur, was twenty-one and his sister-in-law, Henrietta of England, was seventeen. The favorites and the ladies- and gentlemen-in-waiting were young too. They had the grace, heedlessness, and gaiety typical of youth. They must have made an irresistible impression indeed, if Mme de Motteville, spokeswoman for Anne of Austria's old court, could not help but declare, "I had never seen the court looking more beautiful than it appeared to me then."[32]

The King of course set the tone. His love of life equaled his wish to rule. Freed now from the double tutelage of Mazarin and his mother, he could openly devote himself to both passions. He was determined to enjoy himself and to be admired, but he realized that for there to be magnificence combined with grace and etiquette with exquisite manners, the court required a strong female personality. Since his timid Spanish wife was not capable of the task, he turned for help to his brother's wife, who had learned from life's misfortunes at an early age how important it was to make oneself agreeable.

Henrietta was the daughter of Charles I of England and Louis XIII's sister, Henrietta Maria; from childhood on she had suffered terrible ordeals: her father's death on the scaffold, exile, poverty, the charity of the French royal family. Even her brilliant dynastic marriage, arranged when her brother, Charles II, returned to England to claim the throne, was fraught with difficulties. Monsieur, despite his homosexual leanings, proved a jealous, moody husband. "Never has a princess been more touching," wrote the Abbé de Choisy (who shared Monsieur's taste for women's clothes) "nor appeared as much as she did to wish one to be charmed by the pleasure of seeing her. Her whole person was enveloped

---

32. *Mémoires de Mme de Motteville*, Vol. 4, p. 257.

in charm; she was interesting, and one loved her without thinking that one could do otherwise."[33]

Louis was the first to be struck by Henrietta's charms. Anne of Austria, realizing how the honest gallantry of her younger days had developed into a dangerous game, one in which desire was no longer held in check by morality, was much alarmed by the King's understanding with his sister-in-law. In the city as well as at court, respectable, unhappy lovers had become decidedly out of date. Gallantry aside, Henrietta provided the perfect example of that difficult art of pleasing without condescension that had, until now, been much in demand in polite society. Her good taste is confirmed by the protection she afforded Racine and her friendship with Mme de Lafayette. For his part, Louis loved music, dancing, the theater, and opera, while Monsieur himself was a knowledgeable collector of pictures, precious objects, coins, and jewels. At the Louvre and the Tuileries, at the palaces of Saint-Germain, Vincennes, and Fontainebleau, the King amused himself and his itinerant court with festivities, spectacles, and ballets, all of which proved to be at the vanguard of artistic taste. Monsieur and Madame repaid his hospitality with equally extraordinary receptions at Saint-Cloud and the Palais-Royal. The princes of the blood did likewise.

Enchanted, the French nobility could not but admire its sovereign, and even the most blasé foreigners were clearly bowled over. While visiting the gardens at Saint-Cloud in 1668, the Florentine Lorenzo Magalotti was struck by a sight that left him in a state of "blissful ecstasy," which he hastened to report to his master, Cosimo de' Medici, the future grand duke of Tuscany. Magalotti described suddenly seeing "a great number of knights adorned with plumes and ribbons" appear "from every part of the wood and the hillside," followed by the King "on a kind of triumphal chariot, all golden and painted and driven by himself as he sat between Madame and the Princesse de Monaco, with the rest of the chariot filled with ladies . . . and behind it came two other brocaded open carriages filled with ladies and driven by knights."[34]

Four years earlier, on the evening of May 7, 1664, Louis XIV had inaugurated the *Plaisirs de l'Île enchantée* in equally fabulous style, appearing at the head of twelve knights dressed elaborately *à la grecque*, each of whom represented a paladin from *Orlando furioso*.[35] The King had chosen to represent Ruggiero. His heraldic emblem was a sun—"to show that he, like the Sun, was unique"; his motto, *Nec cesso, nec erro*, meant "that, like the Sun, he never tired or erred in his

---

33. *Mémoires pour servir à l'histoire de Louis XIV par feu M. l'abbé de Choisy*, pp. 187–188.

34. Lorenzo Magalotti, *Diario di Francia dell'anno 1668*, edited by Maria Luisa Doglio (Palermo: Sellerio, 1991), pp. 143–144.

35. *Les Plaisirs de l'Île enchantée* (Paris: R. Ballard, 1664), anonymous account reproduced in Molière, *Œuvres complètes*, edited by G. Couton, two volumes (Paris: Gallimard/Bibliothèque de la Pléiade, 1956), Vol. 1, pp. 601–618.

glorious Works."[36] The splendid cortège having filed past, the twelve paladins dismounted and displayed their dexterity in an exhibition of running at the ring. The program of what could be called the first modern theatrical festival, which included the first performance of Molière's *Tartuffe*, continued for five more days with spectacles and every imaginable entertainment.

The *Plaisirs* represented a conscious return to the great pageantry of the Valois, with their ballets, their tournaments, and their mixture of mythological and courtly themes. These were court festivities for the elite, celebrated in the privacy of the royal houses and gardens, in marked contrast to the traditional public festivities on which Louis XIV turned his back. The tournament that took place in Paris to celebrate his marriage in 1662 was, in fact, the last urban festival of his reign. Louis XIV drew on Ariosto, the Italian poet most favored by French nobles, to reintroduce the illusory continuity between feudal custom and the absolute monarchy. In doing so, he turned to his own advantage both the nostalgia of the warrior class and the pastoral fantasy that the nobility had cultivated away from the court and in opposition to it—at the very moment when life at court marked a new stage in the nobility's subjugation. By adopting polite society's rationale of selection and distinction, court festivities were no longer open to everyone. A line of demarcation was drawn between the court and the rest of society, which was excluded. To make it quite clear that he brooked no competition, after Fouquet's disgrace the King summoned to Versailles all the artists the superintendent had employed at Vaux-le-Vicomte to prepare the fatal festivities of August 17, 1661: Molière, the choreographer Théodore Beauchamp, the composer Lully, the writer and librettist Isaac de Benserade, the costume designer Henry Gissey.

Yet in putting aside the insignia of royalty, however briefly, in order to play the role of the prototype valiant warrior Ruggiero, Louis XIV paid homage to the chivalric ideal that was also his. It would be the last time the King of France agreed to descend from the pedestal of absolute monarchy and to appear alongside his knights. Never had the sovereign so gracefully incarnated the person of *premier gentilhomme du royaume*—first gentleman of the kingdom—as on that inaugural night. Thereafter he placed an unbridgeable gap between himself and his subjects. If the Sun King continued to dance "in public" in court ballets with a few chosen courtiers until 1670, this carefully directed display in fact became more and more theatrical. There is an "imperceptible transition," writes Philippe Beaussant, "from the sovereign mingling with his subjects, dancing among and with them, to the sovereign as director of a choreography centered on himself alone. . . . The 'ballet de cour' is nothing but the 'ballet du roi.'"[37] For the next ten years, the lavish festivities with their impossible-to-reproduce series of ephemeral

36. *Gazette de France* (Paris: Théofraste Renaudot, 1643–1672), year 1664, pp. 482–484.

37. Philippe Beaussant, *Le Roi-Soleil se lève aussi* (Paris: Gallimard, 2000), p. 151.

marvels became a sophisticated propaganda instrument for promoting the Sun King's politics. It was their location that made these festivities impossible to reproduce; the gardens at Versailles provided the background and inspiration for the Sun King's entertainments. At one nod from a creator capable of turning the wildest fantasy into reality, nature became pure spectacle; trees became elaborate architecture; fireworks illuminated the night sky; water, brought by the miracles of hydraulic engineering from distant springs, cascaded in streams and fell in jets and sudden gushes and in gentle drops like rain, competing in euphony with the King's violins.

On the last evening of August 1674, the "demiurge" presented himself for the admiration of his subjects. As a finale to the *Divertissements de Versailles* of that year (which had celebrated the conquest of the Franche-Comté), Louis XIV appeared in a gondola in the middle of the Grand Canal. Around him in the night, 20,000 lights illuminated an enchanted landscape. This shimmering watery scene came at the close of the great festivities, but they had accomplished what they set out to do. Less than a decade later, on May 6, 1682, after twenty years of building, Louis settled definitively at Versailles. For the next thirty years the different moments of his day—his *lever*, his *coucher*, mass, mealtimes, walks, audiences, and receptions —would constitute the sole and incomparable spectacle allowed the French court.

What could have illustrated the sovereign's conception of monarchy and his political vision better than the daily presentation of his own life? "We are not as private individuals. We owe ourselves entirely to the public," the King declared. Such a renunciation of privacy in fact demanded an equal sacrifice on the part of the subjects. Obliged to reside at Versailles, the country's elite were invited to participate daily in the spectacle of the court. No longer did they have the freedom or the time to lead independent lives outside the official one, or to cultivate the pleasures of *la bonne compagnie*. Reduced to a mere "province," Paris had ceased to be the social center, and the *esprit de société* went underground, taking refuge in various isolated homes. Charles de Saint-Évremond, exiled for his implication in the Fouquet scandal, rediscovered in London the pleasures of conversation *à la française* with two Mazarinettes: Hortense Mancini, Duchesse de Mazarin, and Marianne, Duchesse de Bouillon. The grand libertine ladies and *esprits forts*—independent minds—were not alone in having to leave France. The large-scale Huguenot emigration represented a terrible denunciation of the Sun King's intolerant politics, but it also "contributed to the Frenchification of Europe," by spreading the French language and culture throughout Germany, England, and Holland.[38]

In his enormous effort to exercise all power himself and in one place, to monopolize society life, and to display the best results of his artistic patronage, Louis XIV was careful to appropriate the entertainments most cherished by the leisured aristocracy. Beginning in the autumn of 1682 the King instituted his

---

38. Louis Antoine de Caraccioli, *L'Europe française* (Paris: chez la veuve Duchesne, 1776), p. 33.

soirées d'appartement. The *Précieuses* had started the fashion of receiving on fixed days in order to avoid clashes between various circles. Louis, however, had no such preoccupations and simply wanted entertainment to be as systematically regulated by the court calendar as were official ceremonies. On Mondays, Wednesdays, and Thursdays, from seven to ten in the evening, the whole court was welcomed in the magnificent reception rooms—the rooms of Apollo, Mercury, Mars, and Diana and the great Hall of Mirrors. Each room had its own particular function, and visitors went according to their whim from the game of hazard to billiards, to dancing and music, to the magnificent vision of pyramids of fruit and dessert and other refined delicacies that anticipated the meal to come. On such occasions etiquette was less strict, and the King, with only one escort, circulated most affably from room to room, behaving like an ordinary host and forbidding his guests to rise as he passed. On the other weekdays leisure time was devoted to the theater. Saturday was set aside for dancing.

Nothing equaled the splendor of those receptions, the beauty of the décor, the elegance of the guests, the quality of the spectacles, and, particularly, the musical performances. Music, which was part of every moment of Louis XIV's day, benefited from both the King's lavish expenditure and his passionate love and talent for it. And nothing, despite his appalling egoism and an idolatrous personal cult, could compare with the King's good manners. Even the Duc de Saint-Simon, his fiercest detractor, had to acknowledge that the sovereign had perfect manners. "He never chanced to say anything disobliging to anyone, and if he had to take someone up, to reprimand or to correct them, which was very rare, he always did so with a more or less kindly air, hardly ever cuttingly, and never with anger.... Never was a man more naturally good-mannered, with such measured, such graduated manners, and so able to acknowledge age, merit, and rank.... But especially with women, no one was his equal. He never passed the humblest coif without doffing his hat, and I am speaking of housemaids whom he knew to be such."

The King's elegance and precision of movement betokened his legendary self-control and a religious respect for etiquette, but they also reflected the agility and grace he had learned from hours spent with dancing masters. As Saint-Simon tells us, he even took his hat off with the virtuosity of a conjuror. "To ladies he took his hat right off, raising it more or less high; to titled people, he half raised it, holding it in the air or level with his ear for a more or less marked instant or two; to gentlemen, he was pleased to touch his hat. He doffed it, as he did for ladies, to princes of the blood."[39]

Nonetheless, this extraordinary theatrical production could not bring to Versailles the *esprit de société* that had animated the aristocratic Parisian circles. The crowded, identical *soirées d'appartement* to which the whole court was invited

---

39. Saint-Simon, *Mémoires*, Vol. 5, pp. 527–528.

lacked the essential conditions of animated society. People associated there because of caste and not because of free choice. How, moreover, could the King's presence be reconciled with that other unshakeable tenet of the aristocratic world: the exclusion of any outside authority from the social dynamic? And how could the euphoric atmosphere and sense of complicity in conversation of a small group be recreated within a throng of courtiers, all of whom were vying with one another? "If someone asked me in what *honnêteté* consisted, I would say that it is no more than excelling in everything regarding life's pleasures and rules of behavior, and on that, it seems to me, the most perfect and most agreeable worldly commerce depends."[40]

Between 1630 and 1660 aristocratic *honnêteté* was grounded in a belief in society's autonomy and the possibility of succeeding in the "art of being oneself." Aesthetic and moral perfection appeared to reflect one another. Beginning in 1682, however, when Louis XIV required the *honnête homme* to renounce his freedom and to learn to serve, the King came face to face with an ideal that was already in crisis. Fortunately, *honnêteté* taught the art of adapting to the world. Unlike Molière's misanthrope, the real *honnête homme* did not pick a ridiculous quarrel with the world around him but knew how to distance himself quietly while retaining his personal inner freedom and expressing himself to others through his personality. Because of this basic ambiguity, the germ of which was always there, the term *honnête homme* was no sooner coined than it became inadequate to describing all the promises it held. Just as the word *esprit* gave rise to numerous adjectives to clarify its exact meaning, so did society with its passion for analysis and classification immediately qualify *honnête homme* with terms such as *homme de bien, homme de qualité, galant homme, habile homme, homme du monde,* or *homme de bonne compagnie,* all of which subtly defy translation. Each new definition reassured and at the same time raised new questions, since nothing could clearly guarantee transparency nor reveal the intentions hidden behind the best manners. In the end, the *honnête homme* was, for Jean de La Bruyère, no more than "someone who does not rob on the highways, who kills no one, whose vices are not, in the long run, scandalous."[41] Although reduced to a mere accessory, courtesy nonetheless retained something of the old ideal. It was the last obeisance paid by vice to virtue. This basic ambiguity was what made it possible during the long final thirty years of the Sun King's reign for the *honnête homme* to adapt to Versailles and fulfill his duties as a courtier without being untrue to himself. In a life where all was pomp and ceremony, where every gesture was designed to glorify the monarch, he could, in his inner conscience, retain his autonomous judgment and remain faithful to the memory of an aesthetic of pure grace and to the art of social perfection as an end in itself.

---

40. Méré, "De la vraie honnêteté," in *Œuvres complètes,* Vol. 3, p. 70.

41. Jean de La Bruyère, "Des jugements," in *Les Caractères,* edited by Louis van Delft (Paris: Imprimerie Nationale, 1998), p. 389.

Throughout his life Louis XIV maintained an almost unchanged calendar of court entertainment, with an inflexible discipline and without regard to family deaths, military defeat, famine, or France's isolation on the political map of Europe. Only in old age did he refrain from attending them in person. But no royal will could prevent the monotony and boredom that resulted from the ever-increasing conformity of Versailles. The monarch had never made a secret of the fact that he resented his guests' desertion, and the terror of incurring his censure was usually stronger than the wish to escape. The first noisy examples of insubordination were manifested from within the royal family, whose members had a better chance of receiving the sovereign's indulgence.

It is hardly surprising that the first to set a bad example were the nephews of Mme de Longueville and the Grand Condé, the young Bourbon-Contis. Not satisfied with scandalizing the court by their irregular behavior, Louis Armand de Bourbon, Prince de Conti, and his brother, François Louis, Prince de La Roche-sur-Yon, defied royal authority and left Versailles without permission to go and fight the Turks in Hungary in 1685. The escapade was doubly reprehensible because the gesture reaffirmed—like a similar gesture in the days of the Fronde—the nobleman's right to take up arms in a just cause; furthermore, however just the defense of Christian Europe might have seemed, it did not accord at all with Louis XIV's pro-Ottoman and anti-Habsburg politics. Nonetheless, this unseasonable romanticism found a following among noblemen who, like the Marquis de Lassay, could not see themselves as courtiers and who sought an answer to existential questions by taking up their hereditary vocation on the battlefield.

The King was already extremely cross even before his *cabinet noir* intercepted the princes' letters, which were written in tones of unheard-of insolence. He did not hesitate to show his displeasure. The Prince de La Roche-sur-Yon was exiled to Chantilly, and the Prince de Conti was denied the privileges of the *grandes entrées*, which had allowed him to attend the most intimate ceremonies of the King's *lever* and *coucher*. This great honor had been conferred on Conti barely a year earlier upon his marriage to Mlle de Blois—the King's daughter by Mlle de La Vallière. Its abrogation was as serious as excommunication.

Things went no better with Louis Joseph, Duc de Vendôme, and his brother, Philippe, Grand Prior of the Temple, who were descended from the legitimized bastard of Henri IV and Gabrielle d'Estrées. *Esprits forts*, known for their scandalous ways, these cousins of the King led an independent life that was in itself an insult to Versailles's official style. In both the château d'Anet and their Parisian palace, built within the walls of the Temple, the Vendômes, protected by the near impunity due to their birth, indulged in radical, boundless hedonism; but they also cultivated a taste for beautiful things, for poetry, and for intellectual discussion, and had gathered around them a small circle of free spirits and unbelievers that included Ninon de Lenclos's devoted admirer the Abbé de Châteauneuf and the

Abbé de Chaulieu, who in his verse expressed the unshakeable conviction that "wisdom is the path to all pleasures."[42] It was at the Temple that La Fontaine, who had never been in Louis XIV's good graces, rediscovered toward the end of his life the free atmosphere of the libertine circles of his youth and sought the Vendômes' support. There, among the habitués dedicated to pleasure and poetry, he also rediscovered the same Marquis de La Fare who had long ago broken Mme de La Sablière's heart.

The lodge of the Temple thus became the stronghold of the spirit of independence of the old princely courts, a place open to new ideas. It symbolized the profound cultural change already taking place at the end of the seventeenth century, defined by Paul Hazard as "the European crisis of conscience." "If libertinage means lack of religious belief on the one hand and, on the other, a taste for voluptuous living—thereby suggesting a double liberty, that of the mind and of the senses—both were undergoing a transformation with time."[43] And just as the freethinkers were no longer satisfied with themselves but embraced various ideas from the great modern philosophical movements, so the *voluptueux* renounced all refinement and moderation and gave way to cynicism and dissolution. Thus in the libertinage that reigned during the young Louis XV's regency, the search for balance gave way to excess, and independence of mind made way to frankly indecent morality.

Caught in the crosscurrent and weary of a philosophical skepticism that dared not theorize, the habitués of the Temple inclined to barefaced libertinage, defying by their behavior the moral and religious conventions of the day. The Abbé de Châteauneuf had probably studied the thought of Epicurus more closely than any of the others, and it was he who in 1706 introduced his barely twelve-year-old godson, François-Marie Arouet, to the Temple. It was an initiation the importance of which, after Châteauneuf's death, would not escape the future Voltaire. It was to the Temple that Arouet returned after his studies in order to acquire a taste for elegant living from the "Great" and, with no need of manuals, to "civilize" learning by shaking the dust of academia from his feet.

During the last ten years of Louis XIV's reign, Temple society went through some difficult times. Philippe de Vendôme was exiled to Lyon; the duke, a real military genius, was killed in Spain during the War of the Spanish Succession; the Abbé Servien was imprisoned at Vincennes; and it was only under the Regency that former ways were allowed to be revived. Despite their years, the old pleasure-seekers had not lost their gaiety. In the company of the Duc de Sully, the Abbé de Courtin, the Abbé de Chaulieu, and the Abbé de Bussy, Voltaire went on a voyage

---

42. Quoted in Paul Hazard, *La Crise de la conscience européenne (1680–1715)* (Paris: Fayard, 1961), p. 118.

43. Hazard, *La Crise de la conscience européenne (1680–1715)*, p. 117.

of discovery of worldly poetry of epicurean inspiration and took his first steps in the art of composing epigrams and impromptus, of which he would soon become master. But the Temple's philosophical dilettantism could hardly satisfy his intellectual curiosity or his ever more imperious demands for answers to the great questions of existence. To discover real philosophy—Locke's sensationism and Newton's scientific revolution—he had later to suffer exile across the Channel and to become "an Englishman in London."[43] Nevertheless his youthful encounter with the old voluptuary poets left a profound mark.

Of all the family defections that took place at Versailles, the most painful for Louis XIV was probably that of the Duchesse du Maine. Contrary to expectation, Anne Louise Bénédicte de Bourbon, the Grand Condé's granddaughter, did not consider it an honor to be married to a royal bastard, the Duc du Maine. Her small stature did not hinder her overweening pride and uncontrollable vivacity, which soon terrified her timid husband. The duke, on the other hand, had been imbued with other qualities by his former governess, Mme de Maintenon, who had lavished the same passionate care on developing his sense of respect and duty as she had applied to nurturing his rickets-ridden infant body.

The young duke was deeply religious, sensitive, cultivated, and paralyzed by a reverential admiration for his royal father in the shadow of whose throne he lived, under the wing of Mme de Maintenon. His wife, on the other hand, knew nothing of obedience and barely tolerated an etiquette that reminded her constantly to give precedence to the legitimate princes. She was, moreover, utterly bored by the implacable repetitiveness of court life. To fight the tedium and an increasing feeling of alienation, the duchess, who was not lacking in the intellectual curiosity of the Condés, took comfort in studying and entrusted herself to the guidance of her husband's old tutor, the learned and amiable Nicolas de Malézieu. Soon, however, like a Nouvelle Héloïse *avant la lettre*, the duchess turned her attention to her teacher. Master and pupil left Versailles for Sceaux, there to create a world in the image and likeness of its chatelaine. In the beautiful château built by Louis's minister Colbert, which she entirely renovated, the duchess, as sole and undisputed queen of her little court, could lead a life entirely dedicated to pleasure.

The theater with its unparalleled illusory powers was of course at the top of the list of entertainments; plays that were being regarded with ever-greater suspicion at Versailles were read out loud at Sceaux and translated impromptu from the Latin and Greek by Malézieu himself. They were staged by professional companies, with Mme du Maine and her guests frequently taking the leading roles. At Sceaux, life itself was disguised as uninterrupted theater where nothing was left

---

44. Letter from Voltaire to Mme du Deffand, April 23, 1754, in *Voltaire's Correspondence*, in *The Complete Works of Voltaire, Correspondence and Related Documents*, edited by Theodore Besterman (Geneva: Institut et Musée de Voltaire, 1975), D5786, Vol. 15, p. 67.

to chance. Festivities of all kinds, masques, *Grandes Nuits*, society games, and poetry competitions allowed the duchess to turn her back on the real world without, however, having to forgo the admiration due to a great princess. Louis XIV had wanted the historian and art critic André Félibien to write an illustrated history of all the great festivals at Versailles so that the other European courts could appreciate his magnificence. In turn, the *Divertissements de Sceaux*, collected by the Abbé Genest in 1712, offered a celebration of the Duchesse du Maine by recording the most ephemeral of her entertainments.

But the real novelty of Sceaux lay in its guests. They came from Versailles and Paris, from the high-ranking nobility and the *noblesse de robe*; they were literati, writers, and ambitious young intellectuals who, together in beautiful surroundings, were rediscovering the pleasures of *sociabilité* and conversation. Overbearing, egocentric, and capricious as she was, the Duchesse du Maine, who insisted on the prerogatives of rank, yielded to the superior spirit that the polygraph Bernard de Fontenelle had come to symbolize. It was an *esprit* quite unlike anything that had come before, capable of confrontation, of examination, and of clarifying the most difficult of problems while preserving the elegance and irony of society language. Such analysis undermined the old certainties but at the same time inspired its admirers with an intellectual euphoria that erased any possible regrets. In the name of *esprit*, Sceaux, although aligned with the Ancients in the *Querelle*, opened its arms to the champion of the Moderns, making Fontenelle its "oracle." Of course there was nothing new about an aristocratic circle expressing respect for a writer, accepting him as a regular guest, and inviting him to take part in its entertainments. And no man of letters had ever had a greater genius for self-promotion than Fontenelle. His success, built up through a formidable network of academic, journalistic, and worldly connections, was such that it spread even to those to whom he was fleetingly well-disposed. Never before had a fashionable man of letters been able to confer a qualification of "wit," thus altering ipso facto a person's social condition.

In her *Mémoires*, Mme de Staal-Delaunay tells of the incident that changed her life. As a poor orphan, albeit unusually intelligent and with an excellent education, Marguerite Jeanne Delaunay entered Mme du Maine's service as a simple housemaid, which is what she would probably have remained for the rest of her life had she not written an amusing note to Fontenelle. Despite his contempt for anything that was not purely rational, the distinguished geometer had disconcerted his friends by showing an interest in a ghost story being circulated by a certain Mlle Tétar, then the talk of all Paris. The subject was even discussed at Sceaux and, quite unexpectedly—since she never addressed a word to her—the Duchesse du Maine asked Mlle Delaunay to tell Fontenelle what was being said about his interest in the tale. She immediately obeyed and sent him a note that for its subtlety, wit, and perfectly measured use of banter and teasing proved to be an ideal example of worldly communication. "Mademoiselle Tétar's adventure," wrote Mlle Delaunay,

> has caused less of a stir, Monsieur, than the attention you have paid it. The various judgments concerning the matter oblige me to address you. People are surprised, and perhaps with some reason, that the destroyer of oracles, he who has overturned the Sybils' tripod, should have fallen to his knees by Mademoiselle Tétar's bed. In vain it may be said that he was captivated by the young lady's charms and not her charm; neither the one nor the other is of any value to a philosopher. So everyone is talking about it. What! cry the critics, this man who has so clearly revealed deceptions fabricated a thousand leagues away and more than two thousand years before his time could not see through a ruse woven in front of his eyes! ... For my part, Monsieur, I suspend judgment until I am better enlightened. I will only remark that the singular attention paid to the least of your actions is incontestable proof of the esteem in which the public holds you; and I find something quite flattering even in its censure, so I do not fear it to be an indiscretion to inform you of it. If you wish to repay my trust with yours, I promise to make good use of it.[45]

She continued with polite, indirect allusions to the critical battle Fontenelle was waging in the context of the *Querelle* and to the alarm it caused within the "devout" party. The duchess's maid thus showed that she knew about the intellectual debate of the moment, referring to it clearly and elegantly but without a trace of pedantry, in the purest tradition of literature and polite conversation. Praised by Fontenelle, her letter was copied, distributed, commented on, and admired. There was an adjective to describe all of its qualities—*à propos*—and it was Mlle Delaunay herself who revealed it. Surprised by the enormous and unexpected success of her letter, she elegantly recounts how she wanted to reread what she had written, taking it into account for the first time. Her assessment has the objectivity of a report. "Its merit clearly depends less on the importance of the things discussed than on its being *à propos*"—that is, apt.[46] Like the *bienséances*, the quality of being *à propos* presupposed a precise assessment of place, person, and circumstance. It was a talent in itself which involved *esprit*, an awareness of opportunity, intuition, quickness, and an ability to enter into perfect harmony with one's interlocutors. And although its field of action included every social circumstance, being *à propos* naturally showed itself off to best advantage in conversation.

---

45. Mme de Staal-Delaunay, *Mémoires*, pp. 91–92.

46. Mme de Staal-Delaunay, *Mémoires*, p. 91.

It was to conversation that Mlle Delaunay owed her rise in society. After the success of her letter, she tells us, "Her Serene Highness lowered herself to speak to me and became accustomed to doing so. She was pleased by my replies and took notice of my approval: I even noticed that she sought it and that often, when she spoke, her eyes were turned toward me to seek my attention." The pleasure appears to have been reciprocal: "I gave it to her wholly and effortlessly, since no one has ever spoken so aptly, so clearly, so swiftly, nor in a nobler or more natural fashion. Her wit has recourse to neither artifice or figuration, nor to anything that might be called invention. Vividly struck by what she sees, she renders it just as a mirror reflects it, adding nothing, omitting nothing, changing nothing. So I took great pleasure in listening to her; and since she realized that, she was gratified."[47]

In order to take full advantage of Mlle Delaunay's gifts without breaking the rules of etiquette, the Duchesse du Maine promoted her to lady-in-waiting and had her marry Jean-Jacques de Staal, one of the Duc du Maine's officers. It was a late, melancholy marriage quite devoid of sentiment. Thus enrolled by authority in what Malézieu called the "galleys of wit," Mme de Staal-Delaunay would have had the honor of contributing by her intelligence to the creation of the first great eighteenth-century social center. But her writing, a detached chronicle of a splendid succession of festivities and entertainments, already betrays that anguished feeling of unreality and emptiness that throughout the century would threaten the euphoria of the privileged. Some decades later, one of her best friends, Mme du Deffand, would bear the most lucid witness to this anguish, and on the eve of the Revolution, Nicolas Chamfort would denounce it with iconoclastic fury for having its roots deeply buried in the very idea of society's perfection.

III. The Revenge of Paris

While the *esprit de société* did not await the passing of the Sun King to be roused from its long lethargy, the Regency allowed for an open and violent rebellion against Louis XIV's principle of order and values. As the rejoicing mob jeered and mocked the funeral carriage with obscene songs as it bore the mortal remains of the aged sovereign to Saint-Denis, Versailles closed its gates and Paris took its revenge.

On September 2, 1715, the day after Louis XIV's death, his nephew, Philippe d'Orléans, assumed the regency and had the Parlement of Paris annul the late King's will; he installed the little Louis XV in the Tuileries and ruled France from the Palais-Royal. As night fell, he withdrew to his private apartments, to dine among friends like an ordinary individual, but reports of his irregular behavior nevertheless became a guaranty for general license. Instead of the *soirées d'appartement*,

---

47. Mme de Staal-Delaunay, *Mémoires*, pp. 95–96.

society men and women masked their faces, mingled with the crowd, and made appointments to meet three times a week at the Opéra ball. They applauded the Italian comedians recalled from exile, and despite all interdictions, fully indulged their passion for the game of hazard. The great aristocratic *hôtels,* which after the decline of the Marais were now concentrated in the boulevard Saint-Germain, relit their lights and reopened their doors. Women abandoned the turreted coiffures of yesteryear, cut their hair and curled and powdered it; they rid themselves of the stiff court crinoline and wore the lightest of Indian silk just floating from the light-weight paniers of their skirts. Freed from its long servitude, French society yielded to all the excesses of a rediscovered freedom. Nobles began to live again, to amuse themselves, to love, and, not least, to converse in broad daylight. "If morality was the loser," wrote the Baron de Benseval, a contemporary witness, "then society gained infinitely. Free from the embarrassment and the cold which the presence of a husband always causes, the freedom was extreme; a vivacious atmosphere was maintained by both men's and women's coquetry, which daily provided for exciting adventures. Languor was banished by the attraction of pleasure, which was fundamental; and the continuous example of the greatest irregularities allowed for the principles of morality and modesty to be challenged."[48]

Once the fever of the Regency was over, the aristocratic world returned, if not to its old values, at least to the punctilious respect of form. It made it a point of honor to disguise its moral laxity behind the delicate veil of *bienséances.* The interval had been too short for a century-old discussion on the art of appearances to be reopened.

Paradoxical though it may seem, it was through society's forced cloistering at Versailles that the national style ultimately became consecrated. "It is to this noble subordination," Talleyrand would later write, evoking the *ancien régime,* "that we owe the art of seemliness, the elegance of custom, the exquisite good manners with which this magnificent age [of Louis XIV] is imprinted."[49] For more than thirty years the French aristocracy had lived in public under the implacable gaze of their King, day after day enacting the same part in the same play, which incorporated all the activities of social life. Elegance of performance was the only free form of expression allowed to individuals, and only through that could they assert their excellence. Those things that had been the distinguishing marks of a small elite—purity of language, extremely refined taste, smiling good manners, and the cult of appearance—became the official style of the French court. Unlike what was happening in other European countries, the French monarch's policy of

---

48. *Mémoires du baron de Besenval sur la cour de la France,* edited by Ghislain de Diesbach (Paris: Mercure de France, 1987), p. 59.

49. *Mémoires de Talleyrand (1754–1815),* edited by Paul-Louis and Jean-Paul Couchoud (Paris: Plon, 1982), p. 74.

centralization during the seventeenth century had concentrated the elite within a small radius of Paris and Versailles, which allowed them to elaborate a shared lifestyle. Obviously an autonomous social life away from the court was impossible for the high-ranking nobility, which could not forgo its rightful posts beside the sovereign, on whom it depended for position, honor, and riches. Thus, with the continuous to-ing and fro-ing between the two worlds, a gradual assimilation of attitudes to behavior was inevitable. With the court installed at Versailles, these ideas were crystallized by the example of the monarch himself into a remarkable synthesis of courtly and society manners, a synthesis that did not entirely survive the Sun King but that unquestionably denoted the beginnings of French hegemony in matters of elegance and manners.

When Louis XV came into his majority in 1723, the court established itself once more at Versailles, but the old monopoly "of grandeur, of manners, of *esprit* and pleasure"[50] had been forever broken. Versailles continued to make a prestigious display of royalty and to be the political and administrative center of the country, but Paris had definitively regained the social and intellectual upper hand. Henceforth, throughout the century, the *ville* rather than the *cour* would provide Europe with the model for a superior art of living. "At Versailles you intrigue, in Paris you amuse yourself," Montesquieu said. Thus, the same nobles, once again free to play both parts, became in turns "courtiers at Versailles and people of the world in Paris."[51]

The court remained a world apart, with its own way of speaking, of dressing, of walking, and of behaving. For all its condescension, however, it could not fail to look at the *ville* with interest, sometimes even finding itself unable to resist the attraction of its fashions. Although he had not wanted in any substantial way to change the daily ceremonial laid down by his great-grandfather, Louis XV disliked performing. Within the corridors of official life, he created a hidden world— the *petits appartements*—which allowed him to lead a double existence. Certainly the choice of a bourgeois mistress strengthened his desire for a private life, the only thing that, according to La Bruyère, Louis XIV had to forgo.[52] Mme de Pompadour knew how to keep the King amused, how to make conversation interesting, and how to preside gaily and graciously over the small suppers for a few friends that took place in the *petits appartements*. She could think up all sorts of surprises and entertainments for the sovereign's sole benefit. In the first place, she initiated the memorable *théâtre des cabinets* in which for four years, from 1747 to

50. *Mémoires de la Comtesse de Brancas, suivis de la Correspondance de Mme de Chateauroux et d'extraits de mémoires pour servir à l'Histoire de Perse*, edited by Eugène Asse (Paris: Librairie des Bibliophiles, 1890), p. 21.

51. *Mémoires de la Comtesse de Brancas*, p. 19.

52. La Bruyère, "Du Souverain ou de la République," in *Les Caractères*, p. 318.

1750, she led a company of dilettante aristocrats as an actress, singer, and leading player. So Versailles, too, welcomed society's passion for treading the boards. Enjoyed by Mme du Maine, the Brancas, Mme d'Épinay, and Mme de Montesson, among others, society theatricals were the entertainments most typical of aristocratic leisure throughout the century. "At least ten of our society ladies," wrote the Prince de Ligne, "can act and sing better than the best actresses I have seen in our theaters."[53] Later, even Marie-Antoinette threw herself into the fray, playing various parts at the Trianon, including Colette in Rousseau's *Devin du village* and Rosine in Beaumarchais's *Barbier de Séville*. A desire for intimacy and friendship and the wish to amuse herself like any young Parisian lady made her reluctant to play the only part suited to her: that of queen. So it was that the aspects of her private life that Marie-Antoinette did not display in public became the subject of speculation and slander. Etiquette might seem a tyranny, but the duties it imposed guaranteed respect of each individual's particular rights. After all, Louis XIV had based the building of Versailles on the reciprocal sacrifice of liberty. Versailles vowed to harbor a merciless grudge against the Austrian queen for cheating it of its raison d'être. The *légende noire* about Marie-Antoinette that would prove so fatal to the *ancien régime* was not started in the city's most progressive circles but in the court's most conservative ones.

IV. The Patriarch of Ferney

"You will say about this century whatever you please," wrote Melchior Grimm to Voltaire in 1770. "Since you created it and it will bear no name other than yours, posterity will willingly grant you the right to do the honors and to say more ill of it than it deserves."[54] In calling him the father of the century, Grimm was not merely adulating Voltaire but was acting as the spokesman of widespread opinion. For most of his contemporaries, the patriarch of Ferney represented the very symbol of the Enlightenment and, more than anyone else, personified critical reasoning, questioning of dogma, hatred of transcendence, faith in progress and science, the belief in a universal morality, the defense of human rights, and the spirit of tolerance. But more than anything else, as Julie de Lespinasse remarked, "He has the tone and the flavor of his century par excellence; he is its delight and its ornament."[55]

---

53. Hippolyte Taine, *Les Origines de la France contemporaine*, two volumes (Paris: Laffont/coll. Bouquins, 1986), Vol. 1, p. 118.

54. Letter from Grimm to Voltaire, December 8, 1770, in Voltaire's *Correspondence*, D16813, Vol. 37, p. 120.

55. Julie de Lespinasse, "Apologie d'une pauvre personne," in *Nouvelles Lettres de Mademoiselle de Lespinasse* (Paris: Maradan, 1820), p. 287.

Yet by both his work and his lifestyle, this champion of the new would bear greater witness than anyone to the continuity of the culture of French polite society long after its traditional view of the world had been overturned. It was Voltaire who, disillusioned by the Regency, rehabilitated Louis XIV's work and laid the foundations for the myth of the *Grand Siècle*. It was Voltaire, too, who right up until his last tragedy defended the cause of the classical language and aesthetic. In both his life and his work he carried the banner of aristocratic taste: a taste for refinement and pomp, for independence and elegant libertinism, for generosity and the *beau geste*. For him, these qualities were personified in the Maréchal de Richelieu, making Louis XV's *aimable vaurien*[56]—"charming good-for-nothing"—into his hero. Such admiration led to mimicry that did not escape the notice of contemporaries like Sénac de Meilhan. "There was the greatest likeness between Voltaire and the Maréchal de Richelieu in both gesture and tone of voice; it was so striking that one could not deny that they imitated one another. The poet had doubtless copied the manners of the man who had the most éclat and most success in society; the courtier had seized upon several expressive gestures of the celebrated writer who combined a gracious wit and a society tone together with the greatest talents."[57]

For Voltaire, who was counted on to preside over public opinion and Paris, the choice of aristocratic style led him to aim for an important post at court too, first as gentleman and historiographer to Louis XV and subsequently as intellectual mentor to the Prussian monarch Frederick II. This most versatile of players was, however, unable to hit the right note with crowned heads. Steeped as he was in snobbery, he refused to understand that sovereigns—be they *bien-aimé* or *philosophe*—would never tolerate familiarity.

More than any other writer, Voltaire knew the art of pleasing society, and never was the mutual attraction greater. But for him—unlike for real socialites—society was not an end in itself. It was a means of social climbing, of literary self-promotion, and of winning elite opinion over to his side. These machinations notwithstanding, society life never ceased to be a fount of joy and entertainment for him. "Earthly paradise is where I am." In the last verse of *Le Mondain* (1736), a poem about luxury and pleasure, Voltaire boldly professed a lifestyle to which he would remain faithful until death. Convinced since youth that "the great and only concern is to be happy,"[58] Voltaire when he was over forty proved himself determined to rise above circumstances and to dominate them rather than to

---

56. Letter from Lord Chesterfield to his son, November 24, 1750, in *Letters*, Vol. 4, p. 1611.

57. Gabriel Sénac de Meilhan, *Le Gouvernement, les Mœurs et les Conditions de la France avant la Révolution* (Paris: de Lescure /Poulet-Malassis, 1862), p. 293.

58. Voltaire to Marguerite-Madeleine du Moutier, Marquise de Bernières [April 1722?], in *Voltaire's Correspondence* (1968), D104, Vol. 1, pp. 116–117.

allow them to dominate him. Henceforth, depending on his mood and fate, he managed time and again to profit from the pleasures offered by society or by studious solitude and to alternate between the weaknesses of the courtier and the courage of the *philosophes*. For him happiness meant, above all, remaining faithful to the changing demands of his own ego.

It was not always so. From the age of about thirty, Voltaire had believed he would find his earthly paradise in the aristocratic world. At the Temple, with the Vendômes, with the Duchesse du Maine at Sceaux, and in the sumptuous *hôtels* of the Villars, the Sullys, the Marquise de Bernières, and the Duc de La Vallière, Voltaire found that elegance, grace, impeccable taste, purity of language, and naturalness of tone and style were not merely the trappings of seventeenth-century literature. They had survived in the daily pastimes of a small elite: the *parfaite bonne compagnie*. "A little separate group," as he himself described it, which "being rich, well brought up, educated, polite, is like the flower of the human race; ... it is to please them that the greatest men have worked."[59]

Drawn to his talent and wit, some of these privileged people opened their doors to him and introduced him to society. In the footsteps of the Blue Room's poet Vincent Voiture, Voltaire—son of the notary Arouet—turned his back on his bourgeois origins and recreated himself as a gentleman by the name of Voltaire. Sainte-Beuve would describe him as "the man of letters with the most naturally elegant taste,"[60] and he mastered the nuances of the complex system of the indispensable *bienséances* with remarkable speed. So determined was he to seduce, to please, and to conquer that he learned to control his impetuosity, to restrain his verve for polemic, and to temper his ferocious irony. By adorning his conversation with all of society's rhetoric, he became a remarkable virtuoso in the art of delicate praise and gallant verbal dueling. He was a master of gaiety, of repartee, of the *à propos*. His talent for conversation was matched by a gift for improvisation; he could recite a hundred lines of impromptu verse and dictate page after page of letters or prose of any kind without ever failing the aesthetics of clarity and brevity.

A century earlier, the Chevalier de Méré had stated that a man of the world should present himself with the awareness and lucidity of an actor. Voltaire was drawn to society's center stage by a passion for drama. At the Duchesse du Maine's court he had been able to observe how closely society and the theater reflected each other. In this small realm where every moment of the day was dominated by a love of theater, he could play every part in both repertories. It was at Sceaux, influenced by a performance of Euripides' *Iphigenia in Tauris*—translated by Malézieu—with Mme du Maine in the leading role, that he first became aware

---

59. Voltaire, "Conversation de l'Intendant des Menus en exercise avec l'abbé Grizel," in *Mélanges III*, in *Œuvres complètes*, Vol. 24, p. 247.

60. Sainte-Beuve, "Lettres inédites de Voltaire," in *Causeries du lundi*, Vol. 13, p. 9.

of his vocation for the theater, and he returned there to give a preview reading of his Œdipe (1717), the play that made his name. Over the years he was there at Sceaux in the guise of dramatist, actor, and spectator, and during intervals between productions he put his talent as a conversationalist, narrator, and poet into Mme du Maine's service. It was solely to entertain her that Voltaire wrote Le Crocheteur borgne and Cosi-Sancta. As he was writing them, he read the final chapters of Zadig aloud to her. In exchange he gathered precious firsthand information from the Sun King's daughter-in-law for Le Siècle de Louis XIV. With Voltaire, anecdote at last became part of history. The anecdote, so dear to society, so essential to the pleasure and variety of conversation and to drawing-room poetry, had hitherto been included only in the -ana collections (such as the Segraisiana). Now it was no longer an exemplum with a moral point, either didactic or contentious, but was used in narrative as a formal part of history writing, simple and discursive. The writer's talent, or rather his genius, allowed him to give the anecdote its full historic value in the general context of the narrative without unnecessary explanation or lengthy argument. In Anecdotes sur Louis XV and Anecdotes sur le Czar Pierre le Grand—both published in 1748—a single phrase, the account of a gesture, or a revealing detail gave the characters psychological veracity and humanized history while stressing its symbolic nature. The reader could thus find himself on familiar ground. Throughout his life, Voltaire was a "gleaner,"[61] fascinated by anecdotes and ready to use them as an inexhaustible source of treasure.

Until 1726 no cloud had overshadowed Voltaire's rise in society. Everything led him to believe that merit and birth spoke the same language. But the Chevalier de Rohan's thrashing brought him back to reality; not one of his noble friends was prepared to avenge his humiliation, and none openly defended him.[62] His mortification would soon turn to defiance, however, and his defiance to victory. Exile in England made the poet into a philosophe. Thereafter he no longer wished to be part of a small class of privileged people but, by his own account, put himself forward quite simply as society's master and guide. With him, the man of letters no longer invoked the protection of the Great. He himself became the guardian angel of the persecuted and the innocent. Precisely because of Voltaire's growing authority over public opinion around the middle of the eighteenth century, the position of the man of letters changed, preparing the way for the writer's apotheosis in the Romantic era. For Voltaire, however, the ideal of the philosophe always existed alongside that of the honnête homme, and throughout his life, he wrote, talked, and acted with the honnêtes gens in mind.

---

61. In Le Siècle de Louis XIV, I, in Œuvres complètes, Vol. 14, p. 421, Voltaire compares anecdotes to "a narrow field where one gleans after history's vast harvest."

62. See Chapter 4 for an account of Voltaire's clash with the Chevalier de Rohan.

Voltaire was admired, courted, and revered and so he continued to love society, not for its mythical protection of his dream of social elevation but as the fount of pleasure and power. He was never a great frequenter of salons, and his name does not appear in the list of Mme de Lambert's or Mme de Tencin's guests. His visits to Paris were short and intermittent, and the time required for the life of the drawing room was incompatible with his work schedule. For him, the aristocratic château life that he knew in his youth was far more congenial. There he could combine the pleasures of a select company and informal conversation with the freedom to write, read, and meditate. This was the formula that Voltaire would adopt first at Cirey with Mme du Châtelet, and later in his years of exile at Ferney. Here on the French border with Switzerland, in his small, elegant château with a chapel, a little theater, and a magnificent library that would attract pilgrims from all over Europe, Voltaire declared with rightful pride: "Having lived with kings, I have become a king in my own home."[63]

Voltaire's true salon was his correspondence, which contains the full display of his worldly wisdom and probably constitutes his greatest masterpiece. A small, well-known painting by Jean Hubert hanging in the Hermitage in Saint Petersburg shows Voltaire having just got out of bed and still busy pulling on his breeches as he dictates a letter—perhaps one of the 16,000 that have survived.[64] The voices of the flower of European nobility are interwoven in an extraordinary correspondence, dictated by urgency. For his audience of emperors and kings, queens, electors and sovereign princes, for dukes, marquises, and counts, Voltaire reproduced with infinite inventiveness an endless spectacle of adulation, provocation, seduction, and challenge.

Neither his naturalness nor the bravura of his improvisation should be allowed to mislead; very little in this great display of fireworks was accidental. Voltaire used each of his correspondents as a pawn in a complicated game of chess, which he moved from a distance in accordance with a particular logic. Here he employs Mme du Deffand to help diminish the scandal caused by the *Lettres philosophiques*; there the Margrave of Bayreuth is inspired to court her brother, Frederick of Prussia, on his behalf; the Duchesse de Choiseul can help him obtain the patents he needs for his factories at Ferney.

Conversing by letter with half of Europe was also a way of drawing attention to his exile, an instrument of moral revenge against the government that had thrown him out. "The great merit of France," he wrote to Mme du Deffand in 1759, "its only merit, its unique superiority, lies in the small number of amiable

---

63. *Mémoires pour servir à la vie de M. de Voltaire: Études et Documents biographiques*, in Voltaire, *Œuvres complètes*, Vol. 1, p. 55.

64. There are two other, smaller versions of the same picture in the Musée Carnavalet in Paris and in the Délices in Geneva.

or sublime geniuses who have caused French to be spoken today in Vienna, in Stockholm, and in Moscow. Your ministers, your supervisors, and your chief clerks have no part in this glory."[65] Yet as he himself had claimed not ten years earlier in *Le Siècle de Louis XIV*, this glory could only be French. "The society spirit is the Frenchman's natural lot; it is a virtue and a pleasure of which other peoples have felt the need. The French language of all languages is the one that expresses with the greatest facility, precision, and delicacy all the subjects of the *honnêtes gens*' conversation; and it thereby contributes throughout Europe to one of the greatest pleasures of life."[66]

---

65. Voltaire to Mme du Deffand, October 13, 1759, in *Voltaire's Correspondence*, D8533, Vol. 20, p. 399.

66. Voltaire, *Le Siècle de Louis XIV*, in *Œuvres complètes*, Vol. 14, p. 421.

I4

THE MARQUISE DE LAMBERT:
THE IDEAL OF THE *HONNÊTE FEMME*

"LAST MONTH I LOST the Marquise de Lambert who, although eighty-six years old, had been my friend for a long time. Scholars and gentlemen [*honnêtes gens*] will remember her for many years to come.... Her house honored all those who were admitted there. I dined there regularly on Wednesdays, which was one of her days; there one conversed but there was no question of cards, as there had been at the famous hôtel de Rambouillet, so celebrated by Voiture and Balzac."[1] In August 1733, with his usual insight, the Marquis d'Argenson described in his *Journal* what it was that made his late friend's house the first intellectual center of the eighteenth century. For over thirty years, the Marquise de Lambert had received visitors twice a week, men of letters and socialites on perfectly equal terms, making it possible for them to "reason" together with mutual respect and to learn from one another. As d'Alembert wrote, "The learned brought knowledge and enlightenment; the others brought those good manners and that urbanity which even the worthy need to acquire.... Men of the world left her house more cultivated and men of letters more amiable."[2] But Mme de Lambert's initiative, which bestowed social standing on writers, philosophers, and scholars and initially formed eighteenth-century *sociabilité*, took its inspiration from the past and came in the wake of a now secular tradition. In comparing conversations held at the marquise's house with those at the hôtel de Rambouillet, d'Argenson was able to pay his old friend the compliment she would have most cherished; by opening the doors of her splendid apartment in the hôtel de Nevers to a chosen circle, Mme de Lambert probably aimed at recreating the atmosphere of the Blue Room.

---

1. *Journal et Mémoires du marquis d'Argenson, publiés pour la première fois d'après les manuscrits autographes de la Bibliothèque du Louvre par la Société de l'Histoire de France*, edited by E. J. B. Rathery, nine volumes (1859–1867; Johnson Reprint Corporation, 1968), Vol. 1, pp. 163–164.

2. Jean le Rond d'Alembert, *Éloge de Saint-Aulaire*, in *Œuvres de d'Alembert*, five volumes (Paris: A. Belin, 1821–1822), Vol. 3, p. 295.

As a widow over the age of fifty, having finished educating her children and having put the family's legal and inheritance affairs in order, the marquise devoted herself to a worldly project that was perfectly in keeping with her aristocratic role and her honor as a gentlewoman. In the last dark, suffocating days of the Sun King's reign, she reacted to the decline in the *esprit de société*, the vulgarization of taste, and the furtive libertinism by making her house into a happy island where elegance and decorum might coexist with intellectual curiosity and moral deliberation. Like Mme de Rambouillet, the marquise turned her back on the court and created, with attention to the slightest detail, a private world in her own image. Like Arthénice, she was wholly virtuous, had a gift for friendship, and cultivated a great variety of interests.

Whereas the Blue Room provided Mme de Lambert with a model for perfect aristocratic leisure pursuits and brought all the power of its legendary reputation to bear on her, in Mme de La Sablière's drawing room she had acquired firsthand experience of a marvelous Abbaye de Thélème, the utopia described by Rabelais. The marquise had been in time to attend the gatherings in the rue Neuf-des-Petits-Champs in person, where she was profoundly struck by the charm of the hostess and by the quality of her guests. Some fifteen years later, her drawing room would adopt the same happy formula: a small group of *honnêtes gens*—men of letters, scholars, and socialites—ready to combine literary pastimes with philosophical and scientific discussion.

Ninon de Lenclos's salon in the rue des Tournelles, which she held in her old age from 1690 to 1705, must have served as the third model to which Mme de Lambert referred when making her own plans. The literary education she had received in youth from her mother's second husband, the libertine writer François de Bachaumont, must have predisposed the marquise to admire the aging courtesan for her superior culture and intellectual elegance. Mme de Lambert shared her refined epicureanism, her belief in the dignity of women, and her ideal of wisdom, and gave her a voice as Ismène in *Discours sur le sentiment d'une Dame*. After Ninon's death, the marquise inherited some of her guests, notably the Abbé Terrasson, who played a large part in the literary life of the first half of the eighteenth century.

With the turn of the century, it was through Mme de Lambert that society culture reasserted the relevance of its ideals and its permanence as a model. Yet in the very act of reestablishing a tradition, the marquise founded another one. Whereas for Mme de Rambouillet the nobility's opposition to intellectualism would have made any kind of organized conversation inadmissible, Mme de Lambert did not hesitate to make her house a *bureau d'esprit* where every Tuesday she welcomed men of letters, scholars, philosophers, and scientists, encouraging them to express their ideas on preestablished subjects according to a classic academic ritual. When, around 1630, Valentin Conrart and his lettered friends took to meeting in the rue Saint-Martin in order to "consult" freely, *en petit comité*, on literary matters close to their hearts, they took the hôtel de Rambouillet as their model.[3] It was not until Cardinal de Richelieu decided to make it official that they became established as an academy. On Mme de Lambert's Tuesdays, however, academic culture took its turn, widening its public to include society people. The hôtel de Nevers's richly decorated rooms thus became the scene of a true revolution. Men of letters were no longer there to serve and entertain the privileged; they became instead teachers and mentors to the *honnêtes gens*. Whereas, for their part, the writers continued to please and never failed in their commitment to clarity, the aristocrats forgot their detachment and threw themselves enthusiastically into learning.

Bernard de Fontenelle's influence certainly contributed to Mme de Lambert's change of direction. Her salon is usually said to have begun around 1698–1700 because those dates coincide with her move to the hôtel de Nevers and with the important part played there by Fontenelle, who was already a member of the Académie française and who, in 1699, was given the important job of permanent secretary to the Académie des sciences.

Born in 1657, Fontenelle was ten years younger than Mme de Lambert, but he too was a perfect example of society culture in the *Grand Siècle*. During the course of his long life, he never betrayed the *Mercure de France*'s description of him when at the age of twenty he began to collaborate with it: "There is no science on which he does not reason solidly; but he does so in an easy manner and one which has none of the rudeness of professional scholars. He likes fine introductions, only to use them as an *honnête homme*; he has a refined, delicate, and gallant mind."[4] The only criticism of him was that he "lacked heart," which might, according to Montesquieu, have helped "to make him more agreeable in society."[5] As an immensely versatile writer with a genius for explaining subjects, Fontenelle nonetheless wanted to be a writer for the elite. "Let us be satisfied with a small, select group," he said to the marquise in *Entretiens sur la pluralité des mondes*, "and let us not divulge our mysteries to the people."[6]

The "small, select group" was of course high society, and throughout his life Fontenelle's influence owed more to "his conversation and his example than to his

---

3. "We are forming a circle of *beaux esprits* where, each week, as on Saturdays at the Hôtel de Rambouillet, we will discuss the offspring of our Muse amongst ourselves"; Charles Pellisson, *Histoire de l'Académie*, quoted in Roger Marchal, *Mme de Lambert et son milieu* (Oxford: The Voltaire Foundation, 1998), p. 349.

4. *Dictionnaire des Lettres Françaises: Le XVIIIe siècle*, revised and updated by François Moureau (Paris: Fayard, 1995).

5. Guillaume Thomas Raynal, *Anecdotes littéraires*, Vol. 3 (1766), p. 269, cited in Robert Shackleton, *Montesquieu: A Critical Biography* (Oxford University Press, 1961).

6. Bernard Le Bovier de Fontenelle, *Entretiens sur la pluralité des mondes habités, sixième soir*, in *Œuvres complètes de Fontenelle* (Paris: Fayard, 1991), Vol. 2, p. 116.

writing. His courtesy, the moderation with which he supported his ideas, [and] his apparent modesty in success attracted even the most susceptible of the *beaux esprits*."[7] His faithfulness to the worldly style of his youth would become more and more evident with the passage of time, and describing him in his ripe old age, the Marquis d'Argenson captured the historic essence of this witness to the past who so flourished in the present:

> He is regarded as one of those masterpieces of delicately and carefully worked art, which one must take care not to destroy because nothing is made like it anymore. He reminds us not only of Louis XIV's resplendent century, so noble and so great, the end of which some of us witnessed, but also of the spirit of Benserade, of Saint-Évremond, the Scudérys, and of the tone of the hôtel de Rambouillet, whose air, one can believe, he breathed in that very place. He has it, that same tone, though gentler, more polished, but in touch with our own century.... His conversation is infinitely agreeable, abounding in the most refined rather than the most striking characteristics and the sharpest of anecdotes, without their being cruel, since they are only about literary or gallant subjects or society bickering [*tracasseries*].[8]

Yet this perfect exponent of a past culture believed only in the present, waged a tireless battle against authority, and believed in modernity as in a religion. His weapons were intellectual lucidity and the ability to write in language that, having rid itself of classical solemnity, acquired the immediacy of the spoken word. Mme de Lambert was the first to admire the naturalness and simplicity of Fontenelle's choice of words and the precision of a language freed of affectation.

Fontenelle loved the times in which he lived and believed that man could find happiness on this earth through the perfection of behavior, taste, reasoning, and knowledge. During the Regency and before it become the property of the *philosophes*, this faith in the progress of the human spirit was known as the *nouvelle préciosité*. This conviction, shared by all the Moderns, was not only about morality, nor was it only to do with women, but like seventeenth-century *préciosité* it believed that culture would overcome prejudice, ignorance, and the brutality of the instincts. And no one was more ready to identify with this new wave of optimism than the Marquise de Lambert, true *précieuse* that she was.

Mme de Lambert's salient characteristics were her sense of duty and her taste for reflection. Having read widely, from Plutarch and Seneca to Montaigne and

---

7. Frédéric Deloffre, *Une Préciosité nouvelle: Marivaux et le Marivaudage* (1955; Geneva: Slatkine Reprints, 1993), p. 17.

8. *Mémoires et Journal inédit du marquis d'Argenson, ministre des Affaires étrangères sous Louis XV*, edited by M. le Marquis d'Argenson, five volumes (Paris: P. Jannet, 1857–1858), Vol. 5, p. 85.

the moralists of Louis XIV's time, the marquise used her learning to help her confront her duties with seriousness and awareness—duties as the wife of a great aristocrat, as a widow in the position of managing the family fortune, as a mother, and as a lady in society. Her own worldview was a personal synthesis of "common ground" taken from the classical *paideia*, the aristocratic ethic, *précieux* feminism, *honnêteté*, and Jansenist thought. Furthermore, her beliefs, developed through deep moral reflection, were ultimately expressed in her writing. The breadth and consistency of her interests can be seen from a glance at the titles of her major works: *Avis d'une mère à sa fille* (1688–1692), *Avis d'une mère à son fils* (1695–1702), *Traité de l'Amitié, Traité de la Vieillesse* (1700–1705), *Discours sur le Sentiment d'une dame, Lettre sur l'Éducation d'une jeune demoiselle* (circa 1715), *Réflexions sur les Femmes* (1715–1723), *Discours sur la différence qu'il y a de la Réputation à la Considération* (1724–1726). Already inclined toward solitary reflection, the marquise gained intellectual confidence and a new boldness from her friendship with Fontenelle, which enabled her, in absolute keeping with the *bienséances*, to converse with the most brilliant men of letters of the day. In turn, this friendship provided Fontenelle with a distinguished setting for exchanging ideas and conducting philosophical discussions. Under Fontenelle's influence, "Mme de Lambert's salon found itself at the heart of literary fashion and became the breeding ground for an ambitious plan whose aim was to unite women, society, the academic institutions, and certain influential political circles in bringing about the triumph of modern ideas."[9]

Mme de Lambert devoted herself to the creation of her salon with the diligence and seriousness of purpose typical of her other decisions in life. Since she minded what society thought and did not wish to be accused of intellectualism, she protected herself by instituting two separate reception days: Tuesdays were for men of letters, and Wednesdays for society. The division of guests was not, however, compulsory. Several went from one gathering to the other, and many—including the Président Hénault, Montesquieu, the Abbé de Choisy, Valincourt, and the Marquis de Saint-Aulaire—claimed right of entry to both. In 1728, for instance, Montesquieu, who was traveling in Italy, asked the marquise to remember him to the guests at both receptions: "Speak of me on Tuesdays, that is to the dearest friends I have in the world; and speak of me on Wednesdays, this day is no less happy than the other when one can delight in it."[10] Not that this prevented Mme de Lambert from presiding over the Tuesdays with the appropriate respect for ritual in mind.

---

9. Marchal, *Mme de Lambert et son milieu*, p. 211.

10. Montesquieu to Mme de Lambert, April 30, 1728, in Montesquieu, *Œuvres complètes*, edited by Louis Desgraves and Edgar Mass, twenty-two volumes (Oxford: The Voltaire Foundation, 1998), Vol. 1, p. 324.

THE AGE OF CONVERSATION

On Tuesdays there were usually no more than about twenty guests who arrived at the marquise's house at midday for the lunch hour. During the meal, the subjects for discussion that afternoon were decided upon, as was the order for reading the manuscripts that writers submitted to the salon for its judgment. Occasionally habitués were asked to offer extracts from works in hand, or newly published books were discussed. Montesquieu was the first to ask the circle for advice. He often brought manuscripts with him "that were infinitely approved by Messieurs de Fontenelle and de La Motte,"[11] and for all its audacity, the *Lettres persanes* was warmly received. At these gatherings, the group's aesthetic orientation and cultural strategy were also decided upon. With the revival of the *Querelle des Anciens et des Modernes*—a real "French crisis of conscience"[12]—the marquise and her guests, finding themselves torn between loyalty to humanist and ecclesiastical traditions and the exigency of the new, naturally sided with Antoine Houdar de La Motte, a regular Tuesday guest and a leading advocate for the Moderns. But once the flames of the first polemic had died down, the Marquise de Lambert suggested a politics of reconciliation, inviting the parties to readopt a tone suited to the gentlemanly exchange of opinions.

The unity and prestige of the group became evident whenever new members were elected to the Académie française; the hôtel de Nevers usually had its own candidates whose success was virtually guaranteed. Contemporaries did not fail to notice Mme de Lambert's personal influence in this academic plotting. "You had to pass by her to get to the Académie française," wrote the Président Hénault in his *Mémoires*.[13] D'Argenson's diary also echoes the sometimes hostile discomfiture provoked by this female appropriation of power in the sanctuary of male culture.[14]

It was no passing achievement, however, for until the end of the century, society women, particularly those with large intellectual salons, interpreted the leanings of their circles and brought much weight to bear on the election of academicians. Certainly the Enlightenment party would never have taken over the Académie so easily without the consistent support of Mme de Lambert, Mme de Tencin, and Julie de Lespinasse.

But on Tuesday evenings erudition gave way to something else. "In the evenings," the Président Hénault recalls, "the scenery changed, and so did the actors. Mme

11. Letter from Mme de Lambert to the Comte de Morville, August 5, 1726, in Montesquieu, *Œuvres complètes*, edited by André Masson, three volumes (Paris: Nagel, 1950–1955), Vol. 3, pp. 1537–1538; quoted in Shackleton, *Montesquieu: A Critical Biography*, p. 53.

12. Marc Fumaroli, "Sur Homère en France au XVIIe siècle," in *Revue d'Histoire Littéraire de la France*, July–August 1973, p. 653.

13. *Mémoires du président Hénault*, edited by Françoise Rousseau (Paris: Hachette, 1911), p. 120. Hénault was called président for his role as a magistrate in the Parlement de Paris.

14. See *Journal et Mémoires du marquis d'Argenson*, Vol. 1, p. 164.

de Lambert gave supper to a more socially exclusive company; it pleased her to receive people who were suited to one another; even though there was no change in her tone; and she preached *belle galanterie* to those who went a little too far: I dogmatized in the morning and sang in the evening."[15]

By returning to the classic rules of aristocratic society, by basing her choice of evening guests on their compatibility, and by adopting a tone of light-hearted *galanterie*, the marquise was once more conforming to a long-thought-out plan by which she intended to defend society's traditional values. Having suffered at length from submission to Versailles, these were now threatened by hedonism, frenzied change, and the Regency's brazen libertinism. At the hôtel de Nevers, it was forbidden to play cards, to get drunk, to fail in the respectful admiration due to the fair sex, or to be ostentatious in clothing, speech, or attitude. The guests on Tuesday and Wednesday evenings supped, conversed, listened to music, and sometimes danced. Each guest brought a collection of novelties, anecdotes, witticisms, improvised verses, and gallant compliments to share with those assembled.

Like Mlle de Scudéry in her day, the marquise claimed that women had a right to be educated and to seek compensation in an intellectual life for the infinite difficulties that fate reserved for them. She also shared Mlle de Scudéry's conviction that the specifically female virtues were modesty, decency, and purity. Yet the marquise shared with La Bruyère—that most misogynist of the classical moralists—the belief that the *honnête femme*, or gentlewoman, had to have the qualities of the *honnête homme*,[16] or, as Ninon de Lenclos claimed, "to make a man of herself." This was not in order to make up for anything lacking in woman's nature, but because loyalty, probity, friendship, and honor were clearly developed from a moral experience shared by both sexes.[17]

From the beginning, aristocratic men and women had been indissolubly tied to the undertaking that was society, but Mme de Lambert added a new meaning to their collaboration. For the marquise, the outward forms of society life acquired an inner dimension. *Politesse* in manners reflected the *politesse* of *esprit*, good speech reflected good thought, and the *galant homme* was also an *homme de bien*—a virtuous man; in effect the *être* (being) came to coincide with the *paraître* (appearance). A hundred years after the Blue Room, another marquise reestablished a utopian ideal of society life promoting *sociabilité* during her own century. "The desire for esteem," Mme de Lambert wrote, "is also the soul of society: it unites us all, the one and the other. I need your approbation, you need mine. By distancing oneself from men, one distances oneself from the virtues necessary to

---

15. *Mémoires du président Hénault*, p. 120.

16. La Bruyère, "Des femmes," in *Les Caractères*, p. 174.

17. La Bruyère, "Des jugements," in *Les Caractères*, pp. 383–385.

society; for when one is alone, one neglects oneself. The world obliges you to look at yourself."[18] For the high-ranking nobility, this rule would become a moral imperative, almost to the point of assuming religious significance. "Nothing was really more Christian, on the human plain, than this *grand monde* vision whereby one lived only by others and for others," wrote Jacques de Norvins in his memoirs.[19] Norvins made his début in good Parisian society on the eve of the Revolution.

The absolute priority given to the business of society could not but relegate religious concerns to second place. In Mme de Lambert's salon, the talk was not, as it had been with Mme de Longueville, Mme de Sablé, and Mme du Plessis-Guénégaud, of predestination, grace, or free will. Instead, her salon laid the foundations for that great quest which would thrive throughout the century and end in terror and a bloodbath: the search for earthly happiness. During the eighteenth century, the idea of the divine seemed to rid itself of tragic connotations, adapting itself to the *bienséances*: society chronicles are no longer filled with accounts of dramatic conversions and exemplary expiation. Fashionable ladies, as Voltaire would observe, changed their clothes according to the season quite naturally: flirtatious in their youth, dedicated to wit and intelligence in maturity, they turned in old age to religion, more in obedience to convention than through fear of God. Even for the Marquise de Lambert, who had only ever worn the clothes of an *honnête femme*, spirituality was limited to morality, and the demands of faith were satisfied by an enlightened deism.

So what were the subjects debated on Tuesdays? Love, friendship, duty, reputation, virtue, taste. These were the same topics that had enlivened conversation in the seventeenth-century salons. Unlike the classical moralists, however, Marivaux, Montesquieu, Fontenelle, and Terrasson were not concerned with defining the immutable character or general laws of human nature as they might be exemplified. They were more interested in diversity of custom, the relativity of moral law, the subjectivity of behavior, and the unpredictability of psychological and emotional life. Other subjects, like "the rejection of injustices born of the organization of a hierarchical society, adherence to the Modern ideal, the progressive secularization of Christian values,"[20] definitely anticipated Enlightenment thinking. But of all the problems discussed, the problem of happiness, everywhere evident in Mme de Lambert's work, probably reveals most about the new conception of social relationships that evolved among the habitués of the hôtel de Nevers. In 1724, an essay by Fontenelle, "Du bonheur," appeared in an edition of his work.

---

18. Mme de Lambert, *Avis d'une mère à son fils*, in *Œuvres*, edited by Robert Granderoute (Paris: Champion, 1990), p. 62.

19. Jacques de Norvins, *Souvenirs d'un historien de Napoléon: Mémorial de J. de Norvins*, edited by L. de Lanzac de Laborie (Paris: E. Plon, Nourrit et Cie, 1896–1897), Vol. 1, 1769–1793, p. 190.

20. Marchal, *Mme de Lambert et son milieu*, p. 477.

Montesquieu had already expounded his theories on the subject in *Mes Pensées*, in which he balances perfectly the two opposing but complimentary eighteenth-century ideas of intense happiness: the perpetual satisfaction of endlessly different desires, on the one hand, and a state of tranquility on the other. During the century, many other writers—from Mme du Châtelet to Helvétius and Diderot—would meditate on the same problem, in the shared belief that happiness was "a natural inclination, invincible and inalienable" and "the only source of... real duty."[21]

The date of the inclusion of Montesquieu's first fragments on happiness in *Mes Pensées* suggests that they may have been notes meant as a point of departure for conversation in Mme de Lambert's house. The marquise had a highly idealistic conception of happiness. For her it was inseparable from altruism and could be sought only in the light of generosity and friendship. "If you wish to be happy on your own," she warned her son, "you will never be happy; everyone will challenge your happiness; if you wish everyone to be happy with you, everything will come to your aid."[22] It was in fact a Tuesday regular, the Abbé de Saint-Pierre, who introduced the word *bienfaisance* into the French language, thus making himself the advocate of a new secular ideal—philanthropy—that, in contrast to the seventeenth-century concept of Christian charity based on inequality, proposed a pragmatic ethic that aimed to reestablish the principle of equality through specific action. *Bienfaisance* thus became the cornerstone of a system in which pleasure and *sociabilité* sustained each other. As Pierre Jean Georges Cabanis, a leading *idéologue*, wrote at the end of the century, "the greatest happiness to which our nature is susceptible undoubtedly lies in the happiness of others."[23] So, for Mme de Lambert, the heart was the new guiding star for the modern *honnête homme*, the "feeling man" (*l'homme sensible*). "The heart is more persuasive than the mind," she wrote, "since our behavior often depends on it.... You can have neither humanity nor generosity without sensibility. A single sentiment, a single movement of the heart affects the soul more than all the philosophers' sentences.... Nothing is so absolute as the superiority of the mind when influenced by sensibility."[24] By turning La Rochefoucauld's famous maxim ("The head is

---

21. Denis Diderot, *Entretiens avec Catherine II*, Chapter 7, in *Œuvres politiques*, edited by Paul Vernière (Paris: Garnier, 1963); quoted in Roland Mortier, "Les réflexions sur le bonheur dans les écrits de Diderot pour Catherine II," in *La Quête du bonheur et l'expression de la douleur dans la littérature et la pensée française: Mélanges offerts à Corrado Rosso* (Geneva: Droz, 1995), p. 251.

22. Mme de Lambert, *Avis d'une mère à son fils*, in *Œuvres*, p. 61.

23. Pierre Jean Georges Cabanis, *Discours de clôture pour le cours sur Hippocrate*, in *Œuvres*, five volumes (Paris: Bossange et Didot, 1823), Vol. 3, p. 24; quoted in Patrizia Oppici, *L'idea di "bienfaisance" nel Settecento francese o il laccio di Aglaia* (Pisa: Libreria Goliardica, 1989), p. 159. Condillac's disciples, the *idéologues*, held up, among other things, the perfectibility of the human race and professed to establish a science of psychology.

24. Mme de Lambert, *Réflexions sur les femmes*, in *Œuvres*, pp. 221–222.

always fooled by the heart"[25]) upside down, Mme de Lambert became the advocate of a new alliance; henceforth, *esprit* and *cœur*, with their names inextricably linked, were destined to illuminate one another.

Of all the marquise's friends, Pierre de Marivaux was the one who excelled in the "metaphysics of the heart" and coined a language that reflected a new type of psychological introspection. Mme de Lambert, however, deserves credit for having shown him the way, whether by the example of her conversation, by her "precious" writing (which Mathieu Marais would refer to as *lambertinage*[26]), or by her portraits.

The literary portrait had come back into fashion with the revival of society life. Saint-Simon, alone in his study, made up for lost time by evoking both the humble and the mighty from the Sun King's court in his celebrated memoirs, his visionary power nourished by hatred. Meanwhile, Mme du Deffand was being admired at the court of Sceaux for her "talent in depicting character, for her portraits, more real than the originals, that made these people better known than would any intimate exchange with them."[27] Mme de Lambert revived the old aristocratic pastime generally designed for the gratification of others, but despite her apparent loyalty to past form, her contributions were innovatory. Her portraits were not concerned so much with appearance and a person's ability to define him- or herself through *bienséances* as with revealing originality and individuality.

In order to describe the psychology and morality of her characters as accurately as possible, in order to express that mysterious *je ne sais quoi*—which evaded Cartesian reasoning but depended only on the writer's sensibility and intuition—the marquise thus made full use of all the language of the "precious" style: neologisms, antitheses and synonyms, substantive adjectives, metaphor, hyperbole. "I do not like to paint with my eyes, only with my mind,"[28] she wrote in her most rigorous portrait, that of the charming old Marquis de Saint-Aulaire—her daughter's father-in-law, and, it was whispered, her secret husband.

In her writing, Mme de Lambert applied one touch of color after another, adding nuance after nuance in an attempt to achieve an analytical precision unknown to classical language. This was something in which only Marivaux would fully succeed, though his mixture of bold inventiveness, subtlety, and stylistic freedom so scandalized the purists as to be branded ironically as *marivaudage*. "I am aware," he admitted, "that there are some troublesome, albeit estimable, readers with whom it is better to leave what one feels than to say it if it can be expressed only in a way that would appear peculiar; this occurs sometimes,

---

25. La Rochefoucauld, Maxim 102, in *Maxims*, p. 50.

26. See Marchal, *Mme de Lambert et son milieu*, p. 481.

27. Mme de Staal-Delaunay, *Mémoires*, pp. 257–258.

28. Mme de Lambert, "Portrait de M de... [Saint-Aulaire]," in *Portraits des diverses personnes*, in *Œuvres*, p. 277.

however, especially in matters where it is a question of rendering what happens in the soul; the soul, which twists and turns in so many more ways than we have power to describe, and to which we should at least allow, if necessary, the freedom to express itself as best it can, so long as its meaning is clearly understood and no other words could be used without diminishing or altering the idea."[29]

Lacking Marivaux's genius and stopping just short of his stylistic revolution, although aware of its necessity, Mme de Lambert showed the master a path forward. As was so frequently the case in society culture—the part played by Mme de Sablé in the genesis of La Rochefoucauld's *Maximes* is a case in point—the taste and leanings of the hôtel de Nevers came to have a profound influence on literary creativity.

With Mme de Lambert, society once again expressed a utopian ideal: by bringing her salon into being with its meticulously contrived ritual, as the great ladies before her had done, the marquise turned her back on the real world and redesigned one more in keeping with her personal aspirations. It was precisely this permanent dialectic between reality and the ideal, between blind conformity and the critical spirit, that gave *sociabilité* renewed drive, keeping it up to date until the end of the *ancien régime*.

If the hôtel de Nevers's intellectual and ethical aims seemed extreme, this was undoubtedly because of society's equally extreme moral decadence during the first thirty years of the century. With the *Lettres persanes* (1721) Montesquieu was the first to show how well narrative lent itself to the analysis of custom. A novel published by Crébillon *fils* in 1736, *Les Égarements du cœur et de l'esprit*, sharply denounced the rampant falseness of the *honnêtes gens* under the Regency. In the well-known conversation in which Versac, the libertine *petit-maître* (a character probably based on the Maréchal de Richelieu), takes off his mask to initiate Meilcour, the young protagonist, into society life, *honnêteté* appears as nothing more than the consummate art of imposture:

> You must learn to disguise your character so perfectly that it would be vain for anyone to try to make it out. And you must add to the art of deceiving others that of seeing through them, and always try to detect beneath the appearance they wish to present to you what they are in fact. But it is a great fault in the eyes of the world to wish to see everything in its true light. Never appear offended at the vices that are revealed to you, and never boast of having discovered those that people think they have concealed. It is often better to give people a poor opinion of your understanding than to show

---

29. Pierre Carlet de Chamblain de Marivaux, *Le Paysan parvenu*, in *Romans, Récits, contes et nouvelles*, edited by Marcel Arland (Paris: Gallimard/Bibliothèque de la Pléiade, 1949), pp. 787–788.

its real strength; to hide your liking for reflection under a careless and irresponsible manner, and to sacrifice your vanity to your interest.... It is only by appearing to give full rein to impertinence oneself that one makes sure of missing none of anyone else's.... I despise it [society's polite tone] but I have adopted it. You must have observed that I never dare to speak to anyone as I have just spoken to you, and if I asked you to keep all that I said absolutely secret, it is because it is of the utmost importance that no one should know what I am and how much I disguise myself. I recommend to you, once more, to imitate me. Unless you condescend to do as I do you will only acquire the reputation of a stiff-necked fellow unfit for society. The more resolutely you refuse to adopt the vices of others the more eagerly will they attribute to you vices of your own. I am not the only one who has concluded that in order not to be thought ridiculous one must become, or at least appear, so.[30]

In explaining his social strategy, Versac takes the themes dear to *honnêteté* and misinterprets them one by one. The perfect understanding of one's interlocutor proposed by the Chevalier de Méré—"one must notice everything that goes on in the hearts and in the minds of those with whom one is conversing, and quickly accustom oneself to discovering what they feel and think from almost imperceptible signs"[31] —was made to serve deceit rather than mutual understanding. Dissimulation was no longer *honnête*, and its aim was not so much to safeguard the self but to dominate. Born of social morality, Versac's anti-morality highlighted the inherent contradictions and extreme frailty of the social morality from which it sprang. And it was hardly surprising that the high point of the old libertine's lesson concerned ridicule.

Fear of ridicule had been one of society's most marked characteristics since, with the decline of heroic morality, aristocratic culture had increasingly tended to perceive honor "as the interiorization of a public judgment concerning the rules of behavior in society."[32] "To be ridiculous is more dishonoring than dishonor itself,"[33] La Rochefoucauld declared, because by either excess or deficiency, by affectation or lack of discernment, it expresses a deviation from the norm, and, as with the *Précieuses ridicules*, an ignorance of true *honnêteté*.

But if the only protection against ridicule was a perfect knowledge of the *bienséances*, and if the *bienséances* had to adapt to people, places, and circumstances

---

30. Claude Prosper Jolyot de Crébillon, *The Wayward Head and Heart*, translated by Barbara Bray, with an introduction by Rayner Heppenstall (Oxford University Press, 1963), pp. 163–173.

31. Méré, "Discours de la Conversation," in *Œuvres complètes*, Vol. 2, p. 107.

32. Dominique Bertrand, *Dictionnaire raisonné de la politesse et du savoir vivre: du Moyen Âge à nos jours*, edited under the direction of Alain Montandon (Paris: Éditions du Seuil, 1995); see "Ridicule," p. 739.

33. La Rochefoucauld, Maxim 326, in *Maxims*, p. 80.

in accordance with the existing rules, then was not Versac right to argue that one had to conform to the *ridicules* of the day? Was that not what exponents of *honnêteté* had maintained in every manual on the subject to date? Among the latest, Morvan de Bellegarde devoted a whole volume to *Réflexions sur le ridicule et sur les moyens de l'éviter*: "When everyone makes the same mistake, no one should be blamed, and however extravagant a fashion might be, a man would be all the more extravagant who refused to obey it."[34]

Infatuated by its own perfection, equilibrium, and its "golden mean," classical culture had never doubted the logic of its moral and aesthetic choices, and so entrusted itself faithfully to the uncompromising cult of appearances, handing down to the next century a highly ambiguous formal code that—with the exception of Pascal—no moralist had questioned in depth. Perhaps even Crébillon failed to do so fifty years later, although, in his first novel, the *Lettres de la Marquise de M*** au Comte de R****, he definitively turned his back on the passions of the *Grand Siècle*. Now, in a degraded, vacuous world that no longer obeyed reason and whose only criteria of success was "anti-excellence,"[35] Versac did not hesitate to affirm his own superiority by denying himself, while secretly still believing in the fundamental rules of classical *sociabilité*: "To be really well-bred a man should have a mind well-furnished but without pedantry, and possess elegance without affectation, be gay without being vulgar and easy without being immodest."[36] As he himself pointed out, he was not the only one to believe this. Others would continue to bear witness to it. Mme de Lambert did so openly.

---

34. Jean-Baptiste Morvan de Bellegarde, *Réflexions sur le ridicule et sur les moyens de l'éviter, où sont représentez les mœurs et les différents caractères des personnes de ce siècle* (1696; Paris: J. Guignard, 1700), p. 271, quoted in Bertrand, *Dictionnaire raisonné de la politesse*; see "Ridicule," p. 729.

35. Claude Reichler, *L'Âge libertin* (Paris: Éditions de Minuit, 1987), p. 42.

36. Crébillon, *The Wayward Head and Heart*, p. 173.

15

MADAME DE TENCIN:
THE ENLIGHTENMENT ADVENTURESS

THE ART OF DISSIMULATION so essential to Mme de Tencin's very possibility of success in no way resembled the social imposture of the Regency's *petits-maîtres*. It was more reminiscent of a great Fronde adventuress. With her "strong, courageous, and resolute soul,"[1] she would not have been out of place in Cardinal de Retz's memoirs; but her moral open-mindedness and agile intellect combined with an inquisitive and versatile intelligence to make her a leading light of the new times in her own right.

The honor, the virtue, and the sense of duty that guided Mme de Lambert had no power over Mme de Tencin's restless soul. To her, such qualities belonged only in novels. The guiding principle of her life was "the right of the individual to choose his own destiny,"[2] and it was to this that the "beautiful, villainous canoness Tencin"[3] subordinated all her decisions.

For the first thirty years of her life, Alexandrine Claude Guérin de Tencin's only aim had been to win her own freedom. Born in 1682, the fourth daughter of a family of minor Dauphinois nobility, she was destined for the nunnery from the cradle. Neither her lack of vocation nor her repugnance for convent life could persuade her parents to change their minds. Although she begged and cried, beseeched friends and relations for help, and even threatened suicide, Alexandrine resigned herself—probably on the advice of a confessor who was sensitive to her charms—to taking the veil. She had, however, been careful to inform a lawyer of

---

1. Marivaux depicted Mme de Tencin as Mme Dorsin in *La Vie de Marianne*; see Marivaux, *Romans, Récits, contes et nouvelles*, p. 258.

2. Raymond Trousson, introduction to Mme de Tencin, *Mémoires du comte de Comminge*, in *Romans de femmes du XVIII* siècle* (Paris: Laffont, 1996), p. 19.

3. Denis Diderot, *Entretien avec d'Alembert*, in *Œuvres complètes*, under the direction of Jean Varloot, with the collaboration of Michel Delon, Georges Dulac, and Jean Mayer; text edited by H. Dieckmann and Jean Varloot (Paris: Hermann, 1971), Vol. 17, p. 95.

her reservations about doing so. The young nun was then fifteen, and when, only seven years later, her tyrannical father died, she at last became mistress of her own destiny and disclosed her desires. Step by step, she demanded—and obtained— not just the annulment of her vows but her share of the family inheritance too.

But freedom gained with such clear-sighted determination brought with it a breath of scandal that Mme de Tencin's subsequent behavior only exacerbated. If her enemies insisted on referring to her as the "Tencin nun," the "sister," or the "defrocked one," it was partly because, starting with her association with Cardinal Dubois, the beautiful Alexandrine's attitude toward religion was beyond profane. The only real affection she is known to have had for anyone was for her brother, Pierre, who was three years her senior and, like his sister, destined for the Church from childhood. She dedicated herself with tireless energy to his career— both as a state minister and cardinal. This transference of ambition, typical of the feminine condition under the *ancien régime*, was not, in Mme de Tencin's case, merely an obligatory expedient dictated by family loyalty and the realization of the impossibility of achieving personal ambition. As Saint-Simon wrote, "The Abbé de Tencin and she were ever only of one heart and one soul, so alike were they; that is, if it can be said that they were possessed of such. He was her confidant all her life and she was his."[4] Contemporaries were so struck by their absolute complicity that the malicious among them spoke of incest. It was also obvious to everyone that it was the sister rather than the brother who called the tune.

Perhaps no eighteenth-century woman provoked as much contempt or admiration as Mme de Tencin. Yet despite all her letters, her novels, and the wealth and variety of evidence about her, the secret of her personality remains a mystery. There are at least three different Mesdames de Tencin, each in open contradiction with the others. There is the unscrupulous adventuress, seen as the symbol of moral depravity under the Regency; there is the woman of letters, loved and respected by the leading intellectuals of the day, the perfect incarnation of committed, cosmopolitan Enlightenment *sociabilité*; and there is the novelist, protected by strict anonymity, whose lucid, elegant stories of love and sacrifice—at first glance closer to *La Princesse de Clèves* than to *Manon Lescaut*—were so successful in the 1730s and 1740s.

Let us take the adventuress first. The list of Mme de Tencin's reputed lovers is certainly impressive, but her choice seems to have depended less on the caprice of *amour-goût*—that password of Regency libertinism—than on political calculation and a desire for power. Among her first definite liaisons was an affair after 1712 with the English ambassador, Matthew Prior, swiftly followed by another with Lord Bolingbroke, English secretary of state and political refugee in France, which earned her a reputation as a spy. In 1714, it was the turn of Philippe, Duc

---

4. Saint-Simon, *Mémoires*, Vol. 7, p. 508.

d'Orléans, who became regent a year later upon the death of Louis XIV. It did not last, and if we are to believe Charles Pinot Duclos, the relationship ended with the unchivalrous duke declaring, "I do not like whores who speak of business between the sheets."[5] This particular habit, however, did not appear to bother Cardinal Dubois, the Regent's former tutor and later his prime minister. He was the very accomplice Mme de Tencin sought.

The infinitely cynical Dubois was astute, tenacious, and indefatigable. With his unlimited craving for power and enormous talent for political realism, he was naturally able to understand perfectly the beautiful adventuress whose impartiality and intelligence he could admire equally. Thanks to him, Mme de Tencin finally came close to the center of power. She pursued business dealings with John Law's bank,[6] while her brother was sent as the King of France's chargé d'affaires to the papal court. The ex-nun and the unbelieving cardinal were so perfectly suited that their relationship, although completely free from any form of sentiment, was to last until Dubois's sudden death in 1723.

To give a full list of all the lovers Mme de Tencin entertained during or after her relationship with the cardinal would take us too far afield, but mention must be made of two who were responsible for the two most infamous episodes of her scandalous existence. One was the amiable and generous Chevalier Destouches, lieutenant general of artillery, who must have represented an entertaining interlude of pure pleasure during a time when she was engaged with two other lovers: the debauched and no longer young Dubois and the old and extremely ugly Marquis d'Argenson (father of the memoir writer), lieutenant of police under Louis XIV and keeper of the seals during the Regency. But even *l'amour-goût* could be risky, and on November 17, 1717, at the age of thirty-five, Mme de Tencin gave birth to a son whom she immediately caused to be left on the steps of the chapel of Saint-Jean-le-Rond, next to Notre-Dame. In fact no very pressing circumstance required her action: she had no husband to whom she would have to explain herself; Destouches loved her and, as he subsequently proved, wished to look after and support the child. She could, moreover, have entrusted the infant to a reliable family and supervised his education in absolute secrecy from a distance. (This is exactly what was done a few years later by the far less independent and less well-off Mlle Aïssé, a beautiful Circassian who was brought up by Mme de Tencin's elder sister, Mme de Ferriol.) But it must be remembered that in Mme

---

5. Charles Pinot Duclos, *Mémoires secrets sur les règnes de Louis XIV et de Louis XV*, in *Œuvres complètes*, ten volumes (Paris: Colnet, 1806), Vol. 4, p. 418.

6. The Scottish-born banker John Law persuaded the government to adopt the use of paper money, convertible into coin through his Banque Générale, established in 1716. This became the Banque Royale in 1720, the same year that Law was appointed controller general of finance. His operations inspired frenzied speculation, and many were ruined in the ensuing collapse. Law fled the country.

de Tencin's day, maternal love was a far less certain commodity; the abandonment of inconvenient children to public charity was, sadly, widespread—we need only recall the choice of that philanthropist Jean-Jacques Rousseau, who sent his children to a foundling hospital. Additionally, the scandal of an illegitimate birth could affect an entire family and, in the case of the Tencins, would surely have damaged the abbé's rising career.

Destouches, who was abroad at the time of the birth, had been kept in ignorance of Mme de Tencin's intentions, but as soon as he returned to the capital, he managed to trace the child and place it in the care of a nurse. He never officially recognized his son, but he saw to his education, established an affectionate relationship with him, introduced him to his family, guaranteed him a small income, and insisted that he change his given name from Jean le Rond (derived from the place where he was found) to d'Alembert.

Mme de Tencin, in contrast, never looked back and never showed the slightest interest in the young genius who in 1743, aged only twenty-six, set out on a dazzling scientific career with the publication of his *Traité de dynamique*. She always avoided meeting him, and she did not even include him in her will. Yet she was not guarding a secret that would have damaged her reputation. By that time, everyone knew that the brilliant *philosophe* who was received in all the fashionable salons (except for his mother's) was Mme de Tencin's son. Diderot mentioned it several times, and Voltaire made a joke of it. The first person to announce it openly was d'Alembert himself, who chose to defy convention and proudly proclaimed his condition as a "child of nature"[7]—or, as Voiture called it a century earlier, "the child of his own deeds."[8] Perhaps it was a way of reminding Mme de Tencin of his existence, or attracting her attention, in the hope of recognition, however late. In her *Mémoires* Mme Suard recounts:

> By entrusting me so much with his confidences, d'Alembert allowed me one day to ask if it was true that, once he had become very famous, Mme de Tencin had sent him a message through a friend to the effect that she would be delighted to see him. "Never," he told me, "has she done anything of the kind." "But, Monsieur, you are credited on this occasion with a very proud reply to a mother who, until you were celebrated, had shown no sign of life, and I have heard many people applaud your refusal as a mark of justified

7. "Portrait de M. d'Alembert par Mme du Deffand," [presumably written in 1755] in *Horace Walpole's Correspondence with Mme du Deffand*, edited by W. S. Lewis and Warren Hunting Smith (Yale University Press, 1939), Vol. 6, p. 94. Walpole's correspondence with Mme du Deffand, with its own internal numbering from 1 to 6, constitutes Volumes 3–8 of *The Yale Edition* of *Horace Walpole's Correspondence*, edited by W. S. Lewis, in forty-eight volumes (Yale University Press/Oxford University Press, 1937–1983).

8. See Voiture's letter to the Abbé Costar, quoted in Chapter 4.

resentment." "Ah!" he said, "I would never have refused the embrace of a mother who reclaimed me: it would have been very sweet for me to recover her."[9]

What then was the reason for such hardness of heart? Perhaps quite simply Mme de Tencin was unable to behave as a mother because she had no maternal feelings; for her, that unwanted son who had threatened her independence had never existed, and continued not to exist. Even though public opinion was determined to attribute him to her, she remained utterly indifferent to the gossip. This charge, however, paled beside another scandal: that her last lover committed suicide in her house, leaving behind him a note that accused her of the worst misdeeds.

Charles de La Fresnaye, a member of the Grand Conseil and a distinguished banker, had already been engaged in an affair with Mme de Tencin for two years when, after a period of success and prosperity, he found himself on the verge of bankruptcy. In order to escape his creditors, he entrusted his mistress with some bonds in his name and asked her for a series of loans with which to embark on new financial ventures. But his affairs only went from bad to worse, and when he turned to his mistress again for help, she refused. Not only did she refuse to advance him additional money, she also declined to return the bonds entrusted to her care, saying that she was keeping them as security for her significant past loans to him. That was the final blow for La Fresnaye, who, in desperation and unable to face the disaster, chose to take his own life—as well as his revenge on Mme de Tencin. On April 6, 1726, just before midday, he made his way to her house and, finding her in the company of several friends, he asked if he might withdraw for a moment to the little study next to her bedroom. There he shot himself in the heart. But that was just the beginning. La Fresnaye had deposited a delirious will with a lawyer in which, "instead of leaving dispositions that he might be prayed for,"[10] he accused Mme de Tencin of wanting to assassinate him, of having robbed him, of having committed all sorts of wickedness, and of entertaining lascivious relations with both the aged Fontenelle and her own nephew, d'Argental.

"No one believes that that woman is guilty of this murder; La Fresnaye's behavior reveals an unbalanced mind," Barbier wrote in his *Journal*.[11] But while the magistrates of the Grand Conseil were busily trying to silence a scandal that involved one of their members, the judiciary police from the Châtelet were

---

9. Mme Suard, *Essaie de Mémoires sur M. Suard*, in Jean-François Barrière, *Bibliothèque des Mémoires relatifs à l'histoire de France pendant le XVIIIe siècle*, edited by M. de Lescure, thirty-seven volumes (Paris: Firmin Didot frères, 1846–1881), Vol. 37, p. 184.

10. Edmond-Jean François Barbier, *Chronique de la Régence et du règne de Louis XV (1718–1763), ou Journal de Barbier*, eight volumes (Paris: Charpentier, 1866), Vol. 1, p. 421.

11. *Journal de Barbier*, Vol. 1, p. 421.

beginning to conduct an investigation. This conflict of the authorities provided a stunning opportunity for a display of strength, so Mme de Tencin was incarcerated in the Grand Châtelet and later taken to the Bastille.

For the next two months, the judiciary police treated the accused like a criminal, subjecting her to the most humiliating interrogations, and even forcing her to spend many hours with La Fresnaye's decomposing body. Then, on June 3, as a result of pressure from the Tencin family, the Conseil du Roi decreed that the matter should be dealt with by the Grand Conseil. The trial ended a month later with La Fresnaye's *damnatio memoriae* and Mme de Tencin's absolute acquittal.

"It is very doubtful that the Grand Conseil's laundering will not have left stains on Mme de Tencin that all the waters of Paris could not expunge," contemporaries remarked. The whole affair had been so sordid that although public opinion saw Mme de Tencin as not guilty, neither did she emerge as entirely innocent. With a concoction of exaggerations, lies, and a few fragments of truth, La Fresnaye had drawn attention to many shadows on the former nun's life, to her innumerable love affairs, her intrigues, and, especially, to her unscrupulousness in business and to the speculations and foreign exchange deals she had made in the time of John Law. She had stolen nothing, but she had kept La Fresnaye's bonds, thus depriving him of a last chance to recoup his fortunes.

The public thus suspended judgment, but it was above all Mme de Tencin herself who gave the impression of being unable to survive after what she had gone through. In fact, on coming out of the Bastille, her health was so poor that she seemed unlikely to live. "Here she is innocent and she is about to die,"[12] Mathieu Marais wrote after having made a note in his *Journal* of the outcome of the trial. But that was a mistaken impression. Religion, politics, and literature were yet to provide Mme de Tencin with the best years of her life. By the following summer, she had already recovered her "devilish spirit"[13] and was throwing herself headfirst into a passionate theological debate.

After a brief interlude with the Duc de Bourbon, Louis XV made the Cardinal de Fleury prime minister, the Regent and Cardinal Dubois having disappeared from the political scene. The old priest Fleury chose the path of prudence and aimed at keeping the peace, a return to moral order, and an end to religious conflict. To these ends, he asked Pierre Guérin de Tencin, who had been made archbishop of Embrun in 1724, to organize a council in his diocese with the intention of putting an end to Jansenist resistance and imposing once and for all the "constitution" of *Unigenitus*—the papal bull promulgated at Louis XIV's request by Pope Clement XI in 1713. The bull, which condemned 101 Jansenist propositions

---

12. Quoted in Jean Sareil, *Les Tencin: Histoire d'une famille au dix-huitième siècle d'après de nombreux documents inédits* (Geneva: Droz, 1969), p. 153.

13. See *Journal de Barbier*, Vol. 1, p. 420.

taken from Pasquier Quesnel's book *Les Réflexions morales sur le Nouveau Testament*, had rekindled old quarrels and, on the orders of the Sun King, had been ratified by the Paris Parlement. The archbishop of Embrun—despite the terrible reputation he had gained under the Regency on account of his loyalty to Dubois, his friendship with the disgraced John Law, and his scandalous sister—had all the necessary qualities to succeed in this difficult task. "Methodical in preparation, clever improviser, insinuating, energetic, and haughty when required, with a severe and imposing physique, a good theologian, admirably able to surround himself with capable men and to profit from their counsel,"[14] he was in fact entirely successful within the space of one month. Jean Soanen, the bishop of Senez, who had written a pastoral letter plainly professing the Jansenist faith, was condemned and removed from his diocese, an act that deprived the Jansenist resistance of one of its most charismatic and inflexible champions.

The Council of Embrun, which ended in 1727, gave Fleury the upper hand over the high-placed Jansenist clergy, allowing him in the years that followed to slap *lettres de cachet*—executive orders—on the more aggressive bishops and to persuade the more moderate ones to adopt the politics of conciliation. There was, however, an unexpected and immediate backlash against the council's decisions from the people, the lower ranks of the clergy, and the reactionary elements in the parlementary world. At the instigation of the *Nouvelles Ecclésiastiques*—a fortnightly publication that was printed clandestinely and distributed in defiance of the police—the Jansenist movement did not hesitate to take advantage of popular suspicion by giving credence to the "hysterics" and to the miraculous cures that had taken place on the Deacon of Paris's tomb in Saint-Ménard cemetery. In so doing, Jansenism turned its back on the spiritual fervor and moral rigor that had so touched the hearts of the *honnêtes gens* in the course of the seventeenth century and became increasingly a movement of political protest and resistance to royal authority.

The violent press campaign following the council gave Mme de Tencin a splendid opportunity to reappear on the scene in a perfectly honorable role as champion of the Church and established authority. Cleverly handled, the Jansenists' furious reaction, which aimed at once again bringing the archbishop of Embrun's findings into question, might become useful for his career. Did not her brother's determination show him to be a true champion of orthodoxy? Did his zeal not make him ipso facto a candidate for a cardinal's hat? And would the cardinal's crimson not make him the elderly Fleury's natural successor as prime minister in the not so distant future?

Mme de Tencin did not merely imagine the future, but set about preparing for it with terrifying energy. While her brother persistently asked Fleury and the Roman Curia to recognize his zealousness on behalf of the faith, she was secretly

14. Sareil, *Les Tencin*, p. 160.

receiving "constitutional" bishops and making her house into the headquarters for an anti-Jansenist countercampaign, commissioning every kind of article, even paying for the printing and organizing clandestine distribution. Her activities were denounced not only by the *Nouvelles Ecclésiastiques* but by Saint-Simon as well, who laughed at these "secret gatherings [that] took place by night at the nun Tencin's house, and to which bishops went in disguise and the poor, stupid, but saintly bishop of Marseille allowed himself to be taken dressed as a cavalier by people who knew the long and the short of it more than he did, and where he was recognized in that strange outfit."[15]

By putting themselves forward so forcefully, the Tencins gave their enemies an opportunity to discredit the council's decisions. No one lent themselves more than they to moral censure, and an avalanche of articles, libels, and satirical verses pointed them out to the public as symbolic of the corruption of the Roman Church. This was exactly what Fleury did not want. His aim was to calm the polemic, not to reignite it. Furthermore, he had no wish to see Tencin made a cardinal; even less did he intend to die. Archbishop Tencin was ordered to publish nothing further without permission—in fact, to keep quiet—and his sister was politely asked by the chief of police to leave Paris. Mme de Tencin quickly obeyed and sent Cardinal de Fleury an obsequious letter in which she maintained that she had received simple acquaintances at her house, and a few old friends "who are perhaps, of all the people in Paris, the most distinguished for their merit and their virtue."[16] Fleury took the opportunity to call her politely but firmly to order by reminding her of the limits imposed on her sex by the *bienséances*: "It is not enough to be intelligent and to belong in good company; prudence demands that a person, especially one of your sex, should be concerned only with things of their sphere."[17]

It is entirely thanks to reports made by the police whose job it was to watch Mme de Tencin's house that we know that Fontenelle, La Motte, and the Abbé de Saint-Pierre were among her visitors of "merit." Mme de Tencin did not wait to be forbidden to meddle in public affairs but gathered a faithful circle of friends around her. From 1728 on, she paid ever more attention to her growing salon, and her apartment in the rue Saint-Honoré became the most liberal and original meeting place in the Paris of the 1730s and 1740s, providing an unparalleled example of intellectual conversation.

Success as a hostess was the whole point of life for many society women who had no horizon beyond society, whereas Mme de Tencin had experience and ambition

---

15. Saint-Simon, *Mémoires*, Vol. 7: *Additions de Saint-Simon au Journal de Dangeau*, p. 921.

16. Quoted in René Vaillot, *Qui étaient Mme de Tencin... et le Cardinal?* (Paris: Le Pavillon Roger Maria Éditeur, 1974), p. 215.

17. Quoted in Vaillot, *Qui étaient Mme de Tencin... et le Cardinal?*, p. 215.

enough for more than one life. Merely holding a salon had never seemed an end in itself. During the forced inactivity following her brush with the Jansenists, however, she discovered that presiding over one could be a source of genuine pleasure. Freed from the iron discipline demanded by ambition, Mme de Tencin, tireless schemer that she was, surrendered to a new, disinterested, recreational pastime: a daily intellectual challenge and conversation's infinite variety. To this century-old game she brought understanding, freedom, and an exceptional knowledge of men, all of which allowed her to regenerate it radically and prepare it for a new era.

Many of Mme de Tencin's literary friends also frequented the Marquise de Lambert's house and, when the latter died in 1733, her habitués all transferred to the rue Saint-Honoré where Mme de Tencin received on Tuesdays, which had become free. By a twist of fate, the social capital of an *honnête femme* dedicated to the cult of virtue and glory passed into the hands of a woman without morals and without honor, and, even more surprisingly, no one appeared to be shocked. It was not that behavior was indiscriminately liberalized, nor that moral judgment was suspended. Rather, beside the already established and cherished social conventions that depended on ethical and aesthetic judgments, eighteenth-century *sociabilité* introduced a new criterion essentially based on intellectual prestige. Society would have continued to conform mainly to the older standards if the intellectuals had not naturally been more interested in the new criterion, but the mutual appeal would be unlimited, with endless compromise on both sides.

Mme de Tencin provided the first and most brilliant example of the victory of intelligence over respectability, a turnaround that did not depend on an abstract assessment of her intellectual ability (which no one doubted in any case) but rather on recognition of its value to society. Once they began to frequent the rue Saint-Honoré, Mme de Lambert's former guests found there a freedom and a complicity unknown to the hôtel de Nevers. Unlike the marquise, Mme de Tencin had no need of programs or rituals to manage the conversation since she possessed a natural authority and certitude of judgment that enabled her to control the threads of a conversation without sacrificing any of the spontaneity or richness of debate. This authority would soon prove to be necessary in those intellectual salons where the *philosophes* came in strength and the dominant tone was no longer the easy, courteous spirit of social leisure but an intense exchange of ideas. Aiming to conquer society, the republic of letters may have needed control from a disciplined outside force in order to stay united for a public it hoped to "illuminate," and not be obscured by polemic and internal quarrels. The women involved in this new and difficult task were not unprepared: for over a hundred years, generation after generation, they had held disciplinary sway by establishing codes of manners and social understanding. It was now a matter of taking the next step. Newcomers had to be taught to follow the essential rules of the old code while being allowed to renew the spirit and the content through shared intelligence.

Mme de Tencin's old friends, however, like Fontenelle, Montesquieu, or La Motte, had no need of initiation and were still perfect gentlemen. Their intellectual audacity went hand in hand with tremendous political prudence but lacked the aggressiveness that would soon typify Enlightenment thinking. Theirs were "conversations in which, to tell the truth, morality [was] accompanied by considerable gaiety,"[18] the ease of which did nothing to prevent emulation. Jean-François Marmontel, who as a provincial young writer was introduced to Mme de Tencin's salon in 1745, famously described these virtuoso conversationalists in his *Mémoires*:

> In Marivaux, an impatience to prove his finesse and sharpness of wit was evident. Montesquieu, with greater calm, waited for the ball to be in his court, but he waited. Maran watched for an opportunity. Astruc did not deign to wait. Fontenelle alone let it come without looking for it; and he made such sober usage of the attention given to listening to him, that his refined words and his pretty tales occupied no more than a moment. Helvétius, attentive and wary, gleaned in order one day to sow.[19]

All the most illustrious people in the fields of learning, letters, and science in the first half of the century were drawn to the salon in the rue Saint-Honoré, with the exception of Voltaire who, in any case, did not even frequent the Marquise de Lambert's salon. The character of the group was determined, however, by a small handful of regulars whom Mme de Tencin laughingly called her *bêtes*. There were first of all the "seven sages" who included, besides Fontenelle and Marivaux, the physician Jean-Jacques Dortous de Mairan, who was a member of the Académie française and Fontenelle's successor as director of the Académie des sciences; Claude Gros de Boze, the well-known numismatist and archeologist, member of the Académie française, and permanent secretary to the Académie des inscriptions; Jean Baptiste de Mirabaud, member of the Académie française and acclaimed translator of Tasso and Ariosto; Jean Astruc, the author of an important treatise on venereal diseases, a ferocious polemicist, and probably Mme de Tencin's last lover; and Duclos, the youngest man of letters in the group, historian, novelist, moralist, and permanent secretary to the Académie française from 1755 on. La Motte and Montesquieu are not listed only because the former died in 1731 and the latter now lived definitively in his château de La Brède, coming only occasionally to Paris.

Mme de Tencin probably owes most of her glory to Montesquieu. He was seven years younger than she, and their friendship went back a long time. After

---

18. Letter from Mme de Tencin to François Tronchin, quoted in Sareil, *Qui étaient Mme de Tencin... et le Cardinal?*, p. 234.

19. Jean-François Marmontel, *Mémoires*, edited by Jean-Pierre Guicciardi and Gilles Thierrat (Paris: Mercure de France, 1999), p. 136.

the publication in 1743 of the *Considérations sur les causes de la grandeur des Romains et de leur décadence*, she had taken to calling him *"mon petit romain"* and their correspondence was affectionate and conspiratorial. When, in the autumn of 1748, *De l'esprit des lois* appeared under the strictest anonymity in Switzerland, the first two copies sent to France were addressed to the Chancellor d'Aguesseau requesting permission for sale in France, and to Mme de Tencin as a mark of esteem. The old lady had already read and expressed her enthusiasm for the manuscript,[20] and she would soon prove herself worthy of the honor bestowed on her.

The Swiss edition of *De l'esprit des lois* was full of errors and arbitrary interventions, which were reproduced in the clandestine edition printed in Paris on the wave of its great success. Faced with a situation that might compromise the book's intelligence, Mme de Tencin reacted swiftly and at her own expense printed five hundred copies of a list of errata. This she publicized in the *Mercure* and the *Journal des Savants* and distributed to bookshops. Then, with the aid of a good copy-editor, she supervised a new French edition, seeing to it that the text was faithful to the original. It was without doubt a fine gesture that showed generosity, a desire for accuracy, and a profound respect for intellectual efforts.

Mme de Tencin's salon was aligned with the Moderns, firmly connected to the academic institutions, and frequented by numerous scholars and scientists. Most of the habitués were men, probably not so much on account of the scandalous past of the hostess as because the intellectual conversation and level of erudition were often inaccessible to many society women. It is hardly surprising that among the few ladies who are usually said to have frequented the rue Saint-Honoré were Mme du Châtelet (a woman of exceptional learning for her times), Mme Dupin (of whose literary ambitions Rousseau writes in his *Confessions*), and Mme Geoffrin, whose intention was to imitate Mme de Tencin and open an intellectual salon of her own.

On leaving the convent, the youthful Alexandrine Claude de Tencin had been introduced to society in the house of her eldest sister, Angélique, who was married to the receiver general of the Dauphiné, Augustin de Ferriol. Angélique, too, was beautiful, unscrupulous, ambitious, and quite cultivated. Among her guests were Fontenelle, the well-known poet Jean-Baptiste Rousseau, and the young Voltaire. But what must have really impressed Mme de Tencin at the time was the discovery of the political and diplomatic worlds, so well represented at the hôtel de Ferriol. In 1712 when the ex-nun went to live with her sister, Augustin de Ferriol's brother, Charles, had just returned a year earlier from Turkey where he had

---

20. "Philosophy, reason and humanity were united in the composition of this work, and the Graces took care to bedeck the erudition." Letter from Mme de Tencin to Montesquieu, December 2, 1748, quoted in Vaillot, *Qui étaient Mme de Tencin... et le Cardinal?*, p. 315.

been ambassador to the Sublime Porte. Mme de Ferriol, although she had recently embarked on a stable relationship with the Marquis d'Huxelles, maréchal de France and an able diplomat, remained on the friendliest of terms with her ex-lover, the Marquis de Torcy, minister for foreign affairs. Both Huxelles and Torcy were involved in the difficult negotiations for the Peace of Utrecht, which began a new era of diplomacy. Through them, Mme de Tencin made friends with Her Britannic Majesty's secretary of state for foreign affairs, Lord Bolingbroke, and with Matthew Prior, the English ambassador to France. This network of acquaintances later supported the nomination of the Abbé de Tencin as chargé d'affaires in Rome. The Ferriols' second son, the Comte d'Argental, would also follow a diplomatic career.

We know how quickly Alexandrine Claude adapted to the world of international diplomacy, so much so that she was suspected of spying, but it would be wrong to think that she was driven by ambition and a lust for power alone rather than by a lifelong and genuine intellectual curiosity. Mme de Tencin was in fact one of the first hostesses to regularly receive foreign visitors. In doing so, she helped to promote the French model of *sociabilité* and set an example for other Enlightenment drawing rooms.

A letter written in French by Lord Chesterfield in 1742 to introduce an English friend visiting Paris to Mme de Tencin gives us the tone of this European society life, which was distinguished by an exquisite courtesy. The English lord dared to permit himself this "indiscretion" since the woman soliciting the honor of being received was "English only by birth, but French by regeneration."[21] The homage to the superiority of the French *bienséances* was the logical prelude to the homage paid to the qualities of heart and intelligence of Mme de Tencin and her friends. How could one deny that a century after the "renaissance" of Vincent Voiture in the purifying waters of the Blue Room, the religion of politeness had adepts throughout Europe? Chesterfield wrote:

> I've gone back and forth, and wavered for a long time, before daring to decide to send you this letter. I felt all the indiscretion of such a step, and how much it was an abuse of the kindnesses you showed me during my stay in Paris to ask you for another; but I was strongly solicited by a woman whose merit sheltered her from refusal, and driven besides to take advantage of the least pretext to recall a memory as precious to me as yours, so that inclination, as almost always happens, has triumphed over discretion, and I am satisfying at the same time my own and the entreaties of Madame Cleland, who will have the honor of giving you this letter. . . . I admit, Madame, that given all that I owe you, it would be wrong to shoulder you

---

21. Lord Chesterfield to Mme de Tencin, August 20, 1742, in *Letters*, Vol. 2, p. 517.

with my compatriots, people scarcely made to spread pleasure in society, and who would find themselves very much out of place in the one that your merit and your good taste creates in your home, and of which you are at once the support and the ornament. But do not fear; I will not push indiscretion to that point. . . . Having thus taken the step, I would like to take advantage of it to explain to you the feelings of gratitude I have, and will always have, for the kindness you showed me in Paris; and I would like to express to you as well all that I think about the qualities that distinguish your heart and your spirit from everyone else's, but that would lead me both beyond the bounds of a letter and beyond my powers. I would wish that Monsieur de Fontenelle might be willing to take care of it for me.[22]

As her response shows, Mme de Tencin was also a virtuoso of the compliment. And since Chesterfield had evoked her and her "society," defining in an exemplary way her virtues as mistress of the house, she answered in the name of her circle and returned the homage. Their English friend had beaten them on their own ground, gathering all the "graces" in a French better than their own. It is probably in the rue Saint-Honoré that "the French spirit of foreigners," of which the Goncourt brothers would speak, revealed its capacity for excellence for the first time.

I wish, Milord, that you could have witnessed the reception of your letter. It was given to me by Monsieur de Montesquieu in the midst of the society that you know. Your flattery prevented me for a few moments from showing it around, but *amour-propre* always finds a way to get its due. My own suggested that it would be an injustice to rob you, on the pretext of modesty, of the praises you deserve.

The letter was thus read, and not just once. I must admit, the effect it produced was much different from what I expected: Monsieur de Fontenelle, who was followed by others, cried, this milord is making fun of us by writing better and more correctly in our language than we do. Let him be content, please, to be the leading man of his nation, to have the insights and the profundity of genius which characterizes it; and let him not return to take over our graces and our kindnesses.[23]

In fact diplomacy and society had been closely interconnected in France for at least a hundred years, and the eighteenth century only wove the web more tightly. While diplomats accredited in France had first of all to ensure they were accepted both at Versailles and in Paris, French ambassadors were generally chosen from the

22. Lord Chesterfield to Mme de Tencin, August 20, 1742, in *Letters*, Vol. 2, pp. 516–517.

23. Mme de Tencin to Lord Chesterfield, October 22, 1742, in Chesterfield, *Letters*, Vol. 2, p. 519, note 1.

nobility, the clergy, or the civil service—in short, from the upper classes. Having no specific professional training, they relied entirely on their education as gentlemen and their knowledge of correct social behavior. Nothing could have prepared them better for the job that lay ahead. Diplomacy was essentially the art of mediation, depending on the spoken word and the glamour of ceremony, and the new society culture derived from formal elegance and the appeal of the spoken word. The importance attached to courtesy and the *bienséances*, and the constant attention to the demands of the *amour-propre* of others, must surely have resulted from the need for reconciliation in a society that had been torn apart for decades by internal strife. It is hardly surprising that François de Callières, a diplomat famous for his negotiating talents who had served the Sun King on several important missions, reflected in his old age on two parallel matters: the qualities and knowledge needed for the modern diplomat's profession, and the science of gentlemanliness, which he considered indispensable to good diplomacy[24]: "This requires a flexible, compliant, insinuating mind, someone who is master of his humors and his movements, who knows how to regulate his behavior according to the kind of mind and the different dispositions of the men with whom he is in commerce, who accommodates himself to their passions, and even to their prejudices and other weaknesses with the intention of making them think again and making them entertain just and reasonable opinions."[25]

The results of such discipline were clear. In *L'Europe française*, published in Paris in 1776, the polygraph Louis Antoine de Caraccioli claimed that with their imperturbable amiability, the French ambassadors had changed the style of European diplomacy. As experienced conversationalists, they possessed, in the highest degree, "the art of appearing to say everything without ever saying anything."[26] And at the height of the Napoleonic era, Mme de Staël, a minister's daughter and a diplomat's wife who had lived through enormous political changes and was a true citizen of Europe, confidently asserted that "the French are the cleverest diplomats in Europe, and these men who are accused of indiscretion and impertinency know better than anyone how to keep a secret and how to captivate those of whom they have need. They never displease unless they wish to, that is to say when their vanity considers itself to be better satisfied by disdain than by courtesy. With the French, the understanding of conversation has singularly developed the more serious understanding of political negotiation."[27]

24. François de Callières, *De la manière de négocier avec les souverains, de l'utilité des négotiations, du choix des ambassadeurs et des envoyez, et des qualitéz nécessaires pour reüssir dans ces employs* (Paris: M. Brunet, 1716).

25. François de Callières, *De la science du monde et des connaissances utiles à la conduite de la vie* (Paris: E. Ganeau, 1717), p. 9.

26. Caraccioli, *L'Europe française*, Vol. 1, p. 62.

27. Mme de Staël, *De l'Allemagne*, Vol. 1, p. 105.

All seventeenth-century society circles included diplomats. Mme de Rambouillet herself was an ambassador's wife, and Vincent Voiture, as we know, had the task of introducing the ambassadors of Gaston d'Orléans. We have seen how the Duc de Longueville and the Comte d'Avaux were involved in negotiations at Münster before the Peace of Westphalia and how Mme de Longueville was hailed as Queen of the Congress. Mme de Maintenon's old friend Guilleragues discussed his *Valentins* at Mme de Sablé's house before leaving France to represent the Sun King at the Sublime Porte; the Marquis Arnauld de Pomponne, who was closely connected to the du Plessis-Guénégauds, corresponded regularly with his distant friends while he was ambassador in Sweden. Mme de Sévigné was friendly with Paul de Barrillon d'Amoncourt, to whom La Fontaine dedicated *Le Pouvoir des fables*,[28] and who was French ambassador to London from 1677 to 1689. Nor was it beneath Mme de Lafayette to act as secret informer to Mme Royale in Turin (which ought to make her far more suspected of spying than Mme de Tencin).

In the eighteenth century, curiosity about everything new, different, and exotic developed into a passion. From its very beginnings, *honnêteté* set itself no boundaries. After all, Mme de Rambouillet had declared, "If I knew that there was a real *honnête homme* in India, without knowing anything else about him, I would attempt to do everything possible to his advantage."[29] It was now a matter of knowing everything about those distant *honnêtes hommes*, and of contacting them, be they in China, in Russia, or on some unknown Pacific island, since cosmopolitanism was establishing itself throughout Europe as a powerful ideal.

With this new and real interest in international politics and alien cultures, foreign diplomats accredited to Versailles were much in demand as guests in the capital's drawing rooms. For its part, the *ville*, having become once again the country's real cultural center as well as the center of public opinion, provided foreigners with an irresistible field of observation for the understanding of France and the French. Visitors would very soon realize that despite the ubiquitous smiling courtesy and apparent uniformity of manners, the salons were far from being identical. Each was distinguished by its own structure and individual cultural and political orientation. None, however, was immune from the attraction of power. Mme Geoffrin's Mondays for artists and Wednesdays for men of letters provided an overall view of Parisian intellectual life; but the social advancement of *philosophie* was accompanied by considerable political prudence. As a mecca for important foreigners, Mme Geoffrin's drawing room was also the obligatory meeting place for Russian and Polish visitors, for it was no secret that the lady of the house had not only a personal relationship with Catherine of Russia but a tender affection for Stanisław Augustus Poniatowski, the King of Poland. Horace Walpole

---

28. La Fontaine, Fable 4, Book 8.

29. Tallemant, *Historiettes*, Vol. 1, p. 444.

and the Englishmen who came after him, on the other hand, preferred the Marquise du Deffand's salon. Despite overtones of aristocratic dilettantism, the marquise's circle was against the *philosophes* and linked to the clan of Louis XV's all-powerful minister, the Duc de Choiseul. Julie de Lespinasse's rival salon, in contrast, passionately supported Turgot's politics of reform.

Welcomed as they were with enthusiasm, courted and vied for, foreign diplomats threw themselves into Parisian life and, having displayed a preference, they allowed themselves to be adopted by this or that group—often by more than one. Returning home felt like exile, and the correspondence they carried on with their French friends was infused with incurable nostalgia. Not only did they miss leading an intellectual and social life unequaled in Europe, but the hospitality they had received had profoundly altered the way they thought and felt. David Hume, in Paris as the secretary to the English ambassador, returned to his native Scotland with an entirely new and original view of France; Domenico Caracciolo, in Paris as the King of Naples's ambassador, subsequently abolished torture in Sicily when he was sent there as viceroy, thereby temporarily triumphing over fanaticism and obscurantism; Carl Frederik Scheffer, the Swedish ambassador, was appointed tutor to the future Gustav III and, with his pupil, promoted the politics of reform, later writing to Mme du Deffand, "Liberty has become my idol, it is upon its altar that I burn all my incense."[30] Not to mention the considerable influence of Paris over the monarchs Gustav III and Stanisław Augustus Poniatowski. Then there was the Abbé Ferdinando Galiani, who, in thrall to his memories of a Parisian sojourn, announced that he lost his intelligence on the way back to Naples:

Now the time has come when I can write to my dear Mme Geoffrin, and she, on reading my letter, will feel not so much regret at having lost me as pleasure at having found me again. Here I am the same as ever, still the abbé, the little abbé, your little plaything. I am installed in my comfortable armchair, waving my arms and legs about like a madman, with my wig all awry, talking nonstop, saying things that were thought to be sublime and that were attributed to me. Ah! Madame, what a mistake! It was not I who said so many fine things. Your armchairs are Apollo's tripods and I was the Sybil. Rest assured that seated on the Neapolitan straw chairs, I talk only nonsense.[31]

30. Carl Frederik Scheffer to Mme du Deffand, March 9, 1754, in *Lettres inédites de Mme du Deffand, du président Hénault et du comte de Bulkeley au baron Carl Frederik Scheffer (1751-1756)*, edited by Gunnar von Proschwitz (Geneva: Institut et Musée Voltaire, 1959); offprint from *Studies on Voltaire and the Eighteenth Century*, Vol. 10 (1959), p. 363.

31. The Abbé Galiani to Mme Geoffrin, October 19, 1771, in Fernando Galiani, *Correspondance avec Mme d'Épinay, Mme Necker, Mme Geoffrin etc. Diderot, Grimm, d'Alembert, De Sartine, D'Holbach etc.*, edited by Lucien Perey and Gaston Maugras, two volumes (Paris: Calmann-Lévy, 1882), Vol. 1, p. 467.

These foreign visitors had been won over by the Enlightenment. What they missed most on leaving Paris was the pleasure of conversation. Intense conversations were not mere social pastimes nor were they designed for the purposes of mutual seduction. They were intellectual confrontations between equals.

If we are to believe Marivaux—the only one who knew how to transform conversation into poetry—it was at the house of Mme de Tencin (portrayed in *La Vie de Marianne* as Mme Dorsin) that this new method of communication took shape, since it was she who made it possible:

> There was no question of rank or condition at her house; no one considered their own importance or lack of it; there were men talking to other men, between whom only the better reasoning prevailed over the weaker; that alone.... There were those for whom titles given them on earth by chance did not count, and who did not believe that their fortuitous positions should either humiliate some or bring pride to others. This was how it was understood at Mme Dorsin's; this is how one behaved with her on account of the impression one received of the reasonable and philosophical way of thinking which I have told you was hers, and which made everyone a philosopher too.[32]

Thus the salon of this adventuress who had been educated in the school of life was, like Mme de Lambert's, a utopian space. In contrast, however, to the hôtel de Nevers's model of *sociabilité*, which was shaped by an ideal of moral perfection and aimed to regenerate society by uniting the values of classical *honnêteté* with the new demands of modern sensibilities, the rue Saint-Honoré experience depended on reason alone (so the author of *L'Île des esclaves* suggests). Far from idealizing society, it implicitly questioned its very basis. In the name of *esprit*, Mme de Lambert welcomed aristocrats and men of letters on an equal footing, inviting them to forget their different social standing for a few hours; but in Mme de Tencin's drawing room, the priority given to intelligence made such differences irrelevant.

Her guests were firm advocates of authority and order and generally careful not to display their philosophical skepticism in public. Encouraged by the lady of the house, however, and supported by the other participants, they were concerned only with following the logic of their argument to its very end, whatever the outcome might be. Thus it was primarily thanks to Mme de Tencin's curiosity, open-mindedness, and lively intelligence that the intellectual adventure destined to threaten the whole established order took off.

Even so, it was not so much through the conversation of a small circle of friends as through her widely read novels, published in strictest anonymity, that

---

32. Marivaux, *La Vie de Marianne*, in *Romans, Récits, contes et nouvelles*, p. 257.

Mme de Tencin launched her attack on *ancien régime* society.[33] She began writing these adventures—five novels in all—in the 1730s (at the time when she was obliged to withdraw from the political scene) and they at first seemed inspired by a desire to escape. Despite appearances, a hidden symmetry linked the writer's own experiences to those improbable tales of unhappy love, renunciation, and expiation described through sieges, duels, abductions, shipwrecks, misunderstandings, and all the most hackneyed means used by novelists, and which end with a moral epilogue to be pondered. In reality, by sacrificing honor, love, and integrity, Mme de Tencin had bought the right to do as she wished; the protagonists of her novels, however, gave themselves up entirely to passion and finally succumbed to it. If she herself was saved through realism, her heroes and heroines were carried away by feelings they were unable to control—even if, on reading between the lines, they, with the author, were ultimately victims of a profoundly perverse system.

The reader should not be misled by the conventional nature of these stories, which seem to be merely the old narrative topoi, cleverly reworked within a new framework. Situations may recur almost identically, but they are observed from a new angle. On closer inspection, passion—which is the individual's only authentic existential quality—is not the real cause of man's unhappiness. That responsibility belongs to the arbitrariness of law and custom. For Mme de Tencin, the problem of unhappiness was not a theological one; it was not to be found in "what transcends humanity, but in humanity itself."[34] Protected by both her anonymity and by literary convention, Mme de Tencin inveighed—albeit less vehemently than her friend and protégé Marivaux—against social, religious, and family institutions, denouncing not only the ills of which she had been a victim, like paternal tyranny, a forced vocation, and religious oppression, but also those that she had practiced herself: avarice and ambition. Her stories leave the reader in no doubt that in her extreme clear-sightedness, Mme de Tencin felt the "mortification of self-knowledge"[35] in her bones, a mortification that tormented her characters and that she evoked in her last novel, *Les Malheurs de l'amour*.

---

33. *Mémoires du comte de Comminge* (1735); *Le Siège de Calais, nouvelle historique* (1739); *Les Malheurs de l'amour* (1747); *Anecdotes de la cour et du règne d'Édouard II, roi d'Angleterre* (unfinished), which appeared posthumously with the third part drawn up by Mme Élie de Beaumont in 1776; *Histoire d'une religieuse, écrite par elle-même*, given to the publisher of the *Bibliothèque universelle des Romans* by the Abbé Troublet and published posthumously in the issue of May 1786.

34. Henri Coulet, "Expérience sociale et imagination dans les romans de Mme de Tencin," in *Cahiers de l'Association Internationale des Études Françaises*, Vol. 46 (May 1994), p. 48.

35. Coulet, "Expérience sociale et imagination dans les romans de Mme de Tencin," p. 50.

16

EMULATION

AS THE BLUE ROOM had done in the seventeenth century, Mme de Lambert's and Mme de Tencin's salons set the tone for eighteenth-century *sociabilité*, providing it with basic models. Under the guidance of equally ambitious and gifted women, many more salons were established with equally important visitors: salons that might ignore one another, make pacts, or declare war on one another, but which, in their multiplicity, were to form such a shining constellation as to attract the eyes of all Europe to Paris. As an indispensable condition of success, every salon had to have its own character, its own style, and its own particular chemistry in the mixture of guests, but none could ignore the novelties of the day or abstain from taking positions.

For decade after decade, this art of being together—this knowledge of "how to live in harmony with men while thinking differently from them"[1]—was to become ever more important and to aim toward perfection. In the seventeenth century, society life flourished during its intervals away from the court and spiritual concerns, by creating precious self-contained worlds to which only a few happy individuals had access. In the following century, society gradually expanded its frontiers to encompass the whole life of the city. Since the Supreme Being seemed to have lost interest in his flock and withdrawn to the heavens to concentrate only on engineering and mechanics, and since Versailles had been reduced to what d'Alembert dismissively described as "a village a few miles from Paris," *sociabilité* had become the elite pastime par excellence, replacing any other. Only through *sociabilité* could the elite amuse themselves, instruct and distinguish themselves, and shine while giving the initiated an intoxicating sense of being at the heart of things and of belonging to a national group that was in the vanguard of progress, taste, literature, and art.

---

1. Pierre Carlet de Chamblain de Marivaux, *Lettres sur les habitants de Paris*, "Notice," in *Journaux et Œuvres diverses*, edited by Frédéric Deloffre and Michel Gilot (Paris: Garnier frères, 1969), p. 9.

This grandiose phenomenon, which was to play such an important part in the country's cultural and political life, followed a double ideal along the two distinct lines laid down by Mme de Lambert and Mme de Tencin: the old ideal of worldly perfection and the new ideal of pure reason. Neither excluded the other. Together, they could be mutually reinforcing, although they could also ignore one another and be diametrically opposed.

In the second half of the century, attention was drawn more to the high bourgeois salons and those associated with the world of finance that had opted for *philosophie*. Helvétius's Tuesdays, Mme Geoffrin's Wednesdays, the Baron d'Holbach's Thursdays and Sundays, and Mme Necker's Fridays offered the Encyclopedists and the whole *philosophe* fraternity a direct contact with the elite to whom they addressed themselves. Here was a precious network of acquaintances and protectors. They also provided an excellent point of departure for both men and ideas. Great writers like Sainte-Beuve and Taine have brilliantly described the meeting of society and *philosophie*, and the elegant utopia born of this union. The *philosophes* took it upon themselves to make learning—science, geometry, philosophy, economics—accessible, attractive, and interesting to a public of women and dilettantes who, captivated by the pleasure of the game, repaid them by investing them with an intellectual and moral authority they had never formerly enjoyed.

But it would be wrong to see the salons as the only sounding boards for new ideas. Despite spying and the police, the academies, literary societies, Masonic lodges, cafés, reading rooms, and both the official and the underground press played a part in spreading the acquired knowledge of *philosophie* in other circles and in other languages. This created a growing public open to the discussion of ideas.

In fact no more than a half-dozen of the great salons, whose regular visitors amounted to a few hundred people, were aligned with the Enlightenment, and their discussions were far from free. The *bienséances*, social convention, and political prudence imposed widespread self-censorship. At home, the Baron Paul Heinrich Dietrich d'Holbach, an atheist and materialist, could only speak freely behind closed doors among intimate friends and never on official reception days. Mme Geoffrin silenced her overbold guests with her famous "*Voilà qui est bien*"—"that's enough for now."[2] In his *Mémoires*, the spirited polemicist and contributor to the *Encyclopédie* André Morellet tells how a company of *philosophes*—which included d'Alembert, Guillaume Thomas Raynal, Claude Adrien Helvétius, the Abbé Galiani, Marmontel, Antoine Léonard Thomas, and himself—having dined with their hostess, would often go to the Tuileries "to meet other friends, to hear the news, damn the government, and philosophize at ease. We made a circle,

2. Jean-François Marmontel, *Mémoires*, p. 207.

sitting under a tree in the big avenue, and gave ourselves over to animated conversation as free as the air we breathed."[3]

A glance at eighteenth-century Parisian society reveals the striking contrast between the stability of the *ancien régime*'s political and social institutions and the wish for change. Not only did fashions succeed one another with monotonous regularity in art and literature as in clothes and entertainment, but the very way of thinking and feeling changed against the unchanging background of privileged life. Even in society, the realm par excellence of caprice and the ephemeral, the passion for novelty lived side by side with a jealous sense of aristocratic tradition and attachment to form and past customs. Generation after generation took the same path and adopted the same ways. A salon could keep its doors open for decades with a fixed weekly agenda, thanks not only to the ambition of the hostess but also to her discipline and forbearance. Mme de Lambert's and Mme du Deffand's salons both lasted thirty years, and Mme Geoffrin's forty.

Ideas changed, but the framework of *sociabilité* remained defined as it had been by Arthénice at the hôtel de Rambouillet. The rituals of dinner, supper, readings out loud, theatrical performances, music, dancing, the exercise of social literary genres, and of course conversation were permanently established by the Marquise de Lambert at the hôtel de Nevers.

Four very different women, linked to one another through complicated relationships involving every feeling from love to hatred, illustrate how society life in Enlightenment Paris could become an obsession that could give rise to insurmountable disagreements even within a single family. It flourished on elective affinities but could provoke ferocious rivalry. Antagonism, however, was no impediment to admiration, and excellence of style sometimes obliged the bitterest of enemies to recognize that they shared a common language.

The four women who represent the four different models of eighteenth-century *sociabilité* at its peak are Mme Geoffrin; her daughter, the Marquise de La Ferté-Imbault; the Marquise du Deffand; and her niece, Mlle de Lespinasse. Their story can be followed through the recollections of Mme de La Ferté-Imbault. Though by far the least intelligent of the four women, the testimony of Mme Geoffrin's daughter is particularly valuable because her viewpoint and her criteria are essentially connected to society. As a victim of her mother's social ambition, Mme de La Ferté-Imbault sought revenge throughout her life by competing in the same field, and in her old age by writing notes, anecdotes, letters, and recollections—all with the intention of affirming her acceptance in society, her friendships, her successes, and her taste.

Marie Thérèse was born in 1715 to François Geoffrin, a rich bourgeois who had made his fortune from the Manufacture royale des glaces of Saint-Gobain,

---

3. André Morellet, *Mémoires de l'abbé Morellet de l'Académie française sur le dix-huitième siècle et sur la Révolution*, edited by Jean-Pierre Guicciardi (Paris: Mercure de France, 1988), p. 97.

and Marie-Thérèse Rodet, a beautiful, devout orphan thirty-four years his junior, who was fifteen years old at the time her daughter was born. Years later, her daughter would describe how domestic peace ended with the appearance of a dangerous neighbor, the ambitious, intriguing, and amoral Mme de Tencin. In visiting her salon, "my mother's devoutness changed into a passion for people of *esprit* . . . [and] the seed of her ambition began to develop rapidly."[4]

It was about 1730. Mme Geoffrin had been married for nearly fifteen years and was just thirty. Conversation at Mme de Tencin's salon in the rue Saint-Honoré had opened the doors on a world unknown to her, making up for the education she lacked, introducing her to the life of the intellect, and showing her an honest way out of the boredom that plagued her existence. She very soon decided to follow that lady's example and, little by little, created her own salon, until finally, on her neighbor's death, she inherited her guests. For a long time M. Geoffrin did everything in his power to oppose his wife's plans, but he was always the loser in the violent arguments that took place over the years. The young Marie Thérèse, witnessing her parents' quarrels and "having exactly his character" and an "automatic aversion" to her mother,[5] suffered from her father's humiliation. In her view, the original sin of sacrificing the family paradise to vanity and ambition was never redeemed by the great undertaking that was the salon. Furthermore M. Geoffrin's reservations about "the failings and virtues of all the great minds, their pride and their lack of friendship"[6] would prevent his daughter from yielding to their intellectual seduction and loving them.

Having won her battle, Mme Geoffrin wanted her daughter beside her on her reception days, and despite her reticence, Marie Thérèse could only have benefited from the extraordinary experience that fate provided to her. Contact with the great intellectuals of the day opened her mind—the writers Fontenelle and the Abbé de Saint-Pierre took her education to heart. She was stimulated by Fontenelle, who made her read Descartes's *Discours de la méthode*, and by the abbé, who, besides teaching Christian virtues and *bienfaisance*, introduced her to the classical philosophers and the great French poets. But the zeal with which the young girl listened to their advice was not entirely innocent: learning was also a tool of revenge against her mother, who had only been taught to read and to count. After she was sixty, Marie Thérèse remembered with satisfaction, "My mother never wanted me to leave her because at bottom she has affection for me, and she

4. Mme de La Ferté-Imbault, "Troisième voyage de ma raison, ce 20 janvier 1770," p. 3, in *Mémoires intéressants de Mme la Marquise d'Estampes de La Ferté-Imbault*, Archives Nationales de France, Fonds d'Étampes, Valençay et Geoffrin (cartons 25–29 contain the Geoffrin family's personal papers, the correspondence and the papers of Mme Geoffrin and her daughter), 508 AP, 27.

5. Mme de La Ferté-Imbault, "Troisième voyage de ma raison, ce 20 janvier 1770," p. 4.

6. Mme de La Ferté-Imbault, "Troisième voyage de ma raison, ce 20 janvier 1770," p. 4.

believes that I can be of use to her in some way, but she could never suffer me to be in her room without being jealous if I made the slightest impression." Despite all her attempts, Marie-Thérèse never managed to banish her obsession with her mother, always seeing her as "the most complicated and the most distinguished person" she had ever known, even attributing a mythical quality to her faults. "Having read in extract the history of all the great men from both ancient and modern times, I have found only two who could compare to her, Alexander the Great and Cardinal de Richelieu. She has the same degree of ambition, the same passion for fame, and the same jealousy of anything that might diminish her brilliance."[7]

Marie Thérèse's accusations and her unlikely comparisons reveal the depth of her resentment but do not explain her mother's success. However great Mme de Geoffrin's ambition, it would have gone nowhere without her entrepreneurial talent, her psychological intuition, and her ability to understand the times she lived in.

In Mme de Tencin's salon, the obscure bourgeoise who had until then socialized with only the religious of the parish discovered not just the intellectual life but also the important part now played in it by women, who sensed that they faced a new phenomenon destined for a great future. The intellectuals now recognized collectively as *philosophes* constituted a new autonomous power quite different from that of the old republic of letters. Unlike Fontenelle, they maintained that truth should not be a prerogative closed to all but a few initiates and sought a place from which to promulgate it. Such a place should not depend on royal authority, as was the case with the academies, but should be opposed to specialization, with its roots in civil society whose mood it could interpret and which allowed for direct communication with public opinion. In exchange for such hospitality, the *philosophes* would freely offer the performance of their intelligence and would guarantee the prestige of whoever received them.

Mme Geoffrin did not hesitate to seize the occasion and, over two decades,[8] cleverly, tenaciously, by carefully choosing her guests and continuously broadening her circle, she succeeded in making her salon "the most complete, the best organized, . . . the best administered of her time," according to Sainte-Beuve[9]—the shop display for the country's intellectual life. The habitués included Mme de

---

7. Mme de La Ferté-Imbault, "Extraits des voyages que ma raison a été obligé de faire pour triompher des devoirs les plus pénibles et les plus variés faits en 1773," p. 4, in *Mémoires*.

8. In one description of her mother in 1772, Mme de La Ferté-Imbault states that Wednesday dinners were "founded" by Mme Geoffrin forty years earlier, that is around 1730, and the Monday ones twenty-five years before, in about 1745. In a letter of condolence written in October 1777 to Mme de La Ferté-Imbault on her mother's death, Cochin claims to have first frequented Mme Geoffrin's house twenty-seven years earlier, in 1750 (See 508 AP, 27).

9. Sainte-Beuve, "Mme Geoffrin," in *Causeries du lundi*, Vol. 2, p. 309.

Tencin's friends—the aging Fontenelle, Dortous de Mairan, Marivaux, the Abbé de Saint-Pierre, the Abbé Trublet, Montesquieu at the height of his fame—and the generation that was gathering around the *Encyclopédie*: Raynal, Duclos, d'Alembert, Helvétius, d'Holbach, Frédéric Melchior von Grimm, Marmontel, Thomas, Jean Baptiste Antoine Suard, Morellet, and François Jean de Chastellux, to name only the best known among them. With great foresight, Mme Geoffrin received not only men of letters but welcomed artists as well to her beautiful house in the rue Saint-Honoré. For the first time painters like Van Loo, Vernet, Boucher, Greuze, Hubert Robert, architects like Soufflot, and engravers like Cochin were received into society and invited to speak about their work. Hitherto, whatever their talent, they had been treated as artisans. Herself a collector, Mme Geoffrin knew the artists personally and used to visit them and talk to them in their studios, but it was the Comte de Caylus who suggested she invite them together to her house once a week. Caylus, the son of Mme de Maintenon's favorite niece—a lady who combined all the graces of *cour* and *ville*—behaved like a misanthrope, hated society life, and loathed the *philosophes*. But he was himself an artist and fascinated by archeology. He was also the most cultivated, most brilliant, and most expert of the connoisseurs, and he presided over the Monday dinners, to which he brought "as many painters as sculptors and amateurs from among his friends," thus making Mme Geoffrin "the benefactress and protectress of young talent, which immediately gave her a reputation in a genre of which she had formerly had no knowledge."[10]

In this way the prestige of Mme Geoffrin's salon was doubled, making it all the more attractive, and by guaranteeing the participation of the best exponents from both worlds, it enabled those worlds to discover each other. The fact that separate days were allotted to each camp did not prevent the Monday guests and the Wednesday guests from sometimes mixing, so that the literati and the artists were able to enlighten each other and discuss their opinions from a common ground of aesthetics and taste. Diderot's art criticism of the *Salons* and numerous other masterpieces of eighteenth-century publishing that developed from the close collaboration between writers, painters, and engravers all bear witness to the accuracy of Mme Geoffrin's judgment. Thanks to Wednesdays in the rue Saint-Honoré, artists could also meet collectors and amateurs and make themselves known to visitors passing through Paris, for diplomats and distinguished foreigners represented a third ace in Mme Geoffrin's hand. These served the dual purpose of adding luster to her salon and of spreading its fame throughout Europe. Marmontel remembered three "who for the allurement of their wit and their abundant understanding

---

10. Mme de La Ferté-Imbault, "6ème Lettre où il est question de ma mère, à Paris, ce 28 mars 1777" (part of a collection of eight letters addressed "*à un homme de mes amis retiré dans sa terre*," June 28, 1776–April 1, 1777), 508 AP, 27.

ceded to none of the most cultivated Frenchmen; they were the Abbé Galiani; the Marquis Caracciolo, later ambassador to Naples; and the Comte de Creutz, the Swedish minister."[11] In fact it was thanks to two of these foreign visitors that Mme Geoffrin "went from notoriety to glory."[12] In 1753 she welcomed to her house a twenty-one-year-old Polish nobleman who had come to Paris for six months to complete his education. The young man whom Mme Geoffrin introduced to her Wednesday dinners and to whom she gave so much advice that she earned herself the affectionate nickname of *maman* was called Stanisław Poniatowski. When eleven years later he was elected King of Poland, he gave proof of his filial affection by inviting her to Warsaw. In 1758, she opened her doors to the Princess of Anhalt-Zerbst, whose daughter, Catherine, soon became Empress of Russia and honored her mother's hostess with a correspondence that lasted for many years.

Did not this extraordinary success in many ways contravene the very principles of aristocratic *sociabilité*? Until now social life had been an end in itself that coincided with aristocratic leisure and was limited to the privileged classes, albeit allowing for, and indeed requesting, the presence of a certain number of writers chosen by virtue of their talent.

Mme Geoffrin, who followed the formula of the Marquise de Lambert's Tuesdays while replacing the hôtel de Nevers's ceremonious tone with Mme de Tencin's freer and more familiar one, did not herself participate in discussions. Lacking the culture of the one and the intellectual gifts of the other, she left the conversation to her guests and merely listened with an attentive air even to arguments that she was not capable of understanding. Her main concern was not for entertainment but for the success of her enterprise, which had to be protected from polemic and scandal. For this reason she took care "to preside, supervise and keep control over these two naturally free societies, to establish the limits to this freedom, and by a word or a gesture rein them in as though by an invisible thread."[13] Her daughter was the first to admire her cleverness: "Her tact is so delicate concerning anything that might cause political inconvenience by going too far that she always changes the conversation when she senses danger; so sublime is her tact that in my youth I have heard Fontenelle and Montesquieu praise her infinitely for that particular gift. For her it takes the place of learning and science, which she could never bear."[14] According to the tradition of polite society, the hostess's tastes defined her salon's cultural boundaries, but in the rue Saint-Honoré, the interests of the guests were paramount.

---

11. Marmontel, *Mémoires*, p. 202.

12. Marguerite Glotz and Madeleine Maire, *Salons du XVIIIe siècle* (Paris: Nouvelles Éditions Latines, 1949), p. 136.

13. Marmontel, *Mémoires*, p. 196.

14. Mme de La Ferté-Imbault, *Mémoires*, August 1774, 508 AP, 27.

Nor can it be said that Mme Geoffrin's guests were chosen for their natural affinity and friendship. Instead, they constituted an intellectual corps that Mme Geoffrin had decided to adopt and that she liked to govern with affectionate authoritarianism. She did not merely welcome writers and artists to her salon, but she took an interest in their careers and private lives, and helped them financially by paying them annuities, buying their works, and occasionally lodging them at her house. In return, she demanded obedience, discipline, and prudence. In the words of Sainte-Beuve, Mme Geoffrin made of her salon "the Encyclopedia of the century in deed and in conversation"[15]—albeit an encyclopedia of her own kind in which anything that might be subversive or disrespectful of institutions was censured. Mme Geoffrin stopped receiving Diderot because she knew the conversation of this man, the most brilliant of the *philosophes*, to be quite beyond control. She preferred to go and see him in his own apartments or to meet him in other people's houses. Yet it was she who came to his aid in 1759 when, as the result of a second verdict, publication of the *Encyclopédie* was halted halfway through, and it found itself on the verge of bankruptcy. Mme Geoffrin's secret gift of at least a hundred thousand écus reassured the printer and allowed Diderot to bring his great enterprise to completion. Clearly it cannot have been ambition and calculation alone that drove her to make her salon into the Enlightenment headquarters.

Until then it had been the hostess who, by virtue of her name and position in society, had lent authority to a salon. In the case of Mme Geoffrin, for the first time it was the salon's success that brought the hostess out of obscurity. With a few rare exceptions, the aristocracy had been in control of high society, but with Mme Geoffrin, a bourgeois house came to represent Parisian intellectual life. Mme Geoffrin's final and most important break with society custom came with her exclusion of women from the Wednesday dinners. Perhaps she wanted, as her daughter claimed, to be the only woman in order to dominate these occasions, or perhaps she wished to prevent female frivolity from interfering with the ordered development of the conversation. Yet her bourgeois practicality would not have carried her so far without the prestige that aristocratic society had accorded women, and had she herself not acquired some of the qualities typical of high society ladies, like naturalness, simplicity, tact, a clear and elegant manner of speaking, a lively and penetrating mind, the ability to tell a tale, and, above all, *savoir vivre*. This last, according to Marmontel, "was her supreme science; about the rest she had only vague and ordinary notions; but in the study of manners and fashion and in her understanding of men and particularly of women, she was profound and capable of giving good advice."[16]

There were plenty of women, however, at the intimate suppers that were the high point of reception days at the house in the rue Saint-Honoré at the end of the

15. Sainte-Beuve, "Mme Geoffrin," in *Causeries du lundi*, Vol. 2, p. 315.

16. Marmontel, *Mémoires*, p. 198.

1750s. As evening drew in, the *philosophes* made way for some aristocratic ladies
—the Comtesse d'Egmont, the Comtesse de Brionne, the Duchesse de Duras, all
young and beautiful—one or two literati, and a few great noblemen. It was these
suppers that assured Mme Geoffrin of her salon's worldly success. She herself had
become an institution.

It must have been difficult to compete with a mother like Mme Geoffrin; but her
daughter tried to do so from childhood. To begin with, it was a "defensive war."[17]
Marie Thérèse had no intention of succumbing to her mother's imperious character and joining the list of her "conquests." As a child she had shown herself to be
disobedient and headstrong, and was encouraged by the fact that Mme Geoffrin
needed her support in her continuous quarrels with her husband. As an adolescent
she liked to embarrass her mother in front of other people with extravagant
expressions of sincerity and sudden outbursts of delight during which nothing
could prevent her from laughing in the face of guests she disliked. But the real
moment of emancipation and revenge came with marriage.

As a beautiful, richly endowed only child, Mlle Geoffrin was an excellent
match, and on the eve of her eighteenth birthday, her parents, allowing snobbery
to prevail over sense, gave her in marriage to Philippe Charles d'Étampes, Marquis de La Ferté-Imbault, the eldest son of a family of the old but impoverished
nobility. The outburst of happiness with which Marie Thérèse greeted his death
four years later leads one to suppose that the marriage had not been a great success. The young marquise embraced widowhood as a happy condition. Mme de
La Ferté-Imbault would continue to live, as she had throughout her short marriage, at the house in the rue Saint-Honoré, but no longer under supervision. She
decided to lead an entirely autonomous existence: a life in keeping with her tastes
and her new social position rather than with her mother's intellectual ambitions.
"Having become free and widowed at twenty-one, I gave myself up to the *Grand
Monde* and to going wherever my fancy led (which I like up to a point), and I went
all around the *cour* and the *ville* with what is called *bonne compagnie*."[18]

Cour, ville, bonne compagnie, Grand Monde: these keywords of polite society
would henceforth guide the existence of the daughter of the Saint-Gobain fac-
tory's former employee. Marriage had introduced her to the world of the high-
ranking nobility and it was there that she sought friendship. Nothing is greater
proof of her success than the list of her new acquaintances. Among the most outstanding names are those of the Duc de Luynes; various members of the great

---

17. Mme de La Ferté-Imbault, *Portrait de ma mère, 1760*, 508 AP, 27.

18. Mme de La Ferté-Imbault, *Mon plan de vie pour ma vieillesse, à commencer dès à présent que j'ai
60 ans. J'espère qu'il sera agréable à ma belle minette* [playful nickname given to her mother]. *Fait à
Paris ce 2 mai 1775*, 508 AP, 27.

Phélypeaux tribe—especially the Marquise de Pontchartrain and her brother the Comte de Maurepas, Louis XV's minister; the Duchesse de Chevreuse; the Duchesse de Rohan-Chabot; the Comtesse de Marsan; the Princesse Louise Adelaïde de Bourbon-Conti, known as Mademoiselle de La Roche-sur-Yon; and the Prince de Condé. The key to the young marquise's success was her cheerfulness. Not the provocative cheerfulness with which she disconcerted her mother's friends, but an effervescent, contagious gaiety—one of the most precious attributes of society life. "When I devote myself to society and to my friends, I like only to laugh, to play, and to forget common sense,"[19] Marie Thérèse would write in her *Plan de vie pour ma vieillesse*—which she penned at age sixty. But her liveliness and exquisite recklessness seemed so seductive only because she never forgot the respect owed to the *bienséances* and the *amour-propre* of others. In both the Parisian and the country houses to which Mme de La Ferté-Imbault was invited, the opportunities for distraction were endless. Surprises, jokes, and disguises were all essential elements of society's agenda, and verse was a vital part of the entertainment. Mme Geoffrin's daughter decided to excel in this aristocratic tradition of the ephemeral.

Her tendency to laugh did not change with age. At fifty she wrote, with obvious pleasure, an "Account of a supper I gave the Prince de Condé in the month of September 1768,"[20] a joke that is very reminiscent of the Blue Room's childish buffoonery. Two of the marquise's women friends offered to take the Prince de Condé, then aged thirty, to have supper with them in a *petite maison*—a place used for gallant encounters—but they took him instead to Mme de La Ferté-Imbault's apartment, which was empty but candlelit:

> The Prince de Condé was astounded to find no one there. Then the ladies told him that he was the god Mars, to whom the three Graces wished to give supper, but that the third was disfigured by a large spot on her nose and so did not dare to show herself. The prince and the ladies came to find me in the little cabinet where I was masked. I arose, took the prince by the hand and sang to him:

> *Dieu terrible, respectez*
> *En la doyenne des trois grâces,*
> *Son gros bouton sur le nez,*
> *Sa dent qui branle et ses grimaces.*
> *Mais pour tous ses autres appas*
> *Grand Dieu ne vous contraignez pas*

---

19. Mme de La Ferté-Imbault, *Mon plan de vie.*

20. Mme de La Ferté-Imbault, "Récit d'un souper que j'ai donné au prince de Condé au mois de septembre 1768," in *Histoire de l'amitié dont Monsieur le prince de Condé m'honore depuis l'année 1762,* 508 AP, 27.

Jouissez-en à votre gré
Avec sa marque sur le nez.[21]

When the Prince of Condé obliged me to unmask, I sang him an old song which goes:

Je n'ai plus assez d'agréments
Pour vaincre un prince qui se défend…[22]

Various other verses followed, sung to different tunes throughout supper by either the ladies, the servants, or the marquise, all of them equally concentrated on the clownish theme of an old woman's unquenchable love for a young prince. Mme de La Ferté-Imbault is known to have felt a maternal affection for the prince, who was so much younger than she, and she was aware that Condé was at the time involved in a passionate and scandalous affair with the Princesse de Monaco. The theme of the old woman in love, which Ninon de Lenclos had brought back into fashion, must have sounded very comical coming from the mouth of the marquise, who was known for her virtue. It is no longer possible to understand the allusions made in Mme de La Ferté-Imbault's comic verses. Nor can we appreciate the musical parody, or imagine the singers' mimicry and the sound of their voices, especially since the marquise has left no hint about the comments, the laughter, or the conversation sparked off by this modest theatrical performance, which must have added to the jollity of the evening.

The same problem arises concerning the avalanche of verse that followed the birth in 1771 of the Sublime Order of Lanturelus, "of which the marquise was both creator, muse, and supreme directress and which was not long in flooding first of all Paris, then France and Europe, with its glory."[23] The Marquis de Ségur was not being ironic. In the eyes of Europe, Paris was not only the Enlightenment capital, but also the home of aristocratic leisure pursuits of which the Order of Lanturelus was a prime example.

The "order" was born one evening when the old Marquis de Croismare, being indisposed, sent a composition in verse in which he dwelt on his ailments to excuse himself from honoring the marquise's invitation to supper. Mme de La Ferté-Imbault immediately refused to accept his excuses. She replied with another composition in verse that ended in the refrain *"Lanturelu, lanturelu, lanturelu."*

---

21. "Terrible God, respect/In the doyenne of the three Graces,/The big spot she has on her nose,/Her tooth that wobbles and her grimaces./But for all her other charms/Great God, do not restrain yourself/Enjoy them as you please/With the mark on her nose."

22. "I have no longer enough charms/To conquer a prince who defends himself."

23. Pierre-Marie de Ségur, *Le Royaume de la rue Saint-Honoré*, p. 180.

This was so successful that it gave rise to the idea of an order entirely devoted to jokes and the exchange of satirical verses between its members. Once a week the queen and her knights met to read their verses out loud and to improvise others. Thanks to the mysterious ways of fashion, this innocent, childish game attracted the greatest variety of people and the most distinguished names, even arousing Catherine the Great of Russia's curiosity. Never had an initiative so in keeping with the eighteenth-century fashion for *sociétés badines*—societies for amusement—been so successful, but the idea of a medieval order that jokingly modeled itself on courtly rites was deeply rooted in tradition, a fact of which Mme de La Ferté-Imbault was certainly aware.[24]

Her passion for putting everything into rhyme also had its roots in society. The improvisation of verse, like singing, dancing, or conversing, was an excellent way to gain admiration while at the same time contributing to the great communal game of self-contemplation. Whether parodies or eulogies, these verses, if only for a moment, reflected and magnified the ephemeral events of society's calendar. The marquise's manuscripts show that rhyming was not her only literary pastime. A series of short portraits of society friends and acquaintances, some anecdotes, a collection of maxims and reflections, some recollections of events she had witnessed during the reigns of Louis XV and Louis XVI, letters of social import, and letters to friends like the Cardinal de Bernis, with whom she corresponded for several decades, all demonstrate Mme de La Ferté-Imbault's engagement, albeit with no great talent, in all the minor literary genres typical of society. But the marquise did not pick up her pen just for amusement: her writing not only amounted to an indirect self-portrait but was also obvious proof of her belonging to the *Grand Monde*.

At nearly sixty, Mme de La Ferté-Imbault was loved and spoiled by high society and no longer needed to compete with her mother, although, of course, Mme Geoffrin was supreme where crowned heads were concerned. In 1766, at Stanisław's invitation, she had made a triumphal visit to Poland, and on passing through Vienna had been presented to Maria Teresa of Austria and treated with the greatest possible respect by Prince von Kaunitz, the Empress's prime minister. In contrast to her daughter, however, the "Geoffrinska"—as she came to be maliciously dubbed—was untitled and could not be presented to the King of France. Thus her own country's court remained a closed world for her.

Mme de La Ferté-Imbault still had the problem of her mother's friends. With the passing of the years, her youthful antipathy for the *philosophes* turned to violent aversion. She was religious, with close ties to both the milieu of the Parlement and the party of the *dévots*, and perfectly understood what her mother had tried

---

24. Arthur Dinaux, *Les Sociétés badines, bachiques, littéraires et chantantes. Leur histoire et leurs traveaux*, two volumes (1867; Geneva: Slatkine Reprints, 1968), cited in Ségur, *Le Royaume de la rue Saint-Honoré*, p. 180.

to conceal: the political significance of the Encyclopedists' "sect" and their challenge to established values. She judged Voltaire and d'Alembert to be "the cleverest apothecaries of new poisons ever to have existed,"[25] and she devoted years to creating her own antidote, which consisted of a vast collection of thoughts taken from the works of the greatest of ancient and modern philosophers, all intended to demonstrate the perennial truth of Christian morality. But when she suggested that her Lanturelus should use this precious collection of wisdom as a starting point for writing an anti-*Encyclopédie*, even the most faithful of knights declined the invitation. Fortunately, thanks to the reputation she had acquired through her excerpts, Mme de La Ferté-Imbault was asked in 1771 to choose the most suitable passages from ancient philosophy for the two little nine- and eleven-year-old royal princesses to read.

It is highly likely that the wish not to leave her aged mother in the hands of unbelievers was a determining factor in persuading Mme de La Ferté-Imbault to make a gesture of reconciliation. It was a *beau geste*, and well advised. On May 2, 1775, a few days before her sixtieth birthday, she drew up *Mon plan de vie pour ma vieillesse* and sent it to Mme Geoffrin. In the first five pages she runs through the main stages in her life in the light of her character, her education, her religious and moral convictions, her intellectual interests, and her friends. Whatever her faults, the simplicity and honesty with which Marie Thérèse recounts her story are in themselves her best justification. But at the end of the fifth page, the rebellious daughter goes much further: she announces that she has written this "little story" for her mother, blames herself for all the past misunderstandings, and expounds her good intentions for the future. "I undertake never to [show] temper either to her or to persons of her society whom I do not like. We have reached an age where the little difference between my mother's and mine draws us together, one to the other, more like sisters than like mother and daughter. The difference in our tastes never having destroyed the solid esteem and friendship that has held sway between us since I reached the age of reason, it can be said that this difference has perhaps served our present happiness."

For all its goodwill, graciousness, and reason, this act of daughterly submission was, however, not enough to disguise the absence of true intimacy. The only passion that Marie Thérèse shared with her mother—probably the only one either had ever really experienced—was the love of society life, and it was to this passion that Mme de La Ferté-Imbault appealed at the time of reconciliation. She did not suggest an unlikely bond of affection with her mother but a worldly alliance, the premise for which already existed. The old antagonisms must be forgotten, one another's successes recognized, and the immense capital accumulated by both combined. "Everyone I frequent has a great regard for my mother and would like

25. Mme de La Ferté-Imbault, *Mémoires*.

to meet her. Her circle and mine then should be seen as a flower bed in which all kinds are to be found. Her visitors and mine constitute, as everyone agrees, Paris's biggest and choicest emporium of *bonne compagnie*. Let us rejoice in the consequences of our characters and in the changes wrought by reason and time, and if life is a path, let us sow flowers on that path."[26]

In fact the marquise's path to reconciliation did not appear to be strewn only with flowers. Her *beau geste* came too late. Her mother dutifully showed her some consideration, but she was unable to disguise the fact that she preferred the company of d'Alembert and Julie de Lespinasse to that of her daughter.

Ten years had already passed since Julie de Lespinasse had been turned out of Mme du Deffand's house and taken under Mme Geoffrin's wing, during which time her influence had grown considerably. Generally speaking, Mme Geoffrin disliked competition from intellectual women. Mme d'Épinay knew all about that, having never been able to recover from not being invited to the rue Saint-Honoré, about which she complained to the Abbé Galiani. But Julie immediately touched Mme Geoffrin's heart and gained her affection. Not only did Mme Geoffrin shower her with gifts, but she also provided her with an annuity by selling two large pictures by Van Loo. She also invited her to her intimate suppers and admitted her (the only other woman besides the Comtesse de Boufflers to have the privilege) to her famous Wednesday dinners.

"Her presence," according to Marmontel, "gave rise to inexpressible interest. A continual object of attention, whether listening or speaking herself (and no one spoke better) without coquetry, she inspired the innocent desire to please; without prudery she made it clear just how free the discussion could be and just how far it could go without offending modesty or violating decency."[27] It is hardly surprising, however, that for all her miraculous powers, Julie's charms were impotent in alleviating Mme de La Ferté-Imbault's hostility. For the marquise, Mlle de Lespinasse was merely a dangerous intriguer who had replaced her at her mother's side and who wished to place a wedge between them. Mme de La Ferté-Imbault would never have been able to get the better of Julie, the interloper, had the latter not died in May 1776, aged only forty-four. Even her demise, however, could not placate the marquise, who left a description of her that was very different from Julie's usual saintly image.

Mlle de Lespinasse is generally thought of as a great tragic figure, the only one of the century until the Revolution forced French noblewomen to rediscover heroism. Julie was not beautiful, but her luminosity was so bright that her lack of beauty went unnoticed. She spoke the pure, elegant French of the classical theater,

26. Mme de La Ferté-Imbault, *Mon plan de vie*.

27. Marmontel, *Mémoires*, p. 201.

but avoided such rhetorical devices as litotes (understatement) and made no effort to temper the intensity of her feelings. Her extreme sensitivity was both her cross and her joy; it was both her *raison d'être* and what led her to the grave. Divided between passion and reason, moderation and excess, delicacy and violence, Julie thrived on her contradictions and lived her life with the same awareness with which she had constructed her persona.

From her letters, her confidences to friends, and through her many admirers, we know the very things Julie wanted us to know about her. We know about her illegitimate birth and the early discovery of the "horrors" that attended it. We also know about her parents' pitiless egotism, her strict dependency on Mme du Deffand, in whose house she served her social apprenticeship, her friendship with d'Alembert, the great success of her salon, her intellectual engagement, her passionate concern for the public good, and her need to love. Her life, which began like a bleak novel, could have ended with her triumphant success in Enlightenment society, but, preferring the stifling atmosphere of tragedy, she chose to die of love for a man—the Comte de Guibert—who did not reciprocate her feelings.

It is hard to imagine two more different characters with two more different stories than Mme de La Ferté-Imbault and Mlle de Lespinasse. The marquise was faithful to tradition and it institutions—the Church, the monarchy, the Parlements—and her idol was the Comte de Maurepas, minister for all seasons. Julie hated corruption, injustice, and the prejudices of the day, and hoped for a reformed future administered by better men. Her idol was the *ministre-philosophe* Anne Robert Jacques de Turgot, who had contributed to the *Encyclopédie* but was minister for only two years. The marquise loved cheerfulness and chose to lead a life ruled by lightheartedness and entertainment. Julie preferred depth to superficiality, which she loathed. The former carefully avoided love; the latter "knew only how to love." The marquise disliked wit as an intellectual value so much that she announced to Voltaire that she would rather to be thought stupid than be tainted by wit.[28] Mme de La Ferté-Imbault abhorred the *philosophes*, preferring the old court nobility to her mother's circle; Julie left Mme du Deffand's aristocratic salon to be welcomed as a privileged guest in Mme de Geoffrin's salon in the rue Saint-Honoré.

Nevertheless, both Mme Geoffrin's daughter and Mme du Deffand's niece belonged to the same worldly culture, shared the same formal code of behavior, and fought with the same weapons. It was a particularly difficult war, precisely because Julie's impeccable manners never allowed Mme de La Ferté-Imbault to gain the slightest advantage. "If la Lespinasse had lived to become mistress of my mother's person, her room, and her money, she would have treated me in so polished and so flattering a fashion that it would have been impossible for me to do

---

28. Mme de La Ferté-Imbault, "Origine de la haine de Mme de La Ferté-Imbault pour Voltaire," in *Anecdotes*, 508 AP, 28.

the situation justice and to play the part of a daughter to my mother, ... and she would also have led d'Alembert in such a way that I could neither have complained, nor waged war against him, which I successfully did."[29]

With the disappearance of her rival, Mme de La Ferté-Imbault decided to settle accounts in a field in which Julie had proved invincible, precisely that of her social standing. As she recounts it, the dramatic and moving tale of Mlle de Lespinasse's life becomes a story of calculation and cynicism with the sensitive, passionate heroine proving to be a vulgar social climber. "La Lespinasse," the marquise recounts, "was the bastard daughter of Mme du Deffand's brother and the Marquise d'Albon; she was ugly, but she was ambitious to play the part of a person of *esprit*, and her *esprit* was of a quality to back her ambition." The initiation into society of the young woman from the provinces took place in the house of the amoral, corrupt Marquise du Deffand, a place of degraded *sociabilité*, where innocent good cheer and delicate *raillerie* had made way for backbiting and spite. "Mme du Deffand, being blind, summoned Mademoiselle de Lespinasse more than twenty years ago to help sustain her salon and her celebrity. At the time Mme du Deffand's circle was made up of all the most brilliant people at court and in Paris and of many distinguished foreigners; this company neither liked nor esteemed Mme du Deffand, nor did they like or esteem one another. They all amused themselves by mocking one another wittily and with finesse, but with a kind of prudence. D'Alembert often went to Mme du Deffand's, and as he is of a mocking nature, the society there pleased him greatly."[30]

Clearly it was not just d'Alembert's talent for parody that made him Mme du Deffand's favorite; the marquise had a deep attachment to him that, through understandable jealousy, would turn to resentment. As soon as Julie arrived in the Saint-Joseph salon, Mme de Tencin's unwanted son began to overlook his old friend in favor of the new arrival for whom fate seemed to have predestined him. "Both without parents," wrote d'Alembert, "without family, and having experienced, since the moment of birth, abandon, misfortune, and injustice, nature seemed to have placed us in the world to find one another, to take the place of everything for one another, to support one another mutually, like two reeds which, battered by the storm, support one another by clinging together."[31] That is what happened. When, after a long story of moods, misunderstandings, and spite,

---

29. Mme de La Ferté-Imbault, *7ème Lettre sur ce qui s'est passé dans la maladie de ma mère, Paris, 10 avril 1777*.

30. Mme de La Ferté-Imbault, *8ème Lettre. L'histoire de Mlle de Lespinasse*.

31. Jean le Rond d'Alembert, "Aux mânes de Mlle de Lespinasse," in *Lettres de Mlle de Lespinasse suivies de ses autres œuvres et de lettres de Mme du Deffand, de Turgot, de Bernardin de Saint-Pierre... et d'une Appendice comprenant les écrits de d'Alembert, de Guibert, de Voltaire, de Frédéric II, sur Mlle de Lespinasse...*, edited by Eugène Asse (Paris: Charpentier, 1918), p. 376.

the storm finally broke, Mme du Deffand turned her niece out for having "stolen" d'Alembert, and the two "love children" never left one another again but ended up living in the same house.

Mme de La Ferté-Imbault's version of what happened is entirely different. According to her, the seed of discord was sown by wounded pride. A letter from Voltaire that Mme du Deffand allowed to be read aloud to her guests without realizing that d'Alembert was present made it clear that the marquise had made fun of her friend.[32] D'Alembert, having been publicly humiliated, "only laughed, while thinking to himself, 'she will pay for that,'" and decided there and then that the instrument of his revenge would be Julie. For her part, the ungrateful niece was looking for an excuse to leave her aunt's home at Saint-Joseph, taking the most distinguished guests with her:

> This Lespinasse, having immediately noticed that none of Mme du Deffand's circle was tied to her by either friendship or esteem, and that they liked nothing better than to discuss her character failings, carefully and subtly became the confidant of all those who were stifling the desire to speak ill of Mme du Deffand. D'Alembert, who, since the incident of Voltaire's letter, was more tormented by that desire than anyone else, became closely involved with Mademoiselle de Lespinasse; she was very flattered and very glad to feel that d'Alembert needed her so badly that if she managed him carefully and took great care of him, she could make him her great supporter... in achieving her great aim, which was to leave Mme du Deffand to begin to set up [her own] little intellectual court.[33]

Julie still had to save face and avoid seeming ungrateful to her benefactress. She succeeded perfectly in this by adopting a suffering air and spreading the news that Mme du Deffand's harsh treatment of her made her "so unhappy that it was impossible for her to live with her without dying of sorrow."[34]

Once banished from Saint-Joseph, Mlle de Lespinasse managed not only to keep the goodwill of Mme du Deffand's guests, but also to acquire that of her enemies. It was hardly by accident that the first person to whom d'Alembert recommended Julie was Mme Geoffrin, who, by Mme de La Ferté-Imbault's own admission, detested Mme du Deffand, and, delighted by the opportunity to avenge herself on her aristocratic rival, welcomed the innocent victim with open arms.

Mlle de Lespinasse's apparently irresistible rise was, according to Mme de La Ferté-Imbault, planned down to the smallest detail with conscious deception,

---

32. There is no trace of this letter in Voltaire's correspondence.

33. Mme de La Ferté-Imbault, *8ème Lettre*.

34. Mme de La Ferté-Imbault, *8ème Lettre*.

marked by hypocrisy and ingratitude. Mme Geoffrin's daughter seems to have persuaded even her mother, albeit in extremis, to admit as much. "My mother told me that she had been duped in every way. When she first made her acquaintance, she had seemed charming because of her wit, her gaiety, her evenness of temper, and because of how she succeeded in pleasing those of the most opposite character whom she often met there; but when she saw how great and rapid was her success and how celebrated she was, [Julie's] head was turned so that she no longer contained her ambition. Her protectresses embarrassed her, she wanted money from all her friends with which to maintain her success, but she did not wish to know from whom these gifts came, and my mother looked at me and said, 'My daughter, would you believe that when I sold my Van Loo paintings to support her, she never thanked me?'"[35]

If Mme de La Ferté-Imbault is to be believed, however, it is hardly surprising that success, having changed Julie's life radically, should also have altered her relationship to others by giving her a new self-image. She had been the protagonist of an unprecedented adventure, and her self-confidence must have increased vastly. For the first time a poor, solitary, less than beautiful woman, with no family support and no social status, had succeeded, by virtue of her intellect alone, in gaining freedom, economic independence, and social prestige. At the beginning of the century, Mme de Staal-Delaunay's life had been changed when it was discovered that she had *esprit* and intelligence, but this had not enabled her to choose her own destiny. Fifty years later, the appreciation of intelligence had become a religion, giving its ministers a supreme authority. Since, due to the presence of d'Alembert at her side, Julie was admitted to the chosen few officiators of the "cult" of the *Encyclopédie* she probably came to think it quite natural that the faithful should contribute to the requirements of their sect. Why should she be grateful for what was morally owed? In selling her Van Loos for a noble cause, Mme Geoffrin primarily served herself. Convinced of the sacred nature of her role as a *femme d'esprit*, Julie seemed to anticipate a belief that would appear again in modern culture: that the "intellectual" is an individual whose special purpose is to enlighten society. Consequently, patronage, whether public or private, is both a duty and an honor for the patron.

Toward the end of 1764, having made the break with Mme du Deffand, Mlle de Lespinasse set herself up in the rue Saint-Dominique in an apartment about a hundred meters away from her aunt, raising "altar against altar."[36] She attracted a large number of Saint-Joseph's regulars to her house. In the large salon lit by four windows framed with crimson taffeta curtains and furnished with elegant pieces given by the Maréchale de Luxembourg, the Comtesse de Boufflers, the

---

35. Mme de La Ferté-Imbault, *8ème Lettre.*

36. Mme de La Ferté-Imbault, *8ème Lettre.*

Duchesse de Châtillon, and Mme Geoffrin, the tone of the circle was dictated not by the guests, but instead by the personality of the lady of the house. The visitors did not constitute a homogenous group; neither were they friends among themselves. They came as much from the ranks of the nobility as from the world of the *Encyclopédie*; there were ministers, diplomats, cardinals, highly placed civil servants, society ladies, famous writers, and young intellectuals starting out in life. According to Marmontel:

> She picked them from here and there . . . but so well matched were they that when they were with her, they found themselves to be as harmonious as the strings of a cleverly strung instrument. To continue the simile, I might say that she played this instrument with an art that touched on genius; she seemed to know what sound the cord she was about to touch would make; I mean that our minds and our characters were so well known to her that in order to bring them into play, she had to say but a word. . . . Her soul's continuous activity was communicated to us, but in a measured fashion: her imagination was the spur, her reason the regulator. And take note that the minds she influenced at her whim were neither feeble nor harebrained; the Condillacs and the Turgots were of their number; and d'Alembert was at her side like a simple, docile child. Her talent for throwing out an idea for debate to men of this caliber, her talent for debating it herself, with precision like them and sometimes with eloquence, her talent for bringing in new ideas and varying the discussions, always with the ease and facility of a fairy who, as she wished, with one wave of her wand, changes the scene of her magic; this talent, I maintain, was not that of a vulgar woman.[37]

Julie's lover, the Comte de Guibert, remarked that in her house, people who had nothing in common discovered themselves to be friends, "united by the same sentiments, the desire to please her and the need to love her." It is understandable that this wonderful harmony came to an end with her and that after she died, the habitués of her salon no longer saw one another. "The words of the Scripture can be applied to ourselves," Guibert went on; "the Lord hath struck the shepherd and the flock is dispersed."[38]

Every day for twelve years, in her apartment overlooking the Bellechasse convent, the *magicienne*—as Mme de La Ferté-Imbault sarcastically dubbed her, although a century earlier the society theorist Méré would surely have admired her "sorcery"[39]—polished her wand and renewed her spells from five to nine in

37. Marmontel, *Mémoires*, p. 260.

38. Jacques-Antoine-Hippolyte de Guibert, "Éloge d'Éliza," in *Lettres de Mlle de Lespinasse*, p. 364.

39. Méré, "Discours de la conversation," in *Œuvres complètes*, Vol. 2, p. 107.

the evening. Spells that amounted to the perfect expression of eighteenth-century *sociabilité* that had reached the finest point of balance between tradition and the demands of the present.

Since the days of the Blue Room, the worldly ideal had been a happy other place, ruled by *bienséances*, good taste, tact, and the wish to charm. A hundred and fifty years later, Julie, in the midst of her circle, appears to have conformed to the same aesthetic, and d'Alembert's compliments were no different from those Mlle de Scudéry might have paid her: "Your mind is pleasing and is bound to please for its many qualities; for your excellence of tone, your correctness of taste, your art of saying the right thing to everyone.... The delicacy of taste that is combined in you with a continual wish to please means that on the one hand, there is nothing far-fetched in you, and on the other, nothing is ever overlooked; so it can be said of you that you are very natural and not at all simple."[40]

Although reassured by praise, Julie was amazed by her ability to perform. "The singular thing is that no one discerns the effort I have to make to appear as I am judged really to be."[41] Yet it was precisely by virtue of a similar effort that the illusion of the *naturel* could take shape according to the classical aesthetic. La Bruyère stated a hundred years before Julie's time: "What art is needed to return to nature!"[42]

Whereas it was Mme du Deffand who initiated Mlle de Lespinasse into this difficult art of balancing instinct and culture, Julie's wish to please was motivated by a tremendous compulsion that went beyond the demands of society. "You do not even refuse to take the first steps when no one else has gone before ... and tedious people do not displease you too greatly, so long as those tedious people are devoted to you,"[43] d'Alembert gently rebuked her. She had soon learned from her illegitimate state in a merciless family that her only hope of improving her position was to trust to her powers of seduction. By overcoming Mme du Deffand's mistrust, Julie avoided the convent and went to Paris. Then, by enchanting the marquise's friends and gathering strength from their support, she managed to gain her independence. By continuously broadening her circle of admirers, she greatly enhanced her worldly position—the only asset on which she could count—and defended it in the marketplace that was Paris. For her, to please was primarily a powerful way of exorcising life's dramas. Seeing herself reflected in the admiration of others, Julie forgot that she was not beautiful, that she lived on charity, could not have a family, and was not loved by the man she loved; her unlimited desire for conquest was there to prevent these thoughts from returning to persecute her.

40. "Portrait de Mlle de Lespinasse par d'Alembert," in *Lettres de Mlle de Lespinasse*, pp. 344–346.

41. Mlle de Lespinasse to Condorcet, May 4, [1771], in Julie de Lespinasse, *Lettres à Condorcet*, edited by Jean-Noël Pascal (Paris: Desjonquères, 1990), pp. 42–43.

42. La Bruyère, "Des jugements," *remarque* 34, in *Les Caractères*, p. 386.

43. "Portrait de Mlle de Lespinasse par d'Alembert," in *Lettres de Mlle de Lespinasse*, pp. 350–351.

"The indifference of whoever it might be," according to her best biographer, "gave rise, almost without her realizing, to an inexpressible malaise, almost a physical pain, and she could not rest until she felt the ice being melted by the rays of her charm."[44]

Only an echo of the conversations that took place in Julie's salon can be gleaned from perusing the four volumes included in the *Manuscrits légués par mademoiselle de Lespinasse*.[45] These 1,676 pages of manuscript (only about twenty of which are in Julie's hand; the rest, with the exception of a few handwritten letters from d'Alembert and Turgot, are by unknown copyists) constitute a collection of a variety of writings by all sorts of different authors: letters, portraits, poems, prose, fragments of criticism, translations, linguistic observations, and thoughts of every kind.

Three hundred years after the invention of printing, the circulation of manuscripts was still a primary source of reading matter and included not only unpublished material but also extracts of various lengths from already published works. The reasons for this phenomenon were not merely economic. Nor did they simply result from mental habit. They satisfied a modern culture that thirsted after the new. The heterogeneity of Julie's documents may imply casualness and a lack of discernment, but the list of texts, drawn up by d'Alembert himself, shows the importance attached to them.

Like the *-ana* of the seventeenth century, this collection of material, for which Julie decided to become the archivist, reflects a fragmented culture that lies halfway between the spoken word and the written one: the purpose was to safeguard the memory of texts threatened by oblivion while, at the same time, offering them as a subject for comment and conversation. The brilliant nucleus of this mass of manuscripts is undoubtedly to be found in the letters, which go to the heart of the intellectual interests of Julie's circle. Nor is it surprising that by far the greatest number of these were from Voltaire, whose bust, with d'Alembert's, dominated the salon in the rue Saint-Dominique. ("Only Voltaire's glory could console me for not having been born English."[47]) In this collection there are more than a hundred letters from him, addressed between 1770 and 1776 to d'Alembert, the Comte d'Argental, and Condorcet, all devoted admirers of Mlle de Lespinasse. These are letters of

---

44. Pierre-Marie de Ségur, *Julie de Lespinasse* (Paris: Calmann-Lévy, 1905), p. 103.

45. See *Manuscrits légués par Mademoiselle de Lespinasse*, reproduced in microfiche by the Voltaire Foundation in Oxford, and the *Portefeuille de Mademoiselle de Lespinasse*, the index to which was published by Charles Henry in *Lettres inédites de Mlle de Lespinasse à Condorcet, à d'Alembert, à Guibert et au Comte de Crillon, publiées avec des lettres de ses amis, des documents nouveaux et une étude par M. Charles Henry* (Paris: Dentu, 1887).

46. In the inventory of her possessions drawn up after Julie's death, the list of books takes only two pages, but the list of manuscripts requires fifty.

47. Mlle de Lespinasse to Guibert, October 30, 1744, in *Lettres de Mlle de Lespinasse*, p. 151.

friendship, of esteem, of intellectual complicity, and letters concerning political strategy or civic duty, and they were doubtless read with emotion in Julie's circle.

Besides Voltaire's letters, the collection includes a broad selection from all the most distinguished Enlightenment figures, from Diderot to Rousseau, Marmontel, Mme Geoffrin, Creutz, Galiani, and Cesare Beccaria, as well as the great enlightened despots like Frederick II and Catherine the Great, who were pleased to court the *philosophes*. The whole of contemporary high society is represented in solemn or cheerful mood somewhere among the hundreds of pages of occasional verse— songs, epitaphs, couplets, madrigals, and *bouts-rimés*—that Julie delighted in collecting over the years. (Fortunately other archivists, through admiration and pity, carefully preserved Julie's letters, which today form a great collection of letters of friendship and love and, together with Mme du Deffand's, prove what the misogynist La Bruyère was forced to admit despite himself: that from the beginnings of polite society culture, women proved that they, more than anyone else, had a talent for conversation, and knew the secret of letter-writing.[48])

In the eighteenth century, psychology had found a platform in the novel, but understanding of it was still essential to social success. Julie appreciated its value as a weapon of both defense and seduction, as well as an inexhaustible subject of conversation. Even the fashion for *questions d'amour*, aphorisms, and literary portraits had become a constant in society culture. Mme de Tencin still delighted in discussing the dilemmas of love with her guests,[49] Nicolas Chamfort used maxims to liquidate the *ancien régime*, and socialites continued to amuse themselves by penning portraits of one another. Mme du Deffand had excelled at this game since her days at Sceaux, Mme de Lambert was just as good, Mme de La Ferté-Imbault also played it, albeit with less talent, and at the end of the century, Sénac de Meilhan and the Duc de Lévis turned to it as a means of reviving the old aristocratic world that had been swept away by the Revolution.

Julie de Lespinasse's collection includes twenty-five portraits—copied from the Cardinal de Retz's *Mémoires* and the Marquis de Lessay's *Recueil*—which describe two generations of the country's aristocracy in all their pride and moral degeneracy, including the princes of the blood. There is also a portrait by Mme du Deffand (her sharp and treacherous portrait of the Abbé Vaubrun, which was "sublime in its frivolity"[50]) and one by Mlle de Lespinasse herself of her secret lover, the

---

48. La Bruyère, "Des Ouvrages de l'esprit," *remarque* 37, in *Les Caractères*, p. 143.

49. Jean Sareil, *Les Tencin*, pp. 234–235.

50. "Portrait de M. l'abbé de Vaubrun par Mme la Marquise du Deffand," in "Galerie de portraits de Mme du Deffand et ses amis," in *Correspondance complète de la Marquise du Deffand avec ses amis le Président Hénault—Montesquieu—d'Alembert—Voltaire—Horace Walpole... Suivie de ses Œuvres diverses et éclairée de nombreuses notes par M. de Lescure*, two volumes (1865; Slatkine Reprints, Geneva, 1971), Vol. 2, p. 742.

Comte de Guibert. It is misleading to compare the latter two with the others, however, because the memoirists wrote for themselves and for posterity and so were free to say what they liked, while the socialites wrote to entertain and surprise their contemporaries, maintaining a delicate balance between credibility and adulation. They might, of course, have used the genre to unmask and ridicule their enemies, but to be successful, unfavorable criticism also had to be credible and entertaining. It was from this topsy-turvy perspective that Julie substituted merciless clarity for good-natured benevolence to carry out her vendetta against Mme du Deffand. Her aunt had shown the way twenty years earlier with her treacherous caricature of Mme du Châtelet (Voltaire's *belle Émilie*). With great bravura she ridiculed a woman who thought that because she was unusual she could ignore the *bienséances* with impunity:

> Picture a tall, dry woman, with heightened color, a narrow face, and a pointed nose; such are the *belle Émilie*'s looks, looks with which she is so pleased that she spares nothing to show them off, curls, pompoms, jewels made of stones and glass, everything in profusion.... She was born with some intelligence, but the desire to appear to have even more caused her to prefer the study of the most abstract sciences to that of more agreeable subjects: she imagines, by such singularity, to gain a greater reputation and a decided superiority over all women.... Madame works so hard to appear to be what she is not that one no longer knows what in fact she is. Even her failings are not natural to her; they could result from her pretensions, from her little regard for being a princess, her aridity with respect to being a *savante* and her heedlessness to being a pretty woman.[51]

Julie's portrait of Mme du Deffand was no kinder, although it struck a different note, exposing the moral baseness of a woman whose worldly success concealed a monstrous egoism and a tragic loneliness even though she was much admired for her intelligence. "She is jealous of neither allure nor intelligence, only of preference and attention, for she can forgive neither those who bestow it nor those who receive it. She seems to say to the people she knows, as Jesus said to his disciples: 'Sell what thou hast and come follow me.' It is more difficult to be on good terms with her than with God; a venial sin forfeits in an instant the merit gained from several years of care. It is to her intelligence alone that she owes the consideration she enjoys. Understanding of her character creates a distance and prevents attachment."[52]

---

51. "Portrait de Mme la Marquise du Châtelet [by Mme du Deffand]," in *Horace Walpole's Correspondence with Mme du Deffand*, Vol. 6, p. 116.

52. "Portrait de Mme du Deffand par Mademoiselle de Lespinasse morte en 1776," in *Horace Walpole's Correspondence with Mme du Deffand*, Vol. 6, p. 70.

For once Julie did not use her psychological acumen to preserve the *amour-propre* of others. But society dictated that hatred should be expressed with the same elegance used to please; it is highly likely that the two sentiments were often closely linked and that constant attention to others generated a secret resentment that only an iron discipline could continue to hide. Perhaps E. M. Cioran was right in maintaining that "the portrait as a genre is born of vengeance and the society gentleman's nightmare of having been too often with his own kind not to detest them."[53]

Since the days of the hôtel de Rambouillet in the seventeenth century, women had been responsible for both teaching the *bienséances* and overseeing the purity of the language. In the Blue Room, Julie d'Angennes was not the only one to become passionately involved in discussions about language and to be known for her perfect French. Her sister, Angélique Clarice, thought to be a prototype *Précieuse*, "fainted whenever she heard a ugly word."[54] More than a century later, Mlle de Lespinasse felt the same way. Morellet recounts that at Mme Geoffrin's, when Julie heard the celebrated naturalist Bouffon use a popular expression like "that's another pair of sleeves" (another kettle of fish), she was completely bowled over and collapsed into an armchair and "did not recover for the whole evening."[55]

Julie's interest in the problems of language is evident, too, from the *Manuscrits légués par Mademoiselle de Lespinasse*. At least 110 pages are taken up with a long reasoned list of seventy-three groups of different synonyms. Enlightenment culture, having turned its back on Cartesian rationalism, was questioning the nature of signs. In his *Discours préliminaire* to the *Encyclopédie*, d'Alembert, inspired by Locke, tried to define "the science of communication" and demanded that "signs be perfected," that the molding of the individual mind be linked to "that of humanity, which from signs came to words, words that designated individuals and then qualities, then abstract words, entrusting to grammar to establish a logic of signs."[56] From this point of view, the precise definition of words was essential, particularly of those words, like synonyms, that might be confused.

In Julie's case, her study of language might also have given her the opportunity to exercise intellectual finesse and psychological acumen as well as a subject of discussion with many possibilities. As the Abbé Girard argued, it involved defining "the subtle difference between those words that, because of a common idea, resemble each other like brothers but that are nevertheless distinguished one from the other by some extra idea particular to each one of them." This precision was

---

53. E. M. Cioran, *Anthologie du portrait: De Saint-Simon à Tocqueville* (Paris: Gallimard, 1996), p. 13.

54. Tallemant, *Historiettes*, Vol. 1, p. 467.

55. *Mémoires de l'abbé Morellet*, Vol. 1, p. 467.

56. Jean-Paul Sermain, "Le code du bon goût (1725–1770)," in *Histoire de la rhétorique dans l'Europe moderne (1450–1950)*, edited by Marc Fumaroli (Paris: Presses Universitaires de France, 1999), p. 921.

necessary in order to "speak accurately." Such accuracy was a "quality as rare as it [was] likeable, capable both of making truth shine and of giving substance to the brilliant."[57]

It is not known who defined the synonyms collected in the *Manuscrits*, but according to Guibert, Julie composed "a great number,"[58] and if this is not enough of an attribution, everything points to their having been read and discussed, if not defined, in her salon in the rue Saint-Dominique. In his commentary on the vocabulary and grammar of the classic style, Hippolyte Taine records that "with admirable scrupulousness and infinitely delicate tact, writers and society people apply themselves to weighing each word and each phrase, so as to determine its sense, to measure the strength of its scope, in order to establish its affinities, its usages, and its alliances."[59] They were all united in the common cause of wishing to construct a rational, clear, and perfect language. Among the many definitions are those that deal with the central theme of authenticity (on which subject Mme de Staal-Delaunay and Devaines, among others, put themselves to the test). Julie herself is given as an example: "The truth is solid and undisguised, candor is sweet and effortless, frankness is simple and without artifice, naiveté is natural and without affectation.... Monsieur d'Alembert possesses frankness.... Mademoiselle de Lespinasse possesses truth, frankness, and candor."[60]

Yet for the Julie who boasted that she had "always been true in everything,"[61] truth was not of one voice, for it expressed the contradictions of a profoundly divided personality. On the one hand, Julie exhibited a genuine vocation for society life and a burning desire to be admired by everyone and to succeed in touching the hardest of hearts. On the other hand, she nourished a secret need to discover herself through an exclusive passion, to be inebriated by her own ability to feel and to love. It was precisely this requirement that drove her to dissimulate and to betray those who loved her most.

Whatever the nature of her relationship with d'Alembert, Mlle de Lespinasse took advantage of his blind trust in her to keep him in the dark about what was obvious to everyone, which was her love affair with the Marques de Mora. D'Alembert only discovered it after his friend's death when putting her papers in order. He was flabbergasted.

José Pignatelli y Gonzaga, Marques de Mora, the eldest son of the Spanish ambassador to Paris, was young, passionate and idealistic, and so deeply infatuated

---

57. Gabriel Girard, "Synonymes français, leurs significations et le choix qu'il faut faire pour parler avec justesse" (Paris: 1736; 1769), pp. vii–ix, quoted in Sermain, "Le code du bon goût," p. 923.

58. *Lettres de Mlle de Lespinasse*, p. 364.

59. Taine, *Les Origines de la France contemporaine*, Vol. 1, p. 143.

60. *Manuscrits légués par Mademoiselle de Lespinasse*, Vol. 2, pp. 101–102.

61. Mlle de Lespinasse to Guibert, October 18, 1775, in *Lettres de Mlle de Lespinasse*, p. 256.

with Julie (who was now forty) that his family, fearing he might do something impulsive, ordered him back to Spain in 1772. Two years later, however, his desire to be reunited with his loved one was so great that despite chronic tuberculosis, he decided to set out for France. He died before realizing his dream. The object of such passion apparently returned it in equal measure. According to Mme de La Ferté-Imbault, Julie, when separated from him, "made a virtue of her despair," forever bothering the unsuspecting d'Alembert, whom she obliged to suffer her changes of mood and whom she made "go to the post to await Mora's letters and to bring them her at once."[62]

No one, neither the spiteful marquise nor Julie's closest friends, could ever have suspected that the romantic love story disguised another, less glorious and more tragic. One winter evening in 1774, in a box at the Opéra, while Mora was summoning the last of his strength to return to her, Julie yielded to the Comte de Guibert, with whom, since the summer of 1772, she had been carrying on a exalted affair that was built on a string of mystification and lies.

Jacques Antoine Hippolyte de Guibert was eleven years younger than Julie and a brilliant officer with literary ambitions and a talent for pleasing intelligent women. Mme de Staël, who knew him when he was older and was briefly his lover, maintained that his conversation "was the most lively, the most animated, the most fruitful [she had] ever known."[63] When Guibert first met Mlle de Lespinasse in 1772, he had just been successful throughout Europe with his *Essai général de tactique*, and Frederick II of Prussia saw him "launching himself on every path to glory."[64] Guibert admired Julie and was flattered by the interest she showed in him; he aspired to her friendship and esteem and put up with her intellectual ascendancy, but he did not reciprocate her feelings. He had had a passing attraction to her, only to find, despite himself, that he was involved in a passionate affair with demands made upon him that he could not satisfy. His real fault was weakness; subjugated by his mistress, he had no idea how to withdraw from the game.

Julie knew how Guibert felt but had no intention of releasing her prey. Without Mora, she needed him to add an appearance of high-flown tragedy to the short time left her by tuberculosis. This emerges from the hundreds and hundreds of letters, however various and however differing in tone, that she wrote to Guibert over three years; there is a need to talk about herself, to shout about her love, to display her capacity for feeling and suffering, obliging him to pay attention. To prevent him from escaping, his victim became a slave driver and revealed herself to be an unscrupulous manipulator. It was Guibert's fault that she had betrayed

---

62. Mme de La Ferté-Imbault, *8ème Lettre*.

63. Quoted in Eugène Asse, "Notice sur Mlle de Lespinasse," in *Lettres de Mlle de Lespinasse*, p. lviii.

64. Ségur, *Julie de Lespinasse*, p. 378.

Mora, Guibert's fault that life had become intolerable and that love had been transformed into a mortal poison. With a perverse subtlety she entangled her kind, foppish, terrified correspondent in an ever-tighter web, moving from disdain to adulation, from blackmail to abnegation. It mattered little if, in so doing, she continuously contradicted herself; and it mattered little that in the meantime Guibert had married a young and beautiful woman and that from then on there was no possible doubt as to his feelings about Julie. Inexorably Julie wanted him to be her witness even unto the very end of a funereal love song.

This frenzy of love did not, however, prevent Julie from carrying on with her everyday life: her friends, her salon, and her intellectual prestige were not only a solace in her desperation but were the most attractive things she could offer Guibert. Whereas in the letters to her lover, Julie seems gradually to withdraw from the world and to have an increasing need for solitude and silence, it is precisely these letters that explain exactly how much time and energy was needed day after day to maintain the tour de force that was her social life. "Society hardly ever interests me, and it always weighs upon me," she wrote; yet a simple account of one of her days, such as she describes them precisely in her very letters, is enough to cast doubt on this claim.[65] Having spent the first half of the morning dressing, reading, and dealing with her correspondence, Julie began to receive her more intimate friends whom she wished to see by themselves. Then, twice a week, she went with d'Alembert to dinner at Mme Geoffrin's, and she was often invited also by either Turgot, Devaines, Mme d'Enville, Mme de Châtillon, the Comte de Crillon, or the Comte de Creutz. "I have dined every day with fifteen people, and that fatigues me," she stated in the autumn of 1774; and dinner was only one part of her daily program.[66]

The early afternoon was often given to visiting: "I began by first going to spend an hour with M. Turgot, and then another hour with Mme Châtillon, which makes for a good many stairs to climb, and when I came home I was dead."[67] But whatever her physical condition, from five o'clock in the afternoon to nine in the evening, and sometimes later, Julie held her salon.

It was the key moment of her day and certainly demanded the most concentration. Until that time, she had lived a sort of double existence, with her mind permanently focused on her lover.[68] Even if her thoughts could turn to Guibert during the readings aloud of the latest literary creation, she could no longer afford to be distracted in the hours set aside for conversation. Mlle de Lespinasse's success was the result of an art that demanded a high degree of concentration. In accordance

65. Mlle de Lespinasse to Guibert, October 26, 1774, in *Lettres de Mlle de Lespinasse*, p. 144.

66. Mlle de Lespinasse to Guibert, October 21, 1774, in *Lettres de Mlle de Lespinasse*, p. 136.

67. Mlle de Lespinasse to Guibert, 1775, in *Lettres de Mlle de Lespinasse*, p. 177.

68. Mlle de Lespinasse to Guibert, October 21, 1774, in *Lettres de Mlle de Lespinasse*, p. 134.

with society tradition, she knew better than anyone how to show the personalities of her interlocutors to their best advantage. Her intellectual curiosity, in harmony with the Enlightenment, was no longer subjected to the *bienséances*. It was also contagious and produced a vivifying effect. "There was nothing which seemed beyond her reach, nothing which did not appear to please her and that she was unable to make agreeable to others. Politics, religion, philosophy, stories, and novels, nothing was excluded from her conversation."[69]

Gained by reading and listening, Julie's vast, self-taught culture was completely without affectation and found its perfect expression in the spoken word. For Julie, the object of conversation was no longer happiness but knowledge. She countered society's euphoria with her own sensibility. For her, society life meant demanding and valuable intellectual exchange. "Some intelligence is not enough; a great deal is needed."[70]

Nor did the day end with the departure of her guests. Julie loved music and often went to the Opéra. For instance, between September 1774 and the following spring, she went to no fewer than seven performances of Gluck's *Orfeo ed Eurydice*. Friends often sent a carriage to collect her and bring her to spend the evening at their house. This impressive social marathon was not an end in itself, for it allowed her to influence the cultural life of the times, to exercise her influence over the election of members of the Académie Française, to help the careers of her young friends who swelled the ranks of the *philosophes*, and clearly to support Guibert's literary ambitions. The last two years of Mlle de Lespinasse's life, years in which sickness and the pains of love seemed to take over her whole existence, making her long for solitude and silence, were the very years in which her prestige was at its highest. On August 14, 1774, one of her best friends, Turgot, Baron de l'Aulne, an economist and distinguished champion of the Enlightenment, was made controller general of finance, thus bringing *philosophie* into government and inaugurating a rigorous politics of reform. His experiment lasted for twenty-one months until he resigned on May 22, 1776, a day before his friend's death. But during those twenty-one months, Julie proudly followed her friend's work; by keeping in close touch with him, her "citizen's soul" could hope for a better future.[71] As Mme de La Ferté-Imbault was obliged to recognize,[72] her influence extended from the intellectual world to the world of politics, from the Académie

---

69. *Correspondance littéraire, philosophique et critique adressée à un souverain d'Allemagne, pendant une partie des années 1775–1776, et pendant les années 1782 à 1790 inclusivement, par le baron Grimm et par Diderot, troisième et dernière partie* [May 1776], five volumes (Paris: F. Buisson, 1813), Vol. 1, p. 201.

70. Mlle de Lespinasse to Guibert, October 21, 1774, in *Lettres de Mlle de Lespinasse*, p. 135.

71. Ségur, *Julie de Lespinasse*, p. 265.

72. See Mme de La Ferté-Imbault, *8ème Lettre*.

to the government, and the first to profit was naturally her lover, who, through her mediation, managed to avoid the expropriation of some family lands.

In her letters to Guibert, evening after evening and apparently without regret, she lays at her lover's feet the triumphs of this existence devoted to society and the pleasure of intellectual exchange. Such denunciation of her daily rounds allowed Julie to lead two profoundly contradictory lives. Whereas her passion for society reinforced her declining strength, making it possible for her to develop the *esprit de société* to ultimate perfection, her passionate love drove her to make a void within herself, obliging her to deny everything that was alien to that love. Thus every night, alone at her desk, a hidden Julie, determined to die for her lover, renounced her daily way of life, offering to sacrifice everything for him, while waiting for the other Julie to return at daybreak and be comforted by the repeated admiration and applause of the most demanding public in Europe. It is pointless to wonder which of the two should be most listened to. Deeply divided within herself, she believed from one moment to another in the truth of that moment, convinced of her sincerity when recounting every second of her life to Guibert: "I have seen, I believe, forty persons today, and I only wanted one, whose thoughts surely did not turn to me,"[73] she wrote to him in the spring of 1774; and a few months later, "I saw a hundred people; and as your letter did my soul some good, I talked and forgot that I was dead."[74]

In view of the irrefutable evidence of the statistics she provided and the energy needed to sustain the extraordinary labor of her social life, it is hard to believe that her tormented thoughts of Guibert were enough to provide her with the strength to continue. Instead it was the therapeutic power of the spoken word that continually revitalized her and reawaked her from her lovesickness and from the lethargy resulting from illness, that restored her, despite herself, to conversation and life.

In the spring of 1776 a combination of tuberculosis and opium abuse led to the last act of Julie's tragic love affair. Some time before she died, her features were horribly deformed by a facial paresis, after which she never wanted to see Guibert again. "Her mouth was so distorted that it nearly reached her ear,"[75] Mme de La Ferté-Imbault noted cruelly. Her last words were for d'Alembert. Moved by the despair of her old friend, who was the only one to sit by her deathbed, she asked him to forgive and forget her.

To forgive her for what? D'Alembert might have found at least a partial answer in Mora's letters, which were among the papers Julie entrusted to him on her death. By a supreme irony of fate, he was to choose Guibert himself as a confidant

---

73. Mlle de Lespinasse to Guibert, 1774, in *Lettres de Mlle de Lespinasse*, p. 66.

74. Mlle de Lespinasse to Guibert, October 5, 1774, in *Lettres de Mlle de Lespinasse*, p. 120.

75. Mme de La Ferté-Imbault, *8ème Lettre*.

in his sorrow. As strange as it may seem, Mlle de Lespinasse's friends had all been as blind as he: no one had ever been aware of her relationship although it had been going on in front of their very eyes for at least four years. In 1766, Horace Walpole remarked of Paris that "it requires the greatest curiosity, or the greatest habitude, to discover the smallest connection between the sexes here. No familiarity, but under the veil of friendship, is permitted, and love's dictionary is as much prohibited, as at first sight one should think his ritual was."[76] Respect for form clearly had the upper hand over both the ambitious young writer's vanity and Julie's exalted love.

Mme Geoffrin's friendship was the only comfort left to d'Alembert, but she too was soon to be a source of sorrow for him. At the end of August 1776, the seventy-seven-year-old lady, whose health was gradually failing, was struck by a serious stroke that left her paralyzed. D'Alembert hurried to her bedside along with her most faithful visitors—Suard, Marmontel, Morellet—only to find it firmly presided over by Mme de La Ferté-Imbault. It was the start of a ruthless war that turned the sickroom into a battlefield. Empowered by her new authority, the marquise intended to be rid once and for all of the *philosophes* and to assure her mother of all the comforts of religion. But the *philosophes*, most particularly d'Alembert, refused to abandon a great friend and protectress when she most needed them and to the mercy of a stupid, bigoted daughter in league with priests. After some violent arguments, excuses, compromises, exchanges of letters, and insults that aligned all the Encyclopedists against the devout party, the Marquise de La Ferté-Imbault won the day, and d'Alembert and his acolytes were finally banished from the house in the rue Saint-Honoré.

It is not known what Mme Geoffrin thought of this unhappy quarrel. In the year left to her, she resorted to her usual good sense and resigned herself to accepting her daughter's decisions. "She never recalled any of those I had sent away; she made her communion at Easter in such a way that her confessor and her priest were happy and my triumph was complete," Mme de La Ferté-Imbault rejoiced some months later.[77] Such joy may well not have been shared. As the curtain fell on her celebrated salon, which she had always wanted to be free from scandal and polemic, Mme Geoffrin must have been aware that her policy of vigilance had failed. The *honnête femme* who had always loved discretion saw her own private world becoming a subject of public discussion. Nothing could now guarantee a respect for *bienséances*.

76. Horace Walpole to Thomas Gray, January 25, 1766, in *Horace Walpole's Correspondence with Thomas Gray*, edited by W. S. Lewis, George L. Lam, and Charles H. Bennett (Yale University Press, 1948), Vol. 2 (Vol. 14 of *The Yale Edition of Horace Walpole's Correspondence*), p. 154.

77. Mme de La Ferté-Imbault, *Mémoires*, quoted in Ségur; *Le Royaume de la rue Saint-Honoré*, p. 376. See also *Lettres et anecdotes sur la maladie de Mme Geoffrin*, 508 AP, 26.

From the depths of her *tonneau*, the famous armchair in which she sat enfolded as in a nest, Mme du Deffand appeared to greet the news of the death of her two rivals with great detachment. "Mademoiselle de Lespinasse died last night, two hours after midnight; once it would have been an event for me, today it is nothing at all."[78] What did the marquise mean by this sibylline phrase? That formerly her niece's death would have brought her sorrow? The event would have been more welcome had it happened sooner? "She should have died fifteen years earlier, and I would not have lost d'Alembert," she is reputed to have said.[79]

Since meeting Walpole in 1765 her existence had changed so radically that she no longer missed her old protégés, although that did not mean she had stopped hating them. She had made the impossible d'Alembert the star of her salon, launched him in the world, imposed him on the Académie, and protected him from the dangers of his own character. She had welcomed Julie into her home, taking her out of obscurity and provincial isolation, trained her for high society, and shared her life and friends with her. In exchange, she had been robbed and betrayed. Insofar as was possible, she condemned her niece to *damnatio memoriae*.

In fact, Mme du Deffand had never been noted for her indulgence. She was as merciless with others as she was with herself and had made perspicacity her strength. Life had tested her early with an ill-matched marriage, a compromised reputation resulting from a brief period of libertinism, and an insufficient inheritance. She reacted by taking a rich lover and cultivating both influential friends and a talent for making herself agreeable. She respected power while recognizing its precarious nature. The plotting that overthrew the Duc and Duchesse du Maine, the Regent's unexpected death, the Duc de Bourbon's disgrace, the Duc de Choiseul's exile—all of these were events that had affected her to different degrees. She knew that she had only her own resources to count on if she were to be influential. In her youth she was beautiful and, according to Mme de Staal-Delaunay, who was no less astute than she, the young Mme du Deffand had an irresistible grace. But her trump card, and the one on which she built her worldly success, was her wit, which even her enemies admired. Her ironic, trenchant wit was more the result of her disenchantment than of any taste for fun. The marquise, who had no illusions and was totally realistic, could capture the ridiculous and the laughable side of life without ever feeling constrained by conventional sentiment.

Sometimes her wit could be caustic and cruel, which no doubt explains in large part her reputation for malice. Cutting irony was characteristic of the aristocratic style and was typical of the great families of the Mortemarts and Condés, for

---

78. Mme du Deffand to Horace Walpole, May 22, 1776, in *Horace Walpole's Correspondence with Mme du Deffand*, Vol. 4, p. 317.

79. Sentence attributed to her by Jean-François de La Harpe; see his *Corréspondance littéraire*, six volumes (Paris: Migneret, Paris, 1801–1807), Vol. 1, p. 388.

example. Probably one of the earliest-known anecdotes about Mme du Deffand should be seen in this light. In 1726 the marquise had wanted to follow Mme de Prie to the country. Mme du Prie, the marquise's "equal in beauty, gallantry, and spite," was involved in the disgrace of her lover, the Duc de Bourbon, who had just been relieved of the post of prime minister.[80] This *beau geste* did not prevent the two friends from "every morning sending each other satirical couplets that they composed about one another. They could imagine nothing better than this entertainment of vipers to counteract the boredom."[81]

Fifty years later, Mme du Deffand could still remember those couplets, which she transcribed for Walpole,[82] but she did not go so far as to claim those that were later attributed to her after Voltaire's mistress, Mme du Châtelet, died giving birth to Saint-Lambert's daughter. She was completing her translation of Newton's *Philosophiae naturalis principia mathematica*:

> *Ici-gît qui perdit la vie*
> *Dans le double accouchement*
> *D'un traité de philosophie*
> *Et d'un malheureux enfant.*
> *On ne sait précisément*
> *Lequel des deux nous l'a ravie.*
> *Sur ce funeste événement,*
> *Quelle opinion doit-on suivre?*
> *Saint-Lambert s'en prend au livre,*
> *Voltaire dit que c'est l'enfant.*[83]

The lines attributed to her by Mme de La Ferté-Imbault about the Duc de Choiseul (whose great friend Mme du Deffand later became) were not so pitiless since they were not aimed at someone who had died, but they were just as virulent:

> *Plus étourdi qu'un éclair,*
> *Plus inquiet qu'un pet en air,*

---

80. Pierre-Edouard Lemontey, *Histoire de la Régence et de la minorité de Louis XV jusqu'au ministère du Cardinal de Fleury*, two volumes (Paris: Paulin, 1832), Vol. 2, p. 261.

81. Lemontey, *Histoire de la Régence*, p. 261.

82. Mme du Deffand to Walpole, March 22, 1780, in *Horace Walpole's Correspondence with Mme du Deffand*, Vol. 4, p. 214.

83. "Here lies one who lost her life/In a double confinement/Of a philosophical treatise/And of an unfortunate child./It is not known precisely/Which of the two stole her from us./On this fatal event,/What opinion must one follow?/Saint-Lambert blames the book,/Voltaire says it was the child." In *Correspondance littéraire, philosophique et critique*, Vol. 6, p. 297.

Plus méchant que Lucifer,
Revenant d'enfer, revenant d'enfer...
Il n'est jamais poire sans ver,
Au dir d'un certain frater.[84]

Satirical verse, which reached its high point and was at its most violent at the time of the Fronde, dogged the French aristocracy like a hidden presence until the end of the *ancien régime*. It was the other face of a *sociabilité* that never stopped observing and talking about itself, but that substituted undisguised brutality for exquisite courtesy, ferocious laughter for euphoric gaiety, and summary execution for the virtuosity of praise. Gone was the noble salon conversation, replaced by a trivial chronicle of gossip, sordid details, insinuations, and true and invented stories that might be funny or defamatory. Anonymous satirical tales were repeated by one person to another, perhaps for political reasons or as part of a vendetta, or for the simple pleasure of laughter. They were secretly copied and embellished by the readers into whose hands they fell.[85]

Mme du Deffand was skilled at improvising verses and songs on the greatest variety of subjects, and her lines on Mme du Châtelet and Choiseul could be said to represent the extreme reaches of her satirical verve. Here perhaps it was not so much malice that made her so pitiless, as many thought, as an inborn mistrust of the whole human race. Her own success had revealed the depths of artificiality of the society of her day, and for her, knowing primarily implied "ripping off the mask."[86] This is probably the source of her capacity to see people as they were and the source of her obsession with the *naturel*, as if stylistic perfection were capable of resuscitating lost innocence.

One of the dramas marking the life of this overly critical, too lucid soul was that she could not do without other people. Although she was used to keeping her personal and inner distance, she could not bear to be alone. In the world of polite society, the dark threat of boredom always hung over the idle privileged: it accompanied the Duchesse du Maine in her theatrical fever at Sceaux; the Regent in his search for pleasure; Louis XV in the exercise of kingship; and even Voltaire in his

---

84. "More crooked than a flash of lightning,/More uneasy than a fart in the air,/More wicked than Lucifer,/Coming back from hell, coming back from hell.../There is no pear without a worm,/According to a certain brother." (According to Mme de La Ferté-Imbault, the last two lines refer to the duke's venereal disease.) In Mme de La Ferté-Imbault, *Mémoires*.

85. Nothing illustrates this eighteenth-century phenomenon better than the *Recueil dit de Maurepas, pièces libres, chansons, épigrammes et autres vers satiriques sur divers personnages des siècles de Louis XIV et de Louis XV*, six volumes (Leyden, 1865). This vast anthology of satire took its name from the minister who was disgraced for a slanderous sonnet about Mme de Pompadour.

86. "Portrait de Mme la Marquise du Deffand par elle-même, fait en 1774," in *Horace Walpole's Correspondence with Mme du Deffand*, Vol. 6, p. 61.

busy life. Ever-greater invention combined with the ever-greater demands of refinement were required if people were to accustom themselves to repetition. By curing the symptoms, the sickness was only temporarily disguised so that its roots became more and more deeply embedded. In her great assessment of the elements that constituted the social aesthetic, Mlle de Scudéry did not fail to point out boredom, or *ennui*, and its inherent dangers. In "Conversation de l'ennuy sans sujet," a dialogue about a young woman who was "restless without reason" and incapable of living fully in the moment, Mlle de Scudéry makes it clear that she is fully aware of the different stages of a "humor" that could damage emotional relationships and upset the inner balance. One character in the dialogue remarks, "It has to be said that *ennui* is borne in one's own heart, and one has to flee oneself in order never to be bored."[87]

While Mlle de Scudéry condemned *ennui* as a troublesome factor in worldly relations, Pascal made it a principle of salvation, denouncing instead the captivating distractions of the world that prevented mankind from being aware of its own misery. In the following century, no one would illustrate more clearly than Mme du Deffand the Pascalian anguish of the void, the impossibility for anyone not sustained by God to remain alone in a room. Although she had been obliged early on to face up to this tragic experience, the marquise never managed to find the metaphysical path, so she opted for temporary oblivion in diversion. Unlike her friend Voltaire, who had raged against Pascal's *Pensées*, Mme du Deffand was not prejudiced against religion. Indeed, she would have liked to have been able to believe, if only—as she would have put it—in order to have something to do. Lacking the gift of faith, however, she found herself obliged to find distractions other than those offered by the Church.

In society life Mme du Deffand found distraction par excellence. Not only did it provide the best therapy for *ennui*, but it also allowed her to pursue the success she needed if she was to protect her interests and her position in society. In fact, it was really her own proud calling that propelled her into society. Her contemporaries were obliged to admit that the *esprit de société* had found one of its most original exponents in her. "She is known by everybody," Mme de La Ferté-Imbault conceded, "and has been judged as she is for forty years, although as she was very much decried in her youth and has since been involved in some very dishonorable stories, it could not have been foreseen that her wit alone would serve her so well, nor that, being blind, not very rich, with no personal importance or family support, she could still be in fashion at her advanced age."[88]

Her wit, elegance, culture, and good taste may have made Mme du Deffand representative of the aristocratic tradition, but her style was unique and unmistakable.

---

87. In *Conversations nouvelles sur diverses sujets*, two volumes (Paris: Barbin, 1684), Vol. 2, p. 461.

88. Mme de La Ferté-Imbault, *Portraits de différentes personnes*, 508 AP, 27.

Like all true socialites, the marquise had an instinctive feeling for the scene but, despite the rules, she did not hesitate to occupy center stage by herself. She thought too little of others to make the effort to bring them out, and she was not patient enough to listen to them. Her ability to attract attention and to soliloquize, her quick and irresistible stories, her lightning repartee, her passing infatuations, her terrible sarcasm, and the certainty of her opinions distinguished her from all the other hostesses and assured her salon of three decades of success. Her old friend the Marquis du Châtel has left a brilliant picture of the marquise's histrionic talent when she set out on her society adventure, having just turned forty. "If there was a question of improvising and executing some plays, it would be to you whom we should turn to. I have often experienced that pleasure by your fireside; there you are admirable. What variety, what contrasting sentiments in both character and in your way of thinking! What ingenuity, what power and accuracy! Even when you are rambling. There is nothing missing, but everything to send one mad with pleasure, impatience, and admiration. You are invaluable to a philosopher spectator."[89]

It is above all in her correspondence with Voltaire that Mme du Deffand's intelligence can still be admired. She can still delight. If these exchanges combine naturalness of tone with style and the perfect use of language, it is because these two conversational virtuosos, who both dictated their letters, wrote as they spoke. They remained as faithful on paper as they were in speech to the technique of improvisation.

The two had known each other since youth, and their friendship was based on mutual admiration. Mme du Deffand recognized Voltaire as the greatest writer of the day, and Voltaire saw the marquise as a perfect example of that aristocratic style that he had always wanted to emulate. At intervals for nearly half a century, they courted one another from a distance, with different ends in mind and without ever reaching an understanding. Mme du Deffand wanted to make Voltaire lead a crusade for the defense of classical taste; Voltaire wanted to persuade Mme du Deffand to support him in his battle for reason and enlightenment. In their tussle, the marquise certainly did not come out the loser. Mme du Deffand never yielded to Voltaire's flattery, displaying instead what Fumaroli has called "the trenchant clarity typical of the libertines of the *Grand Siècle* to whom Pascal had addressed his *Pensées*."[90] She abhorred new ideologies, which she considered more dangerous and more intolerant than the old, nor did she seek for impossible consolation. For her, disgust with life went hand in hand with the terror of death.

---

89. Letter from the Marquis du Châtel to the Marquise du Deffand (1742), in *Correspondance complète de la Marquise du Deffand*, Vol. I, p. 81.

90. Marc Fumaroli, preface to Benedetta Craveri, *Mme du Deffand et son monde* (Paris: Éditions du Seuil, 1999), p. 7.

Indeed, nothing could make up for the misfortune of being born. She did not allow herself to be intimidated for a moment by Voltaire's intellectual authority, appealing instead to Montaigne, that past master of doubt. "Therein one finds everything one has ever thought, and there is no more energetic style; he teaches nothing because he has decided nothing; it is the opposite of dogmatism: he is vain, and are not all men so? ... The 'I' and the 'me' are on every line, but what knowledge can one have without the 'I' and the 'me'?"[91] In an age that idolized happiness, the marquise fearlessly and bravely contemplated the tragic meaninglessness of the human condition.

For Mme du Deffand, the only possible reaction to this unbearable truth lay in the heroism of style: to pretend to do nothing but to practice, in perfect keeping with aristocratic morality, "that liberal art of thinking, speaking, and living against all hope, but gaily and brilliantly among the equals she had chosen and who had chosen her."[92] Hence her correspondence with Voltaire, the "patriarch" of *philosophes*, in which the rigorous exchange of ideas briefly interrupted the virtuoso game of the most hypocritical, playful, and delightful of gallant bantering, which had survived distance, misunderstanding, and age. The end in itself is enough to reveal the tone. In 1778, nearly thirty years after leaving Paris, the eighty-four-year-old Voltaire, returning in triumph to the capital, sent a dazzling note to his "contemporary": "I arrive dead, and I wish to be resuscitated only to throw myself at the knees of Mme la marquise du Deffand."[93]

Mme du Deffand's friends came from the nobility or, like her official lover, the Président Hénault, from the legal profession. She has left admirable portraits of some of them; as in the days of the Grande Mademoiselle, her whole circle was involved in the game of portraits, and she herself inspired more than one piece of bravura. Among her old acquaintances she described the Comte de Pont-de-Veyle, Mme de Ferriol's son, Mme de Tencin's nephew, and an anonymous playwright, whom she described as "sought after by everyone and at ease in all society, is amused by everything and likes nothing;"[94] Here is also Jean Baptiste Nicolas Formont, a dilettante man of letters and friend of Voltaire's, in whose eyes "the world is only a spectacle in which he supposes he has no personal interest," which does not prevent him from "playing his part in the comedy," and who even "becomes excited and animated when the conversation pleases him, to which he

---

91. Mme du Deffand to Walpole, October 27, 1766, in *Horace Walpole's Correspondence with Mme du Deffand*, Vol 1, p. 164.

92. Fumaroli, preface to Craveri, *Mme du Deffand et son monde*, p. 8.

93. Voltaire to Mme du Deffand, in *Voltaire's Correspondence*, in *Complete Works of Voltaire*, edited by Theodore Besterman, D21032, Vol. 45, p. 203.

94. "Esquisse du Portrait de Monsieur de Pont-de-Veyle par Mme la Marquise du Deffand, 1774," in *Horace Walpole's Correspondence with Mme du Deffand*, Vol. 6, p. 82.

then adds point, gaiety, and lightheartedness that make him the best of company."[95] Here, of course, is Charles Jean François Hénault, equally resistant to the heart's impulses ("at times it would be tempting to believe that he limits himself to thinking what he imagines he feels") but no less likeable for that; he too is "the best company in the world."[96] As for women, here is the Maréchale de Luxembourg, one of her oldest friends, who, having excelled first in malice and a libertine life, had imposed herself on her contemporaries as the absolute arbiter of good manners: "She is so perceptive as to make one tremble; the slightest pretension, the least affectation, a tone or a gesture which is not quite natural, all are sensed and judged by her with extreme rigor; the finesse of her mind and the delicacy of her taste prevent anything from escaping her"[97]; and the Maréchale de Mirepoix, for whom Louis XV felt real friendship, and who, unlike the other maréchale, was attractive for her shyness and reserve: "Her desire to please resembles politeness rather than coquetry, besides women see her without jealousy, and men dare not fall in love with her. . . . Her conversation is easy and natural; she does not seek to shine; she allows others to take all the advantage they will without haste, without disdain, without vehemence, without coldness; her countenance and her expressions reflect the fairness of her mind and the nobility of her sentiments."[98]

Still the *grandes dames* who frequented Mme du Deffand's salon were not always treated so benevolently. Certainly the Comtesse de Boufflers—the Prince de Conti's official mistress, so absorbed in narcissistic contemplation of herself— was not: "Her good qualities, for she has several, come from the nullity of her character and the little impression made on her by those around her. She is neither envious, nor malicious, nor dangerous, nor difficult, nor deceptive for the simple reason that she is only concerned with herself and not at all with others."[99] (Yet the Idole du Temple, as Mme du Deffand sarcastically called her, was undoubtedly one of the most fascinating women of her time. Liberal, cultivated, sharing completely the Enlightenment hope for reform, Rousseau's protectress was capable of inspiring the admiration both of an intellectual of David Hume's stature and the

95. "Portrait de Monsieur Formont par Mme la Marquise du Deffand," in *Horace Walpole's Correspondence with Mme du Deffand*, Vol. 6, p. 93.

96. "Portrait de Monsieur le Président Hénault par Mme du Deffand," in *Horace Walpole's Correspondence with Mme du Deffand*, Vol. 6, p. 76.

97. "Portrait de Mme la Duchesse de Boufflers depuis Mme de Luxembourg par Mme la Marquise du Deffand," in *Horace Walpole's Correspondence with Mme du Deffand*, Vol. 6, p. 76.

98. "Portrait de Mme la Marquise de Mirepoix par Mme du Deffand," in *Horace Walpole's Correspondence with Mme du Deffand*, Vol. 6, p. 79.

99. "Portrait de Mme la Comtesse de Boufflers par Mme du Deffand," in *Horace Walpole's Correspondence with Mme du Deffand*, Vol. 6, p. 85.

King of Sweden himself.) The Duchesse d'Aiguillon, who spoke many languages, was fascinated by science, was a friend of Voltaire's and Montesquieu's, and bravely supported the new ideas, fared no better. Mme du Deffand focused on her lack of judgment: "Her mind is as badly designed as her face and is just as conspicuous. Her dominant qualities are abundance, activity, and impetuosity. Without taste, without grace, and without judgment, she astonishes and surprises but she neither pleases nor interests."[100]

In 1747, after a roving existence, Mme du Deffand rented an apartment in the convent of Saint-Joseph, not far from the abbey of Saint-Germain-des-Prés, and made her home there. There, in her famous salon hung with yellow moiré and dotted with fire-red bows, the art of aristocratic conversation found its last sanctuary. Free from the Marquise de Lambert's moral preoccupations and without the intellectual commitment of Mme de Tencin's circle, conversations at Saint-Joseph were of an entirely dilettante nature. With the lightheartedness that often attracts both pessimists and skeptics, the marquise could create around herself an atmosphere of life-enhancing gaiety. Her good cheer, her "imagination," her "vigor and her "grace"[101] were contagious, and, once she had, with her certain touch, started upon *fine raillerie*, her guests were drawn into a game that gradually became both freer and subtler. Mme du Deffand was fully aware of her talent and sometimes let it run to the point of imprudence, leaving more than one person's wounded pride in her wake. But did the chief characteristic of the salon at Saint-Joseph really lie in the systematic pleasure of backbiting, as Mme de La Ferté-Imbault claimed?[102] Or was not it rather that a group of like-minded friends enjoyed an exclusive game that allowed them to judge the world by the standards of their own demanding style and aristocratic tastes?

One need only read the marquise's written portraits to see that despite her irony, conversation still had to obey the rules of the *esprit de société*. So much so that her remarks about the Comte d'Argenson ring almost as self-criticism: "He speaks little; but what he says is always forceful and most just. Ordinarily his wit and his repartee are applauded, but they often embarrass and undermine the conversation so that one leaves [his company] dissatisfied with oneself, and it is often difficult to become accustomed to him."[103] In contrast, the Comte

---

100. "Portrait de Mme la Duchesse d'Aiguillon par Mme du Deffand," in *Horace Walpole's Correspondence with Mme du Deffand*, Vol. 6, p. 81.

101. La Duchesse de Choiseul to Mme du Deffand, June 25, 1767, in *Correspondance complète de Madame du Deffand avec la duchesse de Choiseul, l'abbé Barthélemy et M. Craufurt*, with an introduction by M. le Marquis de Sainte-Aulaire, three volumes (Paris: Calmann-Lévy, 1866), Vol. 1, p. 124.

102. See Mme de La Ferté-Imbault, *8ème Lettre.*

103. "Portrait de Monsieur le Comte d'Argenson par Mme la Marquise du Deffand," in *Horace Walpole's Correspondence with Mme du Deffand*, Vol. 6, p. 109.

d'Argenson's best friend, the Président Hénault, was living proof of a measured *esprit de société*: "His conversation is full of ingenious and clever wit that never degenerates into punning or epigrams and which could embarrass no one."[104] In order to please everyone and upset no one, even the most brilliant wit had accepted respect for the common rules and did not overstep the boundaries of *bienséances*.

Toward the middle of the century, when, having become one of society's most sought-after addresses, the Saint-Joseph salon seemed to have reached its apogee, Mme du Deffand was faced with the most difficult trial of her life. A serious eye disease gave rise to the gradual loss of her vision until eventually, after several years of anguish and of useless cures, she plunged into total darkness. Progressive physical malaise immobilized her, leaving the marquise a prey to herself, unable to resist the attraction of the void within her, which threatened to swallow up her entire existence. In the spring of 1752, in an ultimate attempt to defy this double threat, the marquise left Paris to take refuge in the country. It was a happy choice. Mme du Deffand did not recover her sight at the family château of Champrond, but she met the twenty-year-old Julie de Lespinasse, her brother's illegitimate daughter, who was obliged to live there as a dependent under ambiguous circumstances. She decided to take her back to Paris. Julie's support, enthusiasm, and innocence would distract the marquise from the thoughts that tormented her and make it possible for her to return to Saint-Joseph and take up her usual way of life. Julie had all that was needed to please in society and, with no other choice, she was prepared to be obedient. So in April 1754, after lengthy negotiations, Mlle de Lespinasse joined Mme du Deffand in Paris "to be the happiness and consolation of her life."[105]

The mysteries of initiation into society were once more put into motion in the Saint-Joseph apartment. In Julie the old code of the *bienséances* found another, most original interpreter. Once more, a natural vocation coincided with the right environment: "From the first day you found yourself as free and as little out of place in the most brilliant and most difficult of societies, as if you had spent your whole life there," d'Alembert wrote her of her debut. "You sensed the rules before you knew them, which implies a most unusual precision and refinement of tact, an exquisite knowledge of what is seemly. In a word, you divined the language of what is known as *bonne compagnie*, just as in the *Provinciales*, Pascal divined the French language."[106] Mme du Deffand's influence over her niece must indeed have been definitive if, many years after the break between them, Julie herself was

---

104. "Portrait de Monsieur le Président Hénault par Mme du Deffand," in *Horace Walpole's Correspondance with Mme du Deffand*, Vol. 6, p. 76.

105. Mme du Deffand to Mlle de Lespinasse, April 8, 1754, in *Correspondance complète de la Marquise du Deffand*, Vol. 1, p. 209.

106. "Portrait de Mademoiselle de Lespinasse par d'Alembert," in *Lettres de Mlle de Lespinasse*, p. 344.

still inclined to acknowledge her: "Look at the education I had. Mme du Deffand (since for *esprit* she must be mentioned), the Président Hénault, etc."[107] The marquise had not been content just to form Julie's mind, but saw to it that her niece's naturalness was not compromised by contact with Parisian society, nor that the spontaneity that had so attracted her and to which she never tired of recalling Julie as if to a duty should not be crushed. The young woman entrusted herself meekly to the hands of her Pygmalion. She could surely have done little else, but she had a very real admiration for Mme du Deffand's intelligence, and, like her, she needed to be surrounded by people. For her part, the marquise must have felt an almost maternal pride in her pupil's surprising results and delighted in finding an accomplice in the daily social round. Despite the shared interests, tone, and ways of the two women, who now received together at five o'clock every afternoon, the guests at Saint-Joseph varied greatly among themselves. In the enclosed space of the salon, aunt and niece displayed in an exemplary manner how the *esprit de société* and the *bienséances* could promote two opposite ways of being. Whereas Mme du Deffand wanted to be admired, Mlle de Lespinasse wanted to be loved. The former dominated; the latter charmed. The marquise used her psychological insight to get people's secrets out of them while she distanced herself from them inwardly. Julie tried to "discover everyone's weak point"[108] so as more easily to find her way into their hearts. One was inimitable when she spoke, the other when she listened. Mme du Deffand was skeptical and looked to the past; Mlle de Lespinasse needed ideals and looked to the future. *Ennui*, "like a solitary worm,"[109] consumed Mme du Deffand, causing self-disgust. Her pessimism drove her to a radical denial of every value, inducing her to liken opposites. "To govern a state" was the same as "to play with a top"[110]; "to be an automaton" was equivalent to being "a saint."[111] Devastating nihilism grew from her belief that everything came from "one single misfortune: that of having been born."[112] Julie, on the other hand, was not only in tune with her ego, but had a profound self-respect and a veneration of the sentiments that guided her own life. "I love nothing that is only half, nothing that is indecisive or that is only a little. I do not understand the language of society people; they amuse themselves and they yawn, they have friends and

107. Mlle de Lespinasse to Guibert, September 23, 1774, in *Lettres de Mlle de Lespinasse*, p. 109.

108. "Portrait de Mademoiselle de Lespinasse par d'Alembert," in *Lettres de Mlle de Lespinasse*, p. 346.

109. Mme du Deffand to Walpole, March 17, 1776, in *Horace Walpole's Correspondence with Mme du Deffand*, Vol. 4, p. 285.

110. Mme du Deffand to Walpole, May 3, 1767, in *Horace Walpole's Correspondence with Mme du Deffand*, Vol. 1, p. 288.

111. Mme du Deffand to John Craufurd, February 12, 1774, in *Correspondence complète de Mme du Deffand*, Sainte-Aulaire edition, Vol. 3, p. 83.

112. Mme du Deffand to Voltaire, May 2, 1764, in *Voltaire's Correspondence*, D11853, Vol. 27, p. 352.

they love nothing. That all seems deplorable to me, I prefer the torment that gnaws at my life to the pleasure that benumbs theirs.[113]"

Little by little the Saint-Joseph salon ceased to gravitate around one single person, proving itself to have two different poles of attraction, two different souls. But had not the archetypal model of the Blue Room been the same? Perhaps in order to be the mirror in which all society wished to admire itself, the salon had to be motivated by different energies that could contemplate one another and meld together to form the impetus that was *sociabilité*. For ten years the room hung with yellow moiré was the melting pot in which aristocratic dilettantism, intellectual passion, jealously guarded tradition, reforming spirit, the purity of classical taste, and pre-Romantic sensibilities were melded in a miraculous alchemy. Many Parisian salons were more sumptuous, more brilliant, or more philosophical; some of them counted among their guests more great aristocrats, more powerful men, more illustrious writers, but assuredly none of them incarnated the spirit of eighteenth-century society so much as the Saint-Joseph salon.

Jealousy put an end to this delicate balance by destroying the understanding between aunt and niece. The time had come to "rip off the mask,"[114] even from the innocent Julie, and the marquise realized that her niece was no simple shadow but a perfect double and that the pride of her salon—her favorite d'Alembert —preferred Julie, which put her friendship with him in second place. It only remained for the two women to divide the spoils. Julie could savor the pleasure of opening the doors of a salon that was all her own, while Mme du Deffand disdainfully closed hers to anyone who reminded her of her niece's betrayal or of the triumph of the coterie *philosophique*. Mlle de Lespinasse assumed the role of Egeria to the Enlightenment, Mme du Deffand that of Vesta to the past. Henceforth the ideal of polite society no longer had a privileged place in which to fully express itself.

---

113. Mlle de Lespinasse to Guibert, June 24, 1773, in *Lettres de Mlle de Lespinasse*, p. 20.

114. "Portrait de Mme la Marquise du Deffand par elle-même, fait en 1774," in *Horace Walpole's Correspondence with Mme du Deffand*, Vol. 6, p. 61.

17

THE AGE OF CONVERSATION

I. The Seductions of the Spoken Word

It seems to me that Paris is recognized as the one city in the world where wit and a taste for conversation are most widespread; and what is known as the *mal du pays*, that indefinable mourning for one's country which has nothing to do even with those friends who are left behind, is particularly applicable to the pleasure of discourse, which the French find nowhere to the same degree as at home. Volney[1] recounts how, during the Revolution, the French émigrés wanted to establish a colony and reclaim land in America; but from time to time, so they said, they left what they were doing to go and converse in the town; and this town, New Orleans, was six hundred leagues from where they lived. All classes in France feel the need to converse: the spoken word is not only, as it is elsewhere, a means of communicating ideas, sentiments, and concerns, but it is an instrument that it is enjoyable to play and that, like music with some peoples and strong liquor with others, raises the spirits.[2]

NO ONE UNDERSTOOD the intense nostalgia of French émigrés better than Mme de Staël, who, though born of Swiss parents, was a Parisian through and through. Her outspokenness had earned her Napoleon's animosity, leading to exile in Germany. Moreover, just as she was claiming in her great book of 1814, *De l'Allemagne*, that conversation was central to French culture, she must have realized that she was commemorating a phenomenon that was historically over. How, after the Revolution, could *ancien régime* conversation have survived the

---

1. Constantin-François Chassebœuf, Comte de Volney, *Tableau du climat et du sol des États-Unis d'Amérique. Éclaircissements sur divers articles: Art. IV de la Colonie du Post-Vincennes sur la Wabash*, in *Œuvres*, edited by Anne and Henry Deneys, two volumes (Paris: Fayard, 1989), Vol. 2, p. 314.

2. Madame de Staël, *De l'Allemagne*, Vol. 1, p. 101.

disappearance of the very society of which it was the most original and most ephemeral expression? It was undoubtedly through two centuries of conversation that the *esprit de société* realized its sincerest aspiration: to create a sense of harmonious well-being that could transcend the burden of reality.

As if by magic, the art of conversation radiated a soothing oblivion and created a harmonious atmosphere offering relaxation, entertainment, and instruction while banishing, if only for a few hours, "the troublesome griefs that our life is full of"[3] and life's many dramas. Imbued with a tragic sense of religion and sin, nobles, while committed to defending their own prestige and political power, discovered a fount of joy in conversation among a few. It was, however, a purely social joy, delicately balanced between the new individual aspirations of the day and society's immutable demands, between public and private life. During the seventeenth century, coincidentally with the establishment of the aristocratic art of conviviality, a new notion emerged of the *monde*, or social world. This was not the world in the cosmological sense of antiquity, nor one that corresponded to the traditional Christian view of the human and the secular as opposed to the divine. Rather, it expressed the purely social acceptance of an elite that knew the rules of how to live. In this world the *bienséances* held full sway. But the value of the term varied depending on its context, on religious views, and on the epoch, at times attesting to an aesthetic and moral ideal perfectly in keeping with Christianity, at others to a choice that was incompatible with the demands of faith. To this dialectic between religion and society, society would soon add a number of nuances, as in the *grand monde, beau monde,* and *bonne compagnie,* all of which coincided with the seventeenth-century taste for distinction and which were designed to save the worldly ideal from its practical failings and to reassert its pedagogic and civilizing function.

Guez de Balzac, in dedicating his dialogue *De la conversation des Romains* (1634) to the Marquise de Rambouillet, used the new expression *grand monde* to refer to her circle. He established the noble genealogy of conversation, thereby granting it literary status and restoring it to the great realm of classical rhetoric.[4] It was, however, a disguised, discreet rhetoric whose rules differed from those regulating political oratory. It was designed to serve *otium* rather than *negotium*—private life rather than public life. And it was through conversation that the whole gamut of the meaning of *urbanitas*—the ancient Latin ideal of courtesy, introduced now to France by Balzac—was revealed.[5] Cicero, whom Balzac took as his

---

3. Castiglione, *The Book of the Courtier,* Book 2, Chapter 45, p. 155.

4. Marc Fumaroli, "Premier témoins du parisianisme: le 'monde' et la 'mode' chez les moralistes du XVIIe siècle," in *Littératures classiques,* edited by B. Beugnot (Paris: Klincksieck, fall 1994), Vol. 22, p. 185.

5. See Jean-Louis Guez de Balzac, *Suite d'un entretien de vive voix, ou de la conversation des Romains. À Madame la marquise de Rambouillet,* in *Œuvres diverses* (1644), edited by Roger Zuber (Paris: Champion, 1995), pp. 81–82.

model, had theorized on the necessity and importance of the *sermo convivialis*—convivial exchange—giving an excellent example in his *Familiar Epistles*. But the idea of an open conversation between friends capable, as Marc Fumaroli writes, of "providing somewhere outside time wherein to find the supreme happiness, a search among friends and in the name of love, for divine ideas of truth, beauty, and the good,"[6] goes back much further to the very origins of Western civilization.

The triumph of this ideal in *ancien régime* France resulted first from the nobility's concern for distinction and entertainment. It also reflected the crisis in political oratory and eloquence, which had fallen into desuetude under Louis XIII and Cardinal de Richelieu. Deprived of its essential purpose, rhetoric returned to its older and wider function of studying the words, signs, and gestures that regulated relations between individuals. This drive toward codification (which had its roots in Italian Renaissance treatises) put conversation in a key position, made all the more important by the new approach of writers. Wishing to reach a broader readership in both *cour* and *ville*, they turned to the language of polite society as a sure means of winning over public taste. The society aesthetic developed precisely from the dialectic between literature and life, between the theorizing of scholars and the nobility's taste and style. It is difficult to say who pointed the way for whom; but the two basic texts—Balzac's *De la conversation des Romains*, on the theoretical level, and Vincent Voiture's letters, for the practical application—can both be traced to the Marquise de Rambouillet and her circle's influence.

The central role of conversation, with all that it implied for behavior in society and the importance of its influence on literature, was bound to give rise to a systematic rethinking of its form, its rules, and its aims. On the one hand scholars were concerned with defining rhetoric—making claims either for classical and humanistic precedent or for the absolute originality of the society ideal. On the other hand, experts and writers on varied subjects applied themselves in different manuals to describing the mechanisms of conversation and defining its concepts, only to conclude that no theoretical preparation could take the place of the real thing.

Socialites had no need to turn to "doctrine" to be happily themselves and to practice what Fumaroli calls that "art of living nobly in leisure and in conditions of privacy,"[7] which constituted the essence of *honnêteté*. But this apparent naturalness went hand in hand with an unparalleled awareness and constant self-analysis. It could not have been otherwise from the moment the French nobility chose to define itself primarily through style, making it the touchstone of its superiority.

---

6. Fumaroli, preface to *L'Art de la conversation*, edited by Jacqueline Hellegouarc'h (Paris: Classiques Garnier–Dunod, 1997), p. v.

7. Marc Fumaroli, "De l'âge de l'éloquence à l'âge de la conversation: la conversion de la rhétorique humaniste de la France du XVII⁺ siècle," in *Art de la lettre, art de la conversation à l'époque classique en France, Actes du colloque de Wolfenbüttel*, October 1991, edited by Bernard Bray and Christopher Strosetzki (Paris: Klincksieck, 1995), p. 41.

THE AGE OF CONVERSATION

How could nobles not reflect on their appearance if that was the unmistakable sign of social belonging and individual success? It was precisely through such collective thinking—which encompassed everything from the observation of apparently futile details to the learned study of psychological and moral matters—that society improved itself from one generation to the next. It adjusted its tastes, periodically renewed its main characteristics, absorbed whatever it found attractive along the way, and made and unmade fashion, all the while remaining faithful to its original pledge: to make life into the most elegant of games.

Among the chief instruments of this playful metamorphosis—music, dance, the theater, and literature—nothing could compare to the spoken word's capacity for illusion. Even the Grande Mademoiselle, a princess of the blood who, as a patron, lavishly cultivated all these pastimes, maintained that "the greatest pleasure in life, almost the only one" should be found in conversation.[8] Her belief, widely shared by society's leading lights and echoed by the treatise writers as an unarguable truth, might have seemed exaggerated were it not in perfect keeping with the erotic, exuberant nature of the spoken word and with its ability to disguise reality. If, a hundred years later, in the midst of the Enlightenment, the celebrated hostess Mme Geoffrin (despite her undoubted generosity) had "the tic of detesting unhappy" people, it was because she saw in them a threat to the relaxed and stimulating atmosphere of her renowned salon.[9]

Antoine Gombaud, Chevalier de Méré, was a socialite par excellence and a regular guest in the salons of both Mme de Rambouillet and Mme de Sablé. In old age and in the wake of the Fronde, he established his authority by giving shape to and theorizing on his experiences as a man of the world. To him success in *bonne compagnie* was based on conversation and depended on the ability to please and amuse others by the simple appeal of the spoken word. The art of conversation did not rely only on intuition and improvisation but also presupposed a sum of knowledge and expertise very like what the *honnête homme* required to conform to society without renouncing his autonomous judgment. To please, it was first necessary to "know the world," which involved paying everyone the regard he was due. A regard for etiquette and for different social conditions (such as the forms of respect owed, for example, to women) was an integral part of the *bienséances*; by being aware of the differences, conversation could make these differences less evident, disguise them, and do everything to ensure that each saw himself as the object of the greatest consideration and that no one felt inferior or ill at ease. Rather than indicating the homogeneity of social belonging, the aim was to value individual talent and involve everyone in the pleasure of the game.

---

8. Mademoiselle to Mme de Motteville, May 14, 1660, letter 1, in *Lettres de Mademoiselle de Montpensier*, p. 5.

9. Galiani to Mme d'Épinay, September 18, 1769, in Galiani, *Correspondance*, p. 72.

Méré was the first to point to the importance of intuitively understanding the personality of the person with whom one conversed. This required a sharpened psychological awareness, which helped people to be in tune with their interlocutors and so encouraged them to speak in turn and show themselves at their best. As both La Rochefoucauld and La Bruyère reiterated, the successful conversationalist had first and foremost to allow others to shine—for the best affirmation of the self came from gratifying the *amour-propre* of one's partner.

A talented conversationalist, however, was not satisfied with understanding his interlocutor's psychology in order to be more pleasing but would subject him or her to a Socratic form of questioning. Once encouraged to express themselves, people are revealed to themselves, and thus made to discover qualities that they were perhaps unaware of possessing. In an exchange between equals this "revelation" was by definition reciprocal. "I need to be helped and divined if I am to understand myself,"[10] Méré declared. His friend the Maréchal de Clérambault marveled at his friend's talent: "As soon as I begin to speak...you comprehend me better than I comprehend myself, and if everything you say seems so easy to understand, I often think that I knew it before you told it to me."[11]

As was obvious even to Méré, to lower the mask in a "universe dominated by look,"[12] could be dangerous, and the *honnête homme* had to be careful. Méré's contemporaries held different opinions on this matter. Whereas Torquato Accetto merely advocated "honest dissimulation," the Spanish Jesuit Baltasar Gracián contemplated keeping the "secret" as the basis of a dark strategy of domination. Deprived of its innocent playfulness and no longer safeguarded by a nonaggression pact, conversation became a battleground. The famous Maxim 13 of Gracián's *Oracolo manuale* (1647) sounded like a declaration of war: "Man's life is militia against man's malice."[13] Although sincerity was a forbidden luxury at court, in civil society there were some happy oases where the pleasure of acknowledging one another, the satisfaction of instantly understanding and being able to anticipate one another's thoughts, could be repeatedly experienced through conversation—that same pleasure of which Mme de Sévigné wrote to Bussy-Rabutin, remembering the golden days of their friendship:

> You know well, Monsieur le Comte, that in days gone by we had the gift of understanding one another before we had spoken. One of us answered what

---

10. Méré, "De la vraie honnêteté," in *Œuvres complètes*, Vol. 3, p. 78.

11. Méré, "Cinquième Conversation," in *Les Conversations*, in *Œuvres complètes*, Vol. 3, p. 68.

12. Jean-Jacques Courtine and Claudine Haroche, *Histoire du visage: Exprimer et taire ses émotions XVIe–début XIXe siècle* (Paris Marseilles: Rivages, 1988), pp. 188–189.

13. Baltasar Gracián, *El oráculo manual y arte de prudencia* (1647); French edition, *L'Homme de cour traduit et commenté par le sieur Amelot de la Houssaie* (Paris: chez la veuve Martin, 1687).

the other wanted to say very well; and if we had not wanted to give our-selves the pleasure of easily pronouncing a few words, our minds would almost have done all the business of conversation. When one has under-stood someone so well, one cannot become dull. For me, it is a fine thing to understand quickly: it reveals a pleasing liveliness which is unequaled in its gratification of the *amour-propre*.[14]

Esprit, or wit, was essential to the pleasure of conversation. But what kind of *esprit* in particular? That word, so imprecise, so hard to define, and so changeable in its meaning, appeared everywhere in seventeenth-century usage. In the second half of the century, it was the subject of intense consideration and applied to a whole gamut of human intellectual activity.[15] These problems of definition did not belong in dictionaries and treatises alone but fascinated the whole of society. "In fine conversation, one speaks of nothing else," the influential Jesuit critic Père Bouhours remarked in his *De la manière de bien penser dans les ouvrages de l'esprit*.[16] And for these conversations to be "fine," they had to conform to a par-ticular type of *esprit*: "Nothing is more opposed to *esprit* in conversation than study and business, for, being natural, *esprit* is the enemy of work and of con-straint; we see, moreover, that those who have this talent are ordinarily idle peo-ple, whose principle employment is to pay and to receive visits."[17]

Reflecting the true *honnête homme*, society conversation was idle, its aim none other than the pleasure of conversation for its own sake. It abhorred affectation. Unlike the conversation of *savants*, it made no display of learning, it wished neither to demonstrate nor to persuade, and it avoided quotations, examples, and proverbs. Society people preferred, as Emmanuel Bury writes, "the fire of imagination" to the "weight of memory" and aimed at surprise by showing themselves capable of orig-inal, unexpected comparison, "seizing the occasion, the time and the place with a sure swiftness."[18] "The characteristic of those *esprits* is to speak well and with ease and to give a pleasing twist to everything they say. In company, their repartee is very clever; they always have some very subtle question to put forward, and some pretty tale to tell in order to enliven the conversation or to revive it when it begins to languish; however little they are stimulated, they say a thousand surprising

---

14. Madame de Sévigné to Bussy-Rabutin, May 16, 1672, in Mme de Sévigné, *Correspondance*, Vol. 1, p. 508.

15. See Chapter 4.

16. Quoted in Alain Viala, "L'esprit galant," in *L'Esprit en France au XVIIe siècle, Actes du 28ième Congrès de la North American Society for Seventeenth-Century French Literature*, edited by François Lagarde, Biblio 17 (Paris-Seattle-Tübingen: PFSCL, 1997), p. 54.

17. Bouhours, "Le bel esprit," in *Les Entretiens d'Ariste et d'Eugène*, p. 128.

18. See Emmanuel Bury, "Les lieux de l'esprit mondain," in *L'Esprit en France au XVIIe siècle*, pp. 85–93.

things; above all they understand the art of trifling wittily and of subtle jesting in a humorous conversation, but they also come out well in serious conversations."[19]

Women were the arbiters of conversation in polite society, although the question of whether their physiology was intellectually compatible with *esprit* was much discussed. And since conversation had to please them, *esprit* had to be "gallant," that is, to have a light, even flirtatious, quality. Depending, then, on the art of the spoken word, this "general gallantry which had no objective"[20] became an established element of conversation precisely because of its ability to disguise and embellish reality and, by its very gaiety, to exhilarate. For Méré, this meant making disagreeable things agreeable; for Mlle de Scudéry it was "the art of turning things aside."[21] Ortigue de Vaumorière echoed them both in claiming the need "to find the words with which delicately to wrap the things that we wish to make clear but which *honnêteté* forbids openly expressing."[22] The object of gallant conversation was the same for everyone. Language, "in attenuating malice and aggression [and] moderating or modulating desire," Bury writes, "becomes the repository of a real spiritual exercise (in every sense of that adjective)."[23]

But conversation was not only a means of escape. It was also an education in the world—for many, the only one available. Its usefulness was so obvious that even dictionaries praised it. "Conversation should be loved; it constitutes good society; friendships are formed and preserved through it," claimed Richelet's dictionary. "Conversation brings natural talents into play and polishes them. It purifies and sets the mind to rights and constitutes the great book of the world."[24] In 1690, Mme de Sévigné advised her daughter Mme de Grignan to find a little time to converse with her fifteen-year-old niece, which she claimed would serve the young woman better than any reading.[25] A hundred years later, Mme Necker wanted her child, the future Mme de Staël, to sit next to her on a stool and listen to the conversations taking place in her salon. Conversation not only taught the "beauty of language."[26] It also formed taste and helped one to acquire that eclectic, dazzling culture so necessary to life in society.

19. Bouhours, "Le bel esprit," p. 32.

20. Mademoiselle to Mme de Motteville, letter 3, in *Lettres de Mademoiselle de Montpensier*, p. 74.

21. Mlle de Scudéry, "De la conversation," in *"De l'air galant" et autres conversations*, p. 74.

22. Ortigue de Vaumorière, "De la politesse du Langage, et de la manière de faire un récit," in *L'Art de plaire dans la conversation*, p. 55.

23. Bury, *Littérature et politesse*, p. 109.

24. *Dictionnaire de la langue française, ancienne et moderne, de Pierre Richelet, augmenté de plusieurs additions* (Lyon: Bruyset frères, 1728).

25. Mme de Sévigné to Mme de Grignan, January 15, 1690, in Mme de Sévigné, *Correspondance*, Vol. 3, p. 810.

26. Mlle de Scudéry, *Clélie*, sequel to Part 4, Book 2, Vol. 8, p. 671.

From its very beginnings, society conversation was remarkable for its breadth. Guez de Balzac maintained that the discussions at the hôtel de Rambouillet during the course of one week "would encompass a wider subject matter than is covered by many history books." And such subject matter, he was careful to specify, "was worthy of being heard, it was altogether instructive, and entertaining."[27] Méré, virtuoso that he was, claimed that all subjects were suitable, a statement that accorded perfectly with the *honnête homme*'s dilettantism.[28] What mattered was how these subjects were talked about. In her typically didactic way, Mlle de Scudéry pointed out that conversation "must more often treat of ordinary and gallant things than of great things."

> And yet I hold that there is nothing that may not be included: [conversation] must be free and varied according to the time, the place, and the people present.... Furthermore I would like a certain joyous spirit to preside, which ... would nevertheless inspire in the hearts of the whole Company a disposition to be amused by everything and bored by nothing; and I want great and small things to be spoken of, so long as they are spoken of elegantly; and that one only speaks of that which must be spoken about, without there being the slightest constraint.[29]

Of all the available examples, the seventeenth century's most enchanting illustration of the poetics of conversation is to be found in La Fontaine's verse. In his "Discours à Madame de La Sablière" (1680), La Fontaine suggested the marquise as the perfect example of someone whose conversation, being both profound and lighthearted, provided rich and varied intellectual nourishment:

> La bagatelle, la science,
> Les chimères, le rien, tout est bon. Je soutiens
> Qu'il faut de tout aux entretiens:
> C'est un parterre, où Flore épand ses biens;
> Sur différentes fleurs l'abeille s'y repose,
> Et fait du miel de toute chose.[30]

---

27. Balzac to Chaplain, February 18, 1638, *Lettres familières de Monsieur de Balzac à Monsieur Chapelain*, letter 24, Book 3, p. 281.

28. Méré, "Discours de la conversation," in *Œuvres complètes*, Vol. 2, p. 100.

29. Mlle de Scudéry, "De la conversation," in *"De l'air galant,"* pp. 72–74.

30. "Light matter, learnd information,/Illusions, trifles, all of them are good. I maintain/That in talk no item or subject is vain,/A garden in which Flora spreads blessings like rain./On varied flowers the bee comes to settle, and rests;/It makes honey of all that it ingests"; "Discourse to Madame de La Sablière," in *The Complete Fables of Jean de la Fontaine*, p. 487.

In fact there were many things which could not be discussed, either because they were uninteresting, like private or domestic matters, or because they were dangerous, like religion or politics. Politics in particular, as Robert Darnton writes, "was the king's business, *le secret du roi*—a notion derived from a late medieval and Renaissance view, which treated statecraft as *arcana imperii*, a secret art restricted to sovereigns and their advisers."[31]

So the "great and small things" that came to be densely woven into the conversation by prose or verse were society events and pastimes, however futile or serious. From one visit to another, "idle" individuals who had elegant and natural powers of expression could tell amusing stories or anecdotes, pass on a piece of gossip, describe a successful evening, a hunt, a court ceremony, or discuss the latest fashion, but they could also talk about literature, art, music, the theater, psychology, and morality—anything that was part of everyday life. While remaining faithful to a principle of playfulness, conversation thus unconsciously became an instrument of reflection. Delphine Denis describes how it determined the usages of language, in which "literature in its formative stages is constructed and discussed and the very idea of the writer is elaborated."[32] For Fumaroli, conversation was a genuine "literary institution," which in its own "mediocre" style shaped memoirs, novels, letter-writing, theatrical writing, lyrics, and aphorisms.[33]

With the permanent aim of pleasing, conversation developed a precise strategy involving *politesse*, *esprit*, *galanterie*, *complaisance* (obligingness), *enjouement* (cheerfulness), and *flatterie*. Its application was full of pitfalls, however.

Politesse, for example, did not depend solely on form. In order to be convincing, it had to give the impression of personal involvement. After her conversion, Mme de Longueville's manners remained impeccable but failed to conceal her detachment from society. Her lack of personal involvement did not escape the Comtesse de Maure's practiced eye. "Yesterday I saw Madame de Longueville at last," she wrote to Mme de Sablé. "She is ever as amiable as possible, but she is so cold in herself that it is clear she would not know how to have warmth for others, and the little she shows, she shows out of pure goodness."[34]

If a will to please was obligatory in society, it nonetheless had to avoid appearing indiscriminate lest it arouse the suspicion that it was inspired by self-love rather than a genuine interest (as Mlle de Scudéry had insinuated about Julie d'Angennes). *Complaisance*, too, "is necessary in society, but it must have its

31. Robert Darnton, "Paris: The Early Internet," *The New York Review of Books*, June 29, 2000, p. 42.

32. Delphine Denis, *La Muse galante: Poétique de la conversation dans l'œuvre de Madeleine de Scudéry* (Paris: Champion, 1997), p. 12.

33. See Fumaroli, "La conversation," in *Trois institutions littéraires* (Paris: Gallimard, 1994).

34. Mme de Maure to Mme de Sablé, letter 65, in Barthélemy, *Mme la comtesse de Maure, sa vie et sa correspondance*, pp. 194–195.

limits," as La Rochefoucauld pointed out.[35] In conditions of social superiority or of absolute equality, it was a sign of attention and courtesy to give way graciously to the opinions and wishes of another. But for anyone with a less well defined social position, the slightest nuance could turn *complaisance* to adulation, or even worse, to servility. Mme du Deffand refused, when taking the waters with the Duchesse de Pecquigny at Forges, to yield to her intrusive cordiality. She was, she wrote, "not obliged to flatter her."[36]

Even flattery, although it was the favorite target of writers and moralists, was essential to society. How could courtesy—and, even more so, gallantry—systematically embellish everyday life without the providential aid of a lie? A game in which everyone was complicit must surely be indulged. Mlle de Scudéry was one of the first to confront the tricky problem, concluding that "there is nothing that one forgives more easily than flattery spoken with good grace."[37] Yet in her opinion, flattery could become one of the most shameful vices. However difficult it might have been to tell exactly where to draw the line between amiability and hypocrisy in the wilderness of situations and particular cases, one thing was certain: the only acceptable form of flattery was flattery with an end in itself—that which aimed only at making the flatterer agreeable while excluding any suspicion of an ulterior motive. The best indicator of success was the self-respect of the person being flattered, who after all needed to be able to recognize himself in the admiration of others.

The most dangerous area, however, remained that of *raillerie*, or playful teasing. Castiglione had defined it from the ethical and stylistic point of view, as "the art that belongeth to all this kind of pleasant speech to provoke laughter and solace after an honest sort."[38] French seventeenth-century theorists unanimously agreed that it was essential to society conversation. Even La Bruyère (although ever critical of society's "precious" and euphemistic language) did not hesitate to grant *raillerie* an artistic role: "To joke gracefully and to talk happily about small subjects, too many manners, too much *politesse*, and even too much fecundity are needed; to jest like this is to create and to make something out of nothing."[39] As the brightest star in the constellation of comic devices that included *plaisanterie*, *raillerie*, *bons mots*, the *trait*, and the *pointe*,[40] *raillerie* claimed above all to be the

---

35. La Rochefoucauld, "De la société," in *Réflexions diverses*, II, in *Maximes*, p. 187.

36. Madame du Deffand to the Président Hénault, July 2, 1742, in *Correspondance complète de la Marquise du Deffand*, Vol. 1, p. 16.

37. Mlle de Scudéry, "De la différence du flatteur et du complaisant," in *Conversations sur divers sujets*, two volumes (Paris: Barbin, 1680) Vol. 1, p. 340.

38. Castiglione, *The Book of the Courtier*, Book 2, Chapter 42, p. 150.

39. La Bruyère, "De la société et de la conversation," in *Les Caractères*, p. 203.

40. *Trait* and *pointe* were two different rhetorical figures involving subtle, unexpected wit.

art of gentle mockery, which primarily had to raise a smile from whomever it was aimed at. Possession of this talent was a distinguishing mark of a real man of the world, but it ran considerable risks. One false step could destroy the harmony of the group, which laughter was supposed to unite. Mlle de Scudéry, for instance, devoted two of her most complicated *Conversations* to the topic, listing the instances that should be banned—malicious satire, any *raillerie* that was coarse, "insipid and cold," or extravagant—and describing the correct usages that conformed with gallantry.[41] La Rochefoucauld warned: "*Raillerie* is an agreeable gaiety of spirit, which makes conversation cheerful and which binds the company when it is good-natured but which disturbs it when it is not.... It is a poison which, undiluted, extinguishes friendship and ignites hatred, but which, when tempered by a pleasing mind and flattering praise, makes and preserves friendship."[42]

In the long run, however, the desire to amuse prevailed over scruples of conscience, and the "sweets" in which a drop of acid helped to bring out the sweetness (to quote Hippolyte Taine's metaphor for eighteenth-century conversation) gradually took on a more bitter taste. As the historian and memoirist Charles Pinot Duclos remarked in 1751, "Wickedness today is only a fashion ... it has been reduced to an art; it takes the place of merit in those that have none other, and often earns them respect."[43] Once transformed, so that it systematically hunted out the ridiculous, *raillerie* eventually gave way to *persiflage*. This came into fashion in Paris about halfway through the eighteenth century, and no longer implied a playful irony so much as "continuous mockery under the deceptive guise of approbation ... at the expense of someone who, having been deceived by ordinary expressions of good manners, is unaware of being ridiculed."[44] But there would be no possible equivocation when, on the eve of the Revolution, *esprit* became a real instrument of hatred and resentment. The Abbé Morellet tells in his *Mémoires* how Chamfort's "misanthropic, denigrating" conversation left him with his "soul saddened as though I had just witnessed an execution."[45]

Provided it was amusing, however, *esprit* always held sway, whether sensitive or cruel. According to Saint-Simon, courtiers avoided walking under Mme de Montespan's windows when the King was with her because "nothing was more dangerous than her mockery, which was sharper than anyone else's." To be exposed to her comments was like "facing fire."[46] But Saint-Simon also recognized that

---

41. See the introductory note by Delphine Denis to Mlle de Scudéry, *"De l'air galant,"* pp. 99–102.

42. La Rochefoucauld, Maxim 34, in *Maximes posthumes*, in *Maximes*, pp. 168–169.

43. Duclos, *Considérations sur les mœurs de ce siècle*, in *Œuvres complètes*, Vol. 1, p. 166.

44. Louis-Sébastien Mercier, *Tableau de Paris (1781–1788)*, edited by Jean-Claude Bonnet, two volumes (Paris: Mercure de France, 1994), Vol. 1, p. 384.

45. *Mémoires de l'abbé Morellet*, p. 310.

46. Saint-Simon, *Mémoires*, Vol. 5, p. 538.

that "wicked," "capricious" woman had "a great deal of humor" and an *esprit* "so particular, so delicate, so refined, but always so natural and so agreeable that it distinguished her unique character."[47] Louis XIV's mistress shared the famous "Mortemart family *esprit*" with her sisters, and, like them, possessed "the art of imbuing others with it." That unmistakable tone, "charming and simple," the echo of which Saint-Simon captured from the younger members of their circle, has disappeared without a trace. Proust, imagining what it might have been, created the *esprit des Guermantes*.

To be really effective, the difficult art of speaking needed what came to be called "the eloquence of the body," that is to say, looks, gestures, and facial expression.[48] For theorists of manners who, like Faret, confined conversation to rhetoric, gestures were "the soul of all discourse"[49] and obeyed the logic of oratory *actio*. For society writers who believed in the rhetoric of conversation and who aimed not to persuade but to please, the problem was an ethical and an aesthetic one. The *honnête homme* needed to be remarkable for his self-awareness, the absolute control of his means of expression, and a harmony—at least an apparent one—between the inner and the outer man, the essence and the appearance. "One pleases," La Rochefoucauld wrote, "insofar as one follows the air, the tone, the manners and the sentiments suitable to our situation and our person, and one displeases insofar as one departs from them."[50] Conversation—the very touchstone of *honnêteté*—demanded total spontaneity, an open, cheerful face, a natural, affable manner, an expression of interest and expectation, and the appearance of being at the disposal of others. Mlle de Scudéry, describing the harmony that should exist between the words and the gestures of an ideal conversationalist, praised "the marvelous relationship between the eyes and the spoken word" as that which most contributed toward "making speaking agreeable."[51] What was, of course, even more necessary was what Guazzo in his great treatise called "sweet breathing"—the tone, the modulation, and the volume of the voice.[52] Castiglione had already judged the voice to be very important in shaping the courtier, and Montaigne described it as a distinguishing feature of personality.[53] Interestingly, seventeenth-century treatises touched only fleetingly on the

---

47. Saint-Simon, *Mémoires*, Vol. 5, p. 537.

48. Nicolas Faret, *L'honneste homme ou l'art de plaire à la cour* (1630), edited by Maurice Magendie (Paris: Presses Universitaires de France, 1925), p. 91.

49. Faret, *L'honneste homme*, p. 93.

50. La Rochefoucauld, "De l'air et des manières," in *Réflexions diverses*, III, in *Maximes*, p. 191.

51. Mlle de Scudéry, "De parler trop ou trop peu, et comment il faut parler," in *"De l'air galant,"* p. 93.

52. Guazzo, *La civil conversazione*, Book 2, Vol. 1, p. 88.

53. Montaigne, "Of Experience," in *Essays*, Book 3, Chapter 13.

subject. Although they stressed the need for simple, natural language, devoid of affectation, the period's conversation manuals paid little attention to the voice and its expressive powers, perhaps assuming that such matters go without saying. All the same, the importance of training the voice and of its suggestive force could hardly escape the notice of someone who, like Méré, fully appreciated society's theatricality. In a letter he addressed to Cardinal de Retz's cousin and friend the Duchesse de Lesdiguières, who died in 1656, he praised the duchess as the incomparable performer of a play both written and directed by herself:

> But what pleases me and what I admire [most] is when you sometimes speak at length, beginning always in the tone most suitable to explain yourself, then altering it according to what you have to say, and finding just at the right moment the best expression and the perfect arrangement of words. Thus nothing was ever more agreeably ordered than all that is to be heard in your discourse. This difference of tone does not come so much from raising or lowering the voice, as from using it in an imperceptible way, which nevertheless conforms to what you feel in your heart. . . . To know how to use these tones with such good grace, you must know very well what is suitable. Such knowledge is quite extensive, and few people have acquired it to perfection.[54]

Méré explicitly made the analogy between music and the spoken word, suggesting that the quality of vocal music in the chapel at Versailles could provide a model for conversation, and other virtuosos of society discourse also turned to musical metaphor.[55] La Rochefoucauld, for instance, said, "One can take different paths, have neither the same views nor the same talents, so long as one adds to pleasure in society and remains as true as the various voices of the various instruments in music."[56] Ninon de Lenclos, who had a beautiful voice and could play several instruments, likened conversation to the sound of the flute, of which her father had been a great virtuoso. A century later, Mlle de Lespinasse attributed to Grétry's music "the keenness, the muscle, and the grace of the conversation of a witty man who would always appeal without ever wearying, would have only the degree of warmth and forcefulness suitable to the subject in question, and would appear all the richer for never stepping beyond the bounds dictated by taste."[57] Perhaps when presiding over conversation, Julie de Lespinasse was in fact not unlike a conductor who, mindful of each individual instrument, never lost sight of

---

54. Letter 4 to Mme de Lesdiguières, in *Lettres de Monsieur le chevalier de Méré*, Vol. 1, pp. 20–21.

55. Méré, Discourse II, "De l'éloquence et de l'entretien," in *Œuvres complètes*, Vol. 3, p. 109.

56. La Rochefoucauld, "De la société," in *Réflexions diverses*, II, in *Maximes*, p. 187.

57. Julie de Lespinasse, "Apologie d'une pauvre personne," in *Nouvelles lettres de Mademoiselle de Lespinasse*, p. 277.

the effect of the whole orchestra—or more precisely, of a *symphonie concertante*, a concerto for several soloists that had "an extraordinary vogue" in Paris at the end of the eighteenth century.[58] To her contemporary Mme Necker, the very act of harmonizing with one's interlocutors seemed like a musical phenomenon, although she was not herself a brilliant conversationalist: "One of the charms of *esprit* and of conversation lies in the ability to bow to the *esprit*, the self-respect, and the ideas of others, undulating, if it can be expressed thus, like a musical accompaniment."[59]

Even the hostess's ability to assess the qualities of her guests, inviting them to speak on subjects that pleased them, was like a musical performance. This was certainly the case with Mme Geoffrin. Morellet recounts how, on seeing the often boring Abbé de Saint-Pierre arriving at her house one winter evening, the hostess "led him to subjects about which he spoke very well. As he was leaving, Mme Geoffrin said to him, 'Monsieur l'abbé, your conversation was excellent.' 'Madame,' he replied, 'I am but an instrument on which you have played well.'"[60]

As the manuals on rhetoric, physiognomy, and manners pointed out throughout the seventeenth and eighteenth centuries, conversation consisted of silences as well as words. These were not contemplative or prudent silences but silences full of expression and meaning. "There is an eloquent silence," La Rochefoucauld pointed out, "that sometimes serves to approve or condemn; there is a mocking silence; there is a respectful silence; there are in fact airs, tones, and ways which often make for whatever is agreeable or disagreeable, delicate or shocking in conversation; the secret of how to make good use of this is granted to few."[61] The technique of pausing and suspension was part of rhetorical training. In society conversation, silence contributed to the interlocutors' *captatio benevolentiae*.[62] In 1771, the polemicist and essayist the Abbé Dinouart went so far as to write a treatise on the art of remaining silent, completing La Rochefoucauld's enumeration of

---

58. See Jean Mongredien, *La Musique en France des Lumières au romantisme, 1789–1830* (Paris: Flammarion, 1986): "The *symphonie concertante*, with its oppositions of timbres and all its games of questions and responses from the soloists, offers a picturesque character that seduces the audience, which finds in it precisely that aspect of a 'conversation among many' in music that the French aestheticians of the eighteenth century sought in instrumental music" (pp. 275–276).

59. *Mélanges extraits des manuscrits de Madame Necker*, three volumes (Paris: Charles Pougens, 1798), Vol. 2, pp. 92–93.

60. André Morellet, "Portrait de Madame Geoffrin," in *Éloges de Madame Geoffrin, contemporaine de Madame du Deffand, par MM. Morellet, Thomas, d'Alembert, suivis de Lettres de Madame Geoffrin et à Madame Geoffrin, et d'un Essai sur la conversation, etc., etc., par M. Morellet* (Paris: H. Nicolle, 1812), p. 11.

61. La Rochefoucauld, "De la conversation," in *Réflexions diverses*, IV, in *Maximes*, pp. 193–194.

62. A term from classical rhetoric, meaning "capturing goodwill," and referring to the figure of speech by which a speaker or writer begins by flattering the listerer or reader to ensure that what follows will be heard or read favorably.

various silences with a typology more suited to modern conversation: "An obliging silence not only involves applying oneself to listening to those one wishes to
please without contradicting, but also giving them an indication of the pleasure
one takes in their conversation or their behavior in such a way that looks and gestures all make up for the lack of speech in applauding them."[63]

II. The Deceptions of the Spoken Word

The ethical and aesthetic purpose of conversation was just being defined in lavish
detail with the posthumous publication of Voiture's letters, Méré's theories, and
Mlle de Scudéry's long digressions on various aspects of *sociabilité* in her novels.
Almost simultaneously doubts about its very aims were being raised. The first
edition of La Rochefoucauld's *Maximes* in 1665 and the first performance of
Molière's *Misanthrope* one year later radically called into question the importance
of the art of pleasing, which, as Jean Mesnard writes, "having become social law,
[allowed] for the building of a harmonious society."[64] La Rochefoucauld reduced
aristocratic virtues to "veiled vices" and morality to the simple exercise of *amour-
propre*, while Molière, with the character of Alceste, seemed to denounce the
falseness of *politesse* and the deceit implicit in society flattery:

> *Je veux que l'on soit homme, et qu'en toute rencontre*
> *Le fond de notre cœur dans nos discours se montre;*
> *Que ce soit lui qui parle, et que nos sentiments*
> *Ne se masquent jamais sous de vains compliments.*[65]

At the same time, La Rochefoucauld and Molière were also the first to wish to
please society, and their morality remained supremely ambiguous. Society loved to
admire its own reflection, and even a deformed image could provide an excellent
excuse for considering oneself. Was not the very taste for demystification in its turn
a kind of mystification that legitimized society's way of life? In the long path that
still lay ahead, aristocratic civilization would be the first to examine itself with a
clear and implacable eye without ever forgetting what was at stake. Chamfort,

---

63. Abbé Dinouart, *L'Art de se taire, principalement en matière de religion* (1771), edited by Jean-
Jacques Courtine and Claudine Haroche (Grenoble: Jérôme Millon, 1996), p. 43.

64. Jean Mesnard, "Le Misanthrope," in *La Culture du XVIIe siècle: Enquêtes et synthèses* (Paris:
Presses Universitaires de France, 1992), p. 523.

65. "A man should be a man, and let his speech/At every turn reveal his heart to each/His own true self
should speak; our sentiments/Should never hide beneath vain compliments." Molière, *Le Misanthrope*,
in *The Misanthrope and Other Plays*, translated by Donald Frame (Signet, 1968), Act I, Scene i, p. 35.

that last tragic incarnation of Alceste before the Revolution, told the following anecdote: "M*** was asked, 'What makes one most agreeable in society?' He replied, 'To be pleasing.'"[66]

Even with the most intransigent moralists, criticism of worldly values was motivated from within secular culture itself and did not question the right of man to wish to define himself in relation to others. Many thinkers and churchmen, however, found society's ever-increasing importance and the aspiration to worldly happiness quite incompatible with salvation. "To distance themselves from the commerce of this world is the principal rule of those who wish to live as Christians," held Saint-Cyran.[67] And Pascal, who had personal experience of society life, particularly through his friendship with Méré, denounced its tragically equivocal nature. In their desperate quest for amusement, men were not seeking pleasure but rather oblivion from themselves and from "our weak and mortal condition, so miserable that nothing can console us when we think about it closely."[68] Of all the means most likely to distract from such desperation, Pascal pointed first to "games and the conversation of women,"[69] society activities par excellence. "The mind and the sentiments are formed by conversation, the mind and the sentiments are spoiled by conversation. Thus they are both formed and spoiled by good and bad conversations. It is therefore more important than anything to know how to choose, so as to form and not to spoil [the mind and the sentiments]. And this choice can only be made if they are already formed and not spoiled. Thus a circle is created from which those who escape are most fortunate."[70]

For the Abbé de Rancé, however, there were no "good conversations," since "the purest were not exempt from danger," and the very act of communication was impious.[71] "Company conceals us from ourselves, solitude restores us," thundered another Jansenist writer, François Lamy, as he denounced the alienating effect of conversation.[72] To save himself, man must seek refuge enclosed within

66. Chamfort, "Caractères et anecdotes," no. 968, in *Produit de la civilisation perfectionnée. Maximes et pensées. Caractères et anecdotes*, edited by Geneviève Renaux (Paris: Gallimard, 1970), p. 271. (Chamfort usually refers to himself as M.)

67. Saint-Cyran, "Maximes extraites de Maximes saintes et chrétiennes," in *Moralistes du XVIIe siècle*, p. 73.

68. Blaise Pascal, *Pensée 168*, in *Pensées*, edited by Philippe Sellier (Classiques Garnier–Bordas, 1991), p. 216.

69. Pascal, *Pensée 168*, in *Pensées*, p. 216.

70. Pascal, *Pensée 658*, in *Pensées*, pp. 449–450.

71. The Abbé de Rancé to Mme de Longueville (December? 1657), in Rancé, *Correspondance*, Vol. 1, p. 728.

72. *De la connaissance de soi-même*, five volumes (Paris: Pralard, 1694–1698), Vol. 1, p. 18; quoted in Courtine and Haroche, *Histoire du visage*, Vol. 1, p. 196.

himself, silent in the sight of God. But even such defense, consecrated by long monastic tradition and dear to Jansenist spiritualism, was not safe from profanity. For man discovered the pleasure of conversing with himself. At the end of the sixteenth century, Guazzo had condemned solitude as a "poison," contrasting conversation to it as an "antidote and basis of life."[73] He held that it was pure madness to talk to oneself. A century later, when Mme de Lafayette's novel *La Princesse de Clèves* was published, Bussy-Rabutin criticized the use of internal monologue in the name of verisimilitude, since "it is not usual to speak to oneself."[74] Of course Montaigne, obliged to make a virtue out of necessity, had made solitary conversation the cornerstone of his great essays, but all classical culture was based on the idea of dialogue. However, the writer and freethinker François de La Mothe Le Vayer was already introducing a new note: "He who knows the art of retiring within himself, of conversing with himself internally, who can discover in his mind the order to which one must attain, never needs seek for company elsewhere."[75] This need for internalization and solitude was destined to become more widespread and to serve as an antidote to the ever more tyrannical demands of eighteenth-century *sociabilité*. Rousseau was not the only one to flee the world, to retire into himself, and to converse with his own soul, thus revolutionizing the way his contemporaries felt. In 1762 the Marquis Louis Antoine de Caraccioli, a prolific writer and expert on society, published *De la gaieté* and *La Conversation avec soi-même*, in which he described all the pleasures and advantages of freely conversing with oneself; and in the figure of Julie de Lespinasse, a consummate talent for conversation went hand in hand with the intense drama of interior monologue.

There is no trace of the shadows looming over the seventeenth-century society ideal in François Augustin Paradis de Moncrif's slim volume *Essai sur la nécessité et sur les moyens de plaire*, written when he was flush with social success and published in 1738. Here euphoria reigns supreme. But it is a different kind of euphoria, not one that, trusting only to education and discipline, attempts to transfigure reality, but one that reflects the optimism of a new world vision. In "a century of learning and of sublime knowledge," the desire to please had become essential.[76] *Savoir vivre* and *politesse* were no longer felt as tyrannical and constricting but came from the heart. The wish to please derived from the desire to be loved and was needed because "friendship was necessary to the happiness of a sensitive

---

73. Guazzo, *La civil conversazione*, p. 16.

74. Bussy-Rabutin to Mme de Sévigné, June 26, 1678, in Mme de Sévigné, *Correspondance*, Vol. 2, p. 617.

75. Quoted in Magendie, *La Politesse mondaine*, Vol. 1, p . 126.

76. François Augustin Paradis Moncrif, *Essai sur la nécessité et sur les moyens de plaire* (2nd edition; Paris: Prault fils, 1738), p. 6.

soul."[77] Nevertheless, although the background was changing, the rules and dynamics of *sociabilité* remained the same. Still more efficacious than the written word, "that spoken branch of literature known as conversation"[78] provided a continuously novel and seductive spectacle while, as Moncrif assures us, giving its participants the opportunity to develop their potential, to bring one another out, and to love one another.[79]

The persistence of the society model seems to have been confirmed by the entry on "conversation" that appeared in the second volume of the *Encyclopédie* (published in 1752 and immediately condemned by the Council of State as subversive for including the Abbé de Prades's entry on "certitude"): "The laws of conversation generally discourage leaning too heavily on any subject; it should flow lightly, effortlessly, and without affectation from one subject to another; it should be possible to speak of the frivolous and the serious; it should be remembered that conversation is a relaxation and that it is neither a contest of arms nor a chess game; it must know to be disregarded, more than disregarded if necessary: it must, in a word, give free rein to its wit."[80]

Yet just a year before, Duclos—a protégé of the powerful and very social Brancas clan—denounced the inadequacy of social conversation in *Considérations sur les mœurs de ce siècle*, claiming that it was unable to express the cultural concerns of which the *Encyclopédie* had now become the emblem. For Enlightenment intellectuals, the spoken word needed first and foremost to serve the truth rather than to entertain, and Duclos denounced anyone who used it as a means of achieving merely personal success. That was the ploy of the "agreeable man" who, absorbed by his own frivolous narcissism and indifferent to the public good, often seemed "the least worthy of love." *Bon ton*, or good tone, was an "expression invented only a short time ago, and it is already trivial," describing a purely mannered style of communication, which consisted in "saying nothing [but saying it] agreeably, and not allowing oneself to speak of anything sensible unless one made it acceptable through flowery discourse and by disguising reason when obliged to resort to it."[81] In describing a growing concern, Duclos drew attention to the process of depersonalization to which the rules of propriety subjected the individual, thereby undermining the very foundations of the society aesthetic.

The Marquise du Deffand was not the only one tempted to "tear off the mask." As Mme Necker, who observed the rules of high society behavior with the zeal of

---

77. Moncrif, *Essai sur la nécessité et sur les moyens de plaire*, p. 8.

78. Jacques de Norvins, *Mémorial*, Vol. 1, p. 165.

79. Moncrif, *Essai sur la nécessité et sur les moyens de plaire*, Vol. 1, p. 93.

80. *Encyclopédie*, Vol. 4, p. 165.

81. Duclos, *Considérations sur les mœurs de ce siècle*, p. 165.

a neophyte, maintained, "in this century everybody tries to be alike; therefore, in order to recognize the ridiculous, it is necessary to unravel the differences disguised behind similar masks, as if at the Opéra ball."[82] Even the Duchesse de Choiseul, a perfect example of *honnêteté* who was universally admired for her grace and virtue, was fully aware of the cost to the individual of social conformity: "We wish to please and be agreeable, we wish to be esteemed and we must appear worthy of esteem; thus formed, characters are no more distinguishable than shapes."[83] The Belgian Prince de Ligne, who entered his carriage in the morning in order to spend the evening in Paris, only to return to Brussels the same night, found women in France too alike: "They all have the same way of being pretty, of entering a room, of writing, of loving, and of quarreling. You may change [mistresses] in vain; you still have the impression of always keeping the same one."[84] This rigid uniformity of taste encompassed not only people but places: "Their houses in town are all white and gold, and looking-glass; I never know one from another," observed Horace Walpole on one visit to the capital, whereas the gardens resembled "desserts, with no more verdure or shade. What trees they have, are stripped up and cut straight at top; it is quite the massacre of the innocents."[85]

It would be a mistake, however, to suppose that tyranny of style drove the socialites to really question authority. Uniformity of behavior was, rather, a reason for solidarity: "This model is a meeting point; everyone, by conforming to it, believes himself to be more closely in contact with his fellows. A Frenchman would be as annoyed to be alone in his opinions as in his room."[86]

Some ten years after the publication of Duclos's *Considérations sur les mœurs de ce siècle*, Jean-Jacques Rousseau launched the most vicious attack on conversation in *La Nouvelle Héloïse*:

> One is delighted from the start with the knowledge and reason to be found in discussion, not only with Scholars and men of Letters, but with men of all conditions and even with women; the tone of conversation here is easy and natural; it is neither ponderous nor frivolous; it is knowledgeable but not pedantic, gay but not boisterous, polite but not affected, gallant but not mawkish, bantering but not tasteless. One encounters neither dissertations

---

82. Mme Necker, *Mélanges*, Vol. 1, p. 286.

83. Mme de Choiseul to Mme du Deffand, undated, in *Correspondance complète de Madame du Deffand*, Sainte-Aulaire edition, Vol. 1, p. 4.

84. The Prince de Ligne, *Œuvres choisies, littéraires, historiques et militaires du maréchal-prince de Ligne*, two volumes (Geneva: J.-J. Paschoud, 1809), Vol. 2, p. 13.

85. Horace Walpole to the Countess of Suffolk, Paris, September 20, 1766, in *Horace Walpole's Correspondence*, Vol. 31, p. 49.

86. Madame de Staël, *De l'Allemagne*, Vol. 1, p. 106.

nor epigrams; they reason without arguing; they joke without punning, they artfully combine humor and reason, maxims and witticisms, sharp satire, shrewd flattery, and moral austerity. They talk about everything so everyone will have something to say; they do not explore questions deeply, for fear of becoming tedious, they propose them as if in passing, deal with them rapidly, precision leads to elegance; each states his opinion and supports it in few words; no one vehemently attacks someone else's, no one tenaciously defends his own; they discuss for enlightenment, stop before the dispute begins; everyone is instructed, everyone is entertained, all go away contented, and from these discussions even the wise man can take home with him matters worthy of silent contemplation.[87]

This was merely a first impression: brilliant, elegant, sharp, all-encompassing, witty, and appealing. In fact, beneath its apparent perfection, society conversation concealed egoism, vanity, and deceit; as the supreme expression of what Morellet called society's civilizing process,[88] it could not meet with the approval of someone like Rousseau, who saw the origins of human corruption in the progress of civilization.

Rousseau, who was shy and awkward, had no taste for society life and was fully aware of his own social inadequacy. "A word to be spoken, a letter to be written, a visit to be paid," he admitted to Malesherbes in January 1762, "are for me torture."[89] More to the point, the famous naturalness of society conversation was that of "men who had deviated from nature." Their exquisite courtesy was a means of domination, and their intellectual malleability was a mask for sterility and sophism. As a great admirer of Le Misanthrope, and turning to the typically eighteenth-century metaphor of the automaton, Rousseau, like Alceste, denounced society's artificiality and the duplicity of its actors: "Thus the men to whom you are speaking are not the ones with whom you converse; their sentiments do not emanate from the heart, their perceptions are not in their minds, their words do not represent their thoughts, all you see of them is their shape, and being in a gathering is like standing before a moving tableau, where the detached Spectator is the only creature moving under his own power."[90]

Yet Rousseau did not entirely reject conversation. While awaiting the utopian

87. Jean-Jacques Rousseau, Julie, or the New Heloise, translated by Philip Stewart and Jean Vaché, Vol. 6 of The Collected Writings of Rousseau (University Press of New England, 1997), letter 14, p. 191.

88. "The principle differences that distinguish civilized man from the savage must be attributed to the habit of conversing"; Morellet, Essai sur la conversation, pp. 165–166.

89. Jean-Jacques Rousseau to Malesherbes, January 4, 1762, in Correspondance complète de Jean-Jacques Rousseau, critical edition edited by Ralph Alexander Leigh, fifty-one volumes (Geneva: Institut et Musée Voltaire, 1965–1991), Vol. 10, p. 6.

90. Rousseau, Julie, or the New Heloise, p. 193.

society of his *Contrat social*, he introduced it to the small community at Clarens. Here one or two exceptional beings could both exploit eloquent silences and with reciprocal openness confront not only the problems of the day but also the great moral questions of existence.

Society's self-criticism could be even more merciless than the moralists' accusations, since it offered no possible alternative. For Mme du Deffand, there was no greater torment than to be left to herself. Even the company of automatons was preferable to solitude:

> I was admiring last evening the large gathering at my house; men and women seemed to me like clockwork machines who came and went, talked and laughed without thinking, without reflecting, without feeling; each one played his part out of habit: Madame la Duchesse d'Aiguillon was bursting with laughter, Mme de Forcalquier scorned everything, Mme de la Vallière was prattling about everything. The men were playing no better parts, and I was sunk in the blackest of reflection; I thought I had spent my life in illusion; that I had myself dug all the holes into which I had fallen; that all my judgments had been wrong and rash, always too precipitate, and that in the end, I had known no one really well; and nor had I been known to anyone, and perhaps I did not know myself.[91]

III. The Power of the Spoken Word

With the Enlightenment, the very way conversation was thought about changed; it no longer dealt only with the aesthetic preoccupations of a privileged elite but now addressed the basic problems of the new culture. The spoken word had to serve truth rather than merely provide entertainment. In eighteenth-century debate, writes Jean-Paul Sermain, "conversation was conceived as a group activity to further the advance of reason by offering an open and attentive method of inquiry into the best subjects and as solid reassurance of social cohesion, so as to strengthen a concern for the public good."[92] The great intellectual salons of the era—from the Marquise de Lambert's to Mme Necker's, by way of those of Mme

---

91. Mme du Deffand to Walpole, October 20, 1766, in *Horace Walpole's Correspondence with Madame du Deffand*, Vol. 1, p. 156.

92. Jean-Paul Sermain, "La conversation au XVIIIe siècle: un théâtre pour les Lumières?" in *Convivialité et politesse. Du gigot, des mots et autres savoir vivre. Études rassemblées et présentées par Alain Montandon* (Clermont-Ferrand: Faculté des Lettres et Sciences humaines de l'Université Blaise Pascal, 1993), fasc. 39, pp. 105–130.

de Tencin, Helvétius, the Baron d'Holbach, and Julie de Lespinasse—can be seen as so many possible variations of this unique, ambitious project.

The new responsibilities invested in conversation went hand in hand with the evolution of the idea of *politesse*, which alone made it possible for the *esprit de société* to be fully realized. Whether it was false or sincere, generous or egotistical, *politesse* had, at least in principle, introduced into a society founded on "rank" a criterion of distinction and an assessment of merit that were independent of the established hierarchy. People could thus take part in worldly exchange on an equal footing, and as long as the discourse was regulated and solidarity was guaranteed, no other authority was required. When at the dawn of the eighteenth century *politesse* became the hallmark of the nation and was no longer the distinguishing mark of a gentleman, its pedagogic and moral aims became an integral part of civilization and progress.

As the touchstone of seventeenth-century *politesse*, conversation had adopted its rules in order to guarantee harmony and the free exchange of ideas. Having started life as an idealistic challenge, conversation had gradually developed a system of communication that, by entrusting itself exclusively to the respect for manners, made it possible for society to provide itself with its own forum, what Daniel Gordon calls a "free audience 'behind closed doors,'"[93] where it could express its own opinions. So private conversation made up for the lack of representative conversation, opening itself out to egalitarian dialogue and the confrontation of ideas. Within the absolute state and in more or less explicit controversy with it, "*société* came to signify the ultimate horizon of all individual aspirations, the only domain in which human nature could develop."[94] For the *philosophes* who assimilated its code of behavior and subscribed to it fully, the art of conversation aimed not merely at promoting the Enlightenment and its popularity, but constituted the very dynamics of intellectual thought.

"The development of ideas has, for a century, been entirely directed by conversation,"[95] Mme de Staël maintained at the end of the *ancien régime*. The Abbé Morellet, as an expert in economics, stressed the productive nature of a "commerce" based on an exchange that not only enriched all the participants but also provided a communal investment fund:

> General conversation has this advantage: that in awakening and sustaining the attention of all its participants, it draws a contribution from everyone to the expense and delight of all. It helps, facilitates, and renders more fruitful

---

93. Gordon, *Citizens without Sovereignty*, p. 111.

94. Gordon, *Citizens without Sovereignty*, p. 77.

95. Madame de Staël, *De l'Allemagne*, Vol. 1, p. 102.

the work of the one who has taken the first steps. Very often the one talking has but an incomplete idea, the development of which he has not followed, a principle whose entire consequences he has not appreciated. If he announces it in society, one of those present will be impressed and will perceive the link with one of his own ideas; he will bring them together. This rapprochement in turn excites the first speaker, who sees that his initial opinions can be further developed; and with everyone contributing to the growth of this first fund, the communal contribution will soon be enriched.[96]

For the *philosophes* conversation was primarily a method of thought. According to Morellet, the conversations that took place in the Baron d'Holbach's house were not only "animated" and "instructive" but also quite free, where "matters of philosophy, religion, and government" were concerned.[97] The number of those present varied between ten and twenty.[98] Opinions often differed, but freedom of discussion and strength of argument were always accompanied by great courtesy and "perfect tolerance." "Often only one person spoke, putting forward his theory quietly and without interruption. At other times it was a pitched battle, which the rest of the company quietly observed: a way of listening that I have only rarely found elsewhere." Diderot, the doctor Augustin Roux, and the baron himself "preached absolute atheism dogmatically," whereas the deists (like the Abbé Morellet and the Abbé Galiani) forcefully defended their own opinions "while remaining fond of the atheists in such good company." As on the battlefield where French officers took their hats off to the enemy,[99] or in life's crucial moments when notaries would drink to the health of their expiring clients,[100] so, in theological discussion, *politesse* had the upper hand, and Morellet would turn to his adversary and address him as "Monsieur and dear atheist."[101]

As Daniel Roche has remarked, "What best defined d'Holbach's coterie was the partial rejection of self-censorship by the 'salon.'" However, this "open discussion,

---

96. Morellet, *Essai sur la conversation*, pp. 217–218.

97. *Mémoires de l'abbé Morellet*, p. 130.

98. Morellet has left us a list of the baron's regular visitors: Diderot, J.-J. Rousseau, Helvétius, Barthez, Venel, Rouelle, Roux, Darcet, Duclos, Saurin, Raynal, Suard, Boulanger, Marmontel, Saint-Lambert, La Condamine, Chastellux (*Mémoires*, p. 129); to them can be added "all foreigners of some merit or talent who came to Paris," among them Hume, Wilkes, Sterne, Galiani, Beccaria, Caracciolo, Lord Shelburne, Gustav Philip Creutz, and Benjamin Franklin.

99. See Voltaire, *Précis du Siècle de l'Histoire de Louis XV*, in *Œuvres complètes*, Vol. 15, p. 240.

100. Walpole recounts an anecdote about a dying man whose wife fetched a notary to make his will, after which they "supped by his beside" and the notary raised a glass "*à la santé de notre aimable agonisant*"—"to the health of the our good friend in extremis." Horace Walpole to Lady Ossory, September 9, 1775, in *Horace Walpole's Correspondence*, Vol. 32, p. 260.

101. *Mémoires de l'abbé Morellet*, p. 133.

provocative audacity, true dialogue, and liveliness," which amazed the guests at the rue Royale, were accompanied by great discretion.[102] Members of the coterie knew full well, for example, that d'Holbach had written condemned works, including *Le Christianisme dévoilé*, *Le Système de la nature*, and *La Politique naturelle*, but these were never mentioned, even among themselves. "The idea of the danger incurred to our friend by an indiscretion imposed silence on the most trusted friends," Morellet recalled, adding, "Before the baron's death, not one of us had confided in the others what he knew about this matter, although everyone thought that the others knew as much as he did."[103] The risks of the written word were obvious to everyone and made the freedom of the spoken word all the more precious.

What could be more typical than the case of Diderot, most of whose work was published only after his death? It was in conversation that he enthralled his contemporaries, according to Marmontel, "with his gentle, persuasive eloquence, and his face shining with the fire of inspiration.... When he became animated in conversation and allowed free flow to his abundant thoughts, he forgot his theories and let himself follow the impulse of the moment, then he was enchanting."[104]

Theorists of conversation have always believed in the importance of bringing out the qualities of one's interlocutors, making them discover talents of which they were unaware; Diderot did the same with people's writing. "One of Diderot's fine moments," according again to Marmontel,

> was when a writer consulted him about a work. If the subject was worthwhile, it was good to see him grasp it, penetrate it, and, at a glance, discover the riches and beauty to which it was susceptible. If he noticed that the author had not done justice to the subject, instead of listening to the reading, he worked out in his head what the author had missed. Was it a play? He added scenes, new incidents, character traits; then, believing he had heard what he had dreamed, he praised the work that had just been read, in which, when it came to be published, we found practically nothing of what he had quoted.[105]

For Diderot, however, conversation was, above all, an intellectual necessity, a mental maieutic. "You ask me if I have read the Abbé Raynal. No. But why? Because I have neither the time nor the taste for reading. To read all alone with no

---

102. Daniel Roche, "La coterie d'Holbach, " in *Annales* 7–8 (1978), p. 723.

103. *Mémoires de l'abbé Morellet*, pp. 133–134.

104. Marmontel, *Mémoires*, p. 266.

105. Marmontel, *Mémoires*, pp. 266–267.

one to talk to, no one to argue with, no one to shine in front of, to listen to or to listen to one, is impossible," he confided to a friend.[106] As a proper method of thinking, conversation was, at the time, the most efficient way of disseminating the ideas he wished to promote.

It was no coincidence that Diderot's most audacious philosophical work, *Le Rêve de d'Alembert* (1769), was composed in the form of a conversation: a three-movement dialogue for four voices, about which P. N. Furbank has written an illuminating chapter in his critical biography of Diderot.[107] Significantly, the conclusions reached in the dialogue—a strictly mechanistic and materialistic philosophy of man and the world—do not result from the theorizing of a single individual but appear as the "necessary" result of an exchange of voices. A plurality of points of view integrates and empowers a communal philosophical exploration.

In the first dialogue, Diderot and d'Alembert discuss the thesis that the thinking self does not exist outside tangible matter and that matter regenerates itself, thus engendering the entire chain of being. These problems present themselves again to d'Alembert in the interiorized form of a dream, which gives rise, in turn, to a singular form of conversation. D'Alembert, who dreams he is continuing his discussion with Diderot, is overheard talking in his sleep by his friend Julie de Lespinasse and the cultivated doctor Théophile Bordeu—the author of the *Encyclopédie*'s entry on "crisis." They interrupt and comment upon his remarks. This new dialogue, born of the effort to decipher the earlier one, is no longer a confrontation between philosophers but a process of initiation. Thanks to Bordeu's meditation, which explains and completes what d'Alembert is saying in his sleep, Mlle de Lespinasse opens her mind to philosophical reasoning. What had at first seemed to her to be the sleeper's delirium and folly now becomes something to be questioned, and the brilliant neophyte's words make a new and important contribution to the philosophical inquiry taking place in the *Rêve*. Julie becomes the protagonist in the third and last part of the dialogue. The two philosophers having left the scene, the doctor and the young woman are left to converse tête-à-tête; and just as d'Alembert's dialogue with Diderot converted him to the free play of hypothesis and conjecture, so Julie is freed of her prejudices by her dialogue with Bordeu. Nothing is more rooted in the female mentality than sexual taboo. An increasingly erotic atmosphere contributes to the emancipation of the innocent Mlle de Lespinasse. She feigns not to notice that d'Alembert, envisaging a physical universe in a state of perpetual ferment, and noticing her beside him, finally has an orgasm in his sleep. Meanwhile, the libertine Bordeu's cunning strategy, his compliments, his allusions, and his jokes awaken Julie's curiosity and induce her

---

106. Quoted in Glotz and Maire, *Salons du XVIIIe siècle*, p. 7.

107. P. N. Furbank, "D'Alembert's Dream," in *Diderot: A Critical Biography* (Knopf, 1992), pp. 327–342.

to ask boldly about sex. So here she is with the doctor, launched on a reckless discussion of carnal desire, onanism, homosexuality, and interracial relations. If it is true, as Bordeu maintains, that they are all natural, perfectly acceptable impulses, what becomes of vice and virtue, self-esteem, shame, and regret? The doctor's reply returns to the derisory idea of the self: that it is "puerility based on the ignorance and vanity of a being who ascribes to himself the merit or otherwise of a necessary instant."[108] Once again Diderot, in keeping with libertine thought, used his talent as an erotic writer for intellectual provocation. Once again, sex served as a metaphor in his writing. In her conversation with Bordeu, the fictional Julie showed that she had understood the Enlightenment message at its deepest level: there are no questions that cannot be asked; there are no thoughts that cannot be thought.

The decision to make Mlle de Lespinasse one of the characters in the *Rêve* was probably not based on the demands of verisimilitude alone. It was of course well known that Julie was d'Alembert's closest friend—if not his mistress—and the malicious allusions in the dialogue to their relationship helped to make Diderot's narrative both credible and saucy. Moreover, in choosing Mlle de Lespinasse, a lady known for her refinement and the pure elegance of her speech, he delighted in putting words and conversations into her mouth that were absolutely out of character. It is hardly surprising that the real Julie was horrified to find herself portrayed in such an explicitly intimate scene with d'Alembert, carefully listening to Bordeu's libertine statements and talking to him about physiology and sexual perversion. But what might have seemed like a joke in the worst taste was in fact of great importance to Diderot; and the initiation of his character Julie to "frank talk" was profoundly significant. Society conversation, with its rules and its circumspection, had become a sterile game. The search for truth demanded the sacrifice of social convention.

Fontenelle had claimed at the beginning of the century "that he did not like war because it spoiled conversation,"[109] but for Diderot and those who shared his opinions, conversation itself was becoming an instrument of war. "Opinion, all of whose force for good and for evil you know," he wrote to the minister of finance, Jacques Necker, on June 22, 1775, "originates only from the effect of a small number of men who speak after having thought and who endlessly create, at different points in society, centers of instruction from whence their reasoned truths and errors spread from person to person until they reach the confines of the city where they become established as articles of faith.... What we write influences only a certain class of citizen, our conversation influences everyone."[110]

108. Diderot, *Le Rêve de d'Alembert*, in *Œuvres complètes*, Vol. 17, p. 186.

109. Mme Necker, *Mélanges*, Vol. 1, p. 211.

110. *Choix de lettres du XVIIIe siècle, publiées avec une introduction, des notices et des notes de Gustave Lanson* (Paris: Hachette, 1891), p. 211.

The Swiss banker Necker was one of the first to understand the extraordinary political power of public opinion, on the wave of which he was called three times to rescue France from financial ruin. And knowing that his success depended on opinion more than on the exercise of power, he courted it like no one else. Shortly before he died, long after public opinion had finally abandoned him—and when the French Revolution had proved it to be so brutally fickle—he paid it his last respects: "Public opinion is stronger and more enlightened than the law; it is stronger because it is everywhere present and exercises its empire within society and right into the heart of the family; it is more enlightened because, whereas the law may be the work of one man who might be mistaken, opinion results from the thoughts of nations and centuries."[111] Faithful to her husband's beliefs, Mme Necker recognized the prestige of ideas, but while acknowledging their immense power, she also understood the responsibility that came with this power: "Since opinion has become queen of the world, one must pay a great deal more attention to every word one utters; words soon turn to actions and even take the place and have the strength of the law."[112]

A sense of responsibility did nothing, however, to check the socialites' cheerful experimentalism. Whereas in 1750 Lord Chesterfield was still recommending that his son read Crébillon's novels as an aid to understanding Parisian high society, only twelve years later the critic and playwright La Harpe, writing of *Les Égarements du cœur et de l'esprit* in the *Correspondance littéraire*, claimed that the work was outdated, as were "the originals on whom it was modeled," and "that there were no more characters like Versac, either at court or in the town, because if there had been, they would have been *de mauvais ton*"—in bad taste.[113]

"*Petits-maîtres* are obsolete," remarked Horace Walpole, another Englishman of rank who visited Paris at the time, with a certain disappointment, "but *le monde est philosophe*."[114] Had frivolity really gone out of fashion, or had philosophy become frivolous? Talleyrand was to recall in his memoirs how even the Duc de Lauzun (the *ancien régime*'s last aristocratic dandy), the Duc de Chartres (the future Philippe Égalité), and the Prince de Guémené were introduced to metaphysics by the Marquis de Voyer: "It was ever the soul . . . space . . . the chain of being . . . abstraction . . . matter . . . composites . . . simple . . . without breadth . . . indivisible, etc. All

---

111. *Manuscrits de M. Necker publiés par sa fille* (Geneva: J.-J. Paschoud, "an XIII,") p. 141; quoted in Jean-Denis Bredin, *Une singulière famille: Jacques Necker, Suzanne Necker et Germaine de Staël* (Paris: Fayard, 1999), p. 372.

112. Madame Necker, *Mélanges*, Vol. 2, p. 341.

113. La Harpe, *Correspondance littéraire*, Vol. 2, pp. 10–11. Crébillon's novel *The Wayward Head and Heart* is also discussed in Chapter 14.

114. Horace Walpole to Thomas Gray, November 19, 1765, in *Horace Walpole's Correspondence*, Vol. 13, p. 145.

these words, never defined, and pronounced at intervals with gestures, pauses, in mystical ways, prepared the young adepts to believe. Then they were taught that all sentiment was merely ridiculous, that all scruple was weakness, that justice was prejudice, that self-interest and pleasure alone should determine all our actions."[115]

What shocked Walpole, and even surprised the philosopher David Hume, in the Baron d'Holbach's house was not so much the boldness of opinion or the violent antireligious polemic, as the imprudence with which such matters were publicly discussed: "The French affect philosophy, literature, and freethinking.... Freethinking is for one's self, surely not for society," he wrote to his friend George Montagu, saying he had just dined with a "dozen *savants*" and "though all the servants were waiting, the conversation was much more unrestrained, even on the Old Testament, than I would suffer at my own table in England, if a single footman was present."[116] And a month later Walpole reiterated this impression: "Laughing is as much out of fashion as pantins or bilboquets. Good folks, they have no time to laugh. There is God and the King to be pulled down first; and men and women, one and all, are devoutly employed in the demolition."[117]

But society conversation, beginning with that of the *philosophes*, was by its very nature eclectic and could never be reduced to a single register. On October 20, 1760, in a letter of at least twelve pages to his beloved Sophie Volland, Diderot described certain guests and their "prattling around the fireplace" at the Baron d'Holbach's country house. The company included Mme Geoffrin, the Baron Grimm, and the Abbé Galiani. Realizing that his account included a great variety of subjects, Diderot reflected on the intrinsic logic of such digressions:

> What a singular thing is conversation, especially when the company is numerous. See what digressions we made; a delirious man's dreams could not be more irregular. However, since there is nothing disconnected, either in the head of a man who dreams or in that of a madman, everything also holds together in conversation; but it would sometimes be impossible to find the imperceptible threads that have drawn together so many disparate ideas. A man throws out a word that he has detached from what went before and follows it in his mind; another does the same, then catch it who can. Only one physical quality can guide the mind, which concerns itself with an infinity of different things. Let us take a color—yellow for example: gold is yellow, silk is yellow, care is yellow, bile is yellow, straw is yellow; and to how

---

115. *Mémoires de Talleyrand (1754–1815)*, p. 114.

116. Horace Walpole to George Montagu, September 22, 1765, in *Horace Walpole's Correspondence*, Vol. 10, p. 176.

117. Horace Walpole to Thomas Brand, October 19, 1765, in *Horace Walpole's Correspondence*, Vol. 11, p. 384.

many other threads is this thread attached? Madness, dreaming, the unraveled nature of conversation consists in passing from one subject to another by way of a common quality.[118]

Obviously conversation depending on the association of ideas required remarkably quick reactions and a perfect knowledge of facts and people, without which the point might be missed, just as it was by Horace Walpole—in spite of his dreadful snobbery and passion for gossip. In 1775, on visiting Paris for the sixth time for personal amusement and to see Mme du Deffand, Walpole self-indulgently immersed himself in society life but failed to disguise his British sense of irony. In a letter to the Countess of Ossory, his sarcasm was no longer directed, as it had been ten years earlier, at society conversation's philosophical pretensions, but at its inconsequentiality, of which he gave an example:

> Avez-vous lu des deux Éloges? Ah! Mon Dieu, le petit Cossé est mort; c'est une désolation!—et Monsieur de Clermont qui vient de perdre sa femme!— eh bien, Madame! Et Monsieur Chamboneau qui doit reprendre la sienne— mais c'est affreux—à propos, on dit qu'on vient de nommer deux dames à Madame Élizabeth! si je le sais! Bon; ne voilà-t-il-pas que je viens de me faire écrire chez Madame de Roncherolles! soupez-vous par hasard chez Madame de la Reinière!—This is the quintessence, Madam, of the present state of Paris, Sept. 9, 1775.... You may boast of having the freshest and most fashionable intelligence of what was said last night at half an hour after eight in one of the first houses in this capital.[119]

Yet if, following Diderot, we try to see these apparently unconnected sentences in a topical light pertaining to a communal experience, their apparent disjointedness can be seen, even at a distance of two centuries, to have a logic of their own. The Académie française had announced a competition for a eulogy of the distinguished Maréchal de Catinat, in which one academician—Antoine Léonard Thomas, the undisputed master of the genre—had beaten another, the Comte de Guibert. Anyone wishing to be up to date would have read both eulogies. Walpole's socialites, following the threads introduced by one topical subject, moved from praising a

118. Letter from Diderot to Sophie Volland of October 20, 1760, in Denis Diderot, *Correspondance*, in *Œuvres*, edited by Laurent Versini, five volumes (Paris: Laffont, 1997), Vol. 5, p. 271.

119. "Have you read the two *Éloges*? Oh, *mon Dieu*, the little Cossé is dead! How devastating! And M. de Clermont just lost his wife!—Indeed, Madame, and M. Chamboneau must have his back again—But how horrible!—By the way, they say that two women are being named to Madame Elizabeth [at Court] —Well, I have just been to see Mme de Roncherolles! Are you by any chance dining with Mme de la Reinière?..." Horace Walpole to the Countess of Ossory, September 9, 1775, in *Horace Walpole's Correspondence*, Vol. 32, pp. 258–259.

distinguished, lately deceased gentleman of the *Grand Siècle*, the Maréchal, to regretting two recent deaths. Talk of Mme de Clermont's death led to thoughts of another wife, a lady whose husband wished to be rid of her. Even if the *à propos* that followed escapes the modern reader, the subsequent associations are clear (and must have been absolutely clear to anyone who truly belonged to that world). Two new ladies-in-waiting to Louis XVI's sister were the Marquise de Causans and the Comtesse de Canillac, née Roncherolles, which was probably why one of the interlocutors had just called on her mother, the Marquise de Roncherolles. And since the subject of visits had come up, why would someone else not mention going to sup with Mme de La Reynière? (In order to forget that she was merely a great financier's wife, Mme de La Reynière had made her salon into one of the most brilliant in Paris.)

Walpole's parody reduced the two most typical aspects of society conversation to their bare essentials: speed and the art of moving on. The writer Louis Sébastien Mercier, a chronicler of genius who was not in the least indulgent, admired these very talents only a few years after the Englishman had been so cutting:

> With what delicacy are human opinions tossed about in Paris! . . . But above all, with what ease is one subject moved onto from another, and how many things are discussed in so few hours! It must be admitted that conversation in Paris has been perfected to a point where there is none other like it in the rest of the world. Each flash of wit is like the stroke of an oar, both light and deep. The same subject is not long considered; but there is a general tone whereby every idea is relevant to the matter in question. The pros and the cons are discussed with singular speed. It is a delicate pleasure that can belong only to an extremely polished society that has laid down refined rules that are always observed. A man lacking in this tact, although he has wit, is as dumb as he is deaf. It is impossible to say how the subject changes so rapidly from the analysis of a play to a discussion of [the American Revolution]. The links are imperceptible; but they are there for the attentive listener. The connections, however tenuous, are nonetheless real; and if one is born to think, it is impossible not to perceive that everything is linked, that everything touches everything else, and that a multitude of ideas is needed to produce one good one.[120]

A letter of January 16, 1780, from the Chevalier de Lisle to the Prince de Ligne takes us to the Versailles apartment of the Comtesse Diane de Polignac, the sister-in-law of Marie-Antoinette's dearest friend, Gabrielle de Polignac. No cloud yet threatens the radiant happiness of the young guests, whose heedlessness would

---

120. Mercier, "De la conversation," in *Tableau de Paris*, Vol. 1, pp. 42–43.

soon prove fatal to the French monarchy. The only common ideas running through their disjointed conversations seemed to be a blind optimism and a great *joie de vivre*:

> What a turkey we've just eaten at the countess Diane's! My god, what a fine beast! Monsieur de Poix had sent it from the poultry yard. There were eight of us around him: the mistress of the house, Madame la Comtesse Jules, Madame d'Hénin and Madame de la Force, Monsieur le Comte d'Artois, Monsieur de Vaudreuil, the Chevalier de Crussol, and myself.... Thereupon we spoke of you, and then of Admiral Keppel, then of the turkey, then of the taking of our two frigates, of the Inquisition in Spain, and then of a big Gruyère cheese that our ambassador in Switzerland has just sent to his children, then of the Spaniards' strange treatment of us, and then of Mademoiselle Théodore, who dances, upon my faith, better than ever, and who yesterday charmed us as much by her talent as did Mademoiselle Cécile by her youthful attraction.... The King shows himself every day to be a good husband, a good father, and a good man; one cannot see him without truly liking him, nor without judging him to be the soul of probity; I assure you that we are fortunate to have that particular couple on our throne; may the heavens, who in their goodness placed them there, long preserve them.... We are all going to Paris tomorrow to celebrate the opening of the charming little house that Monsieur le Duc de Coigny has given himself and where we will put... What do you think we will put?... We will put knives on the table for the first time. We will have raillery, proverbs, couplets, fun of every kind; it will be a very fine ceremony.[121]

Naturalness, lightness of touch, a sense of the *à propos*, and the art of moving from one subject to another were all sadly missing in Suzanne Curchod, the young Swiss teacher who in 1764 married Jacques Necker, the rich banker who had moved to Paris from Geneva some time before. Mme Necker was beautiful, cultivated, virtuous, and in love with her husband. She could have been happily herself had she not nurtured the ambition to make her house a social center from which to launch the career of her "great man." In fact Mme Necker dedicated herself to her purpose methodically and with discipline, taking to herself the only day of the week remaining free in the Parisian social calendar—Friday—and creating what was destined to be the last great salon of the *ancien régime*. In the first place, however, as Sainte-Beuve put it, she had to "reshape her mind to suit the people, the circumstances, and the conversation."[122] For all the goodwill, her metamorphosis

---

121. *Choix de lettres du XVIIIe siècle*, pp. 567–569.

122. Quoted in Sainte-Beuve, "Madame Necker," in *Causeries du lundi*, Vol. 4, p. 247.

was not entirely successful. According to Marmontel, who assiduously attended her salon, "one saw her busy making herself agreeable to her guests, concerned to receive properly those she had invited, careful to say what might most please each person; but it was all premeditated; nothing flowed naturally."[123] It was, in fact, so "premeditated" that according to Mme de Genlis, the Chevalier de Chastellux, having arrived early one day, found under an armchair a little notebook in which the mistress of the house had written "all that she must say to the most important invited guests."

> He was himself mentioned in the following terms, "I will talk to the Chevalier de Chastellux about [his] *Félicité publique* and *Agathe*."[124] Then Mme Necker said she would speak to Mme d'Angiviller about love and she would instigate a literary discussion between Messieurs Marmontel and de Guibert. There were further preparations that I have forgotten. Having read this little book, Monsieur de Chastellux was careful to replace it under the chair. A moment later a valet came to say that Mme Necker had left her pocket book in the drawing room. He looked for it and took it to her. This dinner was a delight for Monsieur de Chastellux because he had the pleasure of hearing Mme Necker say, word for word, everything that she had written in her pocket book.[125]

Aware of her failings, Mme Necker made up for her lack of *esprit* and ease of manner with application and study. She was an acute observer and little by little she noted her impressions and opinions with a view to correcting and improving herself, and above all so as to learn the rules of the world she wished to conquer. Meant strictly for her own personal use but published by her husband after her death, her *Mélanges* record the moral tensions of an anxious and demanding person while, at the same time, constituting the last manual of manners to be written in France on the eve of the Revolution:

---

123. Marmontel, *Mémoires*, p. 331.

124. François-Jean de Chastellux, *De la félicité publique, ou Considérations sur le sort des hommes dans les différentes époques de l'histoire*, 1772; *Agathe*, performed in 1775, is one of the five plays Chastellux wrote for the private theater at the château de La Chevrette, formerly owned by Mme d'Épinay's husband, and acquired in 1736 by Charles-Pierre de Savalette de Magnaville, keeper of the royal treasure. With the help of his daughter, Mme de Pernan, and his niece, Geneviève, the future Marquise de Gléon, Magnaville followed Mme d'Épinay's example. In around 1749 she had founded one of the most famous eighteenth-century society theaters at La Chevrette. In the 1770s performances at the château were very successful. See Fanny Varnum, *Un philosophe cosmopolite du XVIIIe siècle: Le Chevalier de Chastellux* (Paris: Rodstein, 1936), pp. 78–81 and 240.

125. Mme de Genlis, *Mémoires inédits sur le XVIIIe siécle et la Révolution française*, Vol. 3, pp. 320–321.

When one receives or makes a visit, one must sit down quietly, have a calm manner, through the eyes express both interest and attentiveness, speak using refined and obliging words, never employing too strong an expression; one must not attempt to show how one is connected to the distinguished people under discussion, nor wish to take over and enliven the conversation; one must tolerate several pauses, await one's turn to speak and not seek it. Thus one shows oneself to be above what one says; but to push oneself forward is to presume that one finds one's thought worthy of admiration. One must not hasten to tell stories; and one must allow oneself to be abandoned in conversation only when carried away by movements of the soul, through pain or indignation and in spite of oneself. Abandon may also be permitted in cases of gaiety; but cold forcefulness always displeases.[126]

The greatest test lay naturally in the role to which Mme Necker most aspired, that of supervising the conversations of others:

The government of a conversation closely resembles that of a state; one must be barely aware of the authority that conducts it. Neither the administrator nor the lady of the house should ever concern themselves with things that work by themselves, but should avoid the ills and inconveniences that arise along the way, remove all obstacles, and revive whatever languishes. The lady of the house must prevent the conversation from taking a boring, disagreeable, or dangerous turn; but she must do nothing so long as the original impetus suffices and does not need renewing; to accelerate too much is to inconvenience.[127]

It is remarkable that rules of behavior elaborated 150 years earlier at the hôtel de Rambouillet were still adhered to in a world in which everything was changing with extraordinary speed. For French noblewomen, these rules had become second nature, but for a provincial Swiss woman to decipher them, as much effort, concentration, and seriousness were required as for the understanding of a new liturgy.

Mme Necker was not always equal to the task she had set herself, and Marmontel recalls how much she minded: "Concerned and anxious, as soon as she saw the scene and the conversation languish, her look searched for the reason in our eyes. She was sometimes even naive enough to complain to me. 'What do you want, Madame,' I said, 'one is not witty at will, and one is not always in a mood to be agreeable. Look at Monsieur Necker himself and see if he is amusing

126. Mme Necker, *Mélanges*, Vol. 2, pp. 239–240.

127. Mme Necker, *Mélanges*, Vol. 2, pp. 1–2.

every day.'"[128] The example can have been of little comfort, since Necker was absolutely "nothing" in conversation and "broke his silence only to subtly mock or to make some sharp witticism about the *philosophes* and men of letters, with whom, in his opinion, his wife was a little infatuated."[129] Not that that prevented the Enlightenment elite from gathering happily in his drawing room to continue with conversations interrupted the previous evening at the Baron d'Holbach's. They were merely careful to avoid the subject of religion, which was incompatible with Mme Necker's fervent Protestantism. In his faraway Naples, Galiani was present on Fridays in spirit, his cheerful banter in the purest style of Vincent Voiture:

To Madame Necker
Naples, August 4, 1770

But it is on condition that you do not reply with a too beautiful or too sublime letter; I want to know from you, Madame, quite simply, quite plainly, how are you? What are you doing? How is Monsieur Necker? What is he doing? Are you amusing yourself? Are you bored? These are the questions about which I am curious. They are natural, since, do not doubt it, there is not a Friday when I do not visit you in spirit. I arrive, I find you sometimes putting the finishing touches to your finery, sometimes listening to this duchess. I sit at your feet, Thomas suffers quietly, Morellet rages out loud, Grimm and Suard laugh good-heartedly, and my dear Comte de Creutz does not notice. Marmontel finds the example worthy of imitation, and you, Madame, cause two of your finest virtues, modesty and *politesse*, to contend with one another, and in suffering thus, you discover me to be a little monster, more embarrassing than odious.

Supper is announced. We leave the room, the others are eating meat, I am fasting, I eat a great deal of that green Scottish cod that I like very well, I give myself an indigestion while admiring the skill with which the Abbé Morellet carves a young turkey. We leave the table and the coffee is served, everyone talks at once. The Abbé Raynal agrees with me that Boston and English America are forever separated from England; and at the same moment, Creutz and Marmontel agree that Grétry is the French Pergolesi; Monsieur Necker finds that good, lowers his head, and leaves.

Those are my Fridays. Do you see me at your house, as I see you? Have you as much imagination as I? If you can see me and if you can touch me,

128. Marmontel, *Mémoires*, p. 331.

129. *Mémoires de l'abbé Morellet*, p. 144.

you will feel that at present I tenderly kiss your hand, but you smile; farewell then, I am content."[130]

In contrast to her mother's social shortcomings, the daughter of the house displayed a talent for the *à propos* at an early age, replying wittily and pertinently to the guests. These delighted in questioning her as, on reception days, Mlle Necker sat up straight on a small wooden stool at her mother's feet. The Neckers' only child was born in Paris in 1766. With a diligence bordering on fanaticism, her mother devoted herself personally to her education. At the age of seven, Germaine could not yet run, but she danced perfectly; she had never had time to play with other children, but she was a walking encyclopedia. Diderot and Buffon took an interest in her studies; Carmontelle described her in one of his famous profiles; Grimm waited to publish her first compositions in his *Correspondance littéraire*.

A terrible disappointment, however, awaited Mme Necker; with the passing of the years Germaine became less and less like the perfect creature of which her mother dreamed but developed instead into a truly extraordinary person, that is to say, beyond and above the normal. The overpowering strength of her intelligence was irresistible, as were the intensity of her emotions and the charm of her speech. Her desire to profit from whatever opportunities life offered was insatiable. Having soon been disappointed in her marriage in 1786 to the Baron de Staël, the Swedish ambassador to Versailles, she embarked on a string of love affairs with a long list of men, giving birth to children from different fathers. Indifferent to scandal, she obeyed only the changing dictates of her own heart. Benjamin Constant, with whom she had a long, dramatic affair, would bear witness to her "perfect good faith" because Mme de Staël had, throughout all her changing feelings and circumstances, "an accent of truth" that defeated her interrogators. Constant had to admit, "Reason, which one thought one possessed, disappears, and one pinches oneself to see if one is still the same being, if one still has the same intelligence one had an hour prior to hearing her speak."[131]

As a girl, Germaine was allowed to attend her parents' dinners on condition that she listen in silence. But no silence was ever more eloquent. "It had to be seen how Mademoiselle Necker listened!" Mme Rilliet-Huber wrote in her memoirs. "Her eyes followed the movements of those who were speaking and seemed to anticipate their ideas. She did not open her mouth and yet seemed to be taking her turn in speaking, her mobile features were so expressive. She was aware of everything, grasped everything, even political subjects which, at the time, were one of the great matters of conversational interest."[132] When the time came for Germaine to

---

130. Galiani to Madame Necker, in Galiani, *Correspondance*, Vol. 1, pp. 227–229.

131. Quoted in Bredin, *Une singulière famille*, p. 371.

132. Catherine Rilliet-Huber, "Notes sur l'enfance de Mme de Staël," in *Occident* 1; quoted in Ghislain de Diesbach, *Madame de Staël* (Paris: Perrin, 1983), p. 37.

speak, the *ancien régime* would find in her the last supreme interpreter of the art of conversation.

For Mme de Staël, born into aristocratic civilization, society life was a necessity, the only way of being in the world and remaining happy. Nothing seemed more terrible to her than the threat of boredom, nothing more painful than solitude and silence. She herself told her husband quite simply that she could not live without her friends and that "animated, intelligent" conversation was indispensable to her. She wrote in De *l'Allemagne*:

> The feeling of satisfaction that characterizes an animated conversation does not so much consist of its subject matter. Neither the ideas nor the knowledge that may emerge within it are of primary interest. Rather, it is a certain manner in which some people have an effect on others; of reciprocally and rapidly giving one another pleasure; of speaking just as quickly as one thinks; of spontaneously enjoying oneself; of being applauded without working; of displaying one's wit through all the nuances of accent, gesture, and look, in order to produce at will a sort of electricity that causes sparks to fly, and that relieves some people of the burden of their excess vivacity and awakens others from a state of painful apathy.[133]

Nevertheless, Mme de Staël was not merely seeking pleasure. She was not content with being the marvelous follower of an epoch but wanted, through the power of speech, to create a new, freer, and more just epoch. Her conversation covered every realm of human knowledge, from literature to politics, from philosophy to economics, history, psychology, and the morality of men and nations. If necessary, she was ready to put her ideas into action. Fate meant that she was able to pit her strength against extraordinary events—the end of the absolute monarchy, the Revolution, the Empire—fortified only by the sovereign authority her reputation brought her. Like her mother and her father, Mme de Staël believed in the cult of freedom and of glory, and she was strengthened in her political affiliations by extreme courage. Nevertheless, when sent into exile by Napoleon for ten years, nothing could console her for her absence from Paris because Paris "was the place in the world where one could best do without happiness."[134]

Never, according to Talleyrand, had "the pleasure of living" been so strongly or so widely felt as in the 1780s in Paris, when Mme de Staël was young and during the last years of the *ancien régime*.[135] "Never," wrote Jacques de Norvins, a

---

133. Mme de Staël, *De l'Allemagne*, Vol. 1, pp. 101–102.

134. Mme de Staël, *De l'Allemagne*, Vol. 1, p. 104.

135. See François Guizot, *Mémoires pour servir à l'histoire de mon temps*, eight volumes (Paris: Michel Lévy frères, 1858–1867), Vol. 1, p. 6.

young friend of Germaine's whom she saved from the firing squad the day after the coup d'état on the Eighteenth of Fructidor (September 1797), "never, I believe, was sociability, for I would not say society, more brilliant, nor did it give more delight than at that period.... Innumerable large houses, hospitable eighteenth-century caravanserais were opened daily in Paris.... Encyclopedists and economists had the upper hand; the Fronde thus sidled into the salons.... Instead of showing themselves to be their protectors, grandees and millionaires paid court to this elite.... No one would have been prepared to contest what might happen to a grandee who forgot himself so much as to lack in respect to a scholar, an artist or an academician."[136] Under the guidance of the *philosophes*, this leisure-loving and highly literate class embarked on the boldest political speculations. Their salons were no longer "Blessed Islands" in which to take refuge from the interference and the brutality of power; they became an agora, in which some of the participants were ready to transform all of France into a utopia.

In addition to being centers of opinion, the salons were also centers of power that royal authority, as it weakened daily, was obliged to take into account. Every important circle had its potential ministers and its network of influence, and it was nearly always the women who held the reins. Their support was essential to a career in whatever branch of administration. It was in this world that the young Talleyrand, still the Abbé de Périgord, began his diplomatic career with single-minded determination.

Received as he was in all the houses that counted, the brilliant young abbé was able to observe high society from the inside in the last decade before the Revolution. He could not avoid seeing it as "a curious spectacle." In blatant disregard of etiquette's most elementary rules, a poet like the Abbé Delille was invited to dine with the Queen at the Comtesse de Polignac's house; a passion for gambling induced a prince of the blood like the Comte d'Artois to sit at the same table with the lowly Abbé Balivière, who had no title at all; the simple functionary Devaines shook hands with the Duc de Liancourt; and, forgetting his own illegitimate birth, the brilliant social climber Chamfort allowed himself to take the Comte de Vaudreuil's arm. "Gambling and the *bel esprit* had leveled everything. Careers, the great supporters of hierarchy and of order, were being destroyed. All young men considered themselves fit to govern. All ministerial action was criticized. What the King and the Queen did personally was subjected to discussion and nearly always met with the disapproval of the Paris salons. Young women spoke pertinently about all aspects of the administration."[137]

Now, Mme Necker complained in around 1788, there was no longer a place for literature in the conversations taking place in her drawing room. "One does

136. Norvins, *Mémorial*, Vol. 1, p. 160.

137. *Mémoires de Talleyrand (1754–1815)*, pp. 75–76.

not suggest playing a game of chess on the edge of a precipice; our attention is turned entirely on other things; and that flower of imagination, the last refuge of decency and delicacy, is lost in our political discussions."[138] But the onetime Swiss schoolteacher took everything too seriously and had no lightness of touch. Political fever had not only struck in the Necker household, with the finance minister being recalled for a third time to work a miracle, but it had spread right through society, bringing with it an exciting feeling of euphoria. The French nobility could remember no more fascinating a game from the mid-seventeenth-century days of the Fronde. Conversation had become openly critical of the government, confrontational, and conspiratorial, without, for all that, losing any of its gaiety, its verve, or its elegance. Talleyrand wrote in his *Mémoires*:

> I remember that at a ball, between two country dances, Mme de Staël was teaching Monsieur de Surgère what the *domaine d'Occident* was;[139] Mme de Blot had an opinion about all the officers in the French navy; Mme de Simiane maintained that no tax should be put on Virginian tobacco.... The Chevalier de Boufflers, who had several letters from Prince Henry of Prussia in his little wallet, was stating that France would regain its political supremacy only if it abandoned its alliance with Austria in favor of one with Prussia.... "Personally, were I in the King's place, I would do such and such a thing," Monsieur de Poix was saying. "In Monsieur le Comte d'Artois's place, I would tell the King...," remarked Saint-Blancard.[140]

Enslaved by its own unlimited power, conversation was betraying its calling for intimacy and private happiness and working toward its own ruin. By 1789 public oratory had taken over the monopoly of the spoken word, which would be revived after a long silence on the benches of the National Assembly.

The lights were soon to go out in the great ballroom where the French nobility was living the last days of the most brilliant of society seasons. The Constituent Assembly still allowed enthusiastic progressives to project the future, but soon events would overtake words, and the Revolution would set out on its path of blood and terror.

And it was precisely in its brutal, tragic epilogue, at the very moment in which it was about to be abolished, that the privileged order revealed its true value and the strength of its civilization. Deprived of everything, the nobility salvaged its style, and thanks to style, its honor. Hippolyte Taine wrote its epitaph in a famous paragraph:

---

138. Mme Necker, *Mélanges*, Vol. 1, p. 157.

139. The term described tax paid on goods coming from America and Canada.

140. *Mémoires de Talleyrand (1754–1815)*, p. 76.

In prison men and women would dress with care, pay each other visits, hold a salon; it would be at the end of a corridor, between four candles; but there they would joke, compose madrigals, sing songs, take pride in being as gallant, as gay, as gracious as before; should you be morose and uncouth because an accident has placed you in a bad inn? Before the judges and on the tumbril, they would retain their dignity and their smiles; women particularly went to the scaffold with the ease and serenity with which they attended a soirée. This supreme characteristic of *savoir-vivre*, built up as a unique duty, became second nature to the aristocracy, and was to be found in its virtues and in its vices, in its abilities and its impotence, in its prosperity and in its fall, adorning it even in death to which it led it.[141]

---

141. Hippolyte Taine, *Les Origines de la France contemporaine*, Vol. 1, pp. 315–316.

Bibliographical Essay

This bibliography makes no claim to be complete and merely indicates the books that gave me pleasure in the course of my work. It only includes modern literary criticism; the primary texts to which I refer in the chapters themselves are identified in the footnotes and are cited, as often as possible, in easily accessible critical editions.

CHAPTER I

On RELATIONS BETWEEN THE NOBILITY AND THE MONARCHY, see Pierre Deyon, "À propos des rapports entre la noblesse française et la monarchie absolue pendant la première moitié du XVIIIe siècle," in *Revue historique* 231 (1964), pp. 341–356; Oreste Ranum, "Richelieu and the Great Nobility," in *French Historical Studies*, Vol. 3 (1963), pp. 184–204, and "Courtesy, Absolutism and Rise of the French State, 1630–1660," in *Journal of Modern History*, Vol. 52, No. 3 (September 1980), pp. 426–451. In his second article, this American scholar shows how Richelieu, "obsessed all his life by both the theoretical and practical study of the relationships between language, gesture, and power" (p. 432), attached considerable importance to the courtesy due to the sovereign, placing it at the center of a plan that was clearly defined in his *Testament politique*.

On the CONFLICTS BETWEEN THE THREE ORDERS, see also Roland Mousnier, "L'évolution des institutions monarchiques en France et ses relations avec l'état sociale," in *XVIIe siècle* 58–59 (1963), pp. 57–72. On Richelieu's dual politics, see Michael Moriarty, *Taste and Ideology in Seventeenth-Century France* (Cambridge University Press, 1988), p. 36.

POLITESSE. The term is used here in the sense indicated by Harald Weinrich in a course he gave at the Collège de France, "L'invention de la politesse dans les langues et les littératures romanes." "Since the Sixties," Weinrich writes, "research into *politesse* has mostly been marked by the distinction between negative and positive *politesse*. This distinction, derived in the final analysis from Émile Durkheim, was developed, as has been noted, by Erving Goffman, who uses it to characterize two 'rituals of interaction': a strategy of avoidance (*évitement*) and a strategy of showing human behavior at its best. In his sociological approach, Goffman clearly favors negative *politesse* and concedes only a marginal place with a healing function to the positive kind. From these methodological premises, it could be inferred that *politesse* is a kind of communicative behavior, verbal or nonverbal, designed to save the 'face' (or social image) of another person against any threatening act ('face-threatening act,' FTA) and to 'restore' that face whenever it was damaged."

On the other hand, taking the opposite method as a point of departure, and taking positive *politesse* as primordial and as of the utmost importance, Weinrich proposes the following definition that is precisely the one to which my work refers: "*Politesse* is a positive form of verbal and nonverbal behavior, designed to discover, envisage, or imagine a certain individual or social excellence in another person, to save his face if that person either cannot or does not wish to excel in that sphere. The act of *politesse* in the history of Romance languages and literatures largely confirms the cognitive importance of positive *politesse*, right from the original act of *politesse* in the European sense of the word: the invention by the troubadours of *courtoisie*, in which *politesse* acquires—in comparison with classical *urbanitas*—a new spiritual center: woman.... In seventeenth-century France, *politesse* again becomes positive and an attempt is made to define the characteristics of politesse that 'makes man appear from the outside as he should be internally' (La Bruyère). This idealized *politesse* is based on the typically French model of the *honnête homme*." (*Annuaire du Collège de France 1993–1994. Résumé des cours et travaux*, 94th year, pp. 891–894.)

For an analysis of the genesis and complex gamut of meanings from which the word *politesse* derives, see Jean Starobinski's important essay "Le mot civilisation," in *Le Remède dans le mal: Critique et légitimation de l'artifice à l'âge des Lumières* (Paris: Gallimard, 1989), pp. 11–59, in English as *Blessings in Disguise, or, The Morality of Evil*, translated by Arthur Goldhammer (Harvard University Press, 1993); and Peter France's "Polish, police, polis," in *Politeness and Its Discontents: Problems in French Classical Culture* (Cambridge University Press, 1992), pp. 53–73.

Inseparable from *politesse*, the BIENSÉANCES comprise the rules that guarantee its application in all of life's circumstances. Dictated by reason, convention, and usage, the *bienséances* guide behavior in accordance with the ancient rhetorical criterion of *aptum*—suitability—and, according to Morvan de Bellegarde, propose "doing so in such a way as to give everyone his due and never to do anything that might displease anyone" (*Les Réflexions sur le ridicule et sur les moyens de l'éviter, où sont representez les mœurs et les differents caractères des personnes de ce siècle*, Paris: J. Guignard, 1695, p. 360). The *bienséances* define the distinctive character of the nobility's style and are indispensable to life in society. Lord Chesterfield, who went to Paris especially to learn the *bienséances*, explained them to his son in a letter of June 13, 1751: "The bienséances are a most necessary part of the knowledge of the world. They consist in the relations of persons, things, time, and place; good sense points them out, good company perfects them (supposing always an attention and a desire to please), and good policy recommends them. Were you to converse with a king, you ought to be as easy and unembarrassed as with your own valet-de-chambre; but yet every look, word, and action, should imply the utmost respect." (*The Letters of Philip Dormer Stanhope, 4th Earl of Chesterfield*, edited by Bonamy Dubrée, six volumes, London: Eyre and Spottiswoode, 1932, Vol. 4, pp. 1750–1751.)

See also on the entry on *bienséances* and the bibliography by Alain Montandon in the *Dictionnaire raisonné de la politesse et du savoir-vivre du Moyen Âge à nos jours*, edited by Alain Montandon (Paris: Éditions du Seuil, 1995), pp. 29–46.

PUBLIC OPINION. See Jürgen Habermas, *The Structural Transformation of the Public Sphere: An Inquiry into a Category of Bourgeois Society* (1962), translated by Thomas Burger with the assistance of Frederick Lawrence (MIT Press, 1991). In describing the genesis in seventeenth-century French noble society of a "public" of readers, spectators, and audience with an ever-growing confidence in its own aesthetic, psychological, and moral judgment, Habermas already sees "modern characteristics" in "the thoroughly aristocratic polite life of these circles," beginning with the hôtel de Rambouillet (p. 31). But he maintains that one can speak of the birth of genuine public opinion only when that "public" became openly critical of established authority—that is, after 1715. It seems to me, however, that on more than one occasion in the seventeenth century, from the unrest of the Fronde to the Jansenist disputes and in literary discussions, French civil society made the force of its beliefs felt. But as Christian Jouhaud points out, the opinion of the times was divided and fragmentarily expressed (see his "Retour aux mazarinades: 'opinion publique,' action politique et production pamphlétaire pendant la Fronde," in *La Fronde en questions*, Actes du XVIIIe Colloque C.M.R., edited by Pierre Ronzeaud and Roger Duchêne, Provence: Publications de l'Université de Provence, 1989, pp. 297–307). Even Louis XIV's absolutism was unable to prevent underground dissent at the heart of the elite, as can clearly be seen from Marc Fumaroli's *Le Poète et le Roi: Jean de La Fontaine en son siècle* (Paris: Éditions de Fallois, 1997), in English as *The Poet and the King: Jean De La Fontaine and His Century*, translated by Jane Marie Todd (University of Notre Dame Press, 2002).

On the FORMATION OF PUBLIC OPINION, see primarily Daniel Mornet's classic study *Les Origines intellectuelles de la Révolution française 1715–1787* (first edition 1933; Paris: Colin, 1967), and Mona Ozouf's essay "L'opinion publique" in *The French Revolution and the Creation of Modern Political Culture*, four volumes (Oxford: Pergamon Press, 1997–1994), Vol. I: *The Political Culture of the Old Regime*, edited by Keith Michael Baker, pp. 419–434. For the significance and genesis of the term in eighteenth-century France, see Keith Michael Baker, "Politique et opinion publique sous l'Ancien Régime," in *Annales*, Vol. 42, No. 1 (January–February 1987), pp. 41–71, and *Inventing the French Revolution: Essays on French Political*

Culture in the Eighteenth Century (Cambridge University Press, 1990). See also Daniel Gordon, "'Public Opinion' and the Civilizing Process in France: The Example of Morellet," in *Eighteenth-Century Studies*, Vol. 22, No. 3 (Spring 1989), pp. 303–328, reprinted in *Citizens without Sovereignty: Equality and Sociability in French Thought, 1670–1789* (Princeton University Press, 1994). Essential in its turn is Roger Chartier's *Les Origines culturelles de la Révolution française* (Paris: Éditions du Seuil, 1991). See also Arlette Farge, *Dire et mal dire: L'opinion publique au XVIIIe siècle* (Paris: Éditions du Seuil, 1992), and *Opinione Lumi Rivoluzione*, edited by Alberto Postigliola, Materiali della Società italiana di studi sul secolo XVIII (Rome, 1993). Robert Darnton's studies, on the other hand, have thrown light on how the desacralization of established authority by clandestine, scandalous, and pornographic publications extraneous to the Enlightenment influenced the people. Of particular interest is the American historian's book written in French, *Éditions et sédition: L'univers de la littérature clandéstine au XVIIIe siècle* (Paris: Gallimard, 1991), but "gossip" and opinion are the subjects of Darnton's essay "Paris: The Early Internet," *The New York Review of Books*, June 29, 2000. On the links between public opinion and polite society, see Daniel Gordon, *Citizens without Sovereignty*, pp. 199–208.

PUBLIC–PRIVATE in the social sphere. Is the salon regarded as a private place, or does it belong in the public sphere? There is a critical assessment of the subject in Erica Harth, *Cartesian Women: Versions and Subversions of Rational Discourse in the Old Regime* (Cornell University Press, 1992), pp. 23–25.

MME DE RAMBOUILLET. There is no study of seventeenth-century French literature, society, or culture that does not devote at least one paragraph to Mme de Rambouillet, beginning with the Comte de Roederer's *Fragments de divers mémoires pour servir à la histoire de la société polie en France* (Paris: Didot, 1834) and *Mémoire pour servir à l'histoire de la société polie en France* (Paris: Didot, 1835). "After reading it, it is no longer permissible to talk of the hôtel de Rambouillet, as happened formerly, with disdain" (Sainte-Beuve, "Roederer," in *Causeries du lundi*, sixteen volumes, third edition, revised and corrected, Paris: Garnier, 1857–1870, Vol. 8, p. 390). Here I will mention only essential reading: Victor Cousin, *La Société française au XVIIe siècle d'après le Grand Cyrus de Mlle de Scudéry*, two volumes (Paris: Didier, 1852); Charles-Louis Livet, *Précieux et précieuses: Caractères et mœurs littéraires du XVIIe siècle* (Paris: Didier, 1859); Maurice Magendie, *La Politesse mondaine et les théories de l'honnêteté en France au XVIIe siècle, de 1600 à 1660* (Paris: PUF, 1925; Geneva: Slatkine Reprints, 1970); Émile Magne, *Voiture et l'hôtel de Rambouillet: Les origines, 1597–1635* (new enlarged, corrected edition, Paris: Émile-Paul frères, 1929), and *Voiture et les années de gloire de l'Hôtel de Rambouillet, 1635–1648* (Paris: Émile-Paul frères, 1912); Georges Mongrédien, *La Vie littéraire au XVIIe siècle* (Paris: Tallandier, 1947), pp. 13–34; Antoine Adam, *Histoire de la littérature française au XVIIe siècle* (1948; Paris: Albin Michel, 1997), Vol. 1, pp. 263–275; Marc Fumaroli, *L'Âge de l'éloquence: Rhétorique et "res literaria" de la Renaissance au seuil de l'époque classique* (1980;

Paris: Albin Michel, 1994). The work of reference on Mme de Rambouillet is, however, Nicole Aronson's biography, *Mme de Rambouillet ou la magicienne de la Chambre bleue* (Paris: Fayard, 1988). Useful and interesting too, is Barbara Krajewska's study *Mythes et découvertes: Le salon littéraire de Mme de Rambouillet dans les lettres des contemporains*, Biblio 17 (Paris-Seattle-Tübingen: PFSCL, 1990), which sets out to "demystify" the celebrated marquise's overidealized image and that of her circle.

EARLIER SALONS AND SALONS CONTEMPORARY WITH THE HÔTEL DE RAMBOUILLET. According to Linda Timmermans, "it was beginning around 1570, and not, as is generally thought, 1620 that salons were widely opened to poets, a new phenomenon at the time. It was also around this time that the salons began to replace the court as places for games of love, conversation, literary entertainment, and gallant and occasional verse." See her *L'Accès des femmes à la culture (1598–1715): Un débat d'idées de saint François de Sales à la marquise de Lambert* (Paris: Champion, 1993), p. 63.

See also L. Clark Keating, *Studies on the Literary Salon in France, 1550–1615* (Harvard University Press, 1941), and Evelyne Berriot-Salvadore, *Les Femmes dans la société française de la Renaissance* (Geneva: Droz, 1990).

The first of the new salons to open in Paris at the end of Henri IV's reign, and to be distinguished by its modern, purist orientation, in contrast to the humanist inspiration of the women's circles flourishing under the Valois, was that of Charlotte des Ursins, Vicomtesse d'Auchy (circa 1570–1646). Tallemant des Réaux dedicated to her one of his *Historiettes* (edited by Antoine Adam, two volumes, Paris: Gallimard/Bibliothèque de la Pléiade, 1960–1961, Vol. 1, pp. 132–137). See Georges Mongrédien, "Une rivale de la marquise de Rambouillet: la vicomtesse d'Auchy," Documents inédits, in *Mercure de France*, April 15, 1931, pp. 355–380; Émile Magne, *La Vie quotidienne au temps de Louis XIII* (Paris: Hachette, 1946), Chapter 7; Barbara Krajewska, "Quelques précisions touchant le salon de la vicomtesse d'Auchy," in *Papers on French Seventeenth Century Literature*, Vol. 19, No. 37 (1992), pp. 415–432. On Marie de Bruneau, Dame des Loges (1584–circa 1641), who also merited one of Tallemant's *Historiettes* (Vol. 1, pp. 606–608), see Jacques Pannier, "Le salon de Mme des Loges," in *L'Église réformée de Paris sous Louis XIII 1610–1621* (Strasbourg: Istra, 1922), pp. 338–343, then in two volumes (Paris: Champion, 1932), Vol. 1, pp. 341–347, Vol. 2, pp. 51–65. For Roger Zuber, Mme de Loges "is the only lady worthy of receiving the letters (and praise) of five different writers: Boisrobert, Godeau, Cosnac, Faret, and Racan" ("Le 'Cabinet d'Oradour': Mme de Loges en Limousin, 1629–1641," in *Le Limousin au XVIIᵉ siècle: Littérature, histoire, histoire religieuse*, Colloque pluridisciplinaire, Limoges, October 9–10, 1976, published in *Travaux et Mémoires de l'Université de Limoges*, U.E.R. des Lettres et Sciences Humaines, 88, p. 248). Thus, as René Bray writes, the Marquise de Rambouillet's salon "was not the first, was not initially the most brilliant, was not the originator of *politesse*, but it was the most renowned and the one that lasted longest" (*La Préciosité et les précieux de Thibaut de Champagne à Jean Giraudoux*, 1948; Paris: Nizet, 1968, p. 108). Of all the salons of the day, mention must at least be made of the one belonging to Mme de Rambouillet's great friend the Marquise de Clermont d'Entragues, which, according to Jean Mesnard, was "one of the main centers of intellectual and social life in Paris between 1620 and 1650" ("Mlle de Scudéry et la société du Marais," in *Mélanges offerts à Georges Couton*, Lyon: Presses Universitaires de Lyon, 1981, p. 173).

The word SALON in the modern sense of a place for social gatherings did not come into use until the end of the eighteenth century. In the sixteenth century, according to Furetière's *Dictionnaire universel* (1690), *salon* had the same meaning as the Italian word *salone* from which it is derived, and described a large room intended for official receptions. Right up until the French Revolution, a variety of words were used to describe both the leaders of society and the places where people met. Among the most common were *assemblée, société, compagnie, cercle, cour, cabale, alcôve, ruelle, cabinet, réduit*. See René Bray, *La Préciosité et les précieux de Thibaut de Champagne à Jean Giraudoux*, pp. 103f. Marc Fumaroli makes the point in the preface to Jacqueline Hellegouarc'h, *L'Esprit de société: Cercles et "salons" parisiens au XVIIIe siècle* (Paris: Garnier, 2000), p. xi, as does Hellegouarc'h in the foreword, pp. 1–2.

Among the numerous publications on SEVENTEENTH-CENTURY SALONS, note: Paulin Paris, *Des salons de Paris vers la fin du règne de Louis XIV* (Paris: Société des Bibliophiles, 1867); Gustave Desnoiresterres, *Les Cours galantes*, four volumes (Paris: Dentu, 1888); Roger Picard, *Les Salons littéraires et la société française (1610–1789)* (Brentano's, 1943); Lucien Brunel, "Les salons, la société, l'Académie," in *Histoire de la langue et de la littérature française des origines à 1900*, under the direction of Petit de Juleville, six volumes (Paris: A. Colin, 1898), Vol. 6, pp. 386–446; Georges Mongrédien, *La Vie de société aux XVIIe et XVIIIe siècles* (Paris: Hachette, 1950); *Au temps des précieuses: Les salons littéraires aux XVIIe siècle*, catalog edited by Jean Adhémar, preface by Étienne Dennery (Paris: Bibliothèque Nationale, 1968). Three excellent contributions to the subject of feminine society and culture come from the United States: Dorothy Anne Liot Backer, *Precious Women* (Basic Books, 1974); Carolyn Lougee, *Le Paradis des femmes: Women, Salons and Social Stratification in Seventeenth-Century France* (Princeton University Press, 1976); and Elizabeth C. Goldsmith, *"Exclusive Conversations": The Art of Interaction in Seventeenth-Century France* (University of Pennsylvania Press, 1988).

On the influence exercised over French literary life by the salons and society from the first half of the seventeenth century, see Alain Viala's important study, *Naissance de l'écrivain: Sociologie de la littérature à l'âge classique* (Paris: Éditions de Minuit, 1985).

On the theme of RETREAT, the most authoritative voice is Bernard Beugnot's, *Le Discours de la retraite au XVIIe siècle: Loin du monde et du bruit* (Paris: PUF, 1996). See also Beugnot's "Y-a-t-il une problématique feminine de la retraite?" in *Onze Études sur l'image de la femme dans la littérature française du dix-septième siècle*, edited by Wolfgang Leiner (Tübingen: Gunter Narr/Paris: Jean-Michel Place, 1978), pp. 25–40. See also Barbara Piqué, "Per una tipologia della 'retraite' nel Seicento," in *Micromegas*, Vol. 15, No. 3 (September–December 1988), pp. 3–14.

If the word CLASS is used, it is because a social mobility existed within the society of the Three Orders, making the use of the word "caste" unsuitable for the nobility. The nobility's attempts to establish itself as a caste have been analyzed by Alexis de Tocqueville, *L'Ancien Régime et la Révolution* (Paris: Gallimard, 1952), Vol. 1, Chapter 9, pp. 147f. On the same subject, see Paul Bénichou, *Morales du Grand Siècle* (1948; Paris: Gallimard, 1980); and Roland Mousnier, *La Vénalité des offices sous Henri IV et Louis XIII* (Rouen: Maugard, 1945), p. 503, and more generally, *Les Institutions de la France sous la monarchie absolue, 1598–1789*, two volumes (Paris: PUF, 1974).

On the NOBILITY'S IDENTITY and CULTURE, see Otto Brunner, *Vita nobiliare e cultura europea* (1949), translated by Giuseppina Panzieri (Bologna: Il Mulino, 1982), and René Bady's classic study *L'Homme et son "Institution," de Montaigne à Bérulle, 1580–1625* (Paris: Belles Lettres, 1964). I found particularly useful Davis Bitton's *The French Nobility in Crisis, 1560–1640* (Stanford University Press, 1969), in which, through fascinating analysis, the American historian reconstructs the contemporary debate about noble identity. The seventeenth-century nobleman's search for a new, aesthetic form of supremacy has been analyzed with great insight by Domna C. Stanton in *The Aristocrat as Art: A Study of the Honnête Homme and the Dandy in Seventeenth- and Nineteenth-Century French Literature* (Columbia University Press, 1980), one of the first studies devoted to the subject. See also François Billacois, "La crise de la noblesse européenne (1550–1650): une mise au point," in *Revue d'histoire moderne et contemporaine* 23 (January–March 1975), pp. 258–277; and Roberto Moro, *Il tempo dei Signori: Mentalità, ideologia, dottrine della nobiltà francese di Antico regime* (Rome: Savelli, 1981). I am also greatly indebted to Ellery Schalk's *From Valor to Pedigree: Ideas of Nobility in France in the Sixteenth and Seventeenth Centuries* (Princeton University Press, 1986), which illustrates the transformation in the nobility's traditional conception of itself, the way it presented itself, and the new importance assumed by the purity of lineage. On the nobility's ethic condemning commerce, see Daniel Dessert's study *Argent, pouvoir et société au Grand Siècle* (Paris: Fayard, 1984), which records the intense financial activity in the highest reaches of society (the Orléans, the Bouillons, the La Trémoilles, etc.) and points out a "congenital" contradiction between the financial organization under the *ancien régime* and caste morality. For the form and content of noble education, see Mark Motley's study *Becoming a French Aristocrat: The Education of the Court Nobility, 1580–1715* (Princeton University Press, 1990).

On the quintessential notion of DISTINCTION and its application to society, as much as to ethics and aesthetics, see Alain Faudemay, *La Distinction à l'âge classique: Émules et Enjeux* (Paris: Champion, 1992), especially the chapter "L'œil, la société, la morale," pp. 113–279, for both the ethical and the social interpretation.

On the changing FASHION IN CLOTHING, note the following: Michèle de Beaulieu's study *Contribution à l'étude de la mode à Paris: Les transformations du Costume élégant sous le règne de Louis XIII, 1610–1643* (Paris: Munier, 1936). For the concept of dress and its evolution from a static, conservative social structure whose purpose was to denote an individual's identity, his role and rank, to the progressive liberalization of fashion that no longer obeyed the transparent dictates of the three orders, see Daniel Roche's important study *La Culture des apparences: Une histoire du vêtement, XVIIᵉ–XVIIIᵉ siècle* (Paris: Fayard, 1989). For further reading, see Anne Hollander, *Seeing Through Clothes* (University of California Press, 1997).

TWO DIFFERENT LINES OF INTERPRETATION ON THE ORIGINS OF CIVILIZATION IN SOCIETY. One line of interpretation, applicable also to the eighteenth century, is to be found in Norbert Elias's well known *The Civilizing Process* (translated by Edmund Jephcott, Blackwell, 1994); and *The Court Society* (translated by Edmund Jephcott, Blackwell, 1983), which points to the court as the only influential center for taste and manners, and the model for *politesse* in classical French culture. For the origins of this thesis, see Roger Chartier's preface to *La Société de la cour* (Paris: Flammarion, 1985). Elias's position can also be found, for example, in Carlo Ossola's excellent *Dal "Cortegiano" all'"Uomo di Mondo"* (Torino: Einaudi, 1987), and in *Miroirs sans visage: Du courtisan à l'homme de la rue*, translated from the Italian by Nicole Sels (Paris: Éditions du Seuil, 1997); and in Peter Burke, *The Art of Conversation* (Polity Press, 1993). Roger Chartier places particular stress on Elias's thesis of "the circulation of cultural models whose dynamic lies in the tension between distinction and popularization"; apropos of which, note Chartier's important essay "Distinction et divulgation: la civilité et ses livres," in *Lectures et lecteurs dans la France d'Ancien Régime* (Paris: Éditions du Seuil, 1987), pp. 45–86.

My book follows another interpretation which, while recognizing the importance of the court model, calls its exclusivity into question by advancing another model. This model depends on the new social culture that developed as an autonomous phenomenon in the heart of the nobility during the first decades of the seventeenth century. The phenomenon is not without polemical connotations, especially concerning the court. Already under Louis XIV, the Chevalier de Méré claimed polite society's judgment to be a superior authority over "the most beautiful court that ever existed," and from Restoration times, with the Comte de Roederer's *Mémoire*, this dualism has never ceased to attract the attention of scholars. Here I will only mention Eric Auerbach's distinguished essay "La cour et la ville" (1951), in *Scenes from the Drama of European Literature* (Meridian Books, 1959), pp. 133–182, and Marc Fumaroli's studies on various aspects of French eighteenth-century society culture. For a critical assessment of these two points of view that sides with the second, see Daniel Gordon's essay "The Civilizing Process Revisited," in *Citizens without Sovereignty*, pp. 86–128. Polite society's autonomous movement away from the court and the emergence of a public space in the time of Louis XIII is apparently also Robert Muchembled's thesis in *La Société policée: Politique et politesse en France du XVIᵉ–XXᵉ siècle* (Paris: Éditions du Seuil, 1998).

FRENCH TRANSLATIONS of *The Book of the Courtier*, *Galateo*, and *Civil Conversation*. There exist three French translations of *Il libro del cortegiano*. 1. *Le Courtisan, nouvellement traduit de la langue italique en français* (the name of the translator is disputed; Paris: chez Jean Longins and Vincent Sertenas, 1537; revised, corrected, and reprinted the following year). 2. *Le Parfait Courtisan du comte Baltasar Castillonois*, translated by Gabriel Chappuis (Lyon, 1580; revised, corrected, and reprinted in 1585 and 1592). Chappuis's translation was recently republished with a "Présentation de Baldassare Castiglione" by Alain Pons (Paris: Éditions Gérard Lebovici, 1987). 3. *Le Parfait Courtisan et la Dame de Cour, Ouvrage également avantageux pour réussir dans les belles conversations, et pour former les jeunes personnes de qualité de l'un et l'autre sexe*, by the Abbé Jean-Baptiste Duhamel (Paris, 1690). On the fortunes of *The Book of the Courtier* in France, see Maurice Magendie, *La Politesse mondaine*, and Pietro Toldo, "Le courtisan dans la littérature française et ses rapports avec l'œuvre de Castiglione," in *Archiv für das Studium der Neueren Sprachen und Literaturen*, Vol. 104, Nos. 1–2 (Braunschweig: George Westermann, 1900), pp. 75–121. The second part of Toledo's article has also been published in Vol. 104, Nos. 3–4, pp. 313–330, and the third and last part in Vol. 105, Nos. 1–2, pp. 60–85. See also Louis van Delft, "La Bruyère et Castiglione," in *La Bruyère moraliste: Quatre études sur les Caractères* (Geneva: Droz, 1971), pp. 80–110.

Galateo was translated into French for the first time by Jean du Peyrat and Jacques Kerver (Paris, 1562), under the title *Le Galathée, ou la manière et façon comme le gentilhomme doit se gouverner en toute compagnie*. The translation by the Abbé Duhamel appeared in 1567; that of Jean II de Tournes, the great Lyon editor, in 1598. The latter was republished by Alain Pons in Le Livre de Poche (Paris: Quai Voltaire, 1988). On the fortunes of *Galateo* in France, see Maurice Magendie, *La Politesse mondaine*, and the study by Mario Richter, *Giovanni della Casa in Francia nel secolo XVI* (Rome: Edizioni di Storia della Letteratura, 1966).

La Civil Conversazione (1574). Two translations of the work appeared in 1579: 1. François de Belleforest's (Paris: chez Cavellat); 2. Gabriel Chappuis Tourngeau's (Lyon: chez J. Bernard). There were nine editions of the book between 1579 and 1592. On the fortunes of *La Civil Conversazione* in France, besides Maurice Magendie, *La Politesse mondaine*, see G. Boccazzi, "Les traducteurs français de Stefano Guazzo," in *Bulletin du Centre d'études franco-italien*, No. 7 (November 1978); "Stefano Guazzo et Guido Bentivoglio témoins de la civilisation et de l'histoire de France," in *La Découverte de la France au XVIIe siècle* (Paris: Éditions du Centre national de la Recherche scientifique, 1980), pp. 203–212; Giorgio Patrizi, *La Civil Conversation, libro europeo, Stefano Guazzo e la Civil Conversazione* (Rome: Bulzoni, 1990).

The Book of the Courtier and *Galateo* did not, however, address the same public. The first offered a model for aristocratic comportment; it was meant for the closed world of the court and difficult to imitate for those who were not part of it. The second aimed at a larger public and expanded urbanity beyond the social frontiers. See Daniela Romagnoli, *La Ville et la Cour* (Paris: Fayard, 1995), and *Rituale e ceremoniale*, under the direction of Sergio Bertelli and Giuliano Crifò (Milan: Bompiani, 1985).

On the great attempt to CODIFY SOCIAL MANNERS and on their legitimization in the Italian treatise, see Alain Pons, "La rhétorique des manières au XVIe siècle en Italie," in *Histoire de la rhétorique dans l'Europe moderne (1450–1950)*, edited by Marc Fumaroli (Paris: PUF, 1999), pp. 411–430.

The PLAYFUL AND NARCISSISTIC CHARACTER of this new polite society is perfectly defined in Jean Starobinski's chapter "On Flattery," in *Blessings in Disguise*.

CHAPTER 2

EVA PRIMA PANDORA. For the iconography of Cousin's painting, I referred to Françoise Borin, "Judging by Images," translated by Arthur Goldhammer, in *A History of Women in the West: Renaissance and Enlightenment Paradoxes*, edited by Natalie Zemon Davis and Arlette Farge, Vol. 3 of *A History of Women in the West*, edited by Georges Duby, Michelle Perrot, et al. (Belknap Press/Harvard University Press, 1993), pp. 187–254. See also Henri Zerner, *L'Art de la Renaissance en France: L'invention du classicisme* (Paris: Flammarion, 1996), pp. 225–234.

COURTESAN. See Adriana Chemello, "Donna di palazzo, moglie, cortigiana: ruoli e funzioni sociali della donna in alcuni trattati del Cinquecento," in *La Corte e il "Cortegiano,"* Vol. 2: *Un modello europeo*, edited by Adriano Prosperi (Rome: Bulzoni, 1980), pp. 113–132. See also Margaret F. Rosenthal, *The Honest Courtesan: Veronica Franco, Citizen and Writer in Sixteenth-Century Venice* (University of Chicago Press, 1992).

Whereas the description "honest courtesan" may seem an oxymoron, it was not originally so. In the Renaissance, "honest" in this context did not signify morally "virtuous," but honored or respected, and indicated a judgment of worth based on the courtesan's ability to make herself agreeable in society.

The FEMALE CONDITION. *A History of Women in the West*, edited by Georges Duby and Michelle Perrot, provides an excellent overall picture; I would particularly like to mention the debt I owe to Natalie Zemon Davis's essay "Women in Politics," in *A History of Women in the West: Renaissance and Enlightenment Paradoxes*, pp. 167–184. I also suggest Margaret L. King, *Women of the Renaissance* (University of Chicago Press, 1992).

On the CORRUPTION OF MORALS IN THE VALOIS COURT, see Ivan Cloulas, *La Vie quotidienne dans les châteaux de la Loire au temps de la Renaissance* (Paris: Hachette, 1983).

The TYPOLOGY OF THE *PETIT-MAÎTRE* and that term's history. (The expression, which took root at the time of the Fronde, described arrogant young noblemen who were followers of the Prince de Condé; it soon came more generally to denote young and fashionable dandies.) See Marivaux's *Petit-Maître corrigé*, edited by Frédéric Deloffre (Geneva-Lille: Droz, 1955): the first chapter of the introduction is entitled "Les petits-maîtres: histoire du mot," pp. 11–18. See Lionello Sozzi's equally interesting Franco-Italian parallel, "Petit-Maître e Giovin Signore: affinità tra due registri stilistici," in *Saggi e ricerche di letteratura francese*, Vol. 12 (1973), pp. 153–230, and "Ancora sul 'Petit-Maître,'" in *L'amabil rito: Società e cultura nella Milano di Parini*, edited by G. Barbarisi et al. (Milan: Istituto ed. Cisalpino, 2000), pp. 483–496.

CONDITION OF WOMEN IN FRANCE. Gustave Reynier, *La Femme au XVIIe siècle: Ses ennemis et ses défenseurs* (Paris: Tallandier, 1929); Gustave Fagniez, *La Femme et la société française dans la première moitié du XVIIe siècle* (Paris: Librairie Universitaire J. Gamber, 1929); Jean Portemer, "Le statut de la femme en France depuis la réformation des costumes jusqu'à la rédaction du code civil," in *Recueils de la Société Jean Bodin pour l'histoire comparative des Institutions*, XII, *La femme, deuxième partie* XXX (Brussels, 1962), pp. 447–497, and "Réflexions sur les pouvoirs de la femme selon le droit français au XVIIe siècle," in *XVIIe siècle* 144 (1984) pp. 189–203; Pierre Ronzeaud, "La femme au pouvoir ou le monde à l'envers," in *XVIIe siècle* 108 (1975), pp. 9–33. On the instruments of feminine culture, see Roger Duchêne, "L'école des femmes au XVIIe siècle," in *Écrire au temps de Mme de Sévigné* (Paris: Vrin, 1981), pp. 77–78. See also Claude Dulong, *La Vie quotidienne des femmes au Grand Siècle* (Paris: Hachette, 1984) and *Amoureuses du Grand Siècle* (Paris: Éditions du Rocher, 1996); Micheline Cuénin, "Les femmes aux affaires (1598–1661)," in *XVIIe siecle* 144 (1984), pp. 203–211; Jannette Geffriaud Rosso, *Études sur la fémininité au XVIIe et XVIIIe siècles* (Paris-Pisa: Libreria Goliardica, 1984); *Onze Études sur l'image de la femme dans la littérature française du dix-septième siècle*; *Onze Nouvelles Études sur l'image de la femme dans la littérature française du dix-septième siècle*, edited by Wolfgang Leiner (Tübingen: Gunter Narr/Paris: Jean-Michel Place, 1984); *Présences féminines: Littérature et société au XVIIe siècle français*, Actes de London (Canada), 1985, edited by Ian Richmond and Costant Venesoen, Biblio 17 (Paris-Seattle-Tübingen: PFSCL, 1987); "Eros in Francia nel Seicento," in *Quaderni del Seicento francese*, edited by Giovanni Dotoli and Paolo Carile (Paris-Bari: Nizet-Adriatica, 1987); Wendy Gibson, *Women in Seventeenth-Century France* (London: MacMillan, 1989); *Femmes et pouvoirs sous l'Ancien Régime*, under the direction of Danielle Haase-Dubosc and Eliane Viennot (Paris: Rivages, 1991); Sara F. Mathews Grieco, *Ange ou diablesse: La représentation de la femme au XVIe siècle* (Paris: Flammarion, 1991); *La Culture des femmes au XVIIe siècle et aujourd'hui: De la précieuse à l'écrivaine*, monographic number of *Papers on French Seventeenth Century Literature*, Vol. 22, No. 43 (1995); Danielle Haase-Dubosc, *Ravie et enlevée: De l'enlèvement des femmes comme stratégie matrimoniale au XVIIe siècle* (Paris: Albin Michel, 1999).

On the EDUCATION OF GIRLS in aristocratic society, see Roger Chartier, Marie-Madeleine Compère, and Dominique Julia, *L'Éducation en France du XVIe au*

XVIIIe siècle (Paris: SEDES, 1976), and Elfrida Dubois, "The Education of Women in Seventeenth-Century France," in *French Studies*, Vol. 32, No. 1 (1978), pp. 1–19. But I wish especially to indicate Paule Constant's fine book, *Un Monde à l'usage des demoiselles* (Paris: Gallimard, 1987), to which I am greatly indebted. See also *L'Éducation des filles sous l'Ancien Régime de Christine de Pizan à Fenelon: Études à la mémoire de Linda Timmermans*, edited by Colette H. Winn, *Papers on French Seventeenth Century Literature*, Vol. 24, No. 46 (1997).

On the FEMALE BODY, see Philippe Perrot, *Le Travail des apparences: Le corps féminin XVIIIe–XIXe siècle* (Paris: Éditions du Seuil, 1984).

On FEMININE CULTURE AND RELIGIOSITY, see Mother Marie de Chantal Gueudre, "La femme et la vie spirituelle," in *XVIIe siècle* 63–64 (1964), pp. 47–77, and particularly the second part of Timmermans's valuable study *L'Accès des femmes à la culture*, concerning "Dévotion et culture féminine."

The importance of Saint François de Sales's *Introduction à la vie dévote* is well explained in Nanda Colombo's Italian translation of that text, edited by Benedetta Papàsogli, with a preface by Henri Bremond (Milan: Rizzoli, 1986); and in René Bady, "François de Sales maître de l'honnêteté," in *XVIIe siècle* 78 (1968), pp. 3–20.

Marc Fumaroli points out how, in *Introduction à la vie dévote*, Saint François de Sales uses the word *monde* not to mean "high society" but "human and profane society in its complexity," see "Premiers témoins du parisianism: le 'monde' et la 'mode' chez les moralistes du XVIIe siècle," in *La Notion du 'monde' au XVIIe siècle*, edited by B. Beugnot, *Littératures classiques* 22 (Autumn 1994), p. 172.

WOMEN'S DOMINION. The homage due to women has been theorized ever since the first seventeenth-century manual on behavior, *L'Honneste homme ou l'art de plaire à la cour* by Nicolas Faret (Paris, 1630), edited by Maurice Magendie (1932; Slatkine Reprints, Geneva, 1970).

On the VARIOUS ASPECTS OF LOVE AND GALLANTRY, there are, first and foremost, two classics: Denis de Rougemont's *L'Amour et l'Occident* (1952; Paris: Editions 10/18, 2001) and Paul Bénichou's *Morales du Grand Siècle*. An analysis of the significance of various nuances of gallantry can be found in Magendie, *La Politesse mondaine*, pp. 424f. Also recommended are Octave Nadal, *Le Sentiment de l'amour dans l'œuvre de Pierre Corneille* (Paris: Gallimard, 1948); Claude Dulong, *L'Amour au XVIIe siècle* (Paris: Hachette, 1969), and *Éros volubile: Les Métamorphoses de l'amour du Moyen Âge aux Lumières*, Actes du Colloque des départements de philologie française et italienne de l'Université de Valence, March 4–7, 1988, under the direction of Dolores Jiménez and Jean-Christophe Abramovici (Paris: Dejonquières, 2000). One may disagree with Jean-Michel Pelous's thesis, which denies the historical existence of the *Précieuses*, seeing them as no more than a satirist's invention, but in my view, his fine book *Amour précieux, amour galant (1654–1675)* remains an important work. See also *Les*

Visages de l'amour au XVIIe siècle, 13e colloque du CMR 17 (January 28–30, 1983), under the patronage of the Société d'études du XVIIe siècle (Toulouse: Université de Toulouse–Le Mirail, 1984); and the study after Micheline Cuénin's literary texts, *L'Idéologie en France (1540–1627)* (Paris: Aux amateurs de livres, 1987). I found two essays by Noémi Hepp particularly useful, "À la recherche du 'mérite des dames,'" in *Destins et enjeux du XVIIe siècle*, edited by Yves-Marie Bercé, Norbert Dufourcq, Nicole Ferrier-Caverivière, Jean-Luc Gautier, and Philippe Sellier (Paris: PUF, 1985), pp. 109–117; and "La galanterie," in *Les France*, Vol. 3 of *Les Lieux de mémoire*, edited by Pierre Nora (Paris: Gallimard, 1992), pp. 745–783.

Recent years have seen an increasing tendency to use the words "gallant" and "gallantry" in the sense in which they were used in the seventeenth century, to indicate the ensemble of values and behavior that constituted polite society's style. The following are important for the definition of a gallant aesthetic: Alain Viala's introduction to *L'Ésthétique galante: Paul Pelisson, Discours sur les Œuvres de Monsieur Sarasin et autres textes*, edited by Alain Viala, with Emmanuelle Mortgat et al. (Toulouse: Société de Littératures Classiques, 1989), pp. 13–46; and his introduction "La littérature galante: histoire et problématique," in *Il Seicento francese oggi: Situazione e prospettive della ricerca*, Atti del Convegno internazionale, Monopoli, May 27–29, 1993 (Paris: Nizet/ Bari: Adriatica, 1994), pp. 101–113; "Le naturel galant," in *Nature et culture à l'âge classique*, under the direction of Christian Delmas and Françoise Gevrey (Toulouse: Presses Universitaires du Mirail, 1997), pp. 61–76. Viala suggests a "current [in] gallantry that is both literary and social, which can actually be found in the second half of the seventeenth century and is historically definable as a form of socialization through the art of conversation and, therefore, as such, susceptible to analysis" ("D'une politique des formes: la galanterie," in *XVIIe siècle* 182, January–March 1994, p. 145). In line with this theory, which refers to gallantry rather than preciosity as a way of broadly describing worldly style, Roger Duchêne's most recent studies have helped to broaden the field of inquiry into the "gallant aesthetic," by very successfully illustrating the wealth of exchanges it established between life and literature in the name of pleasure: "Bourgeois gentilhomme ou bourgeois galant?" in *Création et recréation: Un dialogue entre littérature et histoire, Mélanges offerts à Marie-Odile Sweetser* (Tübingen: Gunter Narr, 1993), pp. 105–110; "Mentalité précieuse ou galante" in *Quaderni del Seicento Francese* 10 (1991), pp. 171–181; Alain Génetiot, *Les Genres lyriques mondains (1630–1660): Étude des poésies de Voiture, Vion d'Alibray, Sarasin, et Scarron* (Geneva: Droz, 1990); Delphine Denis, "Réflexions sur le 'style': une théorization floue," in *Le Style au XVIIe siècle*, edited by Georges Molinié, in *Littératures classiques* 28 (Autumn 1996), pp. 146–158, and her book *La Muse galante: Poétique de la Conversation dans l'œuvre de Mademoiselle de Scudéry* (Paris: Champion, 1977). See also the collection of essays *Du goût, de la conversation et des femmes*, edited by Alain Montandon (Clermont-Ferrand: Association des Publications de la Faculté des Lettres et Sciences Humaines de Clermont-Ferrand, 1994).

LANGUAGE PROBLEMS: Marc Fumaroli, *L'Âge de l'éloquence*; "Le 'langage de la Cour' en France: problèmes et points de repères," in *Europäische Hofkultur im 16.*

und 17. Jahrhundert, Vol. 2 (Hamburg: Dr. Ernst Hauswedell & Co., 1981); "Le génie de la langue française" (1992), in *Trois Institutions littéraires* (Paris: Gallimard, 1994). On the part played by the spoken language of women, see also "Les 'Contes' de Perrault, ou l'éducation à la douceur," in *La Diplomatie de l'esprit* (1982; Paris: Hermann, 1994), pp. 441–478. Equally, "Animus et anima: l'instance féminine dans l'apologétique de la langue française," in *XVIIe siècle* 144 (1984), pp. 233–240. See also Gilles Siouffi's doctoral thesis, "Le 'génie de la langue française' à l'âge classique," (Université de Paris IV, 1995). On the importance of linguistic discussion in polite society, see Peter France, *The Language of Literature in French Literature and its Background*, edited by John Cruikshank (Oxford University Press, 1969).

TRANSLATIO STUDIORUM. The shift in scholarly preeminence from Italy to France is described by Françoise Waquet in *Le Modèle français et l'Italie savante: Conscience de soi et perception de l'autre dans la République des Lettres (1660–1750)* (Rome: École française de Rome, 1989).

HONNÊTETÉ. Within the vast critical literature on the subject—from Maurice Magendie's inaugural study, *La Politesse mondaine*, published in 1925, followed by Paul Bénichou's *Morales du Grand Siècle*, to Emmanuel Bury's *Littérature et politesse: L'invention de l'honnête homme (1580–1750)* (Paris: PUF, 1996), which is the last authoritative analysis of the subject—I would at least like to point to Daniel Mornet, "L''Honnête homme' et la 'Politesse,'" in *Histoire de la littérature française classique 1660–1700: Ses caractères véritables, ses aspects inconnus* (Paris: Armand Colin, 1940), pp. 97–124; André Lévêque, "'L'honnête homme' et 'l'homme de bien' au XVIIe siècle," in *PMLA* 62 (1957), pp. 620–632; Claude Papin, "Le sens de l'idéal de 'l'honnête homme' au XVIIe siècle," in *La Pensée, revue de Rationalisme Moderne, Arts, Sciences, Philosophie*, N.S., 104 (August 1962), pp. 52–83; Bernadette B. de Mendoza, "L'art de vivre de l'honnête homme: éthique ou esthétique," in "Esthétique et société au dix-septième siècle," in *Papers on French Seventeenth Century Literature*, Vol. 1 (1973), pp. 17–26; Jean-Pierre Dens, "L'honnête homme et l'esthétique du paraître," in *Papers on French Seventeenth Century Literature*, Vol. 6 (1976–1977), pp. 69–82; "L'honnête homme et la critique du goût" (Lexington, Kentucky: French Forum, 1981); "L'honnête homme et le dandy," *Études littéraires françaises*, edited by A. Montandon (Tübingen: Gunter Narr, 1993); Domenico Bosco, "'Vertu' e 'Honnête homme': Un tema di morale seicentesca" and "'Honnête homme' e 'politesse mondaine': un tema di morale seicentesca," in *Rivista di filosofia neo-scolastica*, Vol. 71, No. 1 (January–March, 1979), pp. 80–104, and No. 2 (April–June 1979), pp. 326–351; Domna Stanton, "The Aristocrat as Art: Moralistes et mondains au XVIIe siècle," annual congress of the MLA in Washington, D. C., 1984, in *Papers on French Seventeenth Century Literature*, Vol. 13, No. 24 (1989); Francesco Fiorentino, "La prospettiva dell 'Honnête homme,'" in *Il ridicolo nel teatro di Molière* (Turin: Einaudi, 1997) pp. 37–111.

There is an interesting study of FEMMES FORTES by Ian Maclean, *Women Triumphant: Feminism in French Literature, 1610–1652* (Clarendon Press, 1977).

On POULLAIN DE LA BARRE, see in microfiche Bernard Magné's doctoral thesis, "Le féminisme de Poullain de la Barre: origine et signification," Université de Toulouse, 1964. Also by Magné, "Éducation des femmes et féminisme chez Poullain de la Barre (1647–1723)," in *Le XVIIe siècle et l'éducation*, Actes du Colloque de Marseille (1971), supplement to *Marseille* 88 (1973), pp. 117–127. See also Madeleine Alcover's study *Poullain de la Barre: Une aventure philosophique*, Biblio 17 (Paris-Seattle-Tübingen: PFSCL, 1981).

On the influence of feminine TASTE and its effects on literature, see Elisabeth L. Berg, "Recognizing Differences: Perrault's Modernist Aesthetic in 'Parallèle des Anciens et des Modernes,'" in *Papers on French Seventeenth Century Literature*, Vol. 18 (1983), pp. 135–148.

THE SALON AS A PLACE OF SOCIAL MOBILITY. In an important sociological study, *Le Paradis des Femmes: Women, Salons and Social Stratification in Seventeenth-Century France* (Princeton University Press, 1976), Carolyn Lougee, with reference to the names in the second edition of Somaize's *Grand dictionnaire des Prétieuses* (1661), has examined the social condition of 171 women who frequented the best-known salons of the day and established a strong link between social mobility and women's hegemony. Also touching on the influence of women on the culture of polite society, and on the central part in that culture played by the art of conversation, is Elizabeth Goldsmith's book *"Exclusive Conversations,"* mentioned above.

Still on SOCIAL MOBILITY in the eighteenth century and on the process of integration between the nobility and the bourgeoisie, see Guy Chaussinand-Nogaret, *La Noblesse au XVIIIe Siècle: De la Féodalité aux Lumières* (first edition, 1976; Paris: Éditions Complexes, 1984). This process, which was to provoke a reaction from the nobility, is generally said to be of the eighteenth century, but according to Carolyn Lougee, it had already begun in the seventeenth. See also Mathieu Marraud's *La Noblesse de Paris au XVIIIe siècle* (Paris: Éditions du Seuil, 2000), especially the third part, "Dans la société," and the fourth part, "Dans le siècle."

The time has come for a HISTORY OF HISTORIOGRAPHY DEVOTED TO FRENCH WOMEN IN THE ANCIEN RÉGIME. (See *Une histoire des femmes est-elle possible?* under the direction of Michelle Perrot, Paris: Rivages, 1984; likewise Jean-Paul Desaive, Eric A. Nicholson, Michèle Crampe-Casnabet, and Évelyne Berriot-Salvadore, "Di lei, si parla molto," in *Storia delle donne: Dal rinascimento all'età moderna*, pp. 249–394; also Robert Darnton's essay "Cherchez la femme," in *The New York Review of Books*, August 10, 1995, pp. 22–24.) There being no such a history, however, I will merely draw attention here to one or two significant moments. Just as women were making such a mark on the social scene, the nature of French women appears to have become elusive, avoiding too precise an interpretation and showing a different face according to the perspective and times in which it is seen. After a period of oblivion, the nineteenth century rediscovered women and, by a twofold apotheosis, raised them to different heavenly realms. Sainte-Beuve saw them as taking a leading role in defining the essential characteristics of that great uninterrupted conversation in which the critic recognizes the distinctive nature of French literary culture: psychological subtlety, versatility, taste, naturalness, *esprit*. As for Victor Cousin's impressive gallery of portraits of seventeenth-century women, it can be said without irony that it bears moving witness to the misunderstandings into which love can lead even the strictest scholar. In his enormous and pioneering work of documentation, which is essential to this day, Cousin looked at his seventeenth-century ladies with the awareness and prejudices of a nineteenth-century man. He evoked aristocratic heroines who were passionate and virtuous, the reflections of an idealized *Grand Siècle* apology. During those same years, the Goncourt brothers, Edmond and Jules, in a similar way but from a different point of view, praised the cerebral elegance of eighteenth-century women in *La Femme au XVIIIe siècle* (1862; revised and extended by Edmond in 1867) and in their many monographs dedicated to women on various matters typical of the Age of Enlightenment. Their misogyny, and their repugnance for the obtuse, threatening, suffocating, nineteenth-century femininity that was entirely wrapped up in maternal and wifely domestic duties, drove them to seek a remedy in the preceding century. For this see Élisabeth Badinter, "Les Goncourt romanciers et historiens des femmes," preface to *La Femme au XVIIIe siècle* (Paris: Flammarion, 1982), pp. 5–41. Their Enlightenment woman was distinguished by her weightlessness and her gestures, so that, seemingly insensible to the body's weight, her every action obeyed an aesthetic necessity.

Whereas at the end of the nineteenth century it had become obligatory in any historical-cultural reassessment of the *ancien régime* to pay homage to the civilizing part played by women, by the beginning of the twentieth century, feminist historiography had changed radically in its attitude toward the female condition. The privileged position that women enjoyed in elite circles no longer seemed to be the distinguishing mark of the entire nobility, so much as the fruits of a long and difficult battle against the prejudices of a dominant culture. Until Georges Ascoli's pioneering work "Essai sur l'histoire des idées féministes en France du XVIe siècle à la Révolution," in *Revue de Synthèse Historique* 18 (1906), pp. 27–42, 99–106, 161–184 (Bibliography), women appeared as bearers of novelty and change, decidedly aligned with the "Moderns" against traditional culture. Their authority and prestige seemed considerably less than the sacrifices that had been forced upon them, and their reign was seen as a deceptive mask disguising a painful servitude. Women's studies no longer started from the premise of the glorification of women but of their demonization. Despite their being subjugated and dependent, their otherness inspired fear, and they were the victims of male fears, prejudices, and self-interest.

The vast literature produced by the departments of feminist studies in American universities has included several important contributions. For Domna C. Stanton, in

"The Fiction of Préciosité, and the Fear of Women," in *Yale French Studies*, Vol. 62 (1981), pp. 107–134, the *Précieuses* never existed and were merely a satirical male invention designed to discredit various feminist demands being voiced in social circles around the middle of the seventeenth century. As we have seen, with Carolyn Lougee (*Le Paradis des femmes*), male misogyny shifted from the ideological and cultural plane to the social; women were accused of generally encouraging diversity in society, thus threatening its traditional balance, which was based on rank. But for Joan DeJean (*Tender Geographies: Women and the Origins of the Novel in France*, Columbia University Press, 1991), eighteenth-century French noblewomen really set their sights on the planned subversion of both private and public institutions. The Fronde presented them with their great opportunity to exercise political influence and to affect the course of history. Between 1648 and 1653, the Princesse de Condé, the Duchesse de Longueville, and the Grande Mademoiselle, to name but the best-known, had come out ready to challenge the legitimate order; they had conspired, fought, and incited whole cities to rebel against royal authority. But, DeJean points out, these were always individual exploits. The heroines of the Fronde were aristocratic Amazons who knew nothing of female solidarity, which contributed largely to the failure of the revolt. "Had the frondeuses who directed their revolution recreated the legendary state of the Amazons, the most absolute of French monarchies, that of Louis XIV, might have been avoided" (p. 42). With the triumphal restoration of monarchic authority, women were excluded once and for all from playing any direct part in politics and so turned their subversive energies toward literature. Women like Mademoiselle de Montpensier or Mme de Motteville wrote memoirs in which they provided their own version of events, while through romantic literature, they declared war on the patriarchal order. With their old solidarity rediscovered and reunited in the salons and *ruelles* under the banner of *Préciosité*, they were to redefine a protected, isolated space from which to contemplate their destiny. But by telling of the dangers, the suffering, and the deceit involved in marriage, maternity, and love, Mlle de Scudéry, Mme de Lafayette, and Mme de Ville-dieu attacked the very foundations of French society, while gaining a preeminent public position in the world of letters and laying the basis for the modern novel. Erica Harth, in describing the impact that Cartesian philosophy, with its message of equality addressed to both men and women, had on feminine culture, advances a thesis opposing the one held by the Goncourts: "the mind has no sex" (*Cartesian Women*, p. 8). In the seventeenth century, French women contrived a "space of discourse" from which they would be excluded in the following century, when they would merely fulfill the simple duties of lady of the house. Having dominated society culture, guided its tastes, contributed in large measure to the creation of new literary genres, and supported the cause of the "Moderns," women of the Enlightenment simply allowed themselves to become masters of ceremony for male intellectual conversation.

Erica Goodman puts forward yet another hypothesis in *The Republic of Letters: A Cultural History of the French Enlightenment* (Cornell University Press, 1994). She maintains that during the course of the eighteenth century, women's intellectual power increased and constituted a real Republic of Letters, control of which they let slip only on the eve of 1789, with disastrous results. Like Joan DeJean, Goodman enjoys the "ifs" and "buts" of history and advances the hypothesis that if women had not been excluded from political debate, the worst excesses of violence of the Revolution would have been avoided. In the classic style of a solid doctoral thesis, Linda Timmermans's impressive study is both balanced and free of ideology. Timmermans mistrusts extreme interpretations and maintains that "there was nothing subversive in society feminism" (*L'Accès des femmes à la culture*, p. 338). If modernism and feminism seem inextricably linked, it is because their alliance was dictated by mutual convenience. They were primarily united by the same enemies, those *savants* who regarded literature as being for the initiated only, not to be practiced by anyone unlearned in humanistic culture—which included women. Without allowing themselves to be intimidated, women despised the *savants* and banished from the social scene the pedants and scholars who were unable to contribute in any way to their entertainment. But it was not merely for tactical reasons that the Moderns placed themselves under the protection of women and promoted their culture. Their apologia for modern language and literature was inseparable from the apologia for court culture and society culture and could not disregard the influence of women. Women were moreover seen as the genuine guardians of memory and of the really French traditions of which the Moderns saw themselves as defenders (on this point see Marc Fumaroli, "Les 'Contes' de Perrault, ou l'éducation de la douceur," in *La Diplomatie de l'esprit*, pp. 441–478). Did this dense network of interest and exchange create an intellectually equal relationship between the ladies and the literati, the writers and the public? Women's authority was seen to be based not on the strength of reason but rather on a instinctive infallibility in matters of taste, and it can have been no accident that Fontenelle, the most worldly of all the Moderns, devoted space to women in his *Dialogues*, but prevented them from entering the Académie des Sciences (see Alain Niderst's biography *Fontenelle*, Paris: Plon, 1991).

In the history of seventeenth- and eighteenth-century French feminine culture, seen as a long and tiring battle of uncertain outcome against a solidly established male culture, the key words used in women's studies are difference, differentiation, inequality, and separation. Women's condition, their self-assertion on the social scene, and their engagement in the literary world have been and continue to be specialized, richly stimulating subjects of research, to be viewed from many angles. A complex cultural patrimony, partly ignored, often trivialized and oversimplified, and yet, at length, entrusted exclusively to male evaluation, has been repeatedly explored and studied specifically in the light of gender. The wish to reveal what for too long has been confused and unacknowledged is not, however, without risk and can give rise to new misunderstandings. In order to understand the society that flourished in France during the last two years of the *ancien régime*, the things that men and women then felt to be associated and complementary should not now be separated. Jean Mesnard's essay "'Honnête homme' et 'honnête femme' dans la culture du XVIIe siècle," in *La Culture du XVIIe siècle: Enquêtes et synthèses* (Paris: PUF, 1992), pp. 142–159, is enlightening on this point; the distinguished scholar shows that the very ideal of *honnêteté* presupposes that the sexes must be perfectly complementary for them to be properly fulfilled.

The denial of a separate feminine culture—as Timmermans claims—and the belief that the abstract equality of individuals is more important than sexual differentiation are, for Mona Ozouf, the constants that define the "singularity" of French women from the eighteenth century to the present day, as much as the angle from which they are studied in France (*Les Mots des femmes: Essai sur la singularité française*, Paris: Fayard, 1995). Of the ten women in this excellent book—whether aristocratic or bourgeois, militant feminists or convinced believers in the complementary nature of the sexes, writers by vocation, reporters, or those needing to communicate—they all, from Mme du Deffand to Simone de Beauvoir, seem united over and above their many differences by their refusal to turn exclusively to members of their own sex. According to Ozouf, these are "words written by them, written about them, but not written only for them. But for everyone, in the hope of change, in the certainty of a shared language and a common conscience" (p. 397).

In the important concluding essay, which gives the book its subtitle—*Essay on French Singularity*—Ozouf considers the historical reasons for France being spared the resentment and radicalism of English and American feminists, although it was French feminism that in the 1960s and 1970s adopted the most extreme theoretical positions in works such as Luce Irigaray's *Speculum de l'autre femme* (Paris: Éditions de Minuit, 1974); Hélène Cixous, "Le rire de la Méduse," in *L'Arc* 61 (1975); Hélène Cixous, Madeleine Gagnon, Annie Leclerc, *La Venue à l'écriture* (Paris: Union Générale d'Éditions, 1977); and Hélène Cixous and Catherine Clément, *La Jeune-Née* (Paris: Union Générale d'Éditions, 1975).

For Ozouf, the explanation for the attitude of French women who, from whatever their standpoint, generally refute the premise of "difference" is to be found in time and the dual legacy of the *ancien régime* and the Revolution of 1789. Eighteenth- and nineteenth-century French aristocratic civilization was the result of an active collaboration between the sexes, and it accustomed noblemen and noblewomen to living in symbiosis. The Revolution recalled French women to domestic duty and disappointed their hopes of political equality, but at the same time, as Ozouf explains in some very interesting pages, it ignited an irreversible historical process. The principle of universal equality made the exclusion of women from civic and political life theoretically unacceptable and provisional. At the time, republican women, with the all-important duty of providing the country with its future citizens and raising them to be virtuous, retained a central position at the heart of the new society. Thus began a long wait for French women in which the partial gains of Anglo-Saxon feminism were disdained. They were convinced that in a democratic regime based on suffrage as a natural right, the only alternative to exclusion for women was their complete assimilation and absolute equality. Some time before this occurred, French republicanism, concerned with removing women from the influence of the priests and the cult of the past, gave them equality of education and qualified them to teach. School, according to Ozouf, was thus the privileged place of French feminism, a place not only of emancipation but of a strong identification with universal values and national tradition.

The same position taken against the thesis of "writing in the feminine" can be found in Natacha Michel's and Martine de Rougemont's thirteen essays, *Le Rameau subtil: Prosatrices françaises entre 1364 et 1954* (Paris: Hatier, 1993), dedicated to so many other women writers for whom "prose was dear." Replying to Ozouf, Joan DeJean confirms the idea of "writing in the feminine" as being determined by sex and already present in seventeenth-century literature ("Sex, genre et nom d'auteur," in *Le Style au XVIIe siècle*, pp. 137–146).

CHAPTER 3

THE DATE OF THE START OF MME DE RAMBOUILLET'S SALON is the subject of various hypotheses. Barbara Krajewska suggests 1608 as the date of the first meetings at the marquise's house (*Mythes et découvertes*, p. 202). As for the rebuilding of the house in the rue Saint-Thomas-du-Louvre, Nicole Aronson claims that the first stone was laid in June 1618 (*Mme de Rambouillet*, p. 79); but Charles-Louis Livet thinks the work began in 1612–1613 ("it was the eureka of civil architecture," *Précieux et précieuses*, p. 7). The marquise's house perfectly exemplified the nobility's new requirements. As Peter Thornton has written, "the French genius lay in adapting the formal schemes of Italian architectural theory in order to create interiors that were practical and comfortable as well as harmonious and imposing; indeed, this was to be the chief French contribution to European architecture during the seventeenth century, and the influence of women in this development can be scarcely overrated." See his *Seventeenth-Century Interior Decoration in England, France and Holland* (1978; Yale University Press, 1990), p. 10. On the importance of this décor in the art of conversation, see Marc Fumaroli, "La Conversation," in *Trois Institutions littéraires*, p. 128.

On PRIVATE LIFE, see Oreste Ranum, "The Refuges of Intimacy," in *A History of Private Life: Passions of the Renaissance*, edited by Roger Chartier, translated by Arthur Goldhammer, Vol. 3 of *A History of Private Life* (Harvard University Press, 1989), pp. 207–264.

For the meaning of the expression GRAND MONDE (high society), see Emmanuel Bury, "Le monde de 'l'honnête homme': aspects de la notion de 'monde' dans l'esthétique du savoir-vivre," and Marc Fumaroli, "Premier témoin du parisianisme: le 'monde' et la 'mode' chez les moralistes du XVIIe siècle," in *La Notion du "monde" au XVIIe siècle*, in *Littératures classiques* 22 (Autumn 1994), pp. 191–202 and 165–190.

On the importance of the THEATER in French society under the *ancien régime*, in addition, of course, to Antoine Adam, *Histoire de la littérature française au XVIIe siècle*, see Pierre Mélèse, *Le Théâtre et le public à Paris sous Louis XIV (1659–1715)* (Geneva: Droz, 1934); John Lough, *Paris Theater Audiences in the Seventeenth and Eighteenth Centuries* (1957; Oxford University Press, 1965); Maurice Descotes, *Le Public de théâtre et son histoire* (Paris: PUF, 1964); Henri Lagrave, *Le Théâtre et son public à Paris de 1715 à 1750* (Paris: Klincksieck, 1972).

TALLEMANT DES RÉAUX. Born into a family of Protestant bankers, Tallemant des Réaux (1616–1692), poet, lyricist, storyteller, and critic, collected, transcribed, and drew up many documents containing information and anecdotes about the literary and society life of his times, with no thought of future publication. It is significant that the only editorial project in which Tallemant was interested—and which never came to fruition—was a posthumous, annotated edition of Vincent Voiture's work, Voiture having been content to write for a small aristocratic elite without dreaming of publishing his work. As Vincenette Maigne has pointed out in the preface to her critical edition of *Manuscrit 673* (Paris: Klincksieck, 1994, p. 142), Tallemant had no literary ambitions. For him, writing was a form of conversation, and the texts he collected were meant to be read aloud, commented on, and discussed by a whole circle of friends.

Francine Wild's important work on Tallemant ("Tallemant des Réaux et l'écriture anecdotique," 1996)—which I had the privilege of consulting prior to its publication—exactly reconstructs the singular success of a writer who has hitherto been very little studied and long suspected of untrustworthiness. First published in six volumes in 1834, edited by Monmerqué, de Châteaugiron, and Taschereau, the *Historiettes* was shocking for its freedom of tone and for painting a picture of the seventeenth century in rude contrast to the Restoration's highly idealized view of the *Grand Siècle*. Thus the first reaction was to cast doubt on the veracity of Tallemant's stories, an attitude that prevailed until the critical edition of the *Historiettes* edited by Antoine Adam was published in 1960 in Gallimard's Bibliothèque de la Pléiade. In his preface, Adam provided an important list of sources consulted by Tallemant, and from that time, according to Wild, "all the documents unearthed concerning characters written about in the *Historiettes* have confirmed the truth of Tallemant's assertions, and in various cases, historians have been able to establish which manuscripts or printed works he referred to in writing his text" (p. 3). So for us, the *Historiettes* constitutes a doubly valuable source, both for the richness and variety of the historical information provided and because that information came, for the most part, from stories of a confidential nature designed to entertain the circle that constituted Tallemant's audience, and which we in turn propose to evoke.

On Tallemant: Sainte-Beuve, "Tallemant et Bussy ou le médisant bourgeois et le médisant de qualité," in *Causeries du lundi*, Vol. 13, pp. 172–188; J. Barbey d'Aurevilly, "Tallemant des Réaux," in *À côté de la Grande Histoire* (Paris: Lemerre, 1906), pp. 41–56; Rémy de Gourmont, "Tallemant des Réaux," in *Mercure de France 64* (1906), pp. 68–74; Émile Magne's two well-documented volumes, *La Joyeuse Jeunesse de Tallemant des Réaux d'après des documents inédits* (Paris: Émile-Paul frères, 1921) and *La Fin troublée de Tallemant des Réaux d'après des documents inédits* (Paris: Émile-Paul frères, 1922); Edmund Gosse, *Tallemant des Réaux or the Art of Miniature Biography* (Clarendon Press, 1925); Pietro Paolo Trompeo, "Un pettegolo di talento," *L'azzurro di Chartres* (Rome: Sciascia Editore, 1958), pp. 91–98; Giovanni Bogliolo, "Tallemant e l'Italia," in *Studi Urbinati*, Vol. 41, No. 2 (1967), pp. 995–1003; W. Victor Wortley, *Tallemant des Réaux: The Man through his Style* (La Haye–Paris:

Mouton, 1969); Sergio Poli, "La composizione delle 'Historiettes': continuità e analogia," in *La prosa francese del primo Seicento: Ricerche e Proposte*, edited by Cecilia Rizza (Cuneo: Saste, 1977), pp. 195–227; three critical essays by Vincenette Maigne, "Les mots et la chose: historiettes gauloises/bienséances sociales et linguistiques chez Tallemant des Réaux," in *Les Visages de l'amour au XVIIe siècle*, Colloque du CMR 17, Travaux de l'Université de Toulouse–Le Mirail, série A–tome XXIV (1984), pp. 195–203, "Anecdotes en chansons sous le règne de Louis XIV: de la fronde populaire au divertissement aristocratique," in *Cahiers Saint-Simon* 23 (1995), pp. 17–23, and "Le manuscrit comme absolu," in *XVIIe siècle* 192 (July–September 1996), pp. 591–599. See finally *Tallemant des Réaux: Les Historiettes*, edited by Francis Assaf, Actes du XXIVe colloque de la North America Society for Seventeenth-Century French Literature, October 1–3, 1992, Biblio 17 (Paris-Seattle-Tübingen: PFSCL, 1993). This includes contributions by J. F. Gaines, M. Stefanovska, A. Zuerner, M. R. Margiti, N. Aronson, P. Wolfe, M. L. Farrel, and V. Maigne. On Tallemant's technique in literary portraiture, see also Jacqueline Plantié, *La Mode du portrait littéraire en France (1641–1681)* (Paris: Champion, 1994), pp. 516–526.

On the importance of LAUGHTER in social intercourse in society, see Jacques Morel, "Rire au XVIIe siècle," in *Agréables mensonges: Essais sur le théâtre du XVIIe siècle* (Paris: Klincksieck, 1991), pp. 277–288, and Dominique Bertrand's study, *Dire le rire à l'âge classique: Représenter pour mieux contrôler* (Aix-en-Provence: Publications de l'Université de Provence, 1995).

Françoise Bertaut, Dame de MOTTEVILLE (1621–1689) joined Anne of Austria's household in 1643 when the Queen was made regent, and became her confidante. She seems quite soon to have started on her memoirs centered around the Queen, whom she kept informed of her plan. But the text was almost entirely compiled after Anne's death in 1666. Her *Mémoires pour servir à l'histoire de la reine Anne d'Autriche* were published posthumously in 1723 (five volumes, Amsterdam: Changuion). Her intentions as a memoirist are worlds apart from Tallemant's. Whereas the writer of the *Historiettes* takes pleasure in debunking and shocking, Mme de Motteville adopts a calmly detached tone and defends her Queen to the last—while making abundant use of omission. Sainte-Beuve ("Mme de Motteville," in *Causeries du lundi*, Vol. 5, pp. 168–188) is full of praise for "that wise and reasonable spirit of hers which witnessed the events of the day from close up, which appreciated them and described them with such perfect measure, with such pleasing precision" (p. 168). Measure, however, that does not always succeed in disguising the side the writer has taken, or indeed her feelings, in particular her aversion for Cardinal Mazarin. (Apropos of this, see Georges Dethan, "Madame de Motteville et Mazarin," in *Les Valeurs chez les mémorialistes français du XVIIe siècle avant la Fronde*, edited by Noémi Hepp and Jacques Hennequin, Actes du Colloque de Strasbourg-Metz, May 1978, Paris: Klincksieck, 1979, pp. 102–110.) Marc Fumaroli, on the other hand, points out the basically religious and tragic inspiration that makes Mme de Motteville's account of the Queen's life and that of her court an allegory of vanity and death ("La confidente et la Reine: Mme de Mot-teville et Anne d'Autriche," in *Revue des Sciences Humaines* 115, July–September 1964, pp. 265–278).

Although there is still no great critical monograph on Antoine Gombaud, CHEVALIER DE MÉRÉ, the bibliography concerning him coincides with the general bibliography on *honnêteté* (see above) of which he was one of the first and most important theorists: Sainte-Beuve, "Le Chevalier de Méré ou de l'honnête homme au Dix-Septième Siècle" (1848), in *Portraits littéraires*, in *Œuvres*, edited by Maxime Leroy, Vol. 2 (Paris: Gallimard/Bibliothèque de la Pléiade); *Le Chevalier de Méré, ami de Voiture, ami de Pascal, précepteur de Mme de Maintenon: Étude biographique et littéraire, suivie d'un choix de lettres et de pensées du Chevalier* (Niort: Clouzot, 1921); Pierre Viguié, *L'Honnête homme au XVIIe siècle: Le chevalier de Méré* (Paris: Sansot and Chiberre, 1922); J. de Feytaud, "Méré introducteur de Pascal aux 'Essais' de Montaigne," in *Bulletin de la Société des amis de Montaigne* 16 (1960), pp. 42–61; Jacques Benay, "L'honnête homme devant la nature, ou la philosophie du chevalier de Méré," in *PMLA*, Vol. 59 (March 1964), pp. 22–32; Mary Madeline Davitt, "L'art de plaire: une étude des rapports entre l'honnête homme et la société dans l'œuvre du Chevalier du Méré" (doctoral thesis, Rutgers University, 1972); Jean-Pierre Dens, "Méré et la critique mondaine," in *XVIIe siècle* 101 (1973), pp. 41–50, and "'Les agréments qui ne lassent point': le Chevalier de Méré et l'art de plaire," in *L'Esprit créateur*, Vol. 15, No. 1–2 (1975), pp. 221–227; Louise K. Horowitz, "Le Chevalier de Méré," in *Love and Language: A Study of the Classical French Moralist Writers* (Ohio State University Press, 1977), pp. 15–28; Michael Moriarty, "Méré: Taste and the Ideology of Honnêteté," in *Taste and Ideology in Seventeenth-Century France*, p. 105; Barbara Piqué, "I luoghi comuni dello Chevalier de Méré," in *Il confronto letterario*, Vol. 6, No. 12 (November 1989), pp. 347–367.

Méré often refers to the importance of being a good ACTOR in society: see B. de Mendoza, *L'Art de vivre de l'honnête homme: Éthique ou esthétique*, pp. 17–26, and on Méré as precursor to Diderot, "Un 'paradoxe sur le comédien' au XVIIe siècle," in *Revue des Sciences Humaines*, Vol. 38, No. 152 (1973), pp. 541–542.

On WIDOWHOOD, see Roger Duchêne, "La veuve au XVIIe siècle," in *Onze Études sur l'image de la femme dans la littérature française du dix-septième siècle*, pp. 165–181; see also Christian Biet's two articles, "De la veuve joyeuse à l'individu autonome" and "Clarice, veuve et femme libre un moment," both published in *XVIIe siècle* 187 (April–June 1995), pp. 307–330 and 190 (January–March 1996), pp. 33–41 respectively.

On the IMAGE OF SPAIN and the influence of Spanish literature on seventeenth-century France, see Alexandre Cioranescu, *Le Masque et le Visage* (Geneva: Droz, 1983); see also Michel Devèse, *Héroïsme et création littéraire sous les règnes d'Henri IV et de Louis XIII*, Actes du Colloque de Strasbourg (1972), edited by Noémi Hepp and Georges Livet (Paris: Klincksieck, 1974), pp. 91–97.

The INFLUENCE OF ITALIAN LITERATURE. In addition to two classic works, Alexandre Cioranescu's *L'Arioste en France, des origines à la fin du XVIIIe siècle* (Paris: Les Éditions des Presses Modernes, 1939), and C. B. Beall's *La Fortune du Tasse en France* (University of Oregon Monographs, 1942); Roger Lathuillère, *La Préciosité: Étude historique et linguistique*, Vol. 1: *Position du problème—Les origines* (Geneva: Droz, 1969), pp. 264–323, supplement to number 35 of *Studi francesi* 12 (May–August 1968), devoted to *L'Italianisme en France au XVIIe siècle*, and Lionello Sozzi's essay "L'influence en France des épopées italiennes et le débat sur le merveilleux," in *Mélanges offerts à Georges Couton*, pp. 61–73. See also *La France et l'Italie au temps de Mazarin*, texts collected and published by Jean Serroy (Grenoble: Presses Universitaires de Grenoble, 1986).

Honoré d'Urfé, *L'ASTRÉE*. I will restrict myself to recommending only a selection from the vast critical literature surrounding this well-known novel. For a reading of the whole text, see the Vaganay edition (Lyons, 1925; Slatkine Reprints, Geneva, 1966); for selected texts, see Gallimard's recent 1984 reprint, edited by Jean Lafond with an essential bibliography and excellent preface. See also Maurice Magendie, *Du nouveau sur "L'Astrée"* (Paris: Champion, 1927), and *"L'Astrée" d'Honoré d'Urfé* (Paris: Malfère, 1929); Antoine Adam, "La théorie mystique de l'Amour dans 'L'Astrée' et ses sources italiennes," in *Revue d'Histoire et de Philosophie et d'Histoire générale de la civilisation* 4 (1936), pp. 193–206; Jacques Ehrmann, *Un Paradis désespéré: L'amour et l'illusion dans "l'Astrée"* (Yale University Press/PUF, 1963); *Colloque commémoratif du quatrième centenaire de la naissance d'Honoré d'Urfé*, special number of *Diana* (Montbrison, 1970); Giorgetto Giorgi, *"L'Astrée" di Honoré d'Urfé tra Barocco e Classicismo* (Florence: La Nuova Italia, 1974); Maxime Gaume, *Les Inspirations et les sources de l'œuvre d'Honoré d'Urfé* (Saint-Étienne: Centre d'Études foréziennes, 1977); Jean Macary, "Poétique du dialogue dans L'Astrée," in *Papers on French Seventeenth Century Literature*, Vol. 10 (1978–1979), Part 2, pp. 29–73; Erica Harth, "*L'Astrée* and Aristocratic Ideology," in *Ideology and Culture in Seventeenth-Century France* (Cornell University Press, 1983), Chapter 2, pp. 34–48; Louise K. Horowitz, *Honoré d'Urfé* (Boston: Twayne Publishers, 1984).

On the pedagogic and civilizing role of *L'Astrée*, "which granted nobility to the idea of literature itself, thereby offering not only to amuse, but to educate," see Bury, *Littérature et politesse*, p. 93.

VOITURE (1598–1648). Two years after Voiture's death, his nephew Étienne Martin de Pinchêne, with the help of the Abbé Costar, produced a first edition of the *Œuvres de Monsieur Voiture* (Paris: A. Courbé, 1650; the *achevé d'imprimer* is dated November 30, 1649). The first part included the "Lettres," the "Lettres en vieux langage, Lettre espagnole à une dame en luy envoyant le verbe 'J'aime,' Romance." The second included the "Poésies: Élégies, Stances, Sonnets, Chansons, Fragments, Vers burlesques, Rondeaux, Vers en vieux langage." The collection of letters had an ironical epistolary introduction by Pinchêne addressed to Guez de Balzac, in which he claimed that Voiture was the very model of purity, gallantry, and artful letter-writing. It was the start of a great complex polemic that was to be joined by academicians, *savants*, and the "new learned," aimed at legitimizing literary invention and the new society literature. All the important, complex implications of this polemic have been examined by Alain Viala (*L'Esthétique galante: Paul Pellisson, Discours sur les œuvres de Monsieur Sarasin et autres textes*, pp. 18–27). In fact, after Voiture's death, the Abbé Costar instigated a real campaign of apologetics for his late friend, who in his view had been able to reconcile erudite culture with a refined and gallant worldly style, and he had printed, one after the other, *Défense des ouvrages de M. de Voiture* (1653), *Entretiens de M. de Voiture et M. Costar* (1654), and *Suite de la Défense de Voiture, à M. Ménage* (1655). In 1655, as Balzac was bringing his own followers into the fray, Paul Pellisson—an authoritative critic with connections to Ménage and the Scudérys—put forward a different point of view while claiming nevertheless to admire Voiture greatly. Pellisson was a very fashionable writer, in the pay of the Condé family, who had already written *Pompe funèbre de Voiture*, in which praise did not preclude criticism. In the *Discours* that accompanied the posthumous edition of the *Œuvres de Monsieur Sarasin*, he drew up a new literary genealogy based on continuity, which restored Balzac to his position of model and made Sarasin Voiture's equal rather than his imitator. On the importance of Balzac and Voiture in the development of the new French prose, see Bernard Beugnot, "La précellence du style moyen (1625–1650)," in *Histoire de la rhétorique dans l'Europe moderne*, pp. 539–599.

Despite the importance of his work—in particular his letters—in the evolution of the new French prose, Voiture is still surprisingly little studied. Essential from the historical, biographical point of view would be, I suggest, Émile Magne's two books, *Voiture et les origines de l'Hôtel de Rambouillet, 1597–1635: Portraits et documents inédits* (Paris: Mercure de France, 1911), and *Voiture et les années de gloire de l'Hôtel de Rambouillet, 1635–1648: Portraits et documents inédits* (Paris: Mercure de France, 1912). See also V. Fournel, "Voiture et Balzac," in *De Malherbe à Bossuet: Études littéraires et morales sur le XVIIe siècle* (Paris: Firmin Didot, 1885), pp. 24–65; Émile Faguet, "Voiture," in *Histoire de la poésie française de la Renaissance au Romantisme*, Vol. 3: *Précieux et burlesques* (Paris: Bovin, 1927), pp. 55–101; G. Michaut, "Voiture moraliste," in *Mélanges Lanson* (Paris: Hachette, 1922), pp. 210–216; Georges Mongrédien, "Le père spirituel de Voiture, M. de Chaudebonne: documents inédits," in *Mercure de France* 285 (July 15, 1938), pp. 346–365; Antoine Adam, "Voiture," in *Histoire de la littérature française au XVIIe siècle*, Vol. 1, pp. 385–393; R. Lathuillère, "Voiture et le 'bon usage' à l'Hôtel de Rambouillet," in *Cahiers de l'Association Internationale des Études Françaises* 14 (1962), pp. 63–78. A first-class contribution to the understanding of Voiture's poetry is Y. Fukui's study *Raffinement précieux dans la poésie française du XVIIe siècle* (Paris: Nizet, 1964), pp. 186–201, which I found very useful. See also C. F. Davinson, "Cervantes, Voiture, and the Spirit of Chivalry in France," in *Studi Francesi*, Vol. 18, No. 52 (1974), pp. 82–86. Henri Lafay's critical edition in two volumes of the *Poésies* (Paris: Michel Didier, 1974) is important for the rediscovery of Voiture, and I am enormously indebted to Micheline Cuénin's excellent essay "La lettre éducatrice de la sensibilité: l'exemple de Voiture," in *Revue d'Histoire littéraire de la France*, Vol. 78, No. 6 (November–December 1978), pp. 922–939. A. G. Wood, "Epistolary Style in Voiture and Mme de Sévigné," in *Papers on French Seventeenth Century Literature*, Vol. 15 (1988), pp. 229–238; and on Voiture's poetry, Alain Génetiot, *Les Genres lyriques mondains (1630–1660)*.

The Latin suffix -*ANA* appended to the name of a well-known writer often provided the title for a posthumous anthology, a potpourri of opinion, thought, sentences, verse, and anecdotes attributed to that writer. Thus the names of Ménage, Segrais, and Saint-Évremond are at the roots, respectively, of the collections *Menagiana*, *Segraisiana*, and *Saint-Evremoniana*, even though the authors had taken no part in conceiving or producing the works. Francine Wind's doctoral thesis ("Les Ana sous Louis XIV," Université de Paris IV–Sorbonne, 1991)—published ten years after B. Beugnot's essay "Forme et histoire: le statut des 'Ana,'" in *Mélanges offerts à Georges Couton*, pp. 85–101—serves as the primary reference work on this originally humanistic literary genre, which flourished in France from the early years of Louis XIV's reign until the beginning of the Restoration. The editor or editors of the -*ana* were usually disciples or friends of the deceased writer, and the manuscript could be drawn up over a period of time. For example, the five-hundred-page *Menagiana*, with its ten editors, was published in 1693, nine months after the death of Gilles Ménage, the *nouveau docte* who frequented the Blue Room. That collection is not only the genre's most successful example but serves as valuable testimony to a literary and society career and to a mixture of erudition and gallantry that seems to symbolize the culture of the time. Based on real conversations, the -*ana* imitated them by reflecting their wit, diversity, and love of anecdote. See Christoph Strosetzki, *Rhétorique de la conversation: Sa dimension littéraire et linguistique dans la société française du XVII*ᵉ *siècle*, translated by Sabine Seubert, Biblio 17 (Paris-Seattle-Tübingen: PFSCL, 1984), p. 101.

On *OTIUM STUDIOSUM* (learned leisure), see *Le Loisir lettré à l'âge classique*, collected essays by Marc Fumaroli, Philippe-Joseph Salazar, and Emmanuel Bury (Geneva: Droz, 1996). On SOCIAL LEISURE see Marc Fumaroli's "L'empire des femmes, ou l'esprit de joie," in *La Diplomatie de l'esprit*, pp. 321–339, and Alain Génetiot's *Poétique du loisir mondain, de Voiture à La Fontaine* (Paris: Champion, 1997).

CHAPTER 4

On the many interpretations of the word *ESPRIT*, see this book's introduction, Chapters 4 and 15, and the bibliographic notes for Chapter 15, below.

On the evolution of the idea of *STYLE NATUREL*, see Bernard Tocanne, *L'Idée de Nature en France dans la seconde moitié du XVII*ᵉ: *Contribution à l'histoire de la pensée classique* (Paris: Klincksieck, 1978), pp. 371–378. See also Michel Bouvier's

"Le Naturel," in *XVIIe siècle* 156 (July–September 1987), pp. 229–239; Georges Molinier's "La question du style naturel" in *L'Idée de Nature au début du XVIIe siècle*, edited by C. Biet in *Littératures classiques* 17 (1992), pp. 199–204; Emmanuel Bury, *L'Esthétique de La Fontaine* (Paris: SEDES, 1996), pp. 26; Viala, *Le Naturel galant*; Roger Zuber, *Les Émerveillements de la raison* (Paris: Klincksieck, 1997).

GUEZ DE BALZAC (1597–1654). Having enjoyed a great reputation, Guez de Balzac was forgotten for many years until he was rediscovered in the late 1960s as a subject of enormous critical interest. See Bernard Beugnot, *Guez de Balzac: Bibliographie générale* (Montreal: Les Presses de l'Université de Montréal, 1967; completed by *Supplément I*, Les Presses de l'Université de Montréal, 1969, and *Supplément II*, Université de Saint-Étienne, 1979); Frank E. Sutcliffe, *Guez de Balzac et son temps: Littérature et politique* (Paris: Nizet, 1972); H. Frank Brooks, "Guez de Balzac, Eloquence and the Life of the Spirit," *Essays in Memory of Nathan Edelman*, in *L'Esprit créateur* 15 (1975), pp. 59–78; Marc Fumaroli, "Critique et création littéraire: Balzac et Corneille," in *Mélanges offerts à René Pintard, Travaux de linguistique et littéraire*, Vol. 13, No. 2 (1975), pp. 73–79, reprinted in *Héros et orateurs: Rhétorique et dramaturgie cornéliennes* (Geneva: Droz, 1990); also Fumaroli's *L'Âge d'éloquence*, especially pp. 695–706; Jean Jehasse, *Guez de Balzac et le génie romain* (Saint-Étienne: Publications de l'Université, 1977). See also Roger Zuber's *Les "Belles infidèles" et la formation du goût classique* (1968; Paris: Albin Michel, 1995) especially Chapter 4 of part three: "De Balzac à Boileau," pp. 377–411; "Atticisme et classicisme," in *Critique et création littéraire en France au XVIIe siècle*, under Marc Fumaroli's direction, Colloque international du CNRS, 1974 (Paris: Éditions du Centre National de la Recherche Scientifique, 1997), pp. 375–393; "Guez de Balzac et les deux antiquités," in *XVIIe siècle* 131 (1981), pp. 135–148; "Balzac poète? Balzac savant? Les deux originales des 'Lettres de 1636,'" in *Mélanges offerts à Georges Couton*, pp. 147–160; "L'atelier de Chapelain et son invasion par Balzac," in *Les Voies de l'invention aux XVIe et XVIIe siècles*, edited by Bernard Beugnot and Robert Mclançon, in *Paragraphes* 9 (Montreal, 1993), pp. 179–278. Roger Zuber has produced a critical edition of Guez de Balzac's *Œuvres diverses (1644)* (Paris: Champion, 1995).

For the importance of Balzac's Lettres, see Bernard Beugnot's essay "La précellence du style moyen (1625–1650)," in *Histoire de la rhétorique dans l'Europe moderne*, pp. 539–599. First published in 1624 and in nine editions within ten years, the letters were "immediately perceived as the manifesto of the new taste and the new prose art" that was French Atticism and the middle style.

On the figure of the AUTHOR, see Arnaldo Pizzorusso, "L'idée d'auteur au XVIIe siècle," in *Le Statut de la littérature: Mélanges offerts à Paul Bénichou*, edited by Marc Fumaroli (Geneva: Droz, 1982), pp. 55–65.

Mlle de Scudéry expresses herself very clearly on the INCOMPATIBILITY OF THE POLITE SOCIETY FIGURE AND THE AUTHOR. As a woman, she experienced the problem most acutely. See her ten-volume novel *Artamène ou Le Grand Cyrus* (1649–1693; Geneva: Slatkine Reprints, 1972), Vol. 10, Part 10, Book 2, p. 366. On the problems encountered by women writers, see Nathalie Grande, *Stratégies de romancières* (Paris: Champion, 1999).

Society favored EPISTOLARY ART IN WRITING, since it was closely allied to the art of conversation. Voiture, Mme de Sévigné, and Bussy-Rabutin were the genre's most distinguished exponents. But in 1669, with the anonymously published *Lettres portugaises* (penned by the Vicomte de Guilleragues) and with Boursault's *Lettres de Babet*, the form came to be used in novel-writing, and a highly successful literary genre was born. See Bernard Bray's essay *L'Art de la lettre amoureuse: des manuels aux romans (1550–1700)*, inaugural lecture at the University of Utrecht (The Hague: Mouton, 1967). Bray is presently the greatest scholar of the epistolary form, and for his many contributions see his bibliography published in *Sur la plume des vents: Mélanges de littérature épistolaire offerts à Bernard Bray*, edited by Ulrike Michalowsky (Paris: Klincksieck, 1996), pp. 9–19. The essential bibliography to mention here concerns the analysis of the practice of letter-writing as a means of private communication only: Roger Duchêne, "Réalité et art épistolaire: le statut particulier de la lettre," in *Revue de l'Histoire littéraire de la France*, Vol. 71, No. 2 (March–April 1971), pp. 117–194; Bernard Bray, "L'épistolier et son publique en France au XVIIe siècle," in *Travaux de linguistique et de littérature*, Vol. 11, No. 2 (1973), pp. 7–17; Bernard Beugnot, "Débats autour du genre épistolaire, réalité et écriture," in *Revue d'Histoire littéraire de la France*, Vol. 80, No. 2 (March–April 1974), pp. 195–202; *La Lettre au XVIIe siècle*, special number of the *Revue d'Histoire littéraire de la France*, Vol. 78, No. 6 (November–December 1978), pp. 883–1021. Actes du Colloque de la Société d'Histoire Littéraire de France organized by Bernard Bray, Collège de France, November 26, 1977; *Men/Women of Letters*, monographic number of *Yale French Studies*, Vol. 71 (1986); Elizabeth C. Goldsmith, *"Exclusive Conversations"; Roger Duchêne, Mme de Sévigné et la lettre d'amour* (1970), new edition edited by Geneviève Haroche-Bouzinac (Paris: Klincksieck, 1992); *Art de la lettre, art de la conversation à l'époque classique en France*, Actes du Colloque de Wolfenbüttel, October 1991, edited by Bernard Bray and Christoph Strosetzki (Paris: Klincksieck, 1995).

On the custom started by Mme de Sablé and Mme de Maure of writing each other NOTES that dispensed with the usual formulae of respect and manners, see Geneviève Haroche-Bouzinac, "'Billets font conversation': de la théorie à la pratique: l'exemple de Voiture," in *Art de la lettre, art de la conversation*, pp. 341–354.

SALON POETRY. The best reference book for the middle years of the seventeenth century is Alain Génetiot's study *Les Genres lyriques mondains* (1630–1660), and Génetiot, "'Otium literatum' et poésie mondaine en France de 1625 à 1655," in *Le Loisir lettré à l'âge classique*, pp. 212–231. For the eighteenth century and the end of the seventeenth, see Robert Finch, *The Sixth Sense: Individualism in French Poetry, 1686–1760* (University of Toronto Press, 1996).

On the new direction being taken by French poetry, see Bernard Beugnot, "La précellence du style moyen (1625–1650)," in *Histoire de la rhétorique dans l'Europe moderne*, pp. 539–599.

About POETIC IMPROVISATION, see Marc Fumaroli's preface to Françoise Waquet's study *Rhétorique et poétique chrétiennes: Bernardino Perfetti et la poésie improvisée dans l'Italie du XVIIIe siècle* (Florence: Olschki, 1992).

On eighteenth-century impromptu art, see Chapter 5 of Sylvan Menant, *La Chute d'Icare: La crise de la poésie française (1700–1750)* (Geneva: Droz, 1981), pp. 255–272.

VOITURE'S CORRESPONDENCE WITH COSTAR shows how polite society's ways were spreading even among the literati and altering the traditional style of both. As Ortigue de Vaumorière claims in *L'Art de plaire dans la conversation* (1688; Paris: Jean and Michel Guignard, 1701, *Entretien* 9, pp. 139f), manuals suggested that Voiture's model was the right one.

On the complex mechanisms of love and hate, attraction and repulsion, acceptance and confrontation between the literati and society, which form the basis of the *ancien régime*'s last moralist literary masterpiece, Nicolas Chamfort's *Les Produits de la civilisation perfectionné: Maximes et Pensées, Caractères et Anecdotes*, see Claude Arnaud's fine book *Chamfort* (Paris: Laffont, 1988); in English as *Chamfort: A Biography*, translated by Deke Dusinberre (University of Chicago Press, 1992).

DUELING. See, among other studies, Micheline Cuénin, *Le Duel sous l'Ancien Régime* (Paris: Presses de la Renaissance, 1982), and Françoise Billacois, *Le Duel dans la société française des XVIe–XVIIe siècles: Essai de psychologie historique* (Paris: Éditions de l'École des Hautes Études en sciences sociales, 1986).

As Geneviève Haroche-Bouzinac points out in *Voltaire et ses lettres de jeunesse* (Paris: Klincksieck, 1992), Voltaire, who generally disliked Vincent Voiture, "admired [Voiture's] dignified bourgeois behavior when confronting *les grands*" (p. 162).

CHAPTER 5

On the DUC DE MONTAUSIER, see Denis Lopez's monograph *La Plume et l'Épée: Montausier (1610–1690)*, Biblio 17 (Paris-Seattle-Tübingen: PFSCL, 1987).

There is a fine, very well documented modern edition of LA GUIRLANDE DE JULIE, edited by Irène Frain (*La Guirlande de Julie*, followed by a *Dictionnaire du Langage des Fleurs aux fins de chiffrer et déchiffrer vos tendres messages floraux*, Paris: Laffont, 1991).

On the painting of Mme de Rambouillet watching over her dead son, see Victor Cousin, *La Société française au XVIIe siècle d'après le Grand Cyrus de Mlle de Scudéry*, Vol. 1, p. 250; see also *Le Cabinet de Monsieur de Scudéry*, edited by Christian Biet and Dominique Mocond'huy (Paris: Klincksieck, 1991), p. 157.

Julie d'Angennes's marriage to the Duc de Montausier was celebrated on July 15, 1645, by Antoine Godeau, bishop of Grasse. Godeau was a frequent guest at the hôtel de Rambouillet between 1632 and 1636 and Julie's former "dwarf," who later became a man of God. See *Antoine Godeau: De la galanterie à la sainteté*, Actes des Journées commémoratives, Grasse, April 21–24, 1972, edited by Yves Giraud (Paris: Klincksieck, 1975).

CHAPTER 6

On MME DE LONGUEVILLE, see J. F. Bourgouin de Villefore's enlightening biography, *La Véritable Vie d'Anne Geneviève de Bourbon, duchesse de Longueville, par l'auteur des Anecdotes de la Constitution Unigenitus* (Amsterdam, 1739); Victor Cousin's two monographs on her, *La Jeunesse de Mme de Longueville* (1852; Paris: Didier, 1876) and *Mme de Longueville pendant la Fronde* (1859; Paris: Didier, 1881); and Sainte-Beuve's portrait of 1840, "Mme de Longueville" in *Portraits de femmes*, in *Œuvres*, Vol. 2, pp. 1273–1304. Sainte-Beuve paid considerable attention to Mme de Longueville's Jansenist sympathies and to her contribution to the Peace of the Church in his three-volume history of Port-Royal (1860), edited by Maxim Leroy (Paris: Gallimard/ Bibliothèque de la Pléiade, 1953–1955). See also Cécile Gazier, *Les Belles Amies de Port-Royal* (1930; Paris: Librairie Académique Perrin, 1954). More recently, the story of Mme de Longueville's association with the celebrated Jansenist stronghold has been studied by Jacques Émile, "Mme de Longueville protectrice de Port-Royal et des Jansenistes," in *Chroniques de Port-Royal* 29 (1980), pp. 35–83.

On the CABALE DES IMPORTANTS see Michel Pernot, *La Fronde* (Paris: Éditions de Fallois, 1994), pp. 45–50.

The incident of the LOST LETTER has been reconstructed by Noémi Hepp, "Un drame de cour autour de deux lettres perdues: thèmes et variations dans les Mémoires du temps (1643)," in *Sur la plume des vents: Mélanges de littérature épistolaire offerts à Bernard Bray*, pp. 61–62. Anne of Austria's attitude toward the matter has been explored by Simone Bertière, *Les Deux Régentes*, Vol. 1 of *Les Reines de Frances au temps des Bourbons* (Paris: Édition de Fallois, 1996), pp. 389–392.

On the DUC DE BEAUFORT see Cardinal de Retz, *Mémoires, La conjuration du Comte Jean-Louis de Fiesques, Pamphlets*, edited by Maurice Allem (Paris: Gallimard/ Bibliothèque de la Pléiade, 1956), p. 47.

On the CONDÉ FAMILY consult if possible the Duc d'Aumale's monumental seven-volume work *Histoire des Princes de Condé pendant les XVIe et XVIIe siècles* (Paris: Calmann-Lévy, 1886), especially Vol. 3 on Henri II de Bourbon (Monsieur le Prince) and Vols. 4 through 7 on his son, Louis de Bourbon Condé (the Grand Condé). On the latter's Jesuit education and the "occasion of the last literary blaze of magnanimity," see Marc Fumaroli, *Héros et orateurs: Rhétorique et dramaturgie cornéliennes.* See also Gustave Magnon, *Le Grand Condé et le théâtre (1676–1686)* (Paris: H. Leclerc et P. Cornuau, 1899); Henri Chériot, *Trois Éducations princières au XVIIᵉ siècle: le Grand Condé, son fils, le duc d'Enghien, son petit-fils, le duc de Bourbon* (Lille: Desclée de Brouwer, 1896). Also note the following biographies of the Grand Condé: Georges Mongrédien, *Le Grand Condé* (Paris: Hachette, 1959); Pierre Duhamel, *Le Grand Condé ou l'orgueil* (Paris: Perrin, 1981); Marc Blancpain, *Monsieur le Prince* (Paris: Hachette, 1986); Bernard Pujo, *Le Grand Condé* (Paris: Le Grand Livre du Mois, 1995).

The diplomatic negotiations at MÜNSTER have recently been described by Anne-Marie Enaux, "Les plénipotentiares en Westphalie," in *1648, la paix de Westphalie vers l'Europe moderne* (Paris: Imprimerie Nationale, 1998), pp. 125–134.

On the FRONDE, see *La Fronde en questions*; Christian Jouhaud, *Mazarinades: La Fronde des mots* (Paris: Aubier, 1985); Hubert Carrier, *Les Mazarinades*, two volumes (Geneva, Droz: 1989–1991); Michel Pernot, *La Fronde*; Oreste Ranum, *The Fronde: A French Revolution, 1648–1652* (Norton, 1993).

There are various interpretations of the IMPORTANCE OF WOMEN IN THE FRONDE; I will limit myself to recommending two. Joan DeJean maintains that "more than any other conflict in French history, the Fronde can be seen as a woman's war" and that "for nearly six years they dominated French political life in heroic style, forcing a suspension of the *Ancien Régime*'s normal hierarchy of authority" (*Tender Geographies*, pp. 37, 38). Micheline Cuénin, in her essay "La femme et la guerre (1516–1660)," writes that the Fronde gave women their last opportunity to enter the field because "the evolution of methods of warfare and the reorganization of the army instigated by Le Telier made impossible any form of intervention on the part of a woman, be it right or wrong" (in *Présences féminines: Littérature et société au XVIIᵉ siècle français*, p. 317). See also Livet's 1859 essay "Les femmes de la Fronde," in *Revue Européenne* 3 (1859), pp. 529–551, 726–758; see also Dorothy Anne Liot Baker, *Precious Women*, pp. 141–150.

BARBE D'ERNECOURT, COMTESSE DE SAINT-BALMON. In 1634, after the French invasion, Lorraine found itself at the mercy of the imperial and French soldiers and local brigands. While the nobility fled their lands, the countess, in the absence of her husband who was away fighting with Duke Charles IV, organized the defense of the Verdunois, salvaging crops, helping the weakest, and protecting the monasteries and religious places. See the works by Micheline Cuénin and Joan DeJean mentioned above as well as Cuénin's *La Dernière des Amazones: Mme de Saint Baslemont* (Nancy: Presses Universitaires de Nancy, 1992).

MME DE LONGUEVILLE'S POLITICAL WRITINGS were probably collected by Sarasin, the Prince de Condé's secretary, and signed by her. She wrote prolifically during the Fronde of the Princes: *Manifeste de Mme la Duchesse de Longueville* (Brussels, 1650), *Lettre de Mme la Duchesse de Longueville au Roi* (Rotterdam, 1650), *Justification de Messieurs les Princes, contenant les affaires les plus importants qui se sont traictées pour l'ajustement des couronnes* (1650), *Tres humbles remostrances faites au Roy et à la Reyne par Mme et Mademoiselle de Longueville pour la liberté des Messieurs les Princes* (Paris, 1651).

On MME DE LONGUEVILLE's RELIGIOUS CONVERSION, I am indebted to Benedetta Papàsogli's "Ritratto di Mme de Longueville," now in *La lettera e lo spirito: Temi e figure del Seicento francese* (Pisa: Libreria Goliardica, 1986), pp. 77–118. For the significance of the metaphor *fond du cœur* (the bottom of the heart) and its history, I recommend B. Papàsogli's book *Il "fondo del cuore": Figure dello spazio interiore nel Seicento francese* (Pisa: Libreria Goliardica, 1991), a French edition of which was published in Paris by Honoré Champion in 2000.

CHAPTER 7

MME DE MONTBAZON. Tallemant described her in one of his most ferocious *historiettes* (Vol. 2, pp. 217–221), but Mme de Motteville, Cardinal de Retz, La Rochefoucauld, and Mademoiselle de Montpensier also mention her in their memoirs.

On DEATH and THE ART OF DYING WELL in the seventeenth century, I will merely mention here the following important studies: Michel Vovelle, *Mourir autrefois: Attitudes collectives devant la mort au XVIIᵉ et XVIIIᵉ siècle* (Paris: Gallimard-Juliard, 1974); Philippe Ariès, *Essais sur l'histoire de la mort en Occident du Moyen Âge à nos jours* (Paris: Éditions du Seuil, 1975), and Pierre Chaunu, *La Mort à Paris XVIᵉ, XVIIᵉ, XVIIIᵉ siècle* (Paris: Fayard, 1978); R. Chartier, "Normes et conduite: Les arts de mourir 1450–1600," in *Lectures et lecteurs dans la France d'Ancien Régime*, pp. 125–163; *Savoir mourir*, Actes du Colloque international, Créteil, May 21–23, 1992, edited by Christine Montandon-Binet and Alain Montandon, with a postscript by Louis-Vincent Thomas (Paris: L'Harmattan, 1993); Constance Cagnat, *La Mort classique: Écrire la mort dans la littérature française en prose de la seconde moitié du XVIIᵉ siècle* (Paris: Champion, 1995).

On Chateaubriand's *VIE DE RANCÉ*, the genesis of the book, its different editions, and the breadth of literary criticism it provoked, I recommend Benedetta Papàsogli's introduction, biographical note, text notes, and appendix to the Italian edition: *La Vita di Rancé*, edited by Benedetta Papàsogli (Milan: San Paolo, 1993).

On the *GRAND SIÈCLE*'s belief in its own CULTURAL AND ARTISTIC SUPERIORITY, see Françoise Waquet's excellent study, *Le Modèle français et l'Italie savante*. See also

Marc Fumaroli's essay "Les abeilles et les araignées," in *La Querelle des Anciens et des Modernes, XVIIe-XVIIIe siècles*, edited by Anne-Marie Lecoq (Paris: Gallimard, 2001).

RANCÉ. Henri Brémond's brilliant, highly polemical biography, *L'Abbé Tempête, Armand de Rancé, réformateur de la Trappe* (Paris: Hachette, 1929), can be combined with A. J. Krailsheimer's important, balanced study, *Armand-Jean de Rancé, Abbot of La Trappe* (Clarendon Press, 1974). On the *querelle des études* between Rancé and Mabillon, see Blandine Kriegel, *La Querelle Mabillon-Rancé* (1988; Paris: Quai Voltaire, 1992). Roland Barthes' famous preface to Chateaubriand, *Vie de Rancé*, dates from 1965 (Paris: Union Générale d'Éditions, 10/18).

In her fine book *La principessa giansenista: Saggi su Mme de Lafayette* (Rome: Bulzoni, 1981), Gabriella Violato proposes a reading of MME DE LAFAYETTE's masterpiece in the light of JANSENIST teaching.

CHAPTER 8

The first study of MME DE SABLÉ was Victor Cousin's *Mme de Sablé* (1854; Paris: Didier, 1869). It was immediately reviewed in England by George Eliot in a long and penetrating essay, "Women in France: Mme de Sablé," in *Westminster Review* 62 (October 1854), pp. 448–473, now included in *Essays of George Eliot*, edited by Thomas Pinney (London: Routledge and Kegan Paul, 1963), pp. 52–81. There followed Édouard Barthélemy's *Mme la comtesse de Maure, sa vie et sa correspondance suivies des Maximes de Madame de Sablé et d'une étude sur la vie de Mademoiselle de Vandy* (Paris: J. Gay, 1863); *Les Amis de la marquise de Sablé: Recueil des lettres des principaux habitués de salon, annotées et précédées d'une introduction historique sur la société précieuse* (Paris: Dentu, 1865); J. G. A. Crussaire, *Un Médecin au XVIIe siècle: le Dr. Vallant. Une malade imaginaire: Mme de Sablé* (Paris: Vigot frères, 1910); and an extremely well documented study by Nicolas Ivanoff, *La marquise de Sablé et son salon* (Paris: Les Presses Modernes, 1927). See also Giuliana Toso Rodinis, *Mme de Sablé: Les Maximes* (Padua: Liviana Editrice, 1971). From the time of Sainte-Beuve's *Port-Royal* onward, Mme de Sablé has aroused interest primarily because of her connection to the Jansenist movement and for the part she played in the genesis of La Rochefoucauld's *Maximes*. Apropos, see Louis Lafuma's "Mme de Sablé et les dangers de la Comédie," in *Écrits sur Pascal* (Paris: Éditions du Luxembourg, 1959), pp. 117–124; Jean Lafond, "Mme de Sablé, La Rochefoucauld, Jacques Esprit: un fond commun, trois œuvres" and "Mme de Sablé et son salon" in *L'Homme et son image: Morales et littérature de Montaigne à Mandeville* (Paris: Champion, 1996). The *Portefeuilles Vallant* (manuscripts preserved in the Bibliothèque Nationale in Paris) are the documents of the marquise's doctor and secretary that relate to her salon's visitors and the subjects discussed there; they show the importance of Mme de Sablé's position in the culture of the time. Contemporary opinion confirms that Mme de Sablé was a most unusual person. Such sources include Tallemant des Réaux's *historiette* (Vol. 1, pp. 514–521); Mlle de Scudéry's idealized portrait of her in *Artamène, ou Le Grand Cyrus* (Part 6, Book 1, Vol. 6, pp. 71–74), where she is depicted as Parthénie, Princess of Salamis; the Grande Mademoiselle's extremely well known albeit ironical portrait in *Histoire de la Princesse de Paphlagonie* (Bordeaux, 1659, pp. 78–82); and the respective memoirs of Mme de Motteville and Père Rapin, both of which express unqualified admiration for her.

Mme de Sablé's *Maximes* were published posthumously in 1678 by the Abbé d'Ailly with the publisher S. Mabre-Cramoisy in Paris. They can now be found following La Rochefoucauld's *Maximes* in the edition Jean Lafond prepared for Gallimard (1976), as well as, edited by A. A. Morello, in the volume *Les Moralistes du XVIIᵉ siècle*, edited by Jean Lafond (Paris: Laffont, 1992).

On MAXIMS, see Louis van Delft, "Mme de Sablé et Gracián," in *Saggi e ricerche di letteratura francese* 12 (1983), pp. 267–285, and Harald Wentzlaff-Eggebert, "Montaigne, Gracián, La Rochefoucauld, La Bruyère et les Maximes de Mme de Sablé," in *Le Langage littéraire au XVIIᵉ siècle: De la rhétorique à la littérature* (Tübingen: Gunter Narr, 1991), pp. 181–193.

The PART PLAYED BY WOMEN IN RELIGIOUS DEBATE is studied in depth by Linda Timmermans in her *L'Accès des femmes à la culture*, and it is also the subject of an essay by Roger Duchêne, "La théologie expliqué aux dames," in *Hommage à René Fromilhague, Cahiers de Littérature du XVIIᵉ siècle* 6 (1984) pp. 149–162.

On the link between PRECIOSITY AND JANSENISM, see Roger Lathuillère, "Au commencement étaient les précieuses," in *Au bonheur des mots: Mélanges en l'honneur de Gérald Antoine* (Nancy: Presses Universitaires de Nancy, 1984), pp. 289–299; Philippe Sellier, "La névrose précieuse: une nouvelle pléiade?" in *Présences féminines: Littérature et société au XVIIᵉ siècle français*, pp. 95–125; Linda Timmermans, "Une hérésie féministe? Jansénisme et préciosité," in *Ordres et contestations au temps des classiques*, Actes du Colloque CMR 17-NASSCFL I (Paris-Seattle-Tübingen, PFSCL, 1992), pp. 159–172.

Jean Bertaut's VERSE, "Dont malheureuse est l'ignorance/et plus malheureux le savoir," which was quoted in Mlle d'Attichy's letter and appeared in the first edition of 1660, was corrected in the revised edition of 1606 to "Mon mal vient de mon ignorance/Et ma mort vient de mon savoir"; see *Le Recueil de quelques vers amoureux*, edited by Louis Terreaux (Paris: Didier, 1970), p. 142. The verses referred to a lady in whom the poet had placed all his trust and who had unexpectedly betrayed him, thus revealing the incurable inconstancy of the female heart. These quotations, like the ones scattered throughout Mme de Sévigné's letters, show how poetry lived in the memory, nurturing contemplation of morality within polite society.

On the problems of SINCERITY and *POLITESSE*, see Marcel Raymond, "Du Jansénisme à la morale de l'intérêt," in *Mercure de France* 330 (1957), pp. 238–255; Jean Mesnard, "*Le Misanthrope*, mise en question de l'art de plaire," in *La Culture du XVIIe siècle*, pp. 520–545; Roland Galle, "Honnêteté und sincérité," in *Französische Klassik: Theorie, Literatur, Malerei*, edited by F. Nies and K. Stierle (Munich: Fink, 1985), pp. 33–60.

There are several contemporary portraits of the COMTESSE DE MAURE and her husband: Tallemant des Réaux, "Le comte et la comtesse de Maure," in *Historiettes*, Vol. 1, pp. 522–526; "Portrait de Mme la Comtesse de Maure, fait par Monsieur le Marquis de Sourdis," in Mademoiselle's collection *Divers Portraits* (Caen, 1659), pp. 156–160; *Mémoires de Mme de Motteville*, Vol. 2, pp. 395–398.

At the outbreak of the Jansenist dispute, the LETTER in which MME DE MAURE declared herself in favor of papal authority refers, at the beginning, to another letter from Mme de Sablé to the Marquis de Sourdis concerning the problem of grace. In fact, between 1658 and 1659, Sourdis had composed a brief tract designed to unleash the "first civil war at Port-Royal," by which he intended to demonstrate how the five propositions condemned by the Church were in fact really contained in Jansenius's *Augustinus* (see Jean Mesnard, "Récit des discussions avec Barcos," in Blaise Pascal, *Œuvres complètes*, edited by Jean Mesnard, Paris: Desclée de Brouwer, 1964, Vol. 1, pp. 1040f). If Mme de Sablé's letter to Sourdis refers, as seems likely, to the marquis's thesis, it would make it possible to date Mme de Maure's letter to 1658 or 1659.

In this letter the countess discusses the problem of PREDESTINATION, then central to Jansenist polemic, and quotes an Augustinian treatise, *Of Grace*, which in fact does not exist. There are, however, Saint Augustine's *De natura et gratia* (415), *De gratia Christi et peccato originali* (418), *De gratia et libero arbitrio* (426–427), and *De correptione et gratia* (426–427), all of which address the subject of predestination. The one to which Mme de Maure presumably refers is the *De correptione et gratia*, translated into French by Antoine Arnauld in 1644, which contains the key distinction between *adiutorium sine qua non* and *adiutorium quo* (12, 34), which the Jansenists interpreted as meaning that sufficient grace was the opposite of efficacious grace (see Gaetano Lettieri, *Il metodo della grazia: Pascal e l'ermeneutica giansenista di Sant' Agostino*, Rome: Edizione Dehoniane, 1999, pp. 110–113). Sufficient grace is defined by many theologians as the ability to do good, both grace and free will being necessary. For Jansenius, only efficacious grace, otherwise called the act of salvation, was infallible. The passage in *De correptione et gratia* to which Mme de Maure may refer in her letter is one of the many on predestination in which Saint Augustine seems to restrict to the few God's will to save. But to which bull does Mme de Maure appeal? Three bulls appeared during the seventeenth century, all decisively condemning Jansenism: *In eminenti*, promulgated in 1643 by Urban VIII; *Cum occasione*, promulgated in 1653 by Innocent X; and *Ad Sanctam Beati Petri Sedem*, promulgated by Alexander VII in 1656. The main thesis of the second and third is the difference between the Jansenist interpretation of Augustine (summed up in the five famous propositions) and the "true Augustine," which is really a Molinist interpretation of Augustine. The bull referred to by Mme de Sablé could be the *Cum occasione* or the *Ad Sanctam* on account of the attention both attracted in France. Mazarin in fact obliged the clergy, the Parlement, and the Sorbonne to subscribe to them (under the signature "Formulaire").

On *QUESTIONS D'AMOUR*, see Paul Rémy, "Les cours d'amour: légende et réalité," in *Revue de l'Université de Bruxelles* (January–April 1955): pp. 179–197; C. Rouben, "Un jeu de société au Grand Siècle: les Questions et les Maximes d'Amour. Inventaire Chronologique," in *XVIIᵉ siècle* 97 (1972), pp. 85–104; and the section edited by Jean Lafond on *questions et maximes d'amour* and the bibliography in *Moralistes du XVIIᵉ siècle*, pp. 33–54. The problems concerning "questions of gallantry" in Mlle de Scudéry are discussed by Chantal Morlet-Chantalat in her chapter "De l'histoire édifiante à la question galante," in *La Clélie de Mademoiselle de Scudéry: De l'épopée à la Gazette: Un discours féminin de la gloire* (Paris: Champion, 1994), pp. 261–282. For the *questions d'amour* discussed in Mme de Sablé's salon, see Ivanoff, *La marquise de Sablé et son salon*, pp. 138–142; and Louis Lafuma, "Le veritable auteur des 'questions d'amour' des Portefeuilles Vallant," in *Revue d'Histoire littéraire de la France* 62 (1962), pp. 353–362, where authorship of the *questions d'amour* copied down by Vallant is attributed to the Marquis de Sourdis. Also recommended, Corrado Rosso, *Sagezza in salotto: Moralisti francesi ed espressione aforistica* (Naples: Edizioni Scientifiche Italiane, 1991), especially the chapters "Dalle Questions d'amour alle Maximes o un giallo galante nel Seicento francese" (pp. 73–86), and "I 'quiz' di Marie Linage: processo all'amore e formazione delle Maximes" (pp. 87–100).

On the problem of attributing the *LETTRES PORTUGAISES*—and here Leo Spitzer's famous 1953 essay "Les lettres portugaises" should not be forgotten (*Romanische Forschungen* 65, pp. 94–135)—the most important thesis is now that of Frédéric Deloffre, who identified Guilleragues as the author. See the edition edited by Frédéric Deloffre and Jacques Rougeot, *Lettres portugaises, Valentins et autres œuvres de Guilleragues* (1962; Geneva: Droz, 1972); and the puzzling article by Giovanni Macchia, "Un personaggio senza autore," in *Il mito di Parigi: Saggi e motivi francesi* (Torino: Einaudi, 1965), pp. 120–124. Also keep in mind Deloffre's "Guilleragues épistolier: une lettre inédite à Mme de La Sablière," in *Revue d'Histoire littéraire de la France*, Vol. 65, No. 4 (1965), pp. 590–613; "L'énigme des 'Lettres portugaises': preuves et documents nouveaux," in *Bulletin des études portugaises* 27 (1966), pp. 11–27; "'Guilleragues, rien qu'un Gascon': remarques sur quelques particularités de la langue de Guilleragues et des Lettres Portugaises," in *Revue de Linguistique Romane* 20 (1966), pp. 267–278; and finally, the preface to Guilleragues, *Lettres portugaises, suivies de Guilleragues par lui-même*, edited by Frédéric Deloffre (Paris: Gallimard, 1990). See also the beautiful edition of *Lettres portugaises, lettre d'une péruvienne et autres romans d'amour par lettres*, edited by Bernard Bray and Isabelle Landy-Houillon

(Paris: Flammarion, 1983) and Giovanna Malquori Fondi's important study, *Le "Lettres portugaises" di Guilleragues* (Naples: Liguori, 1980). See, finally, Vittorio Fortunati, *Guilleragues autore epistolare: Le "Lettres portugaises" e la correspondance* (Como: Edizioni New Press, 1999).

FRIENDSHIP. Anne Vincent-Buffault, *L'Exercice de l'amitié: Pour une histoire des pratiques amicales aux XVIIIe et XIXe siècles* (Paris: Éditions du Seuil, 1995); *Foi, fidélité, amitié en Europe à la période moderne: Mélanges R. Sauzet* (Tours: Université de Tours, 1995). On the importance of friendship to the Parisian elite around 1650, especially in Fouquet's circle, read Marc Fumaroli's chapter "L'amitié et la crainte," in *Le Poète et le roi*, pp. 159–202. See also the monographic number of *XVIIe siècle* (October–December 1999) devoted to *Amitié*, particularly Sylvie Requemora's essay "L'amitié dans les 'Maximes' de La Rochefoucauld" (pp. 687–728). The debate on friendship that took off in Mme de Sablé's drawing room in about 1661 has been examined by Ivanoff in *La marquise de Sablé et son salon*, pp. 142–147, and by Jean Lafond, "L'amitié selon Arnauld d'Andilly," in *L'Homme et son image*, pp. 267–288. On Robert Arnauld d'Andilly, see too Jean Mesnard, "Jansénisme et littérature," in *Le Statut de la littérature: Mélanges offerts à Paul Bénichou*, pp. 117–135.

On CLASSICAL MORALISTS, from the wealth of criticism available on the subject, I will limit myself here to pointing out several fundamental readings, first and foremost the great inaugural study of 1948 by Paul Bénichou, *Morales du Grand Siècle*, which exists in numerous reprints; Giovanni Macchia, *I moralisti classici: Da Machiavelli a La Bruyère* (1961; Adelphi, Milan, 1989); Corrado Rosso, *Virtù e critica della virtù nei moralisti francesi* (1964; Pisa: Libreria Goliardica, 1971); *La "Maxime": Saggi per una tipologia critica* (Naples: Edizioni Scientifiche Italiane, 1968); Jean Lafond, *La Rochefoucauld: Augustinisme et littérature* (1977; Paris: Klincksieck, 1986); "Littérature et morale au XVIIe siècle," in *L'Homme et son image*, pp. 291–304; *Des formes brèves de la littérature morale au XVIe et XVIIe siècles, Les formes brèves de la prose et le discours discontinu (XVIe et XVIIe siècles)*, edited by Jean Lafond (Paris: Vrin, 1984), pp. 101–121; preface to *Moralistes du XVIIe siècle*, pp. i-xli. Whereas Lafond sees the moralist literature as coinciding with "short form," Louis van Delft—that other great authority on classical moralists—takes another line. He sees the short form as being, together with thematics and point of view, one of the three component parts of the moralist's statute. Van Delft's studies constitute a critical guide and essential methodology for understanding the world of the classical moralists. They include "Qu'est-ce qu'un moraliste?" in *Cahiers de l'Association Internationale des Études Françaises* 30 (1978), pp. 105–120; "La spécificité du moraliste classique," in *Revue d'Histoire littéraire en France* 80:4 (July–August 1980), pp. 540–553; *Le Moraliste classique: Essai de définition et de typologie* (Geneva: Droz, 1982); and *Littérature et anthropologie: Nature humaine et caractère à l'âge classique* (Paris: PUF, 1993). See too Marc Fumaroli's 1994 essay on Montaigne, "Le Protée français et ses moralistes," in *La Diplomatie de l'esprit*, pp. 341–375; *Il prisma dei moralisti: Per il tricentenario* *di La Bruyère*, edited by Benedetta Papàsogli and Barbara Piqué (Rome: Salerno, 1997); the monographic number of *XVIIe siècle* dedicated to *Les moralistes: Nouvelles tendances de la recherche* (January–March 1999); and B. Parmentier, *Le Siècle des moralistes* (Paris: Éditions du Seuil, 2000).

For a critical bibliography of LA ROCHEFOUCAULD, as well as for the critique of classical moralists, I will include here the essential list based on my own reading: Sainte-Beuve, "Monsieur de La Rochefoucauld," in *Portraits de femmes*, pp. 1241–1273 (Sainte-Beuve placed this portrait between one of Mme de Lafayette and one of Mme de Longueville); Paul Bénichou, "L'intention des Maximes," in *L'Écrivain et ses travaux* (Paris: Corti, 1967), pp. 3–37; Jean Starobinski, "Complexité de La Rochefoucauld," in *Preuves* 135 (1962), pp. 33–40; "La Rochefoucauld et les morales substitutives," in *Nouvelle Revue Française*, July 1966, pp. 16–34, and August 1966, pp. 211–229; Jacques Truchet, "Le succès des Maximes de La Rochefoucauld," in *Cahiers de l'Association Internationale des Études Françaises* 18 (1966), pp. 125–137; William G. Moore, *La Rochefoucauld: His Mind and Art* (Clarendon Press, 1969); Enea Balmas, "La bibliothèque du duc de La Rochefoucauld," in *De Jean Lemaire de Belges à Jean Giraudoux: Mélanges d'histoire et de critique littéraire offerts à Pierre Jourda* (Paris: Nizet, 1970), pp. 179–201; Giovanni Macchia, "Il dramma di un moralista," in *Il paradiso della ragione* (1960; Torino: Einaudi, 1972), pp. 111–149, and "L'impassibile arciere," in *Le rovine di Parigi* (Milan: Mondadori, 1985), pp. 34–45; Jean Lafond, *La Rochefoucauld: Augustinisme et littérature*; Philippe Sellier, "La Rochefoucauld, Pascal, Saint-Augustin," in *Revue d'Histoire littéraire de la France*, Vol. 69, No. 3–4 (May–August 1969), pp. 551–575; "La Rochefoucauld et la préciosité," in *La Rochefoucauld, "Mithridate," Frères et sœurs, les muses sœurs*, edited by Claire Carlin, Twenty-Ninth Annual Congress of the North American Society for Seventeenth-Century French Literature, University of Victoria, April 3–5, 1997, Biblio 17, No. 111 (Tübingen: Gunter Narr, 1998), pp. 13–19; "L'Univers imaginaire de La Rochefoucauld," in *Il prisma dei moralisti*, pp. 383–396; Jean Mesnard, "La rencontre de La Rochefoucauld avec Port-Royal" (1984) and "L'esthétique de La Rochefoucauld" (1987), two essays reprinted in *La Culture du XVIIe siècle*, pp. 292–296 and pp. 236–244 respectively; Piero Toffano, *La figura dell'antitesi nelle massime di La Rochefoucauld* (Fasano: Schena, 1989); Maria Teresa Biason, *La massima o il "saper dire"* (Palermo: Sellerio, 1990). By Louis van Delft, I would first recommend the excellent critical assessment "La Rochefoucauld en perspective," in the journal *Op. cit.* 11 (November 1998), pp. 83–92, and "La Rochefoucauld et 'l'Anathomie de tous les replis du cœur,'" in *Littératures classiques* 35 (January 1999), pp. 37–62; the same issue of *Littératures classiques* also contains G. Ferreyrolles's "La Rochefoucauld devant la paresse," pp. 175–194. In addition, I recommend Benedetta Papàsogli's fine textual interpretations of La Rochefoucauld in *Il "fondo del cuore"* and "Socialità e memoria," in *Volti della memoria nel "Grand Siècle" e oltre* (Rome: Bulzoni, 2000), pp. 59–83.

For a bibliographical outline as a whole, see *Images de La Rochefoucauld: Actes du tricentenaire, 1680–1980* (Paris: PUF, 1984), and Jean Lafond's "Dix ans d'études sur les 'Maximes' de La Rochefoucauld (1976–1986)," in *L'Information littéraire* (January–February 1987), pp. 11–16.

On the LAUNCH of *La Princesse de Clèves*, see Maurice Laugaa's reconstruction of events, "Une campagne publicitaire en 1678," in *Lectures de Mme de Lafayette* (Paris: Armand Colin, 1971), pp. 14–40. See also the chapter Roger Duchêne devoted to the novel in *Mme de Lafayette* (Paris: Fayard, 1988), pp. 333–360.

Founded in 1665, on Colbert's initiative, the twelve-page weekly *JOURNAL DES SAVANTS* was meant to shape the opinion of a cultivated and erudite public. See Marc Martin's entry in the *Dictionnaire du Grand Siècle* (Paris: Fayard, 1990).

CHAPTER 9

The most complete and authoritative study of MADEMOISELLE DE MONTPENSIER is Jean Garapon's doctoral thesis, "Le monde littéraire et moral de la Grande Mademoiselle: culture princière et connaissance de soi" (Université de Paris IV, 1994), which provided me with a valuable basis of information and ideas. Garapon had previously published *La Grande Mademoiselle mémorialiste: une autobiographie dans le temps* (Geneva: Droz, 1989). Bernardine Melchior-Bonnet's *La Grande Mademoiselle* (Paris: Perrin, 1985) and Michel Le Moël's *La Grande Mademoiselle* (Paris: Éditions de Fallois, 1994) are both well documented and address a wider public.

La Grande Mademoiselle's romantic life has inspired many biographies over the years, but here I prefer to focus on the main critical studies concerning her: Sainte-Beuve, "La Grande Mademoiselle" (1852), in *Causeries du lundi*, Vol. 3, pp. 503–525; Denise Mayer, "Deux ouvrages de piété de la Grande Mademoiselle," in *Bulletin du Bibliophile* 2 (1980), pp. 170–184; *Mademoiselle de Montpensier: Trois études d'après ses "Mémoires,"* Biblio 17, No. 45 (Paris-Seattle-Tübingen, PFSCL, 1989); Marie-Thérèse Hipp, "Le moi disgracié," in *Mythes et Réalités: Enquête sur le roman et les Mémoires (1160–1700)* (Paris: Klincksieck, 1976), pp. 294–309; *La Grande Mademoiselle (1627–1693)*, Actes de la Journée d'Études tenue le 15 Mai 1993 au Château de Saint-Fargeau, edited by Jean and Marie-Cristine Garapon, *Papers on French Seventeenth Century Literature*, Vol. 22, No. 42 (1995), pp. 11–101; Jean Garapon, "Mademoiselle et l'exil," in *L'Exil au XVIIe siècle*, in *Papers on French Seventeenth Century Literature*, Vol. 21, No. 41 (1994), pp. 345–355; Ginevra Conti Odorisio, "Il viaggio nei 'Mémoires' della Grande Mademoiselle," in *Donne in viaggio*, edited by Maria Luisa Silvestre and Adriana Valerio (Bari: Laterza, 1999), pp. 116–129.

See Jean Garapon, "Le monde littéraire et moral de la Grande Mademoiselle" (pp. 96–118), for a discussion of Mademoiselle's models and the texts dedicated to her and Anne of Austria that emphasize the ideal of the *femme forte*: Père Hilarion de Coste's *Les Éloges et Vies des Reines et des Princesses* (1630), du Gerzan's *Triomphe des*

Dames (1646), Père Le Moyne's *Galerie des Femmes Fortes* (1647), and Gabriel Gilbert's *Panégirique des Femmes* (1650).

On GASTON D'ORLÉANS, see Claude Kurt Abraham's study *Gaston d'Orléans et sa cour: Étude littéraire* (University of North Carolina Press, 1964); and Georges Dethan's biography, *La Vie de Gaston d'Orléans* (Paris: Éditions de Fallois, 1992). On the poets at Gaston's court see Antoine Adam, *Histoire de la littérature française au XVIIe siècle*, Vol. 2, pp. 49–52.

Two interesting articles on the Grande Mademoiselle's HEROISM are Noémi Hepp, "La notion d'héroïne," in *Onze Études sur l'image de la femme dans la littérature du dix-septième siècle*, pp. 9–27, and Micheline Cuénin, "Mademoiselle, une Amazone impure?" in *Papers on French Seventeenth Century Literature*, Vol. 22, No. 42 (1995), pp. 25–36.

For the FRONDE, consult the bibliography provided for Chapter 6.

On Mademoiselle de Montpensier's taste in ARCHITECTURE, see Claude Mignot, "Mademoiselle et son château de Saint-Fargeau," in *La Grande Mademoiselle (1627–1693)*, pp. 91–101, and Denise Mayer, "Mademoiselle de Montpensier et l'architecture," in *Mademoiselle de Montpensier: Trois études d'après ses "Mémoires,"* pp. 93–113.

On the *BALLET DE COUR* see Marie-Françoise Christout, *Le Ballet de cour au XVIIe siècle: Iconographie thématique* (Geneva: Minkoff, 1987).

On MUSICAL CULTURE, see Philippe Beaussant, *Lully, ou le musicien du Soleil* (Paris: Gallimard, 1992). Catherine Massip has written about Mademoiselle de Montpensier as a patron of music in "Le Mécénat musical de Mademoiselle," in *Papers on French Seventeenth Century Literature*, Vol. 22, No. 42 (1995), pp. 79–90.

On Mademoiselle de Montpensier's passion for the THEATER, see "Théâtre et musique," Chapter 4 of Garapon's "Le Monde littéraire et morale de la Grande Mademoiselle," and Georges Mongrédien's studies on the subject: "La Source, le chef des comédiens de la Grande Mademoiselle," in *Mercure de France* 1183 (March 1962): pp. 615–632; *La Vie quotidienne des comédiens au temps de Molière* (Paris: Hachette, 1966); *Les Comédiens français du XVIIe siècle, dictionnaire biographique* (third edition, Paris: Édition du CNRS, 1981).

Mariangela Mazzocchi Doglio has edited the critical work on DORIMOND, providing it with an interesting introduction full of information about the actor's relationship with the Grande Mademoiselle (Nicolas Drouin dit Dorimond, *Théâtre*, Paris: Nizet/Bari: Schena, 1992). On Dorimond, see Giovanni Macchia, *Vita avventure e morte di Don Giovanni* (1978; Milan: Adelphi, 1991) and Enea Balmas, "Il

Don Giovanni di Dorimond," in *Scritti in onore di Giovanni Macchia* (Milan: Mondadori, 1983), Vol. 2, pp. 232–257.

On the LIBRARIES of the nobility, see *Histoire des Bibliothèques françaises: Les bibliothèques sous l'Ancien Régime 1530–1789*, under the direction of Claude Jolly (Paris: Promodis–Éditions du Cercle de la Librairie, 1988).

The great age of French MEMOIR WRITERS began after the Fronde "in a climate of accounts being settled" (Marc Fumaroli, *La Diplomatie de l'esprit*, p. 198); three articles by Fumaroli—"Les Mémoires du XVIIe siècle au carrefour des genres en prose" (1971), "Les 'Mémoires,' ou l'historiographie royale en procès" (1978), and "Retz: des 'Mémoires' en forme de conversation galante" (1981), collected in *La Diplomatie de l'esprit*, pp. 183–215—form essential reading on this literary genre, its historical rationale, and its links to society culture. See too Yves Coirault, "Autobiographie et Mémoires (XVIIe-XVIIIe siècles) ou existence et naissance de l'autobiographie," in *Revue d'Histoire littéraire en France*, Vol. 75, No. 6 (November–December 1975), pp. 937–953, and *Destins et enjeux du XVIIe siècle*, pp. 215–222; Marie-Thérèse Hipp, *Mythes et Réalités: Les valeurs chez les mémorialistes français du XVIIe siècle avant la Fronde*; Michel Baujours, *Miroirs d'encre* (Paris: Éditions du Seuil, 1980); *La Cour au miroir des mémorialistes (1530–1682)*, Actes du Colloque de Strasbourg (Paris: Klincksieck, 1991); Emmanuel Lesne, *La Poétique des mémoires (1650–1685)* (Paris: Champion, 1996). On women's memoirs, see *Revisiting Memory: Women's Fiction and Memoirs in Seventeenth-Century France* (Rutgers University Press, 1990), by Faith E. Beasley, who devotes a chapter to the Grande Mademoiselle, "From Military to Literary Frondeuse: Montpensier's Feminization of History" (pp. 72–128). On Mademoiselle de Montpensier's memoirs, keep in mind Eglal Henein, "Mademoiselle de Montpensier à la recherche du temps perdu," in *Papers on French Seventeenth Century Literature*, Vol. 6 (1976–1977), pp. 37–52. See also Frédéric Briot, *Usage du monde, usage de soi: Enquête sur les mémorialistes d'Ancien Régime* (Paris: Éditions du Scuil, 1994).

On official historiography, for which the memoir writers provide a kind of "descant," I recommend Oreste Ranum, *Artisan of Glory: Writers and Historical Thought in the Seventeenth Century* (University of North Carolina Press, 1980).

The best edition of the *Mémoires de Mademoiselle de Montpensier* is the one edited by A. Chérul in four volumes (Paris: Charpentier, 1858–1859). In 1985 the Librairie Fontaine éditeur (Paris) published the *Mémoires* in two volumes without notes or critical apparatus, with a preface by C. Bouyer.

On the theme of CONVERSATION, see this book's Chapter 17 and its attendant bibliography.

On the COMTESSE DE FIESQUE and the COMTESSE DE FRONTENAC, both *précieuses* and penitent Frondists, scc Miriam Maître, *Les Précieuses: Naissance des femmes de lettres en France au XVIIe siècle* (Paris: Champion, 1999), pp. 167–174. On Mme de

Frontenac, there is also T. P. Bedart's old biography, *La comtesse de Frontenac* (1632–1707) (Paris: Roy, 1904).

On the revival in Paris of HIGH SOCIETY LIFE AFTER THE FRONDE, see Alain Viala, *La Naissance de l'écrivain*, pp. 133f. Linda Timmermans points out the sociohistorical reasons for this phenomenon in *L'Accès des femmes à la culture*: "It is certain that the failure of the Fronde put an end to the political—indeed martial—ambitions of French aristocratic women. Henceforth it would be from the wings and no longer on the public stage that women would participate in affairs of state" (pp. 97f). According to Marc Fumaroli, women's "social and literary authority increased just as male heroism declined" ("Les Mémoires du XVIIe siècle au carrefour des genres en prose," in *La Diplomatie de l'esprit*, p. 204).

On ENJOUEMENT (or *eutrapelia*, which Aristotle defined as a "moderate excess of good education"), see Alain Pons, "La rhétorique des manières au XVIe siècle en Italie," in *Histoire de la rhétorique dans l'Europe moderne*, p. 421. More on this word so fundamental to an understanding of polite society can be found in Delphine Denis, "Conversation et enjouement au XVIIe siècle: l'exemple de Madeleine de Scudéry," in *Du goût, de la conversation et des femmes*, pp. 111–129. On society's gay spirit, see Marc Fumaroli, "L'empire des femmes, ou l'esprit de joie," in *La Diplomatie de l'esprit*, pp. 321–339.

On MADEMOISELLE DE VANDY, see Édouard de Barthélemy, *Mme la comtesse de Maure, sa vie et sa correspondance, suivies des Maximes de Mme de Sablé et d'une étude sur la vie de Mademoiselle de Vandy*.

Exile at Saint-Fargeau, where JEAN REGNAULT DE SEGRAIS went to join his patroness in October 1652 and where he remained until the spring of 1657, proved to be the most prolific period of the writer's life. Not only did he collaborate with the princess on her literary output, correcting her memoirs, supervising the collection of *Portraits* (which were printed in Caen in 1659), and overseeing the publication of Mademoiselle's *Relation de l'Isle imaginaire* and *La Princesse de Paphlagonie* in Bordeaux the same year, he also wrote a pastoral poem, *L'Athys*, light verse—elegies, stanzas, madrigals, songs—eclogues, and, above all, *Les Nouvelles françaises*, which would influence the new narrative trend. At Saint-Fargeau, he also undertook his translation of the *Aeneid*, which he completed in 1681, followed by the *Georgics*. In 1671, however, he was obliged to leave the Grande Mademoiselle's company, on account of having tried to interfere with her relationship with the Duc de Lauzun. As a friend of Mme de Sévigné, La Rochefoucauld, and Mme de Lafayette, he collaborated in *Zaïde*, agreeing to assume the authorship. Collected posthumously in *Segraisiana* (1721), his recollections provide a valuable font of information on intellectual and society life of the times. There is an excellent critical edition of *Les Nouvelles françaises* edited by Roger Guichemerre, two volumes (Paris: Société des textes français modernes, 1990–1992).

See also the *Nouvelles du XVIIe siècle*, edited by Raymond Picard and Jean Lafond (Paris: Gallimard/Bibliothèque de la Pléiade, 1997), which includes Segrais's *Honorine* and *Floridon*.

There are two biographies of Segrais: L. Bredif's *Segrais, sa vie et ses œuvres* (Paris: Durand, 1863), and W. Tipping's *Jean Regnault de Segrais: L'homme et son œuvre* (Paris: Éditions internationales, 1933). Among the critical studies of Segrais the novelist I would draw attention to R. W. Baldner, "The 'Nouvelles Françaises' of Segrais," in *Modern Language Quarterly* 19 (1957), pp. 199–205; Arnaldo Pizzorusso, *La poetica del romanzo in Francia (1660–1685)* (Rome: Sciascia, 1962), pp. 65–78; J.-D. Hubert, "Les Nouvelles françaises de Sorel et de Segrais," and A. Kibedi Varga, "Pour une définition de la nouvelle à l'époque classique," both of which appeared in *La Nouvelle en France jusqu'au XVIIIe siècle*, in *Cahiers de l'Association Internationale des Études Françaises* 18 (1966), pp. 31–40 and 53–65 respectively; René Godenne, *Histoire de la nouvelle française au XVIIe et XVIIIe siècle* (Geneva: Droz, 1970). Two essays to mention in *Les Écrivains normands de l'âge classique et le goût de leur temps*, Actes du Colloque de Caen (October 1980), in *Cahiers des Annales de Normandie* 14 (1982), are J.-P. Collinet, "'Segraisiana,' 'Huetiana': deux écrivains normands devant le goût de leur temps" (pp. 131–143), and Philippe de Lajarte, "'Les Nouvelles françaises' de Segrais ou les glissements progressifs du récit" (pp. 145–159). See also Denise Godwin, *"Les Nouvelles françaises ou les Divertissements de la Princesse Aurélie" de Segrais: Une conception romanesque ambivalente* (Paris: Nizet, 1983).

On the fashion for the SOCIETY PORTRAIT, its inception, typology, and variety, see *Le Portrait littéraire*, edited by K. Kupisz, G. A. Péruse, and J. A. Debreuille, with a preface by P. Michel (Lyon: Presses Universitaires de Lyon, 1982), and above all, Jacqueline Plantié's fundamental study, *La Mode du portrait littéraire en France (1641–1681)*. Regarding Mademoiselle's project, see the chapter entitled "Un jeu de Princesse: Divers Portraits," pp. 185–248.

The theoretical reflection on the painted portrait and the literary portrait in Renaissance Italy is the subject of Édouard Pommier's interesting study, *Théories du portrait: De la Renaissance aux Lumières* (Paris: Gallimard, 1998).

See also J. Lafond, "Les Techniques du portrait dans le 'Recueil des portraits et éloges de 1659,'" in *Cahiers de l'Association Internationales des Études Françaises*, March 1966, pp. 139–148; Sandra Dijkstra, "La Grande Mademoiselle and the Written Portrait: Feminine Narcissism, Aristocratic Pride, or Literary Innovation?" in *Pacific Coast Philology* (October 1978), pp. 19–28; Erica Harth, *Of Portraits in Ideology and Culture in Seventeenth-Century France*, pp. 68–128.

MADEMOISELLE DE SCUDÉRY (1608–1701). Born into a family of the minor provincial nobility, she came to Paris in the wake of her brother Georges—an ambitious writer, poet, dramatist, and polemicist—and was accepted into Mme de Rambouillet's circle. Initially published under her brother's name, her short stories and romansfleuves, particularly *Artamène ou le Grand Cyrus* (1649–1653) and *Clélie, Histoire romaine* (1654–1660), were immensely successful. From 1680, the series *Conversations* was equally successful. Aware of the change in public taste, Mlle de Scudéry regained her popularity in old age by extrapolating dialogues from her old novels that dealt with subjects dear to modern culture—*politesse*, the *air galant*, flattery, conversation, and so forth, and placing them in new settings. It was a last spark, to be followed by years of oblivion for her literary work, if not for herself.

In fact, there was no place for Mlle de Scudéry in the nineteenth-century image of classicism in the *Grand Siècle*, and in studies by that century's scholars, which now provide an important fund of documentation and information, she was seen as an example of a society that lived by rigid rules and as representative of a precious and affected style that bordered dangerously on caricature. I refer to Émile Colombey's *La Journée des Madrigaux* (1856; Slatkine Reprints, Geneva, 1971); Victor Cousin, *La Société française au XVIIᵉ siècle d'après le Grand Cyrus de Mademoiselle de Scudéry*; Rathéry and Boutron, *Mademoiselle de Scudéry, sa vie et sa correspondance* (Paris: L. Techener, 1873); Édouard de Barthélemy, *Sapho, le mage de Sidon, Zénocrate* (Paris: Didier, 1880). The same attitude was adopted in the first half of the twentieth century by Émile Magne in *Le Salon de Mlle de Scudéry ou Le royaume de Tendre* (Monaco: Société des Conférences, 1927), and by Georges Mongrédien in *Madeleine de Scudéry et son salon* (Paris: Tallandier, 1946).

In recent years, however, the view of Mlle de Scudéry has changed radically. No one today would doubt that she was central to seventeenth-century literary debate, nor would they doubt her importance as a moralist or theorist of the society aesthetic. This new, happy era of criticism took its lead from Alain Niderst's study *Madeleine de Scudéry, Paul Pellisson et leur monde* (Paris: PUF, 1976); there followed Nicole Aronson's biography, *Mademoiselle de Scudéry ou le voyage au pays de Tendre* (Paris: Fayard, 1986). As a novelist, she is the subject of René Godenne's excellent analyses, *Les Romans de Mlle de Scudéry* (Geneva: Droz, 1983), and Chantal Morlet-Chantalat's *La Clélie de Mademoiselle de Scudéry*; whereas Delphine Denis has made a brilliant study of her as a moralist and theorist in *La Muse galante: Poétique de la conversation dans l'œuvre de Mademoiselle de Scudéry*. Denis also had the good idea of relaunching some of the writer's more important *conversations*: *"De l'air galant" et autres conversations (1653–1684): Pour une étude de l'archive galante*, edited by Delphine Denis (Paris: Champion, 1998). See also Marie-Gabrielle Lallemand, *La Lettre dans le récit: Études de l'œuvre de Mlle de Scudéry*, Biblio 17 (Tübingen: Gunter Narr, 2000). Of the numerous studies that have appeared in recent years, I will merely mention those by Noémie Hepp ("À propos de la Clélie: mélancolie et perfection féminine," pp. 161–168) and Jean Mesnard ("Madeleine de Scudéry et la société du Marais," pp. 169–188), which both appeared in *Mélanges offerts à Georges Couton*. Of the contributions to *Les Trois Scudéry*, Actes du Colloque du Havre, October 1–5, 1991, edited by Alain Niderst (Paris: Klincksieck, 1993), I would like at least to point out those by Jean Mesnard ("Pour une clef de 'Clélie,'" pp. 371–408), Éva Avigador ("L'honnêteté féminine dans les 'Conversations et les Entretiens,'" pp. 533–540), and Linda Timmermans ("Madeleine de Scudéry et la

préciosité," pp. 611–623). Without doubt, the complete bibliography of Mlle de Scudéry, edited by Chantal Morlet-Chantalat ("Madeleine de Scudéry," *Bibliographie des
Écrivains français*, Paris: Memini, 1997) serves as the most eloquent proof of the critical good fortune that has led, in the past thirty years, to the "Illustrious Sappho's"
rediscovery. See also the published papers from the important international conference
held in Paris for the tricentennial of her death, *Madeleine de Scudéry: Une Femme
de lettres au XVIIe siècle*, Actes du Colloque Internationale de Paris, June 28–30,
2001, edited by Delphine Denis and Anne-Elisabeth Spica (Arras: Artois Presses Université, 2002).

PAUL PELLISSON. See F. L. Marcou, *Études sur la vie et les œuvres de Pellisson suivie
d'une correspondance inédite du même* (Paris: Didier, 1859); Niderst, *Madeleine de
Scudéry, Paul Pellisson et leur monde*; Fumaroli, *Le Poète et le Roi*, pp. 138–153.

The case of the PRÉCIEUSES is one of the most complicated in all seventeenth-century
literature, but Myriam Maître's important study, *Les Précieuses: Naissance des femmes
de lettres en France au XVIIe siècle*, presents a very lucid, learned critique. Interested
readers should consult her revised bibliography.

Starting, then, with Myriam Maître and the basic problem that has divided critics
over the last twenty years, one may ask: Did the *Précieuses* really exist, or were they, as
many would have it, simply a literary invention?

Whether satirical or flattering, seventeenth-century texts concerning the *Précieuses*
(by Molière, Michel de Pure, and Antoine Bodeau de Somaize, among others) always
return to an entirely hypothetical type, since apparently no woman of the day claimed
the terminology for herself. Mlle de Scudéry, said to be "the Queen of the *Précieuses*,"
was careful not to describe herself as such. Nor did she ever use the word *précieuse* to
praise another woman.

It is on the basis of this assertion that, while following very different hypotheses,
scholars like Jean-Michel Pelous (*Amour précieux, amour galant, 1654–1675*) and
Domna Stanton ("The Fiction of Préciosité and the Fear of Women," in *Yale French
Studies*) came to deny the historical reality of the *Précieuses*. Roger Duchêne takes a
middle line and claims that while "it would be wrong to deny totally the historical
existence of the *Précieuses*, . . . it is a mistake to wish to make of them a sociological
reality, a kind of coherent party, that is an active cabal" (Duchêne, "À la recherche d'une
espèce rare et mêlée: les Précieuses avant Molière," in *De la Précieuse à l'écrivaine*,
pp. 331–358).

The *Précieuses*—imaginary creatures, then, born of a satirical literature that flourished for about ten years (1654–1665)—would disappear without a trace with the
passing of the fashion that created them. To start from this premise inevitably means
seeing as methodologically flawed the late-nineteenth-century habit of hypothesizing a
historical reality for the *Précieuses* based solely on literature; but C. Lougee's study *Le
Paradis des femmes* (see the bibliographic notes for Chapter 2) shows how fruitful
research based on both history and literature can be.

There are, however, other, rarer, and less literary seventeenth-century texts that unequivocally attest to the real existence of the *Précieuses*. It is from a systematic reading of them that Philippe Sellier managed to identify about thirty great ladies described as *précieuses* who were generally respected and admired, in "La névrose précieuse: une nouvelle pléiade?" in *Présences féminines: Littérature et société au XVIIe siècle français*, pp. 95–125. Sellier's inquiries led him to fix the date of birth of the *Précieuses* as during the time of the Regency and the hôtel de Rambouillet, that is, well before 1654 (the year in which the *Précieuses* were first spoken of as a "sect"), and to see them surviving throughout Louis XIV's reign.

Welcoming Sellier's findings, Maître successfully pursued the research and brought the number of precious members of the "pléiade" up to 130. She proposes following a third method in her book, however, which "attempts to take the discussion of the *précieuses* as a whole…and invites examination of their possible origins, of their aims and of what was at stake where they were targets of virulent satire or subjects of excessive praise." What justified the violent explosion of satire between 1654 and 1665— that is to say the ten years that immediately followed the Fronde? In order to answer this question, Maître follows two different trails, one of which leads to politics, the other to literature. At the time of Anne of Austria's regency, women valued chastity, purity, refinement of fashion, and "honest gallantry," and built up a network of friendships that centered on the court. If some of them, like Mme de Longueville or Mademoiselle de Montpensier, opted to side with the Fronde, they were granted a royal pardon with the return of peace, and on the whole they had an important part in reconciling former adversaries. But the role played by women in politics made the young King angrier and more jealous the closer he came to taking power. Thus, with the beginning of Louis XIV's personal rule, the court turned its back on the *Précieuses* and they were sacrificed to the Frondists' disappointed resentment and to virulent satire. Like the persecuted minister Fouquet, they became the scapegoats that made it possible for the monarchy to turn the page and regain the popular consensus.

It was through literature, according to Maître, that the *Précieuses* acquired their questionable celebrity. Satire in fact accuses them of exercising a critical tyranny, of preferring lightweight works, and, above all, of wanting to write. The violence with which they were attacked, however, contrasts surprisingly with women's prudence and discretion in the literary field. According to Maître, it did not appear to be the still minor threat of literary competition from women that was at stake, so much as "the very definition of literature": "The more literature, abetted by echoing quarrels, becomes separated from its origins and legitimizes its autonomy, the more ambiguous relations between authors and women who write become: confrontational when women manifest professional ambitions, tinged with both admiration and condescension when they are content to be, with grace and wit, those with whom glory comes to dine" (p. 416). What then is the relationship between the "real" *Précieuses* whose existence has been historically ascertained and the "false" *Précieuses* depicted by satire? Maître has no doubts: never directly called into question by their persecutors, the "real" *Précieuses*, who enjoyed an unassailable social position both at court and in the city, were the first to distance themselves from their caricature and to turn it to their own use: "sensing the danger that lay in bearing such a title, [they] bequeathed it to whoever wanted it" (p. 231).

The interpretive criteria of Maître's vast, ambitious study, which also rejoices in a wealth of documentation, will be without doubt an essential point of reference for any further research on the subject.

The thesis of the determining ROLE OF WOMEN IN THE BIRTH OF THE FRENCH NARRATIVE is passionately argued by Joan DeJean in *Tender Geographies*; her study is accompanied by an important bibliography of women writers from 1640 to 1715 (pp. 201–221).

For MORAL CARTOGRAPHY, consult Paul Zumthor, "La Carte de Tendre et les Précieuses," in *Trivium*, Vol. 6, No. 4 (1948), pp. 263–273; C. Rouben, "Histoires et géographies galantes au grand siècle: 'L'histoire amoureuse des Gaules' et 'La carte du pays de braquerie' de Bussy-Rabutin," in *XVIIe siècle* 93 (1971): pp. 55–73; Claude Filteau, "Le pays de Tendre: l'enjeu d'une carte," in *Littérature* 36 (December 1979), pp. 37–60; E. P. Mayberry Senter, "Les Cartes allégoriques romanesques du XVIIe siècle: Aperçu des gravures créés autour de l'apparition de la 'Carte du Tendre' de la 'Clélie' en 1654," in *Gazette des Beaux-Arts* 89 (1977), pp. 133–134. See above all Louis van Delft, "La cartographie morale," in *Littérature et anthropologie*, pp. 65–86.

On MLLE DE SCUDÉRY'S SALON, see particularly Jean Mesnard, "Mademoiselle de Scudéry et la société de Marais," in *Mélanges offerts à Georges Couton*, pp. 169–188; Barbara Krajewska, *Du cœur à l'esprit: Mademoiselle de Scudéry* (Paris: Éditions Kimé, 1993); Elisa Biancardi, "'Madeleine de Scudéry et son cercle': spécificité socioculturelle et créativité littéraire," in *Papers on French Seventeenth Century Literature*, Vol. 22, No. 43 (1995), pp. 415–430.

The legitimacy of the distinction between FALSE and REAL PRÉCIEUSES—a distinction that was used in seventeenth-century debate and taken up by Victor Cousin as the cornerstone of the polemic (*Société française*, Vol. 2, p. 287)—has been carefully analyzed with contrary results by Roger Lathuillère (*La Préciosité: Étude historique et linguistique*, pp. 201–210) and by J.-M. Pelous (*Amours précieux, amour gallant, 1654–1675*, pp. 359–454), and returned to by Timmermans, *L'Accès des femmes à la culture*, pp. 115–123.

On the EXCHANGE OF LETTERS between the Grande Mademoiselle and Mme de Motteville while they were at Saint-Jean-de-Luz, see Madeleine Bertaud, "En marge de leurs 'Mémoires,' une correspondance entre Mlle de Montpensier et Mme de Motteville," in *Travaux de Littérature, offerts en hommage à Noémie Hepp* (Paris: ADIREL/Belles Lettres, 1990), pp. 277–295; See also the recent *Against Marriage: The Correspondence of La Grande Mademoiselle Anne Marie-Louise d'Orléans*, edited and translated by Joan DeJean (University of Chicago Press, 2002).

CHAPTER 10

Any bibliography, however summary, of MADAME DE SÉVIGNÉ must mention the books about her by Roger Duchêne—to say nothing of his many articles. He edited the three-volume *Correspondance de Mme de Sévigné* (Paris: Gallimard/Bibliothèque de la Pléiade, 1972–1978) and is the chief authority on the marquise: *Écrire au temps de Mme de Sévigné: lettres et textes littéraire* (1981; Paris: Vrin, 1982); *Mme de Sévigné ou la lettre d'amour* (1970; Paris: Klincksieck, 1992); *Chère Mme de Sévigné* (Paris: Gallimard, 1995); *Mme de Sévigné ou la chance d'être femme* (1982; Paris: Fayard, 1996); *Naissance d'un écrivain* (Paris: Fayard, 1996). On Mme de Sévigné as a writer, Bernard Bray's essays are a must: "Quelques aspects du système épistolaire de Mme de Sévigné"—which advances a thesis with which Roger Duchêne disagrees, namely that Mme de Sévigné's "method of letter-writing was knowingly contrived"—in *Revue d'Histoire littéraire de la France*, Vol. 69, No. 3–4 (May–August 1969): pp. 491–505; "Mme de Sévigné et l'art de la narration," in *L'Intelligence du passé: Les faits, l'écriture et les sens. Mélanges offerts à Jean Lafond par ses amis*, collected by Pierre Aquilon, Jacques Chupeau, and François Weil (Tours: Université de Tours, 1988), pp. 295–302; "Une Femme de Vitré: Mme de Sévigné épistolière aux Rochers," in *La Bretagne au XVIIᵉ siècle, Actes du Colloque de la société d'Études du XVIIᵉ siècle*, Rennes, October 14, 1986, edited by Daniel Aris (Vannes: Conseil Général de Morbihan, 1991), pp. 349–368. See also Sainte-Beuve's two articles, "Mme de Sévigné" in *Portraits de femmes*, in *Œuvres*, Vol. 2, pp. 991–1007, and "Mémoires touchant la vie et les écrits de Mme de Sévigné, par M. le baron Walckenaer," in *Causeries du lundi*, Vol. 1, pp. 49–62; Virginia Woolf, "Mme de Sévigné," in *The Death of the Moth and Other Essays* (Harcourt Brace Jovanovich, 1970), pp. 51–57; Jean Cordelier's short but penetrating book, *Mme de Sévigné par elle-même* (1968; Paris: Éditions du Seuil, 1973); Éva Avigador, *Mme de Sévigné: Un portrait intellectuel et moral* (Paris: Nizet, 1974); *Les Lettres de Mme de Sévigné*, Actes du Colloque de Berkeley, edited by H. Allentuch, in *Papers in French Seventeenth Century Literature*, , 2 (1981); M. O. Sweetser, "La lettre comme instance autobiographique: le cas de Mme de Sévigné," in *Autobiography in French Literature* (University of South Carolina, 1987); *Correspondances: Mélanges offerts à Roger Duchêne* (Tübingen: Gunter Narr, 1992).

On the tricentennial of Mme de Sévigné's death, the magazine *Europe* devoted a complete issue to her, *Mme de Sévigné, un féminin pluriel* (January 1996), as did the *Revue d'Histoire littéraire de la France*, Vol. 96, No. 3 (May–June 1996); while the Musée Carnavalet had a beautiful exhibition with a catalog entitled *Mme de Sévigné*, edited by Anne Forray-Carlier and Jean-Marie Bruson (Paris: Paris musées/Flammarion, 1999).

The enormously learned and brilliant polemicist ABBÉ GILLES MÉNAGE published his *Origines de la langue française* in 1650 and, in 1672, his *Observations sur la langue française*, dedicated to the Chevalier de Méré, thus establishing himself as the leader of the *nouveaux savants* (see Viala, *La Naissance de l'écrivain*, pp. 40f). He promoted the minor genres of writing and verse dismissed by Malherbe but brought back into fashion by Voiture and Sarasin. Where the complicated quarrels and alliances that distinguished the literary life of the times were concerned, Ménage seems to have been in line with the circles of Pélisson and Mlle de Scudéry, which Fouquet led against Colbert's protégés Chapelain and Boileau. The prototype of the worldly abbé, Ménage, as Retz's secretary, insinuated himself successfully into society, frequenting the hôtel de Rambouillet and the hôtel de Lesdiguières; he courted both Mme de Sévigné and Mme de Lafayette and became literary mentor to both of them. His rival the Abbé Cotin called him "Pédant coquet" in his *Ménagerie*; Boileau had the line "un galant de notre âge" rhyme with Ménage (*Satire II*, lines 17–18); and Molière modeled on him the character of Magius, who became Vadius in *Les Femmes savantes* (Act III. iii). For his friendship with Mme de Lafayette, see Émile Henriot, "Ménage et Mme de Lafayette," in *Livres et portraits* (Paris: Plon, 1927), Vol. 3, pp. 45–52; Bernard Bray, "Ménage," *Dizionario critico della letteratura francese*, edited by Franco Simone (Turis: UTET, 1972); G. Mouligneau, "'Nostre amitié ne finira que quand nous finirons': Mme de Lafayette et Ménage," in *XVIIe siècle* 109 (1975), pp. 67–91. See the note above on the *-ana*.

For PORTRAITS and MME DE SÉVIGNÉ'S GENEALOGICAL HISTORY, see the catalog for the exhibition "Mme de Sévigné" at the Musée Carnavalet.

On the MARQUISE DE SÉVIGNÉ'S RELIGIOSITY, see Roger Duchêne, *Mme de Sévigné* (Paris: Desclée de Brouwer, 1968).

On ROGER DE BUSSY-RABUTIN, see C. Rouben, *Bussy-Rabutin épistolier* (Paris: Nizet, 1974) as well as that scholar's doctoral thesis, "Bussy, homme de lettres" (McGill University, September 1970); Rouben has also edited Bussy-Rabutin's *Correspondance avec le Père Rapin* (Paris: Nizet, 1982) and his *Correspondance avec le Père Bouhours* (Paris: Nizet, 1986). On these exchanges, see J. P. Collinet, "Un triumvirat critique: Rapin, Bouhours, Bussy," in *Critique et création littéraire en France*, Colloques internationaux du CNRS, No. 557 (Paris: Éditions du Centre national de la Recherche scientifique, 1977), pp. 261–272. Françoise-Antoine Mertens, *Bussy-Rabutin mémorialiste et épistolier* (Louvain-La-Neuve: Cabay, 1984); Elizabeth C. Goldsmith's chapter "History, Social Identity, and Talk: The Writings of Bussy-Rabutin," in *"Exclusive Conversations,"* pp. 77–109; Roger Duchêne, "Bussy épistolier," in *Raboutinages*, edited by D. H. Vincent and the Société des Amis de Bussy-Rabutin (special number, 1988); Jacqueline Duchêne, *Bussy-Rabutin* (Paris: Fayard, 1992). In addition, see Daria Galeteria's afterword to the Italian edition of Bussy's *Histoire Amoureuse des Gaules*, "Castelli in aria," *Storia amorosa delle Gallie* (Palermo: Sellerio, 1992), pp. 201–222; and Bernard Bray, "L'écrire ou le dire: l'expression de l'amour dans 'l'Histoire amoureuse des Gaules' de Bussy-Rabutin," in *Art de la lettre, art de la conversation*, pp. 245–255.

On RELATIONS BETWEEN BUSSY-RABUTIN AND MME DE SÉVIGNÉ, see in particular Roger Duchêne, "Bussy et Mme de Sévigné: une vengeance posthume," and Catherine

Monfort, "Sévigné et Bussy: une relation ambiguë," both published in *Bussy-Rabutin, l'homme et l'œuvre,* Actes du Colloque pour le trois centième anniversaire de la mort de Roger Bussy-Rabutin, Comte de Boissy, July 2–3, 1993, edited by Th. Noblat-Rérolle, J. Quencau, and D.-H. Vincent-Dijon (Société des amis de Bussy-Rabutin, 1995).

Of the literature on FOUQUET, I want to call attention to the following: Urbain Victor Châtelain, *Le Surintendant Nicolas Fouquet, Protecteur des lettres, des Arts et des sciences* (1905; Geneva: Slatkine Reprints, 1971); *Paul Morand, Fouquet ou Le Soleil offusqué* (Paris: Gallimard, 1961); Daniel Dessert, *Fouquet* (Paris: Fayard, 1987); Fumaroli, *Le Poète et le Roi,* pp. 185–237; Jean-Christian Petitfils, *Fouquet* (Paris: Perrin, 1998).

On MME DU PLESSIS-GUÉNÉGAUD, see Urbain Victor Châtelain, "Un salon Janséniste," in *Le Surintendant Nicolas Fouquet,* Chapter 3, pp. 60–67.

The edition of Pascal's LES PROVINCIALES that I refer to is L. Cognet and G. Ferreyrolles's (Paris: Classiques Garnier/Bordas, 1992). For a critical bibliography, see G. Ferreyrolles, *Blaise Pascal: Les Provinciales* (Paris: PUF, 1983), and Roger Duchêne, *L'Imposture littéraire dans les Provinciales de Pascal* (en annexe les Actes du Colloque de Marseille du 10 mars 1984 sur les *Provinciales*) (second edition, Aix-en-Provence: Publications de l'Université de Provence, 1985). Duchêne's book is a polemic that analyzes, letter by letter, the "ruse" with which Pascal, in arguing against theologians and experts, appeals to public opinion and brings the debate to nonspecialist circles.

For the LITERARY AND CULTURAL INFLUENCE OF THE PORT-ROYAL GROUP, Philippe Sellier's important book is essential reading, *Port-Royal et la littérature,* two volumes (Paris: Champion, 1999–2000), Vol. 1: *Pascal;* Vol. 2: *Le Siècle de saint Augustin, La Rochefoucauld, Mme de Lafayette, Sacy, Racine.*

FRESNES. On the importance of country houses in the development of society life and aristocratic sociability, see Marc Fumaroli, "Une 'galanterie' refusée par Louis XIV," preface to *Vaux-le-Vicomte,* edited by Jean-Marie Pérouse de Montclos, photographs by Georges Fessy (Paris: Éditions Scala, 1997), pp. 7–19.

On MME DE MOTTEVILLE, see the bibliographic notes to chapter III.

For more on the distinction between LA COUR ET LA VILLE, see Erich Auerbach's celebrated essay with that title in *Scenes from the Drama of European Literature,* pp. 133–182.

For a critical, biographical, and psychological assessment of MME DE LAFAYETTE, I suggest: Sainte-Beuve, "Mme de Lafayette," in *Portraits de femmes,* in *Œuvres,* Vol. 2, pp. 1206–1241; André Beaunier, *La Jeunesse de Mme de Lafayette* (1921; Paris:

Flammarion, 1927), and *L'Amie de La Rochefoucauld* (Paris: Flammarion, 1927); Émile Magne, *Mme de Lafayette en ménage* (Paris: Émile-Paul frères, 1926), and *Le Cœur et l'Esprit de Mme de Lafayette* (Paris: Émile-Paul frères, 1927); Giovanni Macchia, "La strada di Mme de Lafayette," in *Il paradiso della ragione*, pp. 193–208; Bernaud Pingaud, *Mme de Lafayette par elle-même* (Paris: Éditions du Seuil, 1959); Roger Duchêne, *Mme de Lafayette*. From the vast critical biography dedicated to her work, I would at least like to draw attention to Georges Poulet, "Mme de Lafayette," in *Études sur le temps humain* (Paris: Plon, 1950), pp. 122–132; Benedetto Croce, "Appunti di critica litteraria I: La Princesse de Clèves," in *Quaderni della critica*, Vol. 7, Quad. 19–20 (September 1951), pp. 144–146; Michel Butor, "Sur 'La Princesse de Clèves,'" in *Répertoire I* (Paris: Éditions de Minuit, 1960), pp. 74–78; Arnaldo Pizzorusso, *La poetica del romanzo in Francia (1660–1685)*, pp. 99–130; Jean Rousset, "La Princesse de Clèves," in *Forme et Signification: Essais sur les structures littéraires de Corneille à Claudel* (Paris: Corti, 1962), pp. 17–44; Gérard Genette, "Vraisemblance et motivation," in *Figures II* (Paris: Éditions du Seuil, 1969), pp. 71–99; Jean Fabre, *L'Art de l'analyse dans la "Princesse de Clèves"* (Strasbourg: Presses Universitaires de Strasbourg, 1980); Jean Cordelier, "Le refus de la Princesse," in *XVIIe siècle* 108 (1975), pp. 43–57; Maurice Laugaa, *Lectures de Mme de Lafayette* (Paris: Armand Colin, 1971); Gabriella Violato, *La principessa giansenista: Saggi su Mme de Lafayette*; Pierre Malandain, *Mme de Lafayette: La Princesse de Clèves* (1985; Paris: PUF, 1989); Jean Mesnard, "Morale et métaphysique dans 'La Princesse de Clèves'" (1990), in *La Culture du XVIIe siècle*, pp. 546–555; Jean-Michel Delacomptée, *La Princesse de Clèves: La Mère et le Courtisan* (Paris: PUF, 1990); Henriette Levillain, *La Princesse de Clèves de Mme de Lafayette* (Paris: Gallimard, 1995); Benedetta Papàsogli, "'La Princesse de Clèves' e i poteri della memoria," in *Volti della memoria nel "Grand Siècle" ed oltre*, pp. 159–177.

On the RELATIONSHIP BETWEEN MME DE LAFAYETTE AND LA ROCHEFOUCAULD, in addition to Beaunier's fine book, *L'Amie de La Rochefoucauld*, and the two books by Émile Magne mentioned above, see R. Judrin, "La Rochefoucauld et Mme de Lafayette," in *Nouvelle Revue Française* (1967), pp. 1224–1229; on her relationship with Madame, see Beaunier, *L'Amie de La Rochefoucauld*, Chapter 5; and for a reconstruction of the intrigue surrounding Madame, see Dina Lanfredini, "Mme de Lafayette et Henriette d'Angleterre: l'histoire de Madame," in *Archivo storico italiano* 116 (1958), pp. 178–206, 511–543.

On the FRIENDSHIP BETWEEN MME DE SÉVIGNÉ AND MME DE LAFAYETTE, see Denise Mayer's fine essay, *Une Amitié parisienne au Grand Siècle: Mme de Lafayette et Mme de Sévigné*, Biblio 17 (Paris-Seattle-Tübingen: PFSCL, 1990), to which I am profoundly indebted.

On EDITORIAL CENSORSHIP, see H. J. Martin, *Livre, pouvoir et société à Paris au XVIIe siècle (1598–1701)*, two volumes (Geneva: Droz, 1969); Daniel Roche's chapter "Censures, police et industrie éditorial en France, de l'Ancien Régime à la

Révolution," in *Les Républicains des lettres: Gens de culture et Lumières aux XVIIIe siècle* (Paris: Fayard, 1988), pp. 29–46.

For LA FONTAINE's verses of uncertain date, dedicated to Mme de Lafayette—"À Mme de Lafayette, en lui envoyant un petit billard," see La Fontaine, "Pièces publiées pour la première fois dans les œuvres posthumes" (1696), in *Œuvres complètes*, edited by Jean-Pierre Collinet, two volumes (Paris: Gallimard/Bibliothèque de la Pléiade, 1991), Vol. 2, pp. 742–743.

On LA ROCHEFOUCAULD see the bibliographic notes for Chapter 8.

TASTE. Karl Vossler, *Frankreichs Kultur und Sprache* (1913); Jean-Bertand Barrière, *L'Idée de goût de Pascal à Valéry* (Paris: Klincksieck, 1972); Jean-Pierre Dens, *L'Honnête Homme et la critique du goût*; Michel Moriarty, *Taste and Ideology in Seventeenth-Century France*, especially the chapter "Defining *Goût*: The Dictionaries," pp. 54–82; Claude Chantalat, *À la recherche du goût classique* (Paris: Klincksieck, 1992); *Du goût, de la conversation et des femmes*; Alain Montandon, "Goût," in *Dictionnaire raisonné de la politesse et du savoir-vivre: Du Moyen Âge à nos jours*, pp. 439–449. For the eighteenth century, see Jean-Paul Sermain, "Le code du bon goût (1725–1750)," in *Histoire de la rhétorique dans l'Europe moderne*, pp. 879–943.

On the famous QUERELLE OF THE ANCIENTS AND THE MODERNS, see Giovanni Saverio Santangelo, *La "Querelle des Anciens et des Modernes" nella critica del '900* (Bari: Adriatica Editrice, 1975) and above all, *Querelle des Anciens et des Modernes, XVIIe–XVIIIe siècles*, edited by Anne-Marie Lecoq, preceded by "Les Abeilles et les araignées" by Marc Fumaroli and followed by a postface by Jean-Robert Armogathe (Paris: Gallimard, 2001).

CHAPTER 11

MME DE LA SABLIÈRE. Gustave Desnoiresterres, *Les Cours galantes, l'hôtel de Bouillon, la Folie-Rambouillet, le château d'Anet, le Palais du Temple* (Paris: Dentu, 1860; see the chapter concerning the Marquis de La Fare, Antoine Rambouillet de La Sablière, and Mme de La Sablière, pp. 125–176); Anatole France, "Mme de La Sablière, d'après des documents inédits," in *La Vie littéraire, quatrième série* (Paris: Calmann-Lévy, 1892), Vol. 4, pp. 325–346; S. Menjot d'Elbenne, *Mme de La Sablière, ses pensées chrétiennes et ses lettres à l'abbé Rancé* (Paris: Plon, 1923); André Hallays, "Le salon de Mme de La Sablière," in *Les Grands Salons littéraires (XVIIe et XVIIIe siècles)*, Conférences du Musée Carnavalet (1927) (Paris: Payot, 1928), pp. 49–78; L. Petit, *Mme de La Sablière et François Bernier*, in *Mercure de France* 308 (1950), pp. 670–683. See too Marc Fumaroli's excellent pages on Mme de La Sablière in *Le Poète et le Roi*, pp. 390–403.

CHAPTER 12

NINON DE LENCLOS. Tallemant des Réaux, "Ninon," in *Historiettes*, Vol. 2, pp. 440–449; Sainte-Beuve, "Saint-Évremond et Ninon" (1851), in *Causeries du lundi*, Vol. 4, pp. 170–191. The *Correspondance authentique de Ninon de Lenclos, comprenant un grand nombre de lettres inédites et suivie de la "Coquette vengée"* (1886; Slatkine Reprints, Geneva, 1968) was prepared by Émile Colombey, who had already written *La Cour de Ninon* (Paris: Librairie Centrale, 1858–1867). Émile Magne's biography, *Ninon de Lenclos* (1913; Paris: Émile-Paul frères, 1948), is always interesting and has withstood the test of time very well. See also Roger Duchêne, *Ninon de Lenclos, ou la manière jolie de faire l'amour* (1984; Paris: Fayard, 2000) and Françoise Hamel, *Notre dame des amours: Ninon de Lenclos* (Paris: Grasset, 1998).

There are innumerable contemporary accounts of MME DE MAINTENON, from Mme de Sévigné's letters to Mme de Caylus's *Souvenirs*, edited by Bernard Noël (Paris: Mercure de France, 1965). These also include the Abbé de Choisy's *Mémoires*, edited by Georges Mongrédien (Paris: Mercure de France, 1966); the three volumes of documents about her collected by the Comte d'Haussonville and G. Hannotaux, *Souvenirs sur Mme de Maintenon* (Paris: Calmann-Lévy, 1902–1904), Vol. 1: *Mémoires et lettres inédites de Mlle d'Aumale*; Vol. 2: *Les Cahiers de Mlle d'Aumale*; Vol. 3: *Mme de Maintenon à Saint-Cyr: Dernières lettres à Mme de Caylus*; and finally Saint-Simon's *Mémoires*. In the absence of any critical edition of Mme de Maintenon's correspondence, see the two-volume *Lettres et entretiens sur l'éducation des filles par Mme de Maintenon, recueillis et publiés pour la première fois par M. Th. Lavallée* (second edition, Paris: Charpentier, 1861) and *Mme de Maintenon d'après sa correspondence authentique: Choix de lettres et entretiens*, edited by A. Geffroy (Paris, 1887). The edition of her letters undertaken by Marcel Langlois (Paris: Letouzey, 1935–1939) remained incomplete. See too Sainte-Beuve, "Mme de Maintenon" (1851) and "La Princesse des Ursins" (1852), in *Causeries du lundi*, Vol. 4, pp. 369–388, 401–440; Théophile Lavallée, *Mme de Maintenon et la maison royale de Saint-Cyr (1686–1793)* (Paris: Plon, 1862); Mme Saint-Taillandier, *Mme de Maintenon: L'énigme de sa vie auprès du grand roi* (Paris: Hachette, 1920) and Louis Hastier, *Louis XIV et Mme de Maintenon* (Paris: Hachette, 1957); Madeleine Daniélou, *Mme de Maintenon, éducatrice* (Paris: Bloud et Gay, 1946); Jean Cordelier, *Mme de Maintenon, une femme au Grand Siècle* (Paris: Éditions du Seuil, 1955); Françoise Chandernagor, *L'Allée du Roi* (Paris: Juillard, 1981); Claude Dulong, *Le Mariage du Roi-Soleil* (Paris: Albin Michel, 1986); Georges Couton, *La Chair et l'Âme: Louis XIV entre ses maîtresses et Bossuet* (Grenoble: Presses Universitaires de Grenoble, 1995); André Castelot, *Mme de Maintenon, la reine secrète* (Paris: Perrin, 1996). I particularly wish to record my indebtedness to three recent publications: Simone Berthière's two incisive chapters on Mme de Maintenon ("La gouvernante des bâtards royaux" and "L'épouse non déclarée") in *Les Femmes du Roi-Soleil*, Vol. 2 of *Les Reines de France au temps des Bourbons* (Paris: Éditions des Fallois, 1998), pp. 221–243 and 291–316, respectively; *Mme de*

Maintenon, Mme Caylus et Mme Dangeau: L'estime et la tendresse. Correspondances intimes réunies et présentées par Pierre-E. Leroy et Marcel Loyau, preface by Marc Fumaroli (Paris: Albin Michel, 1998); Mme de Maintenon, *"Comment la sagesse vient aux filles." Propos d'éducation choisis et présentés par Pierre-E. Leroy et Marcel Loyau* (Paris: Bartillant, 1998). See also Alain Niderst, *"L'Enjouée Plotine": Mme de Maintenon, Mme de Scudéry et Ninon de Lenclos*, in *Papers on French Seventeenth Century Literature*, Vol. 27, No. 53 (2000), pp. 501–508.

ON MME DE SÉVIGNÉ'S EVENING AT SAINT-CYR, see Patrick Dandrey, "Pouvoir et séduction: Mme de Sévigné, 'Esther' et le roi," in *Cahiers de Littérature du XVIIè siècle* 7 (Toulouse: Université de Toulouse–Le Mirail, 1985), pp. 23–50.

CHAPTER 13

On the IDEA of FRANCE cultivated by the French and by foreigners, see *La Découverte de la France au XVIIe siècle*, Colloques internationaux du CNRS (Paris: Éditions du Centre national de la Recherche scientifique, 1980).

On the *ESPRIT DE SOCIÉTÉ*, see Marc Fumaroli's essay "L'esprit de société parisien au XVIIIe siècle," the preface to Hellegouarc'h, *L'Esprit de société*.

SOCIABILITÉ. On the extreme importance Enlightenment thought assigned to social life as a distinctive element of the national character and as a characteristic of European culture, see Federico Chabod, *Storia dell'idea di Europa* (Bari: Laterza, 1961). The study of *sociabilité*, a subject already addressed in the nineteenth and twentieth centuries, came into its own historiographically with Maurice Agulhon's research: *La Sociabilité méridionale: Confréries et associations dans la vie collective en Provence orientale à la fin du XVIIIe siècle* (Aix-en-Provence: La pensée universitaire, 1966); *Le Cercle dans la France bourgeoise, 1810–1848: Étude d'une mutation de sociabilité* (Paris: Armand Colin, 1977). The review *Cheiron* devoted an interesting monograph number to sociability as an "object of history" (*Sociabilità nobiliare, sociabilità borghese*, edited by Maria Malatesa, June 9–10, 1989); and among the many contributions in the collection, Daniel Roche's "Sociabilità culturale e politica: gli anni della pre-Rivoluzione" (pp. 19–42) is extremely useful in defining the field of cultural sociability in the eighteenth century. The phenomenon is also central to the essays collected by Daniel Gordon in *Citizens without Sovereignty*, to which we have often referred in this work. See also Margaret C. Jacob, "The Enlightenment Redefined: The Formation of Modern Civil Society," in *Social Research*, Vol. 58, No. 2 (Summer 1991), pp. 475–495; Keith Michael Baker, "Enlightenment and the Institution of Society: Notes for a Conceptual History," in *Main Trends in Cultural History*, edited by Willem Melching and Wyger Velema (Amsterdam-Atlanta, 1994), pp. 95–120. See Louis van Delft, "Les caractères des nations," in *Littérature et anthropologie*, pp. 87–104.

For a definition of the word *POLITESSE*, see the bibliography for Chapter 1, above. After the two fundamental books, Magendie's *La Politesse mondaine*, and Norbert Elias's *The Court Society*, the notion of *politesse* and the vast eighteenth-century literature that accompanied it have, during the last twenty years, increasingly attracted the attention of historians, writers, and sociologists. I should single out the studies by Jean Starobinski, "Le mot civilisation," in *Le Remède dans le mal*, pp. 11–59; Jacques Revel, "Les usages de la civilité," in *Histoire de la vie privée* (Paris: Éditions du Seuil, 1986), Vol. 3, pp. 169–209; and Roger Chartier's "Distinction et divulgation," in *Lectures et lecteurs dans la France d'Ancien Régime*. Concerning the English debate on politeness, which took off at the turn of the seventeenth and eighteenth centuries, see Lawrence E. Klein, "Berkeley, Shaftesbury and the Meaning of Politeness," in *Studies in Eighteenth-Century Culture* 16 (1986), pp. 57–68; Jean-Jacques Courtine and Claudine Haroche, *Histoire du visage: Exprimer et taire ses émotions XVIe–début XIXe siècle* (Paris-Marseille: Rivages, 1988); Michel Lacroix, *De la politesse: Essai sur la littérature du savoir-vivre* (Paris: Juillard, 1990); Philippe Guyard, "Paroles, gestes et conversation dans les traités de civilité et de politesse mondaine d'Erasme à La Salle" (Master's Thesis, Université Paris I–Sorbonne, 1990/1991); Peter France, *Politeness and its Discontents: Problems in French Classical Culture*.

In *Étiquette et Politesse*, edited by Alain Montandon (Université Blaise Pascal, Association des Publication de la Faculté des Lettres et Sciences Humaines de Clermont-Ferrand, 1992), I particularly recommend the following essays: Alain Montandon, "De l'urbanité: entre étiquette et politesse" (pp. 7–18); Alain Pons, "Sur la notion de 'Civilité'" (pp. 19–32); and Emmanuel Bury, "Civiliser la 'personne' ou instituer le 'personnage'? les deux versions de la politesse selon les théoriciens français du XVIIe siècle" (pp. 125–138). See also Emmanuel Bury, "De la Paideia à l'Honnêteté: quelques archétypes antiques de la civilité au XVIIe siècle," in *Convivialité et Politesse: Du gigot, des mots et autres savoir-vivre*, edited by Alain Montandon (Association des Publications de la Faculté des Lettres et Sciences Humaines de Clermont-Ferrand, 1993), pp. 27–47. Equally useful is *Pour une histoire des traités de savoir-vivre en Europe*, edited by Alain Montandon (Centre de recherches sur les littératures modernes et contemporaines, Clermont-Ferrand, 1994); and *Politesse et sincérité*, preface by Harald Weinrich (Paris: Éditions Esprit, 1994). Extremely useful for its excellent contributions is the *Dictionnaire raisonné de la politesse et du savoir-vivre du Moyen-Âge à nos jours*. In addition, see Harald Weinrich, "Due codici contigui: onore e cortesia" (1996), Italian translation by Anna Zagatti, in *Il polso del tempo*, edited by Federico Bertoni (Florence: La Nuova Italia, 1999), pp. 177–192; Emmanuel Bury, *Littérature et politesse*; and also Robert Muchembled, *La Société policée: Politique et politesse en France du XVIe au XXe siècle*. For a philosophical approach, see Camille Pernot, *La Politesse et la philosophie* (Paris: PUF, 1996).

On HUME's relations with France, there is Ernest Campbell Mossner's classic biography, *The Life of David Hume* (Clarendon Press, 1970).

On LORD CHESTERFIELD and FRANCE, see Marc Fumaroli's preface to Chesterfield, *Lettres à son fils, à Paris, 1750–1752* (Paris: Rivages, 1993), pp. 7–54.

On the MARÉCHAL DE RICHELIEU, I refer to my own preface, "Fatti della vita del Maresciallo di Richelieu," in *Vita privata del Maresciallo di Richelieu*, edited by Benedetta Craveri (Milan: Adelphi, 1989), pp. 167–222; published in French by Les Editions Desjonquières, 1993, pp. 5–32.

On the *JE NE SAIS QUOI*, see *Il 'non so che': Storia di una idea estetica*, edited by Paolo D'Angelo and Stefano Velotti (Palermo: Aesthetica edizione, 1997). This excellent essay traces the diffusion of this expression throughout Europe, particularly in seventeenth-century France where it was widely used; there follows an anthology of texts, beginning with *Je ne sais quoi*, the fifth *entretien* in *Les Entretiens d'Ariste et d'Eugène* (1670) by Dominique Bouhours, who was the first to entitle an essay the "je ne sais quoi." For a philosophical approach, read Vladimir Jankélévitch, *Le Je-ne-sais-quoi et le Presque-rien* (Paris: Éditions du Seuil, 1980), Vol. 1: *La Manière et l'Occasion*.

HONORÉ D'URFÉ, see the bibliographical notes for Chapter 3.

LOUIS XIV. There is of course a vast bibliography of works on the Sun King. Two of the best biographies of Louis XIV have appeared in the last twenty years, by François Bluche (Paris: Fayard, 1986) and by Jean Christian Petitfils (Paris: Perrin, 1995), respectively. For an understanding of the complex symbolism that marked the sovereign's "presentation," see Louis Marin, *Le Portrait du Roi* (Paris: Éditions du Minuit, 1981); J. M. Apostolidès, *Le Roi-Machine: Spectacle et politique au temps de Louis XIV* (Paris: Éditions de Minuit, 1981); Nicole Ferrier-Caverivière, *L'Image de Louis XIV dans la littérature française de 1660 à 1715* (Paris: PUF, 1981); *Le Grand Roi à l'aube des Lumières, 1715–1751* (Paris: PUF, 1985); Peter Burke, *The Fabrication of Louis XIV* (Yale University Press, 1992); Gérard Sabatier, *Versailles ou la figure du roi* (Paris: Albin Michel, 1999). The organization of daily life at Versailles is very well described by Jean-François Solnon, *La Cour de France* (Paris: Fayard, 1987), whereas there is an interesting reading of Louis XIV's court seen through Saint-Simon's *Mémoires* in Emmanuel Le Roy Ladurie, *Saint-Simon ou le système de la cour* (Paris: Fayard, 1997). See too Anka Muhlstein, *La Femme soleil: Les femmes et le pouvoir. Une relecture de Saint-Simon* (Paris: Denoël Gonthier, 1976), and Philippe Beaussant, *Le Soleil se lève aussi* (Paris: Gallimard, 2000).

On MADAME, I recommend Jacqueline Duchêne's recent biography, *Henriette d'Angleterre, duchesse d'Orléans* (Paris: Fayard, 1995), and on MONSIEUR, Nancy Nichols Barker, *Brother to the Sun King: Philippe, Duke of Orléans* (John Hopkins University Press, 1989).

The *PLAISIRS DE L'ÎLE ENCHANTÉE* refers to the first three days of royal festivities organized in the gardens at Versailles between May 7 and May 14, 1664. See the official account, *Les Plaisirs de l'Isle Enchantée...à Versailles, le VII May 1664 et continuée plusieurs autres jours* (Paris: Imprimerie royale, 1673). The inspiration came from Ariosto's island of Alcina (*Orlando Furioso*, cantos VI and VII); and the entertainments that followed during the course of the next three days—a ring race on the first day, a performance of the *Princesse d'Élide* on the second, and a ballet on the third—were conceived by the festival's organizer, the Duc de Saint-Agnan, like many other devices arranged by the magician to keep the paladins on the island. For the history and symbolism of the fête I have made much use of my daughter Isabella d'Amico's research, "L'isola di Alcina: Ideologia monarchica e festi agli inizi del regno di Luigi XIV" (degree thesis in modern history at the Faculty of Letters and Philosophy at the University of La Sapienza in Rome, supervisor/examiner Professor Corrado Vivanti, 1994–1995).

On LOUIS XIV'S FIRST LOVE, see Claude Dulong's biography, *Marie Mancini: La première passion de Louis XIV* (Paris: Perrin, 1993). Pierre Combescot has recently written a lively account of the adventurous lives of all seven of Mazarin's nieces, *Les Petites Mazarines* (Paris: Grasset, 1999).

On the friends and habitués of LOUIS JOSEPH DE BOURBON (1654–1712), DUC DE VENDÔME, and his brother, PHILIPPE, GRAND PRIOR OF THE TEMPLE, I refer readers to Desnoiresterres, *Les Cours galantes*, Chapter 5, pp. 177–214, and Chapter 6, pp. 215–285. See also Guilbert Bouriquet, *L'abbé de Chaulieu et le Libertinage au Grand Siècle* (Paris: Nizet, 1972).

There are two biographies of the DUCHESSE DU MAINE: André Morel's *La duchesse du Maine: Reine de Sceaux* (Paris: Hachette, 1928), and Jean-Luc Goudrin's more recent *La duchesse du Maine, Louise-Bénédicte de Bourbon, princesse de Condé* (Paris: Pygmalion, Gérard Watelet, 1999). See too Jacqueline Hellegouarc'h's article "Mélinde ou la duchesse du Maine: deux contes de jeunesse de Voltaire: 'Le Crocheteur borgne' et 'Così-Sancta,'" in *Revue d'Histoire littéraire de la France*, Vol. 78, No. 5 (September– October 1978), pp. 722–735; Adolphe Jullien, *Les Grandes Nuits de Sceaux: Le théâtre de la duchesse du Maine* (1876), reprinted in *La Comédie à la Cour. Les théâtres de société royale pendant le siècle dernier. La duchesse du Maine et les Grandes Nuits de Sceaux. Mme de Pompadour et le théâtre des petits cabinets. Le théâtre de Marie-Antoinette à Trianon* (Paris: Firmin Didot, 1885). See the chapter on Sceaux in my book *Mme du Deffand and her World*, translated by Teresa Waugh (Godine, 1994), pp. 34–59 (originally published in Italian as *Mme du Deffand e il suo mondo*, Milan: Adelphi, 1982).

FONTENELLE. See Alain Niderst's biography, *Fontenelle*; and also *Fontenelle*, edited by Alain Niderst, preface by Jean Mesnard (Paris: PUF, 1989).

On MME DE STAAL-DELAUNAY, see Sainte-Beuve, "Mme de Staal-Delaunay," in *Portraits littéraires*, in *Œuvres*, Vol. 2, pp. 894–908; J. Christopher Herold, "Mme Delaunay de Staal," in *Love in Five Temperaments* (Atheneum, 1961), pp. 119–192;

Gérard Doscot, introduction to *Mémoires de Mme de Staal-Delaunay*, edited by Gérard Doscot (Paris: Mercure de France, 1970), pp. 9–24; Daria Galateria, "Le 'confessioni' di una cameriera," in Mme de Staal-Delaunay, *Memorie*, edited by Daria Galateria (Milan: Adelphi, 1995), pp. 319–353, and Pietro Citati, "Bonheur de la prison," in *Portraits de femmes* (Paris: Gallimard, 2001), pp. 33–40.

On the DUC D'ORLÉANS's lifestyle, see Erlanger, *Le Régent* (1938; Paris: Gallimard, 1985) as well as Jean Meyer, *La Vie quotidienne en France au temps de la Régence* (Paris: Hachette, 1979).

On NOBLE HOUSES, see Natacha Coquery, *L'Hôtel aristocratique: Le marché de luxe à Paris au XVIIIe siècle* (Paris: Éditions de la Sorbonne, 1998).

See Simone de Bertière's excellent pages on LOUIS XV'S LIKING FOR THE PRIVATE LIFE in *La Reine et la Favorite*, Vol. 3 of *Les Reines de France au temps des Bourbons*, pp. 228–232.

On Mme de Pompadour's and Marie-Antoinette's PASSION FOR THE THEATER, see Adolphe Jullien, *Histoire du théâtre de Mme de Pompadour dit théâtre des petits cabinets* (1874), and *La Comédie à la Cour*. There is a reprint edition (Geneva: Minkoff, 1978) of the *Histoire du théâtre de Mme de Pompadour* (1874) and of *Les Grandes Nuits de Sceaux* (1876). Philippe Beaussant has recently returned to the subject in collaboration with Patricia Bouchenot-Déchin, *Les Plaisirs de Versailles: Théâtre et musique* (Paris: Fayard, 1996).

With regard to the black legend about MARIE-ANTOINETTE, see Jacques Revel, "Marie-Antoinette," in *Dictionnaire critique de la Révolution française*, edited by François Furet and Mona Ozouf (Paris: Flammarion, 1988), pp. 286–287.

On VOLTAIRE consult Raymond Naves, *Le Goût de Voltaire* (1937; Geneva: Slatkine Reprints, 1967); the five volumes of *Voltaire en son temps*, edited by René Pomeau (Oxford: The Voltaire Foundation/Taylor Institution, 1985–1994), an intellectual biography and detailed history of Voltaire's life; and Sylvain Menant, *L'Esthétique de Voltaire* (Paris: SEDES, 1995).

On the new PRESTIGE ACCORDED TO MEN OF LETTERS and the process of the writer's sanctification that took place during the eighteenth century, there is Paul Bénichou's classic study, *Le Sacre de l'Écrivain, 1750–1830: Essai sur l'avènement d'un pouvoir spirituel laïque dans la France moderne* (1973; Paris: Gallimard, 1996). Bénichou writes that, in the entry entitled "Gens de lettres" in the *Encyclopédie*, "Voltaire, with his usual acuity, traced, in a few words, the path trodden by men of letters since the Renaissance; from the philologists that they were, he observes, they have become philosophers, men of the world, and guides of the human spirit" (p. 26).

On the seventeenth-century interest in ANECDOTE: Francine Wind, *Les Ana sous Louis XIV*, "Histoire et anecdote," pp. 232–239.

On Voltaire's EPISTOLARY AESTHETIC, see S. S. B. Taylor, *Voltaire letter-writer*, Forum for Foreign Languages Study 21 (1985), pp. 338–348; Introduction to *Correspondance choisie*, edited by Jacqueline Hellegouarc'h (Paris: Livre de Poche, 1990); Geneviève Haroche-Bouzinac, *Voltaire dans ses lettres de jeunesse* (Paris, 1991); *Voltaire et l'Europe*, catalog of the exhibition at the Bibliothèque Nationale de France and the Monnaie de Paris, edited by F. Bléchet and M. O. Germain (Paris: Bibliothèque Nationale de France/Brussels: Éditions complexe, 1994).

CHAPTER 14

THE EIGHTEENTH CENTURY: Paul Hazard, *La Crise de la conscience européenne (1680–1715)* (Paris: Fayard, 1961), has been reprinted several times; André Monglond's two-volume study *Le Préromantisme français* (1930; Paris: Corti, 1966), Vol. 1: *Le Héros préromantique*, Vol. 2: *Le Maître des âmes sensibles* (1930); Ernst Cassirer, *The Philosophy of the Enlightenment*, translated by Fritz C. A. Koelln and James P. Pettegrove (Princeton University Press, 1951); Pierre Trahard, *Les Maîtres de la sensibilité française au XVIIIe siècle* (1931–1933; Geneva: Slatkine Reprints, 1968). Robert Mauzi, *L'Idée du bonheur dans la littérature et la pensée françaises au XVIIIe siècle* (1960; Paris: Albin Michel, 1994), and "Les Maladies de l'âme au XVIIIe siècle," in *Revue des Sciences Humaines*, fasc. 100 (1960), pp. 469f; J. Ehrard, *L'Idée de la Nature en France dans la première moitié du XVIIIe siècle* (1963; Geneva: Slatkine Reprints, 1981); Adolphe Dupront, *Qu'est-ce que les Lumières?* (course held at the Sorbonne in 1962/1963; Paris: Gallimard, 1996); Peter Gay, *The Enlightenment: An Interpretation* (Random House, 1967); Robert Darnton, *The Business of Enlightenment: A Publishing History of the Encyclopédie, 1775–1800* (Harvard University Press, 1979); Michel Delon, *L'Idée d'énergie au tournant des Lumières (1770–1820)* (Paris: PUF, 1988); Lionello Sozzi, "Il Principe e il filosofo: il dibattito sull' 'homme de lettres' dall'Encyclopédie' alla Rivoluzione," in *Il Principe e il Filosofo*, edited by Lionello Sozzi (Naples: Guida Editore, 1988), pp. 45–98; René Pomeau, *L'Europe des Lumières: Cosmopolitisme et unité européenne au XVIIIe siècle* (1991; Paris: Stock, 1995); Didier Masseau, *L'Invention de l'intellectuel dans l'Europe du XVIIIe siècle* (Paris: PUF, 1994).

Of all Daniel Roche's important studies on the cultural, social, and material history of the eighteenth century, I must at least mention *Le Siècle des lumières en province: Académies et académiciens provinciaux (1680–1789)* (1978; Paris: Mouton, 1989); *Les Républicains des lettres: Gens de culture et Lumières au XVIIIe siècle*; *La France des Lumières* (Paris: Fayard, 1993); *Histoires des choses banales: Naissance de la consommation XVIIe–XIXe siècle* (Paris: Fayard, 1997). See Roger Chartier's important works, *Pratique de lecture* (under his supervision) (Paris-Marseilles: Rivages, 1985);

Les Usages de l'imprimé (under his supervision) (Paris: Fayard, 1987); *Lectures et lecteurs dans la France d'Ancien Régime; Les Origines culturelles de la Révolution française; La correspondance: Les usages de la lettre au XIXe siècle* (under his supervision) (Paris: Fayard, 1991); *Culture écrite et société: L'ordre des livres (XIVe–XVIIIe siècles)* (Paris: Albin Michel, 1996); *Au bord de la falaise: L'histoire entre certitudes et inquiétude* (Paris: Albin Michel, 1998).

WOMEN IN THE EIGHTEENTH CENTURY. Edmond and Jules de Goncourt, *La Femme au XVIIIe siècle;* François-Adolphe Lescure, *La Société française au XVIIIe siècle: Les femmes philosophes* (Paris: Dentu, 1881); Pierre Fauchery, *La Destinée féminine dans le roman européen du dix-huitième siècle 1713–1807: Essai de gynécomythie romanesque* (Paris: Armand Colin, 1972); Paul Hoffmann, *La Femme dans la pensée des Lumières* (1977; Geneva: Slatkine Reprints, 1995); Élisabeth Badinter, *Émilie, Émilie: L'Ambition féminine au XVIIIe siècle* (Paris: Flammarion, 1983); *French Women and the Age of Enlightenment,* edited by Samia I. Spencer (Indiana University Press, 1984); A. L. Thomas, *Diderot, Mme d'Épinay, Qu'est-ce qu'une femme? Un débat préfacé par Élisabeth Badinter* (Paris, P. O. L., 1989); Erica Harth, *Cartesian Women;* Mona Ozouf, *Les Mots des femmes.*

The best book about the SALONS is still *Salons du XVIIIe siècle,* by Marguerite Glotz and Madeleine Maire (Paris: Nouvelle Éditions Latines, 1949); see also Roger Picard, *Les Salons littéraires et la société française (1610–1789).* With regard to their influence on intellectual life, Dena Goodman has a novel and certainly bold thesis in "Enlightenment Salons: The Convergence of Female and Philosophic Ambitions," in *Eighteenth-Century Studies,* Vol. 22, No. 3 (Spring 1989), pp. 329–350, and then in *The Republic of Letters.* In her view, it was the salons governed by women that advanced the Enlightenment. They "better supported the new Republic of Letters ... [and] Diderot's project of 'changing the common way of thinking'" (p. 52). (See the bibliography for Chapter 2, above, on the historiography of women.) *L'Esprit de société: Cercles et "salons" parisiens au XVIIIe siècle,* edited by Jacqueline Hellegouarc'h, gives a good overall view of eighteenth-century salons taken from contemporary witnesses.

For an exhaustive bibliography on MME DE LAMBERT, consult Roger Marchal's useful and extremely detailed study, *Mme de Lambert et son milieu* (Oxford: The Voltaire Foundation, 1991), which was a great help to me. I would also like to point to Sainte-Beuve's "Mme de Lambert et Mme Necker," in *Causeries du lundi,* Vol. 4, pp. 217–239; L. P. Zimmermann's "La morale laïque au commencement du XVIIIe siècle: Mme de Lambert," in *Revue d'Histoire littéraire de la France* 24 (1917), pp. 42–64 and 440–466; Paul Hoffmann's "Mme de Lambert et l'exigence de la dignité," in *Travaux de linguistique et de littérature,* Vol. 11, No. 2 (Centre de philologie et de littératures romanes de l'Université de Strasbourg, 1973), pp. 19–32; Jeannette Geffriaud Rosso's *Mme de Lambert* and "Du salon de Mme de Lambert au 'Zibaldone' de Leopardi," in *Études sur la féminité au XVIIe et XVIIIe siècles,* pp. 67–89 and 93–125; Faith E. Beasley's

Anne-Thérèse de Lambert and the Politics of Taste, in *Papers on French Seventeenth Century Literature*, Vol. 19, No. 37 (1992), pp. 337–344. See, too, René de Ceccaty's preface to Mme de Lambert, *De l'amitié* (Paris: Éditions du Seuil, 1999), pp. 1–26.

On the games of influence that determined the election of new members to the ACADÉMIE FRANÇAISE, see Lucien Brunel, *Les Philosophes et l'Académie française au dix-huitième siècle* (1884; Geneva: Slatkine Reprints, 1967).

On MME DE LAMBERT'S RELATIONS WITH MONTESQUIEU, see Jeanette Geffriaud Rosso, *Montesquieu et la féminité* (Pisa, Libreria Goliardica, 1977), pp. 56–66; see also Robert Shackleton, *Montesquieu: A Critical Biography* (Oxford University Press, 1961); and in particular, the discussion on friendship and the duties of friendship in which Mme de Lambert and Montesquieu participated with other guests of the hôtel de Nevers.

On the great eighteenth-century theme of HAPPINESS, see Robert Mauzi's classic *L'Idée du bonheur dans la littérature et la pensée françaises au XVIIIᵉ siècle*, and *La Quête du bonheur et l'expression de la douleur dans la littérature et la pensée française: Mélanges offerts à Corrado Rosso* (Geneva: Droz, 1995). See also Élisabeth Badinter's preface to Mme du Châtelet, *Discours sur le bonheur* (Paris: Rivages, 1977), pp. 9–25.

On the theme of BIENFAISANCE, there is Patrizia Oppici's study, *L'idea di "bienfaisance" nel Settecento francese o il laccio di Aglaia*, preface by Corrado Rosso (Pisa: Libreria Goliardica, 1989).

On MARIVAUX, see Frédéric Deloffre's fundamental work, *Une Préciosité nouvelle: Marivaux et le marivaudage* (1955; Geneva: Slatkine Reprints, 1993). And also David J. Culpin, "La Morale mondaine de Marivaux," in *Marivaux et les Lumières: L'éthique du romancier*, Actes du Colloque internationale organisé à Aix-en-Provence (June 1992), edited by Geneviève Goubier (Aix-en-Provence: Université de Provence, 1996), pp. 183–190.

On the theme of the RIDICULOUS, see Henri Bergson, *Le Rire: Essai sur la signification de comique* (1899; Paris: PUF, 1975); Patrick Dandrey, *Molière ou l'esthétique du ridicule* (Paris: Klincksieck, 1992); Jacques Morel, "Rire au XVIIᵉ siècle," in *Agréables mensonges; Le Rire de Voltaire*, preface by Bertrand Poirot-Delpech, edited by Pascal Debailly, Jean-Jacques Robrieux, and Jacques Van Den Heuvel (Paris: Éditions du Félin, 1994); Dominique Bertrand, *Dire le rire à l'âge classique*, and the entry "Ridicule" in the *Dictionnaire raisonné de la politesse et du savoir-vivre*, pp. 781–800; Francesco Fiorentino, *Il ridicolo nel teatro di Molière*, pp. 67–81; Élisabeth Bourguinat, *Le Siècle du persiflage 1734–1789* (Paris: PUF, 1998).

CHAPTER 15

LIBERTINISM. Jacques Rustin, *Le Vice à la mode* (Paris: Ophrys, 1979); Patrick Wald Lasowski, *Libertines* (Paris: Gallimard, 1980); *L'Ardeur et la Galanterie* (Paris: Gallimard, 1986); Claude Reichler, *L'Âge libertin* (Paris: Éditions de Minuit, 1987); Michel Delon, *Le Savoir-Vivre libertin* (Paris: Hachette, 2000).

Since the famous preface by Étiemble to *Les Égarements du cœur et de l'esprit* (Paris: Club du livre, 1953), when CRÉBILLON FILS was still regarded as a second-rate writer, assessment of the novelist has changed radically. The critical edition of the *Œuvres complètes*, edited by Jean Sgard, two volumes (Paris: Classiques Garnier, 1999–2000), is the culmination of the rediscovery of Crébillon which places him in the tradition of the classical moralists: Bernadette Fort, *Le Langage de l'ambiguïté dans Crébillon fils* (Paris: Klincksieck, 1978); Andrzej Siemek, *La Recherche morale et l'esthétique dans les romans de Crébillon fils*, Studies on Voltaire (Oxford: Voltaire Foundation/Taylor Institution, 1981); Carole Dornier, *Le Discours de maîtrise du libertin: Étude sur l'œuvre de Crébillon fils* (Paris: Klincksieck, 1994); Jean Dagen, *Introduction à la sophistique amoureuse dans les Égarements du cœur et de l'esprit de Crébillon fils* (Paris: Champion, 1995); *Songe, illusion, égarement dans les romans de Crébillon*, under the supervision of Jean Sgard (Grenoble: ELLUG, 1996).

MME DE TENCIN. P.-M. Masson, *Mme de Tencin (1682–1749)* (Paris: Hachette, 1909); J. Christopher Herold, "Mme de Tencin," in *Love in Five Temperaments*; Jean Sareil, *Les Tencin: Histoire d'une famille au dix-huitième siècle d'après de nombreux documents inédits* (Geneva: Droz, 1969); René Vaillot, *Qui était Mme de Tencin... et le Cardinal?* preface by Roland Desné (Paris: Le Pavillon Roger Maria Éditeur, 1974); R. de Castries, *La Scandaleuse Mme de Tencin* (Paris: Perrin, 1986). On Mme de Tencin as a novelist: M. Lévy, "Une nouvelle source d'Anne Radcliffe: 'Les Mémoires du comte de Comminge,'" in *Caliban* 1, Annales publiées par la Faculté de Lettres de Toulouse (January 1964), pp. 149–156; J. Decottignies, "Roman et revendication féminine d'après 'Les Mémoires du comte de Comminge' de Mme de Tencin," in *Roman et lumières au XVIIIe siècle*, Actes du Colloque sous la présidence de MM. W. Krauss, R. Pomeau, R. Garaudy, and J. Fabre (Paris: Éditions Sociales, 1970), pp. 311–320; "Les romans de Mme de Tencin: fable et fiction," in *La Littérature des Lumières en France et en Pologne. Esthétique. Terminologie. Échanges* (Warsaw: Acta Universitatis Wratslaviensis, 1976), pp. 256–266; Chantal Thomas, "Les rigueurs de l'amour: étude sur Mme de Tencin et Stendhal," in *L'Infini* 12 (Autumn 1985), pp. 77–89; Henri Coulet, "Expérience sociale et imagination romanesque dans les romans de Mme de Tencin," in *Cahiers de l'Association Internationale des Études Françaises* 46 (May 1994), pp. 31–51; Françoise Gevrey, "Mme de Tencin et 'La Vie de Marianne,'" in *Marivaux et les Lumières*, pp. 59–70; Raymond Trousson, introduction to Mme de Tencin, "Mémoires du comte de Comminge (1747)," in *Romans de femmes du XVIIIe siècle* (Paris: Laffont, 1996), pp. 3–19; Renée Winegarten, "Women and politics: Mme de Tencin," in *The New Criterion* (October 1997), p. 26–32.

On D'ALEMBERT, see Ronald Grimsley, *Jean d'Alembert, 1717–1783* (Clarendon Press, 1963).

On the RELIGIOUS CONFLICT following the promulgation of the papal bull *Unigenitus* (1713) and the nature of eighteenth-century Jansenism, see Monique Cottret, *Jansénisme et Lumières: Pour un autre XVIIIe siècle* (Paris: Albin Michel, 1998), and Catherine Maire, *De la cause de Dieu à la cause de la Nation: Le Jansénisme au XVIIIe siècle* (Paris: Gallimard, 1998).

On MME DE FERRIOL and her circle, see *Lettere di Mademoiselle Aïssé a Mme...*, edited by Benedetta Craveri (Milan: Adelphi, 1984).

On DIPLOMACY: Lucien Bély, *Espions et ambassadeurs au temps de Louis XIV* (Paris: Fayard, 1990); and, by the same author, *Les Relations internationales en Europe XVIIe-XVIIIe siècles* (Paris: PUF, 1992); Lucien Bély and Isabelle Richefort, *L'Europe des traités de Westphalie* (Paris: PUF, 2000).

On the MARCHESE CARACCIOLI, see Marc Fumaroli, "Louis-Antoine de Caraccioli (1721–1803) et l'Europe française," in *Commentaire* 91 (Autumn 2000), pp. 615–629.

MME DE LAFAYETTE's RELATIONS WITH THE COURT OF SAVOY were researched at the end of the nineteenth century by D. Perrero in "Lettere inedite di Madama di Lafayette e sue relazione colla corte de Torino" in *Curiosità e Ricerche di Storia Subalpina* (Turin), and addressed again by Roger Duchêne in *Mme de Lafayette*.

On STANISLAW AUGUSTUS PONIATOWSKI, see Jean Fabre, *Auguste Stanislas Poniatowsky et l'Europe des Lumières* (Paris: Ophrys, Association de publications près des Universités de Strasbourg, 1952) and Adam Zamoyski, *The Last King of Poland* (London: Weidenfeld and Nicolson, 1997); on his relations with Mme Geoffrin, see the *Correspondance inédite du roi Stanislas-Auguste Poniatowski et de Mme Geoffrin (1764–1777)*, edited by Charles de Mouÿ (Paris: Plon, 1885).

On GUSTAV III OF SWEDEN, see his French correspondence in *Gustave III par ses lettres*, edited by Gunnar von Proschwitz (Paris: Jean Touzot, 1986).

CHAPTER 16

According to the American historian Robert Darnton, the INFLUENCE OF SALONS on eighteenth-century intellectual life and the role of *politesse* in establishing equality among those who visited them give rise to several questions. Charged by Daniel Gordon with a low, "populist" reading of the Enlightenment movement, and by Dena Goodman with minimizing the influence of women, Darnton has defined his position in a brilliant polemic, "Two Paths through the Social History of Ideas," in *The Darnton Debate: Books and Revolution in the Eighteenth Century*, edited by Haydn T. Mason (Oxford: The Voltaire Foundation, 1998), pp. 251–294. *Politesse*, according to Darnton, echoing Rousseau, was certainly a means of advancing oneself socially, but it was also a means of control from above, and snobbery, like *bon ton* and irony, was used to intimidate. As for women and their supposed centrality to intellectual life, Darnton points out "that women published relatively little in the eighteenth century" (p. 274) and that they constituted only 3 to 4 percent of the writers of the day.

On MME GEOFFRIN, see Sainte-Beuve, "Mme Geoffrin," in *Causeries du lundi*, Vol. 2, pp. 309–329; Pierre Marie Maurice Henri de Ségur, *Le Royaume de la rue Saint-Honoré: Mme Geoffrin et sa fille* (Paris: Calmann-Lévy, 1897).

On MME DE LA FERTÉ-IMBAULT, see Constantin Photiadès, *La Reine des Lanturelus: Maire-Thérèse Geoffrin, marquise de La Ferté-Imbault (1715–1791)* (Paris: Plon, 1928); Dena Goodman, "Filial Rebellion in the Salon: Mme Geoffrin and Her Daughter," in *French Historical Studies*, Vol. 16, No. 1 (Spring 1989), pp. 28–47; Didier Masseau, "La marquise de La Ferté-Imbault, reine antiphilosophe des Lanturelus," in *Les Dérèglements de l'art: Formes et procédures de l'illégitimité culturelle en France (1715–1914)*, edited by Pierre Popovic and Eric Vigneault (Montreal: Presses de l'Université de Montréal, 2000), pp. 35–50.

For JULIE DE LESPINASSE, see Sainte-Beuve, "Lettres de Mademoiselle de Lespinasse" (1850), in *Causeries du lundi*, Vol. 2, pp. 121–142; and Eugène Asse, *Études sur le XVIIIe siècle: Julie de Lespinasse et la Marquise du Deffand* (Paris, 1877). Of the numerous biographies, here I will merely mention Pierre Marie Maurice Henri de Ségur's *Julie de Lespinasse* (1905; Paris: Calmann-Lévy, 1931), which is to this day the best. Also see Pierre Trahard, "Une fille spirituelle de Jean-Jacques," in *Les Maîtres de la sensibilité française*, Vol. 3, p. 259–278; J. Christopher Herold, "Mademoiselle de Lespinasse," in *Love in Five Temperaments*, pp. 193–260; Jacques Dupont, "De l'absence au chant: Sur les 'Lettres à Guibert' de Julie de Lespinasse," in *Dix-Huitième Siècle* 10 (1978), pp. 395–404; Bernard Minaret and Claude Arnaud, *Les Salons*, with a preface by Jean-Claude Bonnet (Paris: Lattès, 1885); Dena Goodman, "Julie de Lespinasse: A Mirror for the Enlightenment," in *Eighteenth-Century Women and the Arts*, edited by Frederic M. Keener and Susan E. Lorsch (Greenwood Press, 1988), pp. 3–10; Catherine Blondeau, "Lectures de la correspondance de Julie de Lespinasse: une étude de réception," in *Studies on Voltaire and the Eighteenth Century* 108 (1993), pp. 223–232; Arnaldo Pizzorusso, "Le lettere di Julie de Lespinasse," in *Principi e occasioni della scrittura* (1996; Bologna: Il Mulino, 1999), pp. 111–141; François Bott, *La Demoiselle des Lumières* (Paris: Gallimard, 1997).

By Jean-Noël Pascal, see "Julie romancière," the preface to *Lettres de Mademoiselle de Lespinasse* (Plan de la Tour: Éditions d'aujourd'hui, 1978), pp. 9–15; "Bordeau, Bouvart et Rostain: trois médecins face à la tuberculose en 1772," in *Recherches nouvelles sur quelques écrivains des Lumières*, edited by Jacques Proust (Montpellier: Université Paul Valéry, 1979), Vol. 2, pp. 82–88; "Une exemplaire mort d'amour: Julie de Lespinasse," in *Aimer en France, 1760–1860*, Actes du Colloque international de Clermont-Ferrand, 1977 (Publications de la Faculté des Lettres et Sciences Humaines de Clermont-Ferrand, 1980), pp. 55–63; "Guibert ou le héros du roman de Julie," in *Guibert ou le soldat philosophe*, Actes du Colloque du CERSC (Vincennes: Publications du Centre d'Études et de Recherches sur les Stratégies et les Conflits, 1981), pp. 27–40; "Le rêve d'amour de d'Alembert," in *Dix-Huitième Siècle* 16 (1984), pp. 163–169; "La mort de Mlle de Lespinasse dans les Correspondances littéraires de Grimm et de La Harpe," in *Du baroque aux Lumières: Pages à la mémoire de Jeanne Carriat* (Rodez: Rougerie, 1986), pp. 176–179; Preface to Julie de Lespinasse, *Lettres à Condorcet*, edited by Jean-Noel Pascal (Paris: Dejonquières, 1990), pp. 7–18; "Mlle de Lespinasse: lettres de folie ordinaire," in *Expériences Limites de l'Épistolaire: Lettres d'exil, d'enfermement, de folie*, edited by André Magnan (Paris: Champion, 1993), pp. 185–202; Chantal Thomas, preface to Julie de Lespinasse, *Mon amie, je vous aime* (Paris: Mercure de France, 1996).

On the PORTRAIT AS A LITERARY GENRE, see the bibliographic notes to Chapter 9 above. See also Dirk Van der Cruysse's *Le Portrait dans les "Mémoires" du duc de Saint-Simon. Fonctions, Techniques et Anthropologie. Étude Statistique et Analytique* (Paris: Nizet, 1971). On the eighteenth-century portrait, see above all E. M. Cioran, *Anthologie du portrait: De Saint-Simon à Tocqueville* (Paris: Gallimard, 1996).

On MME DU DEFFAND, see Sainte-Beuve, "Lettres de la Marquise du Deffand" (1850), in *Causeries du lundi*, Vol. 1, pp. 412–431; M. de Lescure, "Mme du Deffand: Sa vie, son salon, ses amis, ses lettres," introduction to the *Correspondance complète de la Marquise du Deffand avec ses amis le Président Hénault–Montesquieu–d'Alembert–Voltaire–Horace Walpole...Suivie de ses Œuvres Diverses et éclairée de nombreuses notes par M. de Lescure* (1865; Geneva: Slatkine Reprints, 1971); Wilhelm Klerks, *Mme du Deffand: Essai sur l'ennui* (Leiden: Universitaire Pers Leiden, 1961); Lionel Duisit, *Mme du Deffand épistolière* (Geneva: Droz, 1963); Benedetta Craveri, *Mme du Deffand and Her World*; Giovanna Macchia, "La mondanità e il nulla," in *Il naufragio della speranza: La letteratura francese dall'Illuminismo all'età romantica* (Milan: Mondadori, 1994), pp. 265–272; René de Céccaty, *L'Or et la Poussière* (Paris: J. C. Lattès, 1996); Chantal Thomas, preface to *Lettres de Mme du Deffand à Voltaire* (Paris: Rivages, 1994); Mona Ozouf, "Mme du Deffand," in *Les Mots des femmes*, pp. 25–51; Marc Fumaroli, "L'aveugle des Lumières," preface to the 2001 Italian edition of my book *Mme du Deffand e il suo mondo* (Milan: Adelphi, 2001).

CHAPTER 17

Since 1970, there has been an increasing interest in CONVERSATION in scholarly circles both in Europe and the United States. Conversation is now seen as a distinguishing mark of French civilization during the *ancien régime*, and research has produced more and more precise works on the literary, historical, sociological, and moral aspects of conversation. Today's bibliography on the subject is remarkable for its richness, rigor, and quality. Some studies I would point to are Bernard Beugnot, *L'Entretien au XVIIe siècle* (Montreal: Presses de l'Université de Montréal, 1971); Jean-Pierre Dens, "L'art de la conversation au XVIIe siècle," in *Lettres romanes* 27 (1973), pp. 977–990; Claudia Henn-Schmölders, "Ars conversationis," in *Arcadia* 10 (1975), pp. 16–33; *La Conversation*, presented by Roland Barthes and Frédéric Berthet, monographic number of *Communications* 30 (Paris: Éditions du Seuil, 1979). Within this issue, I would particularly recommend André Pessel's "De la conversation chez les précieuses" (pp. 14–30) and Évelyne Bachellier's "De la conversation à la conversion" (pp. 31–56); Carlo Ossola, "L'homme accompli: La civilisation des Cours comme art de la conversation," in *Le Temps de la réflexion* 4 (Paris: Gallimard, 1983), pp. 77–89; Christoph Strosetzki, *Rhétorique de la conversation*; Elisabeth C. Goldsmith, *"Exclusive Conversations"*; Mary Vidal, *Watteau's Painted Conversations* (Yale University Press, 1992); Peter Burke, *The Art of Conversation*. My own writings on the subject include "La conversation: les salons et l'esprit de société," in *L'Esprit de l'Europe*, edited by Antoine Compagnon and Jacques Seebacher (Paris: Flammarion, 1993), Vol. 3, pp. 116–127; "The Lost Art," in *The New York Review of Books*, December 2, 1993, pp. 40–43; "Le molte conversazioni di Jean de La Bruyère," in *Il prisma dei moralisti*, pp. 343–360; "Talk!" in *The New York Review of Books*, January 20, 2000, pp. 60–64; *Du goût, de la conversation et des femmes*; *Art de la lettre, art de la conversation*. More studies are: Delphine Denis, *La Muse galante: Poétique de la conversation dans l'œuvre de Madeleine de Scudéry*, and Denis's edited publication of Mlle de Scudéry, *"De l'air galant" et autres conversations (1653–1684)*; *La Conversation: Un art de l'instant*, edited by Gérald Cahen (Paris: Éditions Autrement, 1999); among the various contributions to this volume, I would particularly like to point out Patrick Dandrey, "Le 'commerce des honnêtes gens': Mythe ou réalité?" pp. 84–101. For a theoretical approach to the subject, see Alain Milon, *L'Art de la Conversation* (Paris: PUF, 1999). For conversations of the "learned," see also Peter N. Miller's chapter "Constancy, Conversation and Friendship," in *Peiresc's Europe: Learning and Virtue in the Seventeenth Century* (Yale University Press, 2000), pp. 49–75.

In this happy new era of research into conversation, a special place must be reserved for MARC FUMAROLI. Indeed Fumaroli has, during the last decades, done more than anyone to revive research into *conversation à la française*. He has shown it to be a "literary institution," analyzed its rhetoric and style, thrown light on its historical context and its cultural, artistic, and political implications, reviewed its every aspect, whether social or scholarly. Texts that ought to be consulted are: Marc Fumaroli, "Otium, convivium, sermo: la conversation comme 'lieu commun' des lettrés," in *Bulletin des Amis du Centre d'Études de la Renaissance*, supplement to No. 4 (1990), later published in *Le Loisir lettré à l'âge classique*, p. 29–52; "La 'conversation' au XVIIe siècle: le témoignage de Fortin de la Hoguette," in *L'Esprit et la Lettre: Mélanges offerts à Jules Brody*, edited by Louis van Delft (Tübingen: Gunter Narr,

1991), pp. 94–105; "La conversation," in *Les Lieux de Mémoire*, Vol. 3, pp. 679–743, later published in *Trois Institutions littéraires*; "Le Genre des genres littéraires français: La conversation," in *Zaharoff Lecture for 1990–1991* (Clarendon Press, 1992), and "L'art de la conversation ou le Forum du royaume," in *La Diplomatie de l'esprit*, pp. 283–320; "De l'âge de l'éloquence à l'âge de la conversation: la conversion de la rhétorique humaniste dans la France du XVIIe siècle," in *Art de la lettre, art de la conversation*, pp. 25–45; preface to *L'Art de la conversation: Anthologie*, edited by Jacqueline Hellegouarc'h (Paris: Classiques Garnier, 1997), pp. i–xxix; "Littérature et conversation: La querelle Sainte-Beuve–Proust," in *La Conversation: Un art de l'instant*, pp. 102–121; "L'esprit de société parisien au XVIIIe siècle," Fumaroli's preface to Hellegouarc'h, *L'Esprit de société*, pp. vii–xx; his preface to Pascal, *L'Art de persuader*, preceded by Montaigne's *L'Art de conférer* (Paris: Rivages, 2001).

For the idea of the MONDE: see "La notion du 'monde' au XVIIe siècle," in *Littératures classiques* 22 (Autumn 1994), in which I would particularly recommend Marc Fumaroli's contributions, "Premier témoin du parisianisme: le 'monde' et la 'mode' chez les moralistes du XVIIIe siècle" (pp. 165–190); Emmanuel Bury's "Le monde de 'l'honnête homme': aspects de la notion de 'monde' dans l'esthétique du savoir-vivre" (pp. 191–202); and Roger Zuber's "Balzac et le monde de ses lecteurs" (pp. 203–210).

On the relationship between CONVERSATION and RHETORIC, in addition to the above-mentioned works by Marc Fumaroli, see: Alain Pons, "La rhétorique des manières au XVIe siècle en Italie"; Bernard Beugnot, "La précellence du style moyen"; and Gilles Declercq, "La rhétorique classique entre évidence et sublime (1650–1675)"; three essays included in *Histoire de la rhétorique dans l'Europe moderne*, pp. 629–706. See especially the pages concerning Bouhours's *Entretiens*, "illustration of a new genre, emblematic of French classical eloquence: conversation" (p. 666).

The term URBANITAS introduced by Balzac "places itself on the border of social usage and the practice of language, constituting a demarcation line between two cultures, the academic and the social" (Bernard Beugnot, "La précellence du style moyen," in *Histoire de la rhétorique dans l'Europe moderne*, p. 568). On the concept of *urbanitas*, see also Roger Zuber, "Littérature et urbanité," in *Le Statut de la littérature: Mélanges offerts à Paul Bénichou*, pp. 87–96; "L'urbanité française au XVIIe siècle," in *La ville: Histoires et mythes*, edited by M.-C. Bancquart (Nanterre: Université de Paris X–Nanterre, 1983), pp. 41–57.

On the NEED FOR DIRECT INITIATION into the art of conversation and life in polite society, I will merely recommend four famous theoretical texts. Two are by Mlle de Scudéry, "De parler trop ou trop peu, et comment il faut parler" (1658) and "De la politesse" (1684), both reprinted in Mlle de Scudéry, *"De l'air galant" et autres conversations (1653–1684)*, see pp. 94 and 126, respectively; Ortigue de Vaumorière, *L'Art de plaire dans la conversation*, p. 12; and Bellegarde, *Œuvres Diverses: Les Réflexions sur le Ridicule et sur les Moyens de l'éviter, où sont representez les differens Caractères, les Mœurs des personnes de ce siècle* (1696; fourth edition, Paris, 1699), p. 7.

On the CHEVALIER DE MÉRÉ, see the bibliographic notes for Chapter 3.

On LA BRUYÈRE's ideas on conversation, I invite readers to consult my own essay, "Le molte conversazioni di Jean de La Bruyère," in *Il prisma dei moralisti.*

On TORQUATO ACCETTO, see Benedetto Croce, "Appunti di letteratura secentesca inedita o rara: Torquato Accetto e il suo trattatello 'Della dissimulazione onesta,'" in *Nuovi saggi sulla letteratura italiana del Seicento* (second edition, Bari: Laterza, 1949), pp. 86–94. See also Salvatore Nigro's "Scriptor necans," preface to the edition that he edited: *Della dissimulazione onesta (1641)* (Geneva: Costa and Nolan, 1983), and Louis van Delft's "La notion de 'dissimulation honnête' dans la culture classique," in *Prémices et floraison de l'âge classique: Mélanges Jehasse* (Publications de l'Université de Saint-Étienne, 1995), pp. 251–277.

For BALTASAR GRACIÁN, see Benedetto Croce, "Personaggi della storia italo-spagnuola: Il duca di Nocera Francesco Carafa e Baltasar Gracián," in *Anedotti di varia letteratura* (second edition, Bari: Laterza, 1953), Vol. 2, pp. 136–159; "I trattisti italiani del Concettismo e Baltasar Gracián," in *Problemi di estetica* (sixth edition, Bari: Laterza, 1966), pp. 311–345. Louis van Delft, "La Bruyère et Gracián," in *La Bruyère moraliste*, pp. 111–159. See also Marc Fumaroli's preface to Baltasar Gracián, *La Pointe ou l'art du génie* (Paris: L'Âge d'Homme, 1983), pp. 7–16.

On the IMAGE OF THE COURT IN LITERATURE, read A. Croupie's *De Corneille à La Bruyère: Images de la Cour* (Paris: Aux Amateurs de Livres, 1984).

On the RELATIONSHIP BETWEEN THE ART OF CONVERSATION AND THE ART OF LETTER-WRITING IN MME DE SÉVIGNÉ, see Volker Kapp, "L'apogée de l'atticisme français ou l'éloquence qui se moque de la rhétorique (1675–1700)," in *Histoire de la rhétorique dans l'Europe moderne*, pp. 707–786.

For the idea of *ESPRIT*, turn to the bibliographic notes for Chapter 4 as well as *L'Esprit en France au XVIIᵉ siècle*, Proceedings of the 28th annual Congress of the North American Society for Seventeenth Century French Literature, the University of Texas at Austin, April 11–13, 1996, edited by François Lagarde, Biblio 17 (Paris-Seattle-Tübingen: PFSCL, 1997).

On SARASIN, see the bibliographic notes for Chapter 4.

On *POLITESSE*, see the bibliographic notes for Chapters 1 and 13.

On GALLANTRY, see the bibliographic notes for Chapter 2.

On *COMPLAISANCE* AND FLATTERY, see the bibliographic notes for Chapter 9.

On *RAILLERIE, ENJOUEMENT, BADINAGE, BONNE PLAISANTERIE,* and *BONS MOTS,* see Christoph Strosetzki, *Rhétorique de la conversation;* Claude Chantalat, "Les Ris et les Grâces," in *À la recherche du goût classique,* pp. 163–183; Dominique Bertrand's entry on *"raillerie"* in the *Dictionnaire raisonné de la politesse et du savoir-vivre,* pp. 731–750. On the seventeenth-century juxtaposition of *raillerie* with irony, see Jean-Paul Sermain, *Le Code du bon goût,* p. 934.

The word *PERSIFLAGE* can describe an enigmatic discussion, a double meaning, or a more or less explicit mockery, and made its appearance in 1734. It was much used in society language only to disappear with the Revolution. See Élisabeth Bourguinat, *Le Siècle du persiflage (1734–1789)* (Paris: PUF, 1998).

On the VOICE, see "La voix au XVIIe siècle," in *Littératures classiques* (January 12, 1990); Philippe-Joseph Salazar, *Le Culte de la voix au XVIIe siècle: Formes esthétiques de la parole à l'âge de l'imprimé* (Paris/Geneva: Champion/Droz, 1995); "La voix au XVIIe siècle," in *Histoire de la rhétorique dans l'Europe moderne,* pp. 787–821.

On the ART OF SILENCE, see the Abbé Dinouart, *L'Art de se taire, principalement en matière de religion* (1771), edited by Jean-Jacques Courtine and Claudine Haroche (Grenoble: Jérôme Millon, 1996). Also see Courtine and Haroche's chapter "Se taire et se posséder: une archéologie du silence," in *Histoire du visage,* pp. 215–240. On François Lamy, see Benedetta Papàsogli, "'La scienza del cuore' di Francesco Lamy," in *Volti della memoria nel "Grand Siècle" e oltre,* pp. 85–102, as well as C. Strosetzki, *Rhétorique de la conversation,* pp. 33–36.

During the eighteenth century, the seventeenth-century concept of CONVERSATION as an art of pleasing came into question. Conversation ought not to aim merely at social harmony, but should be THE VEHICLE FOR IDEAS and a means of establishing a collective truth. On the subject, see Jean-Paul Sermain, "La conversation au XVIIIe siècle: un théâtre pour les Lumières?" in *Convivialité et politesse,* edited by Alain Montandon (Clermont-Ferrand: Faculté des Lettres et Sciences Humaines de l'Université Blaise Pascal, 1993), fasc. 39, pp. 105–130; and Sermain, "Le code du bon goût," in *Histoire de la rhétorique dans l'Europe moderne,* pp. 931–939.

On ROUSSEAU's criticism of politesse and conversation, see Peter France, "Lumières, politesse et énergie (1750–1776)," in *Histoire de la rhétorique dans l'Europe moderne,* pp. 989–996.

For the interpretation of *politesse* as an education comparable to an intellectual one, see Daniel Gordon's *Citizens without Sovereignty.*

For a reading of the *Rêve d'Alembert*, I am indebted to P. N. Furbank's interpretation "D'Alembert's Dream," in his important study *Diderot: A Critical Biography* (Knopf, 1992), pp. 327–342.

At a century's distance, the letter sent by DIDEROT to SOPHIE VOLLAND reflects an image of sociability analogous to that which radiates from the letter to Pomponne written at Fresnes by Mme de Sévigné (see my chapter on Mme de Sévigné): the same décor—a magnificent country residence characterized by a refined and sumptuous hospitality—the same atmosphere of freedom and intimacy—a group of people united by friendship and a common way of feeling—the same inexhaustible pleasure of conversing together, even though the cultural climate had profoundly changed.

On the birth about halfway through the eighteenth century of a new literary genre devoted to eulogies of great men, see Jean-Claude Bonnet, *Naissance du Panthéon: Essai sur le culte des grands hommes* (Paris: Fayard, 1998).

On the three NECKERS, see Jean-Denis Bredin, *Une singulière famille: Jacques Necker, Suzanne Necker et Germaine de Staël* (Paris: Fayard, 1999). Among the many writings on Mme de Staël, here I simply recommend J. Christopher Herold's enchanting picture of her in *Mistress to an Age: A Life of Madame de Staël* (Bobbs-Merrill, 1958) and the biography by Ghislaine de Diesbach, *Madame de Staël* (Paris: Perrin, 1983).

On the ABBÉ GALIANI's Parisian success, see Giovanni Macchia, "Galiani e la necessità di piacere," in *Il naufragio della speranza*, pp. 192–206; Francis Steegmuller, *A Woman, a Man and Two Kingdoms* (Knopf, 1991); Ruth Plaut Weinreb, *Eagle in a Gauze Cage: Louise d'Épinay femme de lettres* (New York: AMS Press, 1993). I would like also to point to my own article "Conqueror of Paris," in *The New York Review of Books*, December 17, 1992, pp. 63–68.

On the À PROPOS, see bibliographic notes for Chapter 13 above, the pages concerning Mme de Staal-Delaunay.

Index of Names

Abélard, 124

Accetto, Torquato, born about 1590, lived in Naples, and died toward the middle of the seventeenth century, poet, author of the celebrated tract *Della dissimulazione onesta* (1641), 341, 444

Agnès de Saint-Paul, Mother, Jeanne Arnauld (1593–1671), sister of the Grand Arnauld and of Mother Angélique. Abbess of Saint-Cyr at age six, joined her sister Angélique at Port-Royal des Champs and supported the work of reform there. In the absence of her sister, she assumed the direction of the convent between 1618 and 1623. In 1626, the whole community moved to a new convent in the center of Paris, Port-Royal of the Faubourg Saint-Jacques. She was abbess from 1636 to 1642 and from 1658 to 1661. After Angélique's death in 1661, it was she who led the sisters' resistance to the religious authorities who wanted to force them to subscribe to the "Formula," the declaration of faith that condemned the Jansenist theses, 99, 119

Aguesseau, Henri François d' (1668–1751), chancellor, 287

Aiguillon, Anne Charlotte de Crussol de Florensac (1700–1772), Duchesse d', married in 1718 Armand Louis Vignerot du Plessis-Richelieu, Comte d'Agénois, later Duc d'Aiguillon, mother of Emmanuel Armand, Louis XV's minister, 332, 357

Aiguillon, Marie Madeleine de Vignerot (1604–1675), Marquise de Combalet, Duchesse d', daughter of one of Cardinal de Richelieu's sisters, 37, 38, 70, 109, 138

Aïssé, Charlotte-Elisabeth-Aïcha (1695?–1733), known as Mademoiselle, bought as a baby in the slave market by Charles de Ferriol, French ambassador to Constantinople, brought up in Paris by the count's sister-in-law, Marie-Angélique Guérin de Tencin, Comtesse de Ferriol. Mistress of the Chevalier d'Aydie, 279

Albon, Julie-Claude-Hilaire d' (1695–1746), married in 1711 her cousin Claude d'Albon, Comte de Saint-Michel, by whom she had three sons. Separated from her husband, she secretly gave birth to a son of whom all traces are lost, and a daughter who came to be called Julie de Lespinasse. The father is thought to be Mme du Deffand's brother, Gaspard-Nicolas de Vichy, who in 1739 married his mistress's legitimate daughter, Marie Camille Diane d'Albon, 310

Attichy, Anne d', *see* Maure, Anne Doni.

Aubigné, Agrippa d' (1551–1630), Protestant poet, author of the epic poem *Les Tragiques* (1616),

Aubigné, Françoise d', *see* Maintenon, Françoise d'Aubigné.

Aubry, Françoise Le Breton-Villandry (d. 1634), wife of Jean Aubry, councilor of state, friend of the Rambouillets, 39

Auchy, Charlotte des Ursins (ca. 1570–1646), Vicomtesse d'Auchy, 3, 40, 381

Auerbach, Erich, xiv, 200, 384 426

Augustine, Saint, 116, 126, 150, 411, 412

Aumale, Jeanne d', *see* Haucourt, Jeanne d'.

Aumale, Suzanne d'Haucourt d' (?–1688), second daughter of Daniel d'Aumale, chamberlain to the Grand Condé, wife of Frédéric Armand, Comte de Schomberg, Maréchal de France in 1675. As a confessed Huguenot, Schomberg left France after the Revocation of the Edict of Nantes, 165

Avaux, Charles de Mesmes (1595–1650), Comte d', ambassador to Venice, Denmark, Sweden, and Poland, he participated in negotiations for the Peace of Westphalia, author of *Mémoires touchant les négotiations du traité de paix fait à Münster en 1648* (1674), 77, 187, 291

Bachaumont, François Le Coigneux de (1624–1702), brilliant and independent spirit, coauthor of the celebrated *Voyage de Chapelle et Bachaumont* in verse and prose, father-in-law of the Marquise de Lambert, 264

Bagnols, Anne du Gué, Dame de, Mme de Coulanges's sister, she married in 1672 her cousin Dreux-Louis du Gué-Bagnols, intendant of Flanders and councilor of state, 226

Balivière, Henri-Éléonor Le Cornu (1741–?), Abbé de, socialite, connected to the Polignacs, he built at Royaumont (1784–1789) the last abbatial palace of the *ancien régime*, 373

Balzac, Guez de (1597–1654), writer, 3, 40, 50, 51, 52, 53, 108, 263, 338, 339, 344, 400, 401, 403, 443

Balzac, Honoré de (1799–1850), 31

Barbier, Edmond-Jean François (1689–1771), lawyer at the Parlement de Paris, left a journal of the reign of Louis XV, 281

Barbin, Claude (1629?–1698), the seventeenth century's best-known Parisian printer and bookseller, 121

Barrillon d'Amoncourt, Paul de (1630?–1691), Marquis de Grange, councilor of state, intendant of Picardy, ambassador to England (1677–1689), friend of Mme de Sévigné, Mme de Maintenon, and La Fontaine, 187, 210, 291

Bassompierre, François (1579–1646), Marquis de, grand master of artillery (1617), Maréchal de France in 1622, ambassador to Spain, Switzerland, and England. He took part in the siege of La Rochelle and was imprisoned in the Bastille in 1631 on Richelieu's orders, and was released only on the cardinal's death in 1643. Author of *Journal de ma vie* (1665), 137, 138, 150

Bayard, Jacques de (d. 1677), abbot of Notre-Dame de Bellaigue in the Bourbonnais, childhood friend of the Comte de Lafayette, 199

Bayle, Pierre (1647–1706), scholar and critic. He came from a Protestant family and settled in Rotterdam where, in 1681, he was given a chair in history and philosophy. In 1680 he published *Pensées diverses sur la Comète de 1680* and, from 1684 to 1687, *Nouvelles de la république des lettres*. His *Dictionnaire historique et critique* appeared in 1695, 211

Bayreuth, Sophia Wilhelmina of Prussia (1709–1758), Margravine of, Frederick II's sister and wife of Frederick William, Margrave of Bayreuth, author of *Mémoires*, 261

Beauchamp, Théodore (d. 1695), dancer, ballet master, and choreographer, member of the Royal Academy of Dance founded in 1661, named superintendent of the King's ballet in 1666, 245

Beaufort, François (1616–1669), Duc de, son of César, Duc de Vendôme, bastard son of Henri IV and Gabrielle d'Estrées, and brother of the Duc de Mercoeur, he was a member of the *cabale des Importants* and played a leading part in the Fronde, 74, 90, 91, 143, 406

Beaumarchais, Pierre Augustin Caron de (1732–1799), playwright, 34, 257

Beaussant, Philippe, 245, 416, 432

Beccaria, Angela Bianca, Contessa, dedicatee of Stefano Guazzo's *Ghirlanda*, published in Genoa in 1595, two years after the author's death, 69

Beccaria, Cesare (1738–1794), author of *Dei delitti e delle pene* (1764), published in France two years later, translated by the Abbé Morellet, 316, 359

Bellefonds, Bernardin Gigault (1630–1694), Marquis de, valiant soldier at arms, received a Maréchal de France's baton in 1668 and in 1688 the Order of the Saint-Esprit, 94, 226

Bellegarde, Jean-Baptiste de Morvan de (1648–1734), Abbé de, polygraph and author of manuals of behavior, 23, 275, 378

Benserade, Isaac de (1612–1691), fashionable writer who became, on Voiture's death, the best-known gallant poet of the day. In 1660 he was asked to collaborate with Lully and Lambert and he composed an enormous number of verses for the numerous ballets and court entertainments, 51, 168, 210, 245, 266

Bernier, François (1625–1688), doctor of medicine, prolific writer, Gassendi's pupil; between 1656 and 1659 he traveled widely in the Orient, staying at the court of the Great Mogul. He published a very successful account of his travels in *Mémoires* (1670–1671), 211

Bernières, Marguerite-Madeleine du Moutier, Marquise de, wife of Gilles-Henri Maignard, Marquis de Bernières, president of the Rouen Parlement; in 1722 she had a relationship with the young Voltaire whom she received at her château of La Rivière–Bourdet, 258, 259

Bernis, François Joachim de Pierre de (1715–1794), Abbé and then Cardinal de, protégé of Mme de Pompadour, ambassador to Venice (1752–1755), negotiator of the reversal of the alliance between France and Austria, foreign minister (1757–1758),

Choiseul, Louise Honorine de Crozat du Châtel (1735–1801), Duchesse de, grand-daughter of the financier Crozat, married in 1750 the Duc Étienne François de Choiseul, bringing him an immense dowry, 355

Choiseul-Stainville, Étienne François de (1719–1785), Comte de Stainville, later Duc de. Protégé of Madame de Pompadour, ambassador to Rome (1754–1757) and Vienna (1757). From 1758 until his exile in 1770, Choiseul directed French politics with the authority of a prime minister. He instigated the "family pact," the alliance between France and Austria, 292, 325, 326, 327

Choisy, François Timoléon (1644–1724), Abbé de, traveler, theologian, historian, memoirist. Son of Jeanne Olympe de Choisy, who gave him a taste for transvestism. Tireless and prolific writer, the author of, among other things, *Mémoires* and an account of a trip to Siam, 226, 243, 267

Choisy, Jeanne Olympe de Belesbat de Hurault de L'Hôpital (1600–1669), married in 1628 Jean de Choisy, intendant of Languedoc and Gaston d'Orléans's chancellor. Beautiful and a great intriguer, she held a *"précieux"* salon and was one of the most prominent women in the society of the day, 160

Chrétien de Troyes, 41

Christina of Sweden (1626–1689), only daughter of Gustav Adolphe, she became Queen of Sweden at age six in 1632, and abdicated in 1654. She made two trips to France, the first in 1656, the second in 1657–1658, then settled in Rome, 139, 221, 235

Cicero, 50, 338

Cioran, E.M., 318

Clement XI, Gian Francesco Albani (1649–1721), elected Pope in 1700, 282

Clérambault, Philippe de (1606–1665), named a Maréchal de France in 1653, 341

Clermont-Gallerande, Armand Henri (1688–1776), Comte de, married in 1740 Marie Charlotte de Bragelongne (ca. 1703–1774), 365

Cochin, Charles Nicolas (1715–1790), engraver and art historian, 299, 300

Coigny, Marie François Henri de Franquetot (1737–1821), Marquis and, in 1756, Duc de, governor of Choisy (1748), lieutenant general, and, from 1771 on, the King's first equerry, 367

Colbert, Henriette Louise (1657–1733), the minister's second daughter, married in 1671 Paul, Duc de Beauvillier and Comte de Saint-Agnan, 174

Colbert, Jean-Baptiste (1619–1683), minister and statesman. Trusted by Louis XIV, between 1661 and 1683 he held an impressive number of positions that allowed him to reform the administration, draw up a new economic policy, and carry out an ostentatious program of state patronage of the arts, 251, 415, 425

Coligny, Maurice (d. 1641), Comte de, eldest son of the Maréchal de Châtillon, died from wounds received in a duel with Henri, Duc de Guise, 73, 74, 75

Colonna, Maria Mancini (1639–1715), Principessa, daughter of Michele Mancini and Geronima Mazzarino, niece of the cardinal, inspired a violent passion in the young Louis XIV and in 1661 went to Rome to marry Lorenzo Onofrio Colonna (1637–1689), Duca di Tagliacozzo, Principe di Paliano and di Castiglione, High Constable of the Kingdom of Naples, 138, 242

Gluck, Christoph Willibald (1714–1787), Chevalier, German composer, 322

Godeau, Antoine (1605–1672), habitué of the hôtel de Rambouillet, led the life of a worldly cleric, wrote endless gallant verse before being consecrated as a priest in 1636. As bishop of Grasse, he settled in his distant diocese and devoted himself entirely to pastoral work, turning his tireless pen to the service of religious and moral instruction, 3, 70, 381, 406

Gombaud, Antoine de, *see* Méré, Chevalier de.

Goncourt brothers, 289, 392, 393

Gondi, Jean François Paul de, *see* Retz, Paul de Gondi, Cardinal de.

Gonzaga, Giulia (1513–1566), wife of Vespasiano Colonna, Conte di Fondi, considered one of the most beautiful and cultured women of her time; she had an adventure avoiding abduction by the pirate Barbarossa. She participated in the movement for religious reform developing around Juan de Valdés, 10

Gonzague-Nevers, Marie-Louise de (1611–1667), Queen of Poland, daughter of the Duc de Nevers, later of Mantua, and Catherine de Lorraine-Mayenne, married Ladisław Zygmunt IV Wasa. In widowhood she married her brother-in-law, Jan Casimir V, 35

Gournay, Marie Le Jars (1566–1645), known as Mlle de, Montaigne's *fille d'alliance*, edited the posthumous edition of his *Essais*, author of much literary criticism and moral reflection, 4

Gourville, Jean Hérault de (1625–1703), joined the service of La Rochefoucauld, then went over to Mazarin's side and at the end of the Fronde negotiated his ex-master's pardon, whose sister he married in secret. An important administrative post allowed him to build up an immense fortune, but he was involved in Fouquet's disgrace. Author of *Mémoires*, 186, 204

Gracián, Baltasar (1601–1658), Spanish Jesuit, writer, and moralist, 341, 444

Gramont, Antoine (1604–1678), son of Antoine, like his father was Comte de Gramont, de Guiche, and de Louvigny, Maréchal de France (1641), and Duc (1643). Author of *Mémoires*, 332

Grand Arnauld, *see* Arnauld, Antoine.

Grand Condé, *see* Condé, Louis de Bourbon.

Grande Mademoiselle, *see* Montpensier, Anne Marie Louise d'Orléans.

Grenaille, François de (1616–1680), man of letters, Gaston d'Orléans's historiographer, author of books of morality, 11, 20, 22

Grétry, André Modeste (1741–1813), composer, 349, 370

Greuze, Jean-Baptiste (1725–1805), painter, 300

Grignan, François Adhémar de Monteil (1632–1714), Comte de. From 1663 to 1669 he was lieutenant general in the Languedoc and subsequently governor of Provence, 192, 193

Grignan, Françoise Marguerite de Sévigné (1646–1705), third Comtesse de Grignan, daughter of Mme de Sévigné, 193, 194, 343

Grignan-Rambouillet, Angélique Clarice d'Angennes de Rambouillet, first Comtesse de Grignan (?–1664), daughter of Mme de Rambouillet and sister of Julie d'Angennes, 63, 108, 167, 192, 318

Grimm, Frederick Melchior (1723–1807) Baron von, German by birth and education

years later. Known for the verve of his satirical verse, he gave his name to the *Recueil Maurepas*, a large collection of poetry for occasions of the day, 304, 309, 327

Mazarin, Hortense Mancini (1646–1699), Duchesse de, daughter of Michele Mancini and Geronima Mazzarino, the cardinal's sister, married in 1661 Armand de La Porte, Marquis de La Meilleraye, who on Mazarin's death inherited his fortune and his name with the title of Duc de Mazarin. Her husband's extreme avarice and pathological jealousy caused her to leave France and to travel throughout Europe, 246, 433

Mazarin, Jules (1602–1661) Cardinal. He received the cardinal's hat in December 1641 and succeeded Richelieu as prime minister, a position he held until his death, 70, 72, 74, 79, 80, 81, 90, 103, 114, 131, 137, 138, 141, 142, 182, 183, 185, 186, 242, 243, 398, 412

Meilhan, Sénac de, Gabriel Aimable (1736–1803), man of letters. He had a brilliant career in administration and the army, and emigrated in 1791. In 1795 he published *Du gouvernement, des mœurs et des conditions en France avant la Révolution, avec le caractère des principaux personnages du règne de Louis XVI*, 258, 316

Melson, Charlotte (1630?–1702), Dame Le Camus, 162

Ménage, Gilles (1613–1692), abbé, scholar, linguist, worldly man of letters, 12, 30, 51, 115, 175, 176, 191, 197, 198, 200, 201, 401, 402, 424-425

Menjot, Antoine (b. ca. 1615), Mme de La Sablière's uncle on her mother's side, of Protestant religion, graduated as a doctor in Montpellier in 1636, endowed with encyclopedic knowledge, 210

Mercier, Louis Sébastien (1740–1814), journalist, dramatist, novelist, and critic. His best-known works are *L'An deux mille quatre cent quarante, rêve s'il en fut jamais* (1771) and the *Tableau de Paris* (1781, in two volumes), a broad canvas depicting Parisian life in the 1780s, 366

Mercoeur, Louis de Vendôme, Duc de, 74

Méré, Antoine Gombaud (1607–1684), Chevalier de. In 1644 he entered the service of the young Duchesse de Lesdiguières, whose tutor he became, and he thus frequented Parisian high society. He expounded his ideas on *honnêteté* in *Conversations*, published in 1668, followed by *Œuvres posthumes*, 31, 35, 43, 49, 163, 205, 206, 210, 235, 240, 259, 274, 313, 340–341, 343, 344, 349, 352, 384, 399, 424

Mesmer, Franz Anton (1734–1815), studied medicine in Vienna and moved to Paris to practice healing through magnetism, 213

Mirabaud, Jean Baptiste de (1675–1760), man of letters, translator of Ariosto, 286

Mirepoix, Anne Marguerite Gabrielle de Beauvau-Craon (1707–1791), Maréchale de, married in 1721 Jacques Henri de Lorraine, Prince de Lixin; widowed in 1739, she then married Pierre Louis de Lévis de Lomagne, Duc de Mirepoix, Maréchal de France, 331

Mol, Pieter van (1599–1650), portraitist and painter of historical subjects. Born in Antwerp, worked with Rubens, whose style he imitated. In 1631 he moved to Paris where he painted the frescoes for the Sacred Heart chapel in the Carmelite church. He participated in the founding of the Académie royale de peinture, 70

Molière, Jean-Baptiste Poquelin (1622–1673), so-called, 21, 33, 68, 105, 147, 164, 171, 185, 211, 241, 245, 351, 421, 425

Monaco, Catherine Charlotte de Gramont (1639–1678), Princesse de, wife of Louis Grimaldi, Duc de Valentinois and Prince of Monaco, 244

Monaco, Marie Catherine de Brignole (1739–1813), married Honoré, Prince of Monaco, in 1757 and after his death married Louis Joseph de Bourbon, Prince de Condé, in 1808, 305

Moncrif, François Augustin Paradis de (1687–1770), poet, musician, actor. Elected to the Académie française in 1733, he became reader to Maria Lesczynska, royal historiographer, and director general of the Post. His *Histoire des chats* earned him the nickname of *historiogriffe*, 353–354

Monsieur le Prince, Madame la Princesse, *see* Condé, Henri Jules Bourbon and his wife, Anne of Bavaria.

Montagu, George (1713–1780), friend and correspondent of Horace Walpole, 364

Montaigne, Michel de (1533–1592), 4, 10, 13–14, 127, 195, 220, 266, 330, 348, 353

Montausier, Charles de Saint-Maure (1610–1690), Marquis de, younger brother of Hector and in 1664, Duc de, Pair de France, governor of Normandy (1663), and tutor to the Dauphin (1668–1680), 65–66, 68–70, 117, 405, 406

Montausier, Hector de (d. 1635), 68

Montausier, Julie Lucine d'Angennes de Rambouillet (1605–1671), Duchesse de. First child of Mme de Rambouillet, married Charles de Saint-Maure in 1661, named governess to the royal children and in 1664 lady-in-waiting to the Queen, 30, 33, 45, 53, 56–59, 63, 65–70, 107, 108, 109, 110, 111, 112, 157, 158, 167, 176, 318, 345, 406

Montbazon, Hercule de Rohan-Guéméné (1568–1654), became first Duc de Montbazon in 1595, governor of Paris and the Île-de-France, 89, 98

Montbazon, Marie de Bretagne-Avaugour (1612–1657), Duchesse de, daughter of Claude, Comte de Vertus, and Catherine Foucquet de La Varenne, second wife of the above, 72, 73–74, 89–92, 95, 98, 149, 160, 408

Montdory, Guillaume Gilbert or Desgilbert (1594–ca. 1653), famous tragedian, 33

Montemayor, Jorge de (circa 1520–1562), Portuguese writer, author of *Diana*, famous pastoral novel in Castilian (1559), 41

Montespan, Françoise Athénaïs de Rochechouart (1640–1707), Marquise de, daughter of Gabriel de Rochechouart, Duc de Mortemart, and Diane de Grandseigne, in 1663 married the Marquis Louis Henri de Pardaillan de Gondrin, from whom she separated on becoming Louis XIV's official mistress, 120, 122, 211, 223, 226, 347

Montesquieu, Charles-Louis de Secondat (1689–1755), Baron de, 231, 232, 235, 236, 256, 265, 267, 268, 270, 271, 273, 286, 289, 300, 301, 332, 437

Montesson, Charlotte Jeanne Béraud de la Haie de Riou (1737–1806), Marquise de, widow of the old Marquis de Montesson, married secretly in 1773 the Duc d'Orléans. She wrote poetry, novels, and above all plays, which she staged at the Palais-Royal, 257

Montglas, Cécile Élisabeth Hurault de Cheverny (1618–1695), Marquise de, 153, 161, 179, 185

Roux, Augustin (1726–1776), doctor, named professor at the faculty of medicine in
1771, 359
Rubens, Peter Paul (1577–1640), painter, 139

Sablé, Madeleine de Souvré (1598–1678), Marquise de, daughter of Louis XIII's tutor,
the Marquis de Souvré, lady-in-waiting to Marie de' Medici, married in 1614
Philippe Emmanuel de Laval, Marquis de Sablé, by whom she had four children,
widowed in 1640, xii, 23, 85, 97–99, 101, 105-135, 153, 154, 167, 177, 190, 195,
200, 204, 210, 215, 270, 273, 291, 340, 345, 404, 409–410, 411, 412, 413
Sade, Donatien Alphonse François (1740–1814), Comte de, writer, known as the Marquis de Sade, 89
Saint-Amant, Antoine Girard (1594–1661), Seigneur de, poet, 40, 158
Saint-Aulaire, François Joseph de Beaupoil (1643–1742), Marquis de, lieutenant general
of the Limousin, man of the world, and poet, admitted to the Académie française in
1706, 267, 272
Saint-Balmon, Alberte Barbe d'Ernecourt (1607–1660), Comtesse de, of a noble fam-
ily from Lorraine, defended her lands with an army. Author of a religious tragedy,
Les Jumeaux martires (1650), 80, 407
Saint-Blancard, Charles de Gontaut, Marquis de (b. 1752), captain in the French
Guards, emigrated in 1792 and joined Condé's antirevolutionary army, 374
Saint-Cyran, Jean Du Vergier de Hauranne (1581–1643), Abbé de, friend of Jansenius
with whom he studied Saint Augustine's work for five years, was later greatly influenced by the spirituality of Bérulle, whom he succeeded as leader of the *parti dévot*.
He was much hated by the Jesuits for his attacks on Père Garasse and on the English Jesuits' anti-episcopal theories. In 1636 he took over the direction of the convent at Port-Royal, introducing Jansenist doctrine there. Richelieu, who disliked his
opinions, had him imprisoned in Vincennes without a proper trial. On the cardinal's death Saint-Cyran was freed, but he died soon afterward, having suffered
badly in prison, 99, 104, 126, 352
Sainte-Beuve, Charles Augustin (1804–1869), 61, 78, 99, 129, 259, 296, 299, 302,
367, 392, 398, 406, 409
Saint-Évremond, Charles de Marguetel de Saint-Denys de (1613–1703), writer; impli-
cated in Fouquet's disgrace in 1661, he avoided arrest and took refuge in Holland
and then in England where he spent the next four decades and died without ever
returning to France, xii, 113, 170–171, 205, 206, 220, 222, 229, 246, 266
Saint-Lambert, Jean François (1716–1803), Marquis de, poet and *philosophe*, whose
verse was much appreciated by contemporaries. His most ambitious work, *Les Saisons*
(1769), is a didactic poem in four cantos. Lover of Mme du Châtelet, 326, 359
Saint-Paul, Charles Paris (1649–1672), *see* Longueville.
Saint-Pierre, Charles Irénée Castel (1658–1743), known as the Abbé de, whose extensive works touching on political, administrative, fiscal, pedagogical, and linguistic
problems show him as an idealist reformer with utopian leanings, 271, 284, 298,
300, 350

Saint-Simon, Claude de Rouvroy (1607–1693), Duc de, 94

Saint-Simon, Louis de Rouvroy (1675–1755), Vidame de Chartres, later in 1693, Duc de, son of the above, memoirist, 25, 92, 151, 152, 181, 228, 247, 272, 278, 284, 347–348, 432

Sallust, 61

Salvius, Jean Adler, Swedish plenipotentiary to Münster, 77

Sarasin, Jean-François (1614–1654), gallant poet, introduced by Mlle Paulet to the hôtel de Rambouillet, protégé of Mme de Longueville, secretary to the Prince de Conti. His *Pompe funèbre de Voiture* (1649) was very successful, but he wasn't concerned with publishing his work, which came out posthumously in 1656 as a result of Pellisson's initiative, 11–12, 72, 198, 401, 407, 425

Sauveur, Joseph (1653–1716), distinguished mathematician, member of the Académie des sciences, teacher of the King of Spain and the Duc de Bourgogne, 210, 211, 212

Scarron, Paul (1610–1660), poet, novelist, dramatist, 147, 222

Scarron, Madame, *see* Maintenon, Françoise d'Aubigné, widow Scarron.

Scheffer, Carl Frederik (1715–1786), Count von, Swedish ambassador to France from 1744 to 1751, later senator at the Diet, tutor and adviser to the future Gustav III, 292

Schomberg, Marie d'Hautefort, Maréchale de, daughter of Charles, Marquis de Hautefort, and Renée Du Bellay, lady-in-waiting to Anne of Austria, loved by Louis XIII. Married in 1646 Charles, Duc de Halluin, later de Schomberg, Maréchal de France, 133

Scudéry, Georges de (1601–1667), born at Le Havre where his father was governor, settled with his sister, Madeleine, in Paris in 1639, where he launched himself on a brilliant literary career. His *Observations sur le Cid* (1637) were part of the famous *Querelle*, 68, 70, 157, 169, 419

Scudéry, Madeleine de (1607–1701), born at Le Havre, given an excellent education by an uncle, she followed her brother Georges to Marseilles and then to Paris. In 1641 she published, under her brother's name, *Ibrahim ou l'Illustre Bassa*, which was followed by *Les femmes illustres ou les Harangues héroïques* (1642), the ten volumes of *Artamène ou le Grand Cyrus* (1649–1653), and the ten volumes of *Clélie, Histoire romaine* (1654–1660). She later published a series of *Nouvelles*, and, beginning in 1680, four collections of *Conversations*, and in 1692 the *Entretiens de morale*, 17, 28, 32, 37, 43, 47, 48, 49, 67, 80, 105, 108, 113, 120, 123, 124, 128, 131, 154, 156, 157, 158, 159, 160, 169, 170, 173, 178, 179, 180, 184, 185, 188, 195, 196, 198, 200, 205, 210, 226, 227, 241, 242, 269, 314, 328, 343, 344, 345, 346, 347, 348, 351, 393, 401, 403–404, 410, 419–421, 423, 425

Segrais, Jean Regnault de (1624–1701), poet and novelist, in the service of the Grande Mademoiselle from 1648 to 1674, collaborated with Mme de Lafayette in drafting her novels, 2, 33, 35, 41, 135, 155–156, 158, 159, 198, 200, 402, 418–419

Ségur, Marquis de, 305

Sellier, Philippe, 108, 422

Seneca, 766

Sens, Monsieur de, *see* Bouthillier de Chavigny, François.

Vaugelas, Claude Favre, Baron de Perouges (1585–1650), Seigneur de, grammarian and purist, founding member of the Académie française, directed the undertaking of the *Gran Dictionnaire de l'Académie*; published *Remarques sur la langue française* in 1647, 3, 19, 40, 59

Vaumorière, Pierre d'Ortigue de (1611–1693), novelist, imitator of Mlle de Scudéry, author of an *Art de plaire dans la conversation*, which appeared anonymously in 1688, followed by two revised and enlarged editions (1691–1701), 113, 343, 405

Vega, Lope de (1562–1635), 41

Vendôme, César de (1594–1665), legitimized bastard son of Henri IV and Gabrielle d'Estrées, married Françoise de Lorraine, father of Louis, Duc de Mercoeur, and of François, Duc de Beaufort, 37, 74

Vendôme, Louis Joseph de Bourbon (1654–1712), Duc de, grandson of César de Vendôme and son of Louis, Duc de Mercoeur, and Laura Mancini, lieutenant general in 1668, captain of the galleys in 1694, 249, 250, 433

Vendôme, Philippe de (1655–1727), brother of Louis Joseph de Bourbon Vendôme, Grand Prior of the Temple in 1678, 249, 250, 433

Vernet, Claude-Joseph (1714–1789), painter, 300

Vertus, Comte de, 89

Vertus, Catherine Françoise de Bretagne, Demoiselle de Vertus, Mme de Montbazon's sister. Friend and confidante of the Duchesse de Longueville, she converted to Jansenism and retired to Port-Royal, where she died in 1692, 84, 85

Villarceaux, Louis de Mornay (1619–1691), Marquis de, captain lieutenant of the Dauphiné Lighthorse, lover of Ninon de Lenclos and had a relationship with Mme Scarron, 222

Villars, Claude Louis Hector (1653–1734), Duc de, Maréchal de France, distinguished general, 62

Virgil, 211

Vitry, Marie Louise Aimée Pot de Rodhes (d. 1679), wife of François Marie de l'Hospital, Duc de Vitry, 163

Voiture, Vincent (1598–1648), writer, 30, 38, 39, 43, 45–48, 50–63, 64, 70, 77, 109, 118, 138, 141, 155, 158, 167, 168, 181, 198, 200, 206, 241, 259, 263, 280, 288, 291, 339, 351, 370, 397, 400–402, 404, 405, 425

Volland, Louise Henriette Sophie (1716–1784), known as Sophie, Diderot met her in 1755, developed an amorous relationship with her, and wrote her 553 letters, of which 196 survive, 364, 446

Volney, Constantin François Chassebœuf (1757–1820), Comte de, scholar, traveler, linked to a group of *idéologues*, in 1791 he published his most famous work, *Les Ruines, ou Méditations sur les révolutions des empires*, visited the United States from 1795 to 1798, 337

Voltaire, François Marie Arouet (1694–1788), known as, 17, 32, 34, 52, 62, 213, 223–224, 231, 236, 250, 257–262, 270, 280, 286, 287, 307, 309, 311, 315, 316, 317, 326, 327, 328, 329, 330, 332, 405, 434, 435

Vossler, Karl (1872–1949), 239

Voyer, *see* Argenson, Antoine René de Voyer d'.
Vulteius, Jean, one of the Landgrave of Hesse-Cassel's envoys to Münster, 77

Walpole, Horace (1717–1797), Earl of Orford, fourth son of Sir Robert Walpole. Writer and collector; he launched the Gothic revival with his novel *The Castle of Otranto* (1765) and his house, Strawberry Hill, 17, 125, 291, 324, 325, 326, 355, 359, 363, 364, 365, 366
Watteau, Antoine (1684–1721), painter, 159

Xaintes, Monsieur de, 187